TEXAS RICH

The Hunt Dynasty from the
Early Oil Days through the Silver Crash

HARRY HURT III

W · W · NORTON & COMPANY
New York   London

FIRST EDITION

Portions of this book previously appeared in *Texas Monthly* and *Playboy*.

Library of Congress Cataloging in Publication Data
Hurt, Harry.
  Texas rich.
  1. Hunt, H. L. 2. Businessmen—Texas—Biography.
I. Title.
HC102.5.H86H87 1981   338.092′4 [B]   80-25818
ISBN 0-393-01391-X

W. W. Norton & Company, Inc. 500 Fifth Avenue, New York, N.Y. 10110
W. W. Norton & Company Ltd. 25 New Street Square, London EC4A 3NT

1 2 3 4 5 6 7 8 9 0

For
J.C.H., M.B.H., and H.H. II

CONTENTS

LIST OF ILLUSTRATIONS

"In terms of extraordinary, independent wealth, there is only one man —H. L. Hunt."

—J. Paul Getty (1957)

"The children of H. L. Hunt are richer than their old man ever was."
—Hunt family attorney (1980)

TEXAS RICH

CHAPTER 1

H.L.'S IMAGE

THE old man's ghost howled in from Texas with the worst winter storm in over fifty years. Rain, then sleet, then hail. Volley after freezing volley rumbled down the Red River Valley, lashing Shreveport with a bitter vengeance. Some said the old man used to spend half his life trying to play God and the other half trying to outdo the Devil, but on this stormy January morning in 1978, his spirit seemed to be venting wrath enough for both. As a result of the fury, the outside world had virtually come to a halt. The streets, the bridges, and the Interstate were empty. The airport was closed. The cattle were glued to their feed troughs like plastic toys. About the only motion still visible on the landscape of frozen trees was the occasional sight of a black-iron oil-well pump nodding like a hobby horse in rhythmic indifference to the nasty winds.

Nevertheless, inside the concrete-block federal courthouse at the top of the hill, Frania Tye Lee sat on the witness stand and continued to tell the world how the late H. L. Hunt had bought her off. Whether or not she was telling the whole truth, Mrs. Lee certainly made an excellent witness. She was, as her attorney had described her, "a well-preserved seventy-three," short and graying, but also broad-shouldered and much sturdier looking than the average grandmother. She had put on too much make-up, especially powder, and the harsh courtroom light made her complexion look waxen and unnaturally white. But suggestions of the once-stunning beauty that had attracted young H. L. Hunt still showed through—in her enormous blue eyes, in her wide and yet handsome jaw, in her full-breasted figure. Indeed, the flaws of her old age and her attempts to hide them only made her seem more sympathetic, more victimized.

Holding her chin up and her back straight, Mrs. Lee recounted H.L.'s dramatic attempt to buy her off as if she were reporting the details of a routine family dinner. It was back in January of 1942, she told the court, almost thirty-six years ago to the day. She and Hunt were in Dallas, at the Hotel Adolphus, momentarily alone. All of a sudden, Hunt closed the door to the adjoining room. He shut the transoms and checked the hall outside. Then, satisfied that no one else could hear, he offered her a million dollars to sign a statement saying that she had never really married him.

"That's when I became very angry and screamed that I would never sell my children for all the money he had," Mrs. Lee recalled in an even tone.

Mrs. Lee's attorney interrupted. Why, he asked, did H. L. Hunt want you to sign a statement saying you had never married him?

"So that he would not be revealed as a bigamist," Mrs. Lee replied.

Across the crowded courtroom, the so-called "first" and "second" families of H. L. Hunt listened to Mrs. Lee's testimony with rapt dismay. Prior to the trial, these two Dallas branches of the clan had been the only publicly recognized heirs of H. L. Hunt. Sometimes referred to as "the royal family of Texas," they were actually two distinct groups: the children of H.L.'s first wife, Lyda Bunker Hunt, and the children of his second wife, Ruth Ray Hunt. Different in age, style, and outlook, the two were accustomed to quarreling with each other. But just before coming to Shreveport, the first and second families had temporarily submerged their differences to put up a united front against Frania Tye Lee. Now, sitting together in the same courtroom, they made a remarkable group portrait.

Ray Hunt, the oldest child of the second family, sat at the counsel's table, a few feet away from the rest of his kinfolk, his back to the regular spectators' section. As sole independent executor of the H. L. Hunt estate, Ray was the named defendant in Mrs. Lee's lawsuit. He also bore the most striking resemblance to his father. Blond, broad-shouldered, and fastidiously clean-cut, he had the same square jaw, the same high-boned but puffy cheeks, the same intense blue eyes that had distinguished H.L. in his prime. At thirty-four, Ray was also about the same age H.L. had been when he had first encountered young Frania Tye. Earlier in the week, Ray had been called to the stand to acknowledge that his father was also the father of Frania's four children. After politely confirming that little-known fact, he had returned to his seat to await the defense's turn to argue.

The other Hunts observed the proceedings from a special section of seats directly opposite the jury box. Ray's thirty-three-year-old sister June, the strawberry-blonde professional singer, author, and religious lecturer, sat at the far end of the front row. Then came Swanee, twenty-eight, the youngest, a chubby blonde involved in religious and emotional counseling. Then Helen, twenty-nine, the middle one, a slim brunette with more angular features than the others. A Hunt Oil Company aide sat on one side of the sisters. Ray's blonde wife Nancy sat on the other. With their concerned but innocent expressions, the four Hunt women of the second family looked like a row of supportive angels.

The children of the first family did not look at all angelic. A half generation older than Ray and his sisters, they all had dark hair and less uniform though still unmistakable variations of their father's features. They were also more expressive. Bunker, age fifty-two, the oldest active son, showed his feelings most. Through most of the proceedings, he had slouched back in his chair with his tiny hands folded over the great swell of his belly, his glasses jammed against his forehead by a sullen frown. With the stayless points of his shirt collar bent forward on each side of his tie like tiny white horns, he resembled a spectacled dinosaur caught in a primeval mud bog and brooding over it. Virtually nothing about him hinted that he had once been (and would be again) the world's richest private individual.

Bunker's sister Caroline sat to his right with her graying hair pulled back in a bun, her arms folded, her face wrinkled in a frown approximately half as intense as her brother's. Herbert Hunt, correct and businesslike as always, sat beside his blonde wife, also named Nancy, pensively resting his hand on his cheek. Lamar, age forty-five, the youngest, fidgeted most. Crossing and uncrossing his legs, he would lean forward, remove a gold ballpoint pen from the inside pocket of his habitual blue blazer, examine the pen as if it had mysteriously arrived from another planet, then replace it.

Three more in-laws completed the family portrait: sister Margaret's husband Al Hill; Caroline's husband Buddy Schoellkopf; and Lamar's attractive wife Norma. A slim, vivacious woman with delicate features, big brown eyes, and a great pile of coiffured blonde hair, Norma was easily the most stylish and the most striking of the Hunts, male or female.

The Hunts' show of numbers was impressive. With intermittent arrivals of other relatives swelling their ranks to over twenty strong, the first and second families had enough bodies present to form a full platoon. But this turnout represented less than half the families' total strength. Counting his family by Frania Tye Lee, the late H. L. Hunt had left seventy living direct descendants at his death in 1974. With ten children, twenty-one grandchildren, and twelve great grandchildren, the first and second families accounted for forty-three members of that flock. By the time the Shreveport trial commenced, several more Hunt heirs were being born or conceived. Had each direct descendant come to court with spouse or nursemaid, there would barely have been enough room for the judge and jury. As it was, the Hunt contingent did not even include all of the leading members of the clan.

Of course, those missing were absent for good reasons. H.L.H. Jr., the oldest first-family son, known as Hassie, had not come because of the mental illness that had prevented him from appearing in public for over thirty years. Margaret Hunt Hill, his steel-willed oldest sister, a potential witness for the defense, had chosen to remain in the motel rather than suffer the indignity of waiting outside the courtroom with the other witnesses. Meanwhile, Ruth, the mother of the second family and the last Mrs. H. L. Hunt, had stayed in Dallas on the advice of the attorneys, who feared that if she made the trip to Shreveport, the other side might call her to the witness stand and try to embarrass her with the fact that her own children—Ray, June, Swanee, and Helen—had been born out of wedlock and before the death of H.L.'s first wife, Lyda.

Frania Tye Lee's testimony provided embarrassment enough. As she told the court, Frania had first met H.L. in Tampa, Florida, at the peak of the real-estate boom in 1925. Hunt was then thirty-six years old and the father of a family by his first wife, Lyda Bunker Hunt. Having just sold out of the oil business in Arkansas, Hunt had come to Tampa looking for real-estate investments. Frania, then a stunning twenty-one year old, had left her Polish-Catholic immigrant family back in Buffalo, New York, to seek her fortune as a real-estate salesperson. Their paths crossed when Hunt arrived to inspect a piece of property that was for sale. However, according to Frania, H.L. did not introduce himself to her by his real name. Instead, he used the name "Major Franklin Hunt."

"Everyone just called him Major," Frania told the court.

After describing their stormy "whirlwind" courtship, Frania testified that she and Hunt were married by a justice of the peace in Tampa's Cuban quarter on Armistice Day, November 11, 1925. Mrs. Lee went on to claim that she lived with Hunt for nine years in Shreveport and Dallas before discovering his true identity and the existence of his first wife and family. Following this revelation, Frania moved to Great Neck, New York, and, later, Houston, Texas. Frania claimed that H.L. tried everything from poetry to trickery to induce her to move to Utah and become a Mormon so they could practice bigamy legally. But while she did continue to see Hunt, she refused to acquiesce to his request.

Finally, in 1942, after several more stormy encounters, Frania and H.L. met in Dallas to work out a settlement. Mrs. Lee went on to admit that after the scenes in the Hotel Adolphus, she did sign a statement which omitted any mention of her alleged marriage to Hunt, as well as a document releasing him and his estate from any further claims. She also admitted accepting nearly a million dollars in the form of cash, trust funds for her children, and monthly payments of $2,000, which she continued to receive right through the day of her testimony. However, she said she capitulated only because of Hunt's pressure, his assertion that the court records of their marriage had been destroyed, and, most of all, his promise to recognize her and her children on an equal basis with his first family when he wrote his will. Twelve days after signing the settlement, Frania married a Hunt Oil employee named John Lee, who adopted her four children by H.L. and gave them his name. Frania and John Lee lived together for thirteen years, most of them in Atlanta, then got divorced.

About the same time he was breaking up with Frania, H.L. was taking up with a twenty-one-year-old Hunt Oil secretary named Ruth Ray. Hunt bought Ruth a house in Dallas not far from his first family's home, and she bore him four more children under the assumed name of "Wright." In 1955, H.L.'s first wife Lyda died of a stroke. Two years later, he married Ruth and gave their children his name. After H.L.'s own death in 1974, all three of his families confronted each other over the ocean of his estate.

Up to the time of the Shreveport trial, most of the Hunts' internecine battles had been conducted in private. But by filing suit against the H. L. Hunt estate, Frania Tye Lee had dragged the family feud into the public spotlight. The way Mrs. Lee told it, her decision to sue had been prompted by H.L.'s failure to keep the unwritten promises of recognition he allegedly made to her back in 1942. Mrs. Lee said she had felt secure in those promises until 1973, when Hunt published his autobiographical family histories, *Hunt Heritage* and *H. L. Hunt, Early Days.* The books, she said, had upset her terribly because they did not even mention her or her children. Two years later, when Hunt's will was opened, she discovered that H.L. had left four-fourteenths of some Louisiana oil properties to the "Reliance Trusts" he had set up for her children. But the bulk of his estate was bequeathed to Hunt's other two families. And, like Hunt's books, the will failed to mention her or her children by name. That, she said, was why she had decided to file against the estate.

Mrs. Lee said that shortly after her decision to sue, her son, Hugh Lee Hunt, accompanied her to Florida to look for a marriage license. Although she had looked twice before without finding anything, this time they discovered a voided entry in an old record book that appeared to support her claim. Then, after copies of the document had been made in preparation for the Shreveport trial, someone had come along and sliced the original right out of the record book.

Now Mrs. Lee was asking the court to declare her Hunt's "putative" (commonly accepted) wife. She was also asking for one-half of all the community property H.L. had accumulated between 1925, the year of their alleged marriage, and 1934, the year she claimed to have discovered his true identity, plus all the subsequent fruits of that community property. In a separate but related lawsuit filed in a Baton Rouge court, Mrs. Lee's children were asking to be declared H.L.'s legitimate heirs.

The first and second families opposed Mrs. Lee on several grounds. Though acknowledging her childrens' parentage, they alleged that she and H.L. had never formally married. They challenged her claim of not knowing Hunt's true identity, and they maintained that the 1942 settlement agreement was still valid and that the voided (and now missing) marriage-record entry was a fraud. They also objected to the amount of money Frania wanted. The period between 1925 and 1934 included the time when H.L. had made the famous Dad Joiner deal, the oil lease purchase that proved to be the cornerstone of his great fortune. The fruits of that property amounted to hundreds of millions of dollars. That was one reason attempts at a pretrial settlement out of court had foundered. Mrs. Lee's attorneys had started with a price of $100 million and had refused to come down. But $100 million was simply out of the question, even for the multibillionaire Hunts.

There were also some intangible reasons for the stalemate. Frania's lawsuit involved the most sensitive issues of family life, things like identity, affection, loyalty, and trust. In this case, each dollar at stake had an emotional as well as financial value: how much each family had was in many ways a symbolic measure of how they ranked on the family tree. The confrontation in Shreveport was not just another family squabble, but a three-way shoot-out over love and money and the family name.

As Mrs. Lee's attorney led her over the fine points of her story one more time, the judge, the jury, the families, the spectators, and the press, all seemed transfixed—not just by Mrs. Lee but by an unseen presence from the past. Each person had a separate vision of that presence. But each vision was merely a differently colored image of the same man, the central missing character, Haroldson Lafayette Hunt.

Most people's images of H. L. Hunt came from the media profiles that were done when he was already an old man. They pictured Hunt as a wispy-haired curmudgeon with a lumpy nose, soft blue eyes, and a mischievous grin. He was the man who gleefully admitted to being the world's richest human but insisted on carrying his lunch to work in a brown paper sack. With his habitual bow tie and cheap blue suit, Hunt was a sort of Daddy Warbucks come to life and a near look-alike of fabled Kentucky Fried Chicken founder Colonel Harlan Sanders. He was the Midas who said, "Everything I do, I do for profit," and, at the same time, the irrepressible risk taker who also said, "Money doesn't mean anything to me, it's only the way you keep the score."

Many of those present in the Shreveport courtroom associated this mental picture with eccentric genius. They remembered H.L. for his natural mathematical mind, his propensity to operate on instinct alone, and his incredible luck at finding oil. They also remembered Hunt as an outspoken Christian fundamentalist and the nation's most powerful propagandist of the extreme right, the man who lived in a replica of George Washington's home at Mount Vernon. A few recalled his novel *Alpaca,* which described a utopian constitution that apportioned votes according to how much taxes a citizen paid. But most only thought of his political mouthpieces, Facts Forum and LIFE LINE, whose broadcasts warned of commie-liberal conspiracies behind every tree, and the accusations that Hunt had something to do with the assassination of President Kennedy. The name H. L. Hunt also called to mind the image of a self-described "health crank" who went around hawking HLH-brand aloe-vera products and touting the benefits of a curious exercise he called "creeping." But more than anything else, those present thought of H. L. Hunt as the quintessential self-made man, the last of the true independents. Though hardly typical of other wealthy men in Dallas or elsewhere, he was in many people's minds the personification of the Texas rich.

Frania Tye Lee's testimony conjured warring images of Hunt. She spoke of H.L. as a young man in the prime of life, a strapping six-foot-tall two-hundred pounder with a square jaw and sharp blue eyes. She pictured him as a bigamist and philanderer, a professional gambler, a hypocrite, a con man, and a liar. At the same time, though with less emphasis, she portrayed him as a charmer, a gifted storyteller, a writer of soppy romantic poems and songs, a warmhearted (if often absent) husband and father who amply provided for her material needs and genuinely cared about the health and upbringing of their children. Frania testified that even after their decisive breakup, she taught her children to love and respect Hunt. Frania did not testify much about her own feelings toward Hunt, but she conveyed the definite impression that she had loved H.L. deeply and, despite all that had happened, probably still did. "He was a very unusual man," said Mrs. Lee.

On that point, not even the first and second families could disagree. The truly fascinating, frustrating thing about H. L. Hunt was not the size of his bank account but the richness of his character, the wealth of contradictions that coexisted in the same being. From an early age, Hunt believed that he was special, that the rules governing everybody else simply did not apply to him. And to a large extent, he was right. But in defying the ordinary rules, Hunt also defied the ordinary categories and definitions, making it well nigh impossible for most people to get a grasp on him or what he was really about. As his widow Ruth Ray Hunt once put it, "He was so very, very misunderstood."

Nowhere was Hunt more misunderstood than in his role as a patriarch. Frania Tye Lee's testimony did little to correct that misunderstanding. For reasons of law and litigation, her whole purpose was to show that she had been Hunt's wife, not merely his mistress. But in reality, both terms were irrelevant. H. L. Hunt had a powerful libido, an unquenchable sex drive. But whatever else they may have been, H.L.'s relationships with Frania and, later, Ruth were not just love affairs: they were deliberate attempts to produce families. As he once confided to a business associate, H. L. Hunt thought he carried a genius gene. He believed that by fathering children he was doing the world a favor, providing the human race with its future leaders, even as he provided himself with an ever-increasing flock of self-images.

The results of Hunt's fathering turned out to be mixed. He did create several very bright offspring. Some of his children showed both artistic and financial genius. But H.L. also fathered two children who suffered from incapacitating mental illnesses that even he sometimes feared were inherited straight from him. What's more, Hunt created a three-branched family tree whose members were destined to feud with each other long after he was gone.

However, as the proceedings in Shreveport pointed up, Hunt's most ambivalent legacy was the unanswered mystery of his own life. A loner from youth to old age, H. L. Hunt shared his true thoughts and feelings only with himself. He wrote two autobiographies and gave many interviews about his rise to riches, but not even his wives and children really knew what was going on behind his blue eyes. The first and second families could dispute the specifics of Frania's legal claims, but they could not deny that their late patriarch had led many secret lives. The task of outliving both an oversized myth and an unbelievable reality created constant conflict for all of Hunt's heirs. As one family friend put it, "When they're not fighting each other, they're fighting their old man's image."

At the trial in Shreveport, the three families of H. L. Hunt were fighting both of these battles and an even harder-fought war. For as the testimony progressed inside and the storm raged outside, each was forced to reconcile what he or she heard with what he or she already knew and felt and hoped and believed. Each had to fight within him- or herself to shut out or accept the most elusive image of all: a true picture of H. L. Hunt's life.

CHAPTER 2

HUNT HERITAGE

IN the opening pages of *Hunt Heritage,* H. L. Hunt attributed much of his success to his family heritage. "The Hunts," he wrote, "have long been among the most constructive of the early settlers in this country." H.L. then went on to claim descent from two of America's founding fathers. One of his claimed progenitors was the Reverend Robert Hunt, chaplain of Captain John Smith's Jamestown colony. The other was James Oglethorpe, founder of the Georgia colony. However, since neither Reverend Hunt nor Governor Oglethorpe left any children, both of these claims were impossible. But then pretending descent from the nation's founding fathers was a necessary part of the old man's image as a superpatriot. Or so he believed.

The old man also liked to trumpet his feats as a child prodigy and the special treatment he received as a boy. And he prided himself in what he had been able to accomplish with his special talents. At one point, H.L. even claimed that he was the most famous person ever to have lived in his part of Illinois. Since Abraham Lincoln also lived in the same part of Illinois for several years, that was quite a claim to have to back up. But then the old man was never one for false modesty. What's more, by the time he got around to making all these claims, H. L. Hunt was running Honest Abe a pretty fair second in the fame department.

The saga of the little-boy legend actually began with the Hunt family's trek from the East. Although some of H.L.'s forebears undoubtedly made it to the New World by the late 1700s, his first American ancestor of record was his grandfather, Captain Waddy Thorpe Hunt, who was born in Haversham County, Georgia, in 1821. After farming a 250-acre plot in Haversham County, marrying, and raising six children, Waddy Hunt decided to take the family west to Arkansas in search of new farmland. The year was 1860, and Waddy was a loyal southerner, but at the insistence of his Quaker wife Melissa, he freed the family's slaves when they crossed the Mississippi River. When the war broke out, Waddy joined the Confederate forces by enlisting in the Twenty-seventh Arkansas Infantry at Camp Bragg; he was made a captain and given his own company. That same day Waddy's oldest son enlisted as a private; he was nineteen years old, and his full name was Haroldson Lafayette Hunt, but everyone called him "Hash."

The Civil War nearly ended the Hunt family line before H. L. Hunt, Jr. got a chance to be born. In August of 1864, Waddy Hunt was shot and killed when a band of guerrillas raided the family's farm outside Little Rock. One of Hash's younger brothers was also at the farm during the raid, but his body was never found. The only good fortune in the tragedy was that the rest of the family was away when the raid took place. Three months later Hash was captured by Union troops and thrown into the federal prison in the recently overrun city of Little Rock. Had the war lasted much longer, Hash might well have joined the thousands of other Rebel soldiers who died in Yankee camps. Fortunately, five months after his capture, General Robert E. Lee signed the surrender at Appomattox.

Ravaged and weary, Hash and his family decided to move north to Illinois to escape Reconstruction. For reasons they never made explicit, the family settled in the southern part of the state in Fayette County, near the town of Vandalia. It may well have been that Vandalia was as far north as the Hunts could manage to go on the strength they had left. In any case, conditions there were hardly ideal. There was still plenty of government land available in Fayette County after the Civil War, but the best lots had already been taken by the earlier settlers, most of them Germans and Pennsylvania Dutch who had arrived in the 1820s via the famous Cumberland Road. Much of what was left was open prairie with grass as high as a man on a horse. And compared to central Illinois, even the better sections were not very fertile. The ground was hard. It had to be broken with a horse-drawn plow, and it took a strong man to handle the iron implement capable of doing the job. Eight acres was about the most one man could hope to farm by himself. Barring bad weather or blight, that might be enough for a man to support his family, but it was hardly the quick way to get rich.

Vandalia, (population 5,000), the county seat, was a once great city on a graceful decline. Formerly the state capital, Vandalia boasted a handsome Greek-revival statehouse building in the center of the town square and a legitimate claim as a former home of Abraham Lincoln. But thanks to a bill introduced by Lincoln himself, the Illinois legislature had long since voted to move the capital up to Springfield. Located seventy miles east of St. Louis and about ninety miles west of Terre Haute, Vandalia still served as a depot for several prosperous railroad lines and a market center for the region. But it did not promise to develop much beyond what it already was, and its sons and daughters were already in the process of leaving for the big cities.

Difficult as it was, Fayette County, Illinois, still looked a lot better to the Hunts than the Reconstruction South. With the $1,000 in hard cash she had managed to keep through the war, the widow Hunt purchased an eighty-acre farm north of Vandalia. Now the male head of the clan, Hash eagerly set about the task of making a new life. In December of 1865, fresh out of the Yankee prison in Little Rock, he married a nineteen-year-old local girl named Sarah Jane Wear. The couple had one son they called Thomas. A short time after the child was born, the mother died. In the summer of 1872, Hash, now a thirty-year-old widower with one son and much farm work to do, married again. This time his bride was a widow who also had one young son. Her name was Ella Rose Myers.

Ella was both beautiful and well educated. According to the family genealogy, she was descended from French Huguenot forebears who were "close to the Royal family in Paris" but who were nevertheless exiled from France in the Huguenot purge of the late seventeenth century. Instead of immediately leaving for the New World, the family crossed the border into Germany, where they adopted the name Myers, which derives from the German word for "agriculturalist." Samuel Myers, the first American immigrant, came over in 1797 and settled in Virginia, where he became active in buying and selling land. His son, David Myers, grew up to be a doctor and migrated west to Cincinnati and then to St. Louis, where, on September 30, 1843, his daughter Ella Rose was born.

As a doctor's daughter, Ella was encouraged to acquire a formal education, something most young women of the time were instructed to avoid. She entered Arcadia College in Arcadia, Missouri, at the age of twelve, and graduated in 1859, at the age of sixteen. After teaching school for a short time, she enrolled in the Woman's College at Jacksonville, Illinois, and still later, the Teacher's Normal School at Bloomington, Illinois. In the process, Ella became proficient in Greek, Latin, French, and German as well as in the accepted methods of education.

Ella and Hash were on opposite sides of the Civil War. After her mother died, Ella was raised in Murphysboro, Illinois, by the mother of General John A. Logan, a Union cavalry commander. When the war broke out, she was teaching in Murphysboro and still living with Mrs. Logan. Instead of remaining on the sidelines, she rushed to St. Louis, where her father was enlisting as a chaplain in the Union army. The good St. Louis doctor and his daughter thus set out for the battle lines to attend the sick and wounded. Though attached to opposing armies, Ella and Hash came within twenty miles of each other on several occasions during the fighting, but never met.

After the war and the death of her first husband, Ella gravitated back toward St. Louis. By the time she met Hash Hunt, she was pushing thirty but looked only twenty. She had sparkling blue eyes, a thin, resolute mouth, and thick brown hair that fell to her shoulders in long French spools. She posed for a postwedding photograph in a dark cape with an embroidered collar fastened at the neck with a brooch. Adopting the stiff postures of the day, she was a picture of poise with her back straight and her chin up, one hand holding open a pocket-sized double-frame case that rested on her lap.

Ella's new husband also cut a rather impressive figure. Broad-shouldered and over six feet tall, Hash Hunt dressed in heavy clothes and big riding boots. He had a large, square face, dark hair, dark eyes, and a dark look. With his thick brown beard, he bore a startling resemblance to the archetypal Republican figure of the postwar era, Ulysses S. Grant.

After his marriage to Ella, Hash moved his bride and family to the old Reed family farm at the Carson Township crossroads. The place featured a box-shaped, white, two-story house with an added wing that ran across the rear side, forming a T shape. Nearby, at the crossroad, were twin churches, the little Union chapel and the little Reed family Methodist chapel. As the Hunts settled in, Ella began bearing the first of eight children by Hash. The last of their children was born on February 17, 1889. Named after his father, Haroldson Lafayette Hunt, Jr. had his mother's sparkling blue eyes and creamy complexion. His older brothers and sisters quickly shortened his impossible handle to "Junior," then "Junie," and "June."

June Hunt was too young to remember his most famous childhood feat, but his older brothers and sisters would all insist that it happened in just this way. It was a bright, sunshiny day, and the gently rolling fields of the family farm were like oceans of gold in every direction. Every now and then a horse-drawn wagon would pass like a ship on its way to the muddy crossroads near the family's house. Migrant flocks of Canadian geese kept flying by overhead. Little June was out in the front yard. He was not yet three years old, and he was still wearing one of his baby dresses. His father, whom he called Paw, was arguing with a buyer about the price of hogs.

"Junie," Paw said, "go in my bedroom and bring me the *St. Louis Globe-Democrat*. You'll find it on the desk or the dresser."

June turned around and ran inside the house. A few moments later, he came back with the newspaper and handed it to Paw.

Paw fumbled around as if he could not find his reading glasses. Then he handed the newspaper back to June.

"Junie, read me the St. Louis livestock report," Paw said just as naturally as if his son read it to him everyday.

June nodded. Then he brushed off the front of his baby dress, unfolded the newspaper, and commenced reading the business page.

"Hogs—Receipts, 3,900 head; shipments, 1,500 head; market 10 cents lower; fair to best selected $5.10 and $5.20 . . ."

Paw smiled as if little June's performance was merely routine, but the hog buyer nearly fell off his feet. June's older brothers and sisters were equally stunned. Word about the incredible reading ability of young June Hunt soon spread all over the county.

Shortly after that episode, June Hunt began wearing trousers. In addition to his reading skills, little June demonstrated a precocious talent for numbers. He loved to perform feats of arithmetic, fast computations, and difficult multiplication problems. He was an avid baseball fan, and later delighted in reeling off statistics about his favorite players and teams. But most of all, he loved to apply his numerical talents to playing cards. One of the Hunt children's favorite card games was Authors. Much like a later variation called Fish, the game required a player to empty his hand by matching his cards with cards traced from other players' hands or drawn from the deck. The game called for luck, a willingness to gamble, and a good memory for cards. Little June had all three. In fact, June seemed to have a special memory for cards. After only a brief glance at an upturned deck, he could then name each card in sequence almost without error, for the face of each card would flash in front of his mind's eye like a photograph. Not surprisingly, June quickly proved able to trim his older siblings at Authors or just about any other game they cared to play.

As the baby of a big family, June was automatically pampered and lavished with attention. As a child prodigy, he received even more special treatment. In addition to getting out of most of the farm work, June did not have to attend classes at the schoolhouse with the other children. Instead, he was allowed to stay home from school and take his lessons from his mother. June and his mother had a special relationship. She rewarded his mental feats by allowing him to continue nursing at her breast long after he exchanged his baby dresses for proper trousers. When he became an old man, June would recall his extended breast-feeding in much the same way he recalled his prodigy feats. Although he did not write about the subject in his books, he made it clear in private discussions that he was not ashamed of his overweaning. On the contrary, he saw it as still another indication that he was fundamentally different from other people, innately special, not bound by the ordinary rules of behavior.

Then, one day when June was seven years old, a serpent of sorts entered the garden. According to the story he told a few close confidents many years later, it all began when June was out in the yard flipping cards at the base of a big oak tree. Triumphantly, he called the name of each card out loud before he turned it over.

"Six of spades."

Flip.

"Seven of diamonds."

Flip.

"Queen of hearts."

Flip.

Abruptly, June stopped flipping cards. He listened. He heard a voice. Or thought he did. It was his mother calling his name.

"June . . . Junie . . . Junior."

June gathered up his cards and stuffed them in the pocket of his trousers. Then he started running across the yard toward the house. The house looked very big and very white next to the trees. Up at the crossroads, the twin churches glistened in the sun.

June ran inside the house. It smelled of kerosene and things cooking. He went into the kitchen. He saw his mother kneading dough. That made him feel good. One of the best things about staying home from school was the very special treatment he received from her. Not long before, June's father had caught him at his mother's breast. Paw had said something about how June was getting a little old to keep nursing, but June did not want to stop.

June lifted a small crate from the kitchen floor and carried it over to where his mother was standing. Then he set the crate down, stepped up, and reached for his mother's breast.

His mother smiled. Her crystal blue eyes sparkled. She loosened her blouse and kept on kneading dough.

All of a sudden, there was a heavy sound at the door. Paw strode into the kitchen with his dark beard and big boots.

June was still standing on the crate when his father came into the room. Husband and wife exchanged narrow-eyed looks. Then June jumped down from the crate and ran outside.

With his father's intrusion, June Hunt's breast-feeding stopped, and life around the family farm became increasingly difficult. June still kept getting special treatment and special privileges. He still performed his mental feats. But he no longer reigned as the favored son, the prodigy child who could do no wrong.

Not surprisingly, June's greatest influence continued to be his mother. Although she stopped rewarding his precociousness with turns at her breast, she still allowed him to remain home from school to take his lessons from her. The old man and his mythologizers would later make much of the fact that he lacked much formal education. But he could hardly have gotten better instruction in a rural schoolhouse than what he got from his mother at home. A veteran schoolteacher, Ella Hunt made sure her boy wonder plowed through all the elementary reading primers and took some of the same final exams the other children took. She simply enabled June to do it at home and at a much faster pace than normal.

In addition to developing her son's mind, Ella tried to look after little June's soul. "I remember listening to my mother . . . incessantly reading to me from the Bible in Greek, Latin, French, and German, then translating the passage into English for my benefit," June would write many years later. Ella also taught her son songs from the Methodist hymnal, and saw to it that he was washed and scrubbed and attentive when the family attended Sunday services at the Methodist chapel at the crossroads. Sitting on those hard wooden benches, the little boy heard typically Wesleyan sermons about duty, thrift, responsibility, and love for God and fellow man.

In one of his more selfless moods, June Hunt would later give his mother most of the credit for his highly touted mental capabilities. As he wrote in *Hunt Heritage,* "my mother was the wisest and smartest person and the best teacher I ever knew."

June would not have such glowing things to say about his father. In *Hunt Heritage,* he referred to his father as "a handsome, gentle man who could administer discipline when it was required." However, he confided out of print that he believed his father was a little crazy. He added that he also believed that he had inherited some of that same lunacy himself. June Hunt never elaborated on what in his father (and in himself) he regarded as crazy. When he got around to writing his autobiography, he revealed his inner feelings about his father only by the things he did not say, the praise he did not give. At the same time, though, he also wrote about the lasting examples his father set for him in many areas.

The most important field June's father introduced him to was business. During the period of June's childhood, American farmers were changing from subsistence farming to commercial farming. They were, in short, becoming businessmen. June's father personified the new breed. Though lacking his wife's formal education, Hash Hunt was himself pretty handy at reading, writing, and arithmetic. He also knew how to spot an opportunity. In addition to raising his own crops and livestock, he took advantage of his proximity to the crossroads by starting a kind of midway market. He set up a rack of scales a few hundred feet from the house, and began buying and selling his neighbor's produce. He would then drive the remaining stock up to the railroad connection at the Nichols Prairie junction. Hash got the *St. Louis Globe-Democrat* every day, and kept a careful eye on the prices of the Chicago markets. Every so often, he would take the train up to Chicago and put some of his livestock profits into commodity futures speculations.

Hash's system paid off. By the time he reached mid-life, the former Rebel private had increased his original 80-acre stake to more than 500 acres and was regarded as one of the leading citizens of Fayette County, Illinois. As Hash well knew, his prosperity was assisted by the fact that Ella gave him five boys. Combined with the children from their previous marriages, that brought the Hunt family's total male work force to eight. Hash Hunt had eleven other mouths to feed, but, as his sons grew older, he also had plenty of able bodies to help him manage the family property.

Having shown off his precocious mathematical skill, young June was put to work on the family's market scales. Local farmers would drive up in horse-drawn carts full of hogs, calves, wheat, and corn. Little June would mark the weight on his father's order forms. Then the farmers would drive off, unload, and drive back again to be weighed with their wagons empty. June would mark the weight again, compute the difference, and give the farmer a ticket for his produce. The job made an indelible impression on young June. The family's profit on each wagonload depended on the accuracy of his computations at the scales. And, as June's father did not let him forget, every pound and penny counted. The boy knew he could count on a motherly kiss if he performed one of his mathematical tricks. But he also knew he could count on a fatherly thrashing if he erred at his ticket writing.

Hash Hunt also introduced his boy to what June would later classify as "scientific risk taking." Like his brothers, June eventually got to go along on his father's trips to the Chicago futures markets. There he would watch his father place their bets on futures prices after long consultations among themselves about upcoming crop and weather conditions and anything else under the sun they thought might affect the prices. June loved all the numbers involved and the idea of probabilities. It was all like a giant arithmetic trick. Of course, as June noted to himself, there were a lot of unknown factors involved, a lot of things that could change without warning. Cards were a lot more reliable than commodity futures.

If things seemed to come easily to June Hunt, they had not come so easily to his father. Hash Hunt had ripped his success from the earth, and he never let his sons forget how hard the work had been. At times, when the load got particularly heavy, Hash would curse the unyielding Illinois hardpan, and pine long and loud for the South. In particular, June and his brothers often heard their father mention an area he had fought at during the Civil War, a place in the Mississippi Delta country called Ditch Bayou, Arkansas. There the land was as rich as anywhere on earth, their father said. Farming land like that would not be work, it would be a pleasure.

In addition to passing on his dreams, Hash imbued June with his politics. As he prospered, Hash had joined the Republican party. That in itself said a lot about him and how far he had come since the Civil War. This was the tail end of the Gilded Age, the era when the spoils system dominated government and the robber barons dominated the economy. By the time young June was born, there was mass unemployment in many parts of the country, and strikes were breaking out in all the major industries. Seven-eighths of America's wealth was owned by only 1 percent of the population. Andrew Carnegie was making an income of over $20 million per year from his steel operations, but the average American working man's total *annual* wage was only $500. William Jennings Bryan and the Populists had whipped up the farmers with cries of agrarian reform and free silver coinage, and Grange movements were growing all over the land.

Of course, Hash Hunt had now become more of an agribusinessman than a farmer and had done rather well at a time when many of his fellow countrymen had not. Considering his success the result of hard work and Christian discipline, Hash was naturally attracted to the mainstream conservatism of men like William Henry Harrison and William McKinley. On a local level, he soon became active in Fayette County affairs. In 1889, the year of June's birth, Hash became the first county supervisor from Carson Township. Five years later, in the fall of 1894, he ran for and won the job of county sheriff on the Republican party ticket. As one local historian later remarked, "the main occupation of a county sheriff was to put himself in a position to make some money once he left office." Hash Hunt did just that. Taking typical advantage of the spoils system, he won re-election to a second two-year term in 1896, then returned to his farming interests. A short time later, he opened up a bank in the town of Ramsey, Illinois.

Since the local polling place was at the crossroads a hundred feet from his house, little June could not help but see and hear his father's political action. And since he had a brother who fought in the Spanish-American War, one of the nation's early imperial ventures, he was aware of foreign-affairs development, too. June was also aware that his father's increased prosperity (the opening of the family's bank) followed his tenure as sheriff. And June noticed that his father seemed to become an even bigger and more influential man as he got richer. While there was never any evidence of scandal of corruption in Hash Hunt's politics, the patronage system in his county operated like most other Illinois Republican patronage systems in that period. Fiery-tongued reformers would label that system graft, corruption, the fix. But for practitioners like Hash Hunt, the patronage system seemed like a natural part of the political process, a modern institutionalization of the ancient *quid pro quo*. For June Hunt, that system became the formative political microcosm, his original model of how things worked.

The political talk June heard at home was heavily laced with notions borrowed from the prevailing philosophy of the day. Known as social Darwinism, this world view was based on the simple action "survival of the fittest." Just as Charles Darwin's *Origin of Species* had described biological evolution as an ongoing struggle which the best adapted win, the social Darwinists regarded social evolution as a battle between the strong and the weak. Those who came out on top deserved to win by virtue of being fittest. The haves had a right to their riches because they were clever enough to amass them in the first place. The have-nots' only hope was to keep struggling. Of course, in the social-Darwinist view some groups were innately advantaged, and others were innately handicapped. The former group tended to include mostly white Anglo-Saxon Protestants, the latter blacks, Mexicans, Poles, Italians, and so on. Jews fell into an in-between category. They were advantaged by virtue of their intelligence and financial skill, but they were disadvantaged by virtue of being Jews.

Popularized during the nation's second great wave of immigration, social Darwinism appealed to a broad spectrum of Americans. The poor and the middle class could use it as a justification for their hatred and prejudice against the new immigrants. The rich could use it as a justification for their exorbitant wealth. To the extent that the survival of the fittest depended on hard work, the new philosophy even meshed with the predominant Calvinist morality. But social Darwinism was essentially amoral. Taken to the extreme, it allowed each man to fend ruthlessly for himself while calling it the law of God and nature, not to mention the American way.

Despite being a child prodigy, June Hunt did not recognize himself as one of the world's youngest social Darwinists. But he did read about the theory of evolution, and he could understand a concept like survival of the fittest with no trouble at all. The kind of talk he heard at home—and the kind of life he led with nine older brothers and sisters—fit right in with that way of looking at things. In addition to enhancing his own feeling of specialness by touting the virtues of Anglo-Saxon heritage, this sort of thinking made young June increasingly aware of other people's national, ethnic, and racial backgrounds, and made him prone to generalize about them and their behavior. It was not race hatred per se that he was picking up, but a view of the world that categorized people in much the same way biologists were characterizing plants and animals. Despite its limitations, it was a belief structure young June would carry with him all his life. And, like just about everything else he touched, it was also something he would take well beyond its ordinary limits.

In addition to picking up his father's political beliefs, June also developed an interest in nutrition. Hash Hunt believed that steer meat was more healthful than any other beef. He bought calves, yearlings, and two-year-old steers, grazed them, then put them on a full feed of corn and hay. He fattened his steers for twelve to fourteen months. When they graded prime, he culled out several for family consumption, and shipped the rest to market. Whether or not Hash's theory had any validity, it made his youngest son conscious of healthful and unhealthful food at an early age. This, too, would be something that stayed with him all his years.

Of course, June Hunt hardly spent all his time at his father's knee. Being at the crossroads, the Hunt household was something of a gathering place for young and old. In addition to growing up with a flock of siblings, June was also in frequent contact with children from all over the surrounding countryside. Despite the notoriety he had received for his mental abilities, most of the other children regarded June as just one of the bunch. He went hunting and fishing and horseback riding with them. He came along on the annual trip to Mattoon for the broom corn harvests.

June also explored the pleasures of nearby Vandalia. Though only eleven miles from the Hunt farm, the trip to Vandalia took half a day on horseback when the roads were good. When the roads were muddy, the trip could take much longer. But for June, the trouble was well worth it. There was his father's office in the old statehouse building in the center of town. There were the railroad station and the wagonworks, the baseball team and the never-ending stream of patent medicine salesmen, hucksters, and dream merchants who passed through the town peddling their exotic wares. The new things that were coming to the world came to Vandalia long before they came to the countryside. Things like paved streets and telephones and news of the next new marvel. June Hunt also got a taste of the big-city world from time to time. In addition to accompanying his father on business trips to Chicago, he went on regular family trips to St. Louis, including an outing to the Louisiana Purchase Exposition in St. Louis in 1905.

As he grew older, June continued his feats of prodigy. When he was nine years old, for example, he took the elementary finishing exam given to the eleven- and twelve-year-old groups. Although he had no formal preparation for the test like the other students, June finished second on the test behind only his brother Leonard, who was two years older. Such performances naturally pleased June's mother. So, too, did his fondness for reading. After finishing the first five reading primers, June avidly plunged into the daily newspapers.

At the same time, June became something of a cutup. One of his more charming episodes centered around his remarkable performance on the elementary finishing test. Having scored the second highest on the exam, June found himself bestowed with the dubious honor of giving the salutatorian's speech at the little graduation ceremonies. Though the ceremonies were to be held in the Hunt family house and brother Leonard was the valedictorian that year, June was terrified at the prospect of having to give a speech. Performing card tricks and arithmetic feats were one thing; oratory was another. June handled the situation in a Huckleberry Finn manner by swallowing a wad of tobacco. When the time came, he was simply too sick to speak.

Not all of young June's behavior was so amusing. After the end of his extended breast-feeding, June became more and more a double-natured child. Part of him was still the exuberant child prodigy who was interested in everything and most pleased with himself and his abilities. But another part of June seemed older than his years, and not particularly pleased with himself or anything around him. In this persona, June was stubborn, insistent, authoritarian, and, most of all, distant. Already accustomed to playing by himself while his siblings were at school or work, June became even more withdrawn. He did not talk a great deal, even when there was no graduation speech to give, and he often played alone even when the other children were at home. Increasingly, he became prone to go away by himself for long periods of time. This was not so much shyness (although there was some of that), but a kind of voluntary separateness. June was just a natural loner. Or so it seemed.

As June reached his middle teens, his father grew impatient with him. June was not in school, and he expressed no interest in attending college. What's more, June seemed increasingly disinclined to work on the family farm. He no longer jumped at the chance to operate the market scales, and he seldom volunteered to help his father and brothers with the routine farm chores. He did not even show an interest in the family's new bank. All he seemed to want to do was practice his card tricks. But Hash Hunt, for one, was no longer impressed with his son's precociousness. On the contrary, the former sheriff was coming to regard his youngest son as lazy, the black sheep of the family.

In truth, June was not lazy so much as restless. Operating the family's scales no longer provided an opportunity to show off. Beating his brothers and sisters at cards was also losing its luster. Having been exposed to places like Chicago and St. Louis, June knew that Vandalia was hardly the end of the world. In fact, in reading the local newspapers, he often came across ads like this:

IS BUSINESS SLOW AT HOME?

Then why not investigate what other localities offer?

The chief centers of Southwestern mining, manufacturing, farming, and stockraising industries are found along the Santa Fe Route.

For ticket rates and full particulars of the country, address.

J. W. TEDFORD
General Agent, 108 North Fourth Street
St. Louis, Missouri

While June did not exactly have his mind set on starting a business, he was definitely interested in investigating what other localities had to offer. June had been born at a pivotal time in his country's history. In 1889, the year he was born, the U.S. Army wiped out Sitting Bull and the last of the Indian war parties. In 1890, the U.S. Census brought the nation an equally dramatic piece of news. According to the Census, the West was now "so broken into by isolated bodies of settlement" that it was no longer possible to identify a continuous line of virgin frontier anywhere within the nation's borders. An unorthodox young historian named Frederick Jackson Turner seized upon these events and produced a remarkable new thesis of American history. As he saw it, all of America's history up to that time had revolved around the existence of free land and the westward push of civilization as it filled up that land: "Now, four centuries from the discovery of America, at the end of a hundred years of life under the Constitution, the frontier has gone, and with it has closed the first period of American history."

Historians would later dispute Jackson's thesis, but there was no denying that a transformation was under way. Though the great saga of capturing and taming the continent had come to an end, new frontiers were dawning. Some were in foreign lands, some were above the ground, some below it. Others were in machine shops and test tubes. There were the years of the great world-changing inventions: the electric light, the telephone, the automobile, the airplane. Mass production was becoming the new mode of economic organization, and the United States was establishing itself as a world power. Life in America was changing faster and more dramatically than ever before.

As he wrote later, June Hunt had read Horace Greeley's advice to "go west and grow up with the country." He was as curious as the next lad to get out in the world and take a look for himself before everybody else got there.

June's restlessness also grew from internal sources. One of the boy's central conflicts was his growing rift with his father. As an old man, June would recall that his father and brothers wanted him to qualify as a bank clerk. He wrote later, "This may have added to the lure of the West for me, as I had no interest in the banking business and believed that the borrower always had the much better of transactions between himself and his banker. In later times in my business I seemed always to be the borrower."

A photograph of June Hunt at age sixteen provides some striking insight into the young man's character and conflicts. Dressed in a white shirt and tie, he stands quietly erect with his hands to his sides, his hair parted down the middle and combed back in neat locks at each side of his forehead. His mouth is slightly downturned, his eyes are unsmiling. There is, in the corners of his mouth and the stoop of his shoulders, a suggestion of the arrogant, self-possessed whiz kid. At the same time, his too-short tie and clean, washed face give the impression of a mama's boy still wearing clothes he has long since outgrown.

One fine day in 1905, not long after the photograph was taken, June decided to make his move. He packed up a few clothes, then went down to Vandalia Station and caught a freight train bound for Kansas. His traveling status was "ship, ticket free," which meant he was going to work his way along the trip. Having left home without anyone's permission but his own, June had not one cent to his name. However, in his bedroll there was a deck of cards.

June Hunt hardly looked special just because he was working his way west. America's turn-of-the-century railroad yards bustled with all sorts of other fellows who were doing exactly the same thing. Some were ordinary tramps, bums, and hobos, eternal penniless itinerants never really intending to go anywhere or do anything. But many others were men of purpose, or at least intention, men who really were going west in hopes of starting a new life. In addition to the whites who now considered themselves only American, there was a rainbow of nationalities and races: blacks, Mexicans, Jews, Irish, Swedes, Poles, and on and on. Many still wore the vestments of their former occupations, bankers' suits, butchers' aprons, cowboy hats, farmers' boots, lumberjacks' shirts. Although there were men of all ages on the trains and the railroad gangs, most of the fellows were in their late teens, twenties, or thirties, young men starting out in life.

The only thing that appeared special about June Hunt was his age. At sixteen, he was by no means the babe of the railroad yards, but he was among the youngest of his fellow travelers. At the same time, though, he was getting close to six feet tall. He had broad shoulders and a good back, and, as he later put it, he could "pass for a laborer."

June's first stop was Horace, Kansas, a little depot town about 450 miles west of St. Louis. There he took the first of a string of jobs: dishwasher. His place of employment was the restaurant at the railroad depot. While working there, June was taken in by the wife of the man who owned the railroad yards. The woman mothered him and looked after his diet. He stayed about a month. When he decided it was time to hit the road again, his surrogate mother discreetly passed the word to some of the older hands on the train to keep an eye on the young fellow. When June reached Colorado, the train men told him about the woman's gesture, and he blushed with embarrassment. After that, he determined to be truly on his own.

Near Pueblo, Colorado, June got a job topping sugar beets. Then he moved up to Utah, where he herded sheep into railroad cars at the stockyards. Finally, one of the buyers put him in charge of a shipment on its way to Los Angeles. Upon his arrival, the shipper awarded him one dollar. With that dollar as his first bankroll, June set out on foot for Santa Ana and the great Irvine Ranch, following the railroad tracks like highways.

When he got to the ranch, June signed on as a "long-line skinner." That meant he drove a mule team. There were ten mules to each team, hitched two abreast, and they pulled a "gang plow," which was really five plows nailed together. The job was the toughest June had faced yet. "We worked in the field from sunup to sundown," he recalled later, "and each driver cared for his team of 10, currying them and bedding them down at night in straw, clearing the stalls, and currying them again in the morning before harnessing and treating them as though they were thoroughbred horses." Sometimes the animals could be plenty ornery no matter how much love and care they received. "Nearly every mule would kick at his rider whenever a fair target was offered." They did not have to rear up like a horse and kick with two feet, but some of the mules could strike with one front foot as effectively as a well-trained boxer could strike with one hand.

Later, Hunt was promoted from driving the mule team to driving a "four-up of great horses," hauling carts of olives picked from the ranch's groves by migrant groups of Japanese farm workers. He was also assigned to a crew charged with planting a row of eucalyptus trees as a windbreak against the hot, dry gusts blowing in from the desert. This latter job provided him with a lasting health tip, for by the time he left the ranch he noticed that the oil from the eucalyptus pods was good for relieving coughs and respiratory problems.

After leaving the Irvine Ranch, June headed north to San Francisco, where he twice came close to disaster. The first near miss occurred shortly after his arrival. In need of a place to stay, June followed up on a newspaper advertisement for a rooming house near the bayfront. When he checked into the rooming house, June was put in a room with several other men. He immediately became suspicious. As he had heard, it was notoriously difficult for ship captains to recruit crewmen for long Pacific voyages; as a result, many of the captains resorted to drugs, alcohol, assorted trickery and deceit, and sheer physical force to drag both sailors and inexperienced landlubbers aboard ship to fill out their crews. These tours on the sea sometimes lasted two years or more. During that time, a man was virtually a slave. Many never lived through it, especially those who struggled against their captors. Since the Chinese port of Shanghai was the chief destination on these transpacific voyages, the name for this unsavory form of commercial conscription was "shanghaiing." Fearful that the rooming house he had checked into was a trap for shanghaiing crewmen, June quietly slipped out of his quarters and ran for his life.

Several days later, his courage renewed, June returned to the rooming house to inquire about the other men assigned to sleep in his room. He was told that the men had gone off on a whaling ship.

About this time, June heard about tryouts for a semipro baseball team in Reno, Nevada. He decided to leave San Francisco and take a crack at being an athlete. A few days after his departure, San Francisco was devastated by the earthquake of 1906. As it turned out, June did not make the Reno baseball team. (He later complained that the reason for his failure was a shoulder injury sustained in handling a runaway mule.) But when he heard about the San

Francisco quake, he realized that the baseball tryout may have saved his life.

Following his adventures on the West Coast, June worked his way down to Texas. There he had a rendezvous with his brother Leonard. A lean and sickly young man, Leonard joined June's road trip. The Hunt boys first got jobs planting cattle-feed crops outside the town of Amarillo. Later, they got work in town with a crew laying concrete for sidewalks. Here June displayed some of the take-charge side of himself. The signal incident occurred one day when the concrete-pouring foreman did not show up for work.

"I can run this thing," June announced to the crew, "so let's get on with the job."

The crew followed his instructions, and began pouring the concrete. When the boss finally did show up, he was not impressed. Instead of rewarding June for his initiative, he fired him on the spot. However, before he left, June managed to write his initials in the wet concrete. Years later, as an old man, he would go back to Amarillo, look for that sidewalk, and discover that his initials were still there.

The Hunt boys hung around Amarillo just long enough for June to add one more job to his résumé: chicken cooker. The recipe he used was a simple parboiling process, but it was something that would stick with the young man for the rest of his life. In later years, as he grew to look more and more like the Kentucky colonel who cashed in on his own method of cooking chicken, June Hunt would wistfully regret not capitalizing on what he called "my specialty."

Oddly enough, one of the few types of jobs June did not get in Texas or anywhere else on his journey was a job in the oil fields. Although the 1901 Spindletop well that ushered in the oil age was located near the Gulf Coast, there was plenty of oil-business activity developing in north Texas and California, not to mention in June's home state of Illinois. In fact, back in 1874, a farmer had discovered oil on his property near Mattoon, Illinois, about fifty miles from the Hunt family farm. Two years before June was born, oil was discovered in Terre Haute, Indiana, which was also not too far from the Hunt farm. In the 1950s, there would even be an oil boom less than a dozen miles from June's boyhood home in the Louden field. But as luck would have it, June Hunt would miss out on the oil reservoirs he was born on top of and on many of the yet undiscovered fields he passed in his youthful wanderings.

After the sidewalk-construction episode in Amarillo, the Hunt brothers moved on to the Grand Canyon, then up to the Flagstaff area, where they got jobs as lumberjacks in the San Francisco Timber Reserve. June Hunt was fast approaching his adult height of six feet tall, and he was proud of the physique he was acquiring through his labors. He later wrote in *Hunt Heritage* that his lumberjacking so "built up my arms and shoulders and trimmed down my waist to where it caused considerable comment sometimes in later years." He then went on to brag that a few years later, when he stopped to buy a suit, a group of men approached him and asked if he would agree to be the next white hope to fight against famed Negro boxer Jack Johnson. June declined the invitation but never stopped retelling the story.

What also caused considerable comment during June's years on the road was his remarkable ability at cards. Honing his talent for numbers, he became what he called a "card locator," one of those gamblers who tried to memorize the sequences of the cards played in one hand hoping that if poorly shuffled, the cards would come up again in roughly the same order in the next hand. This method would have been useless in fancy casinos, where the decks were changed with each new hand, but June played his games in railroad yards, flophouses, bunkhouses, farmyards, and logging camps, places where his natural mathematical mind could really stand out. At the same time, these games were maturing. June was no longer playing his brothers and sisters for peer points. He was playing against grown men, most of them strangers, for real money. But, as he found out, June was as good on the road as he had been on the farm. Having made many of his games in the western states, the young man from Illinois eventually picked up the nickname "Arizona Slim."

On occasion, June played cards so well that he got into trouble for winning. One such instance occurred while he was working at a logging camp near Flagstaff, Arizona. The camp was on a railroad branch line worked mostly by a white gang. There was also another branch a few miles away that was being worked by a Mexican gang. June used to go down to the Mexican camp after work and play cooncan, a game played with a Spanish deck missing the eights, nines, and tens. One evening, June was sitting outside with a group of card players, dealing the cards on an overturned crate. After a while, June began to win and win big. Soon, there was a regular procession of men going back and forth to the bunkhouse to get fresh money for the game. June kept on winning. Finally, the money started to dry up. By this time, June had won about $400, and was ready to fold for the evening. He put his winnings in a tobacco sack, stuffed the sack in his pocket, and started heading down the railroad tracks back to his own camp.

Back at the bunkhouse, the Mexican laborers were still chattering excitedly about how much the young gringo had won at cards. A few of them seemed to be gathering around a handcar parked on the tracks June was following.

June kept on walking until he had rounded a curve not far from the camp. Then he ducked into the woods and began running. It was six or seven hard miles back to his camp via the woods, but June knew that if he kept following the railroad tracks, the Mexican gang could overtake him with the handcar and rob him of his winnings. He ran all the way back to camp.

That night, June bedded down without a word to anyone. With heart-pounding sureness, he was convinced that news of his big winnings would make him just as much a target in his own camp as he would have been alone on the railroad tracks. Making his bedroll next to a tree, he stayed awake all night. Several times during the night, he felt hands patting his blankets in the darkness. Or thought he did. The next morning, early, he hit the road again.

In the fall of 1906, June interrupted his odyssey to take a stab at attending college. The way he told it later, the impetus for this seemingly strange decision came from a card game he played during a wheat harvest in the Dakotas. One night, June happened to beat one of his buddies out of $260. That was all the money the fellow had, and since June happened to be fond of him, he tried to get the fellow to take his money back. The man refused. Then Hunt offered to give him back $100 of his winnings, then $50.

"No," the man kept saying, "I don't need it."

"I don't need it either," June said. "What would I do with it?"

Finally, the man said, "You could go to college with it."

"How could I?" June replied. "I've never been to grade school."

June never did get the man to take his money back, but he did start thinking about going to college. He had heard of a school in Indiana and, on an impulse and his card winnings, decided to give it a try.

The name of the school was Valparaiso University, and it was located in Valparaiso, Indiana. June stayed only two semesters. "I tried to take everything," he recalled later. "Latin, algebra, rhetoric, I think they called it, zoology, some kind of history. By the end of the term I was standing second in my class. I was also playing a lot of poker. With those older fellows it was like shooting fish in a barrel. After the start of the second term, though, I got sick. It was a very severe form of tonsillitis that I used to get. Finally, I had to drop out. I went home for a while and never went back."

June Hunt soon hit the road again, traveling to California, Washington, and back to Montana and the Dakotas. He stayed on the road for four more years. All that time, he was working at odd jobs and playing cards. He was up in Canada in the winter of 1910, when he got a telegram from home. His brother Leonard, who had been mysteriously ailing for the past few years, had died. June immediately returned home through the snow. In *Hunt Heritage,* he recalled little of the feelings—if any—he had about his brother's death. Instead, he concluded this episode, and the second chapter of his life story, with a strange, almost emotionless, discussion of how his face froze while he was riding in the sleigh on the way to the railroad station. "The driver stopped the sleigh," he wrote, "and I got out and bathed my face amply in the snow before going on. By the time I got home to Illinois, my face showed no ill effects from freezing and has never given me any problems."

After Leonard's funeral, June struck out for the West again. This time he was on the road about a year when he was called home again. His father had taken ill and was being moved to a hospital in St. Louis. On March 24, 1911, Hash Hunt died at the age of seventy-one. He was buried in a cemetery outside Vandalia.

By prevailing standards, the late H. L. Hunt, Sr. died a comfortably wealthy man. His land holdings amounted to over five hundred acres, he had large stocks of cattle and pigs, and he owned the People's National Bank in Ramsey, Illinois. His worth at the time was in the neighborhood of $100,000. When the estate was divided, June inherited the family house at the crossroads and eighty acres. This was by virtue of the fact that he was the youngest, and could thus be expected to keep the farm in the family for the longest time. June also received $5,000 in cash. Though hardly enough to retire on for the rest of his life, that was no meager sum for a young man to inherit in 1911.

Having spent the better part of six years on the road, June Hunt had to decide where to go next. June's brothers tried to persuade him to stay around the crossroads and help with the family's farm and bank. For a while, he complied, but his heart was not in Illinois. The child prodigy was now an inch over six feet tall and twenty-two years old. He had been a dishwasher, a beet topper, a sheep herder, a mule-team driver, a semipro baseball reject, a crop picker, a concrete pourer, a lumberjack, and a fair roadside gambler. Most of all, he had been an adventurer. He still had no interest in routine farm chores or even banking. But he was far from lazy. Now more than ever he was brimming with unchanneled energy, a drive, a lust, an urge.

As he wrote later, June Hunt interpreted these stirrings as "the urge to get out on my own in the world and start a new venture." After a few months in Illinois, he packed some clothes, withdrew his $5,000 inheritance from the bank, and said good-bye to his family once again. This time, however, he had a specific destination in mind. Remembering his late father's praise for the rich delta soil around Ditch Bayou, Arkansas, June thought he spotted a rare opportunity in the southern farmland. Cotton prices were then soaring. If the land around Ditch Bayou was half as good as his father had portrayed it, June could rush down and make a tidy little sum in no time at all. This would not be just humdrum farming, but full-fledged crop speculation. It would be like cards. It would be gambling.

Thus with visions of easy money dancing in his head, the young man who had already gone west struck out for a new life on the Mississippi. Just before he left, June stopped to pose for a photograph down by the railroad tracks. He was dressed in a brand-new flannel suit, a stiff white collar, a striped bow tie, and shiny black shoes that buttoned on the sides. His brown hair was cut short on the sides with a fall-away lock curling over his forehead. He stood on the platform with his head and shoulders cocked back to his right at a slight angle, his hands gently gripping a round-brimmed boater he held about waist level. When the camera shutter clicked, the lens caught him with a curiously tentative expression on his face, neither smiling nor frowning. Except, perhaps, for the intent look in his eyes and the suggestion of smugness in the turned-down corners of his mouth, there was no hint that he was not just an ordinary railroad passenger, but a young man with a very special future in store.

CHAPTER 3

LUCK, LYDA, AND OIL

THE town of Lake Village, Arkansas, had two things going for it in the fall of 1911: the lake and the land. Unlike the more prosperous city of Greenville, Mississippi, a few miles away, Lake Village was not a river port. However, the little inland town did nestle against the western shore of horseshoe-shaped Lake Chicot. The lake was about a mile wide and about three miles long, with the ends of the horseshoe pointing back to the east toward the Mississippi from whence it came. Most of the lake was muddy and still, edged by flat, unexciting thickets of trees and cane brake, but it was nevertheless much admired by the local citizenry for its "beauty." The lake was also imbued with an air of mystery and adventure. Legend had it that Lake Chicot was the grave of Spanish explorer Hernando de Soto. The name "chicot" was said to be derived from the Moorish word for "unlucky."

Spreading out from the lake shore toward the western horizon was some of the best-looking farmland in North America: low, flat alluvial fields lush with row after row of cotton. One local historian would later claim that the Lake Village area had "by scientific analysis, the richest soil in the world; richer than the valley of the Nile." No one bothered to dispute it. Before the Civil War, the planters of Chicot County had produced 40,000 bales of cotton per year. That was more cotton than was produced by any other county in the United States save one. By the early 1900s, cotton had begun its comeback, and there was a lively land boom in progress on the Greenville side of the river. But on the Lake Village side, where the soil was just as rich, if not richer, land prices were still relatively cheap, and there was plenty of opportunity to get in on the action everyone believed was coming.

By the time June Hunt showed up in town, Lake Village was bustling with the first signs of the expected boom. The population had swelled from 150 to over 1,500, and Main Street was being paved all the way from the new railroad depot to the edge of the lake. Half a dozen stores, seven saloons, and a handful of offices lined the sidewalks. The county courthouse, which stood next to the spirelike Civil War monument at the east end of Main Street, had been completely rebuilt with mortar and brick. The citizenry was now a diverse lot. There was still a tight knot of the old Confederates, but there was also a good number of Yankees who had come down after the war, an occasional Jew, a fairly large contingent of Italians up from New Orleans, and a residue of former slaves. Most of the people lived in modest homes along the lake front or in tumble-down farmhouses and shacks. There were only one or two sizable mansions, and these were in the process of decline. Automobiles had been available for several years now, but everyone in Lake Village still relied on horses and mules.

June took a room in the Lake Shore Hotel with a view of Lake Chicot, and invested most of his inheritance in a 960-acre tract about six miles south of town. The location was called Boeuf Bayou, but it was not far from Ditch Bayou, the site of Hash Hunt's memorable Civil War encounter. June then took the rest of his money to Little Rock, where he bought a freight carload of horses and mules. When he returned to Lake Village, he sold off all but two of the mules (Dolly and Maud) and one of the horses (Spirits), and set to plowing his fields for cotton planting. As he wrote later, "With 960 acres of the most fertile soil in the world, I was ready to make my fortune."

Given the land June had chosen, there was a high probability he would be successful, but there were also a number of inherent pitfalls. As he would recall in later life, many people could appreciate the risks in gambling or drilling for oil, but few could appreciate the great risks in cotton farming. There was, first of all, the risk of too much rain, which could rot the crops, and the risk of too little rain, which could leave the crops dry. There was also the threat of the hated boll weevil and the malicious army worm. Finally, there was the threat that materialized: flooding.

When June arrived in Lake Village, the Mississippi River had not flooded the local area in thirty-five years, but in his first year as a cotton farmer, the river went on a rampage. The problem originated forty miles north of Lake Village at the point where the Arkansas River empties into the Mississippi. Warned of the impending danger, the citizens of both Lake Village and Greenville rallied to the riverbanks and worked feverishly to build up the levees. Their work was to no avail. Although the Mississippi itself stayed below the levee line, the backwaters simply came up behind the levees. Like many other local farmers, June Hunt saw his entire crop wiped out. He waited helplessly as his land remained underwater for three months. The experience led the young man to formulate an axiom that would serve him well in his subsequent business ventures: "Probabilities are not always dependable."

In the meantime, June Hunt determined to make his living by his most tried and true skill: playing cards. As an old man, he wrote that "the Mississippi River plantation owners were among the best poker players in the world, if not the best, and . . . I learned a lot from them." Whether or not that assessment was exaggerated, there is no question that the Mississippi planters also learned a lot from June Hunt. Playing cards became June's all-day occupation. In the mornings and afternoons, he would work the Lake Village side, playing in a little room upstairs above Forte's store on Main Street. In the evenings, he would go up to Luna Landing and catch the ferry to Greenville, where he would play all night. Not surprisingly, he got to be very, very good.

June's easiest marks were the Lake Village folks. Relative bumpkins compared to their Greenville neighbors, the local civic leaders could not help but take a turn at matching wits with the young farmer from Illinois. But the few tricks June had learned as Arizona Slim, the king of the bunkhouse circuit, were too much for the naïve Lake Villagers. The way June bested—and busted—the local mayor exemplified his dominance. Like most of the other Lake Village men, the mayor was one of the tightest card players June had ever come across. When he got good cards, he showed it in his betting. He never bluffed. He just did not seem to have it in him. So when June would bluff him out of a pot, he would "accidentally" throw in his hand so that the mayor could get a glimpse of his hole card. After that happened a couple of times, June sensed that the setup was complete. Having seen June's success at bluffing, the mayor could not help but try the trick himself. The next hand, he shoved out a big stack of chips to cover what appeared to be a straight flush.

"Oh, oh, he's got it," the other players cried, and folded their cards.

June, who showed a pair, did not budge.

"I've got a notion to call you," he said to the mayor, "just for practice."

The other players thought June was crazy—until the mayor flipped over his hole card. He did not have a thing. June reached over and raked in the pot.

The games June played in Greenville did not afford such easy pickings. Then a city of some 10,000 people, Greenville was the busiest cotton loading port between Memphis and New Orleans and one of the most cosmopolitan communities in the South. Many Greenville men had made their money gambling on cotton and land, and learned their card games from the endless stream of riverboat gamblers who passed through town via the Mississippi. They were sophisticated in their betting and bluffing, and proud of their skill. Most of their big games were held at the Planters Club or at the Mississippi Club. Both establishments were located above the shops on Poplar Street. The Mississippi Club, which was the more high-toned of the two, consisted of six different rooms, including one which had an extra-long table for the really big games.

Playing in the big games at the Planters Club and the Mississippi Club was considered a privilege by the betting men of Greenville. The fact that June Hunt, at age twenty-three, gained entry to the big games was itself a measure of how good a card player he was. Every other player at the table was generally ten or twenty years older than he. Here, June could not pull the simple ruses that fooled the mayor of Lake Village and the others back across the river. Instead, he was forced to push his natural mathematical mind and his luck to new limits. If the games in Lake Village provided his bread and butter, the games in Greenville gave him the opportunity to improve himself by losing as well as winning. June suffered innumerable ups and downs. He was flush one day, flat broke the next. But through it all, he developed an ability to remain unruffled, a stoic coolness in the face of boom or bust, that would pay him great dividends for the rest of his life.

When not playing cards, June would go over to the Greenville race track and bet the horses. Here, too, his luck varied, but he kept right on placing his wagers and calculating the probabilities. Later, he managed to gain an edge by entering his own horse in the races.

When not at the card table or the track, June spent a great deal of his Greenville time at a restaurant called Frank's Cafe. Frank's was the town's first counter-style eating place, and it was open twenty-four hours, serving such items as hamburgers for five cents and Irish stew for fifteen cents. The owner, Frank Ciolino, was a member of Greenville's thriving Italian community and a popular local character. As he suffered the vagaries of the gambler's trade, Hunt found Frank's a hardy refuge—mainly because Frank often agreed to carry him on the tab.

One reason Frank Ciolino so readily extended credit to the young gambler was their mutual friendship with one Frank Grego. A swarthy, dark-haired Sicilian whose family had settled in Greenville, Grego was the first in a long line of mysterious sidekicks that would accompany June Hunt through the adventures of his life. Details of Grego's background and occupation were scanty. His sister Louise was an up-and-coming local opera star who eventually made a name for herself in Chicago opera circles. Frank Ciolino was Grego's uncle. By most accounts, Grego operated as a kind of local don in Greenville's Italian community. Remembered as a sincerely good-hearted fellow who was always anxious to do favors for his friends, Grego had helped his Uncle Frank set up his restaurant business and had performed many similar services for the other Italians in town. They, in turn, repaid his favors with free meals and other favors in kind.

Grego and June Hunt met over a card game at the Planters Club. Like the young man from Illinois, Grego considered himself a pretty fair player, but he recognized that the truly exceptional player sat across from him at the table. After the game, Grego and June formed both a friendship and a partnership, June played the role of "the talent," the gifted card shark with all the guts. Grego played the role of "the management," the energetic procurer with all the contacts. In addition to introducing June to the local opera house and his attractive sister, Grego helped arrange for his man to get in the big card games down in New Orleans. Together, the two traveled up and down the river, winning and losing fortunes with each deal of the cards.

Back in Lake Village, June spent a great deal of his nonpoker-playing time hunkered over a checkerboard. In the minds of most of the Lake Villagers, he played so slow it was aggravating. He always had to figure out just where he was going to go before he moved. And he concentrated. Even in checkers, June always played to win. And he usually did win. If poker was his money game, checkers was his ego game. He seldom played checkers for a big pot. In checkers, the prize was pride. In later years, June would boast that he was not only "the checkers champion of Chicot County," but also "the best in the world."

Not surprisingly, everyone in Lake Village soon came to regard the newcomer from Illinois not as a cotton farmer but as what he really was: a professional gambler. However, few people in town looked down on June for his chosen trade. On the contrary, his skill made him a local celebrity. "Although he was a poker player, he never did anything dishonest," remembered Lake Villager Sam Forte. "Somehow he just managed to inspire confidence. People trusted him."

At the same time, June Hunt impressed his elders as being a bit peculiar, a confirmed loner, and mystery man. At the poker table, the other players spent a lot of their time joking and drinking and complaining about their luck. But not June Hunt. A nondrinker, he played seriously and with few words, concentrating instead on remembering what cards had been dealt and calculating the probabilities of what cards would be the next to fall. Away from the poker table, June was much the same: quiet and private.

"You couldn't get a word out of him," his brother-in-law Hal P. Sessions recalled years later. "His conversation wasn't open. He did his own thinking and his own gambling."

June's often-reserved manner made him seem unfriendly to many of the townspeople, who prided themselves on their southern warmth and hospitality. Most of Lake Village addressed the young man formally, calling him "Mr. Hunt" to his face. But behind his back, they sometimes poked fun at his Yankee origins and muttered threateningly about "the blue-bellied slob" who did nothing but play poker all day and all night. These slurs eventually reached June's ears and made a lasting impression. Though he would later emerge as the champion of the far right, though he definitely preferred the South to the North, June never became a flag-waver for the Confederacy.

In truth, young Hunt was not unfriendly so much as wary and wily, an up-and-comer with his eye out for a main chance. He gave a rare clue to the real nature of his quietude one day when a poker-playing buddy finally asked him why he spoke so little.

"What I've learned," he replied, "I've learned by listening."

One of the few times June Hunt did open up a bit was when he got around the young ladies of Lake Village. As he wrote years later, June was "definitely girl-minded" in his Lake Village days, and was pleasantly surprised to find that the little east Arkansas town had more than its share of pretty girls. "I had known cowgirls in the dust storm country," he would recall, "and the comely young ladies of Lake Village with their soft drawl fascinated me."

In contrast to the cowgirl-bunkhouse circuit, the young Lake Villagers' world was a genteel whirl of watermelon parties and ice cream socials. At night, the young "town crowd" would go over to each others' houses, where one would play the piano while the others danced or played cards. Curfew was at 10:00 P.M. In the daytime, one of the most popular recreations was horseback riding.

Already well known around town for his ability at cards, it was on horseback that June liked to show off for the young ladies. Each ride would begin with his horse, Spirits, whom he had trained to buck playfully, putting on a display of rearing up on his hind legs, dipping, and prancing.

"The girls did not know that I had worked with wild horses," June wrote years later, "and they would 'ooh' and 'aah' at my antics in the saddle."

One of those who "oohed" and "aahed" was Mattie Bunker, June's first sweetheart of record. A sprightly, dark-haired lass, Mattie Bunker was one of the most popular girls in Lake Village. She had a fine singing voice and could play the piano as well as any young lady in town. The two met in 1914, when Mattie was eighteen years old. In young Hunt, who was seven years her elder, Mattie saw a fascinating and experienced fellow who could be quite talkative when he wanted to be.

"He had a way about him that captivated people," she remembered. "He had a lot of personality, and he was very popular with the younger set. He had been so many places, and he could tell so many stories."

At the same time, Hunt impressed her as being very different from the southern boys, much more of his own man, eccentric but somehow charming. "He would come in from the farm with mud on his shoes and he wouldn't clean it off," she recalled. "He'd come right out on a date with the mud still on his shoes. He was just different from the other suitors. I don't know any other way to say it."

As fate would have it, young Hunt's special qualities did not go unnoticed by Mattie's older sister Lyda Bunker. Then age twenty-five, Lyda was about one month older than her younger sister's suitor. She was a gentle-natured, well-educated young lady, but not an exceptionally beautiful one. About five feet two inches tall, she had curly brown hair, big brown eyes, and high, regal cheekbones. But she tended to be plump, and this made her features appear overround and puffy. She dressed neatly and conservatively, and, in accordance with the customs of the day, did not wear lipstick or make-up. Having attended high school in Lake Village, Lyda had studied at Maddox Seminary in Little Rock and Potter College in Bowling Green, Kentucky, where she majored in voice. An amateur painter, she was also an accomplished pianist and organist. After finishing school, she had become a schoolteacher in Jonesboro, Arkansas. She sang in the choir at Jonesboro and in the choir at the Methodist Church in Lake Village. Like young Hunt, she was known as a listener rather than a talker.

The original romantic encounter between Lyda and June had its share of obstacles. In addition to June's ongoing relationship with Mattie Bunker, there was Lyda's ongoing relationship with another man. Although Lyda's beau lived twenty miles away in Dermott, Arkansas, the two of them were far along. They were not yet engaged, but it was almost to that point, and it appeared that a wedding announcement might come any day. However, when Lyda came home to Lake Village for summer vacation in 1914, she fell in love with young Hunt. Whatever it was that her sister Mattie had found was so "different" about the rakish gambler-farmer from Illinois took with Lyda Bunker.

Shattering the "love quadrangle" that had now formed, Lyda broke off her relationship with the man from Dermott that fall and engaged to marry Hunt.

June's sudden proposal came at an unusually vulnerable time in his life. In September of 1914, while in the midst of courting Lyda, he received word that his beloved mother had died in Illinois. The favored boy had lost the one who favored him most. If the young man was a loner by nature, he was now more alone than he had ever been, a wandering Yankee without nearby relations or local ties. He had already suffered one major financial disaster in the flood of 1912. He now saw a world of increasing uncertainty. World War I had erupted in Europe in the summer of 1914. Cotton prices were spiraling higher and higher, but June still faced a continuing series of ups and downs in both gambling and planting.

Lyda Bunker offered something June had not enjoyed since boyhood: both emotional and financial security. Like his mother, she was a schoolteacher, an intelligent and cultured woman with a matronly way and a subtle strength of character. She also had the kind of background and lineage he would prize so highly as an old man. The Bunker family not only traced its ancestry back to the whaling captains of Nantucket, but also to the royal family of England and William the Conqueror. But where June's later claims about the Hunt family lineage would turn out to be exaggerated, the Bunker's claimed line of descent would be verified by reputable genealogists. Nelson W. "Pop" Bunker, the father of the bride, was one of the pillars of Lake Village. A wiry, stoop-shouldered man with a white handlebar mustache, Pop Bunker was also a transplanted Yankee and a Republican. He had come to Lake Village after the Civil War to work as a carpenter, and had gone on to prosper as a grocery-store owner, cotton ginner, and landlord. He had also served as the town's postmaster and the commissioner of several local improvement districts, as well as a sort of freelance banker. As one of his relatives put it, "He loaned a lot of money to people, and if you paid him back, you could borrow more."

With the blessing of June's new surrogate parents, the Hunt-Bunker wedding took place on November 26, 1914. It was a simple ceremony in the Bunker family's home on Lake Shore Drive. Lyda's mother served a fried-chicken dinner before the marriage. Then everybody gathered in the parlor. None of June's relatives had come down from Illinois, and he did not have a best man, but there were enough Bunker children and related folk on hand to fill the room. Lyda's sister Mattie played a wedding march on the piano, and the couple joined hands to take their vows. Then the young man who was destined to become the world's richest human being consummated the ceremony by giving his bride a plain gold band.

After the wedding, Lyda and Hunt moved into what one relative later described as "a little old nigger shack" out on the Boeuf Bayou cotton acreage. The place had four rooms and a porch across the front, but the roof sagged and all sides were in need of repair. At Lyda's insistence, the couple soon moved back into town and took up residence in one of Pop Bunker's rent houses next door to the Lake Shore Hotel. This house was a neat frame house, not much bigger than the shack, but far cleaner and better maintained.

Not long after that, Lyda was pregnant. The Hunts' first child, a girl they named Margaret, was born in Lakeview Sanatorium, the only hospital in the area, on October 19, 1915. Two years later, on November 23, 1917, a son was born. His ecstatic father named him Haroldson Lafayette Hunt, Jr., a handle later shortened to "Hassie." Relatives could quickly see that the boy was his father's greatest pride and joy, in part by the fact that instead of naming him H. L. Hunt III, which the child properly was, June literally gave his son his own name.

Despite becoming a father and family man, June Hunt spent the years following his marriage to Lyda in much the same way he had spent the years preceding it. Still a professional gambler by occupation, he continued to make the poker circuit with his sidekick Frank Grego, kept on betting the horses, and kept on spiraling through an endless series of ups and downs. In the summer of 1917, America entered World War I, but June's name was not called in the lottery. Instead of voluntarily going off to war, he stayed in Lake Village and speculated in the long-awaited land boom.

With the wartime economy pushing cotton prices up to a giddy $625 per bale, the land-trading action quickly grew to be faster—and riskier—than the action at the poker tables. The accepted method of deal making required only a small down payment coupled with large promissory notes, a practice that afforded the opportunity to make big profits on very little cash—as long as land prices kept rising. If prices fell, a voracious speculator could find himself in trouble. In order to get out of a deal, the buyer could not simply let the seller repossess his land. He had to find someone else to buy the land at a higher price. Otherwise, the seller could continue to hold him accountable for his promissory notes.

June Hunt took to land dealing like a bee to honey. He had a natural poker player's gift for trading and for sizing up people. Despite his lack of formal education, he also had an easy facility with titles and contracts, which, he once bragged, he could draw up as well as any lawyer. Accustomed to taking big risks, he leveraged his cash as steeply as any man around and managed to get several hundred thousand dollars ahead by the time the war boom began to peak.

Then he made a double miscalculation. Sensing that the boom might soon be coming to an end, June sold all his cotton and sold short on the futures market. His bet was that prices would go down. Eventually, of course, they did, but not before they went up even higher in the few months immediately following June's sellout. June lost everything. When the recession he had predicted finally arrived a few months later, he had no stake left with which he could try to short the market and recover his losses. To make matters worse, June was stuck in what was then a very big land deal for him. The deal involved a 2,500-acre plantation in Louisiana. June and some partners had bought the land with a little cash and plenty of promissory notes. By 1921, cotton had dropped from $625 to $50 a bale, and land prices were plummeting, but the seller of the Louisiana plantation land would not let June and his partners out of the deal.

With his back against the wall, June once again turned to his most reliable source of income: playing poker. The legendary game that saved the family farm took place in New Orleans shortly after June's disaster in the cotton market. Young Hunt had taken his daughter down to New Orleans to have a doctor look at her tonsils. While he was waiting, June wandered over to the Grunewald Hotel and got into a high-powered poker game. Sitting around the table were some of the most fabled card players in the region, men with names like Jinks Miller, White Top, Indian Jack, and John Crow. But the Illinois boy with the poker-playing name Arizona Slim made himself right at home. Wagering the last $100 he had to his name, he started to win and win big. The climax came in a hand that pitted him one on one against Jinks Miller.

When the first up-and-down cards were dealt, June got a small pair. The player next to him had an ace and opened with a moderate bet. Jinks Miller also had an ace showing, and matched the bet, but did not raise. June threw in enough to match, and waited for the next cards. By the time the last card was dealt, there were no pairs showing, but Jinks Miller had a king sitting next to his ace. He made a big bet, and most of the other players threw in their cards.

June thought carefully. The probability was that Miller did not even have a pair, for if he had had an ace or a king in the hole, he would have raised the bet the first time around. June decided to call.

His hunch proved correct. Miller had nothing but the ace and king that showed on the table. June took the pot with a small pair. A few moments later, as the next hand was being dealt, Miller seemed to jerk in his seat as if hit with a sudden realization. As June recalled later, "I knew he had figured out how I knew I had him beat."

June kept on winning into the night. By the time he got up from the table, he had run his original $100 stake into $10,000. He took his daughter Margaret back to Lake Village with his pockets full of cash.

Like his previous big winnings, June's score in the New Orleans game was quickly dissipated by more card games and land-speculation deals. Not surprisingly, his wife Lyda was growing increasingly impatient with her husband's ways. She had returned to teaching school in order to provide the family with a steady income, and she was constantly struggling to make ends meet. At the same time, she realized that her Mr. Hunt was almost congenitally unsuited to anything but gambling and speculating, and that she would probably be destined to spend the rest of her life on a financial roller-coaster ride.

"June," she would say, "why don't you get a regular job?"

June would look at her as if she had just suggested that he cut off his right arm. Without even bothering to reply, he would take off for Greenville or New Orleans and return with just enough cash to tide the family over until the next financial crisis.

Then something happened that changed the Hunts' lives forever. According to his later recollections, the depression of 1921 found June Hunt holding some 15,000 acres of cotton land. Then almost thirty-two years old, he was resigned to holding the land and, despite being short of cash, was on the verge of buying still another tract from a family named Noell. However, as the negotiations for the new acquisition began, one of the Noells began talking about the depression and the way people from all over the country were flocking to the oil boom in El Dorado, Arkansas, a town about seventy miles west of Lake Village. June heard that workers and speculators were overflowing the town just as oil was overflowing the ground, and that people were sleeping in railroad cars and automobiles and just about every other place they could crowd into. At first, June was only mildly interested in the Noells' tales of El Dorado, but as their land transaction dragged on into the late afternoon, the boom talk began to excite him. June excused himself from the negotiating table momentarily and went outside to gaze at the setting sun.

"What is it that you are trying to do?" he asked himself as he stood alone on the porch. "Are you going to bury yourself here for the remainder of your life? If this land ever regains its price, you already have about 15,000 acres and you will be rich. Why not rent out the land and let it come back in price, if it ever will? Why not go to this oil boom instead of investing in more land?"

The more June thought about El Dorado, the more it sounded like the sort of opportunity he had been waiting for. Without further ado, he went back inside the house, and announced to the Noells that he was no longer interested in buying their land. Then he got on his horse and rode back to Lake Village to lease out his plantation land.

Although June held thousands of acres of some of the country's richest farmland, most of his assets other than land were inferior second, third, or fourth mortgage notes. With the depression on, no one had much cash available, least of all June Hunt. June tried to raise a small grubstake from Lake Village's two small banks, but both institutions turned him down. Finally, he managed to arrange a $50 loan from three prominent Lake Villagers: Sam Epstein, the department-store owner he described as "my Jewish pal"; R. D. Chotard, a county official of French descent; and Pete Mulligan, an Irish timberman.

As it developed, none of the men who comprised June's melting pot of investors wanted to accompany him on his first trip to the boom town. Instead, June left Lake Village with his faithful sidekick Frank Grego, his brother-in-law Hal Sessions, and a young merchant named Frank Tushek. The four of them drove out of town in a borrowed Model T Ford, and puttered the twenty miles to the train depot in the town of Montrose. There the flat delta farmland stopped abruptly against the great wall of the south Arkansas forest. June parked the car near the station, and he and his four companions boarded a train for El Dorado.

The railroad cars were packed with other passengers bound for the boom. Like the Lake Village contingent, most of the men aboard the train appeared to have stopped in the middle of whatever they had been doing to join the oil rush. There were farmboys in overalls, blacksmiths with leather aprons, bankers in three-piece suits, cowboys with chaps and spurs and Stetson hats. The scene was heavy with cigar smoke, excited male chatter, and the press of winter-wrapped bodies jammed together in too small a space.

All of a sudden, the train lurched forward, and the day began to darken as the locomotive chugged into the forest and down an endless corridor of giant trees. Through the windows, June and the other passengers could see every kind of tree species imaginable: post oak, red oak, black oak, willowjack, dogwood, mulberry, elm, and loblolly pine. The ground became a deep reddish brown, more claylike and more rolling. Then, about two hours out of Montrose, near the banks of a little stream called Mathis Creek, the forest cleared for El Dorado.

From a distance, El Dorado did not look like much of a town. There was a water tower, a new dome-roofed Baptist temple, a courthouse building, a couple of four-story hotels, and a spreading brownish mass of houses, shacks, and tents. But as if to assuage the doubts of any new arrivals, there was a hand-lettered sign not far from the railroad depot which read: "AS BRIGHAM YOUNG SAID OF THE UTAH VALLEY—THIS IS THE PLACE."

"All I need is a deck of cards and some poker chips."

That was the first thing June Hunt said to his companions when they stopped off the train to look around. It was not hard to see why. By the late January day in 1921 when the Lake Villagers hit town, El Dorado had turned into one of the biggest crap shoots in American history. Once a sleepy little lumber and farm-market center of 4,000 people, "The Place" had taken on a population of 10,000 newcomers in only a few weeks, and hundreds more were arriving every day. Almost every one of the new arrivals had the same objective: to get rich quick. Whatever else it may have been, El Dorado was a professional gambler's paradise.

Most of the action centered around South Washington Street, a two-lane thoroughfare which ran from the railroad depot up the hill to the four-story Garrett Hotel. There were people everywhere on South Washington Street, pressing around the railroad station, spilling over every sidewalk, lobby, and door jam. The boomers had long since overflowed every hotel in town. Now every available hallway, nook, and cranny was packed with sleeping cots. Tents had been thrown up to shelter still more cots in the vacant lots between the buildings. The local citizens were renting out spaces in their own homes for $3 a night. Barber chairs were going for $2 a night.

Even the city fathers had gotten in on the action. First the city council had voted to rent out the town's recently completed city hall as office space for $1,000 an office. Then the council had voted to rent out the sidewalks. The result was Hamburger Row, a rickety line of wooden shacks thrown up on the eastern sidewalk of South Washington Street. In addition to hamburgers, this makeshift shopping center offered everything from hats and shoes to automobiles, oil leases, and fortune tellers. "Cot runners," most of them teenage boys, scurried up and down the row shouting, "Clean beds one dollar."

And still the boomers kept coming. Trains were arriving at the rate of twenty-two per day. Memphis, St. Louis, Shreveport, Chicago, New York. The people came from all over. Some drove into town in brand-new automobiles: Overlands, Fords, Dodges, Saxons, Stars, and Pierce Arrows. One group of boomers arrived in a three-seater airplane direct from Oklahoma City. Still others arrived on horseback or in wagons and buggies. El Dorado boasted five paved blocks around the courthouse square, but the rest of the streets and roads were dirt. With the winter rains and the unprecedented influx of people, many of the thoroughfares in and around town were nothing but mud. At some points, farmers laid down planks of wood across the mud bogs—so-called "Arkansas gravel"—and charged exorbitant tolls to let a traveler cross. At other points, mule skinners positioned their teams to provide passage at 50 cents a pull. Many times, the bogs were so deep that they swallowed up whole teams, driver, skinner, helpers, harness, mules, and all.

As June Hunt and his companions quickly discovered, lawlessness prevailed. In addition to conventional businessmen and speculators, the boom had drawn all manner of hustlers, con men, prostitutes, moonshiners, murderers, and thieves. The situation had long since gotten out of the control of the local police. Vice was becoming institutionalized. The chief centers of lawlessness were the "barrelhouses," combination saloons, gambling halls, and whore houses, so named because drunken customers often had to be hoisted into a barrel and literally rolled away after a hard night's entertainment. The most notorious concentration of barrelhouses was on Pistol Hill, a little knoll a few hundred yards from the center of town that sported such establishments as Dago Red's, Blue Moon, and Smackover Sal's. Dancing cost 25 cents. A six-ounce bottle of moonshine cost $1.25. Prostitutes came in two main varieties: ordinary street hookers, who prowled the barrelhouses and the cot tents on Hamburger Row; and "oil-field doves," who worked the barrelhouses by night and journeyed out to the oil fields to service the workers by day. Many came to town posing as seamstresses or stenographers. They cost anywhere from $2.00 up, the same as barber chairs.

Of course, the main attraction in El Dorado was not the prostitutes nor the poker tables nor the barrelhouses, but black gold. The harbinger of the black-gold boom stood on a gently rolling plot of farmland about a mile southwest of town. It was called the Busey-Armstrong No. 1 well, and it consisted of a rickety wooden derrick about fifty feet tall, some used steel pipe, a gnawed steel drilling bit, and an old-fashioned steam-boiler engine. June and his friends could see the top of the derrick merely by venturing a block or so from the railroad depot. There was a constant flow of traffic back and forth between the well and the town, and a great milling of people about the drill site at all hours of the day and night.

As many of the boomers sensed and hoped and fervently believed, the Busey-Armstrong No. 1 well was ushering in a whole new, horrifying, and magnificent era for Arkansas. By this time, oil had become the lifeblood of the U.S. economy. The ever-industrializing nation was producing over 442 million barrels of oil per year, up from a mere 63 million barrels a year in 1900, and there were now over 9 million automobiles in the land. Although oil sold for only $2 per barrel, it was the way to instant riches. The new addendum to the American dream was to find a reservoir of black gold beneath the family farm. Before the Busey-Armstrong No. 1 well, the people of Arkansas had almost given up hope of sharing in the national oil bonanza. Oil and gas had first been discovered in the vicinity back in 1901, right after the Spindletop discovery in Texas, but none of the strikes had been large enough to develop commercially. Then, in April of 1920, the Constantin gas well blew in on a tract of land about two and a half miles southwest of El Dorado.

The Constantin well produced a little bit of oil and gas and a great deal of panic. Having in effect punctured a huge underground gas pocket, the well set off a series of frightening natural reactions. Amidst a continuing rumble, the earth threw up huge globs of mud. Hundreds of giant craters imploded. The ten acres around the well site became a moonscape. Gas fumes blew everywhere. Crawfish died in their holes. Creeks and water wells as far as four miles away gurgled with the escaping gas. Irate farmers refused to drink the water. A few months later, the well became a holocaust when someone came by and lit a match. The fire killed five people and raged out of control for weeks, lighting up the entire countryside night after night with an awesome yellow-orange flame hundreds of feet high. But for all its horrors, the well was of great importance to the men who drilled it and to its terrified onlookers, for it rekindled hopes that there really was oil and gas in them there pine hills.

The Busey-Armstrong No. 1 well confirmed those hopes with a roar and a rush. It had all began about 4:30 on the afternoon of January 10, 1921, when the well started to rumble. The wooden derrick shuttered violently. The earth shook as if in prelude to an enormous quake. Then, a thick black column of oil, gas, and water shot through the top of the derrick. The great black plume gathered into a giant mushroom cloud, and the wind scattered the spray across the countryside. Sheep on a farm a mile away turned black. In El Dorado, white clothes on the wash lines dripped oil. The whole town bathed in black gold.

With that, the boom was on. By the time June Hunt and his friends made the scene, El Dorado was the mecca for one of the greatest gambles of the twentieth century. Before the year was out, over 50,000 new residents would move to town, and the lives of all concerned would be irrevocably changed.

That first night in El Dorado, June's three companions from Lake Village paid for lodging in a private home. June, however, managed to finagle a room in one of the hotels. This put him in a much better position to look things over, get the feel of the action. He obviously liked what he saw. The next day, Sessions and Tushek were ready to return to Lake Village, but June and his sidekick Frank Grego decided to stay on.

Ignoring the oil and gas trading that was going on all around him, young

Hunt headed straight for the card tables. The way he told it later, this was where he proved that he was "the best poker player in the world." That claim was a combination of brag and fact. The potential in a boom town like El Dorado was not lost on other accomplished professional gamblers, and the Hunt-Grego team did face contingents of high-powered talent from all over the country. Whether or not these players qualified as the best in the world was open to debate, but there were a great many sharpies in the bunch. And by all accounts, Hunt, as everybody knew him, did more than hold his own. Three times he sewed up in the biggest game in town. His competition knew all there was to know about cheating, but as news of his winnings spread, word got out that Hunt was onto some new form of cheating. In actuality, he was just relying on what he rightfully regarded as his "superior skill"—his natural mathematical mind and the poker sense he had honed during his years on the Mississippi. He was also relying on his soon-to-be-famous Hunt luck.

Like any good gambler, Hunt kept looking for a new edge. Before long, he quit being just another poker player and became "the house" by opening up a gambling hall of his own. Located at the lower end of South Washington Street across from the shacks of Hamburger Row, it was a cramped, dimly lit place, but a profitable one for Hunt. A few weeks later, he moved his operation to larger quarters in an old hotel building up the street. The place was basically one big room, about fifty by twenty-five, that was filled with card tables and chairs. There was no bar, no food service, no whoring, no dancing—just poker, blackjack, and dice. Later, Hunt opened up another gambling hall in nearby Junction City.

In the meantime, Lyda and the children remained in Lake Village. Hunt would make the trip home to see them on odd weekends, but he had no intention of moving his family to El Dorado at this stage in the boom. El Dorado was a dangerous place day or night, especially for a man who operated gambling halls. The kind of characters Hunt dealt to and dealt with included not only all sorts of freelance outlaws and rowdies, but members of the Little Rock and Hot Springs gangs and reputed Mafiosi with connections on the East Coast. Even when grown men from Lake Village would arrive to take a look at the boom, Hunt would advise them, "Stay off the streets at night."

Heedless of his own advice, Hunt proved he could hold his own with the slickest of the lot. His most fabled encounter was with Alvin "Titanic" Thompson, a hefty and supposedly unbeatable golfer and gambler with ties to the New York mobs and the Arkansas syndicate. Shortly after the boom began, Thompson came to town and won a pile of money from some local citizens on the golf course and at pistol target shooting, then set up a bookmaking establishment. One day, Hunt placed a large poker bet with Thompson and won. Thompson had to wire his eastern connections to get enough money to cover his losses. Now badly in the hole, Thompson challenged Hunt to give him a chance to win back the money at a game of Hunt's choice. Hunt leaped at the offer.

"I'll take checkers," he said.

Amused at such an unusual selection, the massive Thompson got a checkerboard and began to practice. Then he heard that Hunt had told a friend checkers was his second skill to poker and that he was champion of Chicot County. Fearful of losing still more money, Thompson slinked out of town before the scheduled match could take place. When word of Thompson's ignominious departure got out, Hunt became a kind of folk hero among the gamblers of El Dorado.

Hunt also established a remarkably good reputation among the respectable citizens of the community. Despite being a professional gambler, he was known for his honesty, for being a man of his word. Policemen and other law-enforcement officials frequented his places only to insure order and safety, never to break up the game. Though there was no evidence it was even necessary for Hunt to put the obliging police on his payroll, he was known for spreading his money around thoughtfully. If a local bank ever got a bad check from one of his games, Hunt would personally redeem it with cash. Often he got the cash from a large supply of silver dollars an admiring teller at the National Bank of Commerce secretly maintained for him without even the bank president's knowledge.

Respected as he may have been, Hunt and his gambling halls were as much a part of the general lawlessness of the El Dorado oil boom as were the barrelhouses of Pistol Hill. The boomers brought in a tremendous amount of money, and the local people were willing to tolerate a lot. But after a time, there was a backlash. El Doradoans grew tired of watching the newcomers trample their town and their moral order. In the late summer of 1921, the El Dorado city council finally took the initiative by voting to close down and remove the shacks of Hamburger Row. The city also hired a posse of new lawmen and dispatched them to clean up the barrelhouses.

These official actions were, in turn, accompanied by the enforcement efforts of a number of vigilante groups, most notably the Ku Klux Klan. Like the Klan of early Reconstruction days, the born-again KKK of the 1920s devoted itself to midnight cross burnings and to posting "Nigger, Read and Leave" signs around the countryside. But its "modern" thrust was a more general reaction against moral decay. Its enemies were Catholics, Jews, immigrants, and vice, and its members were often the most respected men in the community. In south Arkansas, the KKK focused its rage on the gambling, drinking, and whoring of the El Dorado oil boom.

One night in 1921, the Klan visited the gambling hall owned by Hunt. A line of twenty or thirty white-robed marchers stood outside as the KKK leaders entered Hunt's place with torches burning. The patrons stopped their card and dice playing and stared in fear and disbelief. Hunt stepped forward to meet the challenge.

"Shut this place down," the Klan leader commanded waving his torch. "Shut it down or else . . ."

Hunt simply stared back at the Klansmen without saying a word. The standoff continued for several very long moments. Then the Klan leader turned with a flourish of his torch.

"Shut it down or else," he said once again and walked out the door.

After the Klan's departure that night, the gaming continued, but Hunt began considering another career change. He was not a man who was easily intimidated. On the other hand, he was not a fistfighter or a gunslinger either. Gambling had been good to him—better, in fact, than any other occupation. But even without the threat of local vigilantes, he was becoming increasingly attracted to the biggest game in town. Shortly after the KKK's midnight visit, Hunt decided that the time had come to try his luck in oil.

As an old man, Hunt and those who knew him would tell at least half a dozen different stories about how he got started in the oil business. The most popular one, which itself had several variations, was that he won his first oil lease in a poker game. But while that story certainly made a good tale, a fitting early chapter in the Hunt myth, it was not quite what happened. What money Hunt had in his early El Dorado days most assuredly came from gambling. That was his profession, his occupation, his primary source of income. During the games at his gambling hall and elsewhere, many a player matched the bet with oil rigs, oil leases, oil production, mule teams, and just about every other available asset. But in Hunt's case, getting into the oil business was a calculated investment of his cash winnings at the poker table, not just another lucky windfall.

The way Hunt told it in *Hunt Heritage,* his quest for black gold began when he and a partner heard that a trader, "Buckshot" Coleman, was selling half-acre leases—the oil-business equivalent of five-acre "ranches" or subdivision "mansions"—on a plot of ground near the Busey-Armstrong well. Since the plots were so small, they made it possible for almost anyone with a little money to get in on the drilling action. Hunt and his partner, whom he identified only as "a trader who was brother-in-law of Texas governor Pat Neff," bought one of the half-acre tracts. A short time later, Hunt bought out his partner and commenced to search for drilling equipment. He found an old drilling rig sitting on the side of the railroad depot because of unpaid freight charges. Hunt paid the freight and the demurrage, and had a teamster haul the rig to the well site about three miles away. Then, drawing on the good credit he had established as a professional gambler, he bought and borrowed the rest of the equipment necessary to make the drilling rig run.

Appropriately, Hunt struck oil with his very first well. This came as no surprise to most of his friends in Lake Village, who were by now familiar with the Hunt luck. When he returned to Lake Village for a family visit after completing the well, Hunt formed a corporation and sold stock in the well to two eager local investors. The prospect, known as the Hunt-Pickering No. 1 well, looked exciting. As Hunt wrote in a letter to one of his backers, the property was "surrounded by splendid flowing wells." Unfortunately, there happened to be too many of these gushers in the vicinity of the Hunt property. After making a few heads of oil, the Hunt-Pickering No. 1 stopped flowing. All the drilling activity in the area had so reduced the reservoir pressures that the oil would no longer "gush" out of the ground on its own. There was still oil in the well, but to get it out, Hunt would have to spend $3,500 on a pumping unit. Unable to finance the equipment, Hunt decided to sell his production to a company that was buying and selling oil for a premium above the posted price, but the company folded before paying up. By any objective measure, the venture ended as a failure, but, as Hunt dryly observed, "it served the purpose of getting me started in the oil business."

Hunt's next oil venture was more profitable and, according to some old-timers, much more illustrative of the way he operated in his early days. Instead of staying bunched in with the other speculators, Hunt moved to the southeast of the Hunt-Pickering well. Except for the obvious fact that being farther from the crowd would put him in an area of higher bottomhole pressure, there was no geological reason for his decision. As Hunt recalled afterward, the leases were simply cheaper to the southeast, and "I liked the direction better."

The way Hunt got his first 40-acre lease to the southeast was mysterious. In later years, he wrote: "Inasmuch as it was proven, Mr. Tom Rowland, the owner of the farm, took my note for $20,000 in payment of the lease. Leases on his farm were in great demand, but Mr. Rowland would not lease to anyone except me, and he did not want to lease to me until he was sure the 40 acres would produce oil."

Hunt apparently managed to convince farmer Rowland to take his note through the good offices of a colorful fellow called "Old Man" Bailey. A short, balding, one-eyed man, Old Man Bailey had helped manage Hunt's gambling halls in El Dorado. He was a little older than Hunt and, in contrast to his boss, a great talker. Like Frank Grego, he acted as a combination friend, flunkie, and procurer for Hunt. Although Hunt never mentioned Old Man Bailey's role in the Rowland lease in *Hunt Heritage,* one veteran of the El Dorado days later claimed that the whole deal turned on Old Man Bailey's fast talking.

"Mr. Hunt didn't have the money to back up his note," the old-timer recalled, "so Old Man Bailey went out to the lease to keep the farmer from cashing the note until Mr. Hunt had time to go back to Lake Village and raise the money to drill the well."

Taking up residence in farmer Rowland's house, the congenial Bailey kept praising the potential of the lease and his boss's ability to get things done. He also kept warning farmer Rowland of the dangers of letting his lease sale to Hunt become public knowledge before the first well was drilled.

"You don't want to take that note to town and cash it," Old Man Bailey would say. "Everybody you know will want to come up and borrow money from you."

Old Man Bailey's logic made sense to farmer Rowland. Instead of taking Hunt's worthless note to town, he decided to hold onto it and bide his time. Meanwhile, Hunt was able to round up the necessary drilling money in $200 and $2,000 lots from several Lake Village businessmen.

Old Man Bailey's stalling and Hunt's hustling proved to be a winning combination. The first well on the Rowland lease came in January of 1922. Two more successful wells followed a few months later. Hunt wrote to one of his investors in March of 1922 that the second well had come in flowing at a rate of 5,000 barrels a day. The output had dropped substantially since the initial gushes, Hunt wrote, and a pumping unit would have to be installed soon. Nevertheless, Hunt told his investor, "indications are that this well will produce for years to come." Hunt's prediction proved to be correct, but the production of the wells on the Rowland leases in 1923 dropped to half the total for 1922, and continued to decline rapidly in each succeeding year. Soon after the wells came in, Hunt sold some of the royalties to his brother James in Illinois.

Although the Rowland wells hardly made Hunt a millionaire, they did get him hooked on the oil business. He closed down his gambling hall and began buying and selling more oil leases. He did not, as he sometimes later claimed, give up playing poker. However, he did settle into a frenetic routine that involved more oil rigs than card decks. He also settled into El Dorado. In late January of 1922, Hunt moved Lyda and the children from Lake Village to a rented bungalow on Peach Street not far from the center of town. On January 23, 1923, the Hunts' third child, Caroline, was born.

Not long after moving into the Peach Street house, Hunt went down to a nearby grocery store to open a family account. The senior clerk in the store looked him over warily. The robust six-footer who stood before him resembled hundreds of other oil boomers. He wore a tattered winter suit, muddy shoes, and a rakish boater hat, but he had an air about him that suggested a certain trustworthiness. The clerk decided to take a chance.

"What's your name and what's your business?" the clerk asked.

"My name is H. L. Hunt," his new customer replied. "By title, I guess I'd be considered a gambler, but I'm fixing to enter the oil business."

CHAPTER 4

MAN WITH TWO FAMILIES

H. L. HUNT never lacked action as an oilman. By the time Lyda and the children got settled in El Dorado, he had eight wells going in the El Dorado field and the East field. Then another oil boom erupted in the nearby town of Smackover, Arkansas. The discovery well came in with such force that when the wind blew from the northeast, the Hunts' porch in El Dorado, some seven miles away, was covered with a reddish sand. Shortly after the Smackover discovery, a fellow named Reuben "Jennie" Jones came to El Dorado looking for Hunt. Jones was a timberman. He knew Hunt from a land deal the two had done on a handshake some years earlier. Believing that his old friend had become an expert in the oil business, Jennie Jones suggested that he and Hunt get together on a joint venture in the Smackover field.

For once, Hunt was cautious. Usually as ready for action as Jones seemed to be, he was now more interested in paying his bills for drilling and equipping his El Dorado wells. Since gas was worth little or nothing at the time and oil prices were depressed, Hunt found it hard to become enthusiastic about entering the Smackover play. But Jennie Jones kept urging him on and offered to advance Hunt's half of each lease block they acquired without security or even a note.

With a deal he could not refuse, Hunt set about looking at maps. He found three 400-acre blocks that could be acquired for little more than the promise of drilling a 2,000-foot test well. Nevertheless, Hunt continued to stall. Jennie Jones went back to his timber interests in Louisiana, and Hunt failed to follow through on the lease acquisitions.

As it turned out, all three leases Hunt had considered produced oil for the men who did buy them. Two of the leases even produced from three different oil-bearing layers of rock or "sands," as the oilmen and geologists called them. Despite the fact that oil prices were depressed, the acreage ended up netting its holders about $10,000 per lease, which, as Hunt later pointed out, was quite a bit of money in the early 1920s. Hunt attributed his failure to cash in on the leases to his own ignorance.

"I failed to make any money at Smackover," he wrote, "simply because I did not know enough about the oil business."

Thanks in part to his early failures, Hunt learned fast. In the beginning, he was what the oil-field hands called a "poor boy." That meant he drilled his wells with very little money and whatever equipment he could beg or borrow. While the major companies like Standard and Shell were using steel derricks, three-cone bits, and platoons of smart-sounding geologists, Hunt and the other "poor boys" were forced to get by with old-fashioned gear, guesswork, and guts. "Poor boying" a well greatly increased the risks involved in finding oil, but it also redoubled the romance and gave an individual a chance to get in on the action for himself. If the rapidly expanding majors were already the Goliaths of the industry, the "poor boys" were the Davids of the oil game or, as they liked to fancy themselves, the Lone Rangers, the last frontiersmen, the true wildcatters.

Following his never-consummated venture with Jennie Jones, Hunt started a well in the Smackover area he called the Lou Ann No. 1. Like many another "poor boy," he used a worn-out rig borrowed from another operator. But after arranging for the lease and the equipment, Hunt did not actually do the drilling work. Instead, he put the operation in the hands of a veteran toolpusher named "Big Boy" Croft. The toolpusher, in turn, hired a crew of seven men to work twelve-hour "tower," or shifts, for $1.50 an hour.

With Hunt riding out on horseback to supervise the operation, Croft and his men first set about clearing a location in the muddy pine forest. That in itself took a couple of days. The trees were tall and thick, and some of the mud bogs were waist deep. Once there was room to move, the crew began assembling the rig. They built the derrick out of pine lumber hauled in by mule from Smackover. The tower rose over seventy feet high, with diagonal and horizontal crosshatching at regular intervals along the way. It took several more days to build. When it was finished, the crew hooked up two rusty steam boilers via a sprocket and chain to a bull wheel on the derrick floor. The bull wheel was then geared into the rotary table, the device which turned the actual drilling bit. The crew then covered the boilers with a frame shack, giving the whole contraption the look of a strangely unfinished pine-wood church.

The well chugged into operation with sputter and grind. As the fishtail bit cut deeper, the crew lined the drilling pipe with a steel casing. Inside the casing, they dropped an elongated bucket called a bailer. This was the tool that actually brought the rock and sand up out of the ground. They had to run water down the hole to keep the bit from getting stuck.

Work proceeded slowly. The bit would burrow down several inches, the bailer would haul up the debris, then the rusty chain would slip off the bull wheel sprocket and the rotary table would spin to a stop. The crew had to keep stopping to reconnect the chain and get the engines going again. The drilling dragged on day after day for several weeks.

Despite the difficulties, Hunt's luck came through. The Lou Ann No. 1 struck oil just below 2,000 feet. Then a new problem occurred. With oil spewing ankle deep all over the derrick floor, the bone-weary crew refused to work anymore. While they went on strike, precious barrels of black gold were being wasted.

Hunt rushed out to the drill site on horseback. When he arrived, he dismounted, rolled up his sleeves, and confronted his crew.

None of the men would recall exactly what it was Hunt said that day. It may have been something about how they were "Hunt men" and could count on being paid if they finished the well and not paid if they quit. It may have been the fact that Hunt indicated he was ready to do the work himself if they would not. But somehow Hunt convinced his oil-soaked men to go back to work long enough to cap the well with a "Christmas tree" valve and connect it to a pipeline.

Once he managed that, Hunt was in pretty good shape with the Lou Ann No. 1. Many operators wasted up to 10 percent of their oil after the original gusher by virtue of having to store it in earthen pits and haul it to market in leaky wooden barrels. The fact that the Lou Ann No. 1 happened to be close to a pipeline hookup was another instance of the Hunt luck. With the connection in place, Hunt could rest assured that most of what he brought up out of the ground would get to market. Still, he had to move fast. As news of his strike got out, other operators would descend upon the area, lowering the pressure by overdrilling. That would mean less oil for H. L. Hunt.

After completing the Lou Ann No. 1, Hunt put his men right back to work. They dismantled the derrick and the engines, and moved the equipment to a second location a few hundred yards away. Big Boy Croft and his crew rebuilt the rig and began drilling another well, the Lou Ann No. 2.

Like its predecessor, the Lou Ann No. 2 was a tough well to work. By now, the engine sprocket was so worn that the chain simply would not stay in place. Hunt had no cash yet, so he had to borrow money from Croft to buy a new sprocket. The crew cut down pine saplings from the lease block to make braces for the drainworks and the shaky, old drilling engine. They had to borrow their surface tools. But these, too, were old and damaged and kept wearing out. The crew kept coming to Hunt with requests for new equipment.

"Can you borrow them?" he would ask.

"Yes," his toolpusher would say, "but I've borrowed so much now that they hate to see me coming."

"Hell," Hunt would say, "tell them you're working for a 'poor boy.' "

Somehow, Hunt and his crew managed to "poor boy" the Lou Ann No. 2 to completion. But by the time they got the well hooked up to a pipeline, the other operators had begun crowding into the vicinity. Unable to afford a longer lease block, there was little Hunt could do to keep them out.

Soon the pressure began to drop, and the Lou Ann wells gradually petered out.

For the next two years, Hunt had to keep "poor boying" his wells, but with each one, he got a little smarter and a little luckier. With drilling costs running to hundreds of dollars per day, he was often unable to pay his men for months at a time. But when his money did come in Hunt always paid up. He knew his men. He would talk to them and listen to their problems. That kept him in good stead when money was tight. Rather than walk out on him, his men developed an abiding loyalty to their boss. It became a thing of pride in the El Dorado oil fields to say "I'm a Hunt man."

Hunt gradually earned a reputation as an honest trader. "A lot of oilmen, if they took a lease with a poor farmer or a nigger and the nearby holes turned out to be dry, why they'd find some fault in the title to keep from paying," recalled one El Doradoan. "Mr. Hunt never did that." Hunt kept borrowing a lot of money, but sooner or later, he always paid it back. He also kept on drilling and drilling.

Hunt's persistence paid off. By late 1924, he accumulated close to 400,000 barrels of oil reserves. At the then-prevailing price of about $1.50 per barrel, that amounted to some $600,000 worth. For the first time in his life, H. L. Hunt had become a man of means. With his wife Lyda pregnant again, he invested a large chunk of money in building a three-story brick house covering an entire block in a nice residential section of El Dorado. Lyda and the children moved out of the bungalow on Peach Street and into the new house just before the baby was born.

As he prospered, Hunt continued to be what he had always been: a loner. He spent most of his time by himself, at the poker table, or in the oil fields. Hunt had no real office. He made his deals in hotel lobbies and in bank offices, on the sidewalks and in the cafés. When he wanted to think, he would go over to the barbershop and sit down on the long brass rail out in front. Sometimes he would sit there all day just staring into space as the traffic passed him by.

Hunt answered to no one and spoke to few. Except for his sidekicks Frank Grego and Old Man Bailey, he did not have any confidants, and even Grego and Bailey were more on the order of employees than friends of equal stature. He could still play the charming storyteller and adventurer—when he wanted to. The rub was that he seldom seemed willing to let that side of himself have free rein. On those occasions when Hunt ventured inside the barbershop for a haircut, he did not socialize. Instead, he would sit in the chair, barely utter a word, get his haircut, pay his money, and leave. Known around the shop as a tightwad, he never left a tip.

Not surprisingly, many of the townspeople regarded Hunt as a little peculiar. His success piqued their curiosity. His honesty inspired their respect. But his silence put them on edge. Hunt became known as a mystery man and, therefore, an even greater curiosity. The menfolk he met in El Dorado wanted to know what was going on behind his piercing blue eyes. But Hunt never volunteered a thing. Finally, Hunt's usual barber could not stand the silence any longer.

"Why the hell don't you say something?" the barber blurted out, expressing in his question the thoughts and feelings of most of Hunt's other El Dorado acquaintances.

Hunt did not even flinch in the chair.

"I don't have anything to say," he replied. Then he fell silent once again.

Hunt's work habits and eccentricities did not make things easy for his wife Lyda. Known around town as a family man who took his wife and children to the movie house on weekends, he was in reality a father who was often away on business. Indeed, as an old man, he would count as one of his fondest memories the Christmas of 1923, which he celebrated with a sack lunch on one of his oil wells. Quiet and unassuming, Lyda was left at home to look after the children, not knowing when her husband would return or how long he would stay. As a result, she learned to cope with El Dorado pretty much on her own.

Despite the extra burdens that entailed, Lyda was kind and gracious to all she met. When delivery boys arrived at the house, she would offer them pies and cookies. She was polite and down to earth, never arrogant or condescending. If her children happened to be cutting up when company was around, she was always very apologetic.

Lyda attended the Methodist church regularly, but she was not a party giver or a socialite. In the evenings, during what little free time she had, she would walk down the street talking to neighbors and shopkeepers. The store clerks would ask after Hunt, and Lyda would almost invariably report that her husband was off on one of his two main pursuits.

"Mr. Hunt's out playing poker," she would say, or, "Mr. Hunt's out on a well."

By herself, Lyda would often sit down in one of the shops just to talk to somebody for a few minutes. Then she would get up and walk back to her house and children. Although she bobbed her hair after the fashion of the day, she dressed simply and did not put on airs. With her round face and matronly figure, she looked like she could have been the wife of the town's most solid citizen, not its most eccentric gambler and oilman.

Beneath her gentle exterior, Lyda harbored unusual strengths of character. As one relative put it, "She was a very determined person. She had that strictness about her, but you couldn't see it on the surface. Her children were brought up to learn that she governed what went on at home." Lyda's only real problem child was her son Hassie. On occasions when he was at home, Hunt lavished Hassie with fatherly attention, often to the exclusion of the other children. Hassie, in turn, often acted like the classic spoiled brat. He seemed to think he could do whatever he pleased, that he was not bound by the same rules that applied to the other children. He was always breaking things and getting into mischief. Lyda did not spare the rod on little Hassie, but despite her attempts at discipline, the boy continued to misbehave.

Lyda also had her hands full with her husband, who seemed to have not an ounce of financial sense whatsoever. He always wanted to risk whatever money he made. He never wanted to put away a nest egg. It was only at Lyda's insistence that Hunt had invested some of his newly made oil money in the family's El Dorado mansion. After more than ten years of marriage, that house was the first solid indication that the Hunts had gone anywhere since the little "nigger shack" out on his Lake Village cotton acreage. Lyda had never approved of her husband's gambling. She had always encouraged him to give up playing poker and make something of himself. Being an oilman entailed gambles enough, but at least it was a respectable occupation. Lyda now strove to imbue her husband with some sense of fiscal responsibility.

Hunt definitely recognized his wife's good intentions. In later years, he would magnanimously credit her with "about 90 percent of our financial success." But in the El Dorado days Hunt remained an incorrigible pupil. Heedless of his wife's advice, he kept on wheeling and dealing as he pleased. In the meantime, his family continued to grow. On February 19, 1925, Lyda gave birth to the couple's fourth child, a girl they named Lyda Bunker Hunt.

Then tragedy struck. On March 20, 1925, the Hunts' one-month-old daughter died. Word got out that this child was asphyxiated by gas fumes when one of the other children tampered with the gas jets in the family's new house. Everyone in El Dorado was stunned. As one old-timer recalled, "It was a terrible thing that happened to the Hunts, and everyone saw how easily the same thing could happen to their children. Everyone was talking about safety measures in the home, and what they could do to prevent that sort of thing from happening again."

The Hunts were devastated. In an attempt to ease the pain, Hunt took Lyda to New York City for the first real vacation of their married life. The two of them went to see several Broadway shows, including *No, No, Nanette* and *Rose Marie.* When they returned to El Dorado, Hunt got Lyda pregnant again.

Then H. L. Hunt began to go through some serious midlife changes. He was now thirty-six years old, successful, but far from satisfied. He still craved action. However, the El Dorado oil boom was peaking out. The best acreage was leased up. The barrelhouses and the gambling halls were closed. The early glamor and excitement were fading into workaday routines. Hunt's old restlessness was stirring again. He liked making money, but he abhorred the humdrum. It would still be years before his oil wells paid out their full return. But he simply could not see settling into the life of a small but steady oil producer. He wanted to find another boom town, a place where he could let all his talents fly and make a fortune fast.

In the summer of 1925, Hunt decided it was time to get out of the oil business and try something new. He sold all his production to a major company for a $600,000 note. Then he discounted the note at the bank for cash, and informed Lyda that he was going off to Florida to try his luck in "that wild real estate boom everybody is talking about."

As Hunt would later observe, "These were romantic years. The country was in a playful mood. It had helped win the world's greatest war in the muddy trenches of France. The Charleston was the dance in vogue and women were wearing short skirts."

In spite of his recent family tragedy, Hunt was in a romantic, playful mood, too. As he boarded a train bound for Tampa, he began composing his own light opera along the lines of the Broadway shows he had just seen in New York City. He entitled one ditty "Whenever Dreams Come True, I'll Be with You." "Up to the time I met you," he hummed, "Life was as drab as can be . . . Something was missing for me . . . You are my love now forever . . . If only in sweet reverie . . ."

Frania Tye came to Florida from a different direction. She was born in Buffalo, New York, on March 8, 1904, the ninth of ten children. Her parents, Andrew and Anastasia Tye (originally Tyburski) were Polish immigrants. Her mother was the daughter of a Polish aristocrat, but her father was a commoner's son, a carpenter who was determined to make it on his own. He kept moving his family from house to house as he built new residences and sold them. Later, he became president of the local carpenter's guild. Frania was the first member of her family to be born in America. Like H. L. Hunt, she had little formal education in her early years. She grew up in Polonia, the Polish section of Buffalo, and attended the Catholic church. A dark-haired, handsome child, she spent her youth mostly in the company of her many brothers and sisters and the other Polish kids in the neighborhood.

The curious circumstances that brought Frania Tye to Tampa began to take shape as she reached her late teens. During this period, Frania's parents were making frequent trips to Poland to visit relatives. While her mother and father shuttled back and forth across the Atlantic, Frania stayed at the Felician Sisters' convent in Buffalo, and grew into a striking beauty. Barely over five feet tall, she had a sculptured jaw and nose, enormous blue eyes, and brows that arched delicately toward her hairline. She also had big breasts and narrow hips. Having grown up in Polonia, she spoke with a bit of an accent that added a sexy edge to her voice. When she wore a curl over the side of her forehead, she looked like a perfect blend of Greta Garbo and the girl next door.

Among the many young men who could not help but notice Frania's charms was one Polikarp Kurzinski. Since his father served as secretary of the local chapter's guild, Paul (né Polikarp) had known the Tyburski family most of the time he was growing up. He first began noticing Frania in 1920 when the two of them were working as salespeople in Goodman's Shoe Store in Buffalo. He was seventeen and she was sixteen. Frania and Paul went out on several dates to ice cream parlors and such. Then Paul left for Cleveland, where he went to work for an egg noodle baking company. Frania stayed in Buffalo. She attended secretarial school for a short time, then held a series of jobs as a department-store beautician and saleslady. Recognizing an asset in her attractiveness, the store also sent her on a trip to New York City to model dress patterns.

What happened next was destined to become shrouded in romantic mystery. According to Frania's version of the story, she and Paul began seeing each other again when the young man would come back to Buffalo to visit his parents. Eventually, she followed him to Cleveland and moved in with his aunt. From the fall of 1923 to the spring of 1924, she worked as a telephone operator with Ohio Bell. During that time, she and Paul became engaged. However, Frania grew homesick and returned to Buffalo.

After several months in Buffalo, Frania got lonesome for her fiancé. In the spring of 1925, she moved in again with Paul's aunt in Cleveland and returned to her job at the telephone company. But by this time, Paul had cooled on the idea of getting married. He broke off their engagement explaining he simply could not afford the financial burden of supporting a wife. Broken-hearted, Frania left Cleveland in the summer of 1925, and went back to Buffalo. A short time after that, Frania headed for Tampa.

Whatever the truth about her past, twenty-one-year-old Frania Tye arrived in Tampa in the summer of 1925 with her father by her side. A wash of stucco white and bay-water blue, the city sparkled in the sunlight like a semitropical jewel. It featured parrots, palm-lined avenues, banana boats, Cuban leaf cigars, and one of the strangest real-estate booms in American history. The boom had actually begun on the east coast of Florida a few years earlier. Over there, the play was in orange groves as income-producing property and in secure homesites in the healthful sunshine. In Tampa, the big action was in transforming reclaimed swampland into subdivisions built around golf courses.

Once a quaint little town of 40,000 people, Tampa was now swelling into a city of over 100,000 inhabitants. But unlike those who flocked to oil-boom towns, most of the newcomers to Tampa were, at least in appearance, relatively clean. When the boomers of El Dorado had arrived in muleskinner's khakis splotched with mud, the hustlers who came to Tampa dressed in knickers and cool cotton shirts like golfers down south for a vacation. With them came carloads of "tin-can tourists," so called because they filled their automobile trunks with enough canned food to last the entire trip. Both the "golfers" and the "tourists" had a common goal: getting in on the land game. Tampa did its best to accommodate them. As one local wag put it, *"Everybody* was in real estate."

So, eventually, was Frania. With her father's help, she first found lodging in the De Soto Hotel in downtown Tampa. Her father put her in the care of the family who ran the hotel, gave her $800 cash, and returned to Buffalo. Frania helped around the hotel for a while, then met some young ladies who were selling a tearoom about three blocks away. She bought the place for $400 cash, operated it for a few weeks, then sold out, and went into the real-estate business as a salesperson for an agent named Bennett. It was while Frania was working in real estate that her life's most incredible adventure began.

The way Frania told it afterward, it all started one bright, sunshiny September day when she was sitting on a park bench near the Tampa Terrace Hotel. She noticed an older man sit down next to her. The older man was bald and gregarious. He started chatting about something—the weather maybe— and mentioned that his name was Old Man Bailey.

"What are you doing here in Tampa?" he asked Frania in the nicest sort of way.

"I'm selling real estate," she replied.

Old Man Bailey then told her that he had a friend who was interested in buying some real estate, and that he would like to put his friend in touch with her. Interested by the prospect of making a sale, Frania gave Old Man Bailey her phone number in the De Soto Hotel.

A short time later, Frania got a telephone call from a man who identified himself only as "Hunt." The man said he was interested in seeing some real estate. Frania agreed to show him some property a few miles outside of Tampa.

The next day, Hunt showed up at the De Soto Hotel in an automobile. He was tall and handsome and quite a bit older than Frania. He was dressed in a suit and tie. Frania gave Hunt directions to the property that was for sale, and the two of them drove out to the site together. Hunt looked over the property but did not make a commitment to buy.

On the drive back to Tampa, Hunt's car broke down and their return was delayed for several hours. Hunt apologized and offered to take Frania to dinner, but she declined the invitation.

A few days later, Hunt called again and asked to see the property a second time. After they returned from this second excursion, Hunt invited Frania up to his hotel room. Shocked by his audacity, Frania slapped his face and flew into a rage.

"No, I will not come up to your room," she told Hunt, and made him understand thoroughly that he was never to make such a proposal to her again.

After that, Hunt left Tampa for several weeks. When he returned in mid-October of 1925, he began asking Frania out again. Forgiving the rocky doings of the past, the two commenced what Frania later described as a "whirlwind courtship." Over the next three weeks, she saw Hunt every day. The two of them would mostly go to restaurants, drink Coke and ginger ale, then go for walks holding hands. Frania thought that at thirty-six he seemed rather old for her but she was enthralled by his charm. Although he was not a dancer, he was an especially good storyteller. He had tales of adventures in the West, sheepherding and lumberjacking, playing semipro baseball and being invited to box as the next "White Hope."

By now, Hunt had introduced himself to Frania as "Major Franklin Hunt." Frania asked if the title had any military significance. Hunt said it did not.

"Everybody in the South is called major or colonel," he told her.

At this point, the twenty-one-year-old real-estate salesperson with the blue moon eyes was not yet in love with Major Franklin Hunt. But she was beginning to feel attached to him. She found him very entertaining, very gentle, very kind, very amusing. When he would go away, she would miss him terribly. When he would come back, she would be very happy.

"Finally, on November 10, 1925, Hunt took her out to dinner and brought the courtship to a climax.

"I can't work properly," he told her. "I've got you on my mind constantly. That's why I've come back to Tampa."

The two stayed up all night and drove to St. Petersburg and back on the new bridge. Their conversation was exclusively about marriage and family. Major Hunt told Frania he was from Illinois and that he had several brothers and sisters. He said he now lived in Louisiana, where he worked in the oil fields.

Frania told Hunt about her Polish-Catholic upbringing in Buffalo. She said later that she never suspected Hunt might already be married and the father of a family: she had been raised in a home where married men do not take out ladies, and she took it for granted that Hunt was not married. However, she was concerned about his religious background.

"If we have any children, I want to raise them Catholic," she informed him.

Hunt replied that he did not care what religion their children were raised in.

"I don't have any religion," he said.

When the couple returned to Tampa at dawn, it was November 11, Armistice Day, a national holiday. Because of the boom, most of the real-estate offices were going to open, but just about everything else was going to be closed. Nevertheless, Hunt wanted to get married right away. Frania asked how he was going to arrange for their marriage license when everything was closed.

"You don't have to have a marriage license to get married in Florida," Hunt told her.

Frania was not satisfied. She kept questioning him on the point. Finally, Hunt told her not to worry about it.

"Old Man Bailey will take care of everything," he said.

About midmorning, Hunt found a pawn shop that was open and bought Frania a simple gold band. Then he informed her that Old Man Bailey had arranged for them to be married by a justice of the peace. Despite her concern about a Catholic upbringing for their children, Frania was apparently willing to allow herself to be married by someone other than a Catholic priest.

Hunt led her to Ybor City, the Cuban quarter. Easily the most romantic section of Tampa, Ybor City was the center of spice, color, and vice. Its brick streets were lined with wrought-iron balconies and bustling with dark-eyed Cuban immigrants. There were fabulous restaurants and nightclubs like the Columbia and El Centro Austriano, where customers ate plantains and pescados and danced the tango. There were fancy gambling halls and speakeasies, where the local mobster contingent entertained the cream of café society. There were blocks and blocks of cigar factories, where Cuban men sat at their desks rolling rich brown tobacco leaves while a reader stood at the front of the room entertaining them with selections from the daily newspaper and the latest Spanish novella.

Old Man Bailey's justice of the peace lived in a white stucco house surrounded by beautiful red flowers. Hunt and Frania went inside. The justice of the peace appeared to be Spanish or Cuban, about forty-five or fifty years old. His wife was there, and so was Old Man Bailey. They were the only witnesses.

Before the ceremony commenced, Frania signed a small ledger with the name Frania Tye. Hunt signed the ledger, too, but she did not see what name he wrote. Then, without ever bothering to ask for a marriage license or any form of identification, the justice of the peace began reading something from the Bible.

"Do you take Frania Tye as your lawful wife?" he asked Hunt.

"Yes," Hunt answered.

"Do you take Franklin Hunt as your lawful husband?" the justice of the peace asked Frania.

"Yes," she said.

The justice then pronounced the couple man and wife, and the ceremony was over.

Frania and Hunt spent the first few days of their honeymoon in a Tampa hotel. Then the couple drove over to Orlando and toured several other Florida towns. When they returned to Tampa, Hunt said that he had to go back to the oil fields on urgent business. Before he left, he and Frania discussed where their new home was going to be. Hunt told her that he wanted to live in Louisiana and that he would send for her to join him soon.

Frania remained in Tampa through the end of the year. Hunt came back to visit, then left again. Finally, in February of 1926, he cabled her to join him in New Orleans, where the Mardi Gras was in progress. Frania boarded a steamboat in Tampa in fine spirits, but as the boat headed out into the Gulf, she began to get ill. When she arrived in New Orleans, she discovered that she was not merely suffering from seasickness; she was pregnant.

Frania and Hunt stayed in New Orleans for a few days to enjoy the Mardi Gras. Then Hunt took her up to Shreveport. At first, the couple lived in a local hotel. Then Hunt moved her to an apartment on Hearndon Street where, as the new Mrs. Franklin Hunt, she settled in to have the baby that was due in October.

H. L. Hunt never wrote about or publicly discussed his romance with Frania Tye. In *Hunt Heritage,* he mentioned his trip to Tampa only as an ill-fated venture in the land options. "It was not long before I became convinced that the Florida land boom was artificial and was set to collapse with disastrous results for those who were strung out with properties," he recalled, "so I allowed my options to lapse unexercised and absorbed my losses of making the play. According to my 1925 financial statement, my total expense for the Florida operation for that year totalled $7,999.20, including my traveling expense."

In years to come, H. L. Hunt would privately deny that he and Frania were ever formally married. But he would never deny that he was the father of her children. If the public side of him played the serious and proper and authoritative Mr. Hunt, the private side played the fanciful and precocious boy wonder with the special privileges at his mother's breast. He was the grown man to whom the ordinary rules did not apply, the mysterious gambler and oilman driven by the unquenchable lust for money and romance, as well as the El Dorado family man. H. L. Hunt's curious relationship with Frania Tye seemed to answer the needs and insecurities of his dual-faced ego. If Lyda was the wife of his right hand, Frania was the wife of his left hand. Regardless of whether or not they were formally and legally married, Hunt and Frania had (at the very least) a kind of morganatic marriage American style. Having a second family was both an outlet for and a reconfirmation of his extraordinary sexual prowess, his unusual personal power. It was also something secret, fanciful, and exciting—a whole new kind of action.

Not surprisingly, Hunt's return from the Florida venture marked the beginning of the most active reproductive period of his life. On February 20, 1926, just about the time he was bringing Frania to Shreveport, Lyda, who was still living less than one hundred miles away in El Dorado, gave birth to a son they named Nelson Bunker Hunt. Eight months later, on October 25, 1926, Frania gave birth to her first child by Hunt, a boy born in Shreveport. The child's birth certificate listed the father as Franklin Hunt and the mother as Frances Tye. Since Hunt was not present at the birth, that information was supplied by Frania. However, according to Frania, the boy's name—Howard Lee Hunt—was arrived at by mutual agreement.

"We both agreed on 'Howard,'" she recalled later, "and he said 'Lee' because in the South it's always 'Lee.'"

Despite the fact that their new infant's initials happened to match the bona fide initials of his father, Frania later claimed that she still did not suspect Major Franklin Hunt's true identity. Rather, she still assumed that she and her husband were like any other ordinary married couple. In the fall of 1927, the two of them went up to her family's home in Buffalo to show off their son. According to Frania, Hunt met everyone in her family as Major Franklin Hunt, not as H. L. Hunt. A few months after they returned to Shreveport, Frania was pregnant again. This child, a girl, was born on October 26, 1928. Although Hunt was not present for the infant's birth, he insisted on calling her Haroldina, which was the feminine equivalent of his own first name.

Five months after Haroldina's birth, Lyda Bunker Hunt gave birth to another boy in El Dorado. The infant was christened William Herbert Hunt, a name taken from his mother's side of the family. He was the couple's fifth surviving child.

Meanwhile, back in Shreveport, Frania was pregnant with her third child by H. L. Hunt. By this time, Hunt had moved her and their children out of the apartment on Hearndon Street and into a picturesque little two-bedroom bungalow in one of the newer residential sections of the city.

Despite having to support another even larger family in El Dorado, Hunt always provided Frania with plenty of expense money. She did not live lavishly, but she did not starve. "He was a cash man," Frania recalled later. "He always had big rolls of money in his pocket." Loathe to carry a billfold, Hunt would simply reach into his suit and pull out $800 or $1,000, whatever was needed to pay the household accounts.

Frania claimed that she thought her husband's income came primarily from his job as an "oil-field worker," but she also knew that he made some of his money from gambling. One day, in fact, Hunt came home to their house in Shreveport, reached into his pockets, pulled out about ten or fifteen thousand dollars in cash, and threw it on the dining-room table. Startled by the sight of so much money, Frania asked where on earth he had gotten all that cash.

"I was playing poker," Hunt replied.

Although her material needs were fairly well taken care of, Frania was not very well provided for in other ways. As in the case of his first family, Hunt played the role of absent father. He was certainly on hand in late January and early February of 1928 and 1930, when the couple's second and third children were conceived, but he usually spent Christmas and other holidays with his first family in El Dorado, not with his family in Shreveport. Many times when he was in town, whether Frania knew it or not, Hunt stayed at a downtown hotel. He never took Frania to meet the members of his own family in Illinois, and never acknowledged the anniversary of their wedding with a card or letter. He did not take her out socially in Shreveport, and he did not invite friends over to their house.

Years afterward, Frania would insist that her husband's extended absences did not give her grounds for suspicion. "I was born in a family where the father worked and he was not there all the time, and I accepted that graciously," she said. At the same time, though, she admitted, "I was very much alone in Shreveport."

Although Frania may not have been suspicious of her husband's behavior, her Shreveport neighbors were. On Gladstone Street, the family whose father did not come home at night became an object of intense curiosity. First, the story went around that Hunt simply traveled a great deal, that he worked out of town and just did not come home very often. Then it was rumored that Hunt had another family living somewhere else. After that, neighbors began referring to what was going on down the street as "bigamy."

In the meantime, H. L. Hunt was becoming well known in both El Dorado and Shreveport. When not fathering more children, he spent most of his waking hours re-establishing himself in the oil business. Prior to taking off for the Florida land boom, he had operated strictly as an individual. On December 28, 1925, in between his last visits to Frania in Tampa, he incorporated his first operating company, H. L. Hunt Inc., and began building something along the lines of a regular organization. Frank Grego and the ubiquitous Old Man Bailey continued to be his main sidekicks and procurers, but they were soon joined by other men whose real expertise and experience was in oil. Among those who became "Hunt men" in the late 1920s were J. F. "Jick"

Justiss, a tall, jug-eared drilling superintendent, and Charlie Hardin, a young oil-field scout. Both were energetic, hard-dealing fellows who craved action almost as much as did Hunt himself.

For better or worse, not one of the "Hunt men" was a qualified geologist. H. L. Hunt and Old Man Bailey prided themselves on being "creekologists." As such, they divined for oil on the basis of the way the hills and valleys rolled and the way the creek beds ran in a particular area. Then, as in later years, geology was far from being an exact science. But the leaders in the field were already of the well-substantiated opinion that what the earth looked like on top was at least a very minor and unreliable indication of what was hidden underneath in the way of oil and gas. Nevertheless, Hunt and Old Man Bailey liked to think that their method was just as professional as any other approach. In reality, of course, they were relying on their intuition and hunches more than anything else. As Hunt himself put it, "With us, it either looked like oil land or it did not look like oil land."

At the same time, Hunt did let his "creekology" get him into many pure wildcatting ventures. The pure wildcatters were those who drilled in virgin, completely unexplored areas. Hunt's custom was to "follow the play" into areas where the presence of oil and gas had already been established. Although this method entailed its share of risks, it also enabled Hunt to reduce the odds. Instead of attempting to discover new fields, he became proficient at jumping into the lease-buying action immediately after a discovery had been made.

If part of Hunt's success depended on his ability to move quickly, an even larger part depended on the job "Hunt men" like Old Man Bailey did in providing him with oil-field intelligence. Bailey and the others made it a practice to befriend other lease hounds, drilling superintendents, and toolpushers who could fill them in on the latest developments in the oil patch. Much of their value to Hunt was in their knack for getting this information and passing it on to their boss before their competitors knew what was happening. Here, as in his days as a gambling-hall operator, he knew how to spread his money around. The result, as one veteran of the era observed, was that "Mr. Hunt always seemed to be around when the first well came in."

As the El Dorado oil boom peaked out, Hunt spent most of his time looking for oil in other parts of south Arkansas and in the newly discovered fields of north Louisiana. He opened a small office in downtown El Dorado, but he also did a great deal of business in Shreveport, operating out of a room in the Washington-Youree Hotel. Then a city of just under 76,000 people and the home base of the fiery, young Huey Long, Shreveport was becoming known as the capital of the Ark-La-Tex, the in-between region formed by the corners of Arkansas, Louisiana, and Texas. On any given day, as many as one hundred oilmen would gather in the great marble lobby of the Washington-Youree to make their deals and sign up their investors. Hunt was usually right in the thick of things, bargaining and bartering with the best of them.

Just as in his days as a full-time professional gambler, Hunt took his work very seriously. Other oilmen liked to make their deals amid plenty of backslapping, guffawing, and general good timing. Hunt was strictly business. Hunt was no great lover of alcohol, but he *was* a firm believer in keeping a clear head. The man with two families had four main vices: gambling, which he continued to do at hotels and race tracks all across the Ark-La-Tex; good-looking women, whom he continued to pursue with vigor even after hooking up with Frania Tye; smoking cigars, a habit he had picked up on his sojourn to Tampa; and eating, which he did with great gusto, often augmenting his main meals with snacks of pecans, which he consumed like an addict. But none of these things, at least to Hunt's way of thinking, clouded his head.

Hunt played the oil game with what the other operators of the day called "class." Once a cotton farmer who came to town with mud on his boots, he now became something of a snappy dresser. Where most other oilmen donned khaki work clothes and riding boots on their trips to the field, Hunt always wore a fedora or a boater and a suit and tie. He would remove his coat once he got to the well site, but he usually kept his shirt sleeves rolled down all the way to the cuffs. He looked virtually the same at his mud-bogged, backcountry wells as he did in the splendid lobby of the Washington-Youree.

Of course, Hunt's taste for suits and ties did not prevent him from getting his hands dirty when the situation called for it. In fact, on one occasion, his very willingness to get down in the dirt and grime helped him make a profit on what at first seemed at most disappointing venture. The well in question was south of Monroe, Louisiana, in the Tullos-Urania field. Hunt's drill bit found oil, but the crude had an asphalt base and was not very popular for use as fuel. It looked like he was going to end up with a lot of oil he could not sell. As it happened, though, Hunt had stayed in the field nearly all the time the well was being drilled, and had been getting the oil on his hands in the course of operating the pump and handling the pipe.

"Getting that black, sticky stuff off was the hardest to do I think I have ever experienced," Hunt recalled, "but when I did get it off, I discovered steady improvement of the skin of both hands, but the hand that accumulated most of the sticky stuff was most improved.

The cosmetic properties of oil were fairly well known by the late 1920s, so it was unlikely that Hunt's "discovery" was much of a breakthrough for anyone but himself. However, it did give him a clue on how to get his money out of the Tullos-Urania field. Instead of trying to market the oil as bunker fuel, Hunt contracted a refining man at Sinclair Oil who was already aware of the crude's cosmetic properties. The Sinclair man gave him an order for 45,000 barrels a day, which was enough to take care of Hunt's well and the wells of most of the other operators in the field. As Hunt noted in *Hunt Heritage,* the deal marked his first venture in the cosmetics field but not his last. Years later, he would get into cosmetics again through his lifelong interest in "cures." For the time being, though, the sale served the more important function of helping him pay the bills.

Thanks to what he now frequently referred to as "the Hunt luck," Hunt gradually became one of the biggest oil operators in the Ark-La-Tex. By 1929, he had more than one hundred wells operating in Arkansas and Louisiana. He was still a long way from any semblance of financial security. Oil was selling for only $1.27 a barrel, and Hunt was plowing most of the money he made back into new drilling ventures as fast as the cash came in and often faster. As he kept on struggling, there were even rumors around El Dorado that Hunt was going to lose his house. But somehow, he always managed to pull through.

About this time, Hunt began to get interested in drilling for oil in Texas. The Lone Star State was hardly undiscovered territory for oilmen. Booms had come and gone and come again along the Gulf Coast, in the Panhandle, and out in west Texas. A great deal of land had already been leased and picked over. But there was also a much more land that was untapped. In 1929, Hunt and Old Man Bailey decided to go prospecting for oil in west Texas. The two of them applied the best of their "creekology," but came up empty-handed. Several months later, an oil boom erupted near the town of Van in east Texas. Once again, Hunt jumped into the action. As it turned out, there was substantial oil production in the area, but Hunt was not able to move quickly enough. By the time he got into the play, major companies like Texaco, Humble, Shell, Pure, and Sun had already tied up the best leases.

Despite these early failures, Texas continued to hold a fascination for Hunt. In the early fall of 1930, just as Frania was about to give birth to the couple's third child, Hunt moved her to Dallas. The move may have been prompted by the rumors about bigamy circulating around Shreveport, or, as Frania later claimed, it may have been because Hunt was "starting a business" in Texas and wanted her to be nearby. In any event, Frania settled into a large, two-story brick house on a corner lot at 4230 Versailles Avenue, in the city's exclusive Highland Park community. Although the place still did not rival Lyda's mansion in El Dorado, it was a definite step up from the bungalows in Shreveport. Curiously enough, the owner of the house as recorded on the deed was Frania's sister Jennie, though the money that paid for it came from Hunt. On October 28, Frania gave birth to a girl named Helen Hilda Hunt. The child was destined to become one of her father's favorites, but, once again, Hunt was absent at the time of birth.

This time, the reason for Hunt's absence was not hard to determine. While the rest of the country was enduring the second year of the Great Depression, H. L. Hunt was embarking on the biggest business deal of his life. The whole thing began in late September of 1930, when Hunt got a telephone call from an El Dorado oil-well-equipment entrepreneur named Judge M. M. Miller. Judge Miller and his brother had developed a drill stem testing device that Hunt had been using successfully in his own operations for some time. Now Judge Miller called his customer with an oil-field tip.

"There's a wildcatter working down in east Texas, and he may have something going," the judge reported. "He might call on us to run a drill stem test on his well, and I thought you might be interested."

Miller added that he thought the wildcatter might have some trouble financing the cost of the test.

Hunt was interested indeed. It so happened that he was short of cash himself at the time, but that hardly unusual predicament had seldom prevented him from going after good deals in the past. He had no intention of letting it stop him now. Hunt's bread and butter was acting on insider information of the type Judge Miller had just given him. If the wildcatter really did have something going, Hunt could get in on the leasing action before the major companies gobbled up the best tracts.

Wasting no time, Hunt quickly contacted his friend Pete Lake. The owner of a prosperous clothing store in El Dorado, Lake was short, skinny, and bald, and always wore a hat. He was also a bachelor who often had extra investment cash on hand. Lake had lent money to Hunt and other oilmen in the past, and Hunt figured that if the deal looked right, Lake would lend him some money again.

Hunt's hunch proved correct. Excited by the prospect of getting in on the ground floor of another big oil discovery, Lake agreed to accompany Hunt on the 150-mile trip to the east Texas well. The two men immediately departed from El Dorado in Lake's car. They stopped briefly in Shreveport to pick up some oil maps. Then they drove across the Texas border toward Rusk County and a rendezvous with destiny in the person of C. M. "Dad" Joiner.

CHAPTER 5

THE DAD JOINER DEAL

COLUMBUS Marion Joiner scurried about the well site like an expectant father. Up on the platform of the Daisy Bradford No. 3, his crew was preparing the hole for the drill stem test. Down on the muddy ground in front of the rig, against a backdrop of towering east Texas pines, Joiner was chattering excitedly with his partners, potential investors, and friends. One by one, he buttonholed each bystander and offered his umpteenth encouraging report.

"We've reached the Woodbine," he told them, referring to the layer of subterranean sand he believed would contain oil. "We'll know if we're really onto something as soon as the tool is in place."

The bystanders nodded their heads, patted him on the back, and wished him good luck once again.

Joiner kept checking and rechecking the progress on the rig.

He did not look like a typical Texas wildcatter. Instead of cowboy boots and a Stetson hat, he wore brogans, slacks, a tie, and a straw boater. He was short and skinny and so stooped at the waist from rheumatic fever that when he walked, he looked like he was fanning his behind. But he was also an oddly handsome fellow. He had a silky smooth complexion (which he attributed to eating carrots), dark bushy eyebrows, silver-streaked hair, lively gray eyes, and remarkable energy for his seventy years.

As most people who met him eventually discovered, C. M. Joiner was quite a talker, quite a womanizer, quite a con man. But somehow it was hard not to be taken in by the old rascal. Charming as well as sly, he always managed to convey the impression that he sincerely believed in the grandiose dreams he peddled. After all, as he often pointed out, he had the same name as the man who discovered America. And for Columbus Marion Joiner, that was ground enough to conclude that he was destined to make a great discovery, too.

Despite his auspicious name, Joiner's voyage to the pine-forested Daisy Bradford lease had been full of rough seas and repeated disappointments. Born in Alabama in 1860, he had been orphaned by the Civil War and reared in Reconstruction poverty. He had gotten his only education from an older sister, who taught him to quote Shakespeare and the Scriptures. As a young man, he had managed to obtain a law degree and had been elected to the Tennessee legislature. Then he had taken off for the land rush in Oklahoma, only to be wiped out by the Panic of 1907. At that point, Joiner had turned to the oil business as a promoter. One of his first wells was a venture in Seminole County, Oklahoma; the drilling had stopped just below 3,100 feet because Joiner ran out of money. A short time later, another wildcatter had drilled 200 feet deeper on a nearby lease and discovered a giant oil field. The same thing had happened to Joiner in Cement, Oklahoma. He had started a well that failed for lack of funds, then someone else had come in and discovered a giant field.

Undaunted by his failures, Joiner had blithely taken credit for discovering the Seminole and Cement fields, and determined to try his luck in Texas. He had first begun buying leases in the area, and leases could be acquired cheaply. Despite the dry holes, Joiner had a hunch that the region contained oil. He wanted to drill some wildcat wells to find out.

For seven years, Joiner had struggled to build up a 5,000-acre block and to find backers for a drilling venture. He had worked out of a one-room office in Dallas and had seldom had more than twenty dollars in cash. He had concentrated his sales efforts on women, particularly widows. Though married and the father of a family living in Oklahoma, he would woo his female clients with dulcet stories and poetic love letters.

"My own darling Heloise," he had written in one such epistle, "my heart warms to every breath of you. I can never feel cast down to earth with the thought of you awakening the sweetest hopes, the highest aspirations."

One of the leases Joiner had obtained was a 975.5-acre section owned by a vivacious fifty-four-year-old widow named Daisy Miller Bradford. Joiner had convinced the good-hearted "Miss Daisy" that the oil discovery he was going to make would mean a new life for the depressed citizenry of Rusk County. He had also persuaded her to relinquish a portion of her royalty interest in return for his promise to drill the first well on her property.

With the Bradford lease thus secured, Joiner had turned to his old friend Doc Lloyd. A veteran of the Seminole and Cement ventures, Lloyd was a most colorful and unusual character. He stood six feet tall, weighed over three hundred pounds, and dressed in khakis, riding boots, and a big sombrero. His real name was Joseph Idlebert Durham, but he had worked under such pseudonyms as Dr. Alonzo Durham and Dr. A. D. Lloyd. A qualified physician and druggist from Cincinnati, he had gone west to become a gold prospector, a patent-medicine salesman, and, finally, an oilman. In the course of his wanderings, he married six times, which was one reason he kept changing his name as he moved from place to place.

Joiner had touted his friend as "Dr. Lloyd, the nationally known geologist," but the title was not quite deserved. Lloyd had no formal geological training, much less national recognition. However, during a stint with the Bureau of Mines in Colorado, he had picked up some of the basic geological terms and had later expanded his knowledge with a little reading. By the time Joiner had called him to Rusk County, Doc Lloyd could talk oil like a geological authority. Since the geologists for the major companies had already discounted the area, Joiner had needed an authoritative statement that Rusk County was indeed a repository of great quantities of petroleum. Doc Lloyd had artfully provided it.

First, Lloyd had drawn a map of the United States showing the nation's established oil fields, then he had inked in lines from all these fields to a single intersecting point—Rusk County, Texas—which he labeled "the apex of the apex." Lloyd had also prepared a geological map of Rusk County. The map pictured a series of salt domes and anticlines, the traditional oil-trapping structures, neatly arranged along a fault line that ran right through Daisy Bradford's property.

Lloyd had then written a report with the impressive title, "Geological, Topographical and Petroliferous Survey, Portion of Rusk County, Texas, Made for C. M. Joiner by A. D. Lloyd, Geologist and Petroleum Engineer." The report discussed the structures drawn in the geological map and spoke of the "thousands of registrations" seismic crews had made in the area. In a letter to Joiner that went along with the report, Lloyd had predicted that Joiner's well would hit the oil-bearing Woodbine sand at 3,550 feet and had flatly stated that Joiner's well was going to open up one of the largest oil finds in the world. Lloyd had concluded his letter by asking Joiner to continue furnishing him core samples from his well, a clear implication that drilling was well under way.

Lloyd's report, maps, and letter were classic examples of con artistry. Although Lloyd had used his geological terms correctly, not a single geological conclusion was based on fact. There were no oil-bearing anticlines in Rusk County, no salt domes, no fault cutting across the Bradford lease. Seismic crews had not made "thousands of registrations" in the area; in fact, they had made none at all. What was more, there was no way Joiner could have continued to send him core samples to analyze because drilling had not even commenced. Nevertheless, Joiner had begun mailing out hundreds of copies of the maps, the report, and the letter to the "sucker list" of investors he had compiled during his years as a promoter. Convinced he had a nose for oil, Joiner more than half-believed in his own con artistry.

"I am sure we're going to make a well," he would tell his prospects. "I am sure of it."

Alas, Joiner's mail-out had brought little response. He then had decided to set an arbitrary figure of $75,000 as the worth of the first well, and had begun selling interests in it for $25 a share; by this formula, each share would be worth 25/75,000 of the total. Once again, his sales effort had brought little response. Finally, Joiner had been able to scrape up about a thousand dollars from some lease and equipment sales made with the help of a local grocer.

In August of 1927, he had managed to set up a pine-wood derrick, and with a "crew" comprised mostly of local farmers, he had begun drilling his first well. A poor boy's poor boy, he had used rusty old pipes turned by a puny 75-horsepower oil boiler and a 50-horsepower cotton-gin engine. Six months and only a thousand feet later, the drill pipe had stuck in the hole. Not even a dynamite charge lowered into the hole could dislodge it, and the well had to be abandoned.

A second attempted well had gotten to 2,500 feet by March of 1929, but once again the pipe had broken and the hole had to be abandoned.

Realizing the handicaps imposed by his shoddy, second-rate equipment, Joiner had hoped to salvage his venture by hiring on a more professional crew. He had hitched a ride to Shreveport and had managed to induce Ed C. Laster, an experienced driller who happened to be out of work, to come to the Daisy Bradford lease and operate a third well for a salary of $10 a day.

On May 8, 1929, Laster had gotten two local farm boys to help him skid the Joiner rig from the site of the second well to a new location about five hundred feet away. But when the rig was just a hundred feet short of the designated new location, a derrick support had caught on a rock and broke. Laster had ordered one of the farm boys to drive over to the sawmill and buy a piece of wood to make a new support. But the young man had informed him that that would be impossible unless he had the $10 needed to buy the piece —in cash.

"The sawmill's cut off Mr. Joiner's credit just like everyone else has," he had told Laster.

Laster had flown into a rage. He had begun kicking the tractor tires and cursing at himself. He had been wary enough about taking on the job when he saw Joiner's poor-boy equipment and heard his meager salary offer. This was the last straw. Suddenly, he looked up and saw the two east Texas farm boys grinning at him. He could not help but stop his tantrum and grin back.

"Oh, hell," he said, "let's get the damn thing leveled off and drill right here."

The drilling had gotten off to a fantastic start. Laster had made it down over 1,200 feet in the first two days. Then another round of problems had set in. The equipment kept breaking down, the members of the crew fell ill, the money for the drillers' paychecks stopped coming in, and a power struggle developed between Laster and Doc Lloyd over how best to handle the drilling. Laster quit in disgust, only to return again more determined than before.

Joiner, meanwhile, had hustled harder than ever. In the process, he had enmeshed himself deeper and deeper in a web of hopelessly entangled financial commitments. He created still another syndicate—his third—and sold certificates at greatly discounted prices all over the countryside. He sold and resold one lease to eleven different buyers. Many of his buyers were special lady friends, for whom he had turned on all of his considerable charms. Joiner had shuttled other prospective investors in from Dallas and had Laster take meaningless core samples while they were present on the well site. Joiner would huddle over the section of earth that had been extracted from the hole and mutter knowingly.

"It seems to me that you're nearing the Austin chalk, Ed," he would say. "The Woodbine can't be too much farther down, according to our geologist."

Such ruses had been sufficient to impress some of the semisophisticated investors who had heard of oil sands like the Austin Chalk and the Woodbine but couldn't really distinguish them from the sand found at a beach. Soon, Joiner had sold well over 100 percent of his venture, but he had little alternative except to keep selling off still more interests in exchange for the cash to keep going.

Finally, on July 20, 1930, thirteen months after the drilling of the Daisy Bradford No. 3 well began, Ed Laster had reached a depth of 3,456 feet, just forty-four feet above the level where Doc Lloyd had predicted their target would be. Laster took a core sample, and brought up nine inches of the best looking Woodbine sand he had ever seen. This sample was no phony—it was saturated with oil. Joiner and his crew at last had a solid indication they were really onto something big.

As fate would have it, a pair of Sinclair Oil Company scouts had been observing the crew's core sample taking from a not too well hidden vantage point a short distance away.

The wily Joiner had noted the presence of the oil-company scouts and determined on a bold course of action. Rather than hide the sample, Joiner ordered his crew to leave a portion of it in a bucket on the derrick floor.

When the crew quit for the evening, the two young Sinclair scouts had taken the opportunity to steal the bucket, just as Joiner had hoped they would. The scouts took the sample back to their superior, who immediately became suspicious.

"Where did you get this?" the supervisor asked.

When the scouts reported that it had been left on the derrick floor, the Sinclair man broke into a grin. Forget about the Joiner well, he told his young employees. The old fox had merely left the core sample on the derrick floor to trick them. It was what oil-field veterans called "salting" a well. Joiner wouldn't be dumb enough to leave the sample there if he had really found oil, the Sinclair man explained. He had left a phony core sample in the bucket so that someone like them would come along and find it and put the word out that he had hit oil. Joiner was probably at the end of his rope, and looking for a way to sell off his leases. The core sample was the key to his fraud.

While the Sinclair people reached this monumentally wrong conclusion, bona fide news about the Joiner well had begun to leak out. Two of the leaks had come from the still embittered Laster. One of them prompted a representative of Shell Oil Company to lease up a thousand acres near the Joiner tracts. Still another leak had come from Judge M. M. Miller, the El Dorado, Arkansas, lawyer and oil man whom Joiner contacted about providing a drill stem test. The man Miller had leaked the news to was H. L. Hunt.

On the morning of September 5, 1930, as Joiner bustled about the well site in anticipation of the drill stem test, Hunt and Pete Lake drove in from Shreveport. They followed the pine-corridored highway six miles past the little town of Henderson, Texas, then turned right down a narrow dirt road that was unusually furrowed by the passage of traffic. They drove for another mile past an open field, around a large pond, then back into the woods again. At last, they reached the small clearing where the Joiner rig stood.

A crowd of maybe twenty or thirty people was gathered around the well. Hunt saw Joiner standing beside some of his investors. Ed Laster and Judge Miller's brother Clarence were up on the derrick floor tinkering with the drill stem testing device. Doc Lloyd, attired in his habitual khakis and a rumpled cowboy hat, was watching over their progress like a mother hen. A convey of interested local farmers stood around the periphery of the clearing, watching over everybody else.

Hunt got out of the car and approached the well. He was wearing his typical oil-field apparel: a long-sleeved white shirt, a tie, a pair of gray slacks, and a straw boater cocked at a jaunty angle. As usual, he was chomping a cigar.

Hunt's arrival caught the attention of drill stem tester Clarence Miller. Climbing down from the rig, Miller rushed over to Hunt and welcomed him to the well site. Then he introduced Hunt to the man of the hour.

"H. L. Hunt, meet C. M. Joiner."

The two men shook hands, and immediately fell into a conversation about the well. They made a curious sight standing there together: the tall, stout, forty-one-year-old H. L. Hunt in his slacks, tie, and boater, and the skinny, stooped, seventy-year-old C. M. Joiner in his slacks, tie, and boater, each man a strange sort of reverse mirror image of the other. But it was quickly apparent that the two took a liking to each other. Joiner seemed to admire Hunt's caginess and salesmanship, and vice versa. Each man sensed in the other something basic in himself.

Hunt's objective was to get a piece of the action if the test proved successful. He knew that in order to complete the well the financially distressed Joiner would have to install a string of cement casing in the hole to keep the walls from collapsing. Hunt's plan was to offer to finance the cost of the casing in return for an interest in the Joiner leases. Joiner's objective, on the other hand, was not to give away too much too fast. He needed money. But he also intended to hold onto what he had—if indeed it were the harbinger of a new oil field. Hunt parried first.

"Mr. Joiner," he asked in a respectful tone, "what are you going to do about casing?"

Joiner's wily gray eyes met Hunt's crystal blue eyes.

"All taken care of, boy," Joiner replied. "Got a string of used casing on the way any time now."

Hunt began to inquire further when their conversation was interrupted by a commotion on the derrick floor. Clarence Miller and Ed Laster were lowering the drill stem tester into the hole. The device consisted of a 12-foot-long stem attached to a steel ball that was, in turn, covered by a U-shaped seat; it was, in effect, like an underground tasting straw. The tool was surrounded by a belted cone which resealed the potential oil sand once the device was pulled back up.

Miller and Laster began to tense as the tool reached total depth. Then a shot of gas rushed up out of the hole. Miller and Laster quickly hauled up the pipe. The rig started to shake and a rumble rose from the earth. One of the derrick supports broke with a loud crack. Then a quick spurt of murky liquid shot up out of the hole and splashed the top of the derrick. A few seconds later, the gushing stopped abruptly and completely.

The crowd hurried over to the derrick floor. Miller and Laster were examining the output of the well and nodding their heads. It contained mud, water, and, yes, oil. The drill stem test was positive.

"It ought to make a pretty good well," Laster reported, "if we can bring it in."

A few yards away, Columbus Joiner was leaning back against a tree with his eyes closed. He opened his eyes and smiled as the farmers rushed up to him with their congratulations.

"Not yet," he cautioned them. "It's not an oil well yet." But he did not refuse to shake their outstretched hands.

Later that day, someone turned up with a camera, and the men responsible for drilling the well lined up in front of the rig for what would turn out to be one of the most famous photographs in the history of the oil business. Joiner and Lloyd stood in the foreground shaking hands. Behind Joiner and Lloyd stood four oil- and mud-splattered members of the drilling crew. Chief driller Ed Laster frowned at the camera from the right side of the picture, holding his hat behind his back. Strangely enough, the group portrait included one man who had not participated in any way in the drilling of the well. This man stood in the background, just to the left of and behind Ed Laster. He was wearing a straw boater and holding a cigar between his teeth. When the camera shutter went down, he had his hands behind his back, and his tie was rippling in the wind. After the picture taking was finished, the man identified himself to the photographer as H. L. Hunt.

News of the drill stem test on the Daisy Bradford spread like a prairie fire. The well had yet to be completed. There was still no final proof that it could produce more than a spurt of oil. The major oil companies were still highly skeptical of the area. But as far as the local farmers and the independents were concerned, the boom was on. People poured in from Louisiana, Arkansas, and all over Texas. A slapdash collection of shacks sprung up where the road to the well intersected the highway, and it became known as the "town" of Joinerville. Newcomers overflowed the hotels in Henderson even at four, five, and six men to a room. Within a month, over two thousand people had arrived to observe the completion of the Daisy Bradford No. 3 and/or to get in on the action for themselves. Hundreds of leases in Rusk County were bought and sold at ever-spiraling prices. New drilling ventures were initiated at all hours of the day and night.

Hunt jumped right into the thick of things. Unable to negotiate a casing-supply deal with Joiner, he took up residence in the Just Right Hotel in Henderson and began buying about 400 acres of leases close to the Daisy Bradford No. 3. Since Joiner and others had already tied up most of the acreage to the north and west of the well, Hunt bought leases mostly to the south and to the east. Then, still keeping an eye out for a way to get a piece of Joiner's action, he brought some of his men over from Arkansas and began making plans to drill some wells of his own.

Meanwhile, C. M. Joiner found himself faced with an excruciating dilemma. News of his successful drill stem test had brought forth an angry swarm of investors who claimed Joiner had defrauded them. If Joiner brought in his well, all his investors would want their share. But Joiner had oversold his venture at least three times. He was sure to lose all he had worked for. His reputation would be ruined. On the other hand, if he failed to bring in his well, he would lose his lease with the widow Bradford and the chance to produce oil for himself and all the people who had supported him for the last ten years.

The situation came to a head in late September when a receivership action was filed against Joiner in state district court in Henderson. But the Joiner camp did not despair. Momentarily taking leave of the work on the Daisy Bradford No. 3, the multitalented Doc Lloyd went around spreading the false rumor that the receivership action was an attempt by the major oil companies to squeeze "the little man" out.

Lloyd's public-relations job was masterful. The depression-ravaged farmers of Rusk County rallied to the cause with pent-up populist fervor. Stories praising Joiner appeared in all the local papers. The headlines transformed Columbus Marion Joiner, the stooped-over old con man, into the "Daddy of the Rusk County Oil Field." Henceforth, he became known to everyone as "Dad" Joiner, the hero of the Daisy Bradford No. 3. The town of Overton held a "Joiner Jubilee." The *Tyler Courier-Times* lashed out at the "slick lawyers" moving in on Joiner and exhorted everyone from the governor on down to see that Joiner got his due. "It's high time the independent operators had their inning," the paper opined, adding, "Now, if this be bolshevism, then we're bolshevists . . ."

On the strength of this outpouring, work on the Daisy Bradford No. 3 continued with new enthusiasm. So did the influx of interested people. By the fifth day of October, a crowd of over 8,000 people had gathered about the well site. The Joiner crew had long since run out of firewood, and they were stoking the boiler with old tractor tires, fuel stock that created a thick black smoke and a terrible stench.

That evening, as driller Ed Laster was swabbing the hole, the pipe began to gurgle. Then the gurgle became a roar. A stream of oil erupted through the top of the derrick, and rained down on the assembled multitude. The crowd danced in the spray like drought-stricken farmers in the year's first thunder-shower.

Laster quickly managed to tame the gusher, and diverted the flow into a nearby storage tank. Then Joiner came over to read the flow gauge. He could hardly contain himself.

"Sixty-eight hundred barrels!" he shouted at the top of his lungs. "Unbelievable!"

The crowd at the well site scattered to spread the news and take advantage of it. Later that day, driller Ed Laster told a reporter for the *Henderson Times*, "I believe we have the biggest thing found in Texas."

Despite the Daisy Bradford's dramatic debut, most of the major oil companies remained skeptical, and with good reason. Five days after the Joiner well came in, the flow dropped from 6,500 barrels a day to about 250 barrels a day. And the flow was not at all steady. Rather, in oilmen's terms, the well was "flowing in heads." It would give up a few hundred barrels of oil, then fall dormant for half a day or longer. This sort of performance gave many experienced operators cause to doubt the greatness of Dad Joiner's great discovery.

H. L. Hunt harbored few such doubts. While the all-important question of the size and shape of the field had yet to be settled, he recognized the quality of the oil coming from the Daisy Bradford No. 3. The stuff was not just another load of asphalt gunk, but one of the best low-sulphur crudes. Dad Joiner was already selling his oil away as boiler fuel, but Hunt knew that the major oil companies would consider the oil ideal for refining into gasoline and other high-grade petroleum products. Having gained some experience in building gathering lines for his oil fields back in Arkansas, Hunt decided to go into the pipeline business. Moving with remarkable speed, he convinced Sinclair Oil Company to build a loading rack for oil deliveries on a branch line of the Missouri Pacific that ran near the Joiner well. Then he began building a line connecting the loading rack to the Daisy Bradford No. 3. On October 20, 1930, he spudded in his own first well in east Texas on his lease to the south of the Joiner discovery.

As Hunt struggled to get a foothold on the field, Dad Joiner struggled to keep what he had found. On October 18, 1930, the receivership action against him came up for a hearing in Judge R. T. Brown's court in Henderson. Sympathetic to Joiner's plight, Judge Brown gaveled for silence, and announced, "I believe that when it takes a man three and a half years to find a baby, he ought to be able to rock it for a while. This hearing is postponed indefinitely."

Upon hearing the judge's ruling, the packed courtroom erupted into a spontaneous celebration. A few days later, the receivership action was dropped.

Unfortunately, Joiner's time for rocking his baby was not destined to last. Another, separate receivership action was filed against him in Dallas. The old man tried to hide in the Hotel Adolphus to avoid being served with the papers, but a lawyer bribed a bellboy to betray Joiner's room number. Joiner had no choice but to appear at the hearing, which was set for October 31.

When the judge called the proceedings to order, Joiner was present and so was a packed house of supporters, onlookers, and angry investors. Among the neutral parties was H. L. Hunt.

To everyone's surprise, Joiner's lawyer rose and presented a petition for a voluntary receivership. Before he could finish reading the petition, a new round of haggling broke out in the courtroom. The investors who had filed for the involuntary receivership were afraid Joiner had found a way to slip out of their clutches. Finally, the parties agreed to appoint Dallas banker E. R. Tennant as the receiver for the Joiner leases. The hearing adjourned with neither Joiner nor his anxious investors certain what the future would bring.

Hunt saw an opening. As Joiner was leaving the courtroom, he approached the old man, and pulled him aside.

"Mr. Joiner," he said, "I'm offering to buy you out lock, stock, and barrel."

"Boy," Joiner replied wearily, "you'd be buying a pig in a poke."

The old man shook his head and just kept on walking.

Hunt refused to be discouraged. Far from considering Joiner's property "a pig in a poke," he now coveted it more than ever. The majors might still be skeptical, but Hunt thought he saw in the "peculiar behavior" of the Daisy Bradford No. 3 a clue to the shape of a great oil field. Hunt still did not subscribe to conventional theories of geology, but the fact that the Daisy Bradford well flowed in heads—that is, flowed and stopped, flowed and stopped—suggested that Joiner may have merely punctured the edge of the Woodbine sand. The intermittent flow could mean that the reservoir Joiner had tapped was being fed by a larger pool located somewhere further along the Woodbine layer. But where?

Hunt had a well-educated hunch. By the time of the receivership hearing, several dry holes had already been drilled to the east of Joiner's discovery well. Hunt surmised that the field—if there was a field—must lie mainly to the west of the Daisy Bradford lease. The well he had begun on his own lease south of the Joiner well would tell him something about the southerly limits of the field. But Hunt's real interest was in the area north and west of the Daisy Bradford No. 3. The firm of Foster and Jeffries had begun drilling a well right in the middle of this area for the Deep Rock Oil Company. The Deep Rock lease was, in turn, surrounded by other leases which Dad Joiner still at least tenuously controlled. Foster and Jeffries was fast approaching the depth at which Joiner had encountered the Woodbine sand. If the Deep Rock well found oil, that would be a most convincing indication that Joiner had indeed stumbled onto a very large oil field.

It so happened that when Hunt approached Joiner in the Dallas courtroom about a buy-out, Hunt did not have the money to come through with such a deal even if Joiner had been willing to discuss it. Having tied up all his money in leases and the pipeline-construction project, Hunt had exactly $109 in cash. As usual, he had made his offer to Joiner on the spur of the moment, intending to worry about such details as cash later. Now he set about finding some financing in preparation for a second buy-out offer.

The first people Hunt approached were Frank Foster of Foster and Jeffries and one of the Deep Rock Oil Company men, but Deep Rock declined to get involved. Then Hunt approached several major oil companies. But they, too, said no. For all the hoopla about Dad Joiner, there was still only one producing well in Rusk County—the Daisy Bradford No. 3—any many geologists still thought that that well was just a freak.

Hunt returned to Henderson in glum spirits. He continued to have enormous faith in the potential of the Joiner properties, but it now looked like he would miss out on them simply because he could not rustle up a partner. As he mused about what to do, Hunt complained of his frustrations to his friend Pete Lake. Lake, in turn, kept urging Hunt to buy Joiner out himself. Hunt reminded Lake that he was somewhat short on cash at the present. Lake nevertheless insisted that Hunt find some way to finance the deal and purchase the Joiner properties himself. Finally, Hunt had heard enough.

"If you're so hot, will you take an interest yourself?" Hunt groused.

That seemed to be the line Lake had been waiting for.

"Hell, yes," Lake replied.

"How much?" Hunt asked.

"I'll take a fourth," the little clothing merchant said.

Hunt could not help but smile. The Hunt luck was coming through again. Wasting no time, he promptly negotiated Lake's interest down to 20 percent. In return for his share, Lake agreed to put up $30,000 in cash toward the purchase of the Joiner leases and out-of-pocket traveling money.

Now Hunt had something to work with. He rounded up three men from his Arkansas operation, and sent them over to east Texas to keep watch on the progress of the Deep Rock well. Then, in late November of 1930, he and Lake drove to Dallas to find Dad Joiner.

Dallas was then the queen city of Texas. The population was over 260,000, the largest of any city in the state save Houston, and the skyline featured over a dozen good-sized skyscrapers, including the thirty-one-story Magnolia Petroleum Building. Dallas boasted both the 46,000-seat Cotton Bowl stadium and the sophisticated fashions of Neiman-Marcus; it had the state's biggest banks, miles and miles of new concrete highways, and transcontinental airline service from Love Field. But as far as the oil fraternity was concerned, most of the city's life centered around the downtown hotels. The hotels were the meeting places and, effectively, the offices for everyone from promoters and investors to pipeline operators, oil-well scouts, lease hounds, and drilling contractors. The two finest hotels were the Adolphus, a magnificent structure with a German baroque façade built by the Busch brewing family of St. Louis, and the Baker, a neat stone-block structure located cater-corner from the Adolphus on Commerce Street.

Hunt and Lake checked into the Baker. Upon their arrival, they discovered that their interests had recently been abetted by some perfectly timed bad news. Two dry holes had recently been reported to the southeast of the Daisy Bradford No. 3. On Sunday, November 23, the *Dallas Morning News* reported that Hunt's well on his south lease had a "showing" of oil in a recent test. However, Joiner's steadily declining discovery well was still the only substantial producer in Rusk County. Lease prices had collapsed. The old doubts had returned.

News of the dry holes did not distress Hunt at all. Since he held to the theory that the field must lie to the northwest of the Daisy Bradford No. 3, he had expected them to be dry. That word of their failure should get out right before he attempted to negotiate with Joiner was a stroke of luck. Hunt still anticipated that the value of Joiner's holdings would skyrocket, provided, of course, that the Deep Rock well came in as expected. But in the public marketplace of the present, Joiner's holdings had just suffered a sudden depreciation in value. The situation could not help but make the old man more amenable to a deal than he had been at the receivership hearing.

Hunt immediately rounded up his acquaintance H. L. Williford. Several weeks before, Williford and Hunt had met on the street when Hunt was in Dallas attempting to find Dad Joiner. At the time, Hunt had just purchased a lease formerly owned by Joiner not far from the Daisy Bradford well. Hunt merely needed Joiner's signature on some papers connected with the transaction, and was going to pay him a $17,000 lease bonus. But because of the creditors on this trail, Joiner has been hiding out. A wispy, balding man with a penchant for wearing snappy vests, Williford had managed to find Joiner for Hunt and helped get the papers signed. After the transaction, Williford had taken Hunt aside and suggested that he buy out Joiner completely.

When Hunt found Williford on this second Dallas trip, he told him that he was now prepared to make that buy-out offer to Dad Joiner. Williford went to Joiner's flea-bag office in the Adolphus Hotel and was informed that the old wildcatter was suffering from a bout with the flu. Nevertheless, Williford managed to find Joiner in one of the hotel's rooms, and dragged him over to the Baker to negotiate with Hunt.

The three men met on the mezzanine. Hunt told Joiner that he would pay him $25,000 in cash and $975,000 in oil payments for his 5,000-acre lease block. Joiner appeared interested and broached the subject of what Williford would get out of the deal. He suggested that Hunt should take care of paying Williford some sort of commission for bringing the two together. Hunt said that sounded fine. The three men talked some more about terms, then Joiner began to get cold feet. Though declining to make a counterproposal, the old man ended the discussion, got up, and left.

After the meeting, Hunt took Williford aside and indicated to him that he would be willing to offer Joiner a little more for his leases if the negotiations were resumed. Hunt also indicated he would pay Williford a $25,000 commission for his trouble.

On Tuesday morning, November 25, 1930, Hunt prepared to meet Dad Joiner in Room 1553 at the Baker Hotel. Room 1553 was an unimposing little corner suite with two windows looking out to the south and one window looking out to the east. The main room of the suite was decorated with gold drapes, a gold carpet, an oak dresser, two twin beds, and some chairs. A door in the middle of the west wall connected to an adjoining bedroom where there were two more twin beds. The place wasn't much, but it was a lot better meeting ground than Joiner's little office in the Adolphus, especially for the purposes Hunt had in mind.

Before Joiner arrived, Hunt set up a chain-call system that would allow him to keep tabs on the progress of the all-important Deep Rock well. The Deep Rock people would be taking a core sample very soon, and Hunt wanted to be the first to know the results. Much of Hunt's communication system depended on his success in convincing drilling superintendent Frank Foster to allow Hunt scout Robert V. Johnson to be present on the drilling platform when the core sample was taken. It was later alleged that Hunt accomplished the task of convincing Foster by offering him $20,000, to be paid at a future date. Although Hunt would deny the charges, he would admit paying the money to Foster for a variety of obscure services whose nature he could never quite seem to pin down. At any rate, Johnson was allowed to be present on the platform of the Deep Rock well. Hunt ordered Johnson to report any developments to Charlie Hardin and Jick Justiss in Henderson. Hardin, in turn, was instructed to relay Johnson's reports by telephone to Hunt in Dallas.

When Joiner arrived at Room 1553 on the morning of November 25, he did not look particularly strong and vigorous. Bent and skinny anyway, he was still suffering the aftereffects of his bout with the flu. He came into the room dressed in his habitual tie, slacks, and boater hat, and sat down on one of the beds. Across from him sat the cigar-chomping Hunt, a bigger, healthier, but almost identically attired replica of Joiner himself. Lake was in the room, and so was H. L. Williford.

"Boy," Joiner began, addressing Hunt like a father to a son, "you're gonna have to pay me more for these leases than what we've been talking about."

"Well, Mr. Joiner, what do you think they're worth?" Hunt replied.

Having heard from H. L. Williford that Hunt was ready to increase his offer, Joiner answered that he thought something like $50,000 would be a more appropriate cash payment than $25,000. Joiner also indicated that he wanted more money in the way of oil payments, too.

For the next thirty-six hours, Joiner spent most of his time in consultation and negotiation with Hunt. The two ate most of their meals in Room 1553 and seldom ventured out of the room for very long. Their haggling continued into the night and on into the wee hours of the morning.

Hunt later claimed that one reason Joiner kept holding out for more money was the fact that Joiner was receiving his own reports on the progress of the Deep Rock well. In fact, on the night of November 25, news swept the lobby of the Baker Hotel that the Deep Rock crew had just encountered a pocket of natural gas. However, Joiner, for his part, later claimed that Hunt kept him so tied up with their negotiations that developments on the Deep Rock well never came to his attention.

In any case, on the morning of November 25, Joiner and Hunt called over Hunt's lawyer J. B. McEntire and a pair of legal stenographers and began dictating an agreement. The work continued through the morning and into the late afternoon. As it was finally hammered out, the deal called for the sale of Joiner's 5,000-acre lease block to Hunt for $1,335 million. Hunt, as trustee for himself and his partner P. G. Lake, agreed to supply $30,000 of the purchase price in cash. The remainder was to be paid out in future oil production from the properties. Two of the three contracts that made up the total deal involved Daisy Bradford leases. The 80-acre tract, which included the discovery well, went for $203,000. Another 500-acre section on the widow's farm went for $153,000. The rest of the purchase price, $979,000, was for over 4,000 acres of leases more in the direction where Hunt figured the field to be. Among them were the leases surrounding the Deep Rock well.

At 4:30 on the afternoon of November 26, just as the stenographers were putting the finishing touches on the sale agreement, Hunt got a telephone call from Charlie Hardin, his man in Henderson. Hardin had important news about the Deep Rock well.

"Mr. Hunt," the scout said, "I think they're right on top of the Woodbine sand now."

Hunt thanked his man for the report and hung up. It would not be long before the Deep Rock crew would be taking a core sample. Then they would know for sure if they had made a well. Excited by Hardin's news, Hunt returned to his negotiations with Joiner.

At 8:30 that evening, Hunt got another telephone call from Hardin.

"Mr. Hunt," the scout reported breathlessly, "they've cored sixteen feet of material from the Deep Rock well, and ten and a half feet of it is saturated with oil."

That was the best and most important news yet. The Deep Rock well looked like a bona fide producer. And that, in turn, meant that Dad Joiner had indeed stumbled onto a sizable field in the location Hunt had figured it to be.

Hunt's next move would be contested for years to come. According to Hunt's version, he immediately informed Joiner of Hardin's report. Hunt claimed that the news only confirmed what Joiner had anticipated himself.

"I was sure all along that they were going to make a well," Joiner supposedly told Hunt.

Joiner's version was much different. According to his recollection, Hunt never told him anything about an oil-saturated core from the Deep Rock well. Rather, Joiner claimed later, Hunt told him the Deep Rock crew had drilled past the Woodbine sand without finding any oil.

In either case, about midnight on the night of November 26, the Hunt-Joiner signing ceremony took place in Room 1553 of the Baker Hotel. The agreement the two men finally settled on was essentially the same deal they had agreed to when the dictating began that morning prior to the reports from the Deep Rock well. Joiner sold out to Hunt for $1.335 million, of which $30,000 was in cash and the rest in future oil payments. Counting the $25,000 commission to Williford and the suspicious $20,000 payment to Foster, that brought Hunt's total up-front cash to only $75,000. In sum, less cash went immediately to Joiner than to the two behind-the-scenes men, a fact Joiner was not apprised of until much later.

Hunt celebrated the occasion by ordering up a plate of cheese and crackers. The way Hunt told it later, Joiner was more than satisfied with the deal. In fact, according to Hunt, Joiner told him over the cheese and crackers, "Boy, I hope you make fifty milion dollars."

News of the Deep Rock core hit the streets before the end of the week. This time, the rush was on again for real. Lease values shot up, and drilling commenced anew. Joiner's holdings now looked better than ever. One company reportedly offered Joiner $3 million for his leases. But as the world soon learned, Joiner was no longer in a position to sell. He had sold. By Sunday, November 30, news of the deal with Hunt bannered the front pages of papers from Dallas to El Dorado: "JOINER SELLS ACREAGE TO HUNT FOR $1,500,000." The oil fraternity was astounded. H. L. Hunt had pulled the business coup of the decade.

Not surprisingly, the closely timed hotel-room sale caused many people to wonder whether Joiner had really known what he was doing when he sold out to Hunt. What had Joiner known about the Deep Rock core? What did Hunt tell him? Why did the old man stay cooped up in the hotel while all these things were going on? Joiner was not much of a drinking man and neither was Hunt. But both of them had an eye for the ladies. Had Hunt provided female companionship to keep them entertained? Had Hunt conned the old con man?

If Dad Joiner thought he had been deceived, he did not say so. At least not at first. Instead, he gave the image of a man enriched and relieved. In taking over Joiner's leases, Hunt had also taken over responsibility for Joiner's legal problems. Dad was not yet home free, but he had a lot less to worry about. Hunt was the one who had to settle all the lawsuits now. With the initial $30,000 cash payments, Joiner received more greenbacks than he had seen in a long, long time. He also had the time to enjoy his money, and he immediately set about doing just that. With his wife and seven children still settled at Ardmore, Oklahoma, Joiner hung around Dallas romancing the young secretary who had stood by him through his east Texas travails. The two spent lavishly on food and entertainment. Dad Joiner was having the time of his life.

H. L. Hunt also had the time of his life, but in a much different way. With the signing of the Dad Joiner deal, he embarked on the most productive period of his career. Like the El Dorado and Smackover booms, the east Texas boom brought with it all sorts of vices and pleasures. But Hunt was strictly business. As he wrote later in *Hunt Heritage:* "While others played, I preferred to work." And with good reason. Hunt quickly discovered that the hardest part of the Dad Joiner deal was still to come: besides the none-too-easy task of bringing in the field, he now had to fight the banks, the major oil companies, the government, the landowners, the hot-oil runners, Dad Joiner's creditors and investors, and even Joiner himself simply to hold onto what he had gotten.

At first, Hunt thought he might never get going at all. After completing the hotel-room purchase in Dallas, he returned home to El Dorado via Shreveport and stopped to talk to a local banker. He presented the banker with a detailed financial statement and an application to borrow $50,000, which was the cost of drilling two wells. The principal asset on Hunt's balance sheet was the Dad Joiner leases. He had little cash.

The Shreveport banker eyed Hunt, looked at his financial statement, and frowned.

"You are broke," the banker said curtly, "and your statement shows you are broke."

"I've got the Joiner leases," Hunt protested. "It's a proven field. There's oil in the ground, and that's a bankable asset."

The banker did not see it that way. As far as he was concerned, the Joiner leases were next to being worthless. He was not about to lend money against something he could not see. To him, Hunt was just another shyster from the oil patch.

"You oil fellows drill a well and it begins to flow, then you take a trip to Europe and buy one or two automobiles, and when it quits flowing, you are broke," the banker railed at Hunt. "I will not lend you fifty thousand dollars, and I do not wish for you to open an account at this bank."

Hunt left Shreveport in a huff and drove back to Dallas. In Dallas, he contacted Nathan Adams, president of the First National Bank. Like Fred Florence at Republic National Bank, Adams was one of the progressive breed of Dallas bankers who recognized early—and very profitably—that oil in the ground was indeed a bankable asset. When Adams looked over Hunt's financial statement, he saw the same figures the banker in Shreveport had seen. But to Adams, the Dad Joiner leases were not worthless at all. Rather, he recognized the Joiner leases as an asset potentially worth millions even if the new east Texas field turned out to be only half of what it was cracked up to be.

"I'll loan you the money," Adams told Hunt.

The two men then shook hands on a banking relationship that would last for the next fifty years.

With his financing thus secured, Hunt hurried to develop his properties. Leaving Lyda and the rest of the family in El Dorado, he picked up his thirteen-year-old son Hassie and took the boy with him to live in Henderson, where they could be close to the Joiner leases at all times. He got some of his men from the Arkansas operations to start drilling the two wells he had financing for, and personally supervised the completion of his Panola Pipeline Company. On December 28, 1930, barely a month after signing the Dad Joiner deal, Hunt's pipeline company sold its first shipment of east Texas oil to Sinclair Oil Company from the loading racks at Friar's Switch.

Meanwhile, the true size and shape of Joiner's amazing discovery began to become clear. Following the Deep Rock well, there were strikes up in Kilgore and Gladewater, some fifteen and thirty miles north of the Daisy

Bradford well. There were also strikes in Smith County, Cherokee County, and Upshur County. Gradually, a pattern emerged. The east Texas field was shaped like a giant bone, long and narrow in the middle with round bulges at each end. It measured over 40 miles from tip to tip and encompassed an incredible 140,000 productive acres. The Daisy Bradford discovery well marked the eastern edge of the field's southern bulge. The leases Hunt purchased were to the west of the discovery well, right smack in the middle of the bulge.

Though the Joiner leases comprised less than 4 percent of the total area of the field, they were a very productive part of an immense reservoir. Within three years of the Joiner discovery, the east Texas field would be pronounced the largest oil field in the world, a title it would hold for over twenty years. No one at the time knew exactly how much the field was capable of producing. Estimates soared from 100 million barrels to 500 million, unbelievable figures for the times. But even those estimates would prove conservative. For over the next fifty years, the east Texas field would produce more than 4 billion barrels of oil.

As the east Texas field came on production, distraught major oil company geologists finally figured out why they had missed the biggest oil find of the early twentieth century. The east Texas field was an anomaly, a freak. Previously, geologists had searched for oil in porous, upwardly bulging rock bubbles called anticlines or in the creases around underground salt domes. The east Texas field represented the first known occurrence of a new kind of oil-bearing structure. The geologists labeled it a "stratigraphic trap." In essence, it was a kind of geological sandwich formed against the shore of a prehistoric island. The bottom layer of the sandwich was composed of nonporous limestone. The top layer was a nonporous rock layer known as the Austin chalk. In between was the oil-bearing Woodbine sand. The oil was capped into the Woodbine not by the arch of an anticline or the edge of a salt dome, but by the layers of limestone below and Austin chalk above.

Never one to bother too long with fancy geological theories, Hunt took note of the new findings and concentrated on drilling more wells as fast as he could. There was good reason for him to make haste. Just as the boom brought the usual gun toting, bootlegging, and whoremongering to the quiet little towns of east Texas, it brought pandemonium to the oil patch. The only law was a kind of institutionalized survival of the fittest. The oilmen called it "the rule of capture." Briefly stated, it held that an operator was entitled to keep whatever he could get out of the ground. But since this relatively simple dictum failed to accommodate the fact that boundaries of leases on the surface of the earth did not necessarily reflect the boundaries of the oil reservoirs underneath, it only increased the potential for havoc. The rule of capture was what compelled the operators of east Texas to drill one well right next to the other. The more wells they drilled, the faster they could get the oil, and the more money they could make. What was more, if an operator failed to keep on drilling, chances were good that his neighbor would get the jump on him and capture a larger share of the oil.

The rule of capture definitely helped stimulate the east Texas oil boom. With all the drilling going on, there were jobs and opportunities for extraordinary wealth at a time when the rest of the nation was suffering through the Great Depression. Families were saved from starvation and poverty. Fortunes of men like Clint Murchison of Dallas and W. A. Moncrief of Fort Worth got their great beginnings. But the boom contained the seeds of a great bust. By promoting overdrilling and overproduction, the rule of capture led to enormous waste. As more wells were drilled, the overall reservoir pressure kept getting lower and lower. That made it more difficult to get the oil out of the ground and decreased the potential amount of oil that could be recovered from the whole field.

At the same time, the rush to production in east Texas contributed to a world oil-price collapse. When the Daisy Bradford No. 3 started flowing, the price of oil was about $1.10 per barrel. Then there was a large strike in South America, and by the spring of 1931, with the east Texas field producing some 160,000 barrels per day, the price of oil had dropped to 15 cents per barrel and 2 cents per barrel on the spot market. Still, the drilling continued as fast and furious as ever.

Increasingly, the east Texas field became a battleground for two groups: the prorationists and the antiprorationists. The prorationists, who were composed largely of the major oil companies and big producers, favored regulated or "prorationed" production, which they claimed would eliminate chaos and promote conservation. The antiprorationists, who were mostly independent operators and other "little men," favored free development of the field according to the rule of capture. The majors had already gobbled up most of the action in other Texas oil booms. The independents regarded prorationing as part of the majors' plot to take over east Texas, too. The majors could afford to sit on their oil. The independents had to produce to survive. They did not favor waste, but they were determined not to get squeezed out once again.

Responsibility for keeping order in the oil fields was in the hands of Governor Ross Sterling and the Texas Railroad Commission. A former president of Humble Oil Company, Governor Sterling was a vacillating politician who seemed surprisingly incapable of applying his business experience or even his prejudices to some sort of solution. The Texas Railroad Commission, meanwhile, was even weaker. The commission had authority to proration and had issued its first statewide proration order two months prior to the Joiner discovery. But the commission had no enforcement ability or powers. Its rulings were widely ignored. Most oilmen considered it a joke.

It was at this point that H. L. Hunt made his first major entry into politics. He came in as a leader of the prorationists. Part of his affinity for the prorationist cause undoubtedly grew out of his early experiences in Arkansas when his first wells went dry from overdrilling in the El Dorado field. Hunt had a genuine notion of the long-term economic importance of conservation. But with 5,000 acres under lease, he was also the largest independent oil operator in the field. His economic interests were really more akin to those of the major oil companies than to those of the "little man." Despite the fact that he was drilling as fast and furious as anybody else, he wanted someone to establish order before the great field was depleted.

As a result, Hunt took the lead in organizing the prorationists into effective political groups, which he referred to as the "East Texas Oil Clubs." One such group, the Gregg and Rusk Counties Proration Advisory Committee, held an emergency meeting in the town of Longview on February 5, 1931. Hunt called the meeting in response to a meeting held by the antiprorationists in Longview earlier that day. By the time Hunt entered the local meetinghouse, every seat was taken and tensions were running high.

Hunt stood up in the front of the room, and waved for the meeting to come to order. Then he began talking about the dangers of overdrilling and overproduction, and the way reservoir pressures and average crude-oil prices were dropping in the east Texas field.

"We don't want rules that favor major companies over independents," he declared. "We want long-term conservation measures that will benefit all operators in the field."

Hunt's remarks brought about loud mutterings of agreement and scattered mumblings of dissent. For a man who did not like to do much talking, he was proving himself a pretty fair country orator.

"I have a proposal," Hunt continued. "I suggest that we immediately send a telegram to the Railroad Commission urging them to proration the east Texas field according to market demand as soon as possible. If we get no response, then I think we should meet again and consider further action."

Hunt's proposal brought another loud cry of agreement from the prorationists in the room. Then a group of antiprorationists crashed the meeting and began causing a verbal ruckus in the back rows.

"Sell-out, sell-out," they shouted. "Hunt's sold out to the major companies."

Hunt stood his ground.

"I haven't sold out to anyone," he replied with remarkable calmness. "I favored prorationing in Arkansas. I favored it in Louisiana. And I favor it in Texas, too."

Once again, Hunt's remarks touched off a furor in the back of the room. The meeting broke up with each side angrily denouncing the other.

Meanwhile, Governor Sterling continued to vacillate, and production in the east Texas field continued to increase to over 500,000 barrels a day. In Oklahoma, a similar prorationing battle finally reached a crisis on August 4, 1931, when Governor William H. "Alfalfa Bill" Murray declared a state of martial law and sent troops into the oil fields to shut down every well. The next day, Governor Sterling of Texas received a telegram urging him to declare martial law in the east Texas field, too. The telegram was signed by H. L. Hunt and thirty-six other east Texas oil operators.

Eleven days later, on August 16, 1931, Governor Sterling issued a proclamation declaring the oil operators of east Texas to be in a state of "insurrection" and "rebellion," and sent in 1,200 National Guard troops to shut down the wells.

The military men arrived in east Texas on August 17 under the command of Brigadier General Jacob F. Wolters. The summer rains had made most of the muddy roads impassable by car, so the troops rode in on horseback. With their billowed riding pants and round-brimmed military hats, they looked like General John J. "Blackjack" Pershing's punitive expedition against Poncho Villa. They also had the air of major-oil-company strikebreakers. General Wolters was a general counsel for Texas, a former leader of the "peacekeeping" force in the Galveston shipping strike, and a veteran "policeman" of oil booms in Borger and Mexia. One of his top aides was an employee of Gulf Oil Company.

Mocked by the locals as "Boy Scouts," General Wolters and his men acted like an occupying army. First, Wolters sent his men into the field on horseback to shut down the wells. Then he began issuing a barrage of orders directed at the general citizenry. He barred the wearing of beach pajamas (a typical prostitute's attire) and prohibited mass meetings within the 600-square-mile boundaries of the military zone. Finally, in an almost laughable attempt to assuage angry tempers, he sent the military band marching up and down the streets of Kilgore to entertain the citizenry.

Martial law achieved little more than an uneasy truce. The shutdown worked, and production came to a halt. But the major oil companies and the big independents like H. L. Hunt kept right on drilling more wells. They could not produce the oil from those new wells yet, but when the shutdown was lifted, they would be able to pump more crude out of the ground than ever. As usual, the ones who suffered most from martial law were the "little men." With production halted, their income was shut off. They did not have the extra resources to keep on drilling like the major companies did. The grounds for imposing martial law were questionable at best: after all, there had been no actual oil-field violence prior to Sterling's order. The independents saw martial law as another step in the major oil companies' plot to cut them out.

On September 5, 1931, the military supervised the reopening of the east Texas field under a new Railroad Commission proration order of 225 barrels of oil per well per day, and the era of the "hot oil" runners commenced. "Hot oil" was the term applied to oil produced in excess of the Railroad Commission allowable. Oil-field legend had it that the name was born one cold fall night when a commission official apprehended a shipment of illegally produced oil and instructed the culprits, "Stand over there by that oil. It's hot enough to keep you warm."

Regardless of how the name came into being, the east Texas field soon became one big hot-oil runners' ring. Operators installed "by-pass" valves on their gathering lines to divert oil into secret storage tanks. Establishing intricate clandestine rendezvous systems, they moved the crude out in wagons, trucks, railroad cars, and every other conceivable means of transportation.

One operator even boarded up the sides of his derrick, built a penthouse on top, declared the whole structure his homestead, so that it would be immune from Railroad Commission inspections, and pumped out his oil through special underground pipes.

"It's my oil," the penthouse well operator declared, expressing the sentiment of his fellow independents, "and if I want to drink it, it's none of your damn business."

H. L. Hunt continued to fight for prorationing throughout the days of the hot-oil running, but he also kept on drilling more wells and producing more oil. According to his own records, he drilled 145 wells and paid Dad Joiner some $700,000 in oil payments between the end of 1930 and the end of 1932. At an average price of 10 cents per barrel, Hunt would have had to produce at least 6 million barrels of oil in that two-year period just to meet his obligations to Joiner. Since Hunt also had to contend with a major oil-price collapse as well as his other personal and financial obligations, it was likely that he produced closer to 12 million barrels of oil in those years, or between 160 and 200 barrels per well per day. Given the periods of price collapse and field shutdowns, it would have been impossible for Hunt to have produced that much oil without violating the prorationing orders at least some of the time. However, Hunt's outfit was convicted of hot-oil running only once, and in that instance he blamed the scheme on some employees who he alleged were trying to steal from him. Innocent or not, he was fined $49,000.

If the size of Hunt's oil production underscored the element of hypocrisy in his prorationist stance, it also showed what a truly remarkable operator he really was. Drilling at the rate he had drilled the Daisy Bradford No. 3, it would have taken Dad Joiner over 145 years to complete the number of wells Hunt drilled in the first twenty-four months of his east Texas operations. Of course, Hunt was no longer just another poor boy. He had fancy bank financing, and he now used steel derricks instead of wooden ones. But he still had to rely on unwieldy steam boilers to power his drilling bits, and he was often stuck with worn-out, second-rate equipment simply because nothing else was available.

He also faced considerable opposition from Mother Nature. Each fall and winter heavy rains fell on the east Texas field. The rain buried the cars and trucks in the mud and brought the mules and blacksmiths out of retirement. Most of the leases were dense with pine trees. The drilling crews had to clear roads to the drill sites, then clear the drill sites themselves. Many times conditions were so bad that not even the mules could make it through. On those occasions, the men had to carry in the pipe and equipment on their backs, wading through water and mud up to their waists.

Although Hunt seldom did the real dirty work, he accomplished, with considerable grace, the none-too-easy task of motivating his men. As in the past, he took care to talk to them and listen to their problems. He was interested, not aloof, and he made them feel proud to be a part of his great enterprise, proud to be "Hunt men." He also knew how to win their loyalty

through their paychecks. In fact, one of Hunt's most remarkable accomplishments in the east Texas field was the creation of what he called "the flexible
work week" plan. Having already created some two hundred jobs by the fall
of 1931, Hunt decided to raise each man's pay 10 percent and to cut the shifts
from twelve hours to six hours. By so doing, he was able to create an additional
two hundred jobs for the depression-racked population of east Texas.

In addition to winning him a reputation as a friend of the poor, Hunt's
"flexible work week" plan won praise at the time from the *Dallas Morning
News*. The paper called Hunt a "pioneer in the share the work movement,"
and gave him credit for instituting his plan long before similar measures were
urged on the public by the Roosevelt administration. Noting that Hunt himself
did not like the term "share the work," the paper went on to report that he
considered his "flexible work week" plan part of "an inevitable universal
reduction in laboring hours." Never one for false modesty, Hunt, the prorationist turned social planner, told the *News* reporter that further adoption of
plans like his was "the solution of unemployment and the way out of the
wilderness of the economic readjustment."

At the same time that he struggled with conditions in the oil fields, Hunt
was constantly engaged in courtroom battles over the titles to the Joiner
properties. In the first two years of his east Texas operation, no less than three
hundred separate lawsuits were filed against him. When the dust cleared, it
turned out that Dad Joiner had actually held clear title to only two acres of
the 5,000 acres he had sold to H. L. Hunt. The legal battles lasted for ten years,
but Hunt and his attorneys, L. L. James and J. B. McEntire of Tyler, managed
to win or conveniently settle every one of the three hundred suits. Their usual
method was to pay the plaintiff $250 and all court costs. In return, the plaintiff
agreed to drop all claims against Hunt and to acknowledge his valid ownership
of the property. Hunt later wrote, "I welcomed these suits which could be
settled with a fee of $250 for they established my claim to the property beyond
a doubt."

The importance of the relatively minimal prices Hunt paid to clear
Joiner's titles could not be underestimated. If all three hundred litigants had
tied him up in lengthy trials and demanded what the properties eventually
proved to be worth, his fortune might well have been dissipated before it ever
got off the ground. That Hunt did dispose of the suits so deftly was testimony
to his own flair as a legal general and to the hardships of the times: $250 was
a lot of money during the depression, especially for a poor farmer who did not
have enough cash to pay a lawyer for a long court fight. A quick settlement
looked like a pretty good deal from both sides of the table—at least in the short
run. In the long run, Hunt's ability to obtain these settlements was worth
inestimable millions in monies he would otherwise have had to pay over in
judgments and legal fees.

Not surprisingly, the man with two families saw relatively little of either
one during his days in the east Texas field. Lyda and the children (except
Hassie) remained in El Dorado the whole time, and Hunt remained close to

his oil wells. He came home for Christmas of 1931, when Lyda conceived still another child, but he was away most of the rest of the time. On August 2, 1932, Lyda gave birth to their sixth surviving child, a boy they named Lamar Hunt, making his initials H. L. backward.

During this period, Hunt continued to visit Frania on some of his many business trips to Dallas, but the two did not have any steadier a relationship than the one they had in Shreveport. They did not cavort in high society, and they did not entertain. In fact, having conceived another child every two years since 1926, Frania failed to become pregnant again in 1932.

Hunt was apparently too busy for much of anything but business. Through the months of 1931 and 1932, he charged ahead at his full-blast best, borrowing, building, drilling, planning, and politicking at all hours of the day and night. By now he was well into his early forties, and no longer the "White Hope" of his youth. He had a paunch on his six-foot, 200-pound frame, and a much rounder, cheekier face. But he was nothing if not dynamic, a vision of energy and drive dashing across the oil fields with his tie flapping in the breeze. What was more, with each new success, he seemed to become even more charged, even more dynamic, both in his own estimation and in observable reality.

Hunt's attention to business definitely paid off in material terms. In his first two years in the east Texas field, he made somewhere close to half a million dollars. And that, of course, was just the beginning. Once the oil payments to Joiner were completed and production really got going, his revenues would soar into the millions. With the prospect of a lasting success more likely than it had ever been at any time in his life, Hunt decided to move Lyda and his first family to Texas. He checked out of the Just Right Hotel in Henderson and bought a fine old mansion in the nicest section of Tyler, the de facto capital city of the east Texas field. Then he opened an office in the People's National Bank building and continued the battle to develop his leases.

Late one rainy night in the fall of 1932, shortly after the move to Tyler, Hunt and one of his men were driving down the highway outside of town when they spotted an overturned car by the side of the road. A crowd of people had gathered, and there were screams of distress. Hunt pulled over and got out to help. He discovered that the driver of the overturned car was trapped beneath it. Swinging into his "White Hope" routine, he rushed to the side of the car and began pushing against it with all his might. Some of the other bystanders joined him in the effort, and finally the car moved. But in the process, something popped in Hunt's back. He left the scene in terrible pain. A short time later, he learned that he would have to spend the next six months in a huge steel brace.

Crippled for the first time in his life and confined to a bed in Tyler, Hunt then learned of a new and potentially more debilitating problem: Dad Joiner was growing extremely dissatisfied with their now-famous deal. Joiner had been testifying on Hunt's behalf in most of the title suits over the east Texas leases. And Joiner had been getting his oil payments with prompt regularity at rates of $30,000 and $50,000 per month. But the money was not enough. Joiner was still having a fling with his young secretary, and had even commenced more highly speculative oil ventures. Lately, he had been coming around to see Hunt about the twentieth or twenty-fifth of each month begging for advances on his oil payments.

"Boy," Joiner would say, "I need you to give it to me a little bit early this month."

Hunt would scold Joiner for his spendthrift ways, then oblige him with a little more money. Joiner would thank him and promise not to bother him again—until he showed up the next month. The Joiner-Hunt relationship had completely reversed its father-son roles.

But despite his genuine affection for H. L. Hunt, Dad Joiner could not help but dwell on the fact that he, the great discoverer, had to go begging for his share of the take, while men like H. L. Hunt reaped fortunes from the great oil field he had found. Joiner had also grown bitter at Ed Laster, his former driller, for revealing the results of the Daisy Bradford core to an agent for the Mid-Kansas Oil Company; Laster's leak had enabled Mid-Kansas to lease up some even better acreage than Joiner had. In early 1932, Joiner filed suit against Laster. Laster threatened a nasty countersuit, and Joiner backed off. Then rumors circulated that Joiner was going to sue H. L. Hunt.

The rumors reached Hunt on November 19, 1932, as he lay in his steel brace in Tyler. Despite his condition, he realized he had to act fast. The statute of limitations was due to run out on November 26, two years from the date of their contract. If Joiner was going to sue, he had to file his petition by then. That gave Hunt one week. Hunt was convinced he could change Joiner's mind or at least stall him, if only he could meet face to face with the man. There was only one course of action available.

"Get me to Dallas," Hunt ordered his men. "I've got to talk to Mr. Joiner."

The two men met in a suite at the Baker. The room looked very much like the room where they had cut their deal. There were drapes, twin beds, some windows, and some chairs. But this time, it was H. L. Hunt who was in ill health and apparently on the defensive. Lying on the bed in his steel brace, he made a most sympathetic figure, the picture of a man needlessly cut down in the prime of life. Joiner, still bent and wheezy himself, sat on the opposite bed commiserating with the fallen Hunt.

The old man and the younger man talked for many hours. Hunt told and retold the tales of his adventures in the West, his Mississippi gambling days, and his struggles in the El Dorado oil boom. Joiner, in turn, recounted the glory days of the Oklahoma land rush and the epic saga of his frustrating quest for oil. As the hours passed, the two discussed just about everything under the sun—except, of course, the rumors that Joiner planned to file a lawsuit. Finally, on the night of November 25, just as Joiner was leaving the suite, Hunt struggled up from his bed and hobbled over to see the old man to the door.

"Mr. Joiner," he said. "I think efforts are being made to get you to sue me. I hope you don't fall for that."

Joiner looked back at Hunt, his eyes welling up with tears. He put his arm on Hunt's shoulder.

"My boy," he said, "I would never do a thing like that. I love you too much."

Then he turned and left.

Hunt returned to his bed with a false sense of security. Despite the risk to his back, the trip to Dallas had been well worth it. Joiner had reassured him. There would be no lawsuit. Or would there? All of a sudden, Hunt became uneasy. He began thinking about why Joiner had gotten so choked about it, why the old man had cried. Then, Hunt realized the truth. Tears had come to Joiner's eyes because he *was* going to sue.

With everything he had worked for hanging in the balance, Hunt quickly formulated an emergency plan. Up to this time, he had managed to obtain credit enough to develop his leases by finding suppliers and bankers who recognized the value of the oil reserves as a bankable asset on his financial statement. But in the course of these arrangements, Hunt had never actually put up any of his property as security or collateral on his indebtedness. This blessing had now become his greatest liability. If Joiner did file suit, his lawyer could also place a lien on Hunt's entire east Texas operation. That would be a powerful inducement for Hunt to come to Joiner's terms.

Hunt called his attorney, J. B. McEntire, in Tyler and told him to get to Dallas with some stenographers. He called his brother Sherman Hunt, also in Tyler, and ordered him to make sure McEntire followed his instructions. Then Hunt called one of his chief equipment suppliers, Continental Supply Company in St. Louis, and asked one of their executives to send down a credit man right away. When the executive learned that Hunt wanted to secure his indebtedness, he answered him, "There's no need for that, Mr. Hunt. We're satisfied with the condition of the account."

"Send him," Hunt commanded. "I don't want to discuss it any more."

Soon Hunt's suite was bustling with lawyers and stenographers, and ringing with the sound of typewriters. Reclining in his bed with the awkward steel brace, Hunt directed a mortgage-writing session that lasted on through the night. By dawn, his hotel room team had finished writing mortgages worth $3 million. Each was properly signed by the Continental Supply Company representative. A squadron of messengers drove the papers over to the courthouse in Henderson.

Hunt's messengers arrived just as the courthouse opened on November 26. One hour later, Dad Joiner's attorney showed up to file suit against Hunt.

Thanks to the hastily prepared lien by Continental Supply, Hunt's oil properties were safe from another lien by Joiner. But it still looked like there was a real battle in store. The main charge in Joiner's suit was fraud. The old man claimed that Hunt had intentionally kept him occupied in the Baker Hotel during their negotiations and had lied to him about the progress of the Deep

Rock well. Joiner further maintained that Hunt had bribed drilling superintendent Frank Foster $20,000 to keep his men informed of the true progress on
the Deep Rock well. Placing a value of $15 million on the 5,000 acres he had
sold to H. L. Hunt, Dad Joiner now claimed that he should have received three
to five times the amount he was paid for the leases.

Suits for fraud were as common in the oil business as dry holes. When
such frauds involved the quickhandedness of some oil scout, public opinion
often scorned the victim as a sucker and praised the accused scout for his
cleverness. Oil-field espionage was seen as glamorous, romantic, exciting. But
the Dad Joiner suit was different. Joiner was still the original wildcatter and,
therefore, in many people's eyes the most righteous hero in the east Texas field.
The fact that he was old and ailing and had apparently been outwitted by a
younger, cagier hustler made Joiner's case another *cause célèbre* for the common folk of Rusk County.

As in the past, the ongoing relationship between Hunt and Joiner remained curious. "I don't have anything against Mr. Hunt personally," Joiner
told reporters on the day he filed his suit. True to his word, Joiner stayed
personally in touch with Hunt and his family, and even sent them a crate of
pink grapefruit for Christmas.

Nevertheless, the battle behind the scenes grew nasty. There were rumors
of witness bribery and intimidation by both sides, and a report that Hunt's
men, under the supervision of his brother Sherman and top aide Roy Lee, were
conducting desk searches and demanding loyalty oaths of Hunt employees.
The wife of Hunt scout Charlie Hardin, the telephone-relay man in Henderson,
claimed that her husband received threatening letters and threatening phone
calls at all hours of the night. When the sheriff finally showed up to serve him
with a subpoena to testify in the *Joiner* v. *Hunt* suit, Hardin was nowhere to
be found.

On December 19, 1932, Joiner's lawyers took Hunt's deposition. He gave
a very uneven performance. Claiming to recall very little of what was said in
the hotel-room negotiations with Joiner, Hunt insisted that he had kept the old
man informed of the true developments on the Deep Rock well just as soon
as he received the news himself. But Hunt also admitted that he had not
actually signed the papers until "three or four hours" after he knew the Deep
Rock crew had cut an oil-saturated core. Then Joiner's lawyer brought up the
subject of the $20,000 payment to Frank Foster, the driller on the Deep Rock
well. Hunt admitted making the payment, but denied that it was made because
of information Foster helped supply concerning the Deep Rock core. Under
questioning, Hunt proceeded to give three completely different stories—in
succession—as to what the payment really was for.

While taking this beating in the witness chair, Hunt fared much better in
the behind-the-scenes negotiations his lawyers had initiated with Joiner's.
Exactly what was said in these negotiations was never revealed. Rumors later
floated out that Hunt promised Joiner a large cash payment if he dropped the
suit. Other unconfirmed reports suggested Hunt had found some counterlever-

age to exert on Joiner. In any event, the two parties suddenly arrived at a secret agreement to settle the suit.

On the morning of January 16, 1933, Judge R. T. Brown entered his Henderson courtroom amid an excited buzz. Every seat was filled, and there were people spilling out into the aisle. Reporters had come in from as far away as Dallas. Many of the major operators in the east Texas field were also on hand. All were expecting a battle royal. Hunt and Joiner sat in the front at the opposing counsels' tables, consulting with their lawyers.

Judge Brown gaveled for order. The case of *C. M. Joiner* v. *Hunt Production Company et al.* was now ready to begin.

Then, to the surprise of everyone but the parties involved, Dad Joiner rose out of his seat and began to read a prepared statement announcing his intention to drop the suit. Explaining that he had filed the suit hurriedly in hopes of getting it in under the statute-of-limitations deadline, Joiner did a complete about-face on his allegations against Hunt: "Since the suit was filed," he told the court, "I have made a thorough investigation and have determined to my satisfaction that the allegations of fraud in my petition are not true. After making such investigation, I reached the conclusion, and hold to that conclusion now, that I was not deceived or defrauded in any manner . . . at the time the contracts in said suit were by me executed."

The courtroom spectators listened to Joiner's droning statement with shocked disbelief. How could the old man be dropping his suit now? What were the conditions of his decision? Had Hunt forced his hand? How could Joiner do a complete turnaround on his story when he was his own chief eyewitness?

The mystery surrounding the Dad Joiner deal only increased as Joiner read through one of the more important middle paragraphs of his statement. In it, Joiner stated, "I am now convinced that the trade . . . was fairly made by all parties to said agreement, and that no oil saturated sand had been recovered from the Deep Rock well prior to the time the sale was made."

The rub here, of course, was that Hunt had already admitted signing the papers after he heard the news of the Deep Rock core. Was Joiner placing a self-contradiction in the record as a clue to what really happened? Or had his settlement with Hunt called for him to rewrite history?

Joiner, for once, was not talking. After finishing his statement, he left the courtroom with no further comment or amplification.

Curiously enough, Joiner's reverse father-son relationship with Hunt continued just as before. In fact, shortly after the trial, Joiner approached Hunt for a $10,000 advance on his oil payments so that he could pay his attorney's fees. Hunt would only agree to give him $3,000.

"He lost the case, didn't he?" Hunt asked Joiner. As Joiner sheepishly nodded his head, Hunt launched into another tirade about Joiner's spendthrift ways.

C. M. "Dad" Joiner spent the rest of his days looking for another great oil field. He concentrated most of his efforts in northeast and west Texas, but the next big strike perpetually eluded him. As in the past, he was always overspending and coming back to Hunt for another advance on his oil payments.

"Boy," he would ask, "could you help me out a little bit? I wouldn't bother you except that I have some checks out."

Hunt would again go through the ritual of scolding him and reluctantly giving in to his request.

On September 8, 1933, Joiner went down to Juárez, Mexico, where he divorced his wife of fifty-two years, and married his young former secretary. Joiner's ex-wife and her children filed some nasty lawsuits against the old man, each claiming a share of the old man's east Texas money. Hunt stepped in and calmed the waters, helping to arrange a settlement acceptable to all sides. Joiner eventually settled into a comfortable house on Preston Road in Dallas, where he lived until his death in 1947. His net worth at the time of his passing was little more than the value of his house and car.

Naturally, Hunt defended the fairness of the Dad Joiner deal until his last breath. "Much has been written about the Joiner deal, and some with overly active imaginations have implied machinations all the way around," he observed in *Hunt Heritage*, "but the fact is it was a sound deal for both Joiner and me, and Joiner received through the cash, notes, and production payments more funds than he would have received by trying to operate the properties in the face of his legal difficulties, and I assumed the risk of proving up his titles."

Hunt might have added that Joiner was hardly a naïve old man. The many lawsuits Joiner faced were a direct result of his own deceitful hustling and overpromoting. His public image may have been that of the lovable, quixotic "Daddy of the Rusk County Oil Field," but his character and modus operandi were as street-wise as anyone's. If Hunt was guilty of fraud, he had committed it in the course of conning a consummate con man. That might not excuse his behavior, but it certainly put it in a different light.

Still, there was little doubt about who came out ahead in the long run. Hunt would later downplay the importance of the Joiner leases, claiming that they did not turn out to be the very best of the very biggest acreage block in the field. This was true. When the dust cleared, Hunt emerged not as the first but the thirteenth largest producer. However, all those ranked ahead of him were major companies like Humble, Gulf, and Shell. Hunt was the largest independent producer in the field and by far the greatest single individual beneficiary. According to the best estimates, Hunt went on to make over $100 million from the Joiner leases. In addition to being Hunt's first really big money, his profits from the Joiner deal proved to be the cornerstone of a fortune eventually worth billions. On a dollar-for-dollar basis, he had outwitted Joiner by 100 to 1.

This lopsided result was enough to prejudice many people against H. L. Hunt forever. Hunt had the kind of wealth made famous by John D. Rockefeller and the robber barons. People called it "tainted money." As one popular saying put it, that meant that the money " 't ain't yours and 't ain't mine." But it also meant that the way the money was obtained—or at least the way people *believed* it was obtained—was through morally questionable means. In Hunt's case, the mysterious hotel-room negotiations and Dad Joiner's sudden decision to drop his lawsuit cast a shadow over the H. L. Hunt fortune that would never completely lift.

CHAPTER 6

THE BEST DAYS

DESPITE the bad publicity that came with Dad Joiner's lawsuit, H. L. Hunt and family were welcomed into Tyler, Texas, with open arms. A pine- and pecan-tree-shaded bastion of the Old South, the Hunts' new home town had always prided itself in being the commercial rose-growing capital of the world. But with Dad Joiner's discovery well and the strikes that followed, Tyler had become the new capital city of the east Texas field. By the time Hunt moved his family from Arkansas, no less than thirty-two other oil companies had established headquarters in town. A number of ten- and fifteen-story buildings were going up around the town square. New residential sections were opening in what had once been pasture and piny woods. The population was swelling from 17,000 to nearly 30,000, and the townspeople were planning civic improvements, ranging from new streets and sewers to new rose festivals.

In the eyes of Tyler, H. L. Hunt's money was no more tainted than that of half the other operators in the east Texas field. Oil was a rough business. The garrisons of Texas Rangers and National Guard troops that stabled in one of the city's barns were sufficient testimony to that. Located more than a dozen miles to the west of the oil field's border, Tyler was eager to share in the wealth and just as eager to keep out the violence and the vice of the boom. The seat of a dry county, Tyler liked to think it attracted the cream of the crop. As one local matron put it, "Those who wanted the open bar went to Kilgore." How a man conducted himself out in the oil field was less important to the gentility of Tyler than how he conducted himself off the field. And for all the accusations about his conduct in the Dad Joiner deal, H. L. Hunt was at least a clean liver. Or so it appeared.

For most people in Tyler, the Hunt character was symbolized not by the Dad Joiner deal, but by the family's new residence, the great Mayfield house at 223 Charnwood. Named for the family who had restored it to grandeur, the

Mayfield house was a big, white Greek-revival mansion, two-and-a-half stories tall, with huge square-cut columns in front, a beveled glass door, a carport, servants' quarters, and a big back yard. The lot was beautifully landscaped with hedges and trees, and there was a white wrought-iron bench bent around the base of a large oak in the front lawn. The front entrance was on a quiet, affluent street paved with V-set bricks, and located only a few blocks from the center of town. The place was, in short, the epitome of genteel respectability, the perfect domicile for a successful oilman with aspirations of becoming a pillar of the community.

For once, H. L. Hunt did not play the role of absent father. Though he still spent plenty of time on the road, Hunt stayed closer to home during his first few years in Tyler than at any other time since the Lake Village days. Part of his extended presence was due to the fact that he was laid up with his back injury for about six months. But mainly, Hunt stayed close to home because his work, the east Texas oil field, was close to home. As a result, Hunt had time to take his children on expeditions for four-leaf clovers (he would award the lucky finder with a quarter) and to tell them stories of his exploits as an oilman. At one point, he packed the brood in the family Oldsmobile and drove all the way out to California for a rare vacation. On Sundays, he would even appear with the family in church, where he would take up the hymnal and sing with gusto.

"The time we lived in Tyler," Hunt would recall years later, "may have been some of the best days we had as a family."

Lyda Bunker Hunt presided over the household with her characteristic homespun dignity. Like other wealthy women in Tyler, she commanded a corps of black servants, but she took personal responsibility for running the kitchen and the cleanups. She did not put on airs or go out of her way to cultivate the friendship of the other ladies of the town. "She had no interest in climbing the social ladder," one friend recalled. "She just wasn't like that." Friends noticed that for all her new money, Lyda always seemed to have holes in her clothes under the arms and mashed-down places at the backs of her shoes. Asked once if she was worried about the impression she may have conveyed, Lyda replied, "Them that knows me will know I've got better, and them that don't know me, I don't care about."

As the other matrons of Tyler could quickly see, Lyda Bunker Hunt's primary concern in life was raising the Hunts' six children. When she arrived in Tyler, Lyda had three teenagers, an eleven year old, a five year old and a newborn infant. Lyda insisted that her children attend the Methodist Church every Sunday, but she generally governed with a loose rein. She allowed her children to turn the third floor of the house into a roller-skating rink, and seldom raised her voice when her little ones raised a ruckus. As one local matron observed, the children of Tyler's new richest family were like FDR's children in the White House: they had the run of the place.

Lyda knew she was sometimes criticized by the other mothers for her light-handed style. But her intention was not permissiveness. Rather, she wanted to make it possible for her children to live a normal childhood. "I'm not trying to manufacture little angels," she complained to a sympathetic friend. "I just want them to be one of the kids."

Hunt had different ideas, at least as far as his oldest son Hassie was concerned. Still his father's runaway favorite, Hassie came to bear a startling resemblance to his father. Tall and broad-shouldered, he had the same bright blue eyes, the same wide jaw and puffy cheeks, and many of the same deliberate mannerisms. The likeness was so strong that Hunt and Hassie won the father-son look-alike contest at Tyler High School and were sometimes momentarily mistaken for each other by some of Hunt's oldest hands.

Hunt tried constantly to fashion his son in his own image. Although Hunt still found relatively little time to devote to his other children, he always had plenty of time—and plenty of fatherly advice—for Hassie. Having taken the boy with him on his first excursions in the east Texas field, Hunt alternately drove Hassie and babied him. At times, he demanded that his son work longer and harder than his regular employees. At other times, he permitted him to lounge around all summer carousing with his friends. Hunt did not let Hassie play football in high school supposedly for fear Hassie would injure his kidneys. Indeed, Hunt encouraged Hassie to take up baseball, his own favorite boyhood sport. But he then sent Hassie off to Culver Military Academy in hopes his son would learn some discipline. Rather than take up baseball, Hassie reacted to the latest paternal dictum by learning to box. One of Hunt's proudest and yet most worrisome moments was the day he visited Culver and found Hassie in the boxing ring giving a good thrashing to "Culver's best pugilist."

In addition to casting Hassie as his new White Hope, Hunt enlisted his son as a fellow creekologist. Hunt believed that Hassie had an almost mystical ability to find oil, a trait the boy had inherited through his paternal line. The two would drive along the back roads and byways of east Texas looking at one lease after another. Finally, Hassie would nudge his father to stop.

"Daddy," he would say, "this looks like a good place to drill."

Hunt usually followed Hassie's advice. Although it was hard to drill a dry hole on his east Texas leases, it was not impossible. And the locations Hassie picked almost invariably turned out to be producers. This, in turn, confirmed Hunt's opinion that his son had special powers.

However, some of the other things Hassie did suggested that he also had special problems. Like his father, he was a double-natured young man, but to even greater extremes. As one friend put it, "There were two Hassies: a calm, controlled one, and one who wanted to be an even bigger boss than his daddy." This other Hassie was lusty and temperamental and prone to violent outbursts. He would be walking around a drilling rig, for example, when he would suddenly reach down, pick up a stray piece of pipe, and send it zinging over the head of one of his father's roughnecks. Or he would be riding through an oil field when he would abruptly jump out of the car and begin rolling around in the mud pits. Or he would be at a high-class cotillion and begin whispering things to his date that one did not say to nicely brought-up young ladies from Tyler, Texas.

Hassie's parents did not know exactly what to make of his actions. Lyda, for one, believed that her son was the victim of too much fatherly pressure. As time passed and Hassie did not improve, she became increasingly concerned that her son's emotional health had been permanently damaged. One reason for her relative leniency with the other children was what was happening to Hassie. As she told her youngest son Lamar when he was old enough to understand her, "I spanked myself out on Hassie. I just don't have any spanking left for you."

Hunt later admitted, "I made a terrible mistake with Hassie." But during the Tyler days, the father had not yet seen the error of his ways. Hunt, on the other hand, believed that Hassie's problems were merely the result of high-spiritedness. He felt certain that Hassie would eventually grow out of his fits of misbehavior in the course of his father's alternating regimes of discipline and indulgence. As Hunt saw it, the whole thing boiled down to the fact that "Hassie needed a lot of action."

Hunt applied some of the same double-edged parental tactics to his other children. For example, when Bunker, the next oldest son, turned eight years old, Hunt let him have his own horse, a mare named Lady. Bunker and the other neighborhood kids liked to jump on Lady four or five at a time, and ride her around the streets of Tyler. Pretty soon Hunt put a stop to Bunker's fun.

"My Dad was scared somebody would get hurt," Bunker recalled afterward. "He sold Lady and got me a bicycle instead."

In this particular instance, Hunt's parental intervention would have enormous repercussions that would only become apparent when Bunker was a grown man with the ability to buy and sell his own horses. But for the most part, Hunt was far easier on his younger sons and on his daughters than he was on Hassie. As Hunt himself put it, "With my other boys I never was so strict as with Hassie. They could do what they wanted."

Of course, H. L. Hunt did not always practice the virtues he seemed to stand for. Living the life of a conventional family man and father was fine as far as it went. And that was certainly the kind of public image Hunt wanted to present to Tyler society and to the outside world in general. But Hunt's private side still operated according to his own double standard. While becoming more and more the personification of bourgeois respectability in his adopted community, Hunt continued to live a very active secret life, the details of which very few Tylerites could even dream of.

At the heart of Hunt's secret life was his Dallas family by Frania Tye. Following the settlement of the Dad Joiner lawsuit, Hunt began seeing Frania a little more often than in his first two years in the east Texas field. How much more often would later become subject to dispute. Frania would claim that Hunt was at their Dallas home "very frequently." He would arrive unannounced, she said, and stay for varying lengths of time—sometimes "a week

or ten days," other times only a day or two. Although Frania admitted that
Hunt was more than usually preoccupied with developing the Joiner leases and
did not seem to remember the back brace he wore for six months, she maintained that he was never away from their home for more than two weeks at
a time.

In any event, Hunt's relationship with Frania continued to follow the
same peculiar pattern that was established back in the Shreveport days. On
those occasions when Hunt was in Dallas, the two did not go out socially and
they did not entertain. At one point, Hunt did take Frania on a trip to New
York to look over offices for an oil importing business he wanted to start. He
also took her on several trips to visit his leases in the east Texas field. But for
the most part, Frania and Hunt spent their time together at home with each
other and their children. Frania, now nearing thirty, was still beautiful, with
flashing blue eyes and a shapely figure. Hunt found her as enticing as ever.

In Hunt's absence, Frania lived with her unmarried younger sister Jennie,
who came down from Buffalo to help with the children. Hunt continued to pay
the bills on the two-story house on Versailles Avenue and to provide Frania
with ample spending money for herself and the children. But in 1932, either
for amusement or extra money or both, Frania and her sister opened a beauty
parlor in nearby Highland Park Shopping Center, which they named Tye's
Beauty Shop. Jennie took charge of the day-to-day operation; Frania, the
investor, kept the books.

Despite the publicity of the Dad Joiner deal and her trips to the east Texas
field with Hunt, Frania later claimed that she still did not know her "husband's" true identity. To her, he was still Major Franklin Hunt, an oil-field
man. She admitted that she had begun to wonder about the relationship
between her Hunt and the H. L. Hunt of Dad-Joiner-deal fame. But she said
that when she asked Hunt about it, he told her that H. L. Hunt was his uncle.

Whether or not Frania knew the truth, Hunt certainly did. So did Hunt's
brother Sherman, whom he introduced to Frania, and several of Hunt's associates, who later claimed to have seen her on trips to the east Texas field. Hunt
went to certain lengths to cover up his second family. The house in Dallas, for
example, remained in the name of Frania's sister Jennie. But according to
former associates, Hunt had no qualms about escorting Frania around the oil
patch or even downtown Tyler, where he would sometimes try to pass her off
as the sister of Frank Grego or some other employee. Hunt also apparently
kept on wanting Frania to bear him some more children, for in early 1934, she
became pregnant with their fourth child.

While increasing the size of his secret family, Hunt carried on more
conventional affairs with several other women in his Tyler days. Or so his office
legend maintained. As one old-timer put it, Hunt and his cronies were "just
beginning to feel their oats." The Hunt offices were well staffed with good-
looking secretaries, and to them the boss was a dashing, romantic figure. As
one former female employee recalled, "He was one of the best-looking guys
you ever saw. He'd come streaking down the hallway with his sleeves rolled

about two-thirds of the way up his arms, his shirt collar open and no tie, and his hair kind of blowing in the breeze a bit."

Hunt's extramarital exploits were abetted by his already well-established custom of conducting his gambling and his legitimate business in hotels. Even when he was in Tyler, Hunt often avoided going into his offices, preferring instead to work out of a suite in the Blackstone Hotel. Many times he would stay at the hotel all night. Eventually, he had an outside staircase built onto the old Mayfield mansion. If Lyda Hunt ever suspected her husband's infidelity, she did not let on. She told friends that Hunt had the staircase built so that he could come and go without disturbing the children, who he claimed also disturbed him. "He's always complaining that he can't get any sleep because the children keep him awake all night with their crying," she would explain.

In Tyler, as elsewhere, Hunt was pretty much of a loner. He talked a little more and dressed more smartly than in the past, but he had few close friends. He traveled with a circle of aides and flunkies—men like Frank Grego, Old Man Bailey, and H. L. Williford—and he socialized primarily with his brother Sherman and his partner Pete Lake. The most important men in terms of the actual operations of the company were Hunt; his hard-fighting lawyers J. B. McEntire and L. L. James; Roy Lee, the short, bald martinet who managed the office; and drilling superintendents Jick Justiss and Sadie Zoller. They were the ones who did or managed most of the critical work. Lake, despite owning a one-fifth interest in the Joiner properties, preferred to leave all the decision making to Hunt. Sherman Hunt, according to one former employee, "drew a thousand dollars a month and didn't have to do anything but draw breath." Known to employees as "Mr. Sherman," he had a reputation as being the wildest member of the triumvirate.

Among the vices Hunt and his crowd enjoyed was booze. Pete Lake reportedly had an inside line on the best moonshine in Tyler, and purchased it frequently in five-gallon oak kegs. Hunt was not much of a drinking man, but he did indulge in some drinking in Tyler. The motivation, while it lasted, apparently had to do with Hunt's longstanding interest in "cures," and the fact that a local doctor had prescribed alcohol for brother Sherman's heart condition. "Nobody had to prescribe a drink for Sherman Hunt," one former employee recalled, "but I think H.L. figured if a doctor said it was good for Sherman, it would be good for him, too." H.L. soon found out differently. Drinking liquor made him sick, not healthy, and he quit the practice after giving it a brief trial run.

The Hunt brothers also spent a good deal of time betting on the horses. Regardless of the thrill and risk of the oil business, gambling was one pastime Hunt could never get out of his blood. Neither was bragging about how well he did with his bets. One of his favorite boasts was his story of winning big money on a 100-to-1 shot named So Rare. As biographer Stanley Brown pointed out, "That probably is an instance when Hunt was gilding one of his lilies, or else found the stupedist bookie in the country, because So Rare was in the money in every race she started in that year."

While Hunt, his brother, and Lake had a good time, they ran the Hunt production company offices on a strict double standard. What went for the top men did not go for the underlings. There were strict rules against employee drinking and gambling. Nevertheless, office workers used to listen in on the bets Hunt and his brother were making and wager on the same horses themselves. Once Sherman discovered that a group of employees had bet on a horse that he and his brother had picked, only to lose their wages when the horse placed second. Instead of getting mad, the Hunt brothers reimbursed the men for their lost money and admonished them not to bet again.

For all his playing around, H. L. Hunt also took care of business. He demanded a great deal from his employees and put in long hours himself. As one employee recalled, "Mr. Hunt was a worker." And it was essential that he should be. For in addition to developing the Joiner leases and defending his ownership of the leases against lawsuits, Hunt had to fight the increasingly violent hot-oil war that raged across the east Texas field.

A major turning point in the hot-oil war came in December of 1932 when the U.S. Supreme Court declared that Governer Sterling's imposition of martial law was "not necessary." A short time later, the governor had to withdraw General Wolters and most of the general's National Guard troops. The military men were replaced by the civilian authority of the Texas Railroad Commission and its new chairman, Colonel E. O. Thompson. Meanwhile, the east Texas operations produced oil faster than ever. The town of Kilgore, one of the centers of the oil boom, became a forest of oil wells. Instead of removing the buildings in the town, landowners simply knocked out the rear twenty-five feet of each one and drilled their new wells right on the spot. Derricks stood so close together that their legs actually touched. One city block contained no less than forty-four separate wells.

Colonel Thompson, whose titled derived from his World War I service rather than from current rank, tried to control the situation. In mid-December of 1932, Thompson and commission engineer E. O. Buck took a pressure reading on the east Texas field. Where the Joiner well had come in with 1,600 pounds per square inch (p.s.i.) in October of 1930, now, only a little over two years later, the pressure had dropped to less than 1,400 p.s.i. in the better parts of the field and to only 700 p.s.i. in the overdrilled sections. Many wells were producing about one-third as much salt water as oil, and the water was encroaching ever more rapidly. The next day, Thompson ordered the field shut down for two weeks. He was able to enforce his order thanks to the help of a few remaining Guardsmen and a contingent of Texas Rangers sent over from Austin. Within seventy-two hours of the shutdown, the pressure in the wells that had shown readings of 700 p.s.i. had returned to a healthy 1,300 p.s.i.

Like H. L. Hunt and the other "conservationists," Thompson realized that unless drastic measures were introduced, most of the east Texas field's great oil riches would be lost in a chaos of overproduction. When the field was due to reopen, he set the new allowable at 350,000 barrels per day for the field and 28 barrels a day for each well. It was by far the most stringent prorationing edict in the history of the Texas Railroad Commission.

Now the "hot oil" controversy became an out-and-out war. Decrying Thompson and the commission, the antiprorationist operators produced their oil faster than ever before. Once again, prices plummeted to a few cents a barrel. But this time the prorationists struck back. Pipelines were dynamited. Oil-field workers and tank-truck drivers were shot at. Well sites were set afire. At last, a state of almost random violence—if not open rebellion and insurrection—existed.

With astonishing timing, a federal court capped off the year by declaring Thompson's per-well prorationing order illegal. The ruling meant that the east Texas field was once again governed only by the laws of nature and the rule of capture. As the *Fort Worth Star-Telegram* editorialized, state regulation in general and the Railroad Commission in particular had been reduced to a "standing joke."

Still a staunch prorationist and an active producer, Hunt felt that the time had come to do something about the war in the east Texas field. Though there was never any evidence that he participated in the bombings and sabotage, he did take a prominent role in pressing for a new regulatory authority. As he knew all too well, the Railroad Commission had been handed control over oil and gas simply because it already had control over the railroads and other common carriers. In Hunt's opinion, the Railroad Commission was both wrongly named and improperly equipped to fulfill its appointed role. So in March of 1933, Hunt drove to the state capital in Austin to lobby for a bill to replace the Railroad Commission with a new Oil and Gas Conservation Commission.

When Hunt arrived in Austin, the prospects for the bill looked good. Governor Sterling had indicated his support, and both houses of the legislature appeared determined to effect passage.

Then a gang of rowdy prorationists (not including Hunt) decided to "celebrate" their apparent victory the night before the bill was to come to a vote. Their celebration included a physical assault on a legislator who favored retaining the Railroad Commission. When the legislator arrived on the House floor in a wheelchair the following morning, the mood of the lawmakers quickly changed. The bill to replace the Railroad Commission was defeated. Much to Hunt's dismay, Colonel Thompson and his heretofore ineffectual squadron of bureaucrats remained the main regulatory force in the east Texas field.

Having narrowly escaped the hatchet in Austin, Colonel Thompson set out to re-exert his authority. First, he ordered all operators to run their wells at full capacity on March 27, 1933, for the purpose of testing the capacity of the field. The results of the test were incredible. They showed that if all the wells were run at absolute full throttle (which not even the greediest operator would actually do for fear of damaging his own reservoir), the east Texas field could produce oil at the rate of 100 million barrels a day. At the time, this was by far the greatest rate of production of any oil field in the world. Still, that was no guarantee the field would last forever. Already the field was producing over 50 barrels of salt water for every 100 barrels of oil. Because of the continuing overdrilling and overproduction, the water continued its relentless encroachment from the west, and the average bottom-hole pressure continued to drop. Thompson realized that something had to be done. But he also realized that it was high time the Railroad Commission issued an order that would hold up in court. Attempting to balance these concerns, he set the new east Texas field allowable at 750,000 barrels per day.

This new proration order may have done more harm than good. Beseiged by lawsuits once again, it was upheld in federal court. However, chaos still reigned in the oil field. Overproduction and hot-oil running continued. Pressure dropped, and so did prices. Mass hot-oil sellers seldom got more than two cents per barrel. More and more salt water came up out of the wells. The bombings and sabotage continued. The east Texas field became an armed camp.

Meanwhile, Hunt and some of the other prorationists split ranks. A few saw the commission's action as a decent attempt to restore order. But Hunt and many others dismissed it as another weak-kneed gesture that would do little to solve the hot-oil and overproduction problems. They gritted their teeth and braced themselves for even more chaos and even lower prices.

Then Governor Sterling's successor, Miriam A. "Ma" Ferguson, called in the Feds. President Roosevelt responded quickly. He issued an order backing the Railroad Commission's authority to block interstate as well as intrastate hot-oil shipments, and announced that new federal affidavits would have to be filed along with all oil shipments. He also dispatched fifty federal agents to Texas to enforce his decree.

FDR's orders brought some fast but short-lived results. The price of oil rose back to one dollar a barrel, the highest it had been in over two years, and for a while some semblance of order returned to the east Texas field. But both the federal agents and their counterparts from the Railroad Commission soon proved incompetent and corruptible. Hot-oil producers bought them off with money and favors, including, in a few cases, jobs in the oil business. In return, hot-oil producers were allowed to get away with signing their federal affidavits with names like "Harold Ickes" (secretary of the Interior) and "F. D. Roosevelt." They were also able to get around the Railroad Commission's well-spacing ordinance by purchasing exceptions for $500 and $1,500 apiece. Through the first half of 1934, the hot-oil runners trafficked their loads more heavily than ever, and both legitimate and black-market production increased monthly.

Ironically, Hunt and some of the other leading "conservationists" were still the ones who drilled the most wells. An inventory taken by Hunt employee Harry Harter on June 15, 1934, showed a total of 13,512 wells in the east Texas field. Nearly two-thirds of those wells belonged to the major oil companies. Humble Oil topped the list with 1,422 completed wells and 22 wells drilling.

But Hunt Production Company ranked thirteenth in the field, with 229 comp-leted wells and 5 wells drilling. Given the fact that his 229 wells were on 5,000 acres of leases, Hunt could not be pegged as a flagrant violator of the well-spacing ordinance, but he could hardly be called a lackadaisical driller either. The way Hunt saw it, the absence of effective regulation made it a case of every producer for himself. As he had observed some time earlier in a telegram to former Governor Sterling, "The majority of the present violators are breaking proration through what they believe a necessity and are for proration if en-forced."

Hypocritical or not, Hunt's flurry of activity was definitely paying off. Taking his number of producing wells as a rough measure of his share in the whole, Hunt could claim a little over 1.5 percent of the production of the east Texas field. That sounded like relatively little until it was remembered that Humble, the largest operator, claimed only 10 percent of the total field. Hunt ranked well below the largest operators, but he was still by far the largest independent in the field. By June of 1934, east Texas had produced nearly 500 million barrels of oil. Hunt's share amounted to about 7.5 million barrels. At an average price of ten to twenty cents per barrel, that translated into a gross income of $750,000 to $1.5 million. Of course, at a dollar a barrel, the gross would have been five to ten times that. It was little wonder why Hunt, like the major companies, wanted controlled production and "stabilized" prices.

While Hunt continued to fight for prorationing, his attention was sud-denly distracted by a problem of a much different nature. This time the trouble emanated not from the east Texas oil field, but from suburban Dallas. Having borne three children and now pregnant with a fourth, Frania wanted out.

The moment of truth arrived one day in the spring of 1934. Frania was sitting in the house on Versailles Avenue talking to her friend Louise Dyer. Frania had met Louise on her first visit to New Orleans years before, and the two had stayed in touch ever since. When Frania wrote to say she was pregnant with a fourth child, Louise had come to visit. Like Frania, Louise had just turned thirty and was a vivacious, good-looking young woman. The two were chatting gaily about a trip they had taken to the 1932 Chicago World's Fair when Louise suddenly turned serious.

"Fran," she said. "I have something to tell you."

Frania stopped and watched her friend's expression grow even more serious.

"Your husband is not Franklin Hunt," Louise said. "His real name is H. L. Hunt, and he has another family living in Tyler."

According to the story Frania told years later, this was the first time she knew the facts about Hunt and his other life. She had heard rumors and innuendos, of course. But it took the words of her friend Louise to make her believe what she did not want to believe.

Frania claimed that a confrontation with Hunt followed a short time after Louise's visit. In that confrontation, Frania informed Hunt that she knew about his real name and his other family. This time, she was not asking him if the rumors she had heard were true; she was telling him she now knew they were.

"He was rather shocked," Frania recalled, "but it didn't take him long to recover. I'd questioned him about H. L. Hunt [on previous occasions], so it was not a surprise."

Frania claimed that in the wake of his shock Hunt finally admitted the truth.

According to the story Hunt family attorneys told years later, Frania's confrontation with Hunt was precipitated by a much different series of events. In a deposition taken years after the fact, Frania admitted being at a party in the spring of 1934 at which one of the guests pointed out to her that H. L. Hunt's oldest daughter Margaret was also in the room. Frania and Margaret did not actually meet at the party, but Hunt family attorneys later alleged that Frania was well aware of Hunt's true identity, and that seeing Margaret at the party caused her to worry that she might be revealed as his mistress.

In any event, after her "confrontation" with Hunt, Frania took a plane back to Buffalo to see her father and ask his advice about what to do. Describing her emotional state at the time as "pretty bad," she said she withheld the truth about her "husband" from her mother until much later. The immediate problem was how to go about rearranging her life.

That rearrangement began as soon as Frania returned to Dallas. With Hunt's assistance, she packed up her belongings and her children and moved to a big white house Hunt bought for her in Great Neck, New York. Frania immediately began calling herself "Mrs. H. L. Hunt" although she realized that she "wasn't Mrs. Anybody." On October 14, 1934, while living in Great Neck, she gave birth to her fourth child by Hunt, a boy who was christened Hugh Lee Hunt.

Hunt did not stop seeing Frania after her departure from Dallas. On the contrary, he paid fairly regular visits to the house in Great Neck, often stopping to gamble at race tracks along the way. According to Frania's former neighbors, Hunt went by the name of "Major Hunt" or simply "Hunt," and seemed to treat Frania like "a normal, loving husband." On occasion, Hunt would even take his second family on traditional family outings, as he did in the summer of 1936 when he and Frania took their brood and some of the neighborhood children on a trip to Coney Island. Hunt also continued to pay Frania's bills, and maintained her comfortably, if not luxuriously, with a car, a couple of servants, and enough money to send their children to private schools.

Frania apparently needed all the support she could get. Following the birth of her fourth child, she was sick for about three years. Combined with the emotional trauma of having to rearrange her life, that illness was especially debilitating. In the winter of 1936, Frania and her children moved to New Orleans in hopes that the warmer climate would restore her health. Her stay in New Orleans lasted about three months and coincided with the city's annual Mardi Gras celebration. Martha Kreeger, a New Orleans resident who befriended Frania during this period, later recalled that she met Hunt as "Major Hunt" and that he and Frania acted as if they were husband and wife. Mrs. Kreeger said that after that first year, Hunt and Frania returned to visit every Mardi Gras. Mrs. Kreeger also said that she subsequently joined Frania, Hunt, and Hunt's brother Sherman on a trip to the New York World's Fair in 1939.

Meanwhile, Hunt evinced his still burning passion for Frania by keeping in touch through a series of letters, telegrams, and poems full of purple prose and verse. One such telegram concerned an upcoming Christmas visit. It was dated December 23, 1937, and was addressed to "Mrs. Fran Hunt." It read:

> Running now a little late
> But hoping to keep our date
> So strong is the urging
> My engine is surging,
> So anxious to see what a family I have
> My hopes are sublime
> To arrive on time.
>
> Love and laughter longingly,
> Daddy

Frania said later that during this period she and Hunt spent a great deal of time discussing what to do about their relationship and their children. She said that Hunt never proposed the idea of divorcing Lyda; instead, he kept trying to induce Frania to become a Mormon because "having two or three wives was normal in that religion." As proof of her claim, Frania provided another piece of Hunt doggerel. It said, in part:

> Fran, when flying over mountains
> To the land of Brigham Young
> She had done a little flitting around
> And by the love bug she was stung.
> She joined a manly man
> A Mormon to become.

Frania declined Hunt's first invitation to fly to Utah. However, a short time later Hunt telephoned her long-distance and told her he was very ill and needed to see her. Distraught about the health of her loved one, Frania immediately boarded a plane and flew out to Utah, only to discover that Hunt's claim of poor health was nothing but a charade.

"When I arrived, he met me at the airport," she recalled. "He took off his hat and started to wave at me. He was not ill. He wanted to introduce me to the Mormon religion."

Hunt did his country-boy best to convince Frania to join the faith of

Brigham Young, but the Catholic girl from Buffalo would not agree.

"No," she told Hunt, "I will never accept it." Then she returned to Great Neck.

Back in east Texas, Hunt continued to fight prorationing of the oil fields. His cause was abetted by the powers in Washington. In the fall of 1934, as Frania was getting resettled in Great Neck, two fiery young enforcement officials arrived on the east Texas scene to represent the Federal Tender Board. One was J. Howard Marshall, a twenty-nine-year-old Justice Department attorney; the other was Thomas "Tough Tom" Kelliher, a twenty-nine-year-old former FBI agent assigned to the Interior Department. Aided by a contingent of Kelliher's former bureau brethren, the two yound feds cracked down on the hot-oil runners with renewed vigor. The hot-oil runners retaliated by taking pot shots at Kelliher, but Kelliher survived unharmed, and the crackdown began to show some tangible results. By October of 1934, hot-oil production had dropped from an estimated 100,000 barrels per day to only 30,000 barrels per day.

Hunt did all he could to aid the federal offensive. Believing that the best way to combat violence was through an impressive show of force, Hunt and three other "conservationist" oil producers came to the feds with an impressive proposal: Why not bring in the Texas Rangers to help with the enforcement effort?

Marshall and Kelliher thought that was a fine idea, but when Hunt and his friends broached their proposal to the powers in Austin, they were rebuffed. The state of Texas, they were told, would not pay the Texas Rangers to do the federal government's job.

Not to be outdone, Hunt and his friends made secret arrangements to finance the Texas Rangers themselves. Within a few days, the FBI agents in the east Texas field were joined by thirty men under the command of Texas Ranger Captain Jim Shown. The oil patch began to look like a Wild West show. Like the National Guard troops before them, the Rangers often had to traverse the muddy fields on horseback instead of by car. But unlike the round-hatted Guardsmen, the Rangers could hardly be mistaken for Boy Scouts. With their Stetsons, six-shooters, and silver stars, their very appearance gave credence to the legend "one riot, one Ranger."

The added muscle helped. By November, the flow of hot oil was down to an estimated 10,000 barrels per day. The Federal Tender Board was no longer a laughing matter.

The antiprorationists still refused to quit. In January of 1935, they won a landmark victory when the U.S. Supreme Court struck down the National Industrial Recovery Act (NIRA) section pertaining to the oil business. The decision was a sign for the small operators and hot-oil producers to open their flow valves full bore. But the production orgy proved to be short-lived. At the behest of the NRA board chairman, Congress moved to draft hot-oil legislation that would hold up in court. The bill that emerged was sponsored by U.S.

Senator Tom Connally of Texas, but its real author was J. Howard Marshall. Known as the Connally Hot Oil Act, the bill closed the legal loopholes of the old NIRA statutes and provided for both fines and jail sentences for violators. It was passed by Congress on February 16, 1935.

There were several more violent skirmishes in east Texas following the passage of the Hot Oil Act, but gradually the hot-oil runners were brought under control. The battle then became a fight between the federal regulators and the state regulators over the jurisdictional right to govern the field. Buttressed by new prorationing regulations passed by the Texas legislature, Colonel Thompson reasserted the Railroad Commission's authority to proration production. He also attacked Interior Secretary Harold Ickes for wanting to run the oil industry as his private domain. The Texas Railroad Commission suddenly became the lesser of two evils in the eyes of the east Texas oilmen, and the two groups began to develop a suspiciously close cooperative partnership for the development of the oil fields that would continue for years to come. The oil industry was tamed at last. Or so it seemed.

No one welcomed the establishment of order more than H. L. Hunt. In later years, Hunt would refer to himself as one of the "fathers" of the Connally Hot Oil Act, and, for once, he would be giving himself only slightly more credit than he perhaps deserved. Although he played no part in the actual drafting of the legislation, he was one of the most vocal prorationists and one of the men who had brought in the Texas Rangers. The end of the hot-oil era was almost as much attributable to the efforts of Hunt and other operators like him as to the enforcement crackdown by the federal government.

As he fought for order in the east Texas field, Hunt also looked to the future of his first family. In 1935, not long after Frania's departure from Dallas, he established the Loyal Trusts for his six children by Lyda Bunker Hunt. Under the terms of the trusts, each child was entitled to spend only the income, not the principal; this provision not only qualified the trusts for tax-free passage through the generations, it also protected them from the fancies of the beneficiaries. Hunt's foresight was apparently prompted by his wife. According to family legend, Lyda did not know yet about the existence of Frania Tye and Hunt's second family. But she was well aware of her husband's historical proclivity for gambling away his money as fast as he could make it. In addition to providing security for her children, the Loyal Trusts offered a measure of protection from the fancies of her husband. A short time after the trusts were formed, Hunt started Placid Oil Company (a name he picked because he believed names beginning with "P" and containing six letters were lucky), and transferred some of his best oil properties into it. Placid, in turn, became the chief asset of the Loyal Trusts and the cornerstone of the first family's fortune.

Not surprisingly, as Hunt's wealth increased so did the family's social status. The social highlight of the Hunts' days in Tyler came in the fall of 1935, when elder daughter Margaret reigned as the queen of the Tyler Rose Festival. The Rose Festival was becoming to Tyler what Mardi Gras was to New Orleans: a celebration of commerce, culture, and society. About to turn twenty years old, Margaret Hunt was the third queen in the history of the festival. Her selection was meant to be as much of an honor for her family as for the girl herself. It was also the first time the name Hunt was associated with "royalty" in public print.

Although he was not one to devote time and energy to social climbing, Hunt nevertheless seemed to take Margaret's coronation seriously. He fussed and fumed over his daughter's appearance and the details of the festival program, and was fit to be tied when Margaret, who was a bit chubby at the time, had trouble wiggling into her newly made gown. As one family friend observed, "You would have thought it was Mr. Hunt being crowned."

Unfortunately, Margaret's appearance as queen of the Rose Festival led to some unpleasant repercussions. Then a student at exclusive Mary Baldwin College in Staunton, Virginia, Margaret was now, next to her father, the highest-profile member of the family. A kidnap threat quickly followed. On the train back to Texas that Christmas, Margaret traveled under the protection of her shotgun-toting brother Hassie and a contingent of security guards. The threatened kidnap attempt never took place, but the episode proved to be the Hunts' introduction to the double-edged fate of being known as Texas rich.

It was about this time that Hunt started feeling restive again. Oil prices had climbed to over a dollar a barrel, and the money was coming in faster than ever. Soon Hunt Production Company would be grossing over $3 million per year from the east Texas field. But Hunt was not content to rest on his riches. Now in his late forties, he had become fleshier, and his hair was beginning to gray. But he still burned with the energy that had driven him across the West, down the Mississippi, and on to El Dorado. The challenges and problems he faced in the oil field and in his secret life with Frania only seemed to drive him harder and compel him to greater accomplishments.

Several years before Hunt made the Dad Joiner deal, John D. Rockefeller had advanced a most curious theory of the acquisition of wealth by declaring, "God gave me my money." Hunt suffered no such illusions. He, more than anyone else around him, realized that his success resulted from courage, cunning, hard work, and, of course, a good dose of the Hunt luck. Rather than increasing his faith in divine guidance, his good fortune, like his sexual exploits, only increased his belief in his own special talents and his personal omnipotence.

H. L. Hunt was a man of contradictions and eccentricities: a bigamist, a family man, a conservationist, a big oil producer, a political mover and shaker, a self-absorbed writer of sentimental love poetry. But, at heart, he was still a gambler. He still craved new action and new opportunities to make money— not because he wanted possessions per se, but because the gambler in him wanted to see if he could run up the score. Specifically, Hunt wanted to pour his profits from east Texas into new drilling ventures, for, as he saw it, "The more wells you drill, the greater chance you have of finding oil."

Hunt's partner, Pete Lake, was not so gung ho. Like Lyda, the former El

Dorado clothing merchant was well aware of Hunt's past proclivity for financial ups and downs. Lake enjoyed the steady stream of income he was now getting from the Joiner leases, and he felt no desire for more. He could easily foresee the complete dissipation of his fortune in a string of dry holes. Rather than run that risk, Lake preferred to settle quietly and profitably into the genteel life of Tyler.

In October of 1936, Hunt and Lake effected an amicable parting of the ways. Having originally invested some $30,000 in the Dad Joiner deal, Lake ended up with five producing leases carved out of the Joiner properties, $1 million in cash, one drilling rig, and one Buick. The value of five leases at that time was thought to be about $4 million, bringing the total worth of Lake's 20-percent share to over $5 million. That made Hunt's remaining share of the partnership worth about $20 million. Though he could hardly be described as the world's richest man, Hunt had done pretty well for a fellow who started the Dad Joiner deal with only $109 in cash.

After splitting with Lake, Hunt incorporated his leases under the name of Hunt Oil Company, and set out to find new fields to conquer. He sent his men to west Texas, to Louisiana, and back into Arkansas, following the plays and scouting for wildcat locations of his own. Hunt prided himself in his ability to move quickly. He and his lawyers equipped Hunt land men with a specially devised questionnaire that allowed them to collect information on local landowners much faster than the major oil companies could do it. Getting the jump on the leasing action was critical in beating the major companies out of the best sections in a new field. Hunt also started Penrod Drilling, his own in-house drilling contractor; composed of a fleet of eleven steam-powered land rigs left over from the Hunt Production Company operations, this new subsidiary gave him the capacity to get into a location and start drilling on his own time schedule instead of some one else's. Soon, Hunt Oil began making new discoveries outside the east Texas field, and Hunt Oil's income began to grow greater and greater.

Hunt also diversified into the refinery business with what some later characterized as typical Hunt tactics. The move began when he became interested in buying into the Excelsior Refining Company. Located in the southern part of the east Texas field, Excelsior was one of many "poor boy" refining operations that converted crude oil to gasoline. Because of the purity of the east Texas oil, the refiners could build their plant for relatively little money (sometimes for as little as $10,000) and make what was known as "Eastex gas." When Hunt first approached the two entrepreneurs who owned Excelsior, he was informed that they were not interested in selling. Then Hunt, who was one of the refinery's major suppliers, made the Excelsior men an offer they could not refuse: if they did not sell him an interest, he told them, he would build another refinery on a plot of land adjacent to theirs. In addition to gaining a competitor, Excelsior would also lose one of its main suppliers.

Faced with that kind of choice, the Excelsior men decided to sell Hunt a one-half interest in their refinery for $150,000. Hunt did not quibble over the price. He listened to the Excelsior men's offer, accepted the terms, and sent over a check for $150,000 signed on his behalf by H. L. Williford. A short time after that, Hunt renamed the operation the Parade Gasoline Company.

Although Hunt chose the new name for his refining company because of his superstition about names beginning with the letter *P,* Parade soon became associated with one of the worst disasters in east Texas history. On March 18, 1937, a Parade waste gas pipeline exploded beneath the New London consolidated school, killing 294 people, most of them schoolchildren. The tragedy was not Hunt's fault. As a later investigation revealed, the school had been illegally tapping in to the Parade pipeline to get gas for heating the classrooms. But within hours of the accident, Hunt was on the scene visiting relatives of the disaster victims. He also had Roy Lee round up Hunt Oil employees not involved in the disaster and dispatched them in pairs to help the victims and their parents. At one home, Hunt himself helped load a casket onto a funeral van, then pulled out a big roll of money, peeled off several $100 bills, and stuffed them into the pocket of the grieving father.

"Here," Hunt said, "you'll probably need this before you get back."

During this period, Hunt acquired a new partner in his quest for oil: Hassie. Still the physical image of his old man, Hassie came into the operation in the wake of a stormy college experience at the University of Texas. Books had not interested the young man. What had interested him was raising hell with his ham radio transmitter. According to a former schoolmate, Hassie would not only jam the programs he did not like, but would break in and criticize them while the programs were still on the air. Hunt had found it difficult to get Hassie out of that, but when he did, Hassie quit school and went into the oil business.

Now more than ever, Hassie found himself under the ambivalent auspices of his father. One of the first tasks Hunt assigned Hassie was to sell the services of Penrod Drilling, the family contractor, to outside customers. But instead of letting the young man learn on his own, Hunt was constantly second-guessing him and revoking his authority. Once, for example, Hassie submitted the lowest of three bids for a job near Longview, Texas. But when the customer called to tell Hassie the good news, Hunt interrupted and informed the customer that the bid was too low and would have to be withdrawn. "I never did think that was the way to raise a boy and teach him to stand on his own two feet," the oilman involved remarked afterward.

Nevertheless, Hunt continued to treat his son as if he were a clay model that could be pressed into whatever shape Hunt wanted. But no matter what Hassie did, Hunt never seemed satisfied. The father kept on goading his son and belittling him and trying to remake him in his image. At one point, Hunt even advised his son to go out to "those poker parlors near Los Angeles and play cards to sharpen your wits."

Hassie did not follow his father's advice. Instead of hitting the card tables, he had his name legally changed from Haroldson Lafayette Hunt, Jr. to Hassie Hunt, and persuaded the courts to remove his disabilities as a minor. Then with a stake of money his father later estimated as "$181," nineteen-year-old

Hassie started buying oil and gas leases on his own and without his father's knowledge. Incredibly enough, he went out and made a big strike near Tinsley, Mississippi, in one of his first solo ventures. The Tinsley field alone accounted for forty producing wells. Other strikes followed, and, by Hunt's own accounting, Hassie was a millionaire in his own right before he reached the age of twenty-one.

Like everything else he did, Hassie's success brought a double-edged reaction from his old man. Hunt seldom raised his voice or got angry in times of stress, even when such behavior might have been called for. But with Hassie, he got most furious indeed, ranting and raving at his son for operating behind his back. At the same time, he could not help but gloat over Hassie's ability to find oil. Even as he criticized Hassie for his insubordination and sloppy paperwork, he took pride over the latest confirmation of his son's mystical oil-finding powers. The Hunts' strange father-son relationship seemed to grow both colder and more intense at the same time.

Meanwhile, Hunt continued to run his life according to his business. By late 1937, his development of the Joiner leases was essentially complete. The Hunt crews had drilled roughly 600 wells, the vast majority of them good producers. There were still some critical problems to attend to, among them the rapid encroachment of salt water throughout the east Texas field. But there was no longer any reason for Hunt to be on the scene of the Joiner leases every day. His interests now ranged across three states, and his operations were growing daily. Communication and transportation became important in his thinking as his operations expanded beyond the east Texas field. Logically enough, he turned to Dallas.

Thanks in part to the east Texas oil boom, Dallas was growing faster than ever. The population was zooming toward the 300,000 mark, and new stores and businesses were opening up every day. The symbol of the city was a giant red neon winged horse atop the thirty-one-story Magnolia Petroleum building. The Pegasus sign weighed 6,000 pounds and contained 1,162 feet of tubing, statistics which purportedly made it the largest revolving sign in the world. Illuminated at night, it made an electric mythic image that could be seen far out into the surrounding prairie. Some sneered that the sign was appropriate to "a one-horse town," but these were words of jealous competitors. Dallas had turned the corner on what historian A. C. Greene called its "deciding years," and with such attractions as Neiman-Marcus and the Dallas Symphony, the city was as sophisticated as any metropolis between New York and Los Angeles. More important, as far as Hunt was concerned, Dallas also boasted the state's biggest banks, a rapidly expanding network of concrete highways, and transcontinental airline service from Love Field.

Hunt determined that Dallas was where his future lay. In December of 1937, Hunt made arrangements to move the Hunt Oil Company offices from the People's National Bank in Tyler to the Cotton Exchange Building in downtown Dallas. Then he sent his trusted aide H. L. Williford to Dallas to find the Hunt family a new home.

CHAPTER 7

DALLAS

EVERYONE called the place Mount Vernon because it was a near replica of George Washington's estate on the Potomac. Built in 1930 by Dallas contractor Thomas Y. Pickett, the house and accompanying swimming pool sat on a ten-acre tract overlooking White Rock Lake. There was a vane-topped crow's nest on the roof and a porch with white columns on the side facing the lake. Though the surrounding lands were far smaller than the plantation acreage Washington commanded, the house itself was slightly larger than the original.* There were fourteen rooms distributed over the two main floors, a basement, and a third floor behind the dormer windows in the attic. The dining-room walls were decorated with hand-painted paper depicting great scenes in American history. Located eight miles from downtown Dallas, the estate was like a refuge of rusticity on the edge of the big city. A cow, a calf, and a handful of deer grazed in the front yard beside chickens, peacocks, and turkeys. Off to the west side of the house were a vegetable garden and a peach orchard. The panorama of the three-mile-long tree-lined lake stretched along the house's eastern side.

Hunt bought Mount Vernon from Pickett on January 1, 1938, for the distressed price of $69,000 cash. Despite later appearances to the contrary, there was nothing especially patriotic in Hunt's decision to purchase the place. Unlike Hunt, Pickett had been ravaged by the depression. He needed cash, and his selling price made Mount Vernon a good buy. Hunt made the purchase on a "move in" basis, which meant that he bought Pickett out lock, stock, and barrel. As their contract noted, the deal included "the sprinkler equipment,

---

*Legend later had it that Hunt's Mount Vernon was ten times the size of Washington's. Tiring of such talk, Hunt hired an engineer to measure his house, and found that it was only "2 percent" larger than the original.

mowers, etc., two peacocks and all chickens except those belonging to Juliet Jane, one cow and calf . . . and all draperies upstairs, downstairs, sun parlors, including curtains in full, etc., also all lighting fixtures."

The Hunts moved in without much fanfare. The only public notice of their arrival was a brief story in the *Dallas Morning News* on January 16, 1938, which reported that "quite the nicest family has come to Mt. Vernon of Dallas to stay." The story went on to list the names of Hunt's wife and children, noting that his daughter Margaret had been queen of the Tyler Rose Festival. The story concluded that Mount Vernon was "the home of real folks in the best American tradition."

Following that auspicious welcome, Hunt had his first run-in with the Dallas establishment. A close-knit and well-coordinated group, the city's business leaders were a club divided into clubs. Money was an important qualification for membership, but it was not the only one. A man had to be willing to "do something for Dallas." R. L. Thornton, a developer who would one day become the city's mayor, expressed the essence of the local conservative boosterism when he said, "Sure, we fight like hell with each other, but when it's for Dallas, it's 'Line up, boys!' "

By the time Hunt moved to town, the Dallas establishment had already formed the Citizen's Council, an organization dedicated to managing the body politic for what its members perceived as the good of Dallas. The establishment had also allied in an ever-proliferating array of charitable boards. Again, Thornton expressed the dominant sentiment of the city's leaders when he was asked to contribute to the Dallas Symphony fund: "The symphony is good for Dallas. I'll be glad to do anything I can to help as long as you don't ask me to attend any concerts."

The Dallas establishment naturally noted Hunt's arrival with interest. Representatives of the city's various charitable projects soon began dropping by the Hunt Oil offices to solicit Hunt's contributions. But the reception they got was hardly the kind they were used to getting. Instead of lining up to "do something for Dallas," Hunt did not donate a penny to the civic drives. Worse, when the solicitors came to call on him, he refused even to see them. Charity after charity made it to the outer office, only to be rejected without a hearing.

Hunt's aversion to charity was both personal and philosophical. Ever the tightwad, he was, as he once put it, "more interested in the acquisition of wealth than its disbursement." He was also an amateur social planner, the man who had introduced the "flexible work week" plan in his east Texas operations. He believed in creating jobs, not charities. To Hunt's way of thinking, being on the public dole undermined a person's will to work and initiative to succeed, and all charities were in some form or another part of the public dole. "The greatest good one man can perform for his fellow man," he wrote later, "is to create gainful employment and opportunities for personal progress through constructive work."

As yet unacquainted with Hunt's beliefs, many of his early Dallas contemporaries regarded his failure to give to the city as stingy and uncooperative.

Hunt came to be unfavorably compared to other self-made millionaires like Clint Murchison, the east Texas oilman who did participate in the city's civic projects. Feeling that Hunt did not care for them, members of the Dallas establishment decided they did not care for Hunt. At Lyda's urging, Hunt applied for membership in Brookhollow Country Club, the city's most exclusive club, and even signed up for golf lessons, but his application was summarily voted down. Hunt eventually gained membership in the slightly less prestigious Dallas Country Club, but he was never invited to join the dance clubs like Idlewild and Terpischorean that formed the backbone of the Dallas social hierarchy. Hunt claimed that he was blackballed by oil-business rivals jealous of his success in the Dad Joiner deal, but the real reason for his social rejection was his disinterest in charity.

In contrast to her husband, Lyda Bunker Hunt was more readily accepted into Dallas society. Never an extravagant entertainer, she did not attempt to turn Mount Vernon into a party palace, but she did join the socially prestigious Highland Park Presbyterian Church, the semiexclusive Dallas Women's Club, and the Marianne Scruggs Garden Club. At the same time, Lyda performed numerous unpublicized acts of charity, ranging from anonymous small gifts to friends and relatives to a large donation toward the construction of a spire for Highland Park Presbyterian Church. Lyda often took care to hide her acts of charity from her husband on practical grounds and generally refrained from taking credit for her generosity on religious grounds.

"Don't let your left hand know what your right hand is doing," she said once in explaining her preference for anonymity. "The Bible teaches us that."

Lyda also took it upon herself to carry the family banner. A few years after the move to Dallas, she commissioned a family genealogy. The work was done by a reputable company and served to remind the Hunts of their long heritage. Lyda's ancestry was traced all the way back to the kings of England and William the Conqueror. Hunt's lineage was traced back to Georgia with possible connections with the Jamestown colony. Lyda had several dozen copies of the genealogy printed up and sent them to all the members of the family.

In Dallas as in Tyler, Lyda governed her children with a loose rein. The three youngest, Bunker, Herbert, and Lamar, held pillow fights in the bedrooms and played football on the lawn. Of the three, Herbert showed the most industry by raising turkeys and chickens in the back yard; his efforts earned his mother's praise as "my little businessman." Bunker, by contrast, did not seem interested in much besides food and sports. When he got old enough to go to work in the oil business, Bunker earned his father's disapproval for things like lying down on the job on hot summer days and going swimming in the well-logging water. Like brother Hassie before him, Bunker was sent off to Culver Military Academy and, later, to the Hill School in Pottstown, Pennsylvania, ostensibly to learn some discipline. By and large, though, the man the three younger Hunt boys knew as Dad, Daddy, or Popsy was easy on them. "I can remember hiding from my father one day because I knew when he came home he was going to teach me to swim," Lamar told a *Sports Illustrated* writer years later, "but I was afraid of swimming, not of him."

The three oldest children entered young adulthood still under the family wing. On October 15, 1938, Margaret married a young Hunt Oil accountant named Albert Galatyn Hill. Her new husband continued to work at Hunt Oil. Margaret also worked for her father as a business aide and confidante, acquiring training available to few other men or women. About this time Caroline went off to college at the University of Texas. She subsequently met and married a college classmate, Loyd Sands, who went to work at Hunt Oil. Hassie, who remained unmarried, operated under the name of Hassie Hunt Production Company but continued to keep his office at Hunt Oil.

True to his original intention, Hunt spent most of his early years in Dallas expanding the size and scope of his operations. A confirmed creekologist, he continued to pick his drilling sites by instinct. He did not employ a single geologist. In fact, few of his employees had more than high-school educations. Hunt was at heart a land man, not a scientist. He got his edge by his natural mathematical mind and by his ability to move quickly. He made decisions individually, not by committee, and he figured his costs in a deal on the back of an envelope using a pencil stub.

"I never saw anything like it before or since," remembered one Hunt Oil secretary. "Mr. Hunt could figure faster with that short little pencil of his than his engineer could figure with a slide rule."

Though he was usually unassuming around the office, Hunt made it clear that he expected his employees to move quickly, too. In those days, Hunt Oil had a reputation for paying better salaries than most other independents and for giving more responsibility to the men in the field. There was also an ever-increasing glamor attached to working for H. L. Hunt, an excitement in helping a rich man in his bid to get even richer, a romance in looking for oil the old-fashioned way. Still haunted by the depression and the fear of losing their jobs for moving too slowly, Hunt's employees gave him their all.

"You had plenty to do, and you moved in a hurry," recalled one Hunt Oil veteran. "I would be up all night. I got a college education in the oil industry working there."

Hunt's business philosophy, as another Hunt employee put it, could be summed up in three words: "Drill, drill, drill." And that was exactly what he did. Opening a new branch office in Shreveport, Hunt concentrated much of his drilling in northern Louisiana. Like his luck at the poker table, Hunt's luck in the oil field ran in streaks. For a while, Hunt Oil drilled nothing but producers, and the rule of thumb for Hunt's competitors was "follow Hunt." Then Hunt drilled a string of seventy dry holes in a row, and the new saying became "follow Hunt and go broke." But overall, the producing wells more than made up for the dry holes, and Hunt's score of successes kept mounting as he found new production in places like Jena and Olla and Cotton Valley and Good Pines.

Hunt also began to go international after the move to Dallas. In 1938, after grabbing some good leases in the Cotton Valley field, he sent Hassie and Williford to Germany. The Germans were then making barter deals involving such incompatibles as canaries and motion pictures. The Hunts made a relatively straightforward trade: oil for steel drill pipe. Hunt Oil also made a deal to export oil to Japan through a California trading company. In making these deals with what were then the world's principal aggressor countries, Hunt was not alone. Many other major and independent oil companies were doing the same thing.

While he expanded, Hunt found that he still had to protect the east Texas production he already had. With the passage of the Connally Hot Oil Act, salt water replaced hot oil as his chief nemesis. The flow of salt water created enormous disposal and environmental problems; there was simply no place to put the stuff without defiling fields and forests or polluting streams, and hauling it away was even more expensive than hauling oil. Even worse, the encroachment of salt water threatened the great oil field with extinction, for the flow of water kept reducing the pressure as well as displacing the volume of crude. But the state of oil-industry science was such that no one knew why the east Texas field was producing so much water or what could be done about it.

Finally a team of geologists assigned to study the east Texas field came up with a remarkable discovery. Unlike the crude in most other oil fields, the crude coming out of east Texas was not driven up from the ground by gas pressure: the driving force was the flow of salt water itself. This salt water had been trapped in the Woodbine layer millions of years before when the area was the shore of an ancient island. It now carried with it what was literally an ocean of oil. The geologists determined that by simply reinjecting the salt water back into the ground, operators could maintain the pressure of the field and solve the waste-disposal problems.

Although Hunt did not invent salt-water injection wells, he was one of the first operators in east Texas to use them widely. The first salt-water injection well was drilled in 1938. Dozens of others quickly followed. Salt water continued to encroach the reservoir, but the new wells slowed the process dramatically. Within four years, the oil wells in the east Texas field were producing only slightly more salt water than oil, and the field pressure had ceased its precipitous decline. As Hunt later observed, "These conservation measures saved the great field from an early death and made it the greatest field ever discovered in North America and the largest in the world up to that time."

In addition to pouring his east Texas profits into more drilling, Hunt also began investing some of his money in real estate. With a steady income from his wells, he had what few others in the depression-ravaged country had—ready cash. In 1937, as he was moving to Dallas, Hunt bought the 7,000-acre Winona Pecan Grove in Smith County, Texas, just outside Tyler. The property was auctioned off at a bankruptcy sale, and Hunt paid only $31,000 for it. The property's greatest feature was its 12,000 pecan trees, for which it claimed the title of "the world's largest pecan grove." That in itself was enough of an attraction for H. L. Hunt, who had by now become virtually addicted to pecans. But the pecan trees covered only 750 acres of the total. Returning to his early roots, Hunt decided to turn the rest of the acreage into a kind of experimental farm. He had his hands plant peaches, plums, blackberries, roses, and acres of improved grasses. The results, he reported later, were proof of his theory that "anything can be grown in East Texas."

As time passed, Hunt grew increasingly lonely for Frania. Although she would not consent to becoming Mormon, neither she nor he wanted to end their unusual relationship. Finally, some five years after their split in Dallas, Hunt told Frania that he wanted her to move back to Texas.

"He said he wanted me to be closer to him," Frania recalled later. "He also said that our children would get a better education in the South than in the North."

Frania was anxious to be closer to Hunt, too. In the fall of 1939, she packed up her four children and left Great Neck for Houston and what she and Hunt evidently hoped would be a new and better life. It did not take long, however, for their hopes to be dashed to pieces in the gravest crisis yet to befall the patriarchy of H. L. Hunt.

Oddly enough, Frania imperiled the chances of her new life from the start. Though she was well aware of the existence of Hunt's first family in Dallas, she arrived in Houston using the name "Mrs. H. L. Hunt." Hunt did not do much to cover his tracks either. Instead of packing Frania away in some obscure little bungalow, he built her a fine new mansion right on River Oaks Boulevard, the main drag of one of the city's best residential sections. Frania then upped the ante by applying for membership in the River Oaks Country Club as "Mrs. H. L. Hunt, femme sole."

Now she was treading on very thin ice. At thirty-five, Frania was a striking beauty. Living in the middle of River Oaks, she was also extremely hard to miss. Houston and Dallas were only 250 miles apart, but the oil business brought the elite of the two cities together every day. With a woman in each place claiming to be Mrs. H. L. Hunt, it was only a matter of time before the inevitable showdown occurred.

The scene was a fancy River Oaks tea party at which Frania was to be introduced to the cream of Houston society. Ruby Matthews, the socially ambitious wife of Houston attorney Wright Matthews, was the hostess. Frania's New Orleans friends Martha Kreeger and Millie Tidmore came over for the party, and Ruby Matthews invited a fine contingent of local matrons, each more elegantly attired than the next.

Then, just as the guests were arriving, Frania received a phone call. The caller had a woman's voice, but she would not reveal her name. She did, however, deliver a very pointed message.

"I know you're not Mrs. H. L. Hunt," the voice said. "You're really his mistress. But if you give me five thousand dollars, I won't tell what I know."

Frania hung up the phone. Someone wanted to abort her new life even as it was being born. Extremely distraught, Frania returned to the tea party and tried to hide what had happened.

Unfortunately, the phone call that spoiled the tea party proved to be just the beginning. "I received at least fifty telephone calls after that first lady was trying to blackmail me," Frania said later. "She notified all these people that I was not Mrs. H. L. Hunt, but a mistress or something."

Frania kept complaining of this treatment to Hunt and urged him to come to Houston to help her. Hunt answered her plea with a letter: "I know you were very much distressed, and I am sorry, but don't let them get your goat. The best of them could never be friends of ours."

Despite his reassuring words, Hunt did not come to Houston. Frania grew more distraught than ever. She was not only being persecuted, she was being abandoned as well. Finally, Frania decided to pack up her children and go to Dallas. She checked into a suite at the Hotel Adolphus and telephoned Hunt at the office.

"These are your children as well as mine," she told him. "Come take them off my hands."

Before Hunt had a chance to say anything, Frania hung up the phone. She put her oldest son Howard, then age fourteen, in charge of looking after his siblings, and left for Houston by herself. As she later acknowledged, her emotional distress was now dominating her reason.

"I don't think I was in a position to think," she recalled. "I just did."

Ill considered or not, Frania's gesture succeeded in getting Hunt's attention. Frania had barely time enough to walk into her house in Houston when the phone rang. It was Hunt.

"Please come back to Dallas and get the children," he pleaded. "We'll make some arrangement."

Frania acquiesced to his request. When she returned to Dallas, she found Hunt in the hotel room along with his daughter, twenty-five-year-old Margaret Hunt Hill. Feeling more despondent than angry, Frania collected the children and went back to Houston.

A short time later, Hunt beckoned her back to Dallas. There followed an extraordinary meeting at which Hunt introduced Lyda Bunker Hunt, the mother of his first family, and Frania Tye, the mother of his secret family. "Hunt did a lot of the talking," Frania remembered. "Lyda and I were strangers. We looked each other over."

The meeting ended with Frania's future still in doubt. Then Frania got a phone call from Lyda. The real Mrs. H. L. Hunt wanted to meet at a restaurant for a woman-to-woman talk. Frania quickly accepted the invitation.

The two women established a rapport. In many ways, their situations were as alike as they were different.

"We talked mostly about the children," Frania recalled. "She said she would help. She was very kind, very sweet, very understanding."

At one point, Lyda even offered to adopt Frania's children. According to

Hunt family sources, Lyda's gesture was at least partly motivated by her desire to protect her own children's share of the family fortune. ("Lyda was a very gracious woman," observed one family member, "but she was not dumb.") At the same time, Lyda also made the suggestion out of genuine magnanimity.

Frania refused Lyda's adoption offer, but left Dallas deeply impressed. "I arrived at the conclusion that Mrs. Hunt was the finest woman I ever met and that every boy and girl would love to have her as a mother," Frania said later. "I was considerably younger than Mrs. Hunt, and I decided I would do everything to leave the family alone regardless of what he would do."

At Hunt's suggestion, Frania moved to Los Angeles, took up residence in the Santa Monica Club, and enrolled her children in private schools, still under the name of Hunt. In 1941, Hunt set up the Reliance Trusts for Frania's four children. Composed primarily of producing oil and gas properties, among them a portion of the Joiner leases, each trust provided a yearly income of roughly $6,000. The "settlor" named for these trusts was Mrs. Frania Tye Hunt.

Frania was still distressed. Part of her distress may have been financial, but the better part was emotional. Her friend Martha Kreeger, who was by now privy to Frania's problems, kept urging her to sue Hunt for bigamy. Frania would hear nothing of it.

"I wouldn't do that," she said. "It would hurt the children."

Frania's friend Martha knew better. Suing for bigamy would not hurt the children, it would hurt Hunt. Frania was still in love.

Hunt tried to placate Frania as best he could, declaring his good intentions over and over. In a letter dated December 13, 1941, and addressed to Frania in Los Angeles, Hunt wrote her, "Never have I wished to antagonize and . . . you won't like this, never have I acted in spite. One doesn't build a business out of spite. I've never done it with my Hardins, Louises, Joiners . . . So why should I do it with . . . you?"

About a month after this epistle, on January 17, 1942, Frania arrived in Dallas to negotiate a settlement. She was accompanied by her friend Martha Kreeger and her attorney Wright Matthews from Houston. Matthews had arranged for Hart Willis, a prominent Dallas attorney, to join him as counsel in the discussions. Frania and her party checked in to a set of suites Hunt had reserved at the Hotel Adolphus. Hunt then showed up with his attorney Ralph Shank.

The talks went on for several days. Sometimes Hunt, Frania, Willis Matthews, and Shank met all together. Sometimes the lawyers met alone. Hunt talked to Willis and Matthews by himself. Hunt and Frania negotiated by themselves. This, as Wright Matthews later acknowledged, was an unusual way to conduct a settlement, but then, as he pointed out, "If you dealt with Hunt, you did a lot of unusual things."

One of the key points of dispute was the marriage license. Frania and her attorney kept asking Hunt to provide a copy, but he allegedly told them that they would never find it because the courthouse in Florida had burned.

The negotiations reached a climax when Hunt managed to get Frania alone again. The way Frania told it afterward, Hunt took special care to see they were alone. First, he closed the door to the adjoining room where Wright Matthews and Martha Kreeger were talking. Then he reached up and shut the transom. He looked up and down the outside hall. Finally satisfied that he could not be overheard, Hunt offered Frania a million dollars to sign a statement saying she had never married him.

Frania became very upset and started to cry.

"I'll never sell my children for all the money you have," she screamed, and ran into the adjoining room.

According to her friend Martha Kreeger, Frania came into the room with tears in her eyes and Hunt in close pursuit. Frania was still screaming, and Hunt was trying to calm her down.

"That's okay," Hunt kept saying. "It's all right. It won't happen again." He stayed only a moment, then left.

Once he was gone, Frania composed herself. "That b—— tried to get me to say I never married him and offered me a million dollars," she told her friends, "but I never said it."

Whether or not things happened exactly as Frania later claimed, her resolve collapsed quickly after Hunt's proposal. The next day, January 24, 1942, she signed a sixty-two-page agreement denying she was married to Hunt and a blanket release indemnifying him from any future claims. In return, Hunt paid Frania $300,000 in cash and another $25,000 for her attorneys. He also agreed to pay Frania $2,000 per month for the rest of her life.

Twelve days after signing the settlement with Hunt, Frania married a Hunt Oil employee and former army colonel named John W. Lee. Rumors circulated that Hunt paid Lee to marry Frania, but no evidence of such a payment ever surfaced. According to Frania's friend Martha Kreeger, Frania and Lee were married in something of a rush, for in the midst of the stormy days before the settlement, the Japanese had attacked Pearl Harbor and Colonel Lee had been called back into the service. One Hunt in-law later claimed that the marriage was a union of convenience between two lovelorn people. "Colonel Lee married her to give those kids a name," the in-law recalled. "He had been very much in love with another girl who was already married with four children. But the girl was a Catholic and she wouldn't get divorced and remarry him because of her religion."

Tall, handsome, and about Frania's age, John Lee made an attractive-looking husband regardless of the circumstances. After the wedding, he and Frania went out to Los Angeles, picked up the children, then moved back across the country to Lee's military post at Fort Benning, Georgia. According to a Houston friend who also wound up stationed in Georgia, the relationship proved to be rather lopsided in Frania's favor. "She dominated him, you could tell. A look. A nod of the head. The way women do."

When the war ended, the Lees invested $50,000 of Frania's settlement money in a large colonial mansion outside the Atlanta city limits, and settled in to raise Frania's four children in semirural peace and quiet.

Meanwhile, Hunt's family life became more complicated than ever. For just as he was breaking up with Frania, Hunt was taking up with a Hunt Oil secretary named Ruth Eileen Ray. Some later suggested that Hunt's involvement with Ruth (and Frania's jealousy over it) was what really prompted the settlement agreement in Dallas in January of 1942. Others contended that the two things happened more or less independently of each other. In either case, it soon became clear that Hunt's romance with Ruth was not just another fling, but a sort of repeat performance of his curious relationship with Frania.

Like the voluptuous real-estate woman of the Florida land boom, Ruth Ray was only twenty-five years old when she met Hunt. Barely over five feet tall, she had curly, reddish-blonde hair, lovely green eyes, a full-breasted figure, and a brightly innocent smile. She came into his life after a depression-strapped childhood in the little southeastern Oklahoma city of Idabel. Ruth's father, Walter "Sing" Ray, was a real-estate and insurance agent who also worked with Choctaw Indian children, taught Sunday school at the First Methodist Church, served as the first city clerk, and loved to sing. He died in 1919, just as he was about to enter the oil business. The youngest of six children, Ruth was only two years old at that time. She grew up in a one-parent family governed by her mother, Grace. Because she proved so adept at running her husbandless family farm, Grace Ray became a kind of local "Dear Abby," the woman the other women in town went to for advice.

"My mother was one of the strongest persons I've ever known," Ruth remarked later. "I never felt like I grew up without my daddy."

Ruth attended grammar school, high school, and the Methodist church in Idabel, then went off to college at Oklahoma A&M in Stillwater. Like her late father, Ruth enjoyed singing and playing the piano, but her real ambition was to be a writer. She had hoped to go to Stephens College in Columbia, Missouri, to study writing. But the depression took its toll on the Ray family's finances.

"We lost everything," Ruth recalled with only slight overstatement. "All we had was each other. We had to give and take and share, make sacrifices for each other."

Ruth discovered that one of the sacrifices was the extra work her older brothers were doing to help put her through school. In 1940, her sophomore year, Ruth decided to make a sacrifice of her own. Without consulting her mother or her brothers, she dropped out of college.

"I didn't tell anyone," she remembered later, "because I knew they would want me to stay in school. I just packed up and came home."

When Ruth returned to Idabel, she found that her older sister Swann and her husband were visiting from Shreveport. Reporting that the prospects for finding employment were far better in Shreveport than in Oklahoma, Swann suggested that her younger sister go back to Shreveport with them to look for work. Ruth accepted the invitation eagerly.

Shreveport was then on the verge of another oil boom, World War II was already well under way, and though the United States had yet to become involved, the tightened world oil market had stabilized prices. Big oil companies were expanding their offices. Independents like H. L. Hunt were opening new offices. Ambitious drilling and production programs were being formulated. There was a flurry of activity all over the oil patch and in the downtown buildings.

Ruth found an opening as a legal secretary for the firm of Blanchard, Goldstein, Walker and O'Quinn. As she later admitted, she was not exactly qualified for the job. "I had taken typing, and I was right in the middle of shorthand when I left school," she recalled. "I was good, but I had never handled legal documents."

Ruth determined to make a success anyway, studying her materials after work to get the hang of legal forms and terminology and telling herself "I can do it—I will."

She apparently did well enough. For when Claude O'Quinn left the law firm to go to work full time for the firm's major client, Hunt Oil Company, he took Ruth Ray with him.

Ruth's new co-workers at Hunt Oil found the girl from Idabel to be nice and cutesy sweet—at times, to a fault. "She was a real baby-doll type," recalled one female co-worker. "She was very bouncy, singing all the time, and very religious. She had a little can on her desk that she put her tithing in. She read the Bible every day."

Ruth's fellow employees were divided over whether or not her sweetness was an act. But all seemed to agree that of all the attractive young women around the Hunt Oil offices, Ruth seemed the least probable one to catch the boss's eye. Despite an occasional low-cut dress, she simply did not come across as a temptress. On the other hand, as one of Hunt's personal secretaries observed, "H.L. didn't like women who came on too strong." Ruth's country-girl naïveté was just the kind of style that appealed to the romantic side of his nature.

Ruth, for her part, apparently fell in love with a living legend. Hunt was the father she never had and the romantic lover of her literary fantasies. She would never forget the first time she heard his name. She was still working back in the offices of O'Quinn's law firm. One of the lawyers and a client were discussing a document Hunt was supposed to sign.

"It doesn't matter to me whether he signs that instrument or not," Ruth heard the client say. "His word is good enough for me."

"That really impressed me," Ruth recalled years afterward. "His word was his bond."

Ruth and Hunt finally met some time after she went to work at Hunt Oil. Although Ruth never discussed the details of their meeting, Hunt later gave a curiously foreshortened account in an unpublished interview with Dallas writer Jane Graham. Hunt said that he first noticed Ruth one day when he was leaving his company's Shreveport office. She was standing on the corner waiting for the bus. Hunt stopped and offered her a ride home.

"We drove out into the country," Hunt recalled with a faraway look in his eyes. "The dogwood was in bloom."

In the midst of his recollection, Hunt's voice trailed off. He snapped out of his rapture and ended his story by saying, "I saw her when it was convenient."

Rumors about young Ruth's developing relationship with Hunt hit the office gossip mill in no time. Ruth complained of feeling ill, and went to see a doctor. The other women in the office nodded knowingly. Then one day in the fall of 1942, Ruth did not show up for work. A letter of resignation came in about a week later. It was postmarked Idabel. Ruth continued to draw paychecks. Then the paychecks stopped. No one in the office heard from her, but nearly everyone surmised the same thing: H. L. Hunt had gotten Ruth pregnant.

Unbeknownst to his first family, Hunt moved Ruth from Shreveport to a fancy apartment in New York City and provided her with a cover story. A short time later, some of Ruth's former co-workers began receiving marriage announcements postmarked from New York. The announcements said that Ruth had wed one "Raymond Wright." Ruth later wrote to say that her husband was with army intelligence and was temporarily on leave to study nutrition at Columbia University. But her story did not take. Ruth's former co-workers cattily predicted that some time during the war, Ruth's husband was going to be missing in action.

Ruth Ray's first child by H. L. Hunt was born on April 6, 1943, in New York City. He was named Ray Lee Wright. A short time after the baby was born, Ruth left for Texas. On the way, she stopped in Shreveport to show off her child to her sister and her former co-workers. One Hunt Oil secretary noted how Ruth beamed with joy throughout her visit, as if she couldn't have been happier. The secretary also remarked on how the infant, with the blue eyes and puffy cheeks characteristic of the Hunt clan, looked exactly like Winston Churchill. The boy's proud mother had no less lofty ambitions for her son.

"He's gonna be president of the United States," Ruth declared proudly.

After stopping in Idabel, Ruth moved to Dallas. Hunt bought her a house on Meadow Lake Avenue, which she occupied under the name of "Mrs. Ruth E. Wright." A one-story brick bungalow with a neat little lawn, the place was situated in a quiet neighborhood bordering White Rock Lake. Its appearance recalled the houses young Frania had lived in during her Shreveport years. But the most incredible thing about the house was that it was located less than a two-minute drive from the Mount Vernon residence of Hunt's first family.

Hunt took advantage of the proximity. Between 1943 and 1950, he and Ruth had three more children, all of them girls. They were named Ruth June, Helen LaKelley, and Swanee Grace. As he later confided to a few close associates, Hunt prolificacy was partly inspired by his ever-escalating opinion of himself and his special powers. In specific, Hunt had come to believe that he carried a "genius gene." He believed that by fathering more children, he was doing the world great service as a producer: he was producing not only future presidents but future leaders in all fields.

Ruth lived comfortably, but not lavishly, on the expense money H.L. provided. Her major luxury was sending the children to private schools. She dressed in neat, not very expensive clothes and kept an eye out for bargains and sales. She played the piano, taught her daughters to sing for their father, became a born-again Baptist, and continued to love, honor, and obey her "Mr. Wright."

The beginning of H. L. Hunt's second secret family coincided with some major turning points for his first family. In the fall of 1942, as Ruth was conceiving their first child, Lyda Bunker Hunt's oldest daughter Margaret presented her father with his first grandchild, a girl named Lyda Hunt Hill. A photograph taken shortly after Lyda Hunt Hill's birth showed the happy, gray-templed grandfather cradling the child in his arms and beaming down at her as if she were his own. Hunt's patriarchy now emcompassed three generations as well as three separate branches. At the age of fifty-four, Hunt still had a long way to go to catch up to King ibn-Saud, but he seemed to be gaining on the Arab ruler in both oil production and people production and was proud of it.

The one major problem in the patriarchy, as Hunt saw it, was the behavior of his son Hassie. The young man continued to find oil with what Hunt believed to be mystical powers. By the age of twenty-four, Hassie claimed ten thousand barrels a day in oil production, enough to give him a tidy gross income of about $4 million per year. But Hassie also began acting more strangely than ever. Sometimes he was a gentle and controlled fellow who wore neat double-breasted suits like his father and acted as good-naturedly as his mother. On other occasions, he was a shy, troubled young man who came into the office barefoot, his shoes hung around his neck by the shoestrings, his hat pulled down over his eyes.

On still other occasions, Hassie was violent. Some of his violence seemed directed at no one in particular. Once, for example, he saw a new car he wanted, threw a rock through the showroom window, then paid cash for the car and the broken glass. But many of his outbursts were aimed at his father. In the course of Hassie's oil-business success, an intense competition had developed between father and son. Hunt was always looking over his shoulder to make sure he had more leases in a particular field than his son had acquired. Hassie was always trying to outfox his father by grabbing only the best leases and by drilling in the most unlikely places. Still able to pull rank when the competition ran against him, Hunt continued to criticize Hassie for his sloppy paperwork and for the high prices he paid for some of his leases. Unable to pull rank, Hassie would make the argument become physical. On several occasions, he and Hunt actually came to blows, jabbing and punching each other and rolling around on the ground like little boys.

"Those two would fight over a copper cent," one Hunt employee of the era recalled.

Finally, Hunt had to assign one of his men to "look after" Hassie full time.

Despite such outbursts, Hunt knew that his son was a "sensitive boy" who was not really violent at heart. When the Japanese attacked Pearl Harbor, Hassie had just turned twenty-four. His age made him prime draft material, but Hunt wanted to keep Hassie out of the fighting. The young man was capable of violent Oedipal tantrums, but, as one of the men assigned to look after him observed, "He would have made a terrible marine."

Unfortunately, Hassie once again became the victim of what his father had wrought. According to one of Hassie's early caretakers, a Hunt competitor who served on the War Board was determined to put the young man into the service. Hunt could probably have had Hassie excused from the service for medical reasons if he had sent Hassie to a doctor, but as far as Hunt was concerned, there was nothing wrong with Hassie that the young man could not outgrow. A medical deferment was simply not to be considered. Instead, he assigned H. L. Williford and Hassie's caretaker Dick Kirkpatrick to keep moving Hassie from Dallas to Shreveport to Jackson, Mississippi, changing draft boards with each move.

"We were keeping him out pretty good," Kirkpatrick recalled. "Finally, we got him a second lieutenant's commission."

Hassie went to Washington, D.C., as a member of the Army Corps of Engineers. His assignment was to "advise" the Chinese nationalist government about oil and gas matters, but his real occupation was sitting out the war in high style. He lived in the Mayflower Hotel right next to the five-star generals, flaunted at least two automobiles, and constantly chased after women. Kirkpatrick, his caretaker, warned that such a good thing would be brought to a crashing end by Hassie's superiors. "If you're smart," he advised, "you'll get yourself out of here."

The army forced the move instead. In 1943, Hassie was transferred to Camp Beauregard near Alexandria, Louisiana. Some later said Hassie was tormented by paranoid ideas that the Rockefellers were plotting to betray him in an oil deal. Others said he feared some of his father's enemies were attempting to get at H.L. by menacing Hassie. Dick Kirkpatrick blamed it on the army. "When he got down to Camp Beauregard, they put him out on the firing field," Kirkpatrick said. "He was so scared he just went beserk."

Hassie wound up in the mental ward of an army hospital near Lake Pontchartrain. He was discharged a short time later.

No longer able to pretend that Hassie would grow out of his problems, Hunt began his long search for a "cure." One of the first places he tried was a psychiatric institution near Andover, Massachusetts, where the doctors administered electric-shock treatments. Hassie remained around Andover as a sort of "outpatient" after his release; his quarters were a small motel Hunt had bought near the hospital. Naturally, Hunt had ideas of his own about how to supplement Hassie's treatment. Part of the remedy called for plenty of "action" with members of the opposite sex.

"Mr. Hunt was keepin' him full of girls, two or three at a time," Dick Kirkpatrick recalled.

After a while, Hunt brought Hassie back to Texas. The two look-alikes went out to the Winona Pecan Grove near Tyler, where Hunt hoped his son would rest and recuperate. But it soon became clear that Hassie was not cured. Instead of becoming better able to cope with the world, he suffered still more delusions and seemed to lose track of such basics as his family relationships.

"You see that woman at the head of the table?" Hassie would ask during dinner. "She's married to that fellow Hunt that you hear about."

On his good days, Hassie could still go down to the office and solve a complex oil-business problem. But on his bad days, he was almost unapproachable.

"You could never disagree with him or ask him questions directly," recalled a Hunt secretary. "If you wanted to know how he was feeling, you had to say things like, 'I wonder how Hassie is feeling today.' You had to be very careful not to upset him."

When he was upset, Hassie would erupt into temperamental fits. He could be especially violent in his attitude toward his father's secretaries. "Mr. Hunt used to introduce the girl friends he traveled with as his secretaries," one former secretary explained. "Hassie, in his mental state, couldn't sort that out. It made him extremely upset."

Hassie directed some of his anger at his mother. Once, for example, he picked up a piece of fruit and threw it at her, breaking her glasses. "There was no reason for Hassie to be angry at his mother," a neutral bystander recalled. "It was just part of his illness."

As in the past, Hassie vented most of his incurable rage at his father. He was always challenging Hunt to fistfights and starting a ruckus whether his challenge was answered or not.

"Hassie got to be pretty tough on his daddy," remembered one Hunt employee. "Mr. Hunt had to be careful because Hassie was strong enough to hurt him."

Hunt still believed that sex might be the answer to Hassie's illness. He dispatched Williford and others to find appropriate female companions for his son. At one point, he called for a "blond German woman with a high I.Q." Later, he ordered his men to find a candidate from the American Airlines stewardess school. Still later, he demanded a psychiatric nurse.

These episodes were usually ill fated. Some of the women quit when they realized that "companionship" required mating with the patient. Others left when they were assaulted and injured during one of Hassie's tantrums. Hunt's aides did their best to pay off the victims and clean up the mess. But when a Dallas doctor concluded that Hassie was "oversexed" and recommended a vasectomy, Hunt replied that having sex was about the only pleasure Hassie had left, and refused to follow the doctor's advice.

Meanwhile, Hunt kept up his quest for a "cure." He called Clare Boothe Luce of Time, Inc. to inquire about the latest medical procedures. He consulted with Dr. Alton Ochsner of New Orleans, the famous cancer specialist. One of H.L.'s former personal secretaries remembered that Hunt must have either contacted or sent Hassie to "every major hospital in the country," including Duke University, the Menninger Clinic, and the Institute for Living in Hartford, Connecticut. At last Hunt found a doctor with a procedure that offered both great danger and great promise. As Kirkpatrick recalled, "He said the operation would either be a success or Hassie would never be the same."

The operation was known as a prefrontal lobotomy. Though later discredited as a form of butchery, lobotomy was, in the late 1940s, one of the latest advances in psychiatric treatment. The procedure essentially involved the insertion of a scalpel beneath the eyebrow to sever the prefrontal lobes from the rest of the brain. Doctors did not know exactly what happened when this procedure was done. Medical science had only a primitive knowledge of the functions of the various parts of the brain. The only thing that seemed clear was that severing the prefrontal lobes calmed hyperactive patients. There were, however, a number of drawbacks. One was that the procedure sometimes calmed patients too much, reducing their personalities to a subhuman level. Another was that once the prefrontal lobe was severed, the correction could never be restored.

Like the electric-shock treatments, the lobotomy was performed by a doctor up East. Unfortunately, the operation did not turn out to be the "cure" Hunt had hoped for. Hassie ceased his violent outbursts, but he did not "get well." He could still walk and talk, but his conversation was more remote and oblique than ever, and he suffered embarrassing lapses of decorum that required twenty-four-hour supervision. Hunt saw no alternative but to send him to a psychiatric institution in New York State, where Hassie could get the kind of constant care he needed.

Putting Hassie away was the worst blow of Hunt's life. One day down at the office Hunt finally realized that his son could not be "cured."

"As I look back on it," he suddenly told his secretary, "my father was a little crazy, and I think I'm a little crazy, too."

Then, for one of the very few times in his life, H. L. Hunt broke down and cried.

Hunt's tearful realization did not last long. The truth was simply too painful for him to bear. When he dried his eyes, Hunt once again set out on a search for a miracle cure. He also insisted on keeping a vacant office right next to his own so that Hassie would have a space to move into when he got better and got back to work. In lieu of Hassie's return, Hunt began giving jobs to persons under treatment for mental and emotional problems in an effort to help their rehabilitation.

While Hassie deteriorated, Hunt's luck in the oil business got better. With the outbreak of World War II, oil prices jumped to $1.20 a barrel, and the demand for petroleum became unquenchable. Having never fought in a war,

Hunt did not volunteer for military service this time, either. Instead, he stopped his trade with Germany and Japan, and did what he considered to be his patriotic duty by staying home and producing oil for America's war machine. Most of the oil was shipped to embarcation points on the East Coast via the 1,400 mile "Big Inch" and "Little Inch" pipelines. In addition to enriching Hunt, this crude was what enabled the Allies to "float to victory on a sea of oil."

Hunt became fond of boasting that the Hunt interests produced more oil during World War II than all the Axis powers combined—"including Romania." Once again, he was giving himself more credit than he deserved, but his accomplishments were still incredible. Between 1941 and 1945, the Axis powers produced about 276 million barrels of oil. During that same period, the east Texas field produced upward of 500 million barrels of oil. Of course, Hunt did not own the entire east Texas field. According to estimates by former top employees, Hunt's 1941–1945 production was a little over 100 million barrels, or about 60,000 barrels a day. About two-thirds of Hunt's production, or an average of 40,000 barrels per day, came from the Dad Joiner leases. The rest came from leases Hunt had acquired after expanding beyond east Texas. In the Dad Joiner deal, Joiner himself had been the wildcatter and Hunt the dealmaker. In the early and middle 1940s, Hunt proved himself an oil finder with the best of them. By 1946, he had a gross income of $1 million per week, and his drilling crews were running sixty-five rigs a day.

"The incredible thing about it was that he did it in only fifteen years," observed one former Hunt man. "Standard Oil never did it so fast."

Still not content to rest on his riches, Hunt kept on drilling for more oil. He hired his first geologist in 1945, but he did not pay much attention to what the man said. Instead, he continued to rely mainly on his creekology and his gambler's guts. He instructed his men to lease the biggest tracts they could in a particular area—60,000 and 70,000 acres at a time—for he wanted to make sure that he got in on the most of whatever oil was there. And he pushed his drilling superintendents to spud in new wells at the rate of over 300 per year.

Hunt's postwar drilling orgy was partly inspired by the tax man. Hunt was in such a high bracket he either had to "drill up" large portions of his income or pay it to the government in taxes. Many times Hunt ordered his men to drill in places where he believed there was almost no chance of finding oil just so he could expense some tax money. And many times Hunt crews would find oil in the very locations where he wanted to drill dry holes. That was the Hunt luck at its damndest.

Following World War II, Hunt opened a refinery in Tuscaloosa, Alabama, and started a chain of gasoline stations in Alabama and Louisiana under the Parade label. That gave him a stake in all major phases of the oil business. He searched for oil under the names of Hunt Oil and Placid Oil. He drilled wells under the Penrod name. He transported oil under the name of Panola Pipeline. He refined it and sold it as gasoline under the name of Parade. No longer just a big fish in the small pond of the Ark-La-Tex, he had operations in five states and was on the verge of expanding to several more. Ever the social planner and innovator, he also established himself as an employee-relations leader by putting his Penrod Drilling men on a five-day (instead of seven-day) work schedule, which was an industry first.

As Hunt's oil production continued to increase, he began to buy more farm and ranch land. In 1944, he bought Lamar Farms in Kaufman County, Texas. The next year he bought several thousand acres in the Powder River Basin in Montana. Three years later, he sent Williford to investigate an even greater purchase: the 250,000-acre Hoodoo Ranches in Wyoming. Hunt was interested in the ranches because Texas farms were being ravaged by a grasshopper plague, and he had heard that Wyoming land was "grasshopper-proof." Williford reported on the property in glowing terms. Among its assets were a vintage log ranch house built in 1893, which Williford described as "one of the finest residences in the state," and "one of the best-watered 'ranges' in the country," which included a variety of lakes and streams and no less than 100 specially constructed stock reservoirs. Nearly the entire property was surrounded with four-wire fences. In addition to the grazing land, there were thousands of acres of forest lands. The livestock included 100 horses, 5,000 cows, 900 heifers, and 10,000 sheep. Herds of antelope and deer roamed about as they pleased.

Hunt wrote that hearing Williford's report "was enough to excite my ranching blood as well as to stimulate my acquisitive interest." He bought the ranch for $1.9 million, and set about turning it into a profit maker. He reported that the ranch eventually held 16,000 head of cattle and turned a profit of nearly $400,000 year. As luck would have it, Hunt found that the land he had bought for a ranch also contained oil. Agriculture remained the primary enterprise of the Hoodoo Ranches, but the oil did help speed up the property's payout.

Hunt seemed as fascinated with the "character" and history of one section of the Hoodoo Ranches—the Palette No. 2—as with the land's great wealth. One of his greatest pleasures was finding ranch founder Colonel A. A. Anderson's autobiography in the ranch house, and reading of Anderson's associations with men like fellow conservationist Teddy Roosevelt, Prince Albert of Monaco, and his neighbor Major General G. E. Pickett, the Civil War commander famous for his charge at Gettysburg. As time passed, the Hoodoo Ranches became one of the Hunt family's favorite recreation spots, a center for horseback riding, pack trips, and camping out.

As Hunt grew wealthier, he also grew more concerned with national and international politics. This was not a sudden change, but a natural evolution. The Republican county sheriff's son did not enjoy campaigning or seeking public office for himself. But he knew when political action served his own best interests. He had recognized the value of political power in the east Texas oil fields when overproduction threatened the leases he had bought. The success of his "flexible work week" plan in the 1930s had confirmed his belief in his own abilities as a social planner. During and after World War II, Hunt began to perceive a larger threat to his universe: the encroachment of socialism and communism.

Like many other successful third- and fourth-generation Americans, Hunt felt strangely dispossessed. The relatively homogeneous America of his boyhood was now even more a land of immigrants. The white western European stock of the first waves of newcomers to the country had been joined by waves of eastern European Jews, Slavs, Poles, Czechs, Irish, Italians, and Mexicans. Blacks were becoming increasingly aware of their rights as citizens. People were leaving the farms and flocking to the cities. The country was modernizing, industrializing, and changing more rapidly than ever before. So was the strife-torn world at large. Marxism, Leninism, and Stalinism were spreading across Europe and Asia. The good old days, such as they had been, were gone.

Although Hunt did not trumpet his views for all to hear, he was one of those who backlashed against this brave new world. He valued the new advances in science and technology, but he also clung to the Calvinist/social-Darwinist world view he had grown up with. As he saw it, the times called for a return to the old America, a renaissance of the old values and the old order. He more than most other men had personally benefited from the policies of the FDR administration—especially Roosevelt's crackdown on the hot-oil runners—but he saw the intervention of the federal government as inherently evil and debilitating.

Perhaps because of his own personal penchant for living secret lives and making secret deals, Hunt's reactionary conservatism was attended by an arch-conspiratorial vision of history and world events. This world view was consistent with what historian Richard Hofstadter described as the "paranoid style." A character of mind prevalent among ideologues on both the extreme left and the extreme right, the "paranoid style" manifested itself in organizations ranging from the Communist party to the Ku Klux Klan. What Hunt had in common with these disparate groups was a belief that almost everything that happened was the result of some great plot, some covert machinations. More often than not, his beliefs were based on his own fantasy and surmise rather than on specific facts. But he was right often enough to think that he was infallible.

Hunt's growing politicization was abetted by a change in the Hunt Oil hierarchy. In 1942, his trusted legal counsel J. B. McEntire died on a golf course. Hunt replaced him with the politically ambitious Sidney Latham. Latham was of medium height and build, with wavy, graying hair, a square jaw, and rimless glasses. A former Hunt secretary described him as "quite good looking in a scholarly fashion," well turned out but with a proper, almost schoolteacherly, air about him. A former state legislator who had been active in passing laws to limit "hot oil" production, Latham was an astute lawyer and a devout Christian conservative. He left the Hunt organization from 1943 to 1945 to serve as secretary of state under Texas governor Coke Stevenson. When he returned after suffering martyrdom in a Democratic party split, Hunt made him a vice president.

More than just a legal troubleshooter, Latham also became one of Hunt's earliest political advisers. Hunt was not the sort of man who could be said to have a mentor. But Latham, whose views were very similar to those of his boss, was able to provide Hunt with intelligence from a wide variety of political contacts. Later, Latham would also help Hunt translate his views into concrete action. It was said that in return, Hunt promised to finance Latham's bid for governor of Texas. If so, it was a promise that was never followed through.

Hunt's most important political project during the mid- and late 1940s was getting General Douglas MacArthur elected president of the United States. Hunt admired no one more than the great Pacific commander and proconsul. In later interviews, he listed MacArthur first among all his heroes and called him "truly the man of this century." MacArthur embodied all the traits Hunt and many other traditionalists held dear about America. The general was a swashbuckling individualist, prone to riling his superiors with flamboyant acts of insubordination as inevitably as he vanquished America's enemies. However, Hunt admired MacArthur for more than just his battlefield exploits and romantic style. What Hunt appreciated most and considered the foremost evidence of his qualification for the presidency was his "rehabilitation of Japan without permitting communist infiltration."

Exactly what Hunt did to help MacArthur in his presidential bids was never fully revealed. A confirmed tightwad, Hunt was always more vocal than generous—at least in his later years. If the reverse was true in the 1940s Hunt never confirmed it. All he said about the matter was that he "supported" MacArthur in 1944 and 1948.

As he broadened his political sphere, Hunt also increased the scale of his gambling. In later years, Hunt would claim that he quit gambling for patriotic reasons during World War II. (He supposedly felt it un-American to tie up the national telephone lines with his wagering business while the country was at war.) But once the fighting stopped, Hunt was back at it like never before. Instead of relying on the bookmakers, he set up his own race-horse handicapping office in Dallas. A maze of telephone lines connected the office to tracks all over the country. The office was staffed by two statisticians, one of whom, according to Hunt, had a degree from MIT. The statisticians' assigned role was to compare their figures with those of the regular bookies and discover the "true" odds on the races. Typically, Hunt would brag about what a "scientific" approach he had devised, then totally disregard the recommendations of his private oddsmakers and bet his hunches.

Hunt conducted his gambling in cash. He customarily assigned his personal secretary to keep a stack of gambling money for him in a cardboard box in her office; he kept another stash in a box in the vault of First National Bank. Hunt's secretary would administer his winnings and/or losses on a daily basis, paying couriers that would come and go, and keeping meticulous records of each transaction.

Although Hunt never released an official tally sheet of his gambling activities, all sorts of legends about his prowess began to circulate. Some said Hunt was so good on his good days that he could break the big East Coast bookies on their home tracks. Others said Hunt's losses offset his winnings and then some. The truth apparently lay somewhere in between. According to one of the secretaries who kept track of Hunt's gambling money, his winnings in one twenty-four-month period shortly after the war amounted to about $135,000. Gradually, Hunt began to increase his wagering, adding more tracks and more races each month on the theory that more bets, like drilling more oil wells, increased his chances of overall success. Whether or not it was as foolproof as he seemed to believe, Hunt's "system" apparently worked, for by the late 1940s he was telling friends that his off-track betting operation was bringing in $1 million per year.

Encouraged by his results, Hunt determined to apply his so-called "scientific" principles of gambling to games of chance. At one point, for example, he liked to frequent Fred Browning's place on the highway between Dallas and Fort Worth, where the game was craps. Hunt would later say that he based his wagering on what he called the "law of consecutivity." He explained that the law held that what the dice were doing at the time, they would continue to do in the short run. Of course, as interviewer Tom Buckley observed, this was merely another way of saying "the dice are cold, the dice are hot." Hunt's "law" was really nothing new. But Hunt seemed to derive great enjoyment— not to mention pride—from tinkering with such formulations and recoining them as his own.

Hunt's favorite form of gambling was his head-to-head encounters with a small group of playing partners in games like poker, gin rummy, and craps. His regular game was with some local Dallas cronies who met in a suite at the Baker Hotel. But Hunt also played with some of the big-name gamblers of the day. One of them was Indiana oilman Ray Ryan, a dark, heavy-set man who dressed with impeccable taste and enjoyed the company of reputed Mafiosi. Renowned gambling figure Jimmy "the Greek" Snyder later wrote of Ray Ryan, "I have known a lot of guys who bet money in my time. That was my life. But I have never—*ever*—known of a higher roller than Ryan." Another Hunt gambling crony was the notorious Frank Erickson, a big-time gangster and bookie heavily invested in the Florida horse-racing scene. Hunt, Ryan, and Erickson would play poker in hotels in Dallas and Chicago, in Ryan's houses in Florida and Indiana, and even on ships crossing the ocean.

"It was a revelation to watch these people gamble," recalled a Hunt secretary who sometimes kept score at their games. "It was all very professional. There was no unnecessary conversation. They gave nothing away by word or expression."

On the strength of his success back in the El Dorado oil-boom days, Hunt still considered himself the best poker player in the world. That opinion of himself was more than a little overblown, but Hunt was apparently able to hold his own with the likes of Ryan and Erickson—at least in poker. Gin rummy was a different story. No matter how hard he tried, Hunt could not seem to master the game. At one point, he even took lessons from recognized world champion Oswald Jacoby, but concluded that Jacoby was overrated.

Hunt's other educational experiences were quite expensive. One of the most costly was a marathon gin-rummy game he played with Ray Ryan. Because of their busy schedule, the two oilmen had a great deal of trouble arranging a time for the game. Finally, they decided to play aboard an ocean liner crossing the Atlantic. When the liner reached foreign shores, Hunt's losses amounted to over $200,000. On another occasion, Hunt lost over $400,-000 to Frank Erickson.

In gaming with men like Frank Erickson and other big-time Mafia bookies, Hunt was consorting with members of major organized crime families. That naturally implied a certain amount of risk in and of itself, but that added element of danger only made gambling more fun for Hunt. There was never any evidence that Hunt did anything besides gamble with the crime figures he knew, no sign that he engaged in side business deals or illegal schemes. Instead, Hunt seemed to associate with these people because they were the highest-stakes gamblers around and because he enjoyed hanging around colorful characters. At the same time, Hunt's gambling cronies were not just charming; they could also be quite mean—especially if a debt was slow in being paid. On one such occasion when Frank Erickson was the winner, Hunt felt compelled to go into hiding for several days for fear Erickson would try to harm him in the collection process. As one secretary observed, "Mr. Hunt had some pretty strange friends."

Of course, Hunt was pretty strange himself. The man with three families lived more than one secret life. How many more was known only to himself. Hunt had a great many acquaintances and associates. He had over a thousand employees. He had plenty of poker-playing buddies. But he had no real friend, no confidant. Still very much a loner, he was more of a mystery man than he had ever been. And yet his dark side was counterpointed with a light side, his air of lawlessness was matched by a curious allegiance to his own internal codes.

"Mr. Hunt was amoral," observed one of his personal secretaries. "He didn't set out to do bad or good. He just was determined to do what he wanted to do."

Hunt's contradictions and eccentricities were also manifest in the way he ran Hunt Oil. He set much of the everyday tone of the office through his right-hand man and office manager Roy Lee. Loyal to Hunt above all else, Lee was a controversial figure. Those who liked the short, bald executive regarded him as brilliant. "Roy Lee could have made a lot of money in the oil business on his own," recalled one former associate. "Instead, he stayed around and made money for Mr. Hunt." Those who disliked Lee, considered him a martinet and complained of his "Gestapo tactics." These tactics allegedly included such things as eavesdropping on employees' telephone conversations and inquiring into their outside business interests. A veteran of the early east Texas days, Lee knew the value of oil-business intelligence and the costliness of unauthorized leaks. His was the unenviable task of insuring that such leaks did not happen at Hunt Oil.

But even as he dispatched Roy Lee to maintain order, Hunt established a kind of ongoing office chaos by employing a mysterious group of personal aides. With Frank Grego and Old Man Bailey now dead, the dean of this crowd was H. L. Williford. Bald, hunched, and obsequious to his boss, Williford had come to be known around the office as "the hatchet man." His assignments ranged from checking out prospective real-estate purchases to arranging for abortions for Hunt's girl friends and keeping them out of sight. Beginning in the late 1940s, Hunt supplemented Williford with a squadron of young men who paraded in and out of the office at seemingly random intervals. Where oil-tool millionaire Howard Hughes had a preference for Mormons, Hunt had a preference for clean-cut, Baptist fellows from small southern towns. These young men had official positions with Hunt Oil Company. They drew salaries, and had cars and expense accounts. But no one except Hunt himself really knew what they did. If anyone questioned their purpose, he or she was told that the young men were "on special assignment for Mr. Hunt."

"A lot of times, the top executive didn't know whether people were supposed to be hired or fired," recalled a former secretary. "I remember once when one of the supposedly young men 'on special assignment' was involved in an auto accident. The woman he collided with said she was going to sue Hunt Oil. Mr. Hunt was away, so a vice president fired the young man. He was worrying about how he was going to replace him, when Mr. Hunt returned. It turned out that Mr. Hunt had never heard of the young man. That kind of thing could happen easily around there."

Hunt expected all employees to be on call twenty-four hours a day. He was particularly demanding of his top employees, whom he would feel free to contact at any hour of the day or night. Likewise, Hunt's top men had instructions to call him about developments on a particular project regardless of when they occurred. Much of this operational style resulted from the demands of the oil business itself. Hunt often had to move overnight to prepare papers securing leases. The drilling and completion of his wells reached critical stages both day and night. Hunt always wanted to be the first to know everything. He wanted every order carried out at once. He was stingy with his compliments and seldom gave anyone extra praise for an outstanding overtime job. Yet, he still managed to push his men harder. As one former employee put it, "He had a way of working the shit out of you and never saying nothing about it."

Most of Hunt's employees lived in fear of him, knowing that if they did not carry out his orders, he would fire them and get someone else. But, remarkably enough, Hunt ran his organization without raising his voice. He was never heard uttering a curse word. Instead of getting hot about things, he simply grew cold. When he wanted to show disapproval of something, he would just say, "That's an all-time low in good thinking" or "I don't think we ought to do it that way," and that was that. When he was especially displeased with someone, he would dismiss them with an icy stare and a curt "That'll be all."

True to form, Hunt complemented his frenetic working pace with slow-moving personal mannerisms and a country-boy style. No longer much of a snappy dresser, he took to wearing conventionally dull gray business suits and a gray Homberg with the brim tipped forward. Because of his bad back, he seemed to tilt backward a bit when he walked. He often came into the office with mud all over his shoes. ("He said it was hard for him to find shoes that fit," one secretary remembered, "so he wore the same pair over and over again.") When he had a lot of dictating to do, Hunt liked to remove his muddy shoes, take off his socks, roll up his pants legs, and prop his feet on the desk. This habit later caused other employees to begin referring to the boss (out of Hunt's hearing, of course) as the "barefoot billionaire."

Although he did not often attend church, Hunt liked to sing gospel songs down at the office. When such moods struck, he would haul out a tattered old hymnal and stand in his office, belting out the strains of his favorite old-time country gospel selection. He knew many of the songs by heart, but he liked to hold the hymnal anyway. Hunt also liked to walk around the office singing Broadway melodies and occasional ditties of his own composition. One of his favorite lyrics went, "I've got a woman who's crazy for me. She's funny that way. . . ."

Hunt was also known to go on peculiar food kicks. For a time, he stopped eating lunch at the office, preferring to work right through the noon hour. Then he began having lunch with his secretary, mooching halves of her peanut-butter sandwiches. "I'll make a deal with you," he told her one day. "You make the sandwiches one week, and I'll make them the next." As might be expected, Hunt's turn never came. Hunt then developed a propensity for late-night meals. Since his wife Lyda reportedly refused to put up with the practice, Hunt would do his cooking at his secretary's house or at Latham's home. "It was nothing for him to come over at ten P.M. and cook, then leave it uncleaned up," recalled one former secretary. On other occasions, at midday Hunt would send one of the girls in the office out to buy barbecue sandwiches; at the time, the sandwiches cost about fifteen cents each, but Hunt often dispatched the girl on her errand with a hundred dollar bill.

Such displays of oilmanly affluence were not always the rule. In fact Hunt had an annoying habit of being out of pocket money. He would borrow five, ten, even a couple of hundred dollars from one of his employees, then forget to pay that person back. Nor surprisingly, most of those he borrowed from would be rather hesitant to ask their boss to pay them back. "He would pay me much more in bonuses than what he borrowed," said one woman who worked for him, but she added that the short-term pinch on her cash reserves often became severe.

Hunt's own office was modestly appointed. In 1945, he moved from the Cotton Exchange Building to a corner suite in the Mercantile National Bank building across from Neiman-Marcus. Hunt's office was dominated by a big mahogany desk, a leather couch, and some leather-upholstered chairs. There was a private bathroom with showers off to one side. However, there was no air conditioning (Mount Vernon and many of the better homes had it in those days, but it was missing from most office buildings), and there were no gilded paintings, grand trophies, expensive rugs, or priceless works of art. The only photograph of any member of the family was a picture of Hassie in an Army uniform. Hunt always drove himself to work in an unimposing Oldsmobile, which he parked a few blocks away across from the White Plaza, where the rates were cheaper than in the middle of downtown.

At the same time, Hunt was not a total tightwad. "Hunt Oil paid good salaries," a secretary from the late 1940s said. "I was hired at two and a half times the going rate." Part of this extra compensation clearly resulted from the "job requirement" of having to put up with Hunt's idiosyncracies all day long. But contrary to some popular misconceptions, Hunt did take a personal interest in seeing that Hunt Oil salaries were commensurate with those at other oil firms. Hunt did not allow his employees to own an interest in Hunt Oil wells or trade privately on Hunt operations. But he did occasionally pass on invest-ment tips to favored employees and associates. There was no profit sharing, no stock options. Employees had to pay their retirement and medical plans themselves. But true to his patriarchal ways, Hunt took it upon himself to "take care of his workers as their needs arose."

"If you were sick, he'd hire a plane and fly you to the Mayo Clinic," recalled one office worker. "He was generous in his way—when it suited him."

Capable of the shrewedest, coldest business calculations, Hunt delighted in performing small kindnesses—giving an employee a ride home, pinning a rose on someone's mother, paying an unexpected bonus. On other occasions, he would look to whomever he was with to provide a sort of paternal care. "I'll never forget the day at the office when he got a chill," a former secretary recalled. "He went in and curled up in his office beneath a blanket. I had to tuck him in just like a baby."

Hunt's reclining moments were rare. His mind seemed to be working twenty-four hours a day. He was always popping up in bed in the middle of the night with some new plan or idea. He was not a gadfly, but a compulsive doer. He pursued each new project with great intensity until he saw it through to what he regarded as its completion. Impulsive as a jackrabbit and apparently unaware of any time schedules or personal commitments other than his own, he was always on the move. His wife, Lyda, managed to anticipate him by having a suitcase packed and ready to go for him at all times. Lyda also learned to expect the unannounced arrival of her husband and any number of unex-pected dinner guests whenever it suited him.

For all his activity, Hunt maintained a remarkably low public profile throughout this period. His name was well known in the oil business and in Dallas financial circles. He was not a recluse in the manner of Howard Hughes. But he was not the sort of fellow people recognized in the street. He did not give interviews; he did not allow newspaper photographers to take his picture. Although Hunt never stated exactly why he wanted to stay out of the public eye, the reasons were obvious. There was the fear of kidnap threats like the one that followed Margaret's appearance as Rose Festival Queen. There was Hunt's desire to avoid being solicited by charitable fund raisers, leeches, and bums. And there was Hunt's desire not to expose his gambling and girl friends and allegedly bigamous families. Hunt was not ashamed of his secret lives and secret families. On the contrary, he was proud of his ability to support more than one wife and family, and he was proud of his exploits at the gambling tables. But he also had sense enough to be aware of the adverse repercussions that would follow if the truth were ever revealed.

Then, in the spring of 1948, something happened to change Hunt's low public profile and, ultimately, his entire life.

CHAPTER 8

THE RICHEST AND
THE RIGHTEST

THE stake-out team waited in the lobby of the Mercantile National Bank building. There were three of them: a man with a camera, a man with a notebook, and a "finger man." It was getting close to four o'clock, and all three men were getting nervous. The man with the notebook had been tipped that H.L. left his office about this time every afternoon to attend a card game in the Baker Hotel. This would be their best chance to shoot him.

The elevator doors opened, and a handful of businessmen walked out. The first one off was a tall, slightly portly man in his late fifties. He wore a tan gabardine suit and a gray fedora. He had jowly cheeks, a large nose, clear blue eyes, and a poker-faced expression; he was neither smiling nor frowning, just looking straight ahead and leaning a little backward as he walked.

The "finger man" nodded as the figure in the gabardine suit passed in front of him. This was their target.

The other two men followed Hunt out of the lobby. It was a windy but clear March day, and the sidewalks of downtown Dallas were crowded with people. Hunt headed west on Commerce Street toward the Baker. At the corner of Ervay Street, across from Neiman-Marcus, he had to stop for a red light. The man with the camera caught up with him. While Hunt waited with the crowd for the light to change, the man with the camera quickly snapped his picture.

Hunt noticed the man taking his picture, but figured he was just another street photographer. He expected the man to rush up and give him a business card, offering six prints for a dollar. But when the light changed, the photographer disappeared. Figuring that the photographer was just shooting the buildings in the background, Hunt kept on walking toward the Baker.

A few weeks later, the bureau chief of *Life* magazine called Hunt's secretary, Allene Pohlvogt, and told her that he had a story about Hunt that he wanted to send over for Hunt's "approval."

Hunt was not in the office when the call came in, but Pohlvogt knew her boss well enough to realize that this news was not good news. She immediately went to Sidney Latham.

"We may have a problem," she began tentatively.

When Pohlvogt related the substance of the telephone call, Latham almost became unglued. Like Pohlvogt, he assumed Hunt would be furious, and that he would somehow blame them.

Those fears proved to be unfounded. When Hunt returned to the office and read the approval copy, he thought it was great. He even appreciated the cleverness of the "enterprising" photographer who had scooped the picture of him.

"I wondered why that fellow never gave me his card," Hunt said with a chuckle.

Then to the amazement of his secretary and his lawyer, the man who had shunned almost all personal publicity for fifty-nine years signed a release agreeing to let *Life* and its sister publication, *Fortune,* run their stories about him. Hunt never bothered to explain why he signed the release or what about the stories appealed to him. Maybe after all these years he wanted public recognition to go with the private confirmation of his accomplishments. Maybe he believed he was so powerful he could now maintain a public profile and his secret lives, too. In any case, those close to Hunt could only shake their heads and wonder if he had suffered a lapse of judgment.

When the stories appeared in print, Hunt's judgment seemed even more suspect. Though they were far from derogatory, both the *Fortune* and *Life* versions consisted of the kind of public identification that Hunt—and many other wealthy men—tried to avoid. The April 1948 issue of *Fortune* said that Hunt was probably "the biggest of the Big Rich, and thus also probably the richest single individual in the U.S." The magazine justified its claim regarding Hunt by reporting, "The Hunt Oil properties have been valued at around $237 million and their daily production of crude estimated at 65,000 barrels. At last year's average price of $2.25 a barrel, this would have given him a gross weekly income of more than $1 million."

The April 5, 1948, issue of *Life* went a step further. In addition to recounting the figures reported in its business-industry sister publication, *Life* ran the photograph of Hunt on the Dallas street corner. Beneath the image of the man in the gray fedora was the caption: "Is this the richest man in the U. S.?"

Typically, the national press began its long and stormy association with H. L. Hunt by making a couple of glaring errors. For one thing, both *Life* and *Fortune* misspelled his first name as "Haralson." The two magazines also came in pretty low with their estimates of his wealth. According to one former top Hunt employee, the total production of Hunt Oil and its affiliates was in fact about 65,000 barrels per day, just as *Life* and *Fortune* reported. But the worth of that production was hard for even Hunt to know, in part because a true valuation depended on such unpredictables as the price of oil, which was steadily going up and the life of his wells, which could average five years, ten years, or even twenty years and more. As Hunt himself would say, "If you know how rich you are, you aren't very rich." Nevertheless, with a gross income from oil and gas of $65 million per year as well as a drilling company and large chunks of real estate, it was likely that Hunt's fortune was by now somewhere in excess of $600 million rather than in the range of $237 million, as *Life* and *Fortune* reported.

Whether or not H. L. Hunt really deserved the title of America's richest man was open to debate. The first John D. Rockefeller had claimed a fortune worth $1 billion in 1913. Though the Rockefeller wealth was by now distributed over three generations, the family still controlled assets worth well in excess of $1 billion. So did the Mellon family of Pittsburgh, which held large interests in a major oil company, a major steel company, and a major bank. The reclusive Howard Hughes was on his way to becoming a billionaire in the late 1940s, as was oilman J. Paul Getty. But thanks to *Fortune* and *Life,* Haroldson Lafayette Hunt had what neither Hughes nor Getty could claim—public recognition as the richest. From now on, everyone knew the identity of the nation's richest individual—he was H. L. Hunt of Dallas, Texas.

Hunt did nothing to discourage his myth makers. A few days after the publication of the *Life* and *Fortune* articles, he granted his first full-fledged personal interview to Frank X. Tolbert of the *Dallas Morning News.* Although Hunt did not confirm or deny the published figures on his wealth, he did posture as every bit the superrich superpatriot his emerging legend would make him out to be.

"Money as money is nothing," he told Tolbert. "It is just something to make bookkeeping convenient."

Hunt went on to say that he had "always attempted to maintain a nonalcoholic and non-Communistic organization," and that his favorite candidate for president was General Douglas MacArthur. Dad Joiner had died in Dallas the year before, but Hunt mentioned the purchase of the Joiner leases only in passing, minimizing its importance to the growth of his fortune. He also avoided mention of the complexities of his family life, though he did credit his wife Lyda with "about ninety percent of our financial successes and the many kindnesses which have been extended to us wherever we have resided."

Apparently more interested in discussing his political philosophy than anything else, Hunt opined that "the healthiest thinking in the United States today is being done on medium-sized farms." He did not mention that he was then in the process of buying up small, medium, and large farms on his way to becoming one of the nation's largest landowners.

Hunt's appearances in the press made him an instant international celebrity. He was deluged with mail from all over the world. So widespread was his fame that one letter addressed to "H. L. Hunt, King of Petrol, U.S.A." was actually delivered to his office from Europe. A few letters simply commended Hunt for his achievements, but the vast majority of them asked for money to finance this or that very special project. Hunt alternately ordered his staff to file letters or just throw them away. He seldom bothered to answer them in writing, much less send the amount requested.

Thanks, no doubt, to the Hunt luck, Hunt did not suffer much serious fallout as a result of his new public profile. On one occasion, he did get a letter from a man who claimed that one night years before, Hunt and a gang of toughs had walked into his gambling hall in El Dorado, Arkansas and had taken over the place, leaving the man on the street without a cent. Hunt called in Sidney Latham for a closed-door conference about the letter, and rumors later circulated around the office that a check had been sent out. But apart from that mysterious incident, there were no major blackmail attempts in the wake of Hunt's publicity, no serious threats to his safety.

Hunt did make two significant financial adjustments following the *Life* and *Fortune* articles. One was to transfer the ownership of Penrod Drilling, the family-owned drilling contractor, to Lyda's sons, Bunker, Herbert, and Lamar. By this time, the original fleet of eleven land rigs was expanding to twenty-seven, making the company worth an estimated $10 million to $15 million. The other significant financial adjustment Hunt made was to set up the Secure Trusts for his family by Ruth Ray Wright. Like the Loyal Trusts for the first family and the Reliance Trusts for Frania's family, the Secure Trusts consisted primarily of producing oil and gas properties. The worth of the Secure Trusts was reportedly in the $1-million range, which was quite a nest egg for the average family but a pittance compared to the wealth accumulating in the first-family trusts. As trustees, Hunt named his gambling buddy Ray Ryan and Ryan's wife Helen.

For Hunt's first family, the publicity was something of a revelation. Up to this time, Lyda and her children had not paid much attention to the fact of being rich. The three youngest children, Bunker, Herbert, and Lamar, though already in their late teens and early twenties, did not even know how wealthy their father really was. But from now on, they would never be able to forget who they were or how much they had. The Hunt children did not mention it to their father, but the whole experience caused them considerable consternation and concern about the future.

Hunt, on the other hand, seemed to regard his new stardom as the crowning confirmation of his special talents. Not only was he worthy of his rank as the nation's richest man, he was also capable of surviving the attendant repercussions without harm. According to former associates, Hunt was now growing more strong-willed and more self-deluded than ever. "He never changed his mind once he made it up," said one. "Once he heard what he wanted to hear, he stopped listening," said another. "He believed the world was the way he wanted it to be, not the way it is," said a third. He also believed even more strongly in his own omnipotence. As one former associate put it with only slight exaggeration, "He thought he was a second Jesus Christ."

Aroused by his publicity in *Life* and *Fortune,* Hunt's savior complex now moved him to become a full-fledged public figure. There were many secrets that he would never reveal, but gradually and with ever-increasing fanfare, H. L. Hunt stepped out of the shadows and into the spotlight.

As Hunt saw it, his motivation in going public was mainly political. The dire world outlook he had been forming since the early and middle 1940s had grown even darker. The world situation seemed to him to have reached crisis proportions despite the end of World War II. Although the causes of this crisis were complex and various, Hunt could and often did sum up his political thought in a single sentence. As he put it, "I believe we are being taken over by the communists."

Hunt considered the threat to be twofold. One part emanated from abroad in the persons and policies of men like Joseph Stalin and Mao Tse-tung. But the other part, the most heinous aspect, emanated "from within," specifically from the New Deal liberalism of the FDR and Truman administrations. By catering to the demand for federal welfare services, the New Dealers were leading America down the road to socialism. But neither major party offered a viable alternative. The Democratic party, except for the Dixiecrat wing, was itself the creator of the New Deal and thus, in Hunt's view, "the instrument of socialism and communism." The Republican party, as presently constituted, displayed what Hunt described as "dangerously radical tendencies."

Hunt was by no means an isolated nut. Although there was a strong populist, liberal, pro–New Deal element in Texas during the late 1940s and early 1950s, the establishment mind was staunchly against the New Deal and staunchly anticommunist. The archetypal figure of the era was Governor Allan Shivers, who served as the state's chief executive from 1949 to 1954. An opponent of "federal interference" in any form, Shivers exemplified the hard line against the communists. At one point, he even urged the state legislature to make membership in the Communist party punishable by death. When the legislature settled for a $20,000 fine and twenty years in jail, Shivers went on record as being "disgusted."

Of course, neither H. L. Hunt nor those other prominent Texans who shared his views were pure ideologues. As Hunt later admitted, "Everything I do, I do for profit." Politics was no exception. The threat Hunt saw in the communists and the New Dealers was largely and directly economic. In addition to wanting to destroy the free-enterprise system that had given him his wealth, the New Dealers also favored federal control of Texas's tidelands and oil fields and opposed the oil depletion allowance. The loss of the tidelands and the depletion allowance could cost Hunt Oil and other producers billions of dollars in potential profits and annual tax write-offs.

Hunt admittedly believed that "patriotism is always profitable." He also believed that he personally could show America the way out of its economic wilderness. After all, he was a producer in every sense of the word, as well as the creator of the flexible-work-week plan that was so successful back in the depression. One of the burning domestic issues of the postwar era was soil conservation and the fight to avoid future dustbowl disasters in the nation's heartland. Returning to his farmboy roots, Hunt had been taking an avid interest in a soil-reclamation project on his ranch in Kaufman County. As the work proceeded to success on an experimental 675-acre plot, Hunt began to observe progress that his fellow Dallas millionaire Toddie Lee Wynne was making on a larger tract of land nearby. He also began getting frequent visits from Louis Bromfield, a Pulitzer Prize–winning novelist and soil-reclamation crusader. Finally, in the early spring of 1950, Hunt came forward with another grand proposal of his own.

He called it his "vast soil conservation plan," but it was much more than a mere agricultural scheme. Rather, it was the brainchild of Hunt's utopian vision. The plan called for recruiting unemployed young men to work in soil-reclamation projects. But learning conservation techniques was only part of the program. Housed in barracks like infantry men, the young recruits would also be indoctrinated in the principles of Americanism and anticommunism.

In March of 1950 Hunt unveiled parts of his "vast soil conservation plan" to a reporter for the *Dallas Morning News,* a mouthpiece for the dominant reactionary sentiments of the day. He said at the time that he was on the verge of getting the project under way on sixteen tracts of land covering 6,000 acres, and that he was willing to back the program up to $25 million.

Although the *News* did not point them out, the remarkable similarities between Hunt's proposed indoctrination farms and the communist collectives he so vehemently opposed did not go unnoticed by some of his associates. As one of his secretaries observed, "He was borrowing from the totalitarian countries, but if you had told him that, he would have been appalled."

A short time after announcing his vast soil conservation plan, Hunt decided to try his hand as an author. His first self-published work was a pamphlet he entitled "A Word to Help the World." The word Hunt offered was "constructive." Hunt proposed the term partly as an alternative to the standard categories "liberal" and "conservative." Although he would never be caught with the label "liberal," Hunt did not consider himself a "conservative" either. ("I don't have a conservative hair in my head," he once told a reporter. "I couldn't have taken a shoestring and run it up as I have done if I were in the least degree conservative.") In Hunt's lexicon, "constructive" combined the best of both sides. He called it "the trademark for the wholesome in government." Best of all, it was a word whose meaning would not be perverted by the communists. As Hunt noted, "It may be said of a person 'too conservative.' It cannot be charged 'too constructive.' "

But "constructive" was more than just a convenient new label. It was also the key to Hunt's sweeping solution for society, his grand vision of how the world should be reordered. And by any other name, that vision was still largely conservative. Although he advocated social security and high pay for teachers, Hunt placed the most emphasis on limiting government in every area except defense. As he put it, "Constructives will work for our government to become fortified with ability and armaments, consistency and character. . . . Constructives will recognize and teach that the government does not produce and therefore cannot provide and that waste and inefficiency would bog down its attempt to produce. . . . Constructives will advocate a government which does not exact a pound of freedom for every service offered."

Disturbed most of all by what he regarded as "public apathy and indifference," Hunt called for "constructives" to organize an "Educational Facts League." The purpose of this organization would be "to secure an impartial presentation of all the news through all the news channels concerning issues of public interest" and to fight for the public's right to "facts on both sides of all issues," not just "the part and kind of news which left-wing workers are willing to let them have."

As it turned out, neither the vast soil conservation plan nor the Educational Facts League ever got off the ground. But Hunt's proposals were not total failures. Rather, they proved to be the genesis of an even more grandiose scheme that did come to fruition. In June of 1951, Hunt gave his new scheme the name that would become known to millions as a catchword for paranoid arch conservatism—Facts Forum.

From its inception, Facts Forum was shrouded in secrecy and deliberate misrepresentation. In order to qualify for status as a tax-exempt foundation, Facts Forum was supposed to be "organized and operated exclusively for religious, charitable, scientific, literary, or educational purposes," and was not supposed to devote itself to "carrying on propaganda or otherwise attempting to influence legislation." In its original application to the IRS, Facts Forum stated that its main activities were "discussion groups, lending libraries, and polls." But in reality, Facts Forum's aims and activities were far more ambitious and political. Its main function was not discussion groups, libraries, and polls, but the circulation of a newsletter and the broadcasting of a fifteen-minute radio commentary show.

Hunt set the tone for Facts Forum in a rare speech he delivered in Dallas in the summer of 1951. In that speech, he declared that the world was locked in a struggle to the death between two divergent groups—the far left and the far right. The Far Left, as Hunt described it, included everyone from "liberal" New Dealers to socialists and communists. The far right was comprised of those Hunt called "constructives." The struggle between these two groups was primary and absolute. The time had come to choose sides. Moderates—or "middle-of-the-roaders," as Hunt called them—would have little effect unless they joined the struggle, too. Facts Forum, Hunt announced, would present a "constructive" airing of "both sides" the issues involved so that the public could be "educated."

"Should we continue to handle Korea as a limited police action?" asked the voice coming out of the radio. "This is Dan Smoot for Facts Forum."

In a moderate and unemotional tone, the voice began the argument for the side that said yes. The voice cited the views of General Omar Bradley and

Adlai Stevenson. "Korea," the voice quoted Stevenson as saying, "is the most remarkable effort the world has ever seen to make collective security work. In choosing to repel the first armed aggression of the Communists, we chose to make bitter sacrifices today to save civilization tomorrow."

The voice continued to present the pro–United Nations view for a few more dry paragraphs. Throughout, the tone remained calm and uninspiring.

Then, with a noticeably more urgent tone, the voice presented the argument for "the other side."

"It is a strange war for a man who has been taught to love the American flag but who now finds himself fighting under a blue flag representing a world organization of which his enemy, the Soviet, is a member," the voice on the radio declared. "It's called a United Nations police action, but the United Nations' only noticeable contribution is the policy of appeasement which keeps the Americans from winning."

Putting the listener on the Korean front lines, the voice continued: "It's cold up here in winter—sometimes thirty below zero. If a boy cries his tears turn to ice. And then there is the enemy, always the enemy. Joe can feel him out there in the blackness, and sometimes he can hear him. And sometimes when a star shell bursts overhead, he can see him—not one, but thousands, moving relentlessly forward. . . .

"Presently, the third assault wave starts . . . then it's the kind of fight that man fought centuries ago; knives and fists, fingers groping for eyes, and teeth seeking a soft spot in the neck. Maybe Joe will die in the slit trench, and maybe he will live, his hands sour and gummy with half-digested rice gruel ripped out of the stomach of a bleeding bundle of rags and bones at his feet. . . .

"Korea: Police action or war? A question for all Americans. This is Dan Smoot for Facts Forum."

True to its promise, Facts Forum programs presented "both sides" of many other issues, but hardly with equal fervor or fairness. The format of the organization's radio slots always involved a single commentator engaged in a one-man debate with himself. The commentator would present the so-called far-left position first. Though actually a jumble of mainstream liberal, moderate, and conservative opinion, the far-left position was depicted as monolithic. The commentator would deliver its message in a bland, unexciting style. Then the same commentator would present the "constructive" side. All of a sudden his voice would become louder and sharper, as he embellished his points with bombastic rhetoric and spurious insinuations about communist influences at home and abroad. Invariably, the "constructive" position was antiwelfare and anti–United Nations.

Many of Facts Forum's early broadcasts were devoted to explaining the unity and goodness of democracy and Christianity. "Democracy is a political outgrowth of the teachings of Jesus Christ," one program declared. "Christianity was essential to the creation of our democracy." In another broadcast, the commentator said, "We in Facts Forum know that American democracy . . . is still the most nearly perfect expression ever made by man in legal and political terms of a basic ideal of Christianity."

However, as Facts Forum grew, it abandoned its defense of American democracy and turned against it, at least rhetorically. "One of the best indications of how far we have slipped is the wide contemporary use by practically all of our intellectual and political leaders of the word 'democracy' to designate our system," said one program. "The American Founding Fathers knew, and Jefferson said in specific terms, that a democracy is the most evil kind of government possible." In the view of Facts Forum and, of course, its founder, H. L. Hunt, the United States was not a democracy but a "Republic." Complaining about a textbook which described America as a democracy, one Facts Forum speaker explained his objection by saying, "Well, you see, Mr. Vishinsky talks about a democracy. Mr. Acheson talks about democracy. Mr. Nehru talks about democracy." He was referring, of course, to the Soviet ambassador to the U.N., the U.S. secretary of state, and the prime minister of India.

Hunt himself did not appear on any of the Facts Forum shows. Preferring to remain anonymous for the time being, he recruited a staff of lawyers and former FBI agents to operate the foundation and its programs. The principal commentator, Dan Smoot, was a broad-shouldered, handsome, former FBI agent and former college English teacher, many of whose listeners came to believe he had some sort of split personality that compelled him to take first one side of an issue and then the other. Smoot's immediate supervisor was Robert Dedman, a conservative Dallas lawyer who handled the foundation's application for tax-exempt status. But while Dedman and Smoot managed Facts Forum's day-to-day affairs, Hunt was constantly looking over their shoulder, advising, suggesting, guiding.

From the summer of 1951 to the fall of 1952, Facts Forum remained a relatively modest organization. The radio broadcasts were carried by only a handful of stations; the newsletter did not circulate widely. The annual budget was only about $100,000, all of which was supplied by contributions from H. L. Hunt. Then, in the fall of 1952, Facts Forum suddenly took off. Outside contributions came pouring in at the rate of nearly $1 million per year. New staff members came on board. Ambitious television programs and other special projects were initiated.

Within a year and a half, Facts Forum claimed a network of 125,000 active "participants" and regular listening and viewing audiences of at least 5 million more. Among its activities were "Answers for Americans," a half-hour weekly panel discussion program carried by 360 radio stations and 22 television stations; two nationwide weekly radio broadcasts—"State of the Nation," which was heard on 315 stations, and "Facts Forum," which was on 222 stations; and a half-hour television version of "Facts Forum," filmed in Washington and carried by fifty-eight stations. Like the radio program, the television version of "Facts Forum" starred Dan Smoot. Authoritatively dressed in a suit and tie, Smoot spoke to the audience from an "office" set decorated with a large desk, bookshelves, a globe, and a wall map of the world. As on the radio program, Smoot engaged in a one-man debate with himself, first taking the far-left position, then switching to the "constructive" side.

Facts Forum's new life, as the nation would soon learn, was largely attributable to the influence of one of America's most notorious political figures, witch-hunting Senator Joseph McCarthy of Wisconsin. The Hunt-McCarthy connection began in April of 1952 when the senator came to Dallas to make a speech sponsored by the American Legion and the Citizens Nonpartisan League. The subject of McCarthy's speech was the American Legion's resolution asking the ouster of Secretary of State Dean Acheson and that Communists be cleaned out of the State Department. But there were also more traditional political issues at hand. This was a crucial time for preconvention maneuvering for the presidential nominations, and McCarthy was still officially uncommitted.

Hunt's interest in meeting the Wisconsin senator was both personal and political. In addition to sharing McCarthy's ideology, Hunt evidently believed that McCarthy's support would be helpful to the presidential aspirations of his beloved MacArthur. So when the senator arrived in town, Hunt put all his resources to work for a successful courtship. Facts Forum began a steady buildup for the speech.

"Facts Forum is pleased to announce that everyone in the Dallas–Fort Worth area now has an easy opportunity to hear Senator McCarthy in person and make his own evaluation of him," said one typical message.

Hunt contacted McCarthy at his suite in the Dallas Athletic Club, and stopped by for a visit. The senator was in a relaxed mood. The American Legion speech was his only scheduled appearance. He had basically come to Texas, he said, to take "a couple of days' vacation."

Hunt told McCarthy about his radio announcements publicizing the speech, and offered the services of "Facts Forum" commentator Dan Smoot to introduce the senator to the audience. McCarthy thanked Hunt for his efforts and accepted the offer.

The two men hit it off immediately, and began laughing and talking like old friends. Before long, they shed their coats and loosened their ties and began playing a game of gin rummy. Then someone called the press. It was later suggested but never proven that that someone worked for H. L. Hunt. At any rate, a gaggle of reporters rushed over to the DAC suite and began interviewing McCarthy and snapping photographs.

Hunt immediately saw an opportunity. Forsaking his customary camera shyness, he stepped forward and asked the reporters to be sure and get the time and place of McCarthy's speech in their stories. Then he went over and pinned a "MacArthur for President" button on McCarthy's lapel. It made a terrific photograph—the senator and the oilman. McCarthy later made sure to remind the press that he was still uncommitted in the presidential race, though he admired MacArthur greatly. Nevertheless, the photograph with a carefully worded caption ran on the front page of the *Dallas News* the next day.

McCarthy and Hunt met again in the fall of 1952. This time they had dinner. Among other things, they discussed Senator McCarthy's political prospects and Hunt's still nascent Facts Forum organization. A short time later, three exceptional new people joined the Facts Forum staff. One was Victor Johnson, a former administrative aide to Joe McCarthy. Johnson, in turn, recruited one Robert E. Lee. An ex-FBI agent who had assisted in compiling a forerunner of McCarthy's infamous list of "205 Communists" in the State Department, Lee had also conducted what a Senate investigating committee called "a despicable 'back street' type of campaign" involving unreported contributions to defeat Senator Millard Tydings of Maryland in the 1950 election. The other new Facts Forum staffer was Jean Kerr, a former researcher for McCarthy who would later become his wife. Kerr had helped assemble the list of "205 Communists" that her boss (and later husband) used in his inglorious smear campaign. She had also assisted Lee in the fund-raising shenanigans in the Maryland senatorial campaign.

Not surprisingly, when Facts Forum suddenly burst onto the scene with a new crop of television programs conceived by a zestful contingent of former McCarthy aides, it was widely rumored that Facts Forum had determined to use its air time and tax-exempt status to promote the political fortunes of Joe McCarthy. Hunt denied that this was the case. "I have no connection with Senator McCarthy whatsoever," he told the press. Dedman backed him up: "Senator Joseph R. McCarthy . . . has no managerial, financial, or policy-making connections with Facts Forum."

Whether or not that was true, McCarthy himself only appeared on Facts Forum once. And investigators were never able to establish a direct financial tie between McCarthy and Facts Forum. But his gin-rummy-playing friendship with H. L. Hunt was close and warm, his influence was immediate and direct, and the essentials of his philosophy were manifest throughout Facts Forum's programming.

Facts Forum also began to use McCarthyite scare tactics in its efforts to influence legislation. A good example was Dan Smoot's argument in favor of the McCarran-Walter Immigration Act. "Those who want to destroy the McCarran-Walter Immigration Act," he told his audience, ". . . want to flood America with people who have been drenched by the socialist propaganda of eastern Europe—people who would swell the tide of socialist votes in our great industrial centers."

Besides just promoting McCarthy and McCarthyism, Facts Forum also promoted racism and anti-Semitism in thinly veiled forms. For example, in presenting the argument against compulsory fair employment practices legislation, the commentator said, "Remember that the Negroes when first brought to America by Yankee and English merchants were not free people reduced to slavery. They were merely transferred from a barbaric enslavement by their own people in Africa to a relatively benign enslavement in the Western Hemisphere."

Facts Forum complemented its broadcast messages with a "free circulating" library program which mailed out hundreds of free copies of specially

selected books and pamphlets to Facts Forum "participants" all over the
country. Four of the books in the original library were devoted to exposing
communism. The other two books were Clarence Manion's *The Key to Peace*
and Joseph Kamp's *We Must Abolish the United Nations.* The Manion book
picked up Facts Forum's emerging antidemocratic theme by attacking the
"tyranny [of] unrestrained majority rule." Kamp's book was a vehement critique of the United Nations from the paranoid perspective. The author of such
works as *Hitler Was a Liberal* and *Behind the Lace Curtains of the Y.M.C.A.,*
Kamp had been quoted as saying, "I pull no punches in exposing the Jewish
Gestapo or any Jew who happens to be a communist." Facts Forum went on
to acquire a tract called *Iron Curtain over America* by John O. Beaty of
Southern Methodist University in Dallas. The Beaty book expounded on "the
problems created in the United States by a powerful minority (Judaized Kha-
zars from Russia) possessed of an ideology alien to our traditions and fired by
an ambition which threatens to involve us in the ruin of a third world-wide
war."

Hunt was unusually sensitive to charges of anti-Semitism. Though prone
to identifying nearly everyone on the basis of his or her ethnic origins, Hunt
denied that he was prejudiced against Jews. In the case of the Kamp and Beaty
books, Hunt even bowed to pressure from the Anti-Defamation League (ADL)
and had Facts Forum drop the books from the "free circulating" library.
However, Hunt went on to have the volumes replaced by McCarthy tracts and
books by other well-known anti-Semites. Among the new titles were
McCarthyism and the Fight for America and *America's Retreat from Victory
—the Story of George Catlett Marshall,* both by Joseph R. McCarthy, *Wings
for Peace* by retired General Bonner Fellers (who once said, "Hitler did
Germany a world of good"), and *Traitors in the Pulpit* by Kenneth Goff.

Facts Forum News picked up where the "free circulating" library left off.
With a claimed circulation of about 60,000, the *News* plugged the library's
recommended reading list and urged subscribers to get on the mailing lists of
various other right-wing national lobbies. The *News* also urged readers to
consult certain "loyalty experts" with any questions they might have about
known subversives. One issue of the *News* named seven people who had
"devoted much of their lives [to] keeping files on un-American activities."
Among those listed was the Reverend Carl McIntire, a Presbyterian minister
who had accused the National Council of Churches of procommunism and the
Roman Catholic Church as a "spy system" for the Vatican. *Facts Forum News*
also published a variety of articles, many of them reprints, attacking communism. One article in *Facts Forum News* was a piece by a young William F.
Buckley entitled "The Liberal Mind." In his essay, Buckley attacked the
liberal mind as the product of "the swollen and irrepressible stream fed for so
many years by the waters of rationalism, positivism, Marxism and utopian-
ism."

By far the most curious feature of *Facts Forum News* was its "Letters to
the Editor" column. As it openly advertised, *Facts Forum News* paid out

hundreds of dollars every month to readers whose letters were printed in the paper. Facts Forum justified these payments on the basis of encouraging citizen discussion of important issues. But the key to getting a letter printed was to pick an appropriate subject and discuss it from the appropriate point of view. A certain J. McCarthy (not the senator) apparently had the knack for Facts Forum letter writing because at least half a dozen of his epistles were printed in the *News*. Most of the J. McCarthy letters were attacks of one sort or another. Among the victims of these attacks were Truman's intervention in Korea, New Dealers, Fair Dealers, high income taxes, Social Security, Dean Acheson, the United Nations, and "international giveaways." Facts Forum paid J. McCarthy $594 and gave him an electric blanket in the first fifteen months of its operations in return for his letters and a song to the tune of "Buckle Down, Winsocki" with lyrics which went, "Wake us up, Facts Forum, wake us up. We can win, Facts Forum, if you'll wake us up." J. McCarthy also received $200 from Facts Forum's Dallas headquarters for starting a neighborhood discussion group.

During the first two and a half years of its operation, Facts Forum paid out a total of almost $4,700 to J. McCarthy and various other letter writers. Of this money, over $3,600 was paid for letters supporting Hunt's and Fact Forum's point of view. Only $439 was paid for letters expressing opposing points of view, while some $596 was paid for letters on nonpolitical subjects. When the one-sidedness of these payments aroused some public controversy, Hunt had Facts Forum announce that in the future it would divide its payments equally between "liberal" and "constructive" letters. However, Facts Forum's own subsequent reports of payments for letters to the editor showed that it kept to its old ways, making payments primarily for those letters that expressed H. L. Hunt's point of view.

Another curious aspect of Facts Forum's overall "educational" program was its monthly "public opinion poll." Unlike the more reliable polling organizations, Facts Forum did not collect its "public opinion" from a random sample of the public so much as a sampling of "informed" opinion—that is, the opinion of Facts Forum participants. Although only one in ten postcards was ever returned, the monthly results were dutifully computed and incorporated into press releases. The press releases were then sent out to some 2,300 newspapers and radio stations and to every member of Congress. The numbers contained in these polls were, of course, "loaded" figures, but the press releases that went out referred to them simply as "public opinion poll," thereby implying that the results were to be regarded just like those of a bona fide survey.

A number of legislators either accepted the Facts Forum polls as genuine samples or wanted them to be accepted as such, for Senators George Smathers of Florida and Homer Capehart of Indiana, among others, inserted results of the polls in the *Congressional Record*. Some of the questions the polls addressed were straightforward; but others, like the opinion sample, were highly biased. One question, for example, asked, "Are internationalists less tolerant of Communism than the average citizen?" Such phrasing, of course, automatically suggested that "internationalists" were not average citizens and would disagree with their views. Other questions asked, "Should we promptly negotiate a stalemate peace?" and "Is the federal payroll large enough to endanger freedom in America?" Not surprisingly, the results of the Facts Forum polls always showed overwhelming support for the Facts Forum/H. L. Hunt position on the question.

More than just another right-wing lobby or consciousness-raising group, Facts Forum provided an entire life style and an instant society for those who felt displaced and disaffected by mainstream society. The model Facts Forum "participant" would be a member of a neighborhood "discussion group." He would have television programs to watch, radio programs to listen to, books to read, letters to the editor to write, and loyalty experts to consult. In short, Facts Forum gave those who felt they could do nothing to change the world things to do. Whether or not those things would actually change the world was a moot point. Doing something, was, for many, a change in and of itself. Unfortunately, the catch was that Facts Forum so distorted and exaggerated the issues that the real dangers of communism were never exposed. By focusing on its own made-up enemies, Facts Forum helped the real villains get away.

Nevertheless, Facts Forum had considerable appeal not only to the little man but also to many rich men, both in Texas and elsewhere. It cost an estimated $4 million per year to keep Facts Forum's radio and TV programs on the air. Of that total about $3 million came from radio stations that carried the programs and some thirty commercial sponsors. The rest came from H. L. Hunt and an estimated 2,000 contributors. Many of these Facts Forum supporters had national reputations. The board Hunt assembled included such luminaries as Norman Vincent Peale, Sears, Roebuck chairman General Robert E. Wood, Texas Governor Allan Shivers, and the very symbol of American masculinity, actor and pro-McCarthy campaigner John Wayne. The list of contributors included such names as Lone Star Steel, Mercantile National Bank, U.S. Steel (Oil Well and Supply Division), Dresser Industries, Republic National Bank, First National Bank, Continental Supply Company, Empire Drilling, Harry Bass Drilling, Brinkerhoff Drilling, and the Ed Cox Foundation. Their contributors ranged from $100 (Harry Bass Drilling) to $35,000 (Continental Supply Company). Also among the contributors were Hunt Oil and its affiliates, and Hunt's children by Lyda Bunker Hunt.

Part of Facts Forum's appeal to wealthy men and their corporations was philosophical. The Texas rich of the early and middle 1950s were among the most arch-conservative in the nation. They held many of the same fears and beliefs that H. L. Hunt did. They also shared a mutual admiration for Joe McCarthy, whose influence so permeated Facts Forum. Giving money to H. L. Hunt's Facts Forum was an indirect way of supporting the philosophies of Joe McCarthy.

At the same time, Facts Forum contributors were attracted to the organization for business reasons. Many of those who gave money to Facts Forum were drillers, contractors, suppliers, or bankers for H. L. Hunt. Giving to Facts

Forum was an indirect way of insuring the continuation of their business relationships. As writer Robert Sherrill later suggested, their donations were a form of tribute money. Because of Facts Forum's tax-exempt status, those donations were tax deductible, a fact Hunt was always quick to remind businessmen when he solicited their donations.

Facts Forum also had some especially close and warm arrangements with its corporate sponsors. One of the most prominent of these was Sears, Roebuck, which sponsored Facts Forum shows on the Texas Quality Network of radio stations and placed Facts Forum promotional placards in fifty-five of its stores. Hunt responded to Sears' generosity by plugging the store in *Facts Forum News*. As one edition of the *News* put it, "It is very appropriate that Sears-Roebuck should be sponsoring Facts Forum. For Sears-Roebuck and its mail order business is as American as the town hall meeting itself. Since Sears-Roebuck is helping us in our fight to overcome apathy and indifference, it might behoove us to express our appreciation and friendship for Sears whenever possible."

Apart from the relationships of the sponsors and contributors to H. L. Hunt, there were several other suspicious things about the finances of Facts Forum. One was that the receipts for "subscriptions" to Facts Forum's newsletter amounted to more than what the newsletter claimed to circulate. In 1955, for example, the total of corporate subscriptions alone was enough to support a circulation of 90,000, which was 50 percent more than the circulation *Facts Forum News* claimed to have that year. But Facts Forum never saw fit to explain the apparent discrepancies on its books or even to give the fully detailed accounting of contributions and expenditures routinely required by law.

Despite its deficiencies, Facts Forum seemed to receive nothing but favorable treatment by the federal government. Year after year, the organization continued to present itself as a nonpartisan "educational" organization qualified for a federal tax exemption. And year after year, the IRS obligingly accepted Facts Forum's misleading self-description and allowed it to maintain its tax exemption. Neither the Federal Communications Commission nor any government agency saw fit to challenge the fairness of Facts Forum's "both sides" format or the blatantly political nature of its attempts to influence legislation. Meanwhile, H. L. Hunt continued to write off every dollar he spent on Facts Forum just as if he had given it away to a charity. In point of fact, though, the only conventional charitable contribution on Facts Forum's books was a $1,000 donation to the Wadley Blood Center. Hunt was not running a charity or even an "educational" organization, but one of the most powerful private-propaganda organs in the history of the United States. Yet, thanks to Facts Forum's tax-exempt status, Hunt and his fellow Facts Forum supporters annually received $4 million worth of air time for their political views—air time that was in effect subsidized by the American taxpayer.

The reasons for the IRS's leniency toward Facts Forum were never fully revealed, but it was no secret that Hunt and Facts Forum had special connections to the FCC. In 1953, former McCarthy aide Robert E. Lee left his job at Facts Forum to become an FCC commissioner. Lee's appointment was made by President Eisenhower, reportedly at the behest of Vice President Richard Nixon. Lee, whose only radio and TV experience was his brief tenure at Facts Forum, joined another McCarthy man at the FCC, Commissioner John Doerfer. About a year earlier, McCarthy had intervened very actively and heavy-handedly in the FCC on behalf of the Hearst interests, and questioners at Lee's confirmation hearings were anxious to inquire about his ties to the Wisconsin senator. In response to the questions, Lee proclaimed that "Senator McCarthy had nothing to do with this appointment. Senator McCarthy is a friend of mine. I like him. I think he is a great guy . . . and I don't think he would ever presume to ask me about anything pending before the commission."

The senators also called Hunt to testify and asked him about Lee's allegiance to Facts Forum. Hunt replied that he did not think that Lee was the kind of man to grant special favors, and he, Hunt, certainly wouldn't presume to ask for them.

The senators apparently accepted these statements, for they confirmed Lee to the FCC. Hunt celebrated Lee's visit to Dallas following the confirmation vote by flying pop singer Pat Boone in from Hollywood to serenade the new commissioner. Hunt also privately revealed (in case there was any doubt) that he did in fact expect Lee to be sympathetic to Facts Forum's approach to "fairness." Hunt wrote of Lee in a memo to one of his employees: "He is a good friend, is a forceful person, so I think that this insures that we will not get nipped in the bud by the commission."

Those words proved to be something of an understatement. Following Lee's appointment to the FCC, Hunt made a personal application for a license for a new television station in Corpus Christi, Texas. Hunt's original application was filed in competition with several other applicants. However, the FCC permitted Hunt to change his application. The commission then granted Hunt an uncontested channel in Corpus Christi. Not surprisingly, two of the votes supporting this decision were made by commissioners Robert E. Lee and John Doerfer.

Some alleged that Hunt's Facts Forum connections resulted in oil-business dividends as well. The greatest of these supposedly came through Facts Forum board member and Texas governor Allan Shivers in the early 1950s, when the Shivers administration auctioned off Texas's tidelands oil leases. Hunt managed to get more than 100,000 acres of tidelands leases at an average price of $6 per acre. Other bidders paid an average price of $78 per acre for their leases. What was more, Hunt and his men entered the only bids on fifty-nine of the sixty-five tracts they acquired. The Texas land commissioner's office, then under Bascom Giles, had the power to reject such uncontested bids but chose to let them go to Hunt.

According to Shivers, the Hunt bids were accepted not because of political favoritism but because of his administration's desire to get drilling activity in the tidelands as quickly as possible. "There was very little development in that area," Shivers recalled. "The thinking was that Hunt would develop them." Shivers added that Hunt "didn't bid on any of the high-priced leases."

As it turned out, the Shivers' administration's hopes were never realized. Hunt did very little development on the leases and eventually let most of them expire.

Not surprisingly, Facts Forum continued to be Hunt's primary political activity throughout the early and middle 1950s. But it was hardly his only major project. Once again, Hunt's admiration for General MacArthur compelled him to try his hand at presidential politics. In 1951, after President Truman recalled MacArthur from his post in Korea, Hunt accompanied the general on a plane flight to Texas for a speaking tour. This time Hunt and fellow oilman Clint Murchison, Sr. were the chief organizers of the pro-MacArthur forces in Texas. Hunt also came through with some money, reportedly spending $150,000 on MacArthur's presidential bid. Exactly how Hunt spent all this money was not known, in part because Hunt later denied having spent it. However, it was known that H. L. Hunt was the largest contributor to America for Americans, a $50,000 fund raised by Sears, Roebuck chairman Robert Wood for the purpose of electing conservative Republican candidates all over the country.

The general, in turn, did not disappoint his financial supporters. If MacArthur was actually a complex man capable of inventive and even liberal social policies (as in his administration of postwar Japan), he chose to make his appeal to what biographer William Manchester called the "McGuffy Reader-ism" of the day. The general thrilled Hunt and the home folks by standing bareheaded in front of the Alamo and praising "that small band of of Texans who stood and died rather than yield the precious concepts of liberty." MacArthur also urged removal of "the burden of taxation" from enterprising men, and charged that this burden was being imposed by "those who seek to convert us to a form of socialistic endeavor, leading directly to the path of Communist slavery."

Hunt later gave his own somewhat dubious version of what caused MacArthur's ultimate defeat and the role he himself played in the prenomination maneuvering. He claimed that shortly after Truman dismissed the general from the Korean command, he set up a meeting in the Waldorf Astoria Hotel between MacArthur, Eisenhower, General Lucius Clay, and former President Herbert Hoover. According to Hunt, MacArthur was reluctant to try for the presidency.

"I told him it had to be him or Ike, but he didn't see it that way," Hunt recalled. "He said it would be Taft, and he didn't want to deprive him of the chance he so richly deserved."

Not to be denied, Hunt set up a MacArthur headquarters in Chicago, the convention site that year, and continued to promote the general's candidacy. Hunt claimed that he kept sending emissaries to a reluctant MacArthur, asking for some encouragement in launching an all-out effort, but the general wouldn't budge.

"He wouldn't let anyone talk to him about it," Hunt said afterward. "It was too bad. He would have made a perfect president."

Hunt later concocted an elaborate story about how he nevertheless came "within two hours of making MacArthur the nominee" by persuading some Taft delegates to switch their votes, only to be betrayed by those same delegates when the crucial roll call was taken.

According to MacArthur biographer William Manchester, the general was not nearly as reluctant as Hunt claimed. As proof, Manchester cited MacArthur's own speechmaking and self-promotional efforts, and the fact that the general angled for and got the privilege of delivering the convention's keynote address. The way Manchester told it, it was MacArthur's decision to adopt the strident rhetoric of the extreme right (à la H. L. Hunt) and some badly bungled convention maneuvering that killed the general's chances for the nomination.

At any rate, Hunt knew better than to ride a dead horse. Although he still loved the general as much as ever, Hunt refused to support MacArthur's third-party candidacy that fall. Instead, he announced that he was switching his support to Dwight Eisenhower, whom he believed had the best chance of ending the Democratic reign he so vehemently opposed. As Hunt explained to the press, "A vote for MacArthur would be the equivalent of half a vote for Stevenson."

Unsuccessful as a kingmaker, Hunt devoted his energies to the passage of the Twenty-second Amendment, which limited an individual's tenure as president to two terms. Claiming that he was "appalled by the stupendous indifference which can result in the failure of this wonderful amendment," Hunt told the *Dallas Times Herald* on January 22, 1951, that the passage of the amendment was necessary to insure the continuation of that great challenge of American life—the fact that mothers and schoolteachers could say to a child, "Some day you may be president." At that time, twenty-four of the necessary thirty-six state legislatures had ratified the amendment. Hunt took full credit for the amendment's ultimate ratification a short time later.

"I alone and single-handed, by telephone, letter, and personal talks whipped the legislatures into ratification," Hunt claimed, adding that "it took me only seven weeks to do it."

As writer Robert Sherrill observed, only Hunt has ever gone on record as crediting Hunt with the ratification of the Twenty-second Amendment. Nevertheless, Hunt later claimed it as "my only public-affairs victory."

Because of his ever-increasing political involvements, Hunt found himself spending less and less time in the oil business. He continued to preside over the Hunt Oil production meetings held in his office each week, and he continued to exhort his men to "drill, drill, drill." But as time passed, he began to entrust more and more responsibility to top associates like W. F. "Dink"

Dalton, head of Placid Oil, and to the sons of his wife Lyda, who were now coming of age.

Hunt engaged in only one attempted foreign-oil venture in the early 1950s, a brief flirtation with the anti-British and anti-American government of Iranian premier Mossadegh. But when the CIA overthrew Mossadegh and replaced him with Reza Shah Pahlevi, the major British and American oil companies got their concessions back and Hunt's venture never got off the ground. Instead of trying other foreign-oil ventures, Hunt turned his attention back to the United States, and began buying up uranium leases in the Southwest on the theory that nuclear power would be the wave of the future.

While Hunt gradually eased out of the oil game, he kept up his lifelong passion for gambling. In 1949, not long after his debut on the pages of *Life* and *Fortune* as America's richest man, Hunt's friend Ray Ryan introduced him to the famous Jimmy "the Greek" Snyder. The three then began placing regular bets against each other on college football games.

"I would call H.L. once a week on Saturday mornings," Snyder recalled in his autobiography. "H.L. loved to bet on games in the Southwest Conference, and my expertise was concentrated in the Southeastern Conference. We would bet fifty thousand dollars a game, head-to-head, with no eleven to ten either way. His accountants would settle up, sending a check to Ryan's office as if it were another expense of the oil business. Or Ryan would send a check to him, which was seldom. H.L. would call Bookie Shaeffer's joint in Chicago and get the line on the games. He would pick three games against the line, giving or taking points, and I would take three the same way."

According to Snyder, Hunt tired of the arrangement several weeks into the first season and suggested a change.

"Young man," he told Snyder, "I think we should delete the Southeastern Conference."

"Well, sir," Snyder replied, "that's your prerogative, but if we delete the Southeastern Conference, I think we should delete another conference of my choice."

"That would be fair," Hunt said.

"All right, then we'll delete the Southwest Conference."

Snyder wrote that this proposal stopped Hunt in his tracks. Since the Southwest Conference was comprised entirely of teams from Texas plus the University of Arkansas, Hunt naturally favored placing his bets on teams he could watch closely. Also, he apparently loved to bet on Dallas-based SMU. Snyder's suggestion of dropping the Southwest Conference from their weekly betting chart would have deprived him of the opportunity to play his favorite —and strongest—teams.

"No," Hunt said at last, "we'll let it go as it is."

Snyder later claimed that he and Ryan were able to "use . . . [an] edge" against Hunt with the help of one of Hunt's own employees. As Snyder recalled it, "Ryan gave me the name of a secretary in Hunt's office to call late in the week. The old man had a habit of jotting his favorite team on a note pad at his desk, and by his top choice he would put a star or two. The secretary could tell me who he liked as a best bet. I would have Ray bet twenty thousand dollars on the team with Bookie Shaeffer, so when Hunt got the line on Saturday, his top choices would be a half a point less [or more]. At other times, when H.L. picked a team I thought was right, I would get Ray to lay off the whole fifty thousand dollars."

These ploys and Snyder's natural talent for betting paid off handsomely. "After two seasons we had [H.L.] for six hundred thousand dollars, of which two hundred thousand was mine per my agreement with Ryan," Snyder recalled. "By then I had other interests, and H.L. didn't seem reluctant to call the arrangement off."

As it turned out, Senator Estes Kefauver's hearings on gambling stopped the party instead. Although Hunt was not fingered in the probe, Snyder and many of his cronies were temporarily put out of business. Reluctantly, "the Greek" had to stop betting on college football, but, as he put it, "I did not forget my old friend H. L. Hunt or his unlisted number."

Apart from his encounters with Jimmy the Greek and Ray Ryan, Hunt's gambling ventures were not always failures. One weekend, for example, he placed a $200,000 bet on a football game and broke all the bookies in Kansas City. On another occasion, he came from a $10,000 deficit to win over $100,000 in a card game with a Las Vegas professional. Another time he won $800,000 from Las Vegas gambler Johnny Drew. Then, too, he kept on bringing in about $1 million per year from his horse-betting operation—or so he claimed. But these winnings were actually curses in disguise. The same flaw that kept Hunt in political blinders also kept him chained to his gambling: he was right often enough to believe that he was infallible. He was, in short, the perfect mark for a real professional.

While he continued to gamble, Hunt did give up one long-enjoyed vice during this period—cigars. Hunt's explanation for his decision to quit smoking was not based on health reasons, as one might have expected, but on considerations of the "profit motive" he claimed was so deeply embedded in him. The way Hunt figured it, just the time he took to unwrap his cigars—time that could otherwise have been spent concentrating on his work—was costing him $300,000 a year. That was enough to make anyone want to quit.

About the time he quit smoking cigars, Hunt began to make attempts to change his diet. He still had a notoriously large appetite for food of all conventional varieties, especially home-cooked food, and he would often plan long automobile trips around the time it took to get from one favored eating place to another. Now he began to take an interest in what would later be called "health foods." Among other things, Hunt believed that white sugar was antinutritional; he also avoided white flour. Many of the foods he began to eat were grown on or near his 7,000-acre farm at Winona—pecans, Deaf Smith County stone-ground wheat bread, fresh vegetables of all varieties. Hunt also became especially fond of apricots, both for their taste and for the health-giving properties he believed the fruit contained. Though described as "health foods," these products were not grown by "organic" methods, but by conventional farming techniques, including fertilizers and insect sprays.

As was his custom, Hunt did not hesitate to preach the virtues of these newly favored foods to those around him. One of his favorite practices was sending a bag of Winona pecans to a friend or a business or political associate. Bags of pecans were sent out to oilmen, gamblers, newspaper editors, politicians, even passing acquaintances. Sometimes Hunt would also send along a jar of apricots or some home-grown Winona product accompanied by a brief note extolling its health-giving qualities. As was also his custom, Hunt did not follow his own advice exactly as he hoped others would. He often departed from his health-food diet to consume great quantities of meat or indulge in sweets. He later admitted with a chuckle, "I don't always practice what I preach."

Nowhere was this more true than in his private life. H. L. Hunt the oilman, gambler, and right-wing propagandist also continued to be H. L. Hunt the inveterate philanderer. In addition to his secret Dallas family with Ruth Ray, Hunt pursued several other extramarital relationships during the early and middle 1950s. According to former associates, his preference was for short, full-breasted, country-girl types in their early twenties. Now a national public figure, he could no longer get away with carrying on under false names, but he had no intention of curtailing his exploits either. Instead, he would merely try to pass off his female companions as "my niece" or as the "sister" of some associate. His ruses rarely fooled anyone but strangers, most of whom could not have cared anyway.

Although he was a high roller with the bookies, Hunt remained a relatively cheap liver compared to other Texas millionaires. Hunt Oil purchased its first plane, a DeHavilland Dove, in 1952. But Hunt's favorite means of transportation was an old Dodge sedan.

At the same time that he pursued his business, politics, gambling, and girl friends, Hunt tried to play the role of patriarch for all three of his families. This he did against great odds and with varying degrees of success. Now in her sixties, his first wife Lyda Bunker Hunt was still a kind and devoted mother and the symbol of family stability, but she was beginning to show the strain of her long marriage. She had suffered the revelation of Hunt's relationship with Frania and had heard rumors of his relationship with Ruth. She had agonized over the mental breakdown of her son Hassie. With the rest of her children now grown up, Hunt's continuing unfaithfulness and eccentricities did not make things any easier for her. "She used to call me to come with her to see a show in Dallas," recalled one friend from the Tyler days. "She always seemed very lonely."

At one point, when Hunt was being particularly difficult, Lyda finally broke down and cried in front of one of her husband's secretaries. Startled by such an uncustomary outburst, the young secretary boldly asked Lyda why she just did not go ahead and divorce Hunt.

"Because I have children to be considered," Lyda replied, "and as long as I live, I'm going to protect them from what's going to happen when I'm gone."

Lyda's children had plenty to endure as it was. After his eldest son's mental breakdown, Hunt kept looking for another Hassie. That was an impossible role for anyone, but it was the fate of Lyda's remaining three sons, Bunker, Herbert, and Lamar, to be expected to live up to it. Hunt did not stay on top of his younger three sons the way he had lorded over Hassie. Nor did he actually sit them down and instruct them in the ways of the oil business. He seemed to give each son a chance to be the next Hassie, then gave up on him almost without warning. Meanwhile, "the boys" themselves seemed to learn from their old man in indirect fashion, as if by osmosis. Though indisputably their own separate personalities, Hunt's sons soon demonstrated such paternal traits as persistence, the ability to think big, and the propensity to trust their instincts.

Bunker, the eldest of the three, had first shot and muffed it. After graduating from prep school, Bunker enrolled at the University of Texas at Austin, but, as he later admitted, he was not exactly a "matriculation star." The final straw came when Bunker heard his geology professor announce that he was in favor of government control of all natural resources. Showing that he had a lot of his old man in him, Bunker promptly dropped out of school and joined the Navy, where he spent the latter days of World War II as a seaman swabbing decks on an aircraft carrier. After the war, Bunker tried one more semester, quit, and went to work for his father.

Considerably overweight and often lackadaisical about his appearance, Bunker impressed some as a rumpled genius and others as an idiotic buffoon. Hunt seemed to favor the latter view. Once, when he put Bunker in charge of the family farm in Kaufman County, Texas, one of the truck drivers stole a load of seed. Although the loss was hardly crippling, it did ruin the farm's chance of making a small profit that year. Hunt was furious. According to a former employee who was present at the time, Hunt, using vile and abusive language, began shouting and raving at Bunker, telling him how stupid he was. Said the employee, "I was actually embarrassed for Bunker."

Nevertheless, Bunker proved himself worthy of the family name by finding a $7-million oil field in Scurry County at the age of twenty-two. His father put him in charge of Penrod Drilling, the family contractor, which soon expanded its fleet to forty-six land rigs. Hunt also gave Bunker special assignments like going to New Mexico and Arizona to buy uranium leases. Here again, Bunker showed he had a lot of his old man in him. He often liked to take time out from his uranium lease buying to fly over to Las Vegas and hit the gaming tables. Though his name, face, and family background eventually became well known in Las Vegas, he did much of his early gambling under the name of the family pilot Jake Cobb.

Despite their similarities—or because of them—Hunt kept finding fault with his second son. One day, he simply up and fired Bunker. The exact circumstances of the firing were never made clear, but the word that got around the office was that Bunker had merely made some routine decision without consulting his father.

In any event, Bunker responded by going out on his own. Believing that the future lay in international oil exploration, he hired University of Illinois geology professor Harold Scott to make a study of the world oil outlook. Scott pointed to three areas of greatest potential: the Middle East, which was already tied up by the major oil companies; North Africa, which was mostly desert; and Pakistan. In early 1955, Bunker announced an ambitious $35-million drilling program in partnership with the Pakistani government. He then proceeded to confirm his father's skepticism by drilling $11-million worth of dry holes.

Meanwhile, Hunt shifted his favor to his next oldest son, Herbert. Neater, trimmer, and in every way more conventional than Bunker, Herbert had attended all four years at Washington & Lee, where he dutifully obtained a degree in geology. After finishing school, he also went back to work for his father. Hunt was afraid that Herbert's geology degree was "going to cost us" because he believed Herbert would drill wells simply to prove a geological theory instead of purely to find more oil. But unlike Bunker, Herbert impressed his father as being able to do things right. He was the kind of young man who could look after details. Hunt gave Herbert increasing responsibilities down at Hunt Oil and soon began to treat him as if he were heir apparent. His mother, whom he favored in appearance, made him the executor of her estate.

Hunt also seemed to have high hopes for his third son Lamar. The youngest of his sports-minded family, Lamar was also the most athletic. After playing high-school football in Dallas, he went on to SMU, where he played third string on a team that included future pro standout Don McIlhenney. Because of his father's wealth, Lamar was stuck with the unimaginative nickname of "Poor Boy." His teammates at SMU used to delight in knocking him down, then stretching out a helping hand, and saying, "Here, Poor Boy, let me help you up." Lamar took it all good-naturedly and did not put on airs, an attitude that made him popular despite his quiet, slightly diffident nature.

Next to his sons, Hunt seemed to favor his son-in-law Al Hill. More than ten years older than Bunker, Herbert, and Lamar, Hill reportedly encountered some initial hostility from Hunt after Hill's marriage to Margaret. But those differences were apparently resolved, for word soon got around the office that Hill had impressed Hunt with his business acumen and was considered a possible heir apparent. What that really meant was that Margaret, Hunt's eldest daughter, was the real heir apparent. Having worked as an aide to her father in the 1930s, Margaret had gotten on-the-job business training available to few men or women. The most conservative of the Hunt children, she avoided her brother Bunker's speculative ventures in favor of investments that grew steadily. Her major project outside the family oil business was developing (with her husband) the Garden of the Gods Club in Colorado Springs, Colorado. A $15-million investment, the Garden of the Gods Club was paying lucrative social and financial dividends as it became a favorite resort for the rich. Back in Dallas, Margaret and Al lived in a large two-story house in Highland Park, and became regulars on the local society circuit. As one Dallas society writer observed, Margaret was "the one who reminded the rest of the family that they were Hunts."

Although none of Hunt's sons by Lyda married into Dallas high society, all three wed nice women and did not smoke or drink—at least not around their father. According to old friends, though, Hunt's sons enjoyed a good time as much as other young men, and used to hold regular secret poker parties at a ranch house near Dallas. There, the men would smoke and drink and bet wads of cash at the card tables while being entertained by some local young lovelies.

If the wild oats that Hunt's sons sowed shocked their father, the truth about Hunt's secret lives stunned them. They had heard rumors, of course, but as late as 1954, when Lamar was getting married, he asked if it was true that his father had a family in east Dallas and a family in predominantly black Oak Cliff. He was told by a family confidant that his father certainly did not have a family in Oak Cliff. Then one day down at Hunt Oil, Herbert came across an oil lease marked for the "Reliance Trusts." When he asked his father about it, Hunt told him the trusts were for his children by Frania. A short time later, the boys also discovered the trusts set up for Hunt's family by Ruth.

Although the revelation of their father's secret families was a strong blow, Lyda's children tried to rationalize the hurt they felt by accepting it as another facet of their father's eccentric nature. Caroline compared her father to King ibn-Saud of Saudi Arabia, the monarch who reputedly fathered some 300 children. "He just likes children," she said, "until they get to be about six or seven years old. Then he isn't interested any more."

Meanwhile, Hunt went on as if nothing unusual had happened. He continued to make regular visits to his secret Dallas family by Ruth Ray, and paid for their children to attend private Greenhill School under the name Wright. Rumor around the neighborhood had it that the Wright children's mysterious father was an agent for the FBI.

Hunt also showed an interest in his family by Frania. Although he did not bring any of Frania's children into the family business, he kept up with their progress through school and after with a certain regularity. Hunt was especially fond of his daughter Helen, who had inherited her father's looks. When Helen graduated from high school, Hunt gave her a mink coat. Later, after Helen graduated from Marymount College in New York and embarked on an acting career, Hunt tried to promote her career through *Time* magazine executive Clare Boothe Luce and other important friends.

For their part, Frania's children found the experience of changing fathers and changing lives a little disorienting. After their mother's marriage to John Lee, they were told to use the last name Lee, even though Lee never formally adopted them. They were told never to use the name Hunt again. At the same time, though, Frania did not tell them to disclaim their father entirely. "She explained that she had married him in Florida," her youngest son Hugh recalled later, "that there was another family that he had, that we were not supposed to use the name, but we were still supposed to respect him as our father and he would take care of us."

Frania herself seemed to plunge into her new life with great zest. Now in her forties, she still had a very pretty face and plenty of style. One Atlanta matron recalled seeing her with her hair tinted blonde and twisted into braids "needing only a dirndl to effect the look of an eastern European maiden." Her husband John Lee was, as Atlanta society writer Yolande Guinn put it, "the best lookin' devil you ever saw, a brunette swarthy lookin' man." Together, the Lees tried to enter Atlanta high society by turning their Flowerland estate in suburban Chambliss into a party palace. "Fran's parties were always very elegant," remembered Atlanta socialite Clarice Geigerman, noting that Frania always hired the city's best caterer. One of the most elaborate of Frania's parties was a debut ball for her daughter Helen at which Frania set the gardens of Flowerland aglow with paper lanterns. The Lees also made the scene at Atlanta's exclusive Capital City Club.

Frania's high-profile social life naturally fueled the gossip mill. Word that Frania was—or at least had been—intimately connected to H. L. Hunt the Texas oilman was leaked to Atlanta society by a newcomer to the city who recognized Frania from her days in Great Neck, New York. Rumors got around that Frania had been Hunt's mistress, that she was living off money she got from him, and that she was using her money to try to "buy into" Atlanta society. In part because of such gossip, Frania did not manage to win acceptance into Atlanta's social elite. Instead, she became a part of what one Atlanta writer described as "a peripheral society of public relations people, press, and hangers on, some of whom were prominent, some of whom were mere pretenders."

Not surprisingly, H. L. Hunt the patriarch and propagandist encountered his share of controversy as time progressed. Most of that controversy concerned Facts Forum. Many prominent public figures who had either supported Facts Forum or agreed to be speakers on its radio and TV programs began to have misgivings when they discovered the true slant of the "both sides" broadcasts. One of those who left was Dr. Norman Vincent Peale, who had sponsored a Facts Forum group address by virulently anti-Semitic speaker in his New York City church. Peale at first defended Facts Forum against the protests of some of his parishioners, but the furor was so great that Peale finally disbanded his Facts Forum group and dropped off the Facts Forum advisory board.

In the fall of 1953, the press got on the trail of H. L. Hunt and Facts Forum. Ironically, Facts Forum actually provoked the first ground-breaking exposé of its political and financial activities by inviting a Washington reporter for the *Providence Journal* to conduct a Facts Forum interview in return for a $125 fee. Former McCarthy aide Victor Johnson, who made the request on behalf of Facts Forum, explained to the reporter that H. L. Hunt was ready to spend some of his fortune to elect "our kind of guy." The *Providence Journal* reporter refused the invitation, but wrote a story about the incident that was picked up by newspapers all across the country. Typically, Facts Forum chose to reprint the version of the story that appeared in New York's socialist *Daily Worker* and mailed copies to Facts Forum subscribers, thereby implying the foundation was the victim of another communist attack. Undeterred, *Providence Journal* reporter Ben Bagdikian followed up his Washington colleague's story with a hard-hitting exposé of Facts Forum's finances and its political, not "educational," character, and its wealthy founder.

By early 1954, Hunt and Facts Forum found themselves embroiled in a feud over tax exemptions. The main protagonists were U.S. Representatives Wayne Hays and B. Carroll Reece. Reece attacked the Rockefeller, Carnegie, and Ford Foundations for alleged grants to "communists" and "socialists." Reece also believed "those people" had prevented Senator Taft from getting the 1952 Republican presidential nomination (thus thwarting Reece's ambitions to be secretary of state). But every time Reece would demand to see the books of the "liberal" foundations, Wayne Hays would demand to see the Facts Forum books. Reece was stalemated. Interestingly enough, when Hays petitioned the IRS to review Facts Forum's tax-exempt status, he was informed that the foundation's books had been misplaced. Nevertheless, the IRS, after making what it described as a "full investigation" pronounced Facts Forum was operating in acceptance with the law.

Hunt did not forget Hays's investigative zeal. In the next election, he contributed $5,000 to Hays's opponent. The contribution proved to be in vain, as Hays won re-election. Perhaps the most significant aspect of the episode was the fact that it marked the first time Hunt had engaged in what was at least indirectly a public political conflict with the Rockefellers. The foundation battle confirmed Hunt's view that the Rockefellers were a part of the great liberal conspiracy that had taken over America, the personification of everything he opposed. Thereafter, Hunt became increasingly obsessed with comparing and contrasting his fortune and beliefs to theirs. The fact that the Rockefellers did not seem to recognize their rivalry with the Hunts only increased H.L.'s anti-Rockefeller fervor.

Despite the criticism he took, Hunt seemed to find such controversies invigorating. He was now reaching what most men regarded as retirement age. His hair was turning white and wispy, he had a growing bald spot on the top of his head, he was stout, and he moved a lot slower than he did in his prime. But he still possessed an extraordinary amount of energy and drive. Nothing could unleash his energy like a good, old-fashioned fight. Hunt's battle against communists and socialists gave him a purpose and mission that could keep him occupied twenty-four hours a day.

Appropriately enough, the man who had once shied from publicity as if it were the plague, celebrated his sixty-fifth birthday on February 17, 1954, by holding a press conference at the Waldorf-Astoria Hotel in New York City.

Before the conference began, a Hunt spokesman announced that Hunt was worth $2 billion and had an after-tax income of $54 million per year. Although the spokesman did not supply any oil-production figures or asset schedules to back up his claim, the assembled press seemed to take the announcement on faith. From that time forward, H. L. Hunt was labeled a billionaire, though, according to former insiders, his wealth at the time was probably less than half of $2 billion.

As the enormity of his fortune was sinking in, Hunt came on and began telling stories about his rise from a family farm in Illinois to his status as the nation's leading oil producer. The press finally managed to steer the questioning toward Facts Forum, but Hunt handled the questions with ease. He denied that Facts Forum was profascist, anti-Semitic, anti-Catholic, anti-Negro, and antilabor. He even denied that the program was slanted toward the conservative side, and claimed that 35 percent of the complaint letters to Facts Forum said the programs were too liberal.

"There is a regular pattern to these charges," Hunt said. "In the *Communist Daily Worker* the motive is obvious for calling us fascists. In responsible publications, I do not think it is due to a deliberate smear, but rather to failure to listen to our programs and understand what we are doing."

Hunt went on to claim that Facts Forum did not start out to be anticommunist, but to be "a positive force *for* freedom." He ventured that Facts Forum was still "a positive force *for* freedom" and would continue to be.

"But if we are anticommunist," he allowed, "people who do not like anticommunists are not going to like us."

Hunt's birthday remarks did not make front-page news, but the *New York Times* dutifully carried a one-column story on page 17 the next day. After all, what H. L. Hunt had to say was newsworthy, for he was the richest man in America and also the rightest.

CHAPTER 9

POPSY AND
HIS PATRIARCHY

LIKE his luck at the poker tables and in the oil fields, H. L. Hunt's life ran in streaks. He would get on a good streak for so long he would seem invincible. Then all of a sudden something bad would happen. Then something else and something else. Soon it would begin to look like his misfortune had no end. Then, miraculously, his luck would change again. Having been rolling along like gangbusters ever since his debut as America's richest man, H.L. hit a bad streak in the spring of 1955.

The bad streak began when his wife Lyda suffered a serious stroke. Hunt did not trust the Dallas doctors to treat her, so he decided to charter a private plane to fly her to the Mayo Clinic in Rochester, Minnesota, where she would get the most advanced medical care. When Lyda's stretcher arrived at the airport in Dallas, Hunt and all the first-family children were there, waiting to board the plane with her. So was Herbert's wife Nancy, who was then due to give birth to her third child. Lyda was too weak to talk. Still, she managed to raise her hand and point to Nancy's stomach, gesturing back and forth with one finger as if to say no, Nancy should not accompany her on the trip in that condition. Nancy took her mother-in-law's advice, and stayed behind. H.L. and the others boarded the plane after Lyda's stretcher.

That was on a Monday. On Friday, May 6, 1955, Lyda Bunker Hunt died at the Mayo Clinic at the age of sixty-six. The child Nancy had been expecting was born three days later on May 9, the day of Lyda's funeral. The infant was named for her grandmother, Lyda Bunker Hunt.

Thanks to the family tax planners, there were relatively few assets in Lyda's estate. The total was valued at less than $5 million. Even allowing for the usual estate-underestimation factor, it amounted to a fraction of the family's total wealth. Having named Herbert her executor, Lyda left her interest in the family home to Lamar, the youngest, and gave her jewelry to her daughters, Margaret and Caroline. She bequeathed her stocks and bonds to the H. L. Hunt Foundation, a small tax-exempt institution the Hunts set up ostensibly for estate-planning purposes in 1954. The rest of her estate was divided among the trusts of her children except for Hassie. Lyda's will excluded Hassie from the estate sharing, noting that he had already accumulated a large estate on his own and needed no further help.

Hunt never wrote about or publicly discussed his reaction to Lyda's death. His true feelings were known only to himself, if known at all. Unlike his children, who later donated to a college and a church in their mother's memory, Hunt never memorialized his wife with a charitable contribution or bequest. But for all his unfaithfulness in life, he did show a noticeable sense of loss, a definite dampening of spirits at her passing.

Things got worse before they got better. For just about the same time Lyda suffered her fatal stroke, Hunt suffered a series of debilitating blows in the political arena. Although Hunt and Facts Forum had managed to come through their first major confrontations with the government and the press with flying colors, adverse public pressure continued. Much of that pressure resulted from the backlash against Senator McCarthy. Once a man who struck fear into the hearts of virtually everyone, McCarthy increasingly came to be regarded as an unscrupulous political blackmailer who did the Republican party and the country more harm than good. McCarthy lost his committee chairmanship when the Republicans lost the midterm congressional elections in 1954, and his communist-hunting scare tactics were subsequently condemned by his Senate colleagues. From that time forward, McCarthy's power declined even more precipitously than it had risen. In the spring of 1957, McCarthy was censured by the Senate for absenteeism. He died several weeks later of a liver ailment at the age of forty-seven.

As his great friend Joe McCarthy suffered his final demise, Hunt's own political fortunes also declined. Journalists and government investigators kept up inquiries into Facts Forum and its curious financial and "educational" activities. Public opinion about Facts Forum, like public opinion about McCarthy, backlashed. Facts Forum was by no means America's recognized public enemy number 1, but it was seriously discredited as an "educational" organization and even as a viable editorial voice. Hunt later claimed that most of the complaints he got about Facts Forum charged that the "both sides" format was "too liberal." In Hunt's view, "people didn't want to hear both sides." Finally, in November of 1956, Hunt had a spokesman announce that Facts Forum was going off the air. The spokesman explained that Hunt had made the decision to close down because "he's tired of fighting for useless and lost causes."

With his first wife gone and his propaganda organ disbanded, Hunt took off on a six-month trip to South America, where, according to his account afterward, he devoted much of his time to studying Latin American government.

Upon his return to Dallas, H. L. Hunt found his house divided between his recognized Dallas family and his unrecognized one. While the first-family children still mourned the death of their mother, Ruth Ray Wright and her children began showing up at Mount Vernon acting just like who they were. Ruth would fuss over the old man and look after the wifely responsibilities of the household. When Hunt got depressed, she would send her daughters over to serenade him with happy songs. The children even began to have their birthday parties at Mount Vernon. Though Ruth and her children still maintained residence at the house on Meadow Lake Avenue, they practically lived at Mount Vernon.

The first-family children saw what was happening and did not like it. Indeed, they privately found fault with Ruth at every turn. She was tacky in her department-store clothes. She was just a little too nice, too sweet, too ingratiating. No matter what she did or how hard she tried to be friendly, the first family continued to think ill of her. They were suspicious of her true motives and embarrassed to be associated with her. They regarded their half brother and half sisters as outsiders, not really members of the same family. Mount Vernon was Lyda's house. Though they were all moved out and grown up with families of their own, they seemed to feel severely displaced by Ruth's presence.

Meanwhile, the man both families called Popsy did not seem particularly concerned with resolving the difficulties developing within his patriarchy. He had no desire to stop seeing Ruth and their children, but he evinced no intention to marry Ruth either.

This uneasy situation lasted for more than two years after Lyda's death. Then, in the fall of 1957, according to the account Hunt later gave a Dallas interviewer, Ruth's son Ray paid his father a visit at Hunt Oil Company. At the time, Ray was fourteen years old and a student at the Greenhill School in Dallas. He had crew-cut hair that was blond like his mother's, but he was in every other way the junior image of his father, broad-shouldered and square-jawed with steely blue eyes. He also had his father's resolve.

"You *will* marry my mother," Ray told his father. "She is a good, religious person, and you *will* marry her."

Hunt later admitted to being somewhat startled by his son's demand. The young man certainly had a lot of nerve. But then he was, after all, the son of H. L. Hunt. Hunt was not one to be forced into anything, but the confrontation started him thinking. On November 2, 1957, he took out a marriage license in Dallas County. Then three weeks passed without a wedding. Finally, a ceremony was scheduled for Sunday, November 24, at 3:00 P.M.

Hunt did not give any advance notice—at least not to the general public or to his first Dallas family. In fact, right up to the day of the wedding, H.L. went about his routine as if nothing special was going on. That afternoon, he even shared a typical Sunday dinner with his daughters Margaret Hunt Hill and Caroline Hunt Sands and their young families at a local Dallas restaurant. Then, about 2:30, Hunt excused himself from the table explaining that he had "an appointment."

The first thing Lyda's children knew about their father's wedding was the six-inch story that appeared in the *Dallas Times Herald* the next day. Under the headline "Oilman H. L. Hunt Marries," the story announced that "Dallas oilman H. L. Hunt, one of the world's richest men, married Mrs. Ruth Ray Wright of 7029 Meadow Lake Sunday afternoon in a quiet ceremony at the home of Mrs. Wright's pastor." After mentioning that Hunt, age sixty-eight, was the father of six children by his deceased wife Lyda, the article reported that "Mrs. Wright has lived in Dallas several years. She is the mother of four children, the eldest about fifteen years old, friends said." The newspaper story went on to note that the couple was "attended by only two close friends," H. L. Williford and Mrs. E. Payson Willard. The article concluded: "In Idabel, Oklahoma, Mrs. Grace Ray, mother of the bride, told the Associated Press that she knew nothing of the wedding. She said her daughter was about thirty-six. Mrs. Ray added that she met Hunt about fifteen years ago in Shreveport, Louisiana, where her daughter was working in a Hunt Oil Company office."

The news of Hunt's marriage did not exactly enhance his public image. Read between the lines, the *Times Herald* story left the impression that H. L. Hunt had run off with his secretary. This, of course, was not really the case at all, but it was the story that became current. Tongues wagged all over gossip-hungry Dallas. Rumors grew on rumors, heads nodded, and knowing looks were exchanged as word got around that there was more to this new Hunt marriage than met the eye. The rumors flew faster than ever when it was revealed that Hunt had "adopted" Ruth's children and changed their last name from Wright to Hunt.

Despite the poor public-relations job, Hunt's marriage to Ruth proved to be the beginning of his late-life attempt to change—or at least moderate—some of his sinful ways. One of the first and most remarkable things he did was quit gambling. The way Hunt told it later, his decision to quit was partly prompted by the fact that he was getting so big he was "getting beat by my own money"; the major bookies, he felt, had begun to conspire to bribe referees and horse jockeys so that they would not have to pay off on Hunt's enormous wagers. But Hunt also claimed that he decided to stop gambling because of a kind of spiritual revelation.

"I found that the clouds and the flowers are a little bit prettier when you don't gamble," he said. "Customs change, too. I used to know of federal judges who bet on the horses, but it ceased to be considered an innocent diversion. It got too troublesome, and anyhow I hated to take the time out from the fight for freedom." He might also have added that he hated to see the way his gambling actually brought his wife Ruth to tears.

There were some other practical considerations as well. In 1958, a federal grand jury began a probe of a gambling syndicate based in Terre Haute, Indiana, one of the stomping grounds of Hunt's friend Ray Ryan. Investigators charged that the syndicate had grossed over $3.5 million that fall on college and pro football betting. In addition to the high stakes, the operation allegedly involved wagers by such prominent names as Zeppo Marx of the Marx brothers comedy team, bridge expert Tobias Stone, the mayor of Terre Haute (who was then running for governor of Indiana), and oilman H. L. Hunt. Although Hunt was among one hundred witnesses subpoenaed in the grand-jury probe, he managed to avoid testifying when a Dallas physician certified that Hunt had a throat ailment. When reporters later cornered Hunt about the timing of his supposed illness, he replied coyly, "If you play a little gin, bridge, or bingo, you are about as much a gambler as I am. And when I do something to turn the tide of world communism, I can't get a word in the papers."

According to allegations made later by an embittered former top employee, Hunt had much more to conceal than "a little gin, bridge, or bingo." At the time of the Terre Haute gambling probe, Hunt reportedly stated in private that his total gambling winnings amounted to over $15 million, and that avoiding the gambling probe saved him as much as $11 million in back taxes he would have had to pay the IRS. Of course, only Hunt himself knew for sure whether or not these statements were accurate, and he never confirmed or denied them publicly. It was possible that Hunt really did come out that much ahead, despite the major losses he suffered at the hands of Ray Ryan, Frank Erickson, and Jimmy the Greek. In any event, shortly after his marriage to Ruth, Hunt shut down his horse-handicapping operation and called in his bets.

About the same time, H. L. Hunt, the sinner who sang country gospel songs but seldom attended church, began to turn to religion. Here, again, the change was partly attributable to the influence of his new wife as well as to certain practical considerations. A sincere and determined woman, Ruth gently insisted that her husband accompany her and her children to church on Sundays, and began inviting church groups to use the living room at Mount Vernon for their meetings and singing sessions. She also switched her attendance from Lakewood Baptist Church to the giant First Baptist Church in downtown Dallas, and enlisted the conversionary help of the powerful Reverend W. A. Criswell. A short and energetic man, Reverend Criswell was the archetypical southern evangelist, a segregationist so conservative he once said, "If I had a liberal hair in my head, I'd pluck it out." As pastor of First Baptist Church, Criswell presided over the St. Peter's of the Southern Baptist Convention. His church claimed the largest (18,500) and the most prestigious membership of any in the land. It was a well-known fact that Billy Graham, himself a resident of North Carolina, was officially a member of Criswell's church. It soon became almost as well known that Reverend Criswell was trying to bring H. L. Hunt, the world's richest man, into the fold.

Thanks to religion, Hunt did experience a rebirth, but it was not exactly the kind of rebirth his spiritual guides intended. Hunt saw religion not as a pathway to heaven but as a means to accomplish some much more earthly ends —namely, the revival of his now dormant crusade against communism. Thus, in the summer of 1958, he resurrected his Facts Forum propaganda apparatus in the form of a new tax-exempt "educational" and "religious" organization called LIFE LINE. Basically a reincarnation of Facts Forum in religious clothing, LIFE LINE (which he always spelled with capital letters) became Hunt's new main passion, his new mission, as well as the means for his personal rejuvenation.

Dedicated to spreading the word via radio broadcasts, LIFE LINE had what Hunt liked to call a "double-barreled appeal." Part of each fifteen-minute program was devoted to hymns, sermons, and discussions of Christian fundamentalism. But at least half, and often more than half, of each show was purely political. In these segments, the commentator concentrated on attacking communism, the United Nations, the State Department, the U.S. Supreme Court, urban renewal, immigration, and unions. When not on the attack, LIFE LINE spent its air time lobbying on behalf of the oil depletion allowance and bills to reform the electoral college. Unlike Facts Forum, LIFE LINE did not even pretend to present "both sides" of these issues. LIFE LINE presented only one side, the "constructive" side.

In some ways, LIFE LINE was ahead of its time. One of the program's main activities was attacking the untrammeled growth of the federal bureaucracy, a theme that would gain widespread popularity among mainstream political groups in the 1970s. "Federal 'empire builders' have placed the government in competition with private business in forty-seven different lines," proclaimed one LIFE LINE script. "As government grows, Freedom shrinks," said another. "Bureaucratic domination is whittling away our personal liberty."

But prescient as they may have been, these warnings were often lost in the jumble of paranoid conspiratorial rhetoric that predominated most of the other LIFE LINE scripts. These scripts characterized any opponents of the "constructive" view as "the mistaken" or as "one worlders," and accused them of being "dedicated to destroy business, Patriotism, and all Freedom." According to LIFE LINE and its founder, the hard core of the mistaken—the truly deliberate communists and socialists—comprised only "two percent of the total population," but many had "skillfully intrigued their way into sensitive positions," thus enabling themselves to exercise power and influence out of proportion to their numbers. It was LIFE LINE's stated goal to expose the mistaken at every turn.

Once again, Hunt showed his faith in the FBI as resistant to communist infiltration by hiring former G-man Gene Scudder as one of LIFE LINE's commentators. But in contrast to Facts Forum, which he literally stacked with bureau men, Hunt also staffed LIFE LINE with fundamentalist Christian ministers and lay apostles. The most prominent was Wayne Poucher, an ordained Church of Christ minister. Before joining LIFE LINE, Poucher's ministerial experience consisted of a one-year stint as pastor of the Owen's Chapel Church in Franklin, Tennessee, and part time preaching at various churches in suburban Washington. His greatest credential was in politics. An unsuccessful candidate for the South Carolina state legislature, Poucher had been the campaign manager for Strom Thurmond's successful write-in campaign for the U.S. Senate. Next to Poucher, LIFE LINE's major voice belonged to James Dobbs, an unsuccessful Texas congressional candidate who was also affiliated with the arch-conservative Church of Christ.

Hunt had LIFE LINE establish its offices on two floors of an old building at 620 Eleventh Street NW in Washington, D.C. The offices were equipped with telephones, typewriters, automatic rotary files, printing presses, and a corps of twenty-eight clean-cut and very conservative young men and women. Each staffer was thoroughly investigated before being allowed to come to work at LIFE LINE. Having spent plenty of time and money spreading the word about communists in government, Hunt wanted to make sure that his own organization was not infiltrated by subversives. Like the minions of Facts Forum, the employees at LIFE LINE spent their time selling right-wing books and pamphlets and putting out a thrice-weekly newspaper called *Life Lines*. But the central focus of LIFE LINE's work was the production of its fifteen-minute radio-commentary slots. Tapes of LIFE LINE's Monday-through-Saturday programs were rented out to radio stations for 20 percent of the fee the station charged the program's sponsor. LIFE LINE's minimum "talent" charge was $5 per week and its maximum was $10 per day. The Sunday program, which was billed as a "nondenominational religious commentary," was distributed free of charge. Tapes were mailed out every two weeks and had to be returned to LIFE LINE after they were used.

In an effort to give his new propaganda organ an aura of prestige, Hunt assembled an advisory board including former Facts Forum board members John Wayne, Robert Wood, and General A. C. Wedemeyer, and a new contingent of Christian ministers led by Dr. W. R. White, president of Baylor University. Hunt desperately wanted singer Pat Boone to join the LIFE LINE board, too. According to one report, he even threatened to use his friendship with filmmaker and right-wing advocate Cecil B. De Mille to force Boone onto the board. But Boone ultimately turned him down.

At first, Hunt publicly downplayed his personal involvement with LIFE LINE. He did not appear on any of the programs and did not even list his name on the LIFE LINE board. But behind the scenes, the founder was more active in the affairs of LIFE LINE than many of the commentators and staffers he recruited to run it. In addition to communicating his advice by telephone and personal contact, Hunt dictated memo after memo instructing LIFE LINE commentators on everything from who to attack and who to praise to the proper style and volume for the hymns. Sometimes Hunt would send out as many as five or six of these memos per day. "Suggest disclosing that there is a practically unrecognized pressure group which is the most evil of all—the big, pink money group—Mistaken Wall Street," he advised in one such memo. "The time is ripe that LIFE LINE could begin putting on a campaign against those who are trying to masquerade in the ministry," he said in another dispatch. "Five percent of the preachers in the country are dedicated Communists." In still another memo, Hunt urged Poucher to write a script "delicately" exposing the way rich people are turned into communists by a "conspiracy" providing them with socialist nurses, socialist playmates, "conspiracy planned marriages, and, for those not available for marriage, lovers."

Wary of being attacked for bigotry as in the Facts Forum days, Hunt urged his LIFE LINE commentators to take an intermediate stance on blacks, Jews, and other minorities. The reason he wanted to avoid a reputation as a bigot, as he expressed it, was strictly pragmatic: "200 genuine anti-Communist organizations, institutions, or movements . . . accomplish little and are of little effect because they handicap themselves by making unwise attacks on minority groups." Later, Hunt suggested that Poucher praise a well-known Jew so that "LIFE LINE would be given the credit of extolling and memorializing a Jew," a credit Hunt evidently believed would help protect LIFE LINE from liberal attack.

As time passed, Hunt became more open about his support for LIFE LINE, though he still denied controlling its internal affairs. One of the more visible and controversial indications of his support was a six-foot-high, twelve-foot-wide, pink and blue LIFE LINE sign he erected on the lawn of his Mount Vernon residence. Hunt was served notice by the city of Dallas on August 1, 1961, that the sign was in violation of a city ordinance forbidding signs in front of buildings in residential areas. When Hunt refused to take down the sign, the city filed suit. Hunt then agreed to remove his sign in return for the city's promise to drop its suit. But no sooner had the sign been taken down than a smaller version of the same message appeared on the side of Mount Vernon's mailbox. It said in hand-painted white letters: "LIFE LINE, 6:15 p.m., dial 1090." As the *Dallas News* pointed out in a story entitled "You Can't Fight City Hall," the score at the end of the LIFE LINE–sign controversy was "One down, and one up."

Meanwhile, LIFE LINE grew and grew. In 1958, its programs were heard on some twenty radio stations. By the early 1960s, LIFE LINE was aired five to seven times per week on 354 stations in forty-seven states; fifty of these stations aired LIFE LINE programs twice a day. LIFE LINE caught on quickest in Hunt's home state of Texas, where it was carried by fifteen radio stations within the first year and a half of its operation. As Wayne Poucher pointed out, "Just about every city in the state of Texas" was in listening range of LIFE LINE programs. The town of Abilene, Texas, a Christian college community, could tune in LIFE LINE programs five times per day. But Texans were not LIFE LINE's only audience. LIFE LINE claimed to have five to six million "dedicated" listeners nationwide and a casual listening audience of many times that number. Whether or not those claims were accurate, there could be no dispute that LIFE LINE was definitely accessible to millions, for by the early 1960s its programs were occupying an estimated 30,000 hours of public-service (i.e., tax-exempt) air time per year.

Most of LIFE LINE's tremendous growth was due to the generosity of a single sponsor. The trade name of that sponsor was HLH Products. Coincidentally or not, HLH Products was often confused with Hunt-Wesson Foods,

makers of Hunt's ketchup and other food items. But HLH Products had
absolutely nothing to do with Hunt-Wesson. The ketchup maker was a conventional marketer based in California and owned by an independent and unrelated group. HLH Products, like LIFE LINE itself, was the brainchild of
H. L. Hunt. Along with LIFE LINE, with which it was clearly intertwined,
HLH Products was also Hunt's greatest passion.

Hunt began his venture in the food business in 1959, when he bought a
$500,000 food-processing plant in Nacogdoches, Texas, and commenced mar-
keting peanut butter and vacuum-packed nuts under the Parade label. The
following year, he created HLH Products as a subsidiary of the Hunt Oil
Company, and embarked on a $15-million expansion program which he an-
nounced at a press conference with eleven-year-old Donna K. Erickson, better
known as "Little Miss Sunbeam," the Sunbeam Bread advertisement girl.
Reaching for national distribution, Hunt bought new plants in Arkansas,
Indiana, Iowa, California, Florida, and Maryland as well as more plants in
Texas. HLH Products' list of product lines expanded to some 1,340 items,
including peanut butter, packed nuts, canned chicken, canned tomatoes, aspi-
rin, vitamins, soft drinks, cattle feed, toothpaste, and transistor radios. Because
of Hunt's dietary habits, the food items sold by HLH Products were widely
mistaken as "health foods." In actual fact, they were ordinary canned vegetables and meats. Everything bore the label HLH. There was HLH Mercuro-
chrome, HLH Rel-E-Hot, HLH Perfection, HLH Tasty, HLH Ringo, and
HLH Gastro-Majic indigestion tablets.

Hunt's decision to go into the food and drug business was prompted in
part by a new personal dream: now reaching his seventies, H. L. Hunt, the
world's greatest independent oilman, wanted to see if he could still build a
business from the ground up. As he later pointed out, Hunt was also drawn
to the food and drug business because of his lifelong interest in "cures" and
his recent increasing interest in "health foods." Then, too, going into the food
business allowed him both a nostalgic return to his farm-boy roots as well as
a chance to integrate an increasingly important component of his existing
wealth, his vast land holdings. Having continued to acquire ranches and farms
through the 1950s, H. L. Hunt was becoming one of the nation's largest
landholders, with an estimated 1 million acres of holdings spread out over
Texas, Louisiana, Arkansas, Oklahoma, New Mexico, Colorado, Montana,
Wyoming, the Dakotas, Kansas, Tennessee, Mississippi, Florida, and California. These lands produced timber, fruit, pecans, poultry, and livestock—much
of which could be processed and marketed by HLH Products. On top of all
this, there was one other major consideration. Some would later say that it was
Hunt's only real reason for starting HLH Products. That consideration was
what HLH Products could do for LIFE LINE—and vice versa.

Hunt had been having sponsorship problems with LIFE LINE from the
beginning. As he wrote in one of his more candid memos, "I simply cannot
get the saphead purchasers of time to use the commercials, except the Hunt
companies and one or two isolated cases. They are afraid of losing their

respectability, I guess. If the sponsors will not begin advertising with the program, we are crippled."

HLH Products solved Hunt's sponsorship problems in a single stroke. With its formation, HLH became LIFE LINE's largest single backer. Although the exact extent of HLH's contributions to LIFE LINE would be obscured in a maze of deliberately inconsistent financial records, there were plenty of indications that HLH gave generously. In a January 1962 memo to the LIFE LINE staff, Hunt reminded his workers that HLH Products was "spending $100,000 a month" to sponsor LIFE LINE programs. That, of course, was the equivalent of $1.2 million per year, or well over $4 million for the first four years of the HLH/LIFE LINE coexistence.

What HLH Products got in return for its sponsor dollars was thousands of hours of national advertising, the expenses of which could be written off against the company's income. In addition, HLH purchased much of its LIFE LINE advertising at discount rates. Amid charges of "self-dealing," Hunt later claimed that the low advertising rates enjoyed by HLH Products were not the result of its "inside position" but the result of good "bargaining." How much "bargaining" Hunt had to do with himself was never disclosed, but LIFE LINE commentator Wayne Poucher subsequently began to complain that HLH Products was delinquent in paying its bills even at the lowered rates. Undeterred by Poucher's report, Hunt merely kept on reminding his commentators to keep plugging HLH Products at the appropriate commercial slots in the program format.

Leaving details of the actual financial and operational management ot subordinates, Hunt devoted his own energies to personally promoting HLH Products at every opportunity. Some of Hunt's promotional work merely consisted of writing letters to business friends like E. J. Hudson of Houston and Humble Oil president Morgan Davis, asking them to ask their employees and families to use HLH Products. But his most eye-catching efforts were at the HLH Products' booths at the Texas State Fair in Dallas and the Louisiana State Fair in Shreveport. There, dressed in his dark-blue business suit, white shirt, and tie, Hunt would personally stand in the booths hawking samples of HLH Products' hottest items. His sales pitch played shamelessly on his image as the Midas of the modern world.

"I'm H. L. Hunt, and I'm the world's richest man," he would crackle, "and these are my products, so you know they must be good."

In an effort to boost Dallas sales, Hunt opened a sandwich shop in the downtown district. Called the HLH, the shop featured nothing but items sold by HLH Products. The soup was made from HLH chicken and vegetables. The sandwiches were made with HLH meats on Hunt's beloved Deaf Smith County stone-ground wheat bread. There were even HLH Gastro-Majik indigestion tablets by the cash register. Hunt made it his business to keep track of the sandwich shop's progress, and checked in at regular intervals every week, sometimes to have a meal and sometimes to help the employee behind the counter sell sandwiches.

Hunt also dabbled in HLH Products' advertising operations, often with comically disastrous results. On one occasion, he composed an ad which declared that "HLH peanut butter is as rich as fertilizer." Hunt's advertising man had to spend a whole afternoon talking him out of using that inauspiciously worded slogan.

On most other occasions, Hunt's advertising problems followed from his attempts to introduce political motifs. He changed the tag line of the LIFE LINE broadcasts from "H. L. Hunt believes patriotism pays" to "HLH Parade and Saxet Products believe patriotism pays." Then he began including pocket samples of HLH Products when handing out LIFE LINE literature, and he began handing out LIFE LINE literature when hawking HLH Products. Soon those interested in HLH Products found they had to swallow the right-wing line along with their canned chicken, a fact which spoiled more than a few appetites.

Undaunted, Hunt set about making plans for one of his grandest advertising ventures: the HLH Products Fun and Food exhibit to open with the 1964 New York World's Fair. Hunt's plans called for an "eastern United States" theme to include small replicas of such historic sites as Mount Vernon, Independence Hall in Philadelphia, and Boston's Old North Church, as well as some amusement rides and food concessions. However, World's Fair czar Robert Moses felt that Hunt's planned amusements would be in poor taste and too high-priced. Moses also feared that, if past were prelude, Hunt would use the occasion of his HLH Products Fun and Food exhibit to distribute right-wing propaganda. Consequently, on October 4, 1963, after a running dispute with H.L. and his staff, Moses ejected the HLH exhibit from the fair. Hunt angrily issued a press release charging that he had been "taken in" by Moses and his World's Fair people. Claiming that HLH was now in the "awkward position" of having to cancel various exhibit contracts, Hunt complained that he was stuck with a carousel of 1900 vintage and a Wild Mouse ride. Leaving New York in a huff, Hunt determined never to have anything to do with another World's Fair.

Despite Hunt's unflagging promotional efforts, HLH Products (which was known simply as "the food division" within the Hunt empire) was a money loser from the day its operations began. Although HLH was grossing over $20 million per year by 1963, annual losses were rumored to be in the range of $1 million, or just about the amount HLH was spending on LIFE LINE. Hunt never gave a full public accounting of HLH's financial difficulties, but it soon became clear that the situation was bad enough to disturb him. As he put it in one LIFE LINE memo reminding the staff to plug HLH Products on the air, "We have done a poor job of running our food business."

If part of HLH Products' problems grew from its political-advertising expenditures, another part stemmed from the inordinate number of product lines the company was attempting to market. The sheer variety of HLH's 1,340 items made processing and marketing decisions extremely complicated and worrisome. Hunt knew a great deal about the oil business, having gained firsthand personal experience in nearly every aspect of the industry. But the food business was a different story. There was a great deal about modern merchandising and packaging (not to mention advertising) that he did not know or have experience in. Besides, Hunt was getting to be an old man. Though he still had the energy of a man many years his junior, it was becoming harder for him to keep on top of things, especially when his food plants were spread out all over the country. This left ever-increasing responsibility in the hands of his aides and plant managers, many of whom were no more experienced in the food business than he was. But rather than close down his operations—in effect admitting failure—Hunt kept pouring more money into HLH in the belief that the operations would eventually turn themselves around.

While HLH Products struggled, LIFE LINE prospered, confirming Hunt's adage that "patriotism is always profitable." LIFE LINE's net worth, which stood at $7,336 in 1960, rose to $142,919 by September 30, 1963. LIFE LINE's report for 1963 showed that after gross income of a little over $500,000 (mostly from tape rentals and "subscriptions") and expenses of a little less than $450,000, the organization had a tidy net profit for the year of $61,377.94.

LIFE LINE's financial success was totally beholden to H. L. Hunt, his family, companies, friends, and business associates. After the Hunt-owned HLH Products, the largest sponsors were Hunt, his first-family children (who gave regular $5,000 tithes), and the operating entities under the Hunt Oil umbrella. Other big givers included a long list of oil-business suppliers, many of whom had also contributed to Facts Forum, and the ever-faithful First National Bank of Dallas, which contributed nearly $70,000 to LIFE LINE directly and through the bank-controlled Bright Star Foundation while lending LIFE LINE another $50,000 for operating expenses.

Like its predecessor Facts Forum, LIFE LINE floated on a sea of funny money. Annual revenues marked "subscriptions" added up to 20 to 30 percent more money than what *Life Lines'* total claimed circulation should have paid for their newspapers. But there was never any explanation or accounting of the difference, where it came from, or what it was used for. More importantly, LIFE LINE continued to masquerade as a nonpolitical, "educational and religious" organization qualified for tax-exempt status. If LIFE LINE's programs had a "double-barreled" appeal, giving to LIFE LINE offered a triple attraction—a donor could do a favor for H. L. Hunt, strike a blow against communism, and claim a tax deduction all at the same time. Of course, that effectively meant that LIFE LINE's real financial backers—willingly or not—were America's taxpayers.

Not surprisingly, LIFE LINE eventually provoked some highly publicized controversy. One of the first public officials to look into the organization was Senator Maurine Neuberger of Oregon. After a preliminary investigation in 1963, she reached what seemed to many to be an obvious conclusion. "There is probably no one," she declared, "who gets more right-wing propaganda for his tax dollar than Haroldson Lafayette Hunt."

In spite of this and other public outcries, the IRS continued to be obliging to LIFE LINE as it had been to Facts Forum. The favoritism apparently came right from the top. After a field investigation in 1962, IRS field agent Angelo Santino wrote that LIFE LINE "does not qualify for exemption as an 'educational organization' because a majority of the Life Line commentaries presented unsupported opinion or did not present sufficient discussion of opposing viewpoints to permit an individual or the public to form an independent opinion." On September 28, 1962, following Santino's report, an I.R.S. official in the Baltimore field office recommended that LIFE LINE's tax-exempt status as an educational organization be revoked. After LIFE LINE filed two more appeals, the case was finally referred to the main office of the IRS in Washington, where it languished for months with no sign of action on the part of top IRS officials. Ultimately, the IRS allowed LIFE LINE to keep its tax exemption.

The Federal Communications Commission was as obliging as the IRS. On September 19, 1963, after LIFE LINE had been operating for four years, the FCC finally ruled that LIFE LINE had made "partisan" broadcasts in a series of programs criticizing the nuclear test ban treaty. But no moves were made to take LIFE LINE off the air, change its format, or punish stations that continued to carry its "partisan" broadcasts. In fact, the FCC even acted to deny a group with views which opposed Hunt's and LIFE LINE's to get equal time on two of the stations that carried LIFE LINE's programs. The FCC's ruling involved a petition by the Citizens Committee for a Nuclear Test Ban Treaty to respond on two Alabama radio stations to a LIFE LINE broadcast that was highly critical of the treaty. The radio stations, which were unwilling to grant such time to the protreaty groups, appealed to FCC secretary Ben F. Waple. Waple ruled that "If it is your good judgement" that the public does not need to hear the protreaty side of the issue, "then your obligation pursuant to the 'fairness doctrine' has been met." By all appearances, the FCC seemed to be saying that there was a double standard in political broadcasting—one that applied to the broadcasts of H. L. Hunt and one that applied to the broadcasts of everyone else.

While Hunt continued to do most of his politicking under cover of religion, the ministers closest to him tried to save his soul. One of the first attempts to make Hunt see the light was ventured by LIFE LINE commentator Reverend Poucher. It occurred one day in 1959, when Hunt was visiting Poucher's suburban Washington home for dinner. The time came for the family Bible reading and prayer, and Poucher asked Hunt if he would like to join in. Hunt replied that he would be a better observer than participant. Poucher brought out a chair and placed it beside one of the children's beds so Hunt would have a place to sit. But as the family kneeled down to say their prayers, Hunt slid off his chair and joined them on his knees. According to Poucher, when the prayers were finished, Hunt's face was streaming with tears.

"I took him to the hotel and for two hours we talked about him and his soul," Poucher recalled. "I finished by telling him that I wanted to take him to the Church building and baptize him."

Hunt was still tearful from the prayer session, but somehow he was not yet ready to be baptized.

"Wayne, I want to," he said, "but I have been an evil person and I don't feel I can ask God to forgive me until I have lived better for a little longer time."

Reverend Criswell, the other major religious man in Hunt's life, apparently convinced him that he had reformed himself enough. For on the first Sunday of 1960, not long after Poucher's unsuccessful conversion attempt, Hunt joined Ruth and their four children in being baptized at First Baptist Church in Dallas. The event was a milestone. The late Lyda Bunker Hunt had always been a religious woman, but she had never managed to get H.L. to attend church with regularity. Ruth and Criswell had performed a minor miracle. Now, for the first time in his adult life, H.L. Hunt was a bona fide member of a church.

With characteristic rhetorical flourish, Hunt later called his baptism "the greatest trade I ever made," because, as he put it, "I traded the Here for the Hereafter." But it soon became clear to those who knew him that he had not completely seen the light. Though he more or less stuck to his decision not to gamble, he continued to commit old sins and new sins with lustful regularity. He also continued to be more interested in religion only as it served his political purposes.

When not promoting or defending LIFE LINE, Hunt engaged in a variety of independent political misadventures of an even less holy nature. More often than not, he was aided in these exploits by two increasingly influential Hunt Oil executives. One was Hunt Oil security chief Paul M. Rothermel. A tall man with square Germanic features, Rothermel was a lawyer and former FBI agent who had come to work for Hunt after leaving the bureau in 1957. By this time, there was a saying around the FBI that former agents had two retirement plans —the bureau's and H. L. Hunt's. But Rothermel was no mere pensioner. In addition to looking after routine corporate security matters and investigating all newly hired Hunt employees, he used his extensive law-enforcement and government contacts to provide Hunt with a continuing stream of political intelligence. Rothermel usually transmitted his reports via typewritten memos, often making provocative allusions to unnamed sources from the White House and the CIA to the Dallas Police Department.

Hunt's other top aide was John Wesley Curington. A tall, skinny fellow with pointed features, Curington talked like a Texas rancher and carried out his boss's orders like a city slicker. A graduate of Baptist-dominated Baylor University in Waco, Texas, Curington had a law degree from SMU. In 1955, as a twenty-seven-year-old attorney, he had gone to work for Hunt Oil in the land department, but by 1960 he was, as he put it, "working directly for Mr. Hunt." By his own account, the things Curington did for Hunt ranged from running HLH Products (the "food division") to covering up tax-evasion schemes, collecting gambling debts, handling matters involving Hunt's secret family by Frania Tye Lee, and carrying out covert political operations.

The most famous Hunt-Curington political caper took place during the 1960 presidential campaign. Hunt arrived in Los Angeles for the Democratic convention as something of a political untouchable. Already familiar with the extremist positions taken by Facts Forum and LIFE LINE, neither of the major mainstream presidential contenders, John F. Kennedy and Lyndon B. Johnson, desired public identification with America's richest man. Jake Jacobsen, then an assistant to Texas governor Price Daniel and later a confidant of LBJ's, ran into Hunt at the hotel the Democrats were occupying for the convention. "I saw old Hunt wandering down the hall, looking like a lost soul," Jacobsen remembered. "I didn't know what he wanted to do, but he didn't seem to be doing much of anything except trying to find somebody who would talk to him. He wandered into Lyndon's suite, which was right next to ours. There were a lot of people in there, but they were all too busy to talk to Hunt, so he wandered on down the hall and talked with me. I thought, "What the hell, here's a man with all that money who can't get anybody to talk to him but me.' "

But Hunt was by no means as pathetic a figure as he appeared. Unbeknownst to Jacobsen and the Democratic powers, Hunt had a covert scheme in the works. Ironically, his scheme was based on one of Reverend Criswell's recent Sunday sermons. In that sermon, the pastor of First Baptist Church had flatly declared, "The election of a Catholic as president would mean the end of religious freedom in America." Hunt's attraction to Criswell's point of view was undoubtedly enhanced by the fact that Kennedy had promised to "review" the oil industry's tax advantages, particularly the oil-depletion allowance.

Believing that Reverend Criswell's pronouncements would hurt Kennedy and therefore help the chances of Texas's favorite son Lyndon Johnson, Hunt had secretly dispatched John Curington to have 200,000 copies of Criswell's anti-Catholic sermon printed up and mailed out to Protestant ministers all over the country. Even as he was being snubbed at the convention, Hunt was confidently waiting for his leaflets to hit the streets, starting a new wave of anti-Catholic hysteria that would knock Kennedy out of the running at the last minute.

As it turned out, the scheme backfired. The Criswell leaflet did become one of the most widely circulated pieces of political literature in the 1960 presidential campaign, but most Protestant ministers and editorial writers rejected Criswell's brand of anti-Catholicism out of hand. Instead of becoming the rally cry for a "dump Kennedy" movement, the Criswell leaflet became the subject of a Senate investigation. This was not just an academic or political inquiry. The Criswell leaflet did not state who had paid for its printing and mailing, and federal election laws specifically prohibited the circulation of such anonymous literature once the campaign was under way. Word soon leaked out that the Senate was focusing its investigation on a prominent right-wing Dallas oil millionaire.

Hunt decided to drop out of sight for a while. He and Curington left Dallas and went out to west Texas, around San Angelo and Lubbock, where they lived for several weeks under assumed names. Curington later claimed that the assumed name Hunt used during the hide out was "Franklin Hunt."

Meanwhile, the Senate inquiry zeroed in. But a Great Neck, Long Island, printer named Ralph B. Raughley testified that Hunt employee John Curington had paid $10,000 to his firm for the printing and mailing of the Criswell sermon. Having put Hunt on the spot, Raughley eased H.L.'s problems by further testifying that the order for the printing had been placed before the close of the Democratic convention that summer. Technically, Hunt's action had been within the law. But that still left plenty of room for public moral outrage, especially since both Hunt and Curington remained underground. Newspapers in Texas and across the country taunted H.L. to come out of hiding. One Texas editorial writer beckoned, "Come Out, Big Daddy, Wherever You Are."

Hunt finally did come out in the fall of 1960. When he faced the press, Hunt claimed that he had not been hiding but had secluded himself in order to write a book. He admitted that he had been the one who paid for the printing and mailing of the Criswell sermon. But he said he had only done it in order to help Lyndon Johnson. That rather lame excuse satisfied neither the public nor the Democratic party, but it was the only explanation that was forthcoming.

Hunt then proceeded to keep a low political profile until four days before the November general election, when he announced that he was supporting the JFK-LBJ ticket after all. This last-minute endorsement was like Big Daddy's kiss of death as far as the Democrats were concerned. Party chairman Henry Jackson quickly called a press conference to repudiate Hunt's endorsement and financial support. In point of fact, Hunt had not offered to contribute any money to the campaign, but Jackson told the press that the Democrats would not accept it if he did.

Hunt's political hijinks did not end with the 1960 election. In a sworn statement made after he left Hunt Oil Company, Hunt's aide John Curington claimed that Hunt continued to make covert campaign contributions long after the furor over the Criswell leaflet died down. Though refusing to specify the amount of these contributions, Curington said that they were "large" and in cash, and generally intended to defeat one of Hunt's political opponents rather than to elect a candidate Hunt specifically admired. Hunt's opponents allegedly included Senator Millard Tydings of Maryland, Senator Alan Cranston of California, and, later, President Lyndon Johnson. Curington also claimed that Hunt secretly gave $25,000 to the USO, $10,000 to "an Arab organization," and $10,000 to "a Jewish organization"—all of which he charged off to HLH Products and Hunt Oil Company as "advertising." But as significant as Hunt's covert contributions may have been, there was never any evidence that they amounted to the millions of dollars contributed by other political fat cats. Nor was there ever any evidence that Hunt's gifts made the difference in the campaign. On the contrary, Hunt's secret gifts seemed to be spent on the losing side more often than not.

Hunt never did become a big spender in the political arena. His largest contribution of record was a $38,000 gift to the Republican party in 1956. Most of his other gifts were in the $250 to $500 range or even lower. Some politicians got even less. In 1962, when George Bush was running for Congress in Houston on the Republican ticket, Hunt beckoned him to Dallas with the words "There's something I'd like to give you." When Bush arrived, Hunt chatted about friends, family—everything but politics and money. Finally, as Bush was getting ready to leave, Hunt handed him a thick brown envelope. Bush opened the envelope expecting to see a large sum of cash. Instead, he saw a thick stack of LIFE LINE literature. Texas congressman Joe Pool, a Democrat, fared even worse. When he went to Hunt in hopes of soliciting a campaign contribution, what he got was a lecture on "constructive" politics and three rolls of HLH Gastro-Majic indigestion tablets.

Few of H. L. Hunt's favorites fulfilled his hopes. In 1962, for example, Hunt began telling friends that retired army general Edwin A. Walker, who had been arrested for allegedly inciting a riot over the enrollment of black student James Meredith at the University of Mississippi, would make a fine governor of Texas in 1962 and a fine president in 1964. But when Walker finished last among six contenders in the 1962 Texas gubernatorial race, Hunt quickly tried to distance himself from the defeated general. As Hunt wrote in a letter to the *New York Herald Tribune,* which had reported that two of the nation's leading right wingers lived in Dallas, "I do not feel you should be attempting to smear General Edwin Walker with me or me with General Walker."

Always more willing to give advice than money, Hunt began to emerge as a public speaker in the early 1960s. His first major address was a speech to the Texas Service Station Operators' annual convention in Houston in 1961. He later made speeches at such occasions as the unveiling of General MacArthur's bust at the Texas State Fair and a meeting of the "Keep Arkansas Christian" society in Little Rock. As Hunt explained, his reasons for mounting the rostrum had to do with America's deteriorating political crisis.

"I'm a notoriety seeker now," he told the press before his Service Station Operators convention speech. "The country is so far gone that I am willing to say anything I can to dispel the apathy of the people."

When not making speeches, Hunt devoted much of his time and energy to writing letters to the editors of newspapers all over the country. Hunt's letters were usually of a reasonable—and therefore printable—length of three or four short paragraphs and were always organized around one or two specific points. Some of Hunt's letters merely trumpeted the virtues of LIFE LINE. Other missives trumpeted Hunt's brand of paranoid anticommunism and apple-pie generalities about America, religion, families, and freedom. "Not more than three percent of the people who have ever lived on this earth have been free," Hunt wrote in one typical letter to the editor. "Love of country,

awareness of unholy fanaticism, attention to public affairs, and belief in the
God have kept men free and made America great."

Hunt sent his letters to publications ranging from the *New York Times*
to the *Duluth Herald News Tribune* and the *Alabama Baptist.* Though the
editors of these and other newspapers turned down many more letters than
they would be able to print in a lifetime, Hunt's steady output made him a
fairly regular contributor to "Letters" columns from coast to coast.

At the same time, Hunt gave his counsel in letters to various national
politicians, among them Richard M. Nixon. Following Nixon's famous defeat
in the 1962 California gubernatorial primary, Hunt wrote Nixon, "I think you
have made many mistakes." Among those mistakes, according to Hunt, were
"yielding to Ike's orders to subside your disclosures" of communists in government, "debating with Kennedy," "wearing the wrong color shirt in the first
television debate," and "reading the conservative and the John Birch Society
out of the party." Hunt went on to console Nixon that he could still become
a statesman like Henry Clay, William Jennings Bryan, Daniel Webster, or
John Calhoun, each of whom failed to achieve the presidency. He ended his
letter by telling Nixon, "You need only to sincerely apologize to the public for
your outburst when under high nervous tension, and start again prosecuting
Alger Hiss and all other Communists or people in public life who are soft on
Communism." There was never any record that Hunt's letter received a reply.

Some of H.L.'s literary output was the work of professional writers he
hired on at Hunt Oil Company, but, according to top former employees, about
90 percent of what was turned out over Hunt's signature was outlined or fully
composed by H.L. himself. Equipped with a bank of secretaries, he would
dictate in rapid-fire style, sending off five and six letters to the editor per day.
Many times he toiled painstakingly with the wording, revising his prose again
and again until he got his meaning down exactly right. He was proud of his
work.

"Except that I am slow," he told one reporter, "I am the best writer I
know."

Hunt's premier literary accomplishment during this period was his novel
Alpaca, which he published himself in January of 1960. Part love story and part
political essay, *Alpaca* presented Hunt's utopian vision in rich detail. The main
character of the book was Juan Achala, a citizen of a mythical Latin American
country called Alpaca. The opening pages of the novel found Alpaca struggling
under the chains of a dictatorship, and Juan setting out to travel the world in
search of a model constitution that would put his country back on the road
to freedom. Juan's travels took him to Switzerland, France, England, and
Italy, where he engaged in dialogue about government with characters representing the American, Austrian, Italian, English, and Polish systems, among
others. In the course of his journey, Juan met a beautiful young opera singer,
also a native of Alpaca, named Mara. Although Mara hailed from an aristo-
cratic background and Juan from the common class, the two fell in love at
once. In the end, Juan got both things he was looking for—Mara and a model
constitution for Alpaca.

Leaving the writing of the romantic passages to a Dallas ghost writer, Hunt devoted his own energies—and most of the novel's pages—to describing Alpaca's new constitution. The essence of the constitution was a system of graduated suffrage in which votes were parceled out according to how much taxes a citizen paid. Those in the highest 10 percent of all taxpayers got seven votes, those in the highest 20 percent got six votes, and so on, down to the highest 60 percent of taxpayers, each of whom got one vote. In addition, "bonus votes" were awarded to citizens who waived 50 percent or more of their government salaries and to citizens who turned down retirement or social security benefits. Attempting to limit the role of the central government, Alpaca's constitution called for government to "conduct its affairs to compete as little as possible with private industry," and to "keep at a minimum its land and real estate ownership." Alpaca's constitution also included bans on freedom of assembly, political parties, and freedom of the press in criticizing the government.

Like most other Hunt ventures, Hunt's novel was designed in accordance with the profit motive. Hunt formed a new company called H. L. Hunt Press to print and market the book. Hunt's new press used one of the cheapest grades of paper (a variety only one step above newsprint) and not very much of it. *Alpaca* had 186 pages, but the pages themselves were only 5 1/2 × 4 inches in size. They were held together by one of the least expensive wax bindings available, the kind that would fall apart after anything more than the most delicate page turning. The front cover was done in a reddish orange with black and white type. The only illustration was a white chain running across the top. The letter *A* of *Alpaca* was enlarged and drawn to a sharp point that split one of the links in the chain. The price of the book, which was fifty cents, was marked in the upper-right-hand corner. The back cover of the book featured a black-and-white photograph of Hunt from his bow tie up. The photograph showed a round-jawed face, neatly trimmed white hair balding at the forehead, large and slightly glassy eyes looking off at a bit of an angle, and an unsmiling mouth with only the suggestion of an expression at the corners. A caption beneath the photograph read: "H. L. HUNT of Dallas." Inside the cover, there was a black and white photograph of Mount Vernon.

Easily the most memorable aspect of *Alpaca*'s publication as far as the public was concerned was the way Hunt hawked his book with the help of his young daughters by Ruth, eleven-year-old Helen and ten-year-old Swanee. The scene that made Hunt's method famous took place at an autograph party for *Alpaca* at Dallas's Cokesbury Book Store. While Hunt signed his copies of his book, his cute, pigtailed daughters sang a little promotional song. The song was done to the tune of "How Much Is That Doggie in the Window?" Its lyrics went, in part:

> How much is that book in the window?
> The one that says all the smart things . . .
> How much is that book in the window?
> The one that my daddy wrote . . .

The sight of the white-haired old oilman smiling away as his daughters warbled to customers of the bookstore was too precious a picture for the local media to pass up. Photographs of the scene ran in the local newspapers the next day and proliferated over the national wire services.

The impact of *Alpaca* itself was less impressive. A salesperson at Cokesbury Book Store in Dallas later reported that the book sold less than 100 copies at the store. Hunt never reported how many copies were in print or how many H. L. Hunt Press sold and/or distributed free of charge to libraries and personal acquaintances of the author. But *Alpaca* never came close to making the national bestseller list or becoming a selection of the Book-of-the-Month Club. Hunt's novel did cause a bit of a stir among liberal readers and reviewers of the *Texas Observer,* the *New Republic,* and the *Washington Post,* who attacked the book with a vengeance. According to H.L., the book also achieved a certain international reception of a more favorable nature.

"In early February [1960] copies of *Alpaca* first reached [A.K.] General Kassem in Baghdad," Hunt asserted in a letter to the editor of the *Washington Post.* "There have since been six or more news releases published in the United States describing constructive movements away from communism in Iraq."

That may have been true at the time Hunt wrote his reply, but General Kassem, who had risen to power by deposing the royal family in July of 1958, turned out to be a most anti-Western leader. Kassem was assassinated in 1963, three years after *Alpaca*'s publication. Hunt later published a long list of mostly perfunctory thank-you notes he had received after mailing copies to government bureaucrats around the world. But there was never any record of any other heads of state or revolutionary leaders adopting Hunt's handbook of governance.

More than anything else, the publication of *Alpaca* confused H. L. Hunt's public image and made him more misunderstood than ever. His novel was widely described as a scheme in which votes were accorded on the basis of how much money a citizen had. (In actual fact, Hunt had called for votes to be accorded on the basis of taxes paid, which was a different thing.) Even though he was one of the few rich men who at least attempted to formulate a utopian vision of any sort, his effort and ideas were summarily dismissed as wacky by the general public. In the end, *Alpaca* seemed to impress most people as just some more evidence of H. L. Hunt's willingness and ability to propagate his own ideas. But Hunt was not discouraged. In fact, he soon began making plans to write a sequel, to be called *Yourtopia.*

True to character, Hunt remained an independent throughout his political and literary escapades. But in later interviews H.L. did credit several personal friends for shaping his thinking. Among them were General Robert E. Wood (ret.), General A. C. Wedemeyer (ret.), General Charles A. Willoughby (ret.), Robert Welch, Reverend Billy James Hargis, D. B. Lewis, and J. Howard Pew. Taken together, these men formed a high council of the right wing, a military-religious-industrial complex of paranoid conservatism. Wood, who was chairman of Sears, Roebuck, and Wedemeyer, who was a former chief

of staff for Chiang Kai-shek, were both board members of Facts Forum and
LIFE LINE and participants in other right-wing groups, most notably, in
Wedemeyer's case, the John Birch Society. Welch, of course, was the founder
of the John Birch Society. Pew was the head of a family reputed to be nearly
as wealthy as Hunt's; the chairman of Sun Oil Company, Pew was also a
member of the advisory committee of the Bircher magazine *American Opinion.*
Willoughby was a former military aide to Douglas MacArthur and a consultant to the right-wing Christian Crusade. Reverend Hargis of Tulsa, Oklahoma, was the head of the Christian Crusade and an outspoken political
right-winger. Lewis was a pet-food producer from California whose right-wing
activities included the sponsoring of further broadcasts by former Facts Forum
commentator Dan Smoot.

Hunt respected these men. He met with them, listened to their advice,
offered his own views, confided in them, corresponded by telephone and by
mail. But, as *Houston Chronicle* reporter Saul Friedman observed, H. L. Hunt
remained "a political movement unto himself." Confident of his mental and
monetary power, Hunt considered himself at the very least the equal of organization founders like Welch and Hargis. He thought much like they did, held
many of the same opinions, but preferred to remain separate, to do his own
thing. He was not about to become anyone's follower. When asked in later
years why he never joined the John Birch Society, Hunt replied, "I always
thought they should have joined me."

Hunt's commitments to LIFE LINE, HLH Products, and the rest of his
utopian anticommunist political activities did not leave him much time for the
oil business. He continued to keep tabs on what his oil entities were up to, but
he did not take an active interest in their day-to-day operations. Instead, he
left his operations in the hands of his sons and long-trusted employees, and
let his companies run on their own momentum. The one exception to this
pattern was in 1958, when Hunt attempted to get an oil concession in Kuwait.
He flew to the Middle East, met all the important sheiks, and lobbied as hard
as he could, but his application was ultimately denied in favor of a Japanese
company. After that, Hunt remained on the periphery of the international oil
game, keeping his eye out for new opportunities but never seeming to find one.

As Hunt withdrew from the oil business, the overall production of the
Hunt companies began to level off. This was due in part to the declining
production of wells that were twenty and thirty years old, and to the introduction of conservation measures in Louisiana. The Hunt companies were still
drilling hundreds of wells per year onshore. Placid was even beginning to drill
offshore in the Gulf of Mexico. But the new finds were barely keeping pace
with the depletion of the family's old fields. By the early 1960s, the Hunts'
estimated total production was still in the 65,000-barrel-per-day range it had
been in the late 1940s. Since oil prices had risen in the intervening years, the
Hunt companies were making more money, but they were not producing much
more oil.

Hunt did not seem concerned. On the contrary, he became more in-fatuated with perpetuating his myth as the world's richest man, regardless of whether or not he really was. The press did its best to abet him at every turn. On the basis of no more hard data than previous news articles and Hunt's sixty-fifth-birthday press conference, the Associated Press bestowed on Hunt the title of the world's richest man. In 1957, the *New York Times* reported Hunt's worth at $2 billion, and ranked him among the five richest men in the world. A short time later, *Fortune* and *Life* reviewed their rankings of the richest, and rated Hunt as second to J. Paul Getty among America's big rich. According to *Fortune,* Hunt's worth was in the $400-million to $600-million category, while Getty's was in the $700-million to $1-billion category. Appar-ently unwilling to bear the burden of being the country's richest man, Getty threw the mantle back to Hunt.

"The corporations in which I own shares are rich enterprises," Getty told the press, "but I am not that wealthy. They hold the property. They control me. In terms of extraordinary independent wealth, there is only one man— H. L. Hunt."

Although Hunt sometimes dismissed reports of his wealth as "stuff and nonsense," he clearly delighted in his various titles as America's richest man and the world's richest man. Even when not using his fame to hawk HLH Products, he would frequently open conversations with new acquaintances by saying, "I'm H. L. Hunt. Some people say I'm the richest man in the world, and some say I'm only the second richest."

One of Hunt's most prized possessions was a letter he received in October of 1957 from a Lorton, Nebraska, garage owner named O. Hunt who wrote in the wake of the 1957 *Fortune* article which ranked Hunt second in wealth behind J. Paul Getty. "Not long ago I see you listed as the top dog financially and was impressed that one with the same name could achieve such distinc-tion," O. Hunt wrote. "What the H—— is the matter? Are you slipping? I see you rated today in the second string list. You get on the ball and get back in the top bracket where you belong, us Hunts don't recognize any second raters!!!"

H. L. Hunt took almost two years to reply to O. Hunt, but when he did, he wrote that the letter was "one of the few pieces of welcome mail which I have ever received as a result of write-ups of this nature." H.L. also disclosed that he "used your letter and these write-ups as a financial report in my negotiations for a fantastic concession in the Middle East." He subsequently reprinted a copy of O. Hunt's letter and his own reply in the back of his novel *Alpaca.*

In contrast to his public image, Hunt's daily routine was relatively mod-est. He would begin the day about 7:00 A.M. by breakfasting on carrot juice and wheat toast at Mount Vernon. In the kitchen, his wife Ruth or one of the cooks would prepare Hunt's lunch in a brown paper sack. The meal generally consisted of HLH brand vegetables, especially carrots, some wheat bread, and maybe a slice or two of meat.

After breakfast, Hunt would take his sack lunch and drive downtown in a 1962 Chevrolet Impala, the successor to his old Dodge. In 1961, Hunt replaced his company's DeHavilland Dove with a remanufactured World War II bomber called a Lockheed Ventura. But neither his new car nor his new airplane was important to him except as a means of transportation. When he arrived at the office, he usually smiled and said good morning to the secretaries, then lumbered down a maze of unmarked corridors to his own corner suite. The front part of the suite was an open area occupied by a bank of three secretaries. Hunt's personal office lay behind an unmarked door.

The office itself was roomy but hardly plush. There were no fancy executive gadgets, no pushbutton wall screens or elaborate communications systems. The walls were dark green, the carpet standard office beige-brown. Hunt's moderate-sized wooden desk commanded a handful of armchairs whose leather was badly cracked and discolored. The carpet had a spot that was worn from Hunt's practice of pitching quarters. The most remarkable furnishings in the room were the symbols of Hunt's dearest endeavors—an eight-inch-high American flag on his desk, a replica of an old-fashioned wooden oil derrick on a side table behind the desk, a display advertisement for Gastro-Majic indigestion tablets, and a small but powerful AM radio receiver that enabled H.L. to listen to LIFE LINE broadcasts twenty-two times per day by rotating the dial from Nashville to Corpus Christi. The only picture on the wall was a photograph of Hunt's son Hassie in his army uniform.

Hunt would sit behind his desk, perhaps take off his shoes and socks, and begin dictating memos or letters in what one former secretary described as a "rapid-fire drawl." At lunch time, Hunt would spread out some newspapers on his desk, open up his lunch sack, and have his meal right on the job. He would usually stay at the office until late afternoon. Most of the office ran on the standard five-day schedule, but H.L. came in six days per week. His favorite day was Saturday, when he would be up in his office alone and free to attend to both his public and private projects.

Of course, Hunt's mind was working twenty-four hours per day. He felt that he was always on call, and he expected his top assistants to be on call twenty-four hours a day also, though his eccentricities on this score did not quite rival those of Howard Hughes. Hunt seldom ordered his men to stand by at some lonely pay phone for six weeks while he deliberated whether or not to call them. But Hunt thought nothing of calling Curington or Rothermel in the middle of the night and ordering them out of bed to perform some urgent task or simply to listen to his latest idea.

Hunt gave more to charity than he usually got credit for, but, relatively speaking, what he gave was not much. At a time when Houston millionaire Hugh Roy Cullen, another oilman and arch conservative, was giving an estimated $200 million to charity, Hunt's one true charitable enterprise—the H. L. Hunt Foundation of Dallas—was making yearly charitable gifts of less than $15,000. As of September 17, 1963, the foundation's net worth was only $1,614,193. Its largest single gift that year was a $7,500 contribution to the

Dallas United Fund. The way Hunt saw it, philanthropy in America had been co-opted by subversive elements. "The mistaken have wormed their way into control of the large charitable and benevolent foundations," he explained once. "Here they use philanthropic dollars to destroy American liberty." Particularly guilty, in his view, were the Rockefeller, Carnegie, and Ford foundations, whose money was devoted to "liberal-socialist" projects. Hunt wanted no part of that.

Hunt had little genuine interest in any of the fine arts. He liked what he regarded as "pretty pictures," but he had poor taste in art. The paintings he purchased, with one or two exceptions, were generally the work of second- and third-rate artists, the output of followers of some "school" of painting rather than works of the masters. As such, they were not even good investments. They could be purchased relatively cheaply, they could cover the wall, they could please the eye of H. L. Hunt. But they had little lasting merit. Hunt's favorite painting was *A Proposal* by Robert James Gordon. It showed a young man and a young woman in pre-twentieth-century garb exchanging romantic looks.

One of the few cultural areas that did seem to attract Hunt, at least in later years, was opera. H.L. had always liked Broadway shows and light musicals; he had even tried his hand at composing his own songs. Opera provided a slightly more mature occasion for musical relaxation. But even here, his presence as a financial contributor was lacking. He did sponsor opera star Lily Pons on her stay in Dallas and was a member of the local opera board, but that was about the only thing he did. On one other occasion, he agreed to sponsor a student production of the *Barber of Seville* at the Music Hall at the Dallas state fairgrounds. The grateful students, fully aware of how rare a display of generosity Hunt's sponsorship really was, asked him to say a few words at intermission. Hunt proceeded to get up on the stage and start hawking HLH Products' Gastro-Majic indigestion tablets, samples of which he began passing out to the audience.

On his good-natured days, Hunt sometimes liked to take a little teasing about his tightfistedness.

"What are you going to do with all your money?" one of his employees would ask. "Take it with you?"

"I'm not planning to go," Hunt would answer only half jokingly.

Not surprisingly, those who were more firmly convinced of H. L. Hunt's mortality continued to be concerned about his flippant attitude, his ongoing sinfulness, and his misadventures with LIFE LINE and other political projects.

Hunt engaged in a running philosophical battle with Reverend Poucher over the nature of life itself. In one memo concerning LIFE LINE, for example, Hunt asserted that "the battle for Freedom is a battle between Communism and the profit motive system." Poucher rejoined that "your life expectancy on this earth is almost used up" so you had better believe "the battle for freedom is not a battle between free enterprise, the profit motive system, democracy, or whatever name we might call it—and communism—but it is

POPSY AND HIS PATRIARCHY

a battle between good, which is God, and evil, which is Satan, for the hearts and minds of men."

As time passed, Hunt's philosophical differences with Poucher grew more personal. Hunt was constantly trying to keep LIFE LINE on a political and commercial track. Poucher, who for all his faults really wanted to preach the gospel, tried to make the show genuinely religious. By the spring of 1963, Poucher realized he was fighting a losing battle. "I have been under increasing pressure from Mr. Hunt to inject his thinking into the program," he wrote to a friend, indicating that he did not know how much longer he could hold out. "Has God sent me to do the work of carrying the Gospel to those who will encounter the greatest difficulty in reaching heaven?"

Finally, on April 6, 1963, Poucher was fired. The reason for his dismissal was his refusal to criticize President Kennedy's tax proposal for the oil industry, as had been suggested by top Hunt Oil lawyer E. D. Guinn. Hunt only aggravated the situation by summarily evicting Poucher from the house he had rented in McLean, Virginia. Poucher then retaliated by suing Hunt for back pay allegedly due him and threatening to wash LIFE LINE's dirty linen in public.

"I am deeply disappointed that I was not able to lead Mr. Hunt to the Lord," Poucher wrote a friend shortly after his firing. Poucher later admitted that even after his four-year association with Hunt, the man and his actions remained unfathomable. "I thought I knew Mr. Hunt, but I didn't," Poucher told a reporter. "No one does."

By this time, Ruth Ray Hunt's good friend and spiritual mentor Reverend Criswell also became concerned about the wealthiest member of his congregation. Criswell had at first been an outspoken supporter of LIFE LINE. In 1959, Criswell declared that he was "convinced of [LIFE LINE's] patriotic and spiritual values" and its ability to strengthen one's "love for Christian principles that have made America great" and its capacity to stem "the terrible erosion of secularism, materialism, and communism." But by the end of 1963, Criswell had changed his tune. LIFE LINE's programs had become too commercial and political even for him. When one news reporter inquired about H. L. Hunt and LIFE LINE, Criswell remarked, "I'd give my soul if I could get Mr. Hunt interested in something else."

That was next to impossible to do. H.L. was nothing if not his own man. Once he had his mind set on something like LIFE LINE and HLH Products, he would not be deterred until he accomplished whatever he considered his goal to be. And before Hunt would save his soul, he had to save the world from communism. It was simply a matter of priorities. His baptism at First Baptist Church notwithstanding, Hunt regarded ministers in much the same way he regarded John Birchers—he always thought they should have joined him.

H. L. Hunt was without doubt a multinatured man. But two main sides predominated. One was his Mr. Hunt side, the persona he showed most often down at the office. As Mr. Hunt, he was the shrewd, tough-trading oilman, landowner, food baron, and right-wing propagandist who loved the glamor of risk-taking even if he no longer gambled the way he once had. The other side of H. L. Hunt was his Popsy Hunt persona. As Popsy Hunt, he was the lovable old eccentric who was always coming up with some improbable new health-giving scheme. Popsy Hunt was the fellow who dropped to his knees on a visit with President Eisenhower at Camp David and began crawling around in the grass looking for four-leaf clovers because he thought it was good exercise. Popsy Hunt was the boss who sincerely recommended Gastro-Majic indigestion tablets when he heard that a child of one of his employees had leukemia. And Popsy Hunt was the white-haired patriarch who presided over one of the most unusual family situations in America as if it were the most natural thing in the world.

The pecking order of Popsy Hunt's patriarchy was mirrored in the corporate structure of Hunt Oil. The parent, which was Hunt's bailiwick, was an oil company with a food-division subsidiary. But it was also a kind of umbrella corporation that provided accounting and other services for the rest of the Hunt companies. Beneath that umbrella were one hundred separate entities—corporations, partnerships, and trusts—which were divided among the members of Popsy Hunt's three families. Sometimes entities associated with the three families acted together, but more often than not they operated independently, with each of the families doing its own thing, pursuing its own interests.

Having already apportioned much of his wealth among the various trusts set up for his fourteen children, Popsy Hunt did not take an active hand in what each of his heirs was doing in business and life, but he did not stay completely out of their affairs either. Especially when things were going poorly for some venture or another, he was fond of poking his nose into his children's activities, if only to leave the impression that he still knew about everything that was going on around him. The impression was transparently false, but that hardly kept Popsy Hunt from trying.

The richest and most active of Popsy Hunt's heirs were his children by Lyda Bunker Hunt. The crown jewel of their portion of the empire was Placid Oil Company, whose production was by this time about twice that of Hunt Oil proper. Owned by the first-family trusts, Placid pumped out about 36,000 barrels of oil per day, or the equivalent of nearly $50 million per year in gross income. Next to Placid in size and importance was Penrod Drilling, a partnership among Bunker, Herbert, and Lamar which owned about twenty-five drilling rigs and was worth over $25 million. In addition, the first family held considerable wealth through their individual accounts and trusts and the subtrusts designated for their children. Each of these individual accounts and trusts was like a separate oil company in its own right. It was run by a Hunt family member or trusted Hunt employee, had a staff of secretaries and accountants, drilled for oil and gas, bought and sold properties of all descriptions, and owned interests in other Hunt companies. A maze of interlocking and interdependent relationships, the Hunt corporate structure was confusing even to employees hired to help operate it. But it was even more confusing to

H. L. Hunt's mother, Ella. COURTESY OF THE HUNT FAMILY ARCHIVES.

Hash Hunt, H.L.'s father. COURTESY OF THE HUNT FAMILY ARCHIVES.

H.L. (left) and his brother, Leonard. COURTESY OF THE HUNT FAMILY ARCHIVES.

H. L. Hunt circa 1911. COURTESY OF
THE BARKER HISTORY CENTER, AUS-
TIN, TEXAS.

A gusher. COURTESY OF THE SMACK-
OVER STATE BANK.

Oil-field mules in the mud, Smackover, Arkansas, 1921. COURTESY OF THE SMACKOVER STATE BANK.

An Arkansas drilling crew circa 1921. COURTESY OF THE SMACKOVER STATE BANK.

Lyda Bunker Hunt circa 1935. COUR-
TESY OF MRS. H. P. SESSIONS.

Young Frania Tye circa 1925. COUR-
TESY OF THE SHREVEPORT JOURNAL.

Dad Joiner congratulates Doc Lloyd after the drill stem test on the Daisy Bradford well. H. L. Hunt (with cigar) is third from the right. Soon afterward, Hunt bought Joiner out, a deal which was to be the cornerstone of the Hunt fortune. COURTESY OF THE BARKER HISTORY CENTER, AUSTIN, TEXAS.

Dad Joiner. COURTESY OF THE BARKER HISTORY CENTER, AUSTIN, TEXAS.

"The richest man in the United States." A 1948 photo of Hunt in *Life*. COURTESY OF THE HUNT FAMILY AR-CHIVES.

Lyda Bunker Hunt, early 1950s. COURTESY OF THE DALLAS TIMES HERALD.

Mount Vernon, H.L.'s home in Dallas. COURTESY OF THE HUNT FAMILY ARCHIVES.

H. L. and Ruth Ray Hunt after their wedding, November 1957. COURTESY OF THE DALLAS TIMES HERALD.

H. L. Hunt and Ruth at the piano, a favorite pastime. WIDE WORLD PHOTOS.

H.L. (left) and his eldest son, Hassie. COURTESY OF THE HUNT FAMILY ARCHIVES.

H. L. Hunt at eighty-three sitting down to a vegetarian lunch in his office. UPI.

H.L. demonstrates his creeping exercise. WIDE WORLD PHOTOS.

Ray Hunt at the *Lee* v. *Hunt* trial, Shreveport, Louisiana. COURTESY OF LEE SHIVELY, THE SHREVEPORT JOURNAL.

Ray Hunt's Reunion project. COURTESY OF HUNT OIL COMPANY.

Lamar Hunt and his wife, Norma. WIDE WORLD PHOTOS.

Frania Tye Lee and her son, Hugh S. Hunt, at the Shreveport trial. COUR-TESY OF ANDY SHARP, THE SHREVE-PORT JOURNAL.

Herbert (left) and Bunker Hunt are sworn in as witnesses before a House subcommittee investigating the collapse of the silver market in 1980. UPI.

outside auditors, and it carried with it numerous tax advantages, including the potential for passing the family wealth down through the generations by means of the trusts.

As the oldest child in the first family, Margaret Hunt Hill still held a certain precedence over her siblings. More socially conscious and more socially accepted than the other Hunts, she and her husband Al Hill were members of the most prestigious clubs in Dallas, including Brookhollow (the country club that had denied H.L. admission) and Terpsichorean, the city's most exclusive dance club. But Margaret was a financial conservative as well as a political conservative, and during the late 1950s and early 1960s, it was her younger brothers who tried to prove themselves money makers in the old man's image by embarking on their own grand-scale wheeling and dealing.

Once again, Bunker tried to lead the way. Undeterred by his $11 million worth of dry holes in Pakistan, Bunker decided to go after the new concessions that were opening up in Libya. That put Bunker, an independent, in direct competition with major oil companies like Esso (Exxon) and Mobil. Rumors began floating around that Bunker was attempting to grease the wheels of the Libyan government with covert payments to key officials, but there was never any proof to substantiate those charges. When the smoke cleared, Bunker wound up with Concession #2, one of the prized coastal tracts, and Concession #65, a remote inland tract hundreds of miles from the nearest harbor. Bunker drilled Concession #2 first and hit oil, but his find was too small to make a commercial well. By this time, his string of dry holes had decimated the income from his trust. In an effort to keep going, Bunker sold half of his interest in Concession #65 to British Petroleum.

Then the Hunt luck came through. In November of 1961, the first Hunt-BP well on Concession #65 came in at an incredible flow of 3,910 barrels per day. That well proved to be the first strike in the biggest oil field in Africa. Known as the Sarir field, it was eventually judged to have reserves in the 8-billion to 11-billion-barrel range, making it nearly three times the size of the great east Texas field. With a one-half share, Bunker had claim to 4 billion to 5.5 billion barrels, or about $6 billion to $8 billion worth of reserves at then prevailing prices. All of a sudden, thirty-five-year-old Nelson Bunker Hunt was, at least on paper, richer than any other private individual in the world, including his daddy.

Ironically, Bunker was also nearly broke. Finding the Sarir field was one thing. Getting the oil out of the ground and to the market was another. Hunt-BP had to lay a 320-mile pipeline from the field to the port of Tobruk, and oil-loading facilities had to be built in the harbor. That would take years. But until the work was completed, Bunker could not sell a single drop of oil. To make matters worse, Bunker suspected that his partner BP, which owned other big international oil concessions, was in no hurry to get the Sarir field on stream for fear of glutting the market and lowering oil prices. Faced with continuing delays, Bunker had no choice but to turn to his father for a loan. Popsy Hunt was still skeptical of his oldest active son's ability as an oil producer, but he reportedly agreed to lend Bunker $5 million until Bunker could get his Libyan oil field on stream.

The next Hunt son to reach for stardom was Bunker's youngest brother Lamar. Tall, lean, bespectacled, and shy, Lamar did not exude the air of a world changer, but that was what he was. Having grown up in a family that played football and bet on it, he saw the game not just as sport but as a lucrative entertainment enterprise that was bound to get bigger as the country's population grew. In early 1959, at the age of twenty-six, Lamar decided to buy a professional football team. His choice was the Chicago Cardinals of the National Football League, but the Chicago owner was not interested in selling out. Neither were the NFL's other team owners. Lamar soon concluded that his best bet of getting into professional football was starting his own league.

On August 14, 1959, shortly after his twenty-seventh birthday, Lamar called a meeting at the Conrad Hilton Hotel in Chicago. Helping him chair the meeting was K. S. "Bud" Adams, Jr., another oil-family scion who resided in Houston. Gathered beside them were hotel heir Barron Hilton of Los Angeles, Denver businessman Robert Howsam, Max Winter, and William Boyer of Minneapolis–St. Paul, and sports-broadcasting czar Harry Wismer of New York. Representing franchises from their six respective areas, the men each agreed to put up $25,000 for charter franchises in the American Football League.

Lamar and his fellow millionaires quickly became known as "the Foolish Club." In the face of an openly hostile NFL establishment, they opened their first season in the fall of 1960, and waited for the crowds that did not come. The biggest attendance at an AFL game that year was only 27,132 at Boston. The lowest was a paltry 4,771 in Denver. Matters were not helped by the fact that the NFL awarded a franchise for the Dallas Cowboys to oilman Clint Murchison, Jr. The scion of another east Texas oil family, Murchison made clear that he and his Cowboys were going to run Lamar's Texans out of town. Total losses that first year were staggering. Denver dropped only $50,000, but Barron Hilton's Los Angeles team lost a whopping $900,000. Lamar lost something on the order of $500,000. With typical exaggeration, the press reported his losses at $1 million and made the whole thing a joke.

"At that rate," remarked one Dallas writer, "he can only afford to lose for the next one hundred years."

Subsequent news stories inaccurately attributed the remark to Lamar's father, but every indication was that Popsy Hunt's attitude was something akin. Lamar's flair and initiative pleased him. And though H.L. remained a little skeptical of the venture, he was not worried about the outcome. Hunt's one visible economy move in response to his son's football losses was to cancel a small but steady advertising contract his Penrod Drilling Company had maintained for some time with the *Oil and Gas Journal.* The surprised *Oil and Gas Journal* account executive was told that the reason for the cut was the fact that Lamar's money-losing football team was under the Penrod name. If the cancellation of a few hundred dollars worth of advertising agreements seemed petty to the journal man, it was vintage H. L. Hunt.

Despite the initial rough going, Lamar showed one of his father's strongest traits: persistence. He counterattacked the NFL with a $10-million antitrust suit, and kept fighting the lopsided battle for the top college players. The AFL ended up losing its antitrust suit, but gradually the tide began to turn. In 1963, Lamar moved his team from Dallas to Kansas City, negotiated a $1-per-year stadium lease for the first two years, and renamed the team the Kansas City Chiefs. The Chiefs drew a healthy opening game crowd of 27,801 that fall. In New York, sports and entertainment genius Sonny Werblin bought the ailing Titans and rejuvenated them as the New York Jets. By the end of the 1963 season, the skeptics were predicting that the AFL might have a future after all. That prediction was confirmed a few weeks later, when AFL president Lamar Hunt signed a $36-million television contract with NBC. The AFL was on the scene to stay, and most of the credit was due to Lamar.

While Lamar made headlines, Herbert, the middle brother, quietly toiled as the heir apparent at Hunt Oil. His official title during much of this period was vice president of Hunt Oil Company, but his actual job was to coordinate all the family interests under the Hunt Oil umbrella. Herbert also acted as the unofficial mediator of internal family disputes. In addition to looking after the family oil interests, Herbert led the Hunt money into more real-estate investments. Among his major purchases were the first tracts in a land package eventually totaling over 6,000 acres in North Dallas and the suburbs of Plano and Richardson. Herbert bought some of these tracts at prices as low as $175 per acre; later he paid up to $40,000 an acre. True to the Hunt good fortune, the land deal Herbert put together later turned out to be worth hundreds of millions.

Far more conventional and sociable than their antipodean father, the children of H. L. Hunt's first family did not follow the typical stereotypes of the Texas rich. Margaret, for example, lived in exclusive Highland Park and was active in the DAR and Dallas high society, while her brother Herbert lived in less prestigious University Park, drove a Chevrolet, and liked to mow his own lawn. Caroline Sands had so low a profile and led so upper middle class a life that most people did not even know she was a Hunt. Bunker was beginning to take an interest in horse breeding, but his main pleasures were eating and watching SMU football and basketball games. Lamar, appropriately enough, liked to shoot baskets in his driveway. Though friends claimed they were not always as pure as they appeared, "the boys" were definitely not playboys. They worked ten-hour days, wore inexpensive and unflashy suits, attended church on Sundays, and raised families. The only one to divorce was Lamar, who remarried a schoolteacher and former Dallas Texans promotional assistant in 1964.

Hunt's secret family by Frania Tye Lee did not fare as well as the children of Lyda Bunker Hunt. For one thing, they did not have nearly as large a financial nest egg. Frania regularly got her $2,000 per month from Hunt Oil as provided by the 1942 settlement agreement. But where the Loyal Trusts set up for the children of Lyda Bunker Hunt were worth hundreds of millions of dollars, the Reliance Trusts set up for Frania's children were worth only a hundred thousand dollars or so and provided yearly incomes of only about $6,000 apiece. Though hardly poverty-stricken, Frania and her brood did not have the kind of money expected of a family of one of the world's richest men.

Frania and her children experienced quite a bit of emotional frustration as well. In the fall of 1956, a little over a year after Lyda Hunt's death, Frania and John Lee separated in Atlanta. A few months later, Frania filed suit against Lee over the title to their Flowerland home and the 747-acre Napier Plantation, both of which had been purchased with Frania's settlement money from H. L. Hunt but were listed in the names of both John Lee and Frania. Frania's attorney in the suit was Griffin Bell, the man who was to become U.S. attorney general under President Jimmy Carter. Lee apparently agreed to sign over the deeds, for a short time later Frania dropped her suit over the titles and filed for divorce. In her divorce petition, Frania complained of "mental cruelty" caused by her husband "continually fussing, nagging, quarreling and staying away from home at extended intervals during which . . . [she] knew nothing of [his] whereabouts." Lee did not contest the divorce, and a decree was entered on June 17, 1957. There was no property settlement.

Since Frania's separation from John Lee happened to take place soon after Lyda Hunt's death, some of those familiar with the unpublicized intricacies of the Hunt patriarchy speculated that the real reason for the breakup was not John Lee's alleged "mental cruelty" but Frania's still burning desire to marry H. L. Hunt. If so, Frania's desires were never realized. Although Hunt was informed of Frania's divorce, there was no record of any contact between them, much less of a proposal of marriage. Instead of becoming Mrs. H. L. Hunt, Frania sold her Flowerland home to the Catholic Church, which turned the property into a girls' school, and bought a large Tudor-style home in Ansley Park, one of Atlanta's finer old inner-city neighborhoods.

Known as the DeGive house for its former owners, Frania's new home became the center for an even more elaborate round of parties than those she held at Flowerland. It also became the center of a public controversy between Frania and her Ansley Park neighbors when Frania proceeded to divide the carriage house into apartment units. While the Ansley Park civic association complained to city hall that Frania was doing her construction without a permit, Frania kept her contractors right on working. By the time the matter could be heard, Frania's apartments were finished. In the end, Frania made peace with and eventually joined the Ansley Park civic association, but she never gained entrée to Atlanta's high society. Instead, amid persistent rumors that she was "monied by H. L. Hunt," Fran Lee remained a member of the same "peripheral society" she had been associating with for years.

Meanwhile, all four of Frania's children showed scars from their unusual family legacy. Frania's oldest daughter Haroldina showed the effects most graphically. A graduate of Agnes Scott College in Decatur, Haroldina was the wife of a local doctor and the mother of seven children. But like her half brother Hassie, she suffered some serious mental problems. The exact nature and source of her problems were not clear, but the family was told that Haroldina's illness may have been a form of schizophrenia caused by a chemical imbalance. Since most of her problems seemed to occur in connection with pregnancy, it was surmised that an overproduction of adrenaline might be to blame. While Haroldina's illness was apparently not as severe as Hassie's, she could not be helped by psychotherapy. She did not undergo a lobotomy, but she did take electric-shock treatments.

In this case, Hunt's peculiar behavior could not be directly blamed for Haroldina's problems. Unlike Hassie, Haroldina was not subjected to an overdose of fatherly attention and demands. And when Haroldina's problems became apparent, Hunt devoted almost as much time to finding a "cure" for her as he did for finding a "cure" for Hassie. But as one of Haroldina's brothers noted, schizophrenia was widely believed to be a "disease of superior people" that was quite possibly inherited. In other words, Haroldina's illness may well have been a case of Hunt's "genius gene" gone awry.

Haroldina's younger brother Hugh displayed a more Oedipal form of reaction to being a child of H. L. Hunt. Tall and broad-shouldered with a square jaw and puffy cheeks, Hugh was the spitting image of his father about the time H.L. made the Dad Joiner deal. Hugh prided himself on his intelligence. "I know my father loved Helen [Hugh's sister] more than he loved me," he said later, "but he liked me because I was smart." After attending Marist College Preparatory School, Hugh went to Georgia Tech. He later spent two years at Harvard Law School, but left without obtaining a degree. He eventually returned to Atlanta, married, and began fathering a family of eight children. But as he later admitted quite candidly, Hugh was beset by "an identity problem." Born in Great Neck, Long Island, after his father's first big breakup with Frania, he was only seven years old when his mother married John Lee. Between childhood and adulthood he went through no less than four name changes from Hugh Richard Hunt to Hue R. Lee to Hue Richard Lee and, later, to Hugh Lee Hunt. Through all these name changes, he seemed to be seeking both the truth about himself and his father's love and recognition.

Unlike their half brothers Bunker, Herbert, and Lamar, neither Howard nor Hugh demonstrated exceptional business talents. After starting out as a roughneck (on non-Hunt oil properties), Howard became an oil investor and a self-employed mechanical engineer. Hugh became a real-estate developer in Atlanta. The conventional wisdom in real-estate circles was that Hugh blew a lot of his mother's money on imprudent investments. True or not, both Howard, who tended to be somewhat sickly, and Hugh, who was physically more robust, eventually found themselves going back to their father to ask for loans of several hundred thousand dollars.

The saddest development in Frania's branch of the family in Hunt's view was what happened to Frania's daughter Helen. After returning to Atlanta from her stint as a New York actress, Helen married a local real estater named William Cartledge, gave birth to a son who was christened Ronald, and founded the Theater Atlanta Women's Guild. On May 9, 1962, Helen and her husband left Atlanta for a month-long Art Association tour of Europe. On June 3, their plane crashed outside of Orly Airport in Paris killing them and 126 other passengers in one of the worst air disasters in history.

Helen's death was both a civic and a family tragedy. The local press eulogized her for her support of the arts and lamented that her death "symbolizes the kind of loss Atlanta has had to absorb since the crash." In her grief, Frania established a memorial to her daughter called the Helen L. Cartledge Excellence Award. Meant as an honor for actors and actresses, the award evolved into a sort of local Tony. Frania also agreed to become a patron of Theater Atlanta, her daughter's favorite performing-arts interest, and took over the care and raising of her orphaned grandson, four-year-old Ronnie Cartledge.

As Frania's surviving children grew older, they began to see their father more regularly than in the past. Their contact was still infrequent and brief, but at least they did see each other two or three times per year. Their gatherings usually took place in Shreveport or Dallas. Sometimes the children would meet their father in a restaurant; on other occasions, they would go right up to Hunt's office. Hugh later recalled visiting Dallas and staying at Mount Vernon. H.L. didn't exactly issue a press release about their arrival, but, as Hugh put it, "he never denied us." Indeed, on a few occasions in the confines of the Hunt offices, Popsy Hunt went out of his way to make clear that he was the Lee children's natural father.

Despite all the family turmoil that had transpired, Frania's children did not find their father an unloving patriarch. "My father was not cold," Hugh said years later, adding that judging Hunt by his actions in scenes like the 1942 settlement-agreement battle in the Hotel Adolphus was like "judging a football player only by what you see him do when he's on the field." Although Hunt was relatively stingy toward the Reliance Trusts, when Howard or Hugh came around asking for a business loan of a few hundred thousand dollars, their father usually complied. And when he received word that his beloved Helen was killed in the Paris plane crash, Popsy Hunt was truly crushed. "He just sat there in a remorsed condition," his aide John Curington recalled afterward. "It really hurt him. It was one of the few times I really felt sorry for him."

Like his secret family by Frania, Popsy Hunt's family by Ruth also had its share of mixed blessings. Known as the "second" family, though they were chronologically Hunt's third, Ruth and her children now had the advantage of being recognized as Hunts. Unlike Frania and her children, they were not a secret. But they did not have the same status as the first family. Dallas society did not buy the myths Hunt put out after his marriage to Ruth. Finally, Ruth decided the best thing for all concerned was to quiet the rumors with the truth. She then let be known what anyone could tell by looking—that her children were not the offspring of a former marriage but the offspring of H. L. Hunt.

Much to Ruth's dismay, gossipers and journalists began referring to Ruth as a former "mistress" and remarking that her children were "born out of wedlock." The sting of these comments was not absolved by the fact that with Hunt's late-life emergence as a political figure, Ruth, at least, was even more frequently identified in public as "Mrs. H. L. Hunt" than Lyda had ever been.

Having lived in unusual circumstances for over fifteen years, Ruth had adopted a happy personal motto: "Bloom Where You Are Planted." She hung the saying on the kitchen wall at Mount Vernon. That was the most major redecoration she made. The gilt-edged mirrors stayed in the front hall, the historic-scenes wallpaper remained on the dining-room walls, and the living room kept its eclectic assortment of couches, chairs, side tables, and paintings, with new pieces being added and old ones deleted mostly on her husband's initiative. Ruth's basic life style also remained remarkably the same. She did not begin putting on airs or wearing fancy clothes. On the contrary, she dressed in inexpensive knits and cottons and hunted for bargains like any ordinary housewife. Her greatest show of opulence was having a governess for the children and a company of cooks and maids to help in the kitchen. She had neither a chauffeur nor a limousine. Like her husband, she drove an ordinary sedan.

When not traveling with her husband, Ruth plunged into the work of the household. She kept the dinner table stocked with the nonsugar, nonflour treats Hunt grew to like, and helped prepare the brown-paper-sack lunches he took to the office. But Ruth was at her best when she would sit down at the piano in the living room and conduct one of the family singalongs Hunt seemed to love so well. Most of the songs were country gospel numbers or traditional American farm ditties or little bits of composition that H.L. had "composed" himself, often by rewriting his own words to an old tune. Ruth had a pleasant voice and she loved to sing, so she began expanding the singalongs to include friends, members of her church, and Hunt Oil Company employees. Like her husband, she abstained from wine and liquor, and served her guests such substitutes as carrot juice and cranberry juice.

Rather than being gifted with some sort of "genius gene" inherited from their father, Ruth's children seemed to be talented overachievers blessed with their mother's kindness of heart. At the time of their mother's marriage in 1957, they were ages fourteen, thirteen, eight, and seven. A short time later, they changed last names, changed schools, and for all intents and purposes changed lives. These changes definitely took their toll, but on the whole, Ruth's children seemed to follow their mother's motto.

The exemplar of the second family was Ray Lee, the oldest child and only son, who had prompted his father to marry his mother. After his mother's marriage, Ray transferred from Greenhill School, a private academy where he had been known as Ray Wright, to St. Mark's, the exclusive Dallas boys' prep school, where he enrolled as Ray Hunt. Ray Hunt proceeded to become Mr. Everything at St. Mark's, compiling a longer list of student activities than anyone else in his class. He was editor of the newspaper, chief photographer for the yearbook, president of the band, and a member of the football and track teams. In his senior year, he was elected class president partly because of the efforts of a good friend and classmate whose life would take a vastly different turn from his own, future rock star Steve Miller. "Ray was not the most popular guy in the class," a long-time friend remembered later. "He was elected because we thought he could get the most done."

Ray worked hard, made good grades, and got into the college of his choice, which was Southern Methodist University. At SMU, he studied economics and met his future bride, Nancy Hunter. During the summers, Ray worked down at Hunt Oil Company. He was a cheerful, unassuming young man, popular with the office staff. Like his father, he seemed to defy the apparel of the rich, preferring instead to appear at work in old suits that were a bit tattered and out of fashion.

Ray's younger sister, Ruth June, also showed herself to be an overachiever. The namesake of both her mother and father, she went by the name June and the nickname "Peaches." Blond and broad-shouldered, she had the almost hawklike features of her father and the Christian disposition of her mother. After transferring to the exclusive Hockaday School for Girls in Dallas as a shy, young teenager, she came out of her shell and excelled as president of the school choir. She also took up the guitar and became active in religious youth work at the First Baptist Church.

June rebelled only when it came time to pick colleges. She wanted to attend predominantly Baptist Baylor University in Waco. Her father wanted her to attend SMU in Dallas. June tried to fail the entrance tests at SMU, and wrote on her admissions application, "I do not wish to attend S.M.U. . . . My father merely wishes me to apply." Alas, June's plan failed. She was rejected by Baylor and accepted at SMU.

"I entered S.M.U. with my personal philosophy, 'Make the best of all situations or they'll get the best of you' (1 June 3:16)," she wrote later. "Surprisingly enough, honors began coming to me early in my freshman year and continued until I graduated. The entry of my name in *Who's Who in American Colleges and Universities,* and receiving the most coveted award for outstanding contribution, and other honors, along with my happiness at S.M.U. served as a verification that God had spoken to me through my father."

June's younger sisters Helen and Swanee had more peculiar parental demands to contend with. As the youngest of all the Hunt children, they received the most pampering, such as it was, but they were also thrust into the public's eye much more prominently than Ray or June. Helen and Swanee, were, in a word, cute. Helen was a slender brunette with beautiful skin and facial features. Swanee was a plump, vivacious blond. Having recognized their potential as advertisers in the course of the family singalongs, Popsy Hunt had pressed them into service with the publication of *Alpaca* and made them sing his silly little promotional jingle. But their father did not stop there. Later, he had his daughters rehearse patriotic songs he would compose to the tune of familiar American folk songs. One such composition, written to the tune of "School Days," went like this:

> Youth days, truth days
> Freedom's golden rule days;
> Join us and take a determined stand
> For freedom and liberty in our land;
> Listen to what our Popsy said,
> Don't give an inch to any Red.
> Give liberty the highest bids
> With the help from a couple of kids.

At first, the girls appeared to enjoy singing Popsy's songs and being the center of attention. But as they grew older, their singing routine became embarrassing. "There were times when I was a teenager," Swanee, the youngest, remarked later, "when I would have given anything to be in a normal family."

Even without such public displays, life with Popsy could be an ambivalent experience all the way around. The house was a whirl of activities whose schedule and character was determined primarily by Popsy's eccentricities. Some of the old man's habits had benign effects. For example, among the most detested of Popsy's penchants—in the eyes of his children—were his belief in the healthful properties of apricot seeds and his belief in the detrimental effects of white sugar. The Hunt children were deprived of ordinary sweets and candy and deluged with apricot-based substitutes. As June recalled, "We had apricot whips and apricot toppings, stewed apricots, just plain apricots, apricot cobbler, apricot jam and jelly, apricot cake—any and all forms of apricots."

The children also sat through special sessions their father would call from time to time to expound on anything from politics to household economics. One of the most memorable of these sessions was Popsy's lecture on electricity usage. Popsy began the seminar by passing out sheets of paper filled with statistics such as the following:

> 1—100-watt bulb cost 4¢ to burn for 1 hour
> 1—150-watt bulb cost 6¢ to burn for 1 hour
> 1—200-watt bulb cost 8¢ to burn for 1 hour

Popsy then commenced to read the statistics aloud so that everyone there would understand how much it cost to use electricity and would therefore be mindful of conserving it in the future. "I can still see us sitting there, holding our papers, while Dad very seriously went over the entire electrical system with us," June recalled years afterward. "I assure you, none of us laughed, yet we didn't take [his] wattage seminar too seriously either."

It was not hard to see why. At the same time that he lectured his children to conserve electricity, the old man had a huge spotlight illuminating the

American flag on the front lawn and, nearby, a tree decorated with hundreds of twinkling white lights. H.L. justified these extravagances in the name of freedom and patriotism. "You see, someone passing by on the street might not see the flag at first, but they'll see the lighted tree and then their attention will be drawn to the flag," Hunt told his children. "It's important they see the flag."

At the same time that he frustrated his children with his eccentricities, Popsy Hunt also compelled them to achieve. Rather than tell them how to do something, he always urged them to go out and find out how things were done. As June wrote later, Popsy demanded more than Ruthie—and he got it.

Popsy Hunt never managed to unite the three branches of his patriarchy. The closest thing to a full Hunt family reunion was a touch football game all his sons (except Hassie) played on the lawn at Mount Vernon one afternoon in the fall of 1960. On one team there were Bunker, Herbert, and Lamar, his sons by Lyda Bunker Hunt. On the other team, there were Howard Lee and Hue Lee, his sons by Frania, and Ray, his son by Ruth. Popsy himself sat up on the porch watching his children play in their stocking feet.

The real game for all three of H. L. Hunt's families during the late 1950s and early 1960s was not touch football, but vying for the old man's love and money. Money had an emotional importance. Being a money maker was not only an end in itself, but a way to earn Hunt's attention and respect. The size of each family's share of the Hunt empire was in more than one sense a measure of their standing in the eyes of the patriarch. Or so many of Hunt's children seemed to believe.

If Frania's family was the most dispossessed on the financial score, the first family felt the most displaced on every score. Lyda's children had, after all, preceded the others. Though Ruth tried to make them feel that Mount Vernon was still their home, too, they could not seem to accept her overtures at face value. Just as in a game of touch football, they interpreted any advance by one of the other sides as a setback for themselves. And in a way, they were right. They had once been the one and only; now, increasingly, they had to share. They had already tied up the greatest portion of the old man's money but they were still insecure, uncertain, and ambivalent about the old man's love. Thus, even more urgently than the other two sides, the first family strove to climb ever higher in the hierarchy of Popsy's affections. One of the more graphic examples of the first family's attitudes was revealed when Margaret Hunt Hill presented a copy of the Hunt-Bunker genealogy to the New York Public Library. Margaret struck through the line on the title page which said "Prepared for Mrs. H. L. Hunt" and wrote in the words "Lyda Bunker Hunt," as if to make sure that the two Mrs. H. L. Hunts would never be confused.

Appropriately enough, the means the first family found to be the most successful in getting closer to the patriarch were politics. Money played a big part in Hunt family politics. The first family and the companies owned by their trusts had been active contributors to Facts Forum. In the late 1950s and early 1960s, they also became active contributors to LIFE LINE and supporters of a range of other right-wing political enterprises. The more money they gave, the more they seemed to rise in the old man's favor.

Margaret's husband Al, who was often mentioned as H.L.'s heir apparent, was also the biggest political giver. As one reporter observed, Hill's contributing grew out of "sincere belief . . . as well as son-in-law diplomacy." By late 1963, Hill had given at least $5,000 to Facts Forum and $5,000 to LIFE LINE, and thousands more to other arch-conservative causes. In 1964, he gave $2,500 to Republican Jack Cox's effort to oust incumbent Texas governor John Connally. The support of Hill, Bunker Hunt, and the Sands was enough to convince Cox to stay in the race, but Cox nevertheless ended up losing badly. H.L.'s aide John Curington later alleged that he also made several large and unreported cash contributions on Hill's behalf.

Hill's political activities were not confined to money giving. In the early 1960s, LIFE LINE sent out a brochure quoting Hill as saying that "New York, headquarters of the Eastern Establishment, is nearer socialist and communist influence than any of the other forty-nine states. . . . Even the most enlightened patriotism is unbearable to the ESTABS. . . . Jefferson, Washington, and Lincoln, who nurtured the thirteen colonies into a great nation and wiped out slavery, were not domiciled in New York."

Hill later devised a project of his own which reportedly made a very favorable impression on H. L. Hunt. The name of Hill's project was "the Prospect Plan." Its aim was to find and recruit talented, right-thinking conservatives for the Republican party. This was to be done not by means of an open forum, but through a secret talent-scout organization of affluent citizens and FBI men. Hill's plan called for the chosen prospects to be educated with LIFE LINE literature, then ushered around to various speaking engagements by their affluent and well-connected sponsor. Billed as a way to "safeguard our nation from a blitz Communist takeover and halt the fatal swing toward Socialism," the Prospect Plan was really an outline for merging H. L. Hunt's political movement unto himself with the Republican party. But for all its ambitiousness, the plan never seemed to get off the ground.

Along with Al Hill, the most active politico in the first family was Bunker Hunt. Bunker's interest in politics was also a combination of sincere belief and family diplomacy. Passed over as the heir apparent, Bunker saw in politics a way to show his father that he, too, had something on the ball. Like the other members of the first family, Bunker contributed generously to H.L.'s pet political projects. According to a report by the House Small Business Subcommittee, Bunker gave $35,000 to LIFE LINE alone between 1957 and 1960. In addition to following in his father's political footsteps, Bunker found a mentor in John Birch Society founder Robert Welch. For Bunker, the John Birch Society seemed to represent a right-minded way to express his political beliefs on his own. Robert Welch became a kind of surrogate ideological father for Bunker, educating him on the Bircher outlook and advising him on how to help the cause. Bunker entertained Welch in his Dallas home and began to contribute what he had the most to offer—money.

At the same time, Bunker did not let his involvement with the Birchers prevent him from participating in his father's political projects. Rather, Bunker saw the two as complementary, and with good reason. In addition to sharing a paranoid right-wing view of the world, both H. L. Hunt and the John Birch Society were vehement critics of President Kennedy. Although Hunt voted for the Kennedy-Johnson ticket in the 1960 election, he had spent much LIFE LINE time and money attacking Kennedy and Kennedy policies ever since. Bunker joined his father's anti-Kennedy bandwagon publicly in September of 1963 when he and Hunt sent letters to the U.S. Senate denouncing the Kennedy-supported nuclear test ban treaty.

As fate would have it, the Hunts' anti-Kennedy letters did not turn out to be the beginning of a new father-and-son intimacy but the beginning of their entanglement in a national tragedy. For a few weeks after the Hunts sent their letters to the Senate, the White House announced that President Kennedy would be making a trip to Texas. Kennedy's trip was not prompted by the Hunts' letters. Rather, it was urged upon him by advisers who feared a schism in the mainstream of the state's Democratic party over the growing unpopularity of Vice President Lyndon Johnson. But the destinies of the Hunts and President Kennedy became irrevocably intertwined when it was revealed that the last stop on the president's swing through Texas would be Dallas.

CHAPTER 10

WELCOME, MR. KENNEDY, TO DALLAS

THE Hunts learned that President Kennedy's visit to Dallas might be greeted with violence nearly three weeks before the president crossed the state line. The warning came from the family's master intelligence man, Hunt Oil security chief Paul Rothermel. In a November 4, 1963, interoffice memo headlined "POLITICS," Rothermel informed his boss that there had been "unconfirmed reports of possible violence during the parade" scheduled to take place when Kennedy arrived in town on November 22. Although Rothermel did not directly identify his sources, it was clear from his memo that he was sharing information the FBI and the Dallas Police Department were getting from informants placed in General Edwin Walker's right-wing political action groups in Dallas and on the campus of North Texas State University in Denton.

"The North Texas informant is reporting information that would indicate that that group may be planning an incident," Rothermel wrote. "There is another report from a left-wing group than an incident will occur with the knowledge of the President whereby the left-wingers will start the incident in hopes of dragging in any of the right side groups or individuals nearby and then withdrawing. The talk is that the incident involving Adlai Stevenson made the present administration hopeful in that if they could get the same thing to happen to Kennedy it could reassure his election."

Given what had been happening in Dallas politics, Rothermel's ominous report did not seem farfetched. A city whose population was as conservative as any in Texas, Dallas had become a kind of capital for the far right. The city abounded with John Birch Society cells, chapters of Young Americans for Freedom, and various better- and lesser-known independent groups like those sponsored by Walker and Hunt. Although they comprised only a fraction of the total electorate, the far-right-wingers were becoming increasingly vocal and increasingly paranoid. Less visible and less numerous were the right-wingers' principal enemies, the left-wingers. Since no more than 20 percent of the city could be accused of voting "liberal" in the traditional sense of the term, the left-wingers had a much smaller pool of potential recruits and sympathizers. But since the right-wingers considered anyone who was in favor of civil rights or the United Nations to be a left-winger, there were always plenty of people and things for the right-wingers to demonstrate against.

In the spring of 1963, the politics of the extremists had turned violent. One night in April, someone had fired a rifle at General Walker as he sat alone in his study working on his income-tax return. The bullet missed Walker by only a few millimeters. Its potential, however, was made clear by the fact that it tore a golf-ball-sized hole in the nine-inch-thick wall of Walker's study; it also shattered the study's window and showered Walker with fragments of glass, bloodying his right arm. To Walker, who had just returned from a right-wing crusade with evangelist Billy James Hargis, the message was clear. The "other side," as he called his political opponents, had tried to assassinate him. When newsmen arrived at the scene, Walker pointed to the hole in the wall and remarked with a derisive laugh, "The Kennedys say there's no internal threat to our freedom." Although Walker's assailant was never apprehended, the incident went down as the year's first act of political violence in Dallas.

Six months after the Walker episode, Dallas had suffered "the incident involving Adlai Stevenson" that Rothermel mentioned in his memo to Hunt. The Stevenson incident took place on October 24, 1963, when the United Nations ambassador was in town for U.N. Day ceremonies. As Stevenson was delivering his speech, a handful of right-wing demonstrators ran up to the podium and spat on him. Stevenson went on to finish his speech despite the disruption, and came out of the incident looking like a hero, but both the right-wing demonstrators and the city of Dallas were stamped with infamy— at least as far as the national public was concerned. To some Dallasites, of course, Stevenson had gotten just what he deserved.

With President Kennedy coming to town so close on the heels of the Stevenson visit, it was not unreasonable to expect disruptions of the sort reportedly being planned by the right-wingers and the left-wingers. But while the local law-enforcement officials had been tipped off to the possibility of a violent demonstration, there had been no publicity about it. As Rothermel pointed out in his memo to Hunt, "If an incident were to occur, the true story of who perpetrated it would never come out." Rothermel, however, had a solution to suggest. "I have thought about the problem," he wrote, "and I am wondering if a few letters to the editor might not be a good way of pre-exposing this if, in fact, there is a planned incident."

Hunt apparently considered his security chief's advice to be sound. Although he did not "pre-expose" the details he had learned about the possible disruptions in the works, Hunt did write a letter to the editor on November 8, 1963. In that letter, Hunt cautioned, "Those who take pride in being 'right of center' may be led astray to demonstrate against speakers for their opposition. A demonstration can be started by some of the less judicious of them. One may even be started by the opposition acting as decoys to rope in patriots to cause them to look ill-mannered. Hostility toward speakers is a very workable way of gaining them tolerance and sympathy. Patriots have the truth and the facts on their side and they need only to get their case stated as widely as possible. They should not build up fireworks which create interest in the appearance of their opponents. They can much better spend their time visiting among themselves or, better yet, making friends with patriots to be found in their church, in school, on the staff of all newspapers, in the entertainment field, and networks and stations."

Exactly where and how widely Hunt circulated this letter to the editor was never revealed. Hunt later reprinted it in a collection called *Old Letters to the Editor,* but he never indicated the publications to which it was sent, and there was no sign of it in either of the Dallas newspapers in the days preceding Kennedy's visit.

Meanwhile, the political operations of H. L. Hunt proceeded with business as usual. Hunt made no effort to arrange a personal audience with President Kennedy or Vice President Johnson and had no special plans to watch the presidential motorcade, which was scheduled to pass down Main Street right below his office window. LIFE LINE, for its part, kept right on broadcasting the same right-wing themes it had always broadcast, and kept on pounding its anti-Kennedy line. Proclaiming that the times demanded "extreme patriotism," LIFE LINE's commentators warned their audience that the Kennedy administration was bypassing the laws of Congress, following policies pleasing to Moscow, suppressing those who spoke out for freedom, and causing American taxpayers to subsidize communism around the world.

On November 4, 1963, the same day Rothermel wrote his memo warning the Hunts of "unconfirmed reports of possible violence" during Kennedy's visit, a group of ambitious young right-wingers was gathering in Dallas to prepare a special welcome for the president. The group consisted of three former army buddies, all of whom were in their mid-twenties. Their names were Larrie H. Schmidt, Bernard W. Weissman, and William B. Burley III, and their long-range goal was nothing less than the unification of right-wing America under their own personal leadership.

While serving together in Munich in 1962, Schmidt, Weissman, and Burley had devised plans to form two secret right-wing organizations to help accomplish their aim. The first was to be strictly political in nature and was called "Conservatism—USA," or "CUSA." The second organization was to be a business entity called "American Business" or "AMBUS." Like the interlocking political and financial organization H. L. Hunt had formed with LIFE LINE and HLH Products, CUSA and AMBUS were envisioned to be mutually complementary organizations, linking patriotism with profit making. But unlike LIFE LINE and HLH Products, CUSA and AMBUS were supposed to keep a low profile—at least in the beginning.

"We knew it would be almost impossible to start from scratch and build a powerful organization," Weissman recalled, "so we planned to infiltrate various right-wing organizations . . . become involved in the hierarchy of these organizations . . . get ourselves elected or appointed to various higher offices in these organizations . . . and eventually take over the leadership of these organizations, and at that time having our people in these various organizations, we would then, you might say, call a conference and have them unite, and while no one knew of the existence of CUSA aside from us, we would then bring them all together, unite them, and arrange to have it called CUSA."

Schmidt, who was the first of the three CUSA-AMBUS founders to finish his stint in the army, had moved to Dallas in October of 1962 to get things rolling. Upon his arrival, he had found a job as a life-insurance salesman, and had become active in various right-wing groups. Schmidt had also written Weissman and Burley with repeated urgings to come join him in Dallas. But after a year had passed, Weissman and Burley still had not come, and Schmidt had grown impatient. On October 1, 1963, some seven weeks before Kennedy was to arrive, Schmidt had written Weissman: "Adlai Stevenson is scheduled here on the 24th on U.N. Day. Kennedy is scheduled in Dallas on November 24th [sic]. There are to be protests. All the big things are happening now— if we don't get in right now we may as well forget it."

The day of the Stevenson demonstration Schmidt had telephoned Weissman with another urging to "hurry down here and take advantage of the publicity, and at least become known among these various right-wingers" so that the three CUSA founders could follow up on the plans they had developed back in Munich. Five days later, Schmidt had written Weissman and Burley again. This time he had told them that as the "only organizer of the demonstration to have publicly identified himself I have become, overnight, a 'fearless spokesman' and 'leader' of the right-wing in Dallas. What I worked so hard for in one year—and nearly failed—finally came through one incident in one night! . . . Politically, CUSA is set. It is now up to you to get AMBUS going."

Weissman and Burley finally took Schmidt's advice and arrived in Dallas in early November of 1963. The two newcomers both found jobs as carpet salesmen. Then, at Schmidt's urging, the three CUSA founders decided to join the local chapter of the John Birch Society. It was at this point that the three became associated with Joseph P. Grinnan, a Dallas independent oil operator who was also the area coordinator for the John Birch Society and an acquaintance of Nelson Bunker Hunt.

A short time after the CUSA-AMBUS founders joined up with the Birchers, Grinnan, Schmidt, Weissman, and Burley got together to consider what they should do regarding President Kennedy's scheduled arrival in Dallas several days hence. The upshot of their meeting was the idea of placing a carefully worded "open letter"–style advertisement in the morning newspaper. "After the Stevenson incident, it was felt that a demonstration would be entirely out of order, because we didn't want anything to happen in the way of physical violence to President Kennedy when he came to Dallas," Weissman explained later. "But we thought that the conservatives in Dallas—I was told —were a pretty downtrodden lot after that, because they were being oppressed by the local liberals, because of the Stevenson incident. We felt we had to do something to build up the morale of the conservative element in Dallas. So we hit upon the idea of the ad."

The principal authors of the advertisement were Grinnan, Schmidt, and Weissman. The text of the ad was taken from a right-wing pamphlet containing fifty questions critical of American policy in general and the Kennedy administration in particular. Most of the questions were highly inflammatory and rhetorical in nature, and focused on U.S. foreign policy and communism. Among the twelve finally selected for the advertisement were the following:

Why do you say we have built a "wall of freedom" around Cuba when there is no freedom in Cuba today? Because of your policy, thousands of Cubans have been imprisoned, are starving and being persecuted —with thousands already murdered and thousands more awaiting execution and, in addition, the entire population of almost 7,000,000 Cubans are living in slavery.

Why have you approved the sale of wheat and corn to our enemies when you know the Communist soldiers "travel on their stomachs" just as ours do? Communist soldiers are daily wounding and/or killing American soldiers in South Viet Nam.

Why has Gus Hall, head of the U. S. Communist Party, praised almost every one of your policies and announced that the party will endorse and support your re-election in 1964?

Why have you ordered or permitted your brother Bobby, the Attorney General, to go soft on Communists, fellow travelers, and ultra-leftists in America, while permitting him to persecute loyal Americans who criticize you, your administration, and your leadership?

Why has the Foreign Policy of the United States degenerated to the point that the C.I.A. is arranging coups and having staunch Anti-Communist Allies of the U. S. bloodily exterminated?

Grinnan, Weissman, and Schmidt typed these and other questions on a sheet of paper below the heading "WELCOME, MR. KENNEDY." Between the headline and the text of the ad, they typed the words, "TO DALLAS," and a series of four lines preceded by ellipses which read:

...A CITY so disgraced by a recent Liberal smear attempt that its citizens have just elected two more Conservative Americans to public office.

...A CITY that is an economic "boom town," not because of Federal handouts, but through conservative economic and business practices.

...A CITY that will continue to grow and prosper despite efforts by you and your administration to penalize it for non-conformity to "New Frontierism."

. . . A CITY that rejected your philosophy and policies in 1960 and will
do so again in 1964—even more emphatically than before.

"MR. KENNEDY," the advertisement continued, "despite contentions
on the part of your administration, the State Department, the Mayor of Dallas,
the Dallas City Council, and members of your party, we free-thinking and
America-thinking citizens of Dallas still have, through a Constitution largely
ignored by you, the right to address our grievances, to question you, to disagree
with you, to criticize you. In asserting this constitutional right, we wish to ask
you publicly the following questions—indeed questions of paramount importance and interest to all free people everywhere—which we trust you will
answer . . . in public, without sophistry."

After finishing the text of the ad, Grinnan, Weissman, and Schmidt
invented a fictitious sponsoring organization, which they dubbed "The American Fact-Finding Committee." As Weissman testified, this was "solely a
name." Nevertheless, it was Bernard Weissman who was listed as "chairman"
of the American Fact-Finding Committee in the space below the questions.
This was done in part to counter charges that Dallas conservatives were
anti-Semitic and in part to afford anonymity to those who might want to help
pay for the ad. As a final touch, Weissman suggested outlining the ad with a
black border so as to draw reader attention to it.

Grinnan then set about raising the $1,400 necessary to run the ad in the
Dallas Morning News. He solicited the money from three wealthy Dallas
businessmen. One was Edgar Crissey, an insurance executive with E. F. White
& Associates. Crissey himself contributed only $15 for the ad, but proceeded
to raise another $135 from "two or three other people" whom he later refused
to name. Grinnan also solicited a contribution from H. R. "Bum" Bright, then
an independent oilman and later chairman of the board of East Texas Motor
Freight, a large trucking concern. Bright later claimed that Grinnan approached him in the company of another individual whom he refused to name.
Bright said that he himself did not have the money to contribute to the
advertisement. However, Bright did put up "$300 or $400" on behalf of his
unnamed friend, considering the money "a loan."

The third businessman Grinnan solicited was fellow John Birch Society
supporter Nelson Bunker Hunt. Having been a friend and supporter of Bircher
leader Robert Welch for some time, Bunker was a likely prospect to help
finance an ad that was basically a rewrite of Bircher literature. According to
later testimony, Bunker did not actually see the text of the ad, but had it
described to him by Joe Grinnan. Concluding that the ad was a "dignified"
way of criticizing the president, Bunker decided to contribute "between $200
and $300" for the ad, which money he peeled off from a fat roll of bills he
happened to have in his pocket when Grinnan dropped in.

On November 18, four days before Kennedy was scheduled to arrive,
Weissman took the ad copy down to the *Dallas Morning News* office and put
up a $500 cash deposit on behalf of "The American Fact-Finding Committee."

The ad-department man at the *Morning News* informed him that the paper did run political ads, but that the content would have to be checked with the paper's lawyers first. Two days later, on November 20, Weissman returned to the *News* to find out what the lawyers had determined. He was told that the advertisement had been approved. At that point, Weissman put up the rest of the $1,400 fee. Everything was set.

The day after Bernard Weissman completed arrangements for the "WEL-COME, MR. KENNEDY" ad, a fat and balding strip-club owner named Jack Ruby drove from suburban Oak Cliff to the downtown offices of H. L. Hunt's son Lamar. Exactly what Ruby was thinking or planning at the time was never disclosed. But according to later testimony, it was a curiously innocent set of circumstances that led to Ruby's trip. Those circumstances were embodied by the passenger sitting next to him in the car, a pretty girl named Connie Trammel.

Ruby had met Miss Trammel the previous April when she and a group of college friends from the University of Texas paid a visit to Ruby's Carousel Club in downtown Dallas across from the Hotel Adolphus. Ruby had been quick to appreciate Miss Trammel's physical charms, and had tried to persuade her to become a stripper. Connie had refused Ruby's invitation, but the two had parted friends.

In mid-November of 1963, having graduated with a degree in public relations from the University of Texas, Connie Trammel had returned to Dallas looking for a job. One day, she had telephoned Ruby and told him that she had an appointment to see Lamar Hunt the following afternoon. Lamar had recently purchased a bowling alley and had announced plans of converting it into a teen club. Connie said she was hopeful of getting a job as the club's public-relations director. She had called Ruby on the chance that he might already know Lamar Hunt and thus be able to advise her on how to approach the interview.

Ruby said that he did not know Lamar, but was interested in meeting him, and asked how Connie had been able to get an appointment to see him. Connie told him that she had found Lamar's home phone number in the telephone directory. She said a maid had answered her call and had given her the number of a direct line to Hunt's office in the Mercantile National Bank building. Knowing that Connie did not have a car, Ruby offered to give her a ride downtown the next day, explaining that he had some business to transact at another downtown bank anyway. Connie gladly accepted his offer.

On the morning of November 21, Jack Ruby picked up Connie Trammel at her apartment and drove her downtown as he had promised. Connie later recalled that during their drive downtown Ruby mentioned that he knew most of the prominent people in Dallas, and could wave at them on the street and be recognized. But Ruby said Lamar Hunt was one man he did not know.

Interestingly enough, Ruby did not say anything to Connie Trammel about the Hunt family's politics. This omission was rather peculiar in light of the fact that only three weeks earlier Ruby had thrown a temper tantrum when he had come across an HLH Products booth at the Texas Products Show in the Dallas Exhibit Hall. As usual, the HLH samples had been displayed along with plenty of LIFE LINE political literature and broadcast scripts. Incensed by the political content of what he read, Ruby had grabbed up a handful of LIFE LINE scripts and rushed over to a friend who was exhibiting at another booth in the Texas Products show.

"I'm going to send this stuff to Kennedy," Ruby had declared, waving the LIFE LINE material in the air. "Nobody has any right to talk like this about our government."

"Well, you just know about it now, but LIFE LINE has been out for some time," Ruby's friend Edward J. Pullman had replied. "That's what Hunt does, and that's how he gets his material around."

"I'm going to do something about this," Ruby had said. "I'm going to see that this is taken up to Washington."

The way Pullman described it, Ruby had become "all excited and red-faced, livid." But then such outbursts were typical of Ruby. According to Pullman, Ruby was always blowing hot and cold, getting mad about something and treating it as if it were the most important thing in the world one moment, then forgetting about it a short time later. As it turned out, the H. L. Hunt booth happened to have been unattended when Ruby threw his fit, so there had been no responsible party on hand with whom he could have registered his complaint. Ruby had simply stuffed the LIFE LINE scripts in his pocket and stalked out of the exhibit hall.

By the time Ruby found himself driving Connie Trammel downtown to Lamar Hunt's office, he had apparently cooled off. The trip progressed with not one discouraging word from Ruby about the Hunts. On the contrary, Connie Trammel noticed that Ruby seemed to be particularly impressed with how much money Lamar Hunt had made. But then, as Pullman would later point out, Ruby's curiously contradictory attitudes toward the Hunts were typical of his "hot and cold" behavior about many things. The drive down to Lamar Hunt's office may have been just another disjointed episode in the life of a man whose mental balance was apparently becoming disjointed as well. Or it may have been part of an elaborate and still indiscernible design to link Jack Ruby with the Hunt family. There was no way to know.

When they reached downtown Dallas, Ruby stopped for a few minutes at the Merchants State Bank on Ross Avenue, then drove Connie the rest of the way to the Mercantile National Bank building. He parked the car in a lot near the building and escorted Miss Trammel into the lobby. Despite his expressed desire to meet Lamar, Ruby did not accompany Connie up to the Hunt offices. Instead, he stopped at the elevator bank and bid her good luck and good-bye.

Connie Trammel never saw or heard from Jack Ruby again. She also failed to get a job at Lamar Hunt's bowling alley.

The twenty-second of November dawned crisp and clear with the north Texas wind whistling through downtown Dallas like a runaway freight train. Editions of the *Dallas Morning News* carrying the black-bordered "WELCOME, MR. KENNEDY" ad were already billowing in the streets. So, too, were copies of a handbill allegedly printed by an associate of General Edwin A. Walker. The handbill, like the ad in the *Morning News,* was essentially a right-wing critique of the Kennedy administration, but the handbill's language was even stronger than the wording of the ad: at the top of the handbill in block letters was the proclamation "Wanted for Treason."

The LIFE LINE broadcast that morning was equally severe. Though the script did not refer to President Kennedy directly, it prophesied that if present trends were allowed to continue, there would come a day when Americans would no longer be allowed to own firearms. The broadcast pointed out that under communism, "No firearms are permitted the people, because they would then have the weapons with which to rise up against their oppressors."

H. L. Hunt arrived at his office that morning carrying his usual brown-paper-sack lunch. He had seen the black-bordered ad in the newspaper and the handbills circulating on the streets. He had listened to the LIFE LINE broadcast. There was every reason to believe that this barrage of Kennedy criticism would leave an impression on the visiting president. It only remained to be seen exactly what kind.

Jack Ruby also noticed the black-bordered "WELCOME, MR. KENNEDY" ad in the *Dallas Morning News,* and was none too pleased. About midmorning, he went down to the *Morning News* office to place an advertisement for one of his clubs. When he reached the newspaper building, Ruby decided to telephone his sister Eva Grant.

"Did you see the ad?" Ruby asked.

"What ad?" his sister replied.

"About the president," Ruby said.

Anxious to get off the phone, Ruby's sister stammered, "Yes, yes."

"Did you read it?" Ruby asked.

"Yes, yes," his sister answered. But her tone was unconvincing.

"Read it," Ruby said. "I'll call you later." Then he hung up. The time was shortly before noon, and Jack Ruby's mental state was becoming increasingly agitated.

A few minutes past noon, the presidential motorcade passed down Main Street, right below Hunt's office. It was then that Hunt realized he was in for a big surprise. He could see the motorcade from his suite, and he could hear the noisy cheering of the downtown crowd as Kennedy waved from the back seat of his open limousine. If the anti-Kennedy propaganda was having any effect, it appeared to be the opposite of what its authors intended. Dallas was giving the president a more tumultuous welcome than even Kennedy's most optimistic supporters could have hoped for.

As the motorcade turned off Main Street and headed up Houston Street, a wave of gratification for the warm reception swept over the passengers in the presidential limousine. Nellie Connally, wife of Texas governor John Connally, expressed everyone's feelings in words.

"Mr. President," she said turning in her seat, "you can't say Dallas doesn't love you."

"That is very obvious," the president replied with a smile.

A few moments later, the motorcade turned onto Dealey Plaza, and the president was assassinated.

The pandemonium that engulfed Dallas swept through the offices of Hunt Oil Company with gale force. Shortly after news bulletins of the assassination started coming over the radio, Hunt's wife Ruth called in. She was at the Phi Delta Theta fraternity house at SMU, visiting Ray. Hunt told her to stay put. Then the FBI called. The bureau man told Hunt what he already knew—that because of his prominence as a Kennedy critic, his own life and the lives of his family would probably be threatened as a result of the president's death. Hunt was advised that it would be better if he did not drive home that day. In fact, the FBI man said, it would be best if Hunt left town as soon as possible.

Hunt objected strenuously. Taking precautions to safeguard his family was one thing. Going into hiding was quite another. But the FBI man was insistent. Hunt had to go. Otherwise, there was no guarantee he would survive the next week.

By this time, Hunt's son Herbert, security chief Rothermel, and several members of the Hunt Oil staff had gathered in Hunt's office. Herbert and Rothermel urged Hunt to follow the FBI's advice. But Hunt could not be persuaded to go undercover.

"I believe I can do better going to Washington to help Lyndon," Hunt said. "He's gonna need some help."

Finally, in the face of Herbert and Rothermel's persistence, Hunt agreed to take his wife and depart Dallas as soon as they could pack their suitcases. Rothermel ordered the Hunts two plane tickets for Washington under assumed names.

Hunt called Ruth at SMU and told her to instruct the children not to come home to Mount Vernon that night. Instead, for their own safety, they were to stay with friends. In the meantime, someone reportedly began shredding most circulating copies of Rothermel's memo of November 4.

Then events took another turn for the worse. On November 24, 1963, Jack Ruby, the strip-club owner who had been so incensed by the anti-Kennedy tone of the LIFE LINE literature he saw at the Texas Products Show and the "WELCOME, MR. KENNEDY" ad he saw in the *Dallas Morning News,* shot and killed accused assassin Lee Harvey Oswald in the basement of the Dallas County Jail. Two of the LIFE LINE scripts Ruby had picked up at the Texas Products Show exhibit were found in his coat pocket when the police grabbed him. Later, the authorities found Lamar Hunt's phone number among Ruby's personal effects.

These things, on top of LIFE LINE's anti-Kennedy broadcasts, were enough to focus the public outcry directly on H. L. Hunt. While most writers stopped short of accusing Hunt himself of pulling the trigger, there was a widely expressed editorial opinion that Hunt and his LIFE LINE commentators were largely responsible for creating the "climate of hate" that had led to Kennedy's death and then Oswald's. An editorial writer for the *New Republic* summed up the essence of the anti-Hunt sentiment when he declared the LIFE LINE broadcast that aired on the day of the assassination "The kind of program . . . that the brooding Oswalds of the left- or right-wing listen to and sometimes act on."

Almost immediately, an informal but widespread boycotting of HLH Products began. So did the threats. Hunt's telephone started ringing in the middle of the night. Nasty letters arrived at the house and at the office. There were even some gunshots fired at Mount Vernon.

Hunt acted as if he were immune to any dangers. Upon arriving in Washington, he and Ruth took a suite in the Mayflower Hotel and lived very visibly. ("I don't get along very well with being scared," he explained later.) After a couple of weeks, Hunt tired of his exile in Washington and told the FBI he was returning to Dallas for Christmas. The bureau protested vigorously, but Hunt would not be deterred. He and Ruth checked out of the Mayflower and celebrated Christmas at Mount Vernon, just as he had told the FBI they would.

Back in Dallas, Hunt was no more cautious than he had been in Washington. He refused to erect a security fence around his house, and he would not hire bodyguards. Consequently, the Dallas police insisted that city detectives ride with him back and forth between home and office, and dispatched another detail to circle Mount Vernon at night. Ruth and the children were grateful that Popsy had the benefit of police protection, but Hunt regarded the detectives as a nuisance. Finally, he informed the detectives their services were no longer needed, or, as he himself said it a few years afterward, "I told them I wasn't going to put up with them anymore."

Impervious to the mounting army of H. L. Hunt critics, Hunt kept on doing the same things he had always done. He allowed both his home and office telephone numbers to remain listed in the directory, and he kept the tree lights and flagpole lights at Mount Vernon burning as brightly as ever. With the exception of the month of December, which he spent mostly in Washington at the Mayflower, Hunt also kept on cranking out his letters to the editor. Although the tone was slightly more defensive, the essential message was the same. H. L. Hunt was not backing down. Only five days after the assassination he wrote, "Grave warnings that patriots are more dangerous and do more harm than communists are outmoded. Toleration of domestic communism and pro-communism is at a low ebb in the U. S. Love of country, when expressed in words and acts 'free from hate,' will no longer be branded divisive nor flip."

As the 1964 presidential campaign got under way, Hunt jumped into the fray with typical style. Believing that President Johnson and Vice President Hubert Humphrey were too "pro-socialist," he spent the primary season trum-

peting the virtues of Barry Goldwater and decrying the alleged eastern-establishment "conspiracy" designed to promote the candidacy of Pennsylvania
governor William Scranton. According to Hunt, even the pollsters, who for
a time ranked Scranton ahead of Goldwater, were in on the plot and had "gone
wild" trying to advance the wishes of "the Eastern Establishment, the Big
Money minority, the 'Invisible Government,' the kingmakers . . . or something
equally sinister."

Not surprisingly, Hunt's appearance at the 1964 Republican national
convention in San Francisco caused a stir. Although this in itself was an
improvement over the lack of notice he had received from the Democrats in
1960, the occasion was not a completely sanguine one. Because of allegations
surrounding the Kennedy assassination and his own higher public profile,
Hunt was much better known, his face more easily recognized, than he had
been in 1960. What's more, it would turn out that this time, Hunt's man would
win. But just as in 1960, Hunt was still excluded from the councils of party
power and generally regarded as a political albatross whose association it was
best to avoid. The press added to Hunt's image problem. It was reported, for
example, that Hunt had rented "a whole suite" at the convention. Other
reports said he had rented a whole floor. Hunt could only do his best to deny
such exaggerations of the fact.

Although Hunt did support Goldwater through the campaign against
LBJ, he was distracted by attacks against his own cause. The national press
profiled him as a bumptious "super-patriot" and cast aspersions on LIFE
LINE's finances and "religious" character. Swarms of fantastic charges and
accusations, each less documented than the one before, began to come at Hunt
from all directions. LIFE LINE's founder soon began to spend increasing
amounts of time denying what he considered to be ridiculous allegations
linking him to the Ku Klux Klan, the Minute Men, black radicals, and even
a comeback attempt by prize fighter Rocky Marciano against heavyweight
champion Cassius Clay. Said Hunt: "The UPI Dispatch 148 quoted a U. S.
Senator (D–Ore.) regarding H. L. Hunt when President Kennedy was assassinated: '. . . If anybody is responsible, he is.' The city desk of a large daily
in New York called me just now to confirm that I am financing the Black
Muslims in rioting in Harlem. Why and for whose benefit do the many reports
like these circulate? Do those who are tolerant of communism and lukewarm
toward the freedom idea get such false and adverse publicity?"

While Hunt complained of his mistreatment in the press, the Warren
Commission pursued its investigation of President Kennedy's assassination.
One of the subjects of the commission's probe was the possible involvement
of certain members of the Hunt family with people or events ostensibly related
to the Kennedy assassination and Jack Ruby's subsequent shooting of Lee
Harvey Oswald. The first Hunt family member to be interviewed was Lamar.
Special Agent Lansing P. Logan of the FBI questioned Lamar in Dallas on
December 17, 1963. The impetus for the interview was the fact that Lamar's

name appeared in a notebook owned by Jack Ruby. Lamar told the FBI man that he had never met Ruby and had no idea why Ruby was motivated to kill Oswald. He went on to say that he could not think of any reason why his name would appear in Ruby's notebook. Lamar also said that he had never met Oswald and did not know of any connection between Oswald and Ruby.

Curiously enough, about this same time, Warren Commission investigators were in the process of discovering some little publicized connections—or at least possible connections—between Jack Ruby and H. L. Hunt. One of the most interesting came out of a volunteered statement by a convicted con man, Harry Hall, also known as Harry Sinclair and Ed Pauley. He had been an informant for the Secret Service's Los Angeles office. Information he had provided had led to the seizure of a counterfeiting plant in the area. When Hall was interviewed by the Secret Service on November 30, 1963, some eight days after Kennedy's assassination, he was serving time at Terminal Island federal prison in California for defrauding a Los Angeles boxing promoter. Through a friend, Hall had advised the Secret Service that he had information concerning Jack Ruby. The Secret Service decided to listen to what Hall had to say because Hall "had been of assistance to other agencies in addition to the Secret Service, and . . . his information in many cases had been reliable."

What Hall had to say certainly was interesting. According to the Secret Service report on the interview, Hall stated that he had first met Jack Ruby in Dallas back in the early 1950s. Using the alias Harry Sinclair, Hall had checked into a Dallas hotel in hopes of getting into some high-stakes gambling games and some wagers on football games and horse races. His method of operation was to drop the names of a few prominent people, ingratiate himself with the local high rollers, then arrange to make a bet. If Hall lost the bet, he would pay off with a bad check and skip town. If he won, he would give 40 percent of his winnings to Jack Ruby. According to Hall, Ruby was given a cut because Ruby had influence with the local police and could insure that Hall would not get arrested.

Hall stated that while he was in Texas on this gambling scam he met H. L. Hunt. Hall said that he and Ruby bet against Hunt on the Cotton Bowl and Rose Bowl games and won a large sum of money, which they split. Hall's anecdote about gambling with Ruby and Hunt seemed like a relatively small thing at the time, but it directly contradicted later contentions by both Ruby and Hunt that the two had never met.

Back in Dallas, the FBI uncovered two other possible links between Jack Ruby and H. L. Hunt. One was Isaiah Howard Haynes. A black laborer and handyman, Haynes had worked for Ruby for sixteen years. His job was to clean up at Ruby's Carousel Club between the hours of 4:00 and 7:00 P.M. But during nine of those years, Haynes had also been employed as a houseman-porter-chauffeur for the Loyd B. Sands family. Although the FBI's report did not mention the fact, Loyd Sands was the son-in-law of H. L. Hunt. Haynes was still employed by both Ruby and the Sands on the day Kennedy was shot. Ruby and the Hunt family also shared another black employee—Andrew

Armstrong. Unlike Haynes, Armstrong did not work for both at the same time. He was employed at the Holiday Hills apartments, which the Hunts owned, from May to December of 1961. Two months later, in February of 1962, he went to work for Ruby as a maintenance man at the Carousel Club. Strangely enough, the Warren Commission investigators questioned Haynes and Armstrong about possible connections or contact between Ruby and Oswald (both said they knew of none), but did not ask them about possible connections between Ruby and the Hunts.

The Warren Commission did inquire into the "WELCOME, MR. KENNEDY" ad that ran in the *Dallas Morning News* on the day of the assassination. This inquiry prompted the FBI to pay a call on Bunker Hunt in the spring of 1964. Hunt Oil security chief Paul Rothermel, himself a former G-man, advised Bunker to "consider not talking with them" and to "insist that there be only one agent" present in the interview "because if there were two, and one lied and the other swore to it, he [Bunker] would be in bad shape." But Bunker decided to submit to the interview in the presence of his attorney Ivan Irwin and his secretary Lois Orahood.

As it turned out, Bunker survived the FBI interview quite handily. He readily admitted having given Joe Grinnan a contribution to place the ad. He described the advertisement as an article which asked "some embarrassing questions" of President Kennedy and a criticism of the president "in a dignified way." Bunker told the FBI men he could not remember exactly how much he had contributed, but said he believed it was $200 or $300. He said he gave the money in cash out of his pocket, and showed the FBI what he meant by reaching into his pocket and pulling out a roll of bills right there in the interview. Bunker went on to say that he did not solicit contributions from any other individuals, and that he did not know Bernard Weissman, whose name had appeared at the bottom of the ad. Bunker also said that he did not know the names of any of the others who had contributed to the cost of the ad, and that he did not know Lee Harvey Oswald or Jack Ruby and had never had any contact with either of them. Then he closed the interview by voluntarily conceding that the timing of the "WELCOME, MR. KENNEDY" ad "was not too good."

Having visited Bunker and Lamar, the FBI and the Warren Commission failed to interview H. L. Hunt about the assassination. There was no effort to follow up on Harry Hall's claim about a gambling connection between Jack Ruby and H. L. Hunt. There was no attempt to discern the significance—if any—of Ruby and the Hunt family sharing two former low-level employees.

Was H. L. Hunt in some way responsible for the shooting of Oswald or Kennedy? Were Hunt and Ruby secret co-conspirators? Were the wispy claims and accusations involving H. L. Hunt actually part of a smokescreen the real assassin (or assassins) had designed to throw investigators off the track? Or were the thin strands apparently linking H. L. Hunt to the events and actors in the assassination drama mere coincidence? The overwhelming lack of evidence against H. L. Hunt suggested the latter two possibilities had the most merit. But without a thorough follow-up of all the leads, it was impossible to reach any firm conclusion one way or another. Yet, instead of investigating H. L. Hunt as alleged conspirator and/or innocent pawn, the FBI and the Warren Commission concerned themselves only with protecting Hunt from threats by "nuts" who were already convinced that he was responsible for Kennedy's murder.

H. L. Hunt did a much better job of investigating the Warren Commission than the commission did of investigating him. Although Hunt did not launch his own independent probe of the assassination, he did keep on top of developments in the case with regularity. Here, credit was due largely to the prowess of Paul Rothermel. The resourceful Rothermel kept his boss apprised of the progress of the commission's investigation and other relevant subjects by means of a steady stream of memos. Often, Rothermel got hold of information long before it reached Chief Justice Earl Warren himself. Rothermel's skill on this score apparently resulted from contacts he made during his days as an FBI agent as well as his ongoing efforts to cultivate sources from the White House and the CIA to the Dallas Police Department.

A great many of Rothermel's memos were devoted to leads and information about possible preassassination connections between Lee Harvey Oswald and Jack Ruby. In his memos, Rothermel often referred to Ruby as "Rubenstein," which was Ruby's real last name. One typical report delivered early in 1964 informed Hunt of rumors that a red convertible that had been stoned by anti-Castro Cubans in a Miami parade by a pro-Castro group with which Oswald was reportedly associated had been seen headed from Oklahoma to Dallas prior to the assassination. "There is a report that the convertible was stashed at Rubenstein's apartment in Oak Cliff," Rothermel wrote, "and was to be used for a get-a-way by Oswald." Rothermel added that the report was being investigated by the FBI, but that no positive identification had yet been obtained. In that same memo, Rothermel also reported a rumor that Ruby/ Rubenstein "had a communist party roommate who was also a homosexual when he lived in Oak Lawn" in Dallas, and that Ruby subsequently rented a room next door to where he lived for Lee Harvey Oswald. "A confidential source is checking out this information at the present time," Rothermel wrote, "and if there is anything to it, we will be advised."

Although none of these particular rumors proved to be true, Rothermel continued to keep tabs on developments great and small in the assassination inquiry. In a provocative memo dated February 6, 1964, he informed Hunt that "Lyndon B. Johnson is mortally afraid of being assassinated and does not trust the Secret Service to protect him. He has ordered the F.B.I. to be present everywhere he goes with no less than two men and more when there is any possibility that he will be exposed. Johnson has confidentially placed a direct telephone line from his office to J. Edgar Hoover's desk."

Four days after the report on LBJ, Rothermel brought his boss some even more stunning news. "There is information that the CIA and the State Department are currently planning a second invasion of Cuba," Rothermel wrote. "A very reliable source reports that the Manuel Ray group, which is extremely left-wing, has been in touch with the CIA and has agreed to a second invasion. The right-wing Cubans are being pressured to join the invasion. The second invasion is being closely scrutinized by John Martino, leader of the right-wing groups, for fear it will be a second Bay of Pigs fiasco."

This time Rothermel's information happened to be on the mark. As later inquiries bore out, the U.S. government and the Cuban expatriates in Miami were engaged in a secret war against Cuba that had commenced well before Kennedy's assassination and continued on a reduced scale well after the assassination. The particular "second invasion" Rothermel's sources reported apparently never got off the ground, but plans for similar military expeditions were being discussed in Miami's Cuban quarter and in Washington both at the time of Rothermel's memo and afterward.

For better or worse, Rothermel and his boss did not come forward with their own detailed theory of the Kennedy assassination while the Warren Commission investigation was in progress. This may have been simply for lack of evidence. Hunt, for his part, was convinced that the president's murder was the work of communists, but even he did not seem to know which communists had done it or how. The thrust of Rothermel's memos suggested that the powers at Hunt Oil Company had some unproven hunches that Oswald and Ruby were somehow in cahoots, and that either pro-Castro or anti-Castro Cubans may have played a part in the assassination also. But without much more to go on than that, Hunt and his security chief had no choice but to wait for the Warren Commission to deliver its own report and hope that the Hunt name would not be further sullied in the process.

The Warren Commission released its report on September 24, 1964. Its central conclusion was that Lee Harvey Oswald was the "lone assassin" of President Kennedy. The commission found no conclusive evidence that indicated Oswald had been acting on behalf of one of many suspected interest groups ranging from the Soviet Union and pro-Castro Cubans to anti-Castro Cubans and the American right-wing. The commission also concluded that Jack Ruby had acted alone in the murder of Lee Harvey Oswald.

The Warren Commission report mentioned the names of three members of the Hunt family—H. L., Bunker, and Lamar—but none was implicated in any wrongdoing. Bunker was cited as one of the financial backers of the "WELCOME, MR. KENNEDY" ad. The report also recounted the details of Jack Ruby's chauffering of Connie Trammel to Lamar's office, and recalled that Ruby had had some LIFE LINE scripts in his pocket when he shot Oswald. But for all the rumors, innuendos, insinuations, and outright public accusations that had followed the tragic events of late November, the Warren Commission report did not link any of the Hunts to the principal figures in the assassination or suggest that members of the family were even indirectly involved. Indeed, H. L. Hunt's name was mentioned only in passing.

The Hunt family's reaction to the Warren Commission report was highly ambivalent. On the one hand, the Hunts were relieved that the report had not accused them of bankrolling or inciting Kennedy's murder. But that was at best a sort of backhanded victory as far as they were concerned. The Hunt name had been bandied about in the press for months; the family reputation had been irrevocably tarnished by all the rumors and loose accusations. The family had become the subject of threats, HLH Products had been boycotted. To be cleared—or, rather, not accused—of something they did not do was all well enough, but plenty of damage had been done in the process. The Hunts decided that it was best to keep their opinions of the Warren Commission to themselves for the time being. But privately, they felt that they had once again been the victims of an eastern liberal smear.

"A strenuous attempt was made to blame the assassination of our gallant young president on patriots by calling them 'extremists' and 'hate groups,' " Hunt wrote in an inner-office memo that was at best a thinly veiled gesture of self-defense. "Thinking people know patriots had nothing to gain by this vile deed. Following the tragic assassination, the Warren Commission of seven was appointed to investigate. Without disclosing a motive, its report has been released less than forty days before November 3. To help whoever would gain." Hunt stopped short of saying exactly who he thought the Warren Report would benefit on November 3, but the logical inference was that the beneficiary would be Lyndon Johnson, who was running against Republican Barry Goldwater for the presidency.

Miraculously enough, Hunt did eventually change his public position on the Kennedys. The man who had been responsible for the circulation of Reverend Criswell's anti-Catholic sermon and the broadcasting of dozens and dozens of anti-Kennedy scripts on LIFE LINE suddenly became one of the late president's greatest admirers. In a column entitled "The Assassination Must Not Be Forgotten," Hunt wrote, "The assassination of President Kennedy was the greatest blow ever suffered by the cause of freedom. Throughout the land, citizens were stunned into helplessness over the tragic death of our vibrant young President. The balancing effect of the two opposing political parties was lost. This is part of the legacy left Americans by the Marxist assassin, and being a Marxist he would have wanted it that way. For the continued progress of the country he so courageously served, the assassination of President Kennedy should not be soon forgotten and should be openly and often reviewed, discussed and analyzed. The tragic event and its catastrophic results will be with us for years. The better it is understood, the less paralyzing the tragedy will be; and John F. Kennedy would be the last to desire that blame be ascribed to anyone who is blameless."

Hunt went even further in praising Kennedy in a 1965 interview with *Playboy* magazine. "I was for practically everything that Jack Kennedy did in public life," Hunt told his surprised interviewer. Maintaining that "Catholics are known for being anti-Communist," Hunt attributed Kennedy's success in part to the "constructive" philosophy of his father. He went on to praise

Kennedy for deploring "the betrayal of China to the Communists" and for a speech in which Kennedy said, "What our young men had saved, our diplomats and our Presidents have frittered away." When the *Playboy* interviewer insisted that Kennedy's liberal Democratic policies must have conflicted with Hunt's conservatism, Hunt was unable to enumerate specific mistakes he thought Kennedy made. "Unless there is a turn toward constitutional government and a decrease in pro-Socialist legislation forced through the Congress," he declared, "the Kennedy Administration is likely to appear highly constructive when compared to the Administrations yet to follow."

Hunt's conversion to pro-Kennedyism to the point of conveniently forgetting the record of his own virulent anti-Kennedy actions may have been an old man's way of working out guilt over defaming the martyred president before he died. Or it may have been a subterfuge for getting the growing army of Kennedy assassination investigators off his back. Or it may have been merely another example of Hunt's political eccentricity. In any case, Hunt got his wish. The Kennedy assassination was not forgotten. But it was not remembered in the way Hunt would have preferred. Instead of laying to rest public doubts, both the Warren Report and Hunt's own pronouncements only aroused new questions about the murder of President Kennedy. Assassination investigators, both amateur and professional, proliferated from coast to coast and overseas. The farther away from the scene of the crime the investigators resided, the more byzantine—and the more certain—were their theories. And before long, H. L. Hunt, the Kennedy-hater turned Kennedy-eulogist, found himself the prime suspect in several new Kennedy assassination probes.

The most serious and threatening investigation emanated from New Orleans in early 1967. The leader of the probe was Jim Garrison, a flamboyant and controversial New Orleans district attorney who was a local legend in his own time. Garrison was able to get a group of wealthy New Orleans businessmen to finance his reopening of the Kennedy assassination case by convincing them he could prove the plot had been hatched in New Orleans. Rumors about the targets of the Garrison probe first hit the streets in early 1967, when Garrison ordered the arrest of a retired New Orleans businessman and admitted homosexual named Clay Shaw. In the wake of Shaw's arrest, some stories contended that Garrison was going after a ring of New Orleans homosexuals. Other stories said Garrison was after the CIA. Still other stories had it that Garrison was pinning Kennedy's assassination on a "wealthy Texas businessman." Not surprisingly, the "wealthy Texas businessman" most often connected with the rumors was H. L. Hunt.

Just as in the days of the Warren Commission probe, Hunt's security chief Paul Rothermel did a first-rate job of keeping his boss informed. One of Rothermel's earliest reports on the Garrison investigation came on August 23, 1967, when he informed Hunt that *Life* magazine was due to "come out with a big spread blasting Garrison and his probe of the Kennedy assassination." Rothermel went on to say (correctly, as it turned out) that *Life* would link

Garrison to reputed mafia chief Carlos Marcello of New Orleans through over $5,000 worth of hotel and gambling credit extended to Garrison on a visit to Las Vegas. "In addition, *Life* will try to show that Bobby Kennedy and the Kennedy family are opposed to Garrison's probe," Rothermel continued.

Seven weeks later, Hunt received a much more unsettling memo from Rothermel. "I have information that Garrison is referring to either you or Bunker as the wealthy oilman in his probe," the security chief wrote. Rothermel's memo did not elaborate beyond that. He did not say exactly how Garrison planned to tie in Bunker and/or H.L., and he did not suggest what course of action should be taken.

From that time forward, the progress of the Garrison probe became a matter of consuming interest for the Hunts and their security chief. Rothermel pumped his sources for constant updates on the probe, and kept Hunt informed of the increasing dangers he already faced as a result of the affair. Among other things, Rothermel advised Hunt not to go to New Orleans for fear that he "might either be arrested or subpoenaed." Hunt elected to heed Rothermel's warning at least for the time being, and on December 6, 1967, canceled a scheduled meeting in New Orleans with his friend Senator Russell Long.

At some point Rothermel got hold of a hand-drawn chart which purportedly detailed Garrison's theory of the assassination. The chart consisted of a series of name boxes and circles connected by dotted lines and arrows. At the top of the chart was the name "H. L. Hunt" and below that the notation "screened three times by Rothermel." Directly below Hunt's name were lines emanating to the Dallas police, Jack Ruby, the FBI, Oswald, a Texas congressman, and several lesser-known New Orleans and Texas characters. The chart did not explain exactly what all the lines and boxes were supposed to mean or the supposed scenario of what took place, but the implication was clear: Garrison and/or his investigators apparently believed H. L. Hunt had had a hand in Kennedy's murder.

The Hunts and Rothermel continued to fret over the Garrison probe for the rest of that dreary winter. Then the spring brought a chain of welcome news. On April 3, 1968, Rothermel reported in a terse note that "A C.I.A. agent in Houston, Texas has indicated that an effort is being made to have a lunacy hearing on Jim Garrison, the New Orleans District Attorney. The informant said he did not know who would push the lunacy charges but that the C.I.A. seems concerned enough to be behind the movement." Now it appeared that the tide was turning—against Garrison.

Remarkably enough, the Hunts received from one of Garrison's investigators the very next day an apology and reassurance that they were *not* the targets of the Garrison probe. Once again, the message came in through Rothermel. According to a Rothermel memo of April 4, 1968, the bearer of the message was one Bill Wood, a "former C.I.A. man and investigator for Garrison," who was in Dallas doing some legwork. Wood first apologized for rumors that his research was focusing on Hunt. Wood said that Garrison had become "extremely provoked" over the rumors and had sent him "hat in hand to explain that Garrison was in no way concerned with Mr. H. L. Hunt." Wood added that Garrison wanted Rothermel's "personal cooperation" because Rothermel had given him "valuable information" in the past.

Wood went on to say that Garrison "will prove the assassination was a plot by officials in the Federal Government and consisted of C.I.A., Secret Service, F.B.I., and one or two military men." Allowing that Garrison had "done himself a great disservice" through his "outbursts" to the press as the investigation had progressed, Wood said he hoped Rothermel and Hunt realized that "Garrison had to come forward with statements that would bring him both leads for investigation and throw off the C.I.A. which was trying to thwart his investigation."

Despite Wood's reassurances, Rothermel and the Hunts remained wary. Rumors continued to circulate that Garrison was trying to indict the Hunts after all. It was 1968, a presidential campaign year, and a most divisive one at that. Lyndon Johnson had chosen not to run for re-election. The war in Vietnam raged hopelessly out of control. There was violence and craziness in the air. Anything could happen, it seemed, especially with a character as unpredictable as Jim Garrison.

While Hunt tried to escape blame for the Kennedy assassination, his name was dragged less extensively through the mud in the wake of two more national tragedies in 1968. Ironically, Hunt kicked off 1968 by writing in his syndicated column in January an article entitled "Less Hate in '68." In that column, he counseled, "One emotion that freedomists should absolutely rule out of their hearts and minds during the New Year in 1968 is hate, including hate for those who seek to destroy freedom. The freedom fight is a joyous and constructive crusade. It has no place for destructive hate. . . . The best weapon to use against the enemy is truth."

Once again, Hunt's advice went unheeded. On April 4, 1968, the Reverend Martin Luther King, Jr. was assassinated as he stood on the balcony of a Memphis motel. On June 4, 1968, Sirhan Sirhan killed presidential candidate Robert Kennedy in the kitchen of the Ambassador Hotel in Los Angeles. All of a sudden, the Hunts had two more assassination allegations to be concerned about. Although suspicion of the Hunts never achieved quite the same level as it had with the John F. Kennedy assassination, the slayings of King and the younger Kennedy brought immediate responses.

The threats on the Hunts began anew. There were more phone calls and letters, many every day at first, then an average of about one per month. At one point, someone even sent a pair of trained dogs to attack and kill the handful of deer Hunt liked to keep around Mount Vernon. Such viciousness was the exception, but there was now even more reason for concern about Hunt's physical safety and, for that matter, for the safety of every member of the family.

In the wake of all this, Hunt changed his public opinion of both Robert

Kennedy and Martin Luther King. Prior to the assassinations, Hunt had been as critical of what Robert Kennedy had stood for as he was of what John F. Kennedy had stood for. As for King, Hunt said he shared FBI director J. Edgar Hoover's opinion—to wit, that King was a liar without any regard for "the truth, religion, sincerity, peace, morality, or the best interest of the Negro people." But after the Kennedy and King assassinations, Hunt expressed his grief and blamed both their deaths on communist plots. "I do not feel that these sad events prove that our Nation is sick," Hunt wrote in one of his columns. "I think they result from the privileges granted to Communists in the United States or those who are coming to our country. Communism and crime go hand-in-hand, and the U. S. Supreme Court should take cognizance of this fact."

As if pointing the finger at the communists were not enough, Hunt went on to write a column endorsing Edward M. Kennedy for the 1968 Democratic presidential nomination. Noting that "Ambassador Joseph Kennedy Sr. was sufficiently constructive that he was disapproved of by FDR," Hunt began his endorsement by cataloguing the Kennedy family tragedies and disclaiming any responsibility for the assassinations on behalf of all constructives. "The atheists —whether Marxist, Maoist, W.E.B. Dubois members—are the assassins, but apparently the public wants to believe the assassins are patriots who love our country too devoutly," Hunt wrote. "The U. S. State Department furnished Lee Harvey Oswald the funds to bring his Russian wife to the U. S. from the Soviet Union. The United Nations furnished accused Sirhan Sirhan funds to come to the United States from Jordan." Hunt went on to say, "The Democratic party should nominate for President Edward M. Kennedy and choose for the Vice Presidential nomination one with similar philosophies who is a proven vote-getter representing an area outside the East with a high percent of the presidential electors. Pleasant and persuasive Ted Kennedy should not accept a Vice Presidential nomination."

Meanwhile, new problems developed on the John F. Kennedy assassination front. In November of 1968, Rothermel managed to obtain an advance copy of a book called *Farewell America.* As Rothermel described it, *Farewell America* was a book about the Kennedy assassination that was "highly derogatory of Mr. Hunt." The thrust of the book and an accompanying chart was that H. L. Hunt and several other notables had had something to do with the alleged grand conspiracy resulting in the assassination of John F. Kennedy. Full of innuendo but short on documentation, *Farewell America* was the kind of book that might normally have been dismissed out of hand, but its publication happened to coincide with the opening of Garrison's first Kennedy assassination trial in New Orleans.

As it turned out, however, the target of Garrison's prosecution was not H. L. Hunt, but Clay Shaw, the homosexual businessman Garrison had arrested at the outset of his probe. Testimony in the Clay Shaw trial lasted six weeks. During that time, Garrison attacked the Warren Report's vulnerable "lone assassin" theory. He also tried to prove that Shaw, using the alias "Clay Bertrand," plotted the assassination of President Kennedy in September 1963 with Lee Harvey Oswald and a pilot named David Ferrie. But the witnesses Garrison put on the stand resembled a parade of circus performers. One man recanted earlier incriminating statements he had made about Shaw by confessing that what he had said was a "figment" of his imagination. Another man, purported to be the "mystery witness" who saw Shaw meet with Oswald, shattered his own credibility by testifying that he had been hypnotized by fifty to sixty "enemies" over the past few years who planted wild ideas in his mind. This "mystery witness" also cast some doubt on Garrison's good judgment when he said that he had told the district attorney and his staff of his hypnotic experiences before taking the stand. In the face of all this, attornies for Shaw, who denied any involvement in the assassination, put on substantially more credible evidence that Shaw had never seen or met Oswald or Ferrie.

On February 28, 1969, Clay Shaw was acquitted of charges of conspiracy to murder President Kennedy by a New Orleans jury. Although Garrison vowed to prosecute Shaw for perjury, he was forced to announce that his investigation of the Kennedy assassination had come to an end. A wily and adroit politician, Garrison managed to win re-election as district attorney, but the show at Clay Shaw's trial and Shaw's acquittal served generally to discredit him as a Kennedy assassination investigator.

Unfortunately for H. L. Hunt, Garrison's demise did not quell public interest in the Hunts' possible involvement with the events of November 1963. One of the more persistent Kennedy assassination investigators who crossed Hunt's path was a Washington attorney named Bernard Fensterwald. Fensterwald founded an organization dubbed the Committee to Investigate Assassinations (CIA), which was devoted to doing just that by pooling information on the assassination from all available sources. In the summer of 1969, some five months after Clay Shaw's acquittal, Fensterwald visited Rothermel in Dallas.

At first, Fensterwald's inquiry seemed not to center on the Hunts, but on several other mysterious characters not previously implicated in the assassination who had conducted some oil dealings with the Hunts. On June 2, after first meeting Fensterwald, Rothermel wrote a contact in the Dallas Police Department that he was "not overly impressed with Fensterwald." Rothermel described a packet of Fensterwald material sent by his police contact as "highly enlightening and amusing." But by July of 1969, Rothermel felt the need to sound the alarm once again. "It may be possible," he wrote Hunt, "that Fensterwald is going to write a new book, pointing the finger at the Hunts."

As it turned out, though, a California television newsman named Peter Noyes wrote a book, *Legacy of Doubt*, which allegedly implicated non-Hunt people.

After the Noyes book, assassination theories involving the Hunts continued to dog the family for years. None of the theories proved able to stand up under close scrutiny. To be sure, the Warren Report and other investigations left plenty of loose ends to explore and plenty of unanswered questions to look into. But for all the continued hoopla, there was not a shred of solid evidence implicating H.L., Bunker, or any other member of the family to the murders of Kennedy and Oswald. Still, the Hunts found themselves having to deny one new allegation after another with almost seasonal regularity.

True to character, Hunt did not shrink from his "constructive" positions. His endorsement of Ted Kennedy in 1968 was his one major concession to the nation's postassassination mood. Otherwise, he literally stuck to his guns politically and philosophically. "No matter how deeply we regret the assassination of important public figures," he wrote in a July 1968 column, "we must not allow our emotions to rule our reason. A government which is concerned with protecting the innocent from the law breaker has no need to fear private ownership of weapons. A government that is seeking to control the private lives of its citizens cannot allow those citizens to own the means of self-defense."

As *Dallas Times Herald* editorial writer A. C. Greene observed at the time, there was something almost quaint about H. L. Hunt and his seemingly ominous pronouncements. "If he had more flair and imagination, if he weren't basically such a damn hick," Greene told one visiting reporter, "H. L. Hunt could be the most dangerous man in America." But as Greene well knew, H. L. Hunt, the boy wonder, wanderer, gambler, oilman, polygamist, health nut, and propagandist, was, in the end, exactly that—a hick. This characteristic in and of itself would not be enough to absolve him of the Kennedy assassination in the face of hard incriminating evidence. But in lieu of such evidence, it was certainly enough to allow him to be considered innocent until proven guilty. It was also enough to keep him engaged in one peculiar adventure after another throughout the middle and late 1960s, even as all the assassination allegations swirled about him.

CHAPTER 11

JUST PLAIN FOLKS

H. L. HUNT liked nothing better than sitting on the porch at Mount Vernon with his wife Ruthie. Up above, they had the bright shining stars and the yellow Texas moon, "the show," as Hunt liked to call it. In front of them, they had White Rock Lake, a pocket in time protected from advancing Dallas by a backdrop of trees and low hills. Sometimes Popsy and Ruthie would just sit together, hand in hand, without saying a word, the farm boy from Illinois and the small-town girl from Oklahoma. As daughter June observed, "They had been together a long time, and words were not always necessary for conversation between them." But every so often, as the mood struck them, Mr. and Mrs. Hunt liked to sing their favorite song. The title of the tune was "Just Plain Folks," but Popsy and Ruthie referred to it as "our song."

"To a mansion in the city . . ." they would sing, "came a couple old and gray . . . to see the son who left them years before. . . . He had prospered and grown wealthy . . . since a youth he left his home . . . now his life was one of pomp and show. . . . But coolly did he greet them . . . for his friends stood by his side . . . who'd heard him speak of home so grand. . . . As the old man gazed at him . . . he said with simple pride . . . while he gently took his dear wife by the hand . . . 'We are just plain folks . . . your mother and me . . . just plain folks . . . like our own folks used to be. . . . As our presence seems to grieve you . . . we will go away and leave you . . . we are sadly out of place here . . . 'Cause we're just plain folks.' "

Singing "Just Plain Folks" often brought tears to H. L. Hunt's hard blue eyes. For as he warbled the words, Hunt simultaneously believed them and realized once again that they were not and could never be true. Hunt had turned seventy-five on February 17, 1964. His quest for success had led him far away from the rural beginnings he so romanticized in memory. The things he had done, the things he had been made it impossible for him to be considered just plain anything. H. L. Hunt was a most complex person. But he still longed for a simple self and a simple time. Looking out over White Rock Lake at night, he could reach that self and time through fantasy and song.

During the day, Hunt had to live alongside his own overgrown myth. To the press and, therefore, to the public, H. L. Hunt was still the world's richest man, the archetypal right-wing Texas oil billionaire. Washington columnist Jack Anderson expressed some of the nation's typical misconceptions about Hunt when he wrote that Hunt "has become symbolic of the lusty Texas tycoon who flashes $1000 bills, drapes his women in mink, and turns in his Cadillacs when they get dirty." Apart from being accurately described as lusty, no image of H. L. Hunt could have been further off base. At the same time, though, the myths others made of him and the myths he made of himself had a certain reality.

Symbolic of the crosscurrents in Hunt's life was his decision to move Hunt Oil Company and most of the other family accounts out of the aging Mercantile Bank building and into the brand-new First National Bank building in early 1965. The First National Bank building was the place to be. Fifty stories of glass and steel trimmed with vertical stripes of outside lighting, it was the tallest building in town and the headquarters of the biggest bank in Texas. The Dallas Petroleum Club occupied the top floor. The businessmen who came in and out of the First National building looked a little sharper, a little more successful, a little more Ivy League than their counterparts across downtown. The secretaries were pretty and more Neiman-Marcus in style. The First National building was a manifestation of the "new Dallas," the city on its way to greatness despite the stigma of the Kennedy assassination.

The Hunt Oil Company executive offices were on the twenty-ninth floor of this sparkling new edifice and yet were oddly in keeping with Hunt's "just plain folks" image. There were no fancy Oriental rugs, elaborate wood inlays, or high-priced wall hangings. The twenty-ninth floor featured a large switchboard and a small reception area near one end of the elevator bank. Long, undecorated hallways led off in two directions. There were no special signs or distinctive markings, not even a brass plate that said Hunt Oil Company. The carpets were a standard tan synthetic; the walls were space-divider white. Hunt's suite was at one corner. There was an open space large enough for three secretaries in front. Hunt's own office and the offices of his top aides, Paul Rothermel and John Curington, were adjacent to the secretarial pool. There was also a furnished but unoccupied office next to Hunt's with the name "Hassie Hunt" on the door plate.

Hunt's office was spacious but hardly extravagant. He had it furnished with the same old leather-topped desk and cracked leather armchairs that had adorned his office in the Mercantile building. He had his high-powered radio, but no fancy gadgets. Just as before, a miniature American flag was atop his desk. But now Hunt had a truly remarkable view through the office's giant plate-glass windows. Unlike the view from the porch at Mount Vernon, there was no illusion of being out in the country. The ever-growing city of Dallas sprawled in all directions. The landscape was dotted not only with the down-town towers nearby, but with high-rise apartment buildings, offices, industrial plants, shopping centers, and housing tracts which extended from the lush green creek beds on the Park Cities to the treeless suburbs that seemed to be stretching all the way to Oklahoma.

With the move to the First National building, the empire of H. L. Hunt embarked on a new round of prosperity and a new round of serious problems. In 1965, Placid Oil Company discovered the giant Black Lake field in south-central Louisiana. Placid managed to lease up an estimated 12,000 acres in the field, and with typical aplomb Hunt, upon learning of the discovery, castigated one of Placid's executives for not leasing up even more acreage. "The trouble with you," Hunt said, "is you don't know how to think big." Such criticism not withstanding, Placid had a strike that was big by any standard. Production at Black Lake was estimated at 25,000 barrels of oil per day, or enough to double Placid's previously discovered oil production, and there were huge quantities of natural gas in the field as well.

The discovery of the Black Lake field made the Hunts bona fide bil-lionaires for the first time. Added to the production of the other Hunt interests, Black Lake brought the Hunts' companies' total average output to nearly 100,000 barrels per day. With oil prices in the neighborhood of $3 per barrel, that translated into an annual gross income of about $100 million and proven and probable reserves in excess of $1 billion. Bunker's great strike in Libya had a much grander potential, but the Libyan production had yet to come on stream and would always be subject to the changeableness of international politics. Black Lake was not in the middle of some foreign desert, but snugly within the borders of the state of Louisiana, a proverbial bird's nest on the ground. With the income generated by the Black Lake field, Placid was able to make some new investments with enormous future potential, including the purchase of offshore leases in the North Sea.

There was only one hitch to all this as far as H. L. Hunt was concerned. Although Placid Oil definitely counted as one of the Hunt family's interests, none of that production belonged to Hunt himself. Owned by the trusts of his six living children by Lyda Bunker Hunt, Placid was the property of the first family. The discovery of the Black Lake field did a great deal to increase the wealth of Margaret, Hassie, Caroline, Bunker, Herbert, Lamar, and their heirs, but it did not, strictly speaking, add to the personal fortune of H. L. Hunt or to the production total of Hunt Oil Company.

Meanwhile, the interests that Hunt did personally own were encountering considerable financial difficulties. Most of those difficulties involved HLH Products. By the middle 1960s, Hunt had spent upward of $15 million on HLH Products for the acquisition of various processing plants in Texas, Florida, Arkansas, Iowa, Indiana, and California. HLH Products had gross annual sales of $23 million. But the food division kept right on losing money just as it had from day one. In the beginning, these losses were running at about $100,000 per month, or a little over $1 million per year. But instead of reversing themselves as the company became established, the losses were continuing to mount.

While some of the food division's difficulties were caused by what appeared to be poor salesmanship and sloppy management, much of the continuing downtrend seemed to result from HLH Products' ongoing support of LIFE LINE and other H. L. Hunt political projects. In order to make up for its losses, the food division had to fall back on the oil and gas division of Hunt Oil Company. But as he had become consumed with his political projects and his food and cosmetic ventures, Hunt had neglected the oil and gas division. Hunt Oil salaries, once on a par with any in the industry, had begun to fall behind those paid by other companies. Saddled with the burden of backing HLH Products, the oil and gas division was now drilling fewer and fewer wells, both because of Hunt's declining interest in the oil business and because the ever-increasing cash demands of HLH Products left less and less money for the drilling budget. Hunt Oil Company, the flagship of the empire, was getting caught up in a vicious circle of declining productivity on the oil and gas side and increasing deficits from the food-division side.

Hunt's money-losing activities were by this time becoming a source of much consternation for the children of his first family. Though they were as powerless as anyone else to contradict the old man's will, they believed that their father had gone overboard with his politics and his food business, and they made their feelings clear. At the most basic level, the first family's misgivings were an expression of concern about their father's welfare as well as his wealth, but Hunt did not see it that way. To him, his children's meddling was just that—meddling, or worse. Fearing that his own offspring were out to deprive him of the things he really enjoyed, Hunt became more paranoid than ever. Finally, one day just prior to the move to the new offices in the First National building, his fear and hostility erupted.

The person on the receiving end happened to be his son Herbert, who was then vice president and head of production at Hunt Oil and the reigning heir apparent. According to one version by former Hunt insiders, it all started when Herbert tried to insulate the first family from his father's wasteful ways by instituting some new policies. In the past, when an oil deal came into the office, it was first passed to Hunt Oil. Then, if Hunt Oil rejected the deal or could not handle it, the deal was passed on to Placid and the other companies beneath the Hunt Oil umbrella. Herbert reportedly reversed the process, directing that deals first be sent to Placid and then routed to Hunt Oil.

When Hunt found out, he was furious. According to one account of the incident, he literally grabbed Herbert by the collar and escorted him to the elevators shouting, "You're no son of mine."

Another less sensational insider version of the episode had to do with Herbert's decision to borrow from one of the other first-family trusts (his sister Margaret's) in order to finance a real-estate venture. According to this version, Hunt called Herbert out to Mount Vernon and ordered him to "tell everyone you're not running things anymore. If you don't tell them, I will." In either case, the bottom line was the same: Herbert, like his brother Bunker before him, was on the outs with his father.

Hunt's rupture with Herbert marked a turning point in his relationship with the first family. Having grown even further apart since the discovery of Hunt's secret families and his marriage to Ruth, the first-family children and their father were now truly estranged. Hunt did not disinherit the first family. His children did not completely stop speaking to him. Herbert even held onto his title as a vice president of Hunt Oil. But real communication between them reached an impasse. In Herbert's place, Hunt appointed his nephew Tom Hunt, a first-family cousin, as head of production at Hunt Oil. But for all intents and purposes, he remained isolated from the first family in a world of his own. His closest confidants were not his sons, but his aides Curington and Rothermel. In fact, in order for Hunt's children or anyone else to see him, they had to first pass by Rothermel's office on the right or walk through Curington's office on the left.

Having reasserted his control over Hunt Oil Company, Hunt spent very little time tending to matters of oil and gas. When not fending off allegations about the Kennedy assassination, he devoted most of his time to his politics, his food business, his writing, and his philosophizing. He was the first to admit that he was a dreamer—a dreamer of "constructive dreams," he would say— but more and more he seemed to live in his dreams. His vision of reality, like his visions of utopia, was defined by his growing dictionary of neologisms, the words he made up to describe everything from political philosophy to indigestion tablets. To his first terms "constructive" and "mistaken" he added "freedomist" and "anti-freedomists" (terms that described the same two conflicting sides), "Fabians" (a pseudonym for the so-called eastern establishment), and "Republic USA" (which Hunt preferred to "democracy" when referring to America). These words came to define his reality, the world according to H. L. Hunt.

Hunt concluded early on that the communists showed no signs of mellowing, and he was determined not to mellow either. He kept dictating letters to the editor, and kept writing daily and weekly newspaper columns which harped on the same anticommunist, anti-U.N., anti–Supreme Court themes that had always dominated his political statements. At their peak, Hunt's columns were carried by thirty-six dailies and twenty-two weeklies. Subscribers were mostly small-town papers such as the *Shreveport* (Louisiana) *Journal,* the *Kilgore* (Texas) *News-Herald,* the *Elizabethtown* (Pennsylvania) *Chronicle,* and the *Colorado Springs Gazette.* In his columns, Hunt decried the increasing "permissiveness" of American society and spoke out against drugs and civil disobedience. He assured his readers time and again that it really was possible to rekindle and spread the good old values that had made America great. As he put it in one column, "We *Can* Turn Back the Clock."

Despite his complaint that he was a slow writer, Hunt was nothing if not prolific. Between 1964 and 1970, he wrote ten books, all of which he published under the HLH Products label. Six of these books were collections of newspaper columns and letters to the editor Hunt wrote during the period. But the other four were full-length works in their own right. In addition to his speechmaking primer *Why Not Speak?*, these books included *Fabians Fight Freedom,* his alliterative analysis of how the eastern establishment was leading the United States down the road to communism, and *Gobiernate A Ti Mismo (Govern Thyselves),* a proposed South American constitution which he had translated into Spanish in the hopes that it would encourage the "Spanish descendants" living in Latin America to achieve self-government. Still intrigued with the utopian system he had created in his 1960 novel *Alpaca,* Hunt wrote a sequel, entitled *Alpaca Revisited,* in which he incorporated several minor refinements that had occurred to him since *Alpaca*'s publication. Just as before, votes were distributed according to how much taxes a citizen paid.

Hunt was not shy about touting his literary efforts. "*Alpaca Revisited* will have a profound effect in the formation and life of nations," Hunt wrote in a newspaper column devoted to plugging his new book. He went on to say that the book "may be the most worthwhile in Latin America," where he hoped it would help people to "reject tyranny in favor of its detailed provisions enabling freedom loving people to govern themselves." Hunt also ventured that *Alpaca Revisited* might be useful to the many states in the United States that were in the process of revising their state constitutions.

Unfortunately for Hunt, neither the countries of Latin America nor the states of the Union shared his assessment of *Alpaca Revisited.* Like its predecessor novel, it became merely another signal to mainstream politicians that H. L. Hunt was a little wacky. The same was true of most of Hunt's other political writings. Given his prolificness and the unwelcome prominence accorded to him by the fallout from the Kennedy assassination, Hunt did gain a national reputation as a spokesman for the far right. But he never gained the kind of local or national influence he seemed to desire. *Dallas Times Herald* editorial writer A. C. Greene frequently got telephone calls from reporters for out-of-state and national publications inquiring as to what H. L. Hunt's position was on some particular issue. Greene's standard reply: "No one knows, and no one particularly cares." For those few who did care, finding the answer was simple enough. As Greene would helpfully point out, all an industrious reporter had to do was call Hunt at home or at the office (both phone numbers were listed) and ask. More often than not, H. L. Hunt himself would come to the phone and reply in person.

Not the sort of man who accepted rejection with grace, Hunt sometimes tried to pressure newspapers into running his columns and letters to the editor. The main form of pressure was the sheer volume of material Hunt sent in for publication. Dozens and dozens of letters and columns would arrive in an editor's mail, followed by a personal telephone call from the author himself. Hunt would remind the editor of the Hunt Library output that was crossing his desk, and suggest that the material was highly printable. If the editor happened to disagree, Hunt would inform him that it was costing upward of

a thousand dollars per week to turn out the letters and columns. That informa-
tion sometimes made an impression and sometimes did not. In the case of the
Dallas Times Herald, it did not. Greene, for example, told Hunt that he
appreciated the costs involved but asserted, "we still can't just run all H. L.
Hunt." Though Hunt never did seem to understand why not, he accepted
Greene's verdict and hung up.

Undaunted by his critics, Hunt was constantly dreaming up new gim-
micks for promoting his political views. One of his dearest projects was his plan
for an organization of Youth Freedom Speakers. Convinced that "adjust and
other young people will listen more intently to youth and be more responsive
to what they have to say," Hunt determined in 1966 to organize and train
groups of young people to give three-and-a-half-minute "pro-freedom"
speeches to various organizations and groups. The groups began, not surprisingly, with Hunt's three daughters by Ruth—June, age twenty-one, Helen, age
seventeen, and Swanee, age sixteen—who had been singing patriotic songs for
their father for several years now. Hunt later wrote a column about taking his
daughters and four other recruits on a trip to Los Angeles in the summer of
1966. Hunt was pleased with but not uncritical of their performance.

"On this first trip, they depended on emphasis and voice inflection," he
wrote, "but in the short time, none of them developed the ability to induce
joyous laughter and a minute later a shedding of a few tears. In L.A., the most
expert in the entertainment and publicity fields said the performance of the
girls was definitely 'a show,' and their fresh, amateurish delivery made their
message more appealing." Hunt went on to report that when the girls returned,
they began to accept invitations to speak at "service club luncheons, break-
fasts, at prayer meetings and small gatherings."

Hunt claimed his goal was to build the original organization of 6 speakers
into 300, then 1,000, then 10,000 strong. At that point, he declared, the Youth
Freedom Speakers would "begin realizing their goal of cutting the crime wave
in half." Hunt further ventured that when the speakers numbered 50,000, it
would be possible to bring U.S. soldiers home from Vietnam, and that when
the YFS's ranks swelled to 100,000 worldwide, "wars may become a thing of
the past and communism collapse."

At one point, Hunt's plans for his YFS team came to include an ambitious
anti-Castro program to be co-sponsored by the Roman Catholic Church.
According to Hunt's version of the story, the Vatican approached him in 1966
with the idea of sending 1,000 YFSers to Latin America for the purpose of
counteracting incipient procommunist organizers. The project was slow to get
off the ground, but by 1969, an initial group of seven girls was selected to make
the trip. Plans at that time called for an eventual expenditure of $11 million
on the program, which journalists had now labeled the Children's Crusade.
Hunt promoted this and other YFS projects in press conferences, columns, and
letters to the editor, but the YFS never realized its founder's grandiose objec-
tives, in part because the organization never managed to attract more than a
handful of regular participants.

While he experimented with YFS, Hunt also tried to encourage the formation of various ad hoc groups devoted to spreading his political message. These included such specialized groups as "Vacationers for Freedom," Hunt's suggestion for a concerted effort by vacationing Americans to speak up for their country while enjoying their time off. In Hunt's mind, all this was part and parcel of his dual belief that while patriotism should be profitable, freedom should also be fun.

When not promoting new patriotism projects, Hunt spent a good portion of the middle and late 1960s defending old ones, particularly LIFE LINE. One of LIFE LINE's sharpest foes was Texas congressman Wright Patman, chairman of a House banking committee investigating foundations that exploited loopholes in the tax laws for other than charitable purposes. Convinced that LIFE LINE, in violation of the law, was a political—not an educational—organization, Patman found that investigators for the Internal Revenue Service had concluded the same. But curiously enough, the highest levels of the IRS seemed committed to rejecting or simply not acting upon the staff's recommendation to end LIFE LINE's tax exemption. In late 1963 and into 1964, Patman publicized his own findings about LIFE LINE and tried to prod the IRS to take what he considered the appropriate action.

Hunt counterattacked in his columns and letters to the editor. Here he showed that he was still just plain shrewd as well as just plain tough. "The I.R.S. is not 'cracking down' on LIFE LINE, but is carefully evaluating the content of its radio program," Hunt maintained in one letter. "Wright Patman, chairman of a House Subcommittee, has been defaming LIFE LINE and, at the same time, putting pressure on the I.R.S." After making some personal attacks on Patman, Hunt went on to say, "LIFE LINE is entitled to present the point of view it considers to be educational. . . . LIFE LINE should be commended and not condemned because it is opposed to communism. It consistently campaigns for a better way of life and what it says is quite free from being a 'hate message.'"

In the end, Hunt proved the victor. Despite Patman's pressure, the IRS decided to allow LIFE LINE to maintain its tax-exempt status. Still classified as a "religious" organization, LIFE LINE achieved even greater audience penetration. By 1969, LIFE LINE was carried on 547 radio stations nationwide.

When not defending LIFE LINE, Hunt spent a good deal of his time orchestrating political attacks and counterattacks on such figures as Senator Thomas Kuchel of California and Senator J. William Fulbright of Arkansas. Hunt opposed Kuchel and Fulbright for their views on foreign affairs, which in his estimation were far too accommodating to the Russians and thus dangerous to Republic USA. Another strike against Fulbright was the fact that he had been a Rhodes scholar, something Hunt considered a prime indication that Fulbright was allied with the "Fabians" of the eastern establishment. Kuchel's defeat in the 1968 Republican primary counted as one of Hunt's few political victories. An editor in the *Arkansas Gazette* later claimed that "a few short days before the Arkansas balloting," Hunt "confessed cheerfully that, yes, he was out to 'get' Senator Fulbright, by any means . . . just as he said he had already helped 'get' Senator Thomas Kuchel in California." Hunt subsequently denied having used the word "get" in reference to either man and informed the *Gazette* that his opposition to the two men was not something to be "confessed" but something to be proud of. Hunt's aide John Curington later claimed that Hunt augmented his verbal attacks on Fulbright with large secret cash contributions to his opponent.

Hunt loosed what could only be described as just plain venom in a spat that commenced with columnist William F. Buckley, a former contributor to Facts Forum. According to Hunt, the once-enlightened Buckley, who had recently distinguished his brand of conservatism from that of the so-called far right, had lost his way. "Papers which publish his column have called him an outstanding conservative spokesman," Hunt wrote in one letter to the editor dated January 11, 1968, "but in recent years he has been making virulent attacks against well-known disciples of the truth side." One of the "well-known disciples" Hunt referred to was himself. "He says the books I write are silly, and catalogs them, hoping his followers will find them as silly as he says they are," Hunt said candidly in another letter to the editor. This he presented as final factual proof that Buckley was merely "masquerading as a conservative."

One of the few press profiles Hunt liked was a *Playboy* interview that ran in the magazine's August 1966 issue. Since the story mainly consisted of him talking about his right-wing views and telling a few stories about himself, there was not much that the old man could find objectionable. Besides, being in *Playboy* with all the good-looking women appealed to him. Hunt immediately ordered his aides to produce thousands of reprints of the article, which he then offered for sale at twenty-five cents per copy.

When not on the attack, Hunt liked to play cagey with the press, if only to keep their attention focused on him. Once, for example, a rumor began circulating that Hunt had purchased the *Saturday Review* magazine. Dallas reporter A. C. Greene called up Hunt and asked if the rumor were true.

"Well, I don't know," Hunt replied.

"What do you mean, you don't know?" Greene asked.

"I don't know whether I've bought it or not," Hunt said.

Hunt kept up his "maybe I have and maybe I haven't" line for several more minutes. Greene finally hung up, concluding that Hunt had not in fact purchased the magazine. Greene was right. The purchaser was the California-based Hunt-Wesson Foods, an unrelated firm that H. L. Hunt did not own.

When not being cagey, Hunt tried to show that he was a true "constructive" with positive things to say. In one column, for example, Hunt tried to counter charges that he was a racist by going on record in praise of a black leader. His choice was Moise Tshombe, the recently deposed prime minister of the Congo. Beneath the title "Plight of the Heroic Negro," Hunt wrote that "a Negro freedomist like Tshombe is more than a hindrance to communism; he is a threat, for communism must set race against race, particularly in the

USA, before its plans for world enslavement can reach fruition." Hunt also wrote a praiseful piece about Jews. On his rounds promoting HLH Products, Hunt would carry the piece with him to show to Jewish merchants and brokers. "I'm not prejudiced," Hunt would declare, drawing the column from his pocket, "and this proves it."

Alas, Hunt's professions of good-heartedness were mostly just that— professions. The old man loved to be serenaded by groups of local black schoolchildren on his birthday, but he was still every bit as prejudiced as his critics maintained. "H.L. hated niggers," one former employee recalled. "It pissed him off that they could cancel his vote."

Hunt also tried to offer "constructive" suggestions to America's major political parties, especially at election time. In 1968, he even attempted to have a say in the nomination of both the Republican and Democratic presidential candidates. His Democratic choice, of course, was Ted Kennedy, whom he suggested in the wake of Robert Kennedy's assassination. But his real interest was in the Republican candidate. Hunt's favorite was Michigan congressman Gerald R. Ford, and though Ford himself had not encouraged it, Hunt went to the Miami convention for the express purpose of placing Ford's name in nomination. "In the event of a deadlock," Hunt declared, "he might become the best nominee for president the Republicans could select." Hunt later claimed that when it become apparent Richard Nixon would be nominated on the first ballot, Ford and other party leaders discouraged his plan to nominate Ford. Two weeks after the convention, Hunt wrote, "When Nixon made his great acceptance speech, I was delighted that the idea of nominating Ford had been abandoned."

Hunt spent much of the middle and late 1960s engaged in a series of clandestine projects and ongoing secret adventures. Paul Rothermel's counterinvestigations of the Warren Commission and the Jim Garrison probes of the Kennedy assassination were two of the most important such episodes. But Rothermel and John Curington also provided their boss with intelligence on subjects ranging from new employees and local elections to the activities of radical groups of foreign students and the activities of members of Hunt's own family. Always the sort of man who wanted to know what was going on around him at all times, Hunt was growing extremely distrustful of people at almost all levels of his empire. As a result, he perpetuated a system of spying and counterspying that was confusing even to those who were supposed to be in charge of it. As Curington put it later, "We had so many guys spying on each other at one time you almost had to wear a badge."

Much of the Hunt spying was aimed at threats—or perceived threats— to the safety of Hunt and his family. One such threat involved a group of left-wing Libyan exchange students who were attending school in Dallas in the late 1960s. At this time, Hunt's son Bunker was trying to bring his massive Libyan oil production on stream, and there was a growing element of the Libyan population favoring nationalization of the country's oil fields. The Libyan students in Dallas were among the members of that segment. Curington provided Hunt with a startling report of one student meeting. Curington delivered his report in a memorandum filled with code names. "X" designated an Arab man. "MC" designated "my contact," which was Curington's source. The essence of the memo was that the Libyan students, which the report described as "left-wing nationalists," were contemplating some type of action against the Hunts because Bunker was, in their words, "stealing" oil from the people. The report did not say exactly what the Libyan students might do, but it did mention that one of the parties involved was a homosexual. As it turned out, the Libyan students' reported threat never materialized. But it was the kind of thing that kept the Hunt paranoia pumping hard and fast. That paranoia, in turn, helped fuel the system of spy and counterspy.

While his aides gathered intelligence through generally conventional overt and covert means, Hunt began to delve into more mystical methods. In part because of his abilities as an oil finder, Hunt came to believe that he might possess powers of extrasensory perception. He also began to place great faith in the psychic powers of forecaster Jeane Dixon. Mrs. Dixon's capabilities came to Hunt's attention in 1967, when he heard that she had correctly predicted the winner of that year's Kentucky Derby. Hunt subsequently began consulting her on everything from the numbers to bid on oil leases to the outcome of investigations of the Kennedy assassination and Hunt's still-continuing attempts to find a "cure" for his lobotomized son Hassie. Though the full record of Mrs. Dixon's predictions was never revealed, she was said to have pleased Hunt considerably with her prediction that Hassie would one day recover.

Hunt also drew on the counsel of several mysterious and highly controversial brain trusters. One of the most prominent of these advisers was Benjamin Harrison Freedman. A Jew based in New York, Freedman was a known contributor to several allegedly anti-Zionist organizations and propaganda sheets. According to a later sworn statement by John Curington, Hunt ordered Curington to furnish Freedman with unspecified amounts of cash "with instructions for the funds to be used to create an unfavorable image for Jews." On a more general level, Hunt relied on Freedman, whose anti-Zionist views enhanced his connections to the Arab world, as his Middle East watcher. Having been unsuccessful in previous attempts to gain concessions in Iran and Kuwait, Hunt nevertheless kept an eye out for an opportunity to get into the Middle East oil action throughout the early and middle 1960s. Although he was never able to put together a Middle East oil deal of his own, Hunt used the advice of Freedman and others about the volatile political situation in the Middle East as the basis for his decisions regarding such things as the purchase of farmland in the United States, the price of which he believed would be affected by developments overseas.

Ever the tightwad, Hunt dispersed money about as freely as a professional gambler might give away a royal straight flush. He paid his top men low salaries (Rothermel and Curington, for example, made less than $30,000 per year) and was known to dispute such inconsequential items as a $30.16 bill two black waiters submitted for a full day's work at a rare party at Mount Vernon. According to Rothermel, Hunt would even shortchange his own aides when ordering them to make under-the-table cash contributions to politicians. "He'd call me in and say, 'Here is five thousand dollars. I want you to deliver it to Mr. X,' " Rothermel recalled. "I would count it, and there would be only four thousand. I was one of the few people who could holler at him, and I'd tell him, 'You only gave me four thousand. Where's the other thousand?' And he'd tell me, 'You make up the difference.' "

Besides dispatching his aides on political projects, Hunt also entrusted his top men (particularly Curington) with the administration of matters pertaining to his publicly secret family by Frania Tye Lee and his now recognized family by Ruth Ray Hunt. These tasks included routine business deals for both the Reliance Trusts (for Frania) and the Secure Trusts (for Ruth). But according to Curington, they also included "causing certain [oil and gas] farmout agreements to be transferred among the various entities after production had been obtained, and backdating them," presumably to avoid taxes.

Although Hunt no longer gambled, he had several items of unfinished business left over from the old days. One was an $800,000 debt owed to him by Las Vegas gambler Johnny Drew, which, with Curington's help, he tried unsuccessfully to collect year after year. According to Curington and others, Hunt also had a number of unpaid debts of his own. One was a $430,000 debt he allegedly owed to the notorious Frank Erickson. In this case, Curington was assigned to "protect" Hunt from Erickson's efforts to collect, presumably by helping Hunt get out of town and keeping his whereabouts a secret when Erickson came asking for his money. Still another outstanding debt was $70,-000 Hunt owed to his old football-betting crony Jimmy "the Greek" Snyder. One day, after being busted by the Justice Department and with his daughter deathly ill, "the Greek" called up Hunt in an effort to collect the debt.

"I hear Johnny Drew is still alive," Hunt said. "Why don't you get it off him."

"H.L., you know Johnny isn't going to pay me," Snyder replied.

"Well, Jimmy," Hunt said, "you know I've always fulfilled my obligations But I got screwed by Drew and I'm just not going to pay."

"In a way, I can't blame you," Snyder admitted. "But it really isn't fair to put your problems on me. If someone didn't pay me, and I laid off some of your bets, I'd still be responsible to you."

"I'll think about it," Hunt said. But in the end, he never paid off.

Taken separately or as a whole, the elements of Hunt's universe hardly amounted to a world of "just plain folks." But for all the continuing craziness and incessant activity, there were also signs that the old man was mellowing. His personal habits were almost spartan, especially compared to earlier years. He did not lapse into gambling or smoking cigars, and he stuck ever more religiously to his special diet. Though he often kept Ruth's dinner time busy with a swirl of unannounced last-minute guests, many of them political friends, his night life was basically his porch sitting and singalongs. Ruth was constantly sharing the house and the swimming pool with visiting church groups. She extended an open invitation to Hunt employees to join in the regular singalongs, and she tried to make Mount Vernon the home of both Dallas families, especially at times like Christmas. But H.L. and Ruth did not all of a sudden start giving big parties or attending the charity balls that were the highlights of Dallas high society. They were usually in bed by 10:00 P.M.

One of Hunt's favorite recreations at Mount Vernon was feeding the handful of deer he kept in a large pen in back of the house. Hunt knew all the deer by name, and loved to stroll among them, petting each one and handing it a carrot or a crumb. "Here, Sweetie," he would chirp, "have a bite."

A self-described "billionaire health crank," Hunt also enjoyed sharing the wisdom of the "just plain folks" medicine he practiced on himself. Thus, Hunt filled the back pages of his political books with such things as cold remedies and instructions on how to place long-distance telephone calls. For respiratory attacks, Hunt advised, "Place a wool or flannel cloth about 8″ x 10″ inside undershirt or pajama top to cover chest, with Vicks applied generously to the inside of the cloth. If throat is sore, use a wool sock pinned around the neck in addition to the cloth on chest. The Vicks fumes resulting from the body heat are inhaled and are very helpful." Hunt also prescribed Panalba capsules ("Upjohn preparation"), Histady 1, and Ephedrine Number 2 ("a Lilly preparation"), vitamin C, and, of course, three HLH products—HLH One-A-Day Multi-Vitamins, HLH Brewers Yeast, and HLH Natural Vitamins. Hunt also advised cures for ailments ranging from "nausea and vomiting" to "spots on the back of the hand."

Hunt's favorite cure-all was aloe vera. He had heard of aloe vera for years, but his interest in the plant's curative properties was renewed "in late 1967 or early 1968," when he heard the late great farm broadcaster Dewey Compton mention it on a Saturday-morning radio show. Hunt sent three of his men to investigate aloe vera, and they reported back that the plant's curative properties were not just old wives' tales. Hunt opened an entire HLH Aloe Vera cosmetics line. Among the top of the line were HLH Aloe Vera Suntan Lotion and HLH Aloe Vera Hand Lotion, a bottle of which Hunt always kept on his desk. Hunt promoted aloe vera with the same style and enthusiasm with which he promoted his other HLH products, often making personal visits to drug and department stores in an effort to persuade them to carry his aloe-vera-based goods. At home, Hunt hawked aloe vera and his other health tips to all his guests, often handing out aloe vera samples and copies of his books as if they were afterdinner mints.

Hunt's other great new health passion in the late 1960s was his Indian Hot Springs resort in west Texas. Hunt bought the 1,900-acre resort in 1967 after hearing of the health-giving qualities of its mineral waters. Once the stomping grounds of Apaches, who discovered the hot springs centuries before, the resort was in a state of decline and disrepair. Hunt had the adobe buildings around the springs restored, and installed whirlpool jets to enhance the effects of the mineral waters. In what was certainly one of his more bizarre projects, Hunt also ordered his men to dig up some old Indian graves that were discovered in the area, and had them moved onto his property as a tourist attraction.

When not looking for new health potions and "cures," Hunt often looked back on the adventures of his life and times with nostalgia and sentiment. He began to talk about his past—or, rather, his own sanitized version of his past —in life-story-style interviews for newspapers and magazines. He also wrote columns about such subjects as the Dad Joiner deal, his life on the Mississippi, his experiences in the El Dorado oil boom, and his mother. On one occasion, Hunt even sacrificed profit to sentiment. This occurred when the Daisy Bradford No. 3, the original discovery well on the Dad Joiner leases, had just about given out. The well was still coughing up a barrel or two per day, but the cost of keeping the pumping equipment on the well was greater than the revenue from the oil it was producing. Under ordinary circumstances, the well would simply be shut in and chalked up as another depleted hole. But Hunt just hated to see it go. "There must be some way we can keep it producing," he suggested to his field man. Taking the hint, the field man kept the pumps in place and allowed the Daisy Bradford No. 3 to keep yielding a little more oil each day.

H. L. Hunt the tightwad also delighted in performing small and unexpected kindnesses for relatives, friends, and employees. These ranged from adding on a room at Mount Vernon so that his wife's mother would have a place to stay on her visits to Dallas to paying sick calls on the children of old cronies and offering occasional investment opportunities to the men who worked for him. Though still adverse to charities, Hunt also maintained his interest in opera.

Although he had ceased being a big-time gambler, Hunt still liked to play a game of checkers from time to time. Most of all, he liked to drop in unannounced at the general store in some small town and get in a game with the local porch sitters. It was a most nostalgic scene—H. L. Hunt, the white-haired oilman with his blue suit and bow tie, sitting barrel by barrel with a bunch of rustic old-timers in their suspenders and straw hats, plotting strategies across the checkerboard as if a fortune hung in the balance. And in a way, a fortune did hang in the balance. For H. L. Hunt still considered himself both the world champion of checkers and the checkers champion of Chicot County, Arkansas. His pride was at stake. He always played to win. And usually he did win.

The greatest joy of Hunt's life during the middle 1960s was the return of his beloved son Hassie. The motive force behind Hassie's return was Ruth. In the eastern mental institution where he had been staying, Hassie was under twenty-four-hour supervision, but, as Ruth recalled, "to see him there alone wasn't like being in a home environment." Ruth finally went to Popsy and suggested, "Why don't we bring him home? We can keep nurses with him around the clock." Hunt agreed, and in early 1965 Hassie Hunt came back to Mount Vernon.

Hassie's homecoming was not without its difficulties. As Ruth recalled, "We did make adjustments, and the children made adjustments." Although

Hunt could never give up hope for his favorite son's full recovery, Hassie was still seriously ill. The lobotomy had muted Hassie's violence, but it had also left him a middle-aged man with a childlike mentality. There was not much Hassie could do besides walk around the grounds of Mount Vernon, take his meals, and sit in on the family singalongs. Often, Hassie stayed off to one side of the room by himself, without saying (or singing) much of anything. When he stood up, he often stood at attention, military style. His demeanor was neither sullen nor sad so much as strangely stiff, as if he were in a trance.

For the first few years after his return, Hassie lived right on the grounds at Mount Vernon in specially constructed quarters fashioned from the pool house. Then a mansion adjacent to Mount Vernon went up for sale. Hassie's trust bought the house, and Hassie moved in. Hunt saw to it that a flagpole was erected in the front yard so that Hassie, like his father, could fly the flag at all times. Both at Mount Vernon and at his new home, Hassie was supervised on a twenty-four-hour basis by staffs of male and female nurses.

Hassie Hunt was still a big name in the oil business. At Hunt Oil, no less than three separate entities, two trusts, and a production company bore his name. Those entities had been drilling wells and operating in the oil business just like ordinary companies for all the years of Hassie's illness. During that time, the Hassie Hunt interests had built up production estimated to be worth more than $200 million. Not counting Bunker's huge strike in Libya, this was still more oil than all the other Hunt sons had found. Hunt occasionally took Hassie down to the Hunt Oil offices for a visit, but Hassie was in no shape to resume command of his empire within the empire upon his return from the hospital. Still, the trusts operating under his name continued to drill, drill, drill, and Hassie's income kept flowing in, just as if the founder's instinctual luck had rubbed off.

Occasionally, in nonbusiness situations, Hassie would surprise everyone but his father with a display of something akin to the "mystical" powers Hunt still attributed to him. Once, for example, Hassie, Hunt, and John Curington were sitting on the back porch at Mount Vernon. It was a clear evening, but Hassie turned to his father and said, "They're having a terrible storm in Waco right now." The next morning's paper proved Hassie was right. Waco, which was about one hundred miles from Dallas, had indeed suffered a terrible storm. On another occasion, Hassie showed an even eerier form of foresight. It all began when Hunt advised Curington to inform Hassie that he had just fired one of Hassie's male attendants for being a spendthrift. "He was just too rich for my blood," Hunt confided to Curington, "but I think Hassie was rather fond of him, so try to break it to him easy." Curington walked out to the pool house to tell Hassie the bad news only to find that Hassie already knew what had happened. Before Curington could even speak, Hassie said, "I'm glad Dad got rid of him. He was too rich for my blood." As Curington noted in amazement, Hassie had used almost the same words to describe the fired attendant as his father had used.

Despite the "adjustments" the Hunts had to make, Hassie's homecoming seemed to make Hassie feel a little better, and it definitely made Hunt feel better. Even if Hassie could not rejoin him in the oil business or some other venture, Hunt could still enjoy just sharing the company of his son. One of their favorite pleasures was to go on long walks down the driveway at Mount Vernon and along the little strip of parkland that formed the bank of White Rock Lake. Now nearly fifty years old, Hassie was still the spitting image of his father. He was a little thinner and more gray-haired than white-haired, but he had the same jaw and eyes, the same general height and build, even, it seemed, the same walk as his old man. The sight of the two of them strolling together on a cloudless spring afternoon, each in a blue suit, white shirt, and blue bow tie, was enough to make the average passerby think that he or she was seeing double.

Walking with Hassie, sitting on the porch with Ruthie, carrying brown-paper-sack lunches to work, driving his own car—these habits of H. L. Hunt never failed to impress media interviewers with the old man's simplicity and frugality. *Playboy, Esquire,* the *Houston Chronicle,* the *Dallas Morning News,* the *Dallas Times Herald* all sent those writers and reporters who were struck by Hunt's "just plain folks" side to Hunt's house. None could really believe that the world's richest man could enjoy living the way he did. But Hunt had the same reply to all their doubts. As he put it, "I feel like I'm living high."

While their father lived in the world according to H. L. Hunt, the three active sons of Lyda Bunker Hunt made big names and big money for themselves in a variety of fields. Nelson Bunker Hunt once again went through the most sensational (if not the most highly publicized) swings. The fulcrum for Bunker's seesaw ride was his multibillion-barrel Libyan oil play. Like his father's battle to buy and maintain the Dad Joiner leases in the east Texas field, Bunker's adventures in Libya developed into a saga of epic proportions, involving, among other things, a primal conflict between majors and independents. But where Hunt's drama was set in the east Texas piny woods with wildcatters, con men, hot-oil runners, Texas Rangers on horseback, and the hardships of the depression, Bunker's modern oil drama was played out in the deserts of North Africa and the corporate towers of Dallas and London with an aging king, a radical young army colonel, international politics, socialist revolution, and CIA intrigue.

The first and foremost problem Bunker faced in Libya was getting his great oil field on production. By December of 1965, four years after the discovery of the Sarir field, not a single drop of Sarir crude had found its way to market. The main reason was that the 320-mile pipeline from the field to Tobruk harbor on the Mediterranean was still unfinished. Building the pipeline was a massive job, but it should not have taken as long as it did. Bunker suspected that the cause for the delays was not so much the adverse desert conditions, but the foot dragging of his partner, British Petroleum. As an independent oil producer still strapped by his string of prior dry holes, Bunker was anxious to get the Sarir field on stream as quickly as possible so as to start realizing some income. But British Petroleum, as a major oil company with plenty of other producing fields in its inventory, looked at Libya in the context of world market conditions. World oil prices were then in the under-$2-per-barrel range, and British Petroleum was not anxious to drive the price further downward by flooding the European market with Libyan crude.

To make matters worse, there was political trouble brewing in Libya. Aging King Idris ruled over a triethnic nation most of whose 1 million citizens lived in abject poverty. Now that Hunt–British Petroleum and several other companies had made big oil discoveries in Libya, radical populist and socialist movements were demanding that the government share the country's new oil wealth. King Idris and his ministers made an effort to respond to what was being said in the streets. Having allowed the oil companies themselves to draft the country's original petroleum law, the king decided in 1966 to put a new petroleum law into effect. The new law was still highly favorable to the oil companies, but it did call for doubling the effective tax rate and for the hiring of more Libyan nationals to work in the oil fields. For Bunker, the new law meant that per-barrel production costs, which were already higher than those in the Persian Gulf countries, would be considerably higher by the time the Sarir field did come on stream.

About this time, the Central Intelligence Agency entered the picture. Given the popular movements growing in Libya, the State Department had become concerned over the prospects of political upheaval. The CIA, apparently in an effort to monitor the situation, wanted to place an agent in Bunker's Libyan operation. Bunker refused. The reason he could not allow it, he told the CIA, was not lack of patriotism, but his concession agreement with the Libyans which specifically prohibited him from representing a foreign government. According to Bunker, the CIA asked twice more for Bunker's cooperation and was refused twice more. Then the CIA went ahead and covertly placed an agent in his operations anyway.

In January of 1967, the long-awaited day finally came. British Petroleum opened the pipeline between Sarir and Tobruk, and the oil began flowing at a rate of 100,000 barrels per day. But as prodigious as this output was, it accounted for less than one-quarter of the field's estimated capacity, or at least what Bunker estimated the capacity to be. Bunker's partner, British Petroleum, kept playing down the significance of the Sarir production. One official spokesman even told the press that the Sarir field would "never do more than 150,000 barrels a day." This statement infuriated Bunker. To him, it was more evidence that British Petroleum preferred to hold down its Libyan production in favor of pulling oil from its interests in the Persian Gulf.

In an attempt to get British Petroleum to increase production, Bunker leaked information to the *Oil and Gas Journal,* which suggested that the true capacity of Sarir was three times the highest estimate British Petroleum was giving out. Being half owned by the British government, British Petroleum now faced the embarrassing predicament of having to explain itself to the British public. BP's defenders would later deny giving out any deliberately low estimates or engaging in any effort to limit the field's production below its capacity. But after Bunker's leak to the *Oil and Gas Journal,* production from Sarir increased dramatically. By the end of 1967, the field was pumping out over 300,000 barrels a day, or more than double BP's original public estimate of the field's total capacity.

Bunker was impatient for even more production. At his own expense, he constructed another $20 million worth of production facilities to complement the $160 million worth of pipeline and equipment BP had installed. Eventually, production from the Sarir field rose to 470,000 barrels per day. After deductions for BP's interest and oil due them as payment for being the operator of the field, Bunker's share came to about 220,000 barrels a day, or more than twice the daily production of all the other Hunt-family oil interests combined. His net profit, after deductions for royalties and expenses, came to about 40 cents a barrel. Thus, by the time Sarir was producing at peak capacity, Bunker was taking home approximately $30 million per year, all of which, because of the foreign tax credit, was exempt from U.S. taxes. Bunker had not only gotten himself out of debt, but appeared to be well on his way to becoming richer than his father had ever been.

As the Hunt luck would have it, Bunker's fortunes in the horse business turned upward about the same time that his Libyan production finally came on stream. Though not nearly as sizable an investment as his oil gambles, Bunker's stake in horses was something he took seriously. He personally studied the bloodlines and racing statistics of his horses and established a numbering system to keep track of each one. Able to reel off the figures on his horses from memory, he operated straight from the hip, a fact that led him to make every beginner's mistake in the book. But Bunker also developed some innovative new ideas of his own. One was purchasing Peruvian mares, which he found he could acquire much more cheaply than American or European horses. Early on, Bunker decided to concentrate his racing efforts in Europe rather than the United States. As he later explained, "I had lots of business in Europe and spent quite a bit of time there. Also, living in Texas, I was in a sort of neutral area as far as racing is concerned. To see my horses run involved a rather sizable plane trip, anyway, whether they were racing here or in Europe. Also, horses stand training better in Europe. We had a good bunch of two year olds . . . and so many of them went wrong. There was the humanitarian aspect of just hating to see the horses get hurt and there also was the financial aspect."

Bunker's strategies began to pay off. In 1967, his horse Gazala II won the French 1,000 Guineas and French Oaks, becoming Bunker's first real champion. That same year, at Tattersall Farms' December sales in Kentucky, Bunker acquired the progenitor of his success as a horse breeder with the purchase of a British-bred colt called Vaguely Noble. Bunker bought a half interest in Vaguely Noble after it was auctioned for $342,720, then the record bid for a horse at a public auction. Vaguely Noble went on to win four of five races in Europe, including the prestigious Arc de Triomphe. But Vaguely

Noble's true worth began to tell when Bunker acquired a majority interest in the colt and brought him to Kentucky to stud. Over the next several years, Vaguely Noble sired a line of champion thoroughbreds that would bring their owner his original investment back dozens of times.

Dollar for dollar, the horse business would prove to be one of Bunker Hunt's most profitable enterprises. This was partly because of the tax advantages afforded by the accelerated depreciation of race horses, and partly because Bunker ran his horse business like a business and did well at it. But the sport had an added appeal for Bunker that he did not always find in oil and other businesses. As he put it, "Nearly everyone I meet in racing is interesting." Among the interesting people Bunker met in the course of his racing endeavors were Queen Elizabeth, the Queen Mother, and a long list of other European nobles and big-business figures. But Bunker was no snob. He also took the time to chat with horse trainers, jockeys, grooms, and every other level of person associated with his sport. Besides gaining him a next-door-neighbor-style image, this practice also helped him glean the best information as he built his string to over two hundred horses.

Judging from his personal and financial involvement, Bunker also found right-wing politics interesting. Bunker did not have as high a profile as his father did during the 1960s, but he was nonetheless one of the largest political contributors in the country. Reporters frequently accused H. L. Hunt of being a financial backer of the John Birch Society, an accusation the old man repeatedly and truthfully denied. But what Hunt never seemed to get around to explaining amid his denials was that his son Bunker was one of the John Birch Society's largest contributors. Exactly how much money Bunker gave the Birchers over the years was never disclosed, but Bunker's close associates maintained that his donations were substantial. The first public indication of Bunker's financial commitment came in 1965, when the Bircher-owned *American Opinion* magazine filed a statement of ownership with the Post Office as required by law. Bunker Hunt was listed as owner of 1 percent or more of the stock in the magazine; only two other individuals were listed with Bunker. Bunker gave a rare public indication of his ideological fervor one day in 1965, when a Dallas reporter, trying to contact Bunker's father for a comment, informed Bunker that Barry Goldwater, Clare Boothe Luce, Karl Brandt, and a handful of other notables had formed a conservative organization called the Free Society Association. "Those don't strike me as any so-called conservatives," Bunker told the reporter. "They're not Robert Welch or H. L. Hunt."

In addition to backing the Birchers, Bunker actively supported a number of other controversial right-wing organizations. Along with his brother-in-law Al Hill, he was an "endorser" of the arch-conservative Manion Forum, which (like LIFE LINE) devoted itself to spreading right-wing political messages by means of radio and television, and a member of the Southern States Industrial Council, an organization opposed to unions, civil rights, foreign aid, and the Tennessee Valley Authority. But Bunker's strangest association by far was with the International Committee for the Defense of Christian Culture

(ICDCC). Founded in the early 1960s by an ex-Nazi turned anticommunist, the ICDCC claimed the support of German chancellor Konrad Adenauer, French premier Antoine Pinay, segregationist Oklahoma preacher Billy James Hargis, Major General Charles A. Willoughby (an arch-conservative friend of H. L. Hunt's), and Nelson Bunker Hunt. In addition to being dedicated to the defense of Christian culture, the ICDCC claimed to be devoted to "resistance against regimes and political concepts" contrary to its own. Exactly what the organization did toward its goals was never fully revealed, but it apparently disbanded in 1964. Its significance for Bunker may only have been that the ICDCC was like LIFE LINE on a global scale and marked one of his first attempts to support capitalism and Christianity with a united thrust.

A member of Highland Park Presbyterian Church in Dallas, Bunker subsequently became involved with Campus Crusade for Christ, an avowedly nondenominational born-again organization founded by layman Bill Bright. In those days, Campus Crusade was primarily a U.S. organization devoted to "spreading the word" on the nation's campuses. But like the ICDCC leaders, Bright had some more global plans in mind for the future, plans in which Bunker Hunt would figure prominently. Just as Robert Welch was Bunker's surrogate political father figure, Bill Bright became Bunker's surrogate religious father.

Bunker's political activities also extended into more mainstream associations. Though larger than most of his father's contributions of record, many of Bunker's political gifts were of moderate size. Campaign finance records show that Bunker contributed $1,000 to Senator Strom Thurmond's 1964 campaign and $1,000 to Harrison Thyng's 1966 campaign in New Hampshire. In 1967, Bunker gave $2,500 to a group backing Thurmond and Ezra Taft Benson for president and vice president in 1968.

Bunker reserved his biggest political money for the 1968 presidential campaign of George C. Wallace. At one point, a disgruntled Wallace supporter charged that the John Birch Society was trying to "take over" the Wallace campaign in Texas. The Wallace campaign officially denied the charge, but as things developed, it became clear that at least one John Birch Society member —Nelson Bunker Hunt of Dallas—exercised a significant financial influence over the campaign. Three years after the campaign was over, it was disclosed that Bunker had given General Curtis LeMay a $1-million investment fund as an incentive to become George Wallace's running mate. The fund was reportedly set up so that LeMay would be compensated for whatever career and financial losses he might suffer while campaigning for the vice presidency. Once again, the Hunt-supported candidates lost the race, but Wallace did make a very strong showing. While most of Wallace's success was attributable to his personal appeal, platform, and political skill, there was little doubt that Bunker Hunt's financial support was an important boost to the Wallace-LeMay ticket.

By the spring of 1969, the world of Nelson Bunker Hunt was blossoming at last. His Libyan oil production had been on stream for over two full years, his race horses were doing better and better, he had four healthy children, and his twentieth wedding anniversary was just around the corner. All this seemed to call for a celebration. Though they lived in a fine French-provincial-style house in Highland Park, Bunker and his wife Caroline were not known as socialites. But one weekend in May of 1969, they decided to give a party for five hundred people at London's prestigious Claridge's Hotel. The entertainment consisted of no less than three bands, including Woody Herman and his orchestra, whom the Hunts flew over from the United States for the party. The fact that the Hunts staged their party in England, not in Texas, was appropriate. No longer just his father's son, Bunker had a notable list of accomplishments in his own right. But Bunker's greatest successes were outside the United States. His biggest oil deal was his partnership with British Petroleum in Libya. His winning race horses were in France and England. Despite his wealth and political escapades, Nelson Bunker Hunt was not very well known in his own country, and he was definitely not considered much of a social lion. But with the party at Claridge's he seemed to be showing the world that he had arrived. News of the Hunts' social doings filled the gossip pages of the London dailies.

Then, just as things seemed to be going so well, trouble broke loose in Libya. On September 1, 1969, four months after Bunker's big bash in London, a twenty-seven-year-old Libyan army colonel named Muammar al-Qaddafi led a coup which deposed the aged King Idris and established himself as the new Libyan head of state. An avowed socialist, al-Qaddafi was loudly hostile toward the foreign oil companies who were exploiting his country's rich petroleum resources. It seemed inevitable that he would make much larger demands on the oil companies. The question was: How much larger? Would al-Qaddafi merely insist on increased royalty and tax payments? Or would he also move to nationalize the oil industry? Until the new regime established a petroleum policy of its own, the answers to these questions were unknown. What was certain was that the staying power of Bunker Hunt and the other oil companies with interests in Libya would be put to a severe test in the coming months. There was nothing to do except wait and see.

Meanwhile, Bunker became more and more paranoid. He took great pains to keep his business projects and personal comings and goings as little known as possible. When he traveled by commercial airline, he generally made several reservations on different flights at different times and did not tell anyone which flight he actually planned to take. "You would never know what plane he was coming in on," complained a former overseas business associate. Though this practice obviously caused some inconvenience for Bunker's friends, it was justified, in Bunker's eyes, by the confusion it caused his enemies. The specific identity of those enemies was always hard to determine. The CIA, the Warren Commission investigators, government regulators, business rivals, foreign political agitators—Bunker hinted at all of these potential villains at one point or another. Sometimes the "threats"—that is, the possible embarrassments, worrisome investigating, and so forth—were real. But on many occasions they seemed, even to some of his most sympathetic friends, to be largely imaginary. Real or imaginary, Bunker genuinely seemed to love intrigue and mystery and was prone to coming and going without notice to anyone even on the most routine occasions.

While Bunker did his international wheeling and dealing, his younger brother Herbert, now in his mid-thirties and also on the outs with his father, set about increasing his own share of the family fortune. Although Herbert operated more quietly and with less flair than Bunker, he, too, took some sizable risks. After the falling out with his father at Hunt Oil Company, Herbert began to concentrate on expanding Penrod Drilling, the drilling contractor he owned in partnership with Bunker and Lamar. At this point in time the biggest gamble going was the future of offshore drilling around the world. New plays were opening up or due to open up in the North Sea, Alaska, the Canadian Arctic, and other exotic locations around the globe. There was a prospect of huge profits for offshore contractors if the expected drilling boom materialized. But there was also the risk of tremendous losses for overextended contractors if the boom turned out to be a bust.

Herbert decided to bet that the offshore drilling boom would pan out. Over the next several years, he poured an estimated $100 million of family money into Penrod, adding five expensive new jack-up rigs to Penrod's fleet, while the company reduced its fleet of land rigs from forty-six to twenty-three. Where H. L. Hunt had first drilled with 50-foot-tall pine derricks powered by wheezy old steam boilers, the new jack-up rigs Herbert bought were set on retractable steel-girdered legs that were over 400 feet tall and included not only powerful combustion engines to drive the rig, but a helicopter pad, an excursion boat, and complete galley and living quarters for the crew. Towed to location by tugs, the jack-up rig floated on a large triangular hull with its legs pulled up. When it reached the drilling site, the rig anchored its legs on the sea floor, and jacked up the hull above the water, where it became the drilling platform. Measuring over 200 feet in length and width and weighing over 21 million pounds, the average cost of these rigs at the time was over $20 million, and that cost was destined to escalate sharply in years to come.

Dispatching the rigs to the Gulf of Mexico, Herbert found that the drilling boom was real. Thanks to a steady stream of business both from Hunt family and from outside accounts, Penrod prospered. In 1969, the company went international, sending its first jack-up rig to drill in the Dutch sector of the North Sea. Appropriately enough, the well was drilled for Placid Oil and turned out to be a big producer.

Like brother Bunker, Herbert shared the Hunt family's congenital arch conservatism, but he was not as active in political affairs as his brother or his father. An elder of the Highland Park Presbyterian Church, Herbert instead played a greater role in conventional civic affairs. He was active in the Boy Scouts, in which his son was a member, and went on to become president of the International Association of Oilwell Drilling Contractors, the Dallas Petroleum Club, and the Wadley Institute of Molecular Medicine. More conventional than Bunker in appearance, dress, and style, Herbert served as the Hunt family's official representative to the outside world.

Although Bunker and Herbert dealt with the biggest money, the real star of the Hunt family in the eyes of most of the American public was Lamar. By the middle 1960s, Lamar's tall, trim figure, bespectacled face, and L-shaped jaw were becoming familiar to millions of football-conscious Americans. Lamar's enterprises were the kind the public could see and enjoy. The Kansas City Chiefs and the American Football League were in the newspapers and on radio and television every day during the pro-football season and almost every day during the off-season. Many of those who had only read about Lamar Hunt still considered him a rich man's son. But those who dealt with Lamar firsthand—in the oil business or in the sports business—quickly realized that he had much more going for him than his last name and his trust fund. Lamar was proving himself a shrewd and insightful businessman, a dreamer who could make his dreams become reality, and during the middle and late 1960s, Lamar took his dreams even further.

Lamar's blossoming actually began with his second marriage, which took place on January 22, 1964. Lamar's new bride, Norma Lynn Knobel, then age twenty-five, was a beauty. She had short brown hair, beautiful big brown eyes, and a bone structure that combined the best features of a top fashion model and the girl next door. She and Lamar had met a few summers before when Norma was selling tickets and doing promotional work for the old Dallas football team. The newspapers made much of the fact that Norma was a schoolteacher (she taught history at suburban Richardson High School) who was marrying a millionaire. But Norma was no ordinary suburban school-teacher. An honors graduate of North Texas State University, she had been president of her sorority, Top Coed on Campus, Woman of the Year, and one of those listed in *Who's Who among Students in American Colleges and Universities.* She was also quite a football fan. According to the newspaper article announcing her wedding, she had seen some thirty games during the 1963–1964 season.

The wedding took place on a Wednesday morning at the home of Norma's parents. After the ceremony, the thirty-one-year-old sports magnate and his bride flew off to Austria to see the 1964 Winter Olympics. Upon their return to Dallas, Norma Hunt seemed to bring her once shy husband out of his shell. She was good at handling people and publicity and appeared to be able to put Lamar more at ease in public. The two of them made a most striking couple, especially after Norma dyed her hair blonde and began wearing designer fashions. Thanks to Norma, Lamar began to exhibit what was popularly referred to as "style."

Thanks to Lamar, the world of professional sports proceeded to go through some of the most important transformations in its history. Pro football was the first to be affected. By the end of the 1964 season (its first under the five-year $36-million contract with NBCO), it was apparent that the AFL was not just a play-by-night operation, but a rapidly maturing organization whose

franchises were beginning to show solid profit-making potential. Competition
with the NFL grew fiercer than ever. In 1965, the competition escalated to the
level of a war when the New York Jets of the AFL signed highly touted
University of Alabama quarterback Joe Namath. The bidding over Namath
and the $400,000 contract the young quarterback was able to negotiate con-
vinced many team owners in both leagues that unless something was done,
money wars over highly sought players could drive them all into bankruptcy.
The two leagues continued to do financial battle through the 1965 season, but
the idea of negotiating a merger between the two leagues began to be discussed
more and more seriously.

Then in April 1966, while hurrying through the lobby of the Dallas airport
to catch a plane to Houston, Lamar Hunt bumped into Tex Schramm, general
manager of the Dallas Cowboys. Standing beneath the statue of the Texas
Ranger that dominates the Love Field lobby, the two men began talking
football. Their discussion quickly turned to the subject of an NFL-AFL
merger. Lamar decided to delay his flight to Houston. Instead, he and
Schramm walked out to Schramm's car, got inside, and sat there talking
merger for an hour and a half. That talk proved to be a decisive one. More
formal negotiations ensued, and two months later, on June 8, 1966, Hunt,
Schramm, and NFL commissioner Pete Rozelle announced in New York that
the NFL and AFL would merge in stages to be completed over the next four
years.

The AFL remained in image and in fact the weak sister of the two leagues
in the early years. NFL teams won most of the interleague games and the first
two Super Bowls. Then in Super Bowl 3, the New York Jets of the AFL, led
by the flamboyant Joe Namath, defeated the Baltimore Colts of the NFL. The
Jet's victory proved to the NFL and to the fans that the AFL had truly come
of age. The next year's Super Bowl was the last one prior to the final merger
between the two leagues. This time, the Kansas City Chiefs of the AFL, owned
by Lamar Hunt, beat the NFL's Minnesota Vikings 23–7. After the game, a
slightly tattered Lamar Hunt stood in the middle of the dressing room to
accept the championship trophy, his eyes welling with tears of happiness.

Lamar's stewardship of the AFL proved that he had sharp business
acumen and staying power. His next big sports venture—the creation of a
professional tennis circuit—proved that he was innovative as well. The idea
for the venture actually came from Dave Dixon, a New Orleans friend who
had previously expressed interest in bringing an AFL franchise to his city. Like
many other sports enthusiasts, Dixon could see that world-class tennis was a
badly mismanaged hypocrisy. The sport was controlled by the amateur organizations, whose full-time players made a living only by taking money under the
table. Professional tournaments, such as they were, offered little prize money
and drew few spectators. Dixon recognized that tennis was "a great sport that
was not being handled correctly." He also realized that between 1957 and 1967,
close to one hundred fine sports arenas had been built in the United States,
arenas that would welcome a sport like tennis when their other occupant sports

were out of town or off-season. Viewing tennis as "a brand-new opportunity," Dixon turned to someone with the staying power to make his idea work. That man was Lamar Hunt.

"I like it," Lamar remarked when Dixon explained his idea for a pro-tennis tour one day in 1967. One of the selling points was that, unlike football, Lamar would not have to buy a franchise. In addition, the tennis tour would not have to compete with a powerful, established professional league. The players, unaccustomed to the high salaries common in other pro sports, could be contracted for relatively little.

"Let me think about it," Lamar said. About a week later, he informed Dixon that he was ready to go ahead with the idea. Dixon agreed to put up 50 percent of the starting capital. Lamar put up 25 percent and his nephew Al Hill, Jr., Margaret Hunt Hill's son, put up another 25 percent.

From the beginning, Lamar was the driving force. He thought up the name for the new enterprise—World Champion Tennis (WCT)—and the new style that should go along with it. In making tennis a mass spectator sport, it was essential to move it out of the country-club atmosphere—not just physically, but in every other way. Thus, he decided to replace the traditional tennis whites with colored clothing and to stage the tournaments in public arenas as much as possible. He instituted rules changes like the seven-point tie breaker in an effort to add to the excitement and to keep match times within manageable limits. More importantly, he also signed up the tour's first players. His strategy was simply to go after the four male semifinalists at Wimbledon that year. The four happened to be John Newcombe, Roger Taylor, Tony Roche, and Nicki Pilic. When the players left the stadium, Lamar met them with American Football League contracts that had been revised to apply to tennis and offers of $40,000 each. Taylor and Pilic signed up on the spot; each received a suit of clothes from a Saville Row tailor as a bonus. Newcombe and Roche agreed to turn pro a short time later. These first four were later joined by Dennis Ralston, Cliff Drysdale, Butch Bucholz, and Pierre Barthes, who filled out the nucleus of first pros known as the "Handsome Eight."

As Dave Dixon recalled with only slight exaggeration, the signing of these four top players virtually "wiped out amateur tennis." The WCT lost $300,000 its first year, and Dixon eventually dropped out of the venture, but Lamar stuck with it. He kept signing the top amateur players, fighting the bans the amateur organizations put on the pros and competing against the rival pro-tennis organization that sprung up after WCT. In time, he won. WCT became a moneymaker, and the professionals of tennis came to dominate the amateurs.

About the same time he was getting the WCT going, Lamar got involved in still another new sports venture—bringing professional soccer to America. The idea seemed like a natural. Though confined mainly to prep school and elite college leagues in the United States, soccer was the largest drawing sport in the world. Why not in America, too? Two pro-soccer leagues, the National Professional Soccer League and the United Soccer Association, got going in 1968. Lamar joined the United Soccer Association, which had been founded by Los Angeles sports czar Jack Kent Cooke, and named his team the Dallas Tornado. He approached his new enterprise with high hopes. "I only paid twenty-five thousand dollars for a franchise," Lamar recalled afterward. "There were no promotional dollars, the operating cost was low, and we had dreams of quick success when the leagues merged the next year." But success did not come as easily as it had in pro football. All but five of the original seventeen teams dropped out of the league. Attendance averaged a paltry 4,500 people per game. The Dallas Tornado, like all other teams, lost money, but Lamar, with a persistence that could only have been inherited from his father, stuck it out. As he remarked later, "I was too hardheaded to give in."

Lamar did not confine his new projects to sports. A showman at heart, he viewed his sports enterprises not just as athletics, but as entertainment. Thus, it was natural that Lamar should begin to move into more traditional segments of the entertainment industry as well. One of his first big projects was his proposal to turn Alcatraz into a tourist attraction. Lamar offered to buy the island for $2 million from the city of San Francisco and promised to spend another $4 million to "retain and restore all the historic buildings, plant new trees and flowers and construct a shopping area like San Francisco of the 1930s." He also said he would build an underground space museum. Lamar's plans had the backing of Mayor Joseph Alioto, but after receiving tentative approval from the city supervisors, the plan drew over 10,000 citizen protest letters.

Lamar eventually abandoned the Alcatraz project, but he did not give up his desire to expand in the entertainment industry. He went on to buy an amusement park in Kansas City called Worlds of Fun. Lamar stocked his park not only with the usual assortment of thrill rides but also with *"objets d'art"* like the giant Humpty Dumpty parade float (a veteran of the famous Macy's Thanksgiving Day parade) he bought at an auction for $4,000.

Quietly and with great care, Lamar also invested in fine art. His was not a family of great collecting tradition. H.L. had acquired a few good Oriental rugs, a lesser Remington, and some decidedly second-rate realist paintings. Bunker had developed some interest in Western art (including a Frederick Remington bronze) and pictures of fine race horses, the latter being the principal and practically only adornment to his small downtown office. But Lamar developed a taste for fine American paintings, especially works by landscape artist Thomas Moran. Art was to Lamar what race horses were to his older brother. He personally studied each painting before buying it, learning its history and the components of its value. He hung some of his purchases in his home; others decorated the executive suites of the Kansas City Chiefs at Arrowhead Stadium. But at all times, Lamar took pains to make his purchases in such a manner so as not to attract any publicity. Though he enjoyed art, he did not want to become known as an art collector for fear of the problems that would create for the security of his purchases and his family. He bought paintings only through third parties or at private sales.

Of all the Hunt brothers of the first family, Lamar generally impressed outsiders as the one most in touch with the world around him, the one most attuned to new things and new ideas. Within the family empire, Lamar tended to keep to his own projects, taking an interest in some of his brothers' oil and real-estate ventures but remaining mostly in his own world of sports enterprises. At the same time he showed that he had plenty of Hunt traits in him. Like the others, Lamar was very private, even secretive. As one of his friends put it, "He doesn't like to talk about what he's doing. He likes to handle everything himself." That description sounded like no one more than H. L. Hunt.

Despite the many ways in which they resembled their father, "the boys" were full of ambivalent feelings toward him. The pain of discovering his secret families, the pain of witnessing Hassie's deterioration, the pain of the old man's relative emotional neglect of them were evident to many of those around them. But so, too, was "the boys' " not always conscious desire to please H.L. and be close to him. Theirs was a love-hate relationship. Hunt's sons saw their father as a "phenomenon," but they knew all too well that living with a phenomen was not easy. Often during the middle and late 1960s, their negative feelings predominated.

Hunt did not help the situation. Still fearful that his sons were somehow out to deprive him of his politics and his food business, he sent his aides to spy on them and look into their business dealings. Other times, Hunt himself would insist on sitting in on one of his son's business meetings and putting in his ear on a deal or subject he knew nothing about. His sons usually intercepted their father's infiltration attempts at the start. Many times, one of the aides their father had sent to spy on them would simply confess at the outset that that was his mission. On occasions, when Hunt would sit in on business deals, "the boys" would send discreet hand and eye signals around the table, alerting the people present not to take what the old man said as the final word on the deal under discussion. Unable to work with their father, his sons worked around him.

"The boys" also worked around their half brother Ray, Ruth's eldest son. Blond, blue-eyed, and half a generation younger than the first-family sons, Ray started working full-time at Hunt Oil in 1965, after graduating with a business degree from SMU. He seemed the outgoing campus-leader type on the surface, but he was really shy. He had many acquaintances but very few friends. In those few, Ray sometimes confided that he thought he had a lot of his old man in him. Yet, he also seemed to be insecure, ambivalent about being a Hunt, and anxious to prove that he would be worth knowing even if his last name did not have what he later called that "peculiar spelling."

Bunker, Herbert, and Lamar did not welcome Ray's arrival with open arms. "Bunker and his brothers just looked at Ray as different," one insider recalled. "He made them feel uncomfortable, and vice versa. They could never seem to accept each other as brothers. The three older ones always worked together, but they never brought Ray in with them. He was always the little guy. They always left him out in the cold."

Another Hunt Oil executive friendly to the first family's side remembered that Ray had found it difficult to get interested in the company in his early years. "One summer they had him in leasing, but he didn't show much enthusiasm about that. When he got out of college, he used to ask his relatives to let him sit in when they made an executive decision. The problem is that you just can't plan ahead when you're going to make executive decisions in the oil business, but Ray didn't seem to grasp that. He also never quite seemed to be able to make it to the weekly production meetings they held in Tom Hunt's office. Even old H.L. somehow managed to show up for those."

These early criticisms of Ray ultimately proved petty and exaggerated. Whatever problems Ray may have had in the beginning, he eventually got some profitable oil and real-estate deals under way in a few short years by operating from the Hunt Oil offices and using money from his trust fund. The true significance of the derogatory remarks that were made about him was not what those comments revealed about Ray, but what they said about the growing internal problems in the patriarchy and business empire of H. L. Hunt.

Not surprisingly, H. L. Hunt himself was at the center of the difficulties. As he reached his eightieth birthday, he began to show his age. Although he still possessed uncommon health and vigor, his eyesight was failing, but he did not like to wear his glasses except for reading, and he insisted on driving himself wherever he had to go. His speech would tend to ramble, making the answer to an ostensibly easy question into a wide-ranging diatribe on the profit-motive system and the evils of communism. On other occasions, such as at a press conference announcing his Youth Freedom Speakers project with the Vatican, Hunt's discussions of politics would degenerate into a potpourri of anecdotes and advice, stories about his early days in the oil business, tips about the benefits of aloe vera, and lessons from the slow-aging Hunzukuts of Baluchistan. His genius and his eccentricity merged with his senility, and it became increasingly difficult to tell which was which. As one of Hunt's grandchildren observed, "Some days he would be perfectly normal and on top of everything. Other days it didn't seem like he was all there."

Nowhere did Hunt seem to be failing more than in his stewardship of the food business. By the late 1960s, the food division had grown to include 5,000 employees, or about five times the number of employees in Hunt Oil's oil and gas division. But the creature that had outgrown its creator was not carrying its own weight. On the contrary, HLH Products was draining funds from the oil and gas side at an alarming rate. The food division's annual losses had now escalated from $1 million per year to over $5 million per year, and the losses were getting worse with each passing month. Long-time Hunt employees like Controller John Goodson tried repeatedly to call Hunt's attention to the situation, but to no avail. Hunt would simply acknowledge that there were problems and shrug them off, confident that the losses would eventually be reversed.

As the losses at the food division persisted, the first family became concerned about their aging father's estate. By this time, the first family had
inherited the bulk of the Hunt fortune through their trusts. The largest of their
companies was Placid Oil, which was by now over twice the size of Hunt Oil
Company itself. The first family also owned Penrod Drilling, vast tracts of real
estate, and 18 percent of the stock of Hunt Oil. All together, their share of the
empire amounted to over $1 billion. Hunt's share consisted mainly of an
80-percent interest in Hunt Oil. Although still the flagship of the family
fortune, Hunt Oil's oil and gas, real-estate, and foods properties were worth
only about $100 to $150 million at the time. The Secure Trusts, which Hunt
had set up for Ruth and the second-family children, were worth only about
$3 million.

Despite having already gotten most of their father's money, the first
family felt increasingly displaced by the second. Ruth was now Mrs. H. L.
Hunt, and Mount Vernon was her home, not theirs. The second family had,
in a sense, captured the castle. The first family now seemed worried that the
second family would get a larger share of the Hunt fortune, too. The second
family, on the other hand, was increasingly sure of Hunt's love, but still
uncertain about what Popsy intended to leave them in his will or what the first
family might do to deprive them of their rightful inheritance.

Then, toward the end of 1968, unsubstantiated rumors began circulating
among the first family that Hunt's security chief and adviser Paul Rothermel
was allied with Ruth in trying to influence H.L. to leave the bulk of his estate
to the second family. Those rumors were fueled in part by a visit that first-
family cousin Tom Hunt paid to Hunt at Mount Vernon on Christmas Day,
1968. According to Tom, Hunt was hardly his spry old self that Christmas.
"H.L. sounded so weak I though he was doped up," Tom recalled later. What
Hunt had to say was even more disconcerting to Tom than his weakened
condition.

"They're trying to get me to change the will," Hunt reportedly told his
nephew.

Although Hunt did not specify who "they" were, the first family took
"they" to mean Rothermel and Ruth.

The second family later denied the rumors, but the first family was not
satisfied. The first family's suspicion and distrust grew stronger.

Meanwhile, Hunt himself seemed blithely unconcerned. In February of
1969, he celebrated his eightieth birthday by consenting to an interview with
hard-questioning Mike Wallace of the CBS news-magazine show "60 Minutes." As it turned out, Wallace pinned Hunt down on a few incisive points
about his politics, but most of the show was devoted to charming scenes of the
white-haired old wildcatter taking his sack lunch to work, looking over his
cattle in a cowboy hat, and singing "Just Plain Folks" at home with his wife
Ruthie. The highlight of the show came when Wallace tried to get Hunt to tell
how rich he was.

"Give us a horseback guess as to how much H. L. Hunt is worth,"
Wallace asked.

"Well, it would be so . . . so misleading no one would believe it, so let's don't do it," Hunt replied.

"What do you mean—why misleading?" Wallace said.

"Well, you see, they talk about that I have an income of a million dollars a week," Hunt began.

"Yes . . ."

"And that is a lot of percent erroneous."

"It is erroneous? It's bigger or smaller than that?" Wallace asked.

"As far as I know," Hunt replied, "I would starve to death with an income of a million dollars a week."

Hunt's appearance on "60 Minutes" provoked a typically double-edged reaction. Some viewers apparently found him to be an engaging old curmudgeon they would not mind having for a grandfather, money and all. But other viewers reacted strongly the other way, and Hunt began to receive a spate of hate mail in reaction to his statement that he would "starve to death with an income of a million dollars a week." One letter called Hunt "you f——ing pig mother f——er" and warned that the author would kill Hunt—in fact, the author was going to beat up Hunt and then kill him. The letter was signed "A human being." Another author signed his threat letter less hypocritically, "Tommy Beserk."

Fortunately for Hunt, neither "A human being" nor "Tommy Beserk" made good on his threats. But another sort of trouble did materialize. And unlike the hate mail, it came not from without but from within.

CHAPTER 12

THE WIRETAP CAPER

H. L. HUNT convened Hunt Oil Company's March 1969 annual meeting two weeks after his eightieth birthday party, but no one in the twenty-ninth-floor conference room was in a mood to celebrate. Herbert and Lamar, who held vice-president's titles, sat on one side of the long conference table, fidgeting anxiously with their pens. Production manager Tom Hunt, general counsel George Cunyas, and secretary-treasurer Bill Beeman sat on the other side of the table wearing looks of serious concern. Hunt himself hunched at the end of the table looking dour and curiously distant. Just as at his eightieth birthday at Mount Vernon, Hunt was wearing his habitual blue suit, white shirt, and blue bow tie, his white hair slightly tousled, his blue eyes constantly in motion. But instead of being serenaded with "Happy Birthday" or "Just Plain Folks," Hunt was about to hear some different tunes.

The first man up was HLH Products executive W. R. Butterfield. Though he ranked below food-division manager John Brown and Hunt's aide John Curington, Butterfield had been selected to deliver that year's report on the food division. One of the subjects his report addressed was HLH Products' continuing losses. Butterfield acknowledged that there were problems at HLH Products, problems he did not bother to go into in much detail, but he predicted that the subsidiary's losses could and would be turned around. Then he ended his report.

The next man to speak was John Goodson. A gaunt, white-haired man, Goodson was Hunt Oil's chief financial officer and one of Hunt's most loyal employees. He had joined Hunt Oil's bookkeeping department in 1938, and had handled the numbers and most of the major tax decisions ever since. He was one of the few men outside the family who really knew and understood the Hunts' interlocking maze of trusts and corporations, and how much all of it was probably worth. Even more than the penurious H. L. Hunt himself,

Goodson was responsible for Hunt Oil Company's reputation as a tight ship.

In sharp contrast to the Butterfield report, what Goodson had to say was alarming. According to his account, H. L. Hunt was rapidly going broke. Hunt Oil Company was teetering on the brink of financial disaster. There was not enough cash on hand to pay the bills. The company was no longer finding any oil. Long-time Hunt Oil employees were openly worrying about the security of their jobs and their pension. The Hunt family empire was facing one of the gravest crises in its history.

To an outsider, Goodson's report would have sounded preposterous, outrageous, impossible. Had Mike Wallace announced similar news in his "60 Minutes" piece on H. L. Hunt, he might have been laughed off the air. Hunt acted like he did not believe it all himself. But Goodson's cold, hard statements were not lies. Hunt Oil Company was in serious trouble. And most of the problems were emanating from the food division and its incredible losses.

Unlike the previous speaker, Goodson did go into detail. Since its inception in 1960, he told the meeting, HLH Products had suffered cumulative operating losses of more than $30 million. That was an average of nearly $4 million per year over the life of the company. And things were getting worse instead of better. In 1968, the total annual loss was over $7.9 million. The food division's losses were now running $1 million a month, or roughly $30,000 a day. After record losses in 1968, it appeared that HLH Products was going to lose up to $12 million more in 1969 alone. That would bring the food division's total lifetime operating losses to over $42 million. And that $42-million figure did not include another $35 million worth of capital Hunt had tied up in processing plants and land. All told, HLH Products was an albatross, costing nearly $80 million.

"We are getting to the point where we definitely need to do something about these losses," Goodson intoned.

The way Goodson told it, the losses at HLH Products had crippled the oil and gas division of Hunt Oil Company. Strapped with the burden of having to absorb the food division's losses, the oil and gas division no longer had sufficient capital to keep searching for more oil and gas. The company's exploration arm, its true bread and butter, had virtually shut down. Representatives of billionaire J. Paul Getty's mammoth Getty Oil Company had recently asked Hunt Oil to join in a consortium to bid for leases on Alaska's North Slope, but the way it looked now, Hunt Oil would not have enough cash to participate. The losses being picked up from the food division were causing the company to miss out on the greatest American oil play since the days of the east Texas field. For the first time since its formation in 1936, Hunt Oil's income was based solely on production that had been found in years past. There were no new fields coming on stream, no new wildcat wells being drilled.

As if all this were not enough, Goodson continued, Hunt Oil faced a severe cash crisis. Income from old oil production was averaging about $1 million per month, but that was barely enough to cover the $1-million monthly losses at HLH Products. In October, the Hunt Oil bookkeepers had found it necessary to hold up the company's checks to vendors and suppliers so that Hunt Oil could first meet the payroll of its office employees and field personnel. Considerably more drastic measures might have to be taken if the losses at HLH Products persisted. Moreover, the Hunt Oil employees' pension plan, which had been instituted only seven years earlier, was not yet fully funded. By this time, more and more Hunt Oil employees were aware of the company's financial problems, and there was increasing fear that the company was going to fold. If that happened, Hunt would still have his first family and their rich entities like Placid Oil and Penrod Drilling to take care of him, but Hunt's most faithful employees would be left without jobs or retirement money.

Goodson pointed out that the problems at HLH Products were not part of his official responsibilities. The food division kept a separate set of books from the oil and gas division and the rest of the company. Operational responsibility for the food division was in the hands of division manager John Brown and Hunt's aide John Curington. But the oil and gas division was picking up the food division's losses. And that was Goodson's responsibility. Put simply, if Hunt Oil Company kept on picking up food-division losses at the current rate, it would fold.

"It is essential," Goodson concluded, "that we stop or reduce these losses immediately."

Hunt acted as if he had not really heard what Goodson had been saying. When Goodson finished his presentation, Hunt began to move the meeting on to the next item on the agenda, as if what he had just listened to had been a routinely dull report on steady interest rates. Goodson's report on Hunt Oil's critical situation did not seem to affect him in the slightest.

But Hunt's son Herbert and his nephew Tom would not let him continue. As Hunt tried to take up the next order of business, Herbert and Tom cut him off. They wanted to stay on the subject of the losses at HLH Products. While Hunt might be willing to ignore the problems at the food division, Herbert and Tom wanted to get to the bottom of the trouble, investigate the matter for themselves.

"We want to look at it," Herbert insisted.

Hunt did not give in easily. He glowered at Herbert and Tom and grumbled that the two of them just might be talking out of turn. He gave them each a look of disdain, a look that said, "I can still find more oil with a road map than you boys could find with all the geologists in Texas." But Herbert and Tom would not be shaken. Fully aware that Hunt had used the food division as a funnel for his political contributions, they knew they might be opening up a can of worms. Undoubtedly, some of the losses at HLH Products were the result of Hunt's political contributing. But not $30 million worth. There was no way that H. L. Hunt was going to be that generous to any politician. Like most of the other men in the room—they believed—rightly or wrongly —that the main cause of HLH Product's problems was festering mismanagement on the part of Hunt's subordinates, and they were determined to do something about it before Hunt Oil collapsed.

After some dangerously pointed discussion, Hunt finally relented. He still did not believe that there was anything wrong at the food division that could not be taken care of on its own. But he would let Herbert and Tom take a look for themselves. If they found out what the matter was, they could tell him.

Hurriedly, the Hunt Oil board of directors formed a "Committee of Four." The members of the committee were Herbert Hunt, Lamar Hunt, Tom Hunt, and secretary-treasurer Bill Beeman. The committee's mission was to investigate the losses at HLH Products and, if possible, to find a way to reverse them. The investigation quickly focused on H. L. Hunt's three closest aides, Rothermel, Curington, and Brown. Of the three, only Rothermel was destined to emerge relatively unscathed.

The man who took charge of the "Committee of Four" investigation was Tom Hunt. He was a natural for the task. A short, garrulous fellow with a balding head and a phenomenal memory, Tom was only a cousin of the first family, but he was regarded as the first family's official historian. Having been Hunt's personal aide in the late 1940s and the production manager of Hunt Oil since Hunt's rupture with Herbert in the mid-1960s, Tom knew most of the old man's major secrets and could recognize almost every Hunt Oil employee from the highest executives to the lowliest tool pushers. Tom was also much closer to Hunt than Bunker, Herbert, and Lamar. If Curington and Rothermel were Hunt's closest confidants, Tom was next in line. In fact, Hunt spoke more frequently with Tom than he did with his sons. The two of them were on the telephone discussing business at least twice each day, and usually more. As Tom put it, "If H.L. woke at 4:30 in the morning, he knew I got up early, he would call me."

Tom began his investigation by going through the entire food-division file. He reviewed the cost and date of each major acquisition and gathered a sense of the division's history and structure. Among other things, he learned that the food division had fifteen separate plants located in Dallas and in various farm towns all over the country. According to the reports in the file, these plants were supposed to be the most efficient and up-to-date units available. That only made the company's staggering losses an even greater mystery. Tom decided he ought to pay some unannounced visits to their food plants and look at the operation firsthand. Before departing Dallas, Tom revealed his intention to only one person—H. L. Hunt.

"Fine," Hunt said. "Go on out."

The first plant Tom chose to visit was in Oxnard, California, just outside Los Angeles. But when Tom's plane arrived at the L.A. airport, his name was being paged at the Delta ticket counter. John Curington was on the phone from Dallas. Now Curington was suggesting that Tom first visit the company's plant at Whittier, California, some sixty miles in the opposite direction from Oxnard. The suggestion struck Tom as suspicious, not to mention annoying. He hung up the phone. He was now more determined than ever to see what was waiting at Oxnard.

The Oxnard plant turned out to be quite a surprise. As Tom later testified, "I expected a modern plant. I found nothing. I couldn't even find the manager. Nothing was being done. I found that we didn't even have an adequate sewage line to process produce. An empty warehouse—that is what I found."

Tom reported finding similar situations when he visited other food-division plants. There was the pecan plant in Tyler, Texas, that had never operated since the day it was purchased. This, as Tom discovered, was because the machinery in the plant was so obsolete that the FDA would not allow it to be operated. There was the plant in Bloomsburg, Pennsylvania, that was supposedly the most modern food-processing installation in the country. Tom learned that despite its expensive acquisition price, the plant did not even have an adequate sewer system. To install one would cost another $1 million.

In addition to these peculiarities, Tom began uncovering a trail of what seemed to be suspicious side deals apparently related to the company's losses. These side deals involved a number of brokerage and trading companies with vague-sounding names. Tom suspected that these companies were controlled by Paul Rothermel, John Curington, food-division manager John Brown, and their close friends.

Tom related his initial findings to H. L. Hunt and the other members of the Hunt Oil board. Hunt told him to close the inoperable plants. Tom set out to do just that, but ran into opposition from Rothermel and Curington. While Tom was on his way to Indiana, for example, they told Hunt that the company would have to pay off $400,000 worth of growers' contracts if the Bloomsburg plant closed. Hunt called Tom from Dallas and instructed him to hold off.

"Fine," Tom said, "but we are going to lose a million dollars if we operate. Let's negotiate with the farmers. It's been frosty here this morning, and they haven't put their crops in yet."

Hunt would not listen. Rothermel and Curington had his ear. Or so Tom Hunt would allege. "Unfortunately, they were there" in the Dallas office "and they prevailed," Tom testified later. "We operated that plant and lost one million one hundred thousand dollars that year."

As his investigation progressed, Tom kept running across other suspicious schemes allegedly connected with the food-division losses. Many of the schemes were complicated. One involved reduced price sales of HLH food products that had been falsely labeled as distressed merchandise. Other transactions involved exorbitant or extraordinary sales commissions, the purchase of overpriced real estate, and different types of kickback arrangements. Though the form of the scheme varied, in each instance, the pattern was virtually the same: HLH Products would make a money-losing deal and one or more Hunt Oil insiders would allegedly pocket a percentage.

Tom saw only the tip of the iceberg when he began his cleanup of the food division in the spring of 1969. The scope of the alleged misdoings in the food division and the nature of all the various schemes and side deals involved would not become clear for many months. Indeed, the name of the game was finding enough evidence to prove what he suspected. Still Tom already felt sure that there were some massive embezzlements involved in the food division's losses, and that the problems at the Oxnard and Bloomsburg plants were merely representative of the larger malaise.

When he returned to Dallas, Tom pleaded with his uncle to take drastic action at once. The food division was a sham and in shambles, Tom said, and blamed Rothermel, Curington, and Brown.

Hunt still refused to listen.

Hunt's attitude only gave John Goodson and other long-time Hunt Oil employees further cause for alarm. They importuned Tom to get Bunker, Herbert, and Lamar involved in the effort to make Hunt see the light. "You have got to make the boys get in with this," Goodson argued. "They have got to forget about their own oil activities and help on this problem with Hunt Oil Company."

As it happened, Tom was keeping Hunt's sons posted on his investigation, and they were planning to act. One afternoon in early June, all the active children of the first family—Margaret, Caroline, Bunker, Herbert, and Lamar—gathered in Lamar's office at Hunt Oil. Tom Hunt and Margaret's husband Al Hill were standing by. The group waited until about 5:30, when most of the employees had left for the day, then they got up and trooped down the hall to Hunt's office.

The old man received them guardedly. Everyone found a seat. Then Herbert and Lamar, who were the family representatives on the "Committee of Four," brought up the baleful purpose of their mission.

"Dad," Herbert began, "we have reached the point where the food division is literally breaking the company." The situation was even bleaker than it had been back at the time of the annual meeting in March. Herbert continued. The company's deterioration had reached a new crisis point. Herbert stated the matter as plainly as he could. "We have reached the point," he said, "where we have to borrow money to keep going."

But that was hardly the worst of it. The bank, the tried-and-true First National Bank of Dallas that had stuck by H. L. Hunt for all these years, had refused to make Hunt Oil Company a loan.

The shock of Herbert's statement was paralyzing. Herbert himself could hardly believe his own words. But that was the situation. First National had informed the Hunts that there was no way the bank could justify lending money to a company that was losing money as badly as Hunt Oil. The bank even went so far as to suggest that if Hunt Oil really needed money, the company should probably consider selling off some of its oil assets. As Herbert noted later, this was the first time Hunt Oil had ever been turned down at a bank. The mere embarrassment of such a thing was nearly as painful as the monetary losses plaguing the food division.

"Obviously the food company is grossly mismanaged," Herbert continued. "But the problem can't be all mismanagement. There has to be theft involved. We have to look into this thing and bring the situation under control."

Hunt asked who Herbert and Lamar thought was doing the stealing.

"We don't have any concrete proof," one of them said, "but we think that Rothermel and Curington, being the two closest to the operation, have to be involved in it. . . . Along with other people. . . . Obviously, they can't do it all by themselves."

"Well, you'll have to prove it to me," Hunt replied. "I can't believe that Rothermel and Curington would steal from me or from the company. I owe my life to Paul Rothermel. There is just no way he could be involved."

The sons and daughters of H. L. Hunt could only shake their heads in frustration and dismay. Their father seemed determined to ignore the truth that was so plain to them. Nothing short of signed confessions appeared capable of changing his mind. Margaret, Caroline, Bunker, Herbert, and Lamar trooped out of Hunt's office more discouraged than ever.

Meanwhile, each passing month brought more losses and more startling revelations. One of the more upsetting episodes occurred when Tom Hunt learned that, as he put it, "there was a Mafia member on our payroll." The man he was referring to was none other than John Brown, one of the chief suspects in the investigation of the food division. Furious that Rothermel had allowed such a man to make it past the employee background check, Tom stormed into the security chief's office demanding an explanation.

Rothermel told Tom he knew all about John Brown's connections with the Mafia. Brown was not really criminal, but a paid informant working for the FBI, Rothermel explained. Brown's job was to keep watch on a neighbor reputed to be a high-ranking member of the syndicate.

Rothermel was telling the truth. John Brown was indeed a paid informant for the FBI. But to Tom Hunt, hot on the trail of what he believed to be a massive embezzlement, Rothermel's story defied belief. Tom relayed the tale to H. L. Hunt, George Cunyas, Bunker, and Herbert as still more evidence that the situation in the food division had reached crisis proportions. As Tom recalled afterward, "I was mad."

But Tom's anger provoked little change in Hunt's attitude. On the contrary, the old man seemed more inclined than ever to follow the counsel of Rothermel and Curington over the conflicting advice of his own family. For example, early in the game, a food-division employee was fired for alleged theft. But Hunt subsequently rehired him on the advice of Paul Rothermel and John Curington. When Tom Hunt learned of Brown's alleged involvement with the reputed Mafioso, Hunt nevertheless decided to keep Brown on the payroll, also.

"He gave everyone too many chances," Tom observed later. "That was Mr. Hunt's nature. If you had a man with a drinking problem, you had to give him three chances."

H. L. Hunt also continued to put his trust and faith in Paul Rothermel and John Curington. According to Tom Hunt's later testimony, H. L., at the insistence of Rothermel and Curington, even made his nephew promise to stay out of the day-to-day operation of the food business, though he agreed to let

Tom continue his investigation of the losses and/or "thefts" still racking the company. After all, in spite of the continued hoopla about alleged embezzlements and secret schemes, Hunt had yet to be presented with any solid, convincing proof that his top men were guilty of any disloyalty or illegality whatsoever.

By this time, Tom and "the boys" were growing increasingly frustrated. As the summer dragged on, it became necessary for them to prepare their bids on the North Slope leases in Alaska that were due for auction in September. They were all getting too busy with their own projects to carry the food-division investigation forward themselves. According to Tom, Herbert was now of a mind to let H. L. Hunt clean up his own mess. The financial future of Hunt Oil Company was ultimately of relatively little consequence to the first family, who had Placid, Penrod, Libya, and their trusts to fall back on. If Hunt Oil collapsed because of H. L. Hunt's stubbornness, it would be too bad, but the first family would remain fabulously wealthy no matter what happened. Herbert had tried to warn his father of the food division's spendthrift ways back in 1965 when he and H.L. had their falling out. The way Herbert saw it, the first family had been doing their best to alert their father to the troubles within his empire ever since. If Hunt still refused to listen, it was his own fault.

Bunker, however, was more soft-hearted. Their father was stubborn—there was no doubt about that. But he had to be protected—even if it was from himself. Bunker insisted that "the boys" find a way to keep the food-division investigation going despite their preoccupation with other matters.

As Tom looked on, Bunker and Herbert began thumbing through the yellow pages for listings of security firms that might be able to do the job on their behalf. They settled on the Burns Agency. According to Bunker, the Burns Agency had a better investigative image than the Pinkertons, who had a reputation as mere plant guards.

"Burns is a national outfit," Bunker said. "They can spot-check the plants in a hurry, and maybe get this thing to a head in a hurry, too."

So saying, Bunker dispatched Herbert, the detail man, to make the necessary arrangements with the Burns Agency.

Having brought the Burns Agency onto the case, Herbert and Tom turned their full attention to the Alaskan lease bids. Here, again, they were basically making up for the problems caused by the food-division losses. Hunt Oil Company was supposed to be part of a consortium that included Getty Oil, Marathon Oil, Amerada Hess, and Louisiana Land and Exploration Company. Each company had a one-fifth interest in a bidding fund of $250 million. But because of the losses in the food division, there was no way that Hunt Oil Company itself could come up with its $50-million share. Consequently, Herbert and Tom had to raise the money for Hunt Oil's contribution from the other family accounts.

As the deadline for the bids approached, it was decided that Herbert would fly to Alaska to handle the last-minute details. Tom would stay in Dallas to coordinate their strategy. The two planned to talk back and forth on the telephone until the final bid was in. Both Herbert and Tom were aware of the need for security. High stakes were involved in the Alaskan bid—hundreds of millions of dollars—and prior knowledge of the Hunt consortium's bid could be bought and sold for considerable sums. A leak could cost the consortium a fortune. As a result, Tom and Herbert spoke back and forth in a prearranged code.

Then, just before deadline, Tom called Herbert with some chilling news. As Tom later testified, he told Herbert he had found a jumper wire connecting his phone at Hunt Oil Company to Paul Rothermel's phone. To Tom, the questions raised by his discovery were most ominous. Was someone leaking information about the Alaskan bids? Were the same men who were allegedly bilking the food division now turning on the first-family interests as well? Were months of planning and millions of dollars about to go down the drain? It was too late to know before the bidding closed. Herbert and Tom could only pray that their conversations had been protected by their code.

As it turned out, the Hunts' bid was safe. The Getty-Hunt consortium managed to get some of the choicest property on the North Slope, and the first family became part owner of one of the last great oil fields in North America, a field that promised to return the original $50—million investment many times over. But the Hunts' elation over their successful bids was cut short by the reminder of the jumper wire to Rothermel's phone and the continuing problems at the food division.

For Tom and the others, the fall of 1969 was rife with questions. Was Rothermel trying to monitor Tom's conversations with H. L. Hunt? Was the security chief trying to undermine Tom's investigation of the food division by anticipating where Tom would look next? Rothermel and Curington had been openly jealous of each other for years, but was their enmity really just a clever charade? Were Rothermel, Curington, and Brown perpetrating what was possibly the biggest private embezzlement in Texas history? Or were H. L. Hunt's aides as innocent as they claimed? Were Rothermel, Curington, Brown, et al. actually just carrying out one of their boss's more peculiar secret schemes?

The detective agency Hunt's sons had hired to find out was coming up with few answers. The Burns Agency men had been concentrating on uncovering side deals—real-estate transactions and the like—involving the three chief suspects, Rothermel, Curington, and Brown. But the agency was able to come up with only one major lead, which was a deal involving a farm in Maryland, and even that prospect soured. The farm's owner indicated that he would be willing to cooperate in the Hunts' investigation; then he left the country for a few months. When the farmer returned, he wrote Tom Hunt a letter in which he indicated a drastic change of heart—apparently out of fear. "I am not afraid of the devil himself," the farmer wrote, "but I do not see any special reason why I should assume the personal risk that this thing could involve me in. I know you are going to be disappointed in me." Thus, by November of 1969, after nearly six months on the job, the Burns Agency had virtually no hard evidence against Rothermel, Curington, Brown, or anyone else.

Bunker and Herbert grew more impatient. They reckoned that one of the reasons the three suspects remained so elusive was that Rothermel had learned about the Burns investigation within a week to ten days after the agency had been hired. (The tip-off, they believed, was a pay voucher for Burns that Rothermel had been informed of by one of his many sources in the Hunt organization.) One thing seemed certain: the Burns Agency, despite its national reputation, simply was not capable of matching wits with them.

Then events took an unexpected turn. On November 14, 1969, Paul Rothermel resigned from Hunt Oil Company. The same day, John Curington also resigned. That was on a Friday. Both resignations were made effective on Saturday, November 15. The following Wednesday, November 19, John Brown called Hunt on the telephone to express his resentment of Tom Hunt's inquiries about the food division. Brown told Hunt that he, his secretary, and his chief assistant would resign "if you people up there, and particularly Tom, don't quit interfering."

Hunt hung up and called Tom. "What do you want to do?" he asked.

Tom replied that the best thing to do would be to send another accountant out to the food plant and let Brown make good on his threat. Hunt followed Tom's advice, and that afternoon Brown resigned.

All of a sudden, all the supposed arch villains were out of Hunt Oil Company. But the Hunts' problems were far from over. Tom later testified that on the Saturday following their resignations, Rothermel and Curington removed "file after file" of food-division records from the Hunt Oil offices. The Hunts had all the office locks changed on Monday, but by then it was already too late. There was one computer run of food-division records that was not removed, but for the most part, the paper trail the Hunts had hoped to follow was gone.

Tom and the others realized it would now be harder than ever to convince Hunt that his aides had betrayed him.

About this time, Bunker recalled a conversation he had had a few years before with his friend K. S. "Bud" Adams, Jr. of Houston. Like Hunt's sons, Adams was a second-generation independent oilman. His friendship with Bunker went back to their days as schoolmates at Culver Military Academy. Recently, Adams had co-founded the American Football League with Lamar. He owned the Houston Oilers football team, vast acres of ranches and commercial real estate, and many head of cattle. He was, in short, a man well seasoned in the unpublicized difficulties of being an absentee owner and a manager of great wealth. Bunker remembered that on a visit back in 1965 Adams had told him about a theft problem inside the Adams organization. The way Adams had related it, the manager of one of his ranches had been operating a kickback scheme on cattle sales that had resulted in heavy losses to Adams. Adams had told Bunker that he did not have any luck in catching the culprit until he hired a private investigation agency from Houston to wiretap his ranch manager's telephone. Thanks to the wiretaps, the private eyes were able to make recordings of the ranch manager plotting his crooked deals. Adams had confronted his ranch manager and sent him packing. The key, Adams had said, was having the tape-recorded proof. With the tapes, there could be no denying what had been done.

Bunker reckoned that wiretapping might be the key to the food-division case, too. He believed that if he could get Curington and the others on tape, his father would have to see how they had been stealing from him. But what was the name of the agency Adams had used? Willis? Williams? Bunker could not remember. He decided to give Adams a call.

"Clyde Wilson," Adams told him. "Clyde Wilson Associates." The firm was top-rate, Adams said. In fact, since uncovering the thefts on Adams's ranch, the Wilson agency had taken on a whole range of security responsibilities for Adams, everything from his oil business to his pro-football team. Adams suggested that Bunker contact Wilson directly. Adams also reiterated his belief in the efficacy of wiretapping, and stated that the only way Bunker and his brothers would catch the thieves was by obtaining tape recordings of their actual negotiations.

Bunker allowed that Adams was probably right, thanked his friend for the name and advice, and hung up. Now, he thought, there was a way of bringing the situation to a head.

The call came into the offices of Clyde Wilson Associates on a crisp November morning. The voice at the other end of the line asked to speak to proprietor Wilson. Wilson was not in, so his associate W. J. Everett took the call.

"This is Mr. Smith," the caller said when Everett came on the line.

Everett identified himself as Clyde Wilson's associate. Could he be of some assistance?

Hopefully so, said the caller, because he had a problem within his company in Dallas.

The caller went on to say that the situation called for a certain job to be done, and that his friend Bud Adams had recommended the Wilson agency as being able to handle that job. The caller did not identify the type of job he wanted the Wilson agency to do. Instead, he simply asked if Everett and Wilson could come up to Dallas to discuss the matter further.

Everett replied that he would have to check with Wilson about it, but allowed that such a meeting could probably be arranged.

Good, said the caller, because the matter was of utmost urgency. Then, the caller revealed that his real name was not "Mr. Smith," but Nelson Bunker Hunt.

Everett could not help but make the connection immediately. Nelson Bunker Hunt was the son of H. L. Hunt the Dallas oilman, and the brother of Lamar Hunt the sports magnate. This might mean a big-money client. The Wilson agency already had a long string of them: Bud Adams, Tenneco, Continental Can. One more never hurt. His interest was perked.

Bunker gave Everett his home phone number and address and the two made plans to get together in Dallas the following week.

Nelson Bunker Hunt and W. J. Everett met in the den of Bunker's house on Lakeside Drive. They were a contrast, to say the least. A short, broadshouldered man in his late thirties, Everett wore a crew cut and spoke with a slow east-Texas drawl. He was a poor boy trying to make good. Before becoming a private investigator, Everett had been chief deputy sheriff of Brazos County for five years. He had joined Clyde Wilson in 1966, and three years later wound up with a share in the company and the title of president. Wiretapping was one of many investigative services he had performed along the way.

Bunker Hunt, on the other hand, was the archetypal rich man's son. Overweight and overendowed, he had first gone out to prove that he could increase his father's money by his own wit and willingness to take risks. Now he had to find a way to protect his father's money from the old man's own overspending. Ironically, it was their mutual predilection for secrecy and intrigue as a means to their separate ends that brought Bunker Hunt and W. J. Everett together.

Bunker explained the situation to Everett in outline form. His father's company was suffering huge losses. He and his brothers felt certain that the losses were the result of an embezzlement being perpetrated by some employees and ex-employees, including a former FBI man. The problem was that the embezzlement was so sophisticated that it was difficult for the average private investigator or even very bright people in the company to figure out what was going on. Bunker told Everett that he had hired the Burns Agency several months earlier, but that very little had been turned up in the way of conclusive proof. In fact, within a week or ten days after Burns got on the case, former security chief Paul Rothermel, who was one of the suspects, had found out about their investigation. Bunker said he had now concluded that the only way to catch the people who were stealing was to put taps on their telephones.

Everett nodded his head, but suggested that possibly there was another way an investigation of the thefts could be handled.

No, Bunker said, he preferred to go the wiretap route. Part of the problem had to do with convincing his father that an embezzlement was going on. The suspects involved were very close to Hunt, and his father could not believe that they were stealing from him. Bunker said he wanted to get tape recordings that he could play back for his father as proof of the thievery. Bunker then gave Everett the names of the three chief suspects—Rothermel, Curington, and Brown. Theirs were the telephones he wanted to have tapped.

"Well, there may be other people involved," Everett suggested.

Bunker replied that there was no indication of that so far. There appeared to be some co-conspirators in some of the food plants, but no one else in the main office.

"Who are the people closest to your father?" Everett asked.

Bunker gave him two more names: George Cunyas, the company's general counsel, and Juanita Edwards, who was Hunt's personal secretary. Later, Tom Hunt's name was added to the list.

Everett took down the names, addresses, and phone numbers, and told Bunker that he would have to look into it. There were some problems. He would have to check with the agency's electronics expert and get back to him. Then he asked Bunker if the Hunts wanted to prosecute the thieves or just get their money back.

"I don't know," Bunker answered. "That will have to be taken up with other people."

Before concluding their meeting Bunker and Everett discussed the method of payment. Bunker informed Everett that he had paid the Burns Agency with a company check, and that Rothermel had probably found out about the Burns investigation when the check was processed. The two men then agreed that the best way to prevent that from happening again would be to make all payments in cash. Then, according to Everett's later recollection, a most important exchange occurred.

"Mr. Hunt," Everett supposedly said, "if we do this and get caught, we could all be in trouble, criminally and civilly."

"We aren't concerned about that," Bunker purportedly replied, adding that the family could take care of any legal problems that might arise. Then, almost as an afterthought, Bunker asked if Everett knew of anyone who had ever gone to jail for wiretapping.

Everett replied that he did not know of anyone.

According to Bunker's later recollection, none of the preceding conversation segment ever occurred. There was no warning from Everett of possible criminal or civil liability as a result of the wiretapping, no remark by Bunker that his family could take care of the potential legal problems involved.

These disputed points would become important because Bunker would later claim that he did not know at the time that wiretapping was illegal. In his defense was the fact that when he first discussed the subject of wiretapping with Bud Adams back in 1964, wiretapping was not illegal. The Omnibus Crime Act of 1968, which made wiretapping a federal offense, only went into effect on January 1, 1969, approximately eleven months prior to Bunker's meeting with Everett. Although the FBI, the CIA, and the Nixon White House were secretly indulging in illegal wiretapping themselves, the soon-to-be famous burglary of the Democratic National Committee headquarters had not even been conceived yet, and the word "Watergate" was not due to become part of the public consciousness for three more years. There was, in short, plenty of circumstantial evidence to support Bunker's claim of being ignorant of the law.

In any event, Bunker and Everett ended their meeting with Everett promising he would check back in a few days and let Bunker know if the Wilson agency could take the job.

Upon his return to Houston, Everett went to see his firm's electronics expert. That expert's full name was Patrick Willard McCann III, but those who had known him as a youth called him "Sparky." A short, wiry fellow in his late twenties, McCann was a classic electronics whiz. As a child, he had played with electricity and electrical gadgets as naturally as the young Mozart played the piano, and with commensurate affection. As an adult, he had outfitted his room with all sorts of gizmos and gadgets—devices for opening and closing the curtains, alarms, light switches, buzzers, remote units, and central control panels for operating it all. McCann had never finished college, he had no fancy degrees or high level training, but by the fall of 1969, he was at the top of his field. That field, of course, was wiretapping.

McCann first got into wiretapping prior to the passage of the 1968 Omnibus Crime Act. In those days, there were only vague and loosely enforced restrictions on the use of electronic surveillance devices. Wiretapping was a growth industry, especially in booming sunbelt cities like Houston. There was an increasing number of applications in industrial espionage, corporate security, and law enforcement. McCann's initial experience in wiretapping involved a case where some employees were stealing from his own father, who was the proprietor of a small business. Later, McCann began building and selling special transmitters—that is, "bugs"—to be used in telephone surveillance operations. Before long, he became one of the nation's leading manufacturers of wiretapping equipment.

Among McCann's best customers were the police, particularly the Houston police, whose predilection for wiretapping would become almost as well known as their mistreatment of minorities. Like a number of other law-enforcement agencies in Texas and elsewhere, the Houston police kept right on wiretapping without court orders even after the passage of the Omnibus Crime Act. In fact, between 1968 and 1973, the Houston police used unauthorized wiretaps on as many as half of all their major narcotic cases and in the surveillance of certain political figures. Many of the bugs the Houston police used were made in the station by police electronics men, but many other HPD bugs were the handiwork of Pat McCann.

In wiretapping without court orders after January 1, 1969, the Houston police were breaking the law. So were McCann's private-sector clients. So was operator/manufacturer McCann. Unlike Bunker Hunt, McCann later admitted that he knew right from the start that what he was doing was illegal. But, McCann also pointed out that certain "in house" wiretaps were legal and that the whole subject of wiretapping law was "a gray area." After all, the cops were doing it right and left to catch crooks. It only seemed reasonable that private citizens could do the same.

Everett outlined the Hunt case for McCann, and told the electronics expert that he wanted an estimate of what the job would cost. A few days later, McCann and Everett flew to Dallas, rented a car, and drove around surveying the residences of the various people Bunker wanted to wiretap. The two of them rolled up nearly 100 miles on the rent-a-car going from location to location. Then Everett and McCann returned to Houston, where McCann worked up his cost estimate. The next day, McCann telephoned Bunker Hunt. Naturally McCann taped the call.

"I just got the pricing worked out on all of this stuff, but some of it is going to take some rather complex equipment," McCann told Bunker. "What I really need to do is find out how urgent the timing is on the situation."

"We need to get going," Bunker replied. "I think . . . if possible, say the first of next week. Is that possible?"

McCann said that depended on which way they went about it. The approach he preferred would involve designing what he referred to as "some custom deals to go on the line." These specially made transmitters would be able to transmit the voices "a couple of blocks or so," and thus allow the operation to be "discreet" and "not take any chance." Just the equipment cost on this job would be $2,850, McCann explained. Then, too, there would need to be one man on the job in Dallas full time to change the tapes and the batteries and make sure the equipment remained functional.

"This equipment would probably take a couple of weeks to fabricate because it is rather complex equipment," McCann explained. "Now if we have some real urgency we could go second-rate and use conventional devices that are on the lines." McCann advised that it would take more manpower to operate these "conventional devices" and that installing such devices was "kind of ticklish." But he also said that this "second-rate" plan could be ready "sometime next week."

"Yeah, I understand," Bunker said, pausing only a moment. "Well, I think the charges will be all right. I think I would prefer to get going sooner."

A few moments later, Bunker and McCann finished their conversation, and plans to execute the speedier but decidedly "second-rate" wiretapping scheme were set in motion.

Bunker was scheduled to be out of town on business when the wiretappers arrived, but before he left, he confided his plan to brother Herbert. He put Herbert in charge of giving the wiretappers a cash down payment when they arrived and overseeing the operation in his absence. Bunker later claimed he did not inform Lamar of his plan. "Lamar isn't interested in the oil business too much," Bunker explained afterward, "so I didn't want to bother him."

At some point, Bunker did reportedly discuss the matter with Ray. Exactly what happened between Bunker and Ray would later become subject to hot dispute. The first family's side of the story was that Ray not only refused to participate in the wiretapping, but also refused to investigate the alleged embezzlement at all. Ray's side of the story was that he simply informed his half brothers that he did not want to take part in their investigation, but would confine his efforts to assisting the official Hunt Oil investigation that Tom and the Burns Agency were conducting.

By any objective reasoning, there was good reason for Ray to proceed with caution. Although he was the oldest child and only male in the second family, Ray had just turned twenty-six when the investigations of the alleged embezzlements got under way. He was caught between the demands of his half brothers, who had been openly hostile to his branch of the family, and his loyalty to his father, who still believed that Rothermel and the others were trustworthy. Ray wanted to see the losses stopped. Both he and his mother had been pleading with Hunt to look into the food-division and the possible role Hunt's top aides might have played in its problems. But Ray's instincts must have told him that joining Bunker and Herbert in a wiretapping operation was unwise.

In any case, Bunker and Herbert were furious. The way they saw it, the money at stake was money their father would probably bequeath to the second family, at least in part. And yet, the first family had spearheaded the investigation of the food-division losses all along. Ray had hardly lifted a finger. Already estranged from their half brother and his branch of the family, Bunker and Herbert no longer saw any hope of bridging the rift between them. In a huff, Bunker and Herbert decided to proceed on their own. Ray could just look out for himself.

Sparky McCann returned to Dallas in late November in the company of W. J. Everett and two young associates. Since Bunker Hunt had left town on business, McCann drove to Herbert Hunt's house to pick up their initial $2,000 down payment. McCann announced his arrival by calling Herbert's home from the mobile telephone in his car. As they were getting ready to hang up, McCann informed Herbert that he was driving up his driveway.

Herbert met him at the door. The two men went inside. McCann told Herbert that he and his associates were checked in at the Royal Coach Inn and ready to start. He explained that it would take a few days to get the tapes operational, then collected the money, and left.

McCann had not exaggerated when he told Bunker that installing the wiretapping equipment would be "kind of ticklish." The operation was rife with the danger of exposure. In fact, there was only one relatively safe and easy tap in the bunch. That was Tom Hunt's phone. Tom lived in an apartment complex where all the phone lines fed into and out of a central equipment room. His phone was thus amenable to a pure wiretap, what McCann called a "hot-line recording."

McCann, Everett, and their assistants Jon Kelly and Morgan Watson simply rented another apartment in the same complex, got access to the phone wires via the office, and installed a jumper wire connecting Tom's phone to a phone they placed in the attic of their newly leased apartment. The attic phone, in turn, was wired to a voice-activated recorder (McCann preferred a Craig model 2603) whose reels could be checked and changed without detection by whomever was assigned to stay in the apartment below. To a layman, this operation might not seem so easily accomplished. But for an experienced wiretapper like McCann, the Tom Hunt job was basically a piece of cake.

The other jobs, which were all at private homes, were not so simple. They involved "bugging" as opposed to pure wiretapping. Instead of merely installing a jumper wire physically connecting one phone line to another, a tiny transmitter, or "bug," had to be placed on the line to be tapped. The bug itself was about the size and shape of the preprocessed butter pats served in most commercial restaurants. According to the setup McCann preferred, the bug package included a conventional nine-volt battery to power the transmitter, an alligator clip to attach the bug to the telephone line to be tapped, and a thirty-inch antenna wire to enable the bug to transmit the conversations it picked up. Also, part of the system was an FM receiver of the type found in any ordinary stereo. Positioned some distance away from the phone line being tapped, the receiver would pick up the signals transmitted by the bug. Instead of being tuned to regular radio broadcasts in the 88- to 108-megacycle range, the receiver was tuned down to a frequency between 85 and 88 megacycles, just below the commercial band. As McCann explained later, this was done "so that someone accidentally tuning their FM radio in the vicinity of the transmitter wouldn't actually detect the transmitted signal and alert someone that something snoopy was going on." The FM receiver was, in turn, wired to a voice-activated tape recorder which taped the calls as they come in.

The "ticklishness" of the operation was in direct proportion to the type of bug being used. The most commonly available bugs could transmit only 800 feet or so. That meant that the FM receiver cum tape recorder had to be positioned no more than 800 feet from the target house. In addition, whoever was supervising the operation would have to venture that close to the house at regular intervals to change reels. Chances of being detected by curious neighbors increased drastically. That was why McCann had wanted to devise some special bugs that could transmit farther than the usual mode, what he had called "custom deals" in his conversation with Bunker. But building a transmitter from scratch took a little time, and Bunker had said he was in a hurry to get the tapes going.

McCann and his crew went about the task of installing the bugs with as much discretion as possible. First, they rented a big yellow panel truck of the same type the telephone company leased when it needed extra trucks on the job. McCann and Watson, who happened to be a telephone installer in Houston, strapped on big leather tool belts that looked like regulation telephone company equipment, which in fact they were. Then McCann and his helpers drove around from location to location, working in broad daylight just like ordinary telephone-company repairmen. Since all but one of the neighborhoods involved had modern underground phone lines, they did not have to do much telephone-pole climbing. Instead, they merely installed the bugs on the short steel poles that stuck up out of the ground in the easements behind the houses.

Once the bugs were in place, the real fun began. McCann and Kelly, a rookie private eye who worked for the Wilson agency, blackened their faces with shoe polish, put on dark clothes, and drove around from location to location in the dark of night dropping suitcases in the bushes. The suitcases were painted with brown and green camouflage colors just like an Army battle jacket. Inside each suitcase was a Blaupunkt FM receiver and a Craig model 2603 voice-activated tape recorder. McCann and Kelly made their drops like commandos installing land mines. Running low and quiet, they scurried from drainage ditch to drainage ditch, bush to bush, trying to keep out of sight of insomniac neighbors. For Kelly, a thin, blond twenty-five year old who bore a faint resemblance to the actor David Soul of "Starsky and Hutch," this was an experience he would not forget. "It was just like in a movie," he remembered later. "We really got into it."

By the end of the first week in December, all six tapes were in operation. McCann, Kelly, Everett, and Watson stayed in motels nearby. They kept switching motels every few days so as not to arouse suspicion. The Holiday Inn on Central, the Royal Coach, the Rodeway, the North Park Inn. They also had to keep going back to the wiretap locations every day or so to check on the equipment and change the reels of tape.

After about a week, McCann, Everett, and Kelly met Herbert Hunt in the North Park Inn to hear the first batch of tape recordings. The results were disappointing. The tapes did pick up a few cryptic conversations between the suspects, but much of the reels were wasted on extraneous conversations by other callers. Herbert listened only to the relevant portions of the tapes. He instructed the wiretappers to keep on going.

A few days later, Herbert and the wiretappers met again at another motel. This time, the tapes were more provocative. There was talk among some of the suspects about bringing in "a leg breaker," discussions of "a bag daddy" who would pick up kickbacks. Herbert later characterized the language as "what you would expect from a Mafia bunch." Herbert paid the wiretappers a few thousand dollars more and instructed them to keep going.

Then things began to get hot. Everett got word through one of the Wilson agency's many police sources that Rothermel had been checking with the Houston police about the Wilson agency's background. How Rothermel found out that the Hunts had hired the Wilson agency was not known, but it appeared that there was some sort of leak in the Hunt Oil ranks. A short time later, Kelly got a tip that the Dallas police were suspicious of the wiretappers. That was enough to make Kelly want to clear out. Kelly left all the bugs in place, but hurriedly gathered up the camouflaged suitcases with the receivers and tape recorders inside and went back to Houston.

In Houston, Kelly and McCann rented a motel room and set about editing the wiretap tapes. They edited out what they later called the "private" conversations of various family members that the tapes had picked up. They saved especially conversations involving Rothermel, Curington, and Brown.

Kelly then brought the edited tapes back up to Dallas. By this time, Bunker had returned from out of town and was anxious to hear the results. Kelly played the tapes for him. The evidence on the tapes was still sketchy, but on the whole Bunker's suspicions were being confirmed. According to Kelly's testimony, there was talk on the tapes of gold bullion stashed in

Mexico, discussions about schemes to sell fur coats, and comments about H. L. Hunt entertaining underworld characters at the Garden of the Gods Club in Colorado. Kelly noted that mention of this last item visibly upset Bunker.

Kelly also claimed later that Bunker was extremely intent on conversations pertaining to Hunt's will and estate, including Hunt confiding to Tom Hunt that he thought his sons were going to try to have him committed and a discussion between Tom Hunt and Al Hill, Sr. about the possible contents of Hunt's will. Kelly said all this caused him to conclude that the real struggle going on was a power play for control of the Hunt empire, not just an attempt to catch some alleged thieves.

Kelly also noted that Bunker seemed to be much more caught up in the intrigue of the caper than brother Herbert. Kelly claimed Bunker asked if there were any contingency plans for being discovered. Kelly replied that he always kept a bucket of acid in his car and that if caught, he would dunk the tapes in the acid. "I was lying to him about the bucket of acid," Kelly said later, "but it sounded like a good story, and Bunker really seemed to like it."

Kelly left the tapes with Bunker and went back to Houston for Christmas. But before he left, Kelly collected another $3,000 in cash from Bunker. Kelly later claimed with an amused grin that Bunker always seemed quite clumsy at handling his money. "He tried to count out the money in hundred-dollar bills, and he came up with a different total each time," Kelly recalled. "Finally, I took his wad of bills and counted out the money myself." The total bill for the wiretapping operation was now approaching $11,000.

About the same time, the aboveground investigation of the food-division affair was starting to pick up. Herbert released the Burns Agency, and hired a Dallas private investigation firm called Dale Simpson Associates. The Simpson agency advertised itself for what it was: an association of former FBI agents. If anyone could catch a crook, it seemed that this firm of former G-men could do the job. Herbert told Simpson everything he knew about the problems at the food division and what had developed in the case so far. But Herbert did not say anything to Simpson about the Wilson agency's involvement in the case or the wiretaps. Bunker and Herbert wanted to keep their electronic-surveillance operation a secret. They still believed that tape recordings of the thieves in action was the only form of proof that would convince their father of the betrayal they believed was going on all around him. And they felt that the only way to get those tapes was by maintaining strictest secrecy.

After Christmas of 1969, the Hunt brothers called Everett again and requested that he and his men return to Dallas to resume the wiretaps. Everett was reluctant. He told the Hunts he thought the Dallas police were suspicious about their operation. With Rothermel's extensive law-enforcement contacts, that raised the possibility that either Rothermel might have tipped the police or that the police might have tipped Rothermel. Everett suggested that the Hunt brothers' own telephones might be bugged. Nevertheless, he agreed to send Kelly and McCann back to Dallas to get the operation going again.

Upon their return to Dallas, McCann and Kelly first met with Bunker and

Herbert in the Hunt Oil Company offices. The two wiretappers checked the Hunts' telephones for bugs and swept the offices in search of wall- or ceiling-mounted electronic listening devices. They found nothing. Then Kelly, McCann, and the Hunt brothers sat down to discuss how they were going to go about starting their wiretapping operations again. Kelly told the Hunts that he and McCann were going to try something different. Instead of leaving their receiver/recorder suitcases in the bushes, they were going to rent cars and park them near the residences whose phones were being tapped. Kelly said he and McCann planned to rotate the cars and their locations every few days so as not to arouse suspicion.

The Hunts told Kelly and McCann that it was now time to focus the investigation. The tapes on the telephones of Juanita Edwards, George Cunyas, and Tom Hunt should be abandoned. What had been gathered thus far suggested that none of the three was involved in the alleged embezzlement. The Hunts instructed the wiretappers to concentrate on the three men they had suspected from the beginning—Rothermel, Curington, and Brown, an order which suggested that the Hunt brothers were not in fact vying for a larger share of their father's estate but trying to protect him as they claimed. Since Bunker was once again scheduled to go out of town, Kelly and McCann were told to report their progress to Herbert.

For the next couple of days, Sparky McCann and Jon Kelly went around to the wiretap locations disguised as telephone-company repairmen. The nine-volt batteries powering the transmitters had run down by now and needed to be changed. McCann and Kelly also went by Bunker's house and swept the place for wiretaps and bugs. They found nothing. Then, they rented some cars, placed the camouflage-painted suitcases on the floor mats beneath piles of newspaper, parked the cars in place, and started recording conversations again.

Once things were operational, McCann returned to Houston. Another Wilson agency employee named Ron Adams replaced him. Adams was not an electronics expert. He had not helped build or install the wiretapping equipment. He was merely on hand to help Kelly rotate the parked rent cars. And that is what Adams and Kelly did day after day as the New Year came and turned cold. Kelly also checked in with Herbert Hunt at least three or four times during the first two weeks of January 1970. Whenever he called, Kelly used the code name "Kirkland."

Meanwhile, Kelly was becoming increasingly paranoid. Once, when he had last changed the car parked near Paul Rothermel's house in suburban Richardson, Kelly had found a white chalk mark on one of the tires. It seemed like a sure sign that someone—most likely a cop—was now checking on the mysterious car that was parked all day on the neighborhood street.

Kelly quickly told Herbert about the chalk marks, and said that he was afraid the police were on to them. He suggested that the tapes be discontinued.

Not to worry, Herbert said. He and his brothers owned most of the land in that part of Richardson and were in the process of building another subdivision. The chalk marks were probably made by the security guard who worked for the Hunts. There was no need to be alarmed about him, Herbert said. He instructed Kelly to continue the wiretaps.

On the afternoon of January 16, Kelly returned to Rothermel's neighborhood to move the red Ford Mustang that he had parked on the street behind Rothermel's house. His partner, Ron Adams, dropped him off a few blocks from the Mustang. Kelly covered the rest of the distance on foot, trudging up a slight hill to where the car was parked. It was only about 4:30 or 4:45, but because it was winter, the shadows were already beginning to lead the way into darkness. Kelly stood beside the Mustang for a second, then walked around and looked at the tires to see if there were more chalk marks. The tires looked okay. Kelly got into the car and started the engine.

Then Kelly noticed a Richardson police car in his rearview mirror. The police car was parked in a driveway just down the hill, in the opposite direction from which Kelly had come. The cop inside the car appeared to be lighting a cigarette. Kelly's nerves screeched, but there was nothing he could do except try to drive away normally.

Kelly began to guide the Mustang down the street at about twenty-five miles per hour. The police car followed. The street curved and came to an intersection. There was a stop sign at the intersection which marked the entrance to the subdivision. Kelly later swore that he stopped at that stop sign, then turned out of the subdivision. He made sure to stop, he said, precisely because he knew he was being followed by a police car.

George Taylor, the Richardson cop, later swore that Kelly did not stop at the stop sign. Not that it really mattered. A short time earlier, one of the neighbors had reported the mysterious car-switching on the street to the Richardson police. Taylor's supervisor had ordered him to go out and watch the car. Taylor had told his supervisor he was going to stop the car if anyone came to pick it up. He said he would have a talk with the driver and find out why the cars were being switched. Thus, when Kelly passed through the stop sign, Taylor turned on his flashing lights.

Kelly pulled over. He got out of the Mustang, and started walking back toward the police car. Taylor had stopped his car, and started walking toward Kelly. The two men met halfway between their vehicles.

"Let me see your driver's license," Taylor demanded.

Kelly obliged.

Taylor then began asking Kelly a series of routine questions about where he was from and how he had gotten into the neighborhood.

Kelly responded to Taylor's questions with one-word answers or with silence.

Taylor grew more suspicious. There had been some suggestion back at the station that the police might have stumbled onto a private investigator engaged in a perfectly lawful investigation. Taylor still thought this might be the case, but the man he had stopped was being a little too evasive.

"We've been watching this car," Taylor told him, "and we would like to know what's going on."

Kelly remained silent.

Taylor left Kelly where he was standing and approached the red Mustang. He looked in the windows and saw the pile of newspapers on the right floorboard.

Taylor reached into the newspapers, pulled out the camouflage briefcase, and looked inside. He saw a receiver, a speaker, and a tape machine.

"Have you been doing some wiretapping?" Taylor asked.

Again, Kelly remained silent.

"Are you a private investigator?"

"Yes," Kelly replied.

"Are you out here working on a divorce case or something?" Taylor asked.

The fact that Kelly was a private investigator at once suggested a legitimate explanation for the suspicious car switching. Taylor later testified that if Kelly had said that he was working on a divorce case, he, Taylor, would probably have written him a ticket for running a stop sign and let him go.

But Kelly did not think to offer up such a ready explanation. Instead, he panicked.

"I think I'd better talk to my attorney," Kelly said.

Taylor was suspicious once more. He decided that he better take Kelly down to the station and let him talk to the chief.

"There are some questions we want to ask you," he told Kelly. "As soon as you answer them, you'll be able to leave."

A short time later, Jon Joseph Kelly was booked into the Richardson city jail under a suspicious-persons ordinance, and the Richardson police were calling in the FBI.

Herbert Hunt found out about the trouble he and Bunker could be in only hours after Kelly's arrest. If, as he later claimed, Herbert really had not known that wiretapping was illegal, he soon discovered different. The Richardson police were merely charging Kelly with a traffic violation, a ticket for running the stop sign. But the Richardson cops had listened to portions of the tapes in Kelly's car, and had recognized Paul Rothermel's name and his former association with H. L. Hunt. They had also recognized that wiretapping was a federal crime and had turned over the tapes in Kelly's car to the FBI. It appeared that the case was going to be brought before a federal grand jury.

Herbert called Bunker, who was in New Zealand on business.

"One of the detective people, Jon Kelly, has been arrested with a traffic violation," Herbert told him. "In the process of the arrest, they found a tape recorder on him, and they're filing charges in relation to the tape recorder."

"Well, that doesn't concern us," Bunker replied. "I don't think we're involved in that at all."

"Apparently it's more serious than you think," Herbert said. "There might be a violation on our part."

Bunker later claimed that this call was the first indication to him in the entire wiretapping caper that wiretapping might be illegal. True or not, Bunker

soon discovered, wiretapping was indeed illegal and carried a penalty of up to
four years in prison and a fine of up to $10,000, or both. He and Herbert also
learned that Kelly's continued silence was one of the main things that stood
between the Hunt brothers and a possible criminal indictment for wiretapping.

Exactly what Bunker and Herbert did after Kelly's arrest would later
become as disputed as what they did before his arrest. But, Kelly would claim,
and the U.S. government would charge, that the Hunt brothers and a list of
some of the most prominent attorneys in Texas now embarked on a conspiracy
to cover up the Hunt brothers' illegal wiretapping as best they could. According to the government, Herbert Hunt took the first step in the cover-up
conspiracy when he allegedly destroyed some of the tapes the wiretappers had
made. Then, according to Kelly and Kelly's cousin and attorney, Jerry
Patchen, Herbert Hunt and long-time Hunt Oil attorney Ralph Shank attempted to insure Kelly's silence.

The first key meeting allegedly occurred about two weeks after Kelly's
arrest. The Hunts would later point out that Kelly and Patchen had been the
ones who initiated the conference when Kelly complained that the attorney his
official employer, Houston private eye Clyde Wilson, had hired to defend him
seemed interested only in saving Wilson's skin, not Kelly's. But according to
Kelly, Herbert and Shank quickly put Kelly in the same sort of situation he
was trying to escape. Herbert allegedly told him there was "nothing to worry
about" and that "everything" had been "taken care of." There appeared to be
a way to get out of the mess without any indictments, Herbert supposedly said.
He added that if there were any indictments, the Hunts would pay Kelly's legal
fees.

According to Kelly, Herbert and Shank indicated that Will Wilson, a
Texan then serving as head of the Justice Department's criminal division, was
their high-level contact. Herbert and Shank also recommended that Kelly hire
noted Dallas attorney Charles Tessmer to defend him in the traffic-ticket case.
Kelly later claimed that he wanted to hire another attorney named Bill Walsh,
but that the Hunts and Shank insisted he hire Tessmer, and proceeded to
contact Tessmer on Kelly's behalf.

The Hunts, for their part, later denied trying to "silence" Kelly, but they
did not deny paying for Charles Tessmer to represent him.

While all this was going on, W. J. Everett claimed to have received a
telephone call from Bunker Hunt. According to Everett, Bunker told him
everything was being taken care of "up the country." Everett said he took "up
the country" to mean Washington.

Although much of what happened next would be clouded by conflicting
versions of events, the Hunts' long-time family friend, Senator James Eastland
of Mississippi, later admitted that he did try indirectly to contact Will Wilson
on the Hunt's behalf early in 1970. Eastland said he called Texas congressman
George Mahon to ask that Mahon call his nephew Eldon Mahon, then an
assistant U.S. attorney in Dallas. Eastland wanted the congressman to ask his
nephew to contact Deputy Attorney General Richard Kleindienst, who in turn

would presumably contact Will Wilson.

George Mahon later claimed he told Eastland he did not want to get involved in the case and would not call Eldon Mahon. George Mahon said Eastland then told him he did not want him to discuss the case with Eldon, but only to ask that Eldon call Kleindienst. Mahon admitted that he did call his nephew and ask him to call Kleindienst, but added "that was all."

Eastland, for his part, claimed that he was only trying to get a status report on the case, not fix it. "They will tell anybody if they're under investigation," Eastland said.

The legal battle began auspiciously. On March 4, 1970, Jon Kelly appeared in Richardson, Texas, municipal court to answer charges of running a stop sign. Kelly's attorney Charles Tessmer managed to get the case dismissed. Unfortunately, the dismissal of the traffic ticket did not close the matter. Even as Kelly left the Richardson court a free man, the government was determined to press forward with its investigation of Kelly's wiretapping activities.

In the meantime, the Hunts pressed forward with their investigation of the alleged thefts at the food division. Tom Whitaker, an ex-FBI agent working for the Dale Simpson agency, spearheaded the effort. Bunker and Herbert had not informed the Simpson agency of their wiretapping activities, but Whitaker's investigation did not stop with Kelly's arrest. On the contrary, Whitaker stayed on the case for fifteen months after the wiretappers were discovered. He built up thick files on the details of various alleged embezzlement schemes and traced trails of checks through brokerage companies with names like Tri-Point Brokerage, Empire American Trading, and Marion Salvage. According to Whitaker's investigation, these companies, just as Tom Hunt had suspected earlier, had been set up by Rothermel, Curington, and Brown.

Among other things, Whitaker claimed to have found evidence of nearly $50 million of food-division losses caused by the alleged culprits. He estimated that as much as $5 million of these losses went directly to Rothermel, Curington, and Brown. Whitaker later testified that Curington and Brown were continuing to receive checks from their alleged schemes even after their resignations from the Hunt organization.

Hunt enemies later claimed that the family's estimates of the losses were purposely exaggerated in an effort to discredit Rothermel, Curington, and Brown. And in point of fact, the Hunts never did sue for all the money they claimed to have lost. In July of 1970, the Hunts filed their first report with the bonding company, claiming losses of over $500,000. In November of 1970, Hunt Oil filed suit against Rothermel, Curington, and Brown for $932,227, or barely a fraction of the alleged total embezzlements. But the family's defenders later claimed that their failure to sue for more damages resulted from the fact that the true extent of those damages did not become clear until many months later.

H. L. Hunt's position and influence in all this waffled from day to day.

For all their effort and risk, Bunker and Herbert were never able to let Hunt hear the tapes they thought would convince him that his closest aides had betrayed him. Hunt did become convinced enough to sign the report to the bonding company in July and to authorize Hunt Oil's damage suit against Rothermel, Curington, and Brown in November. Some company insiders said that Bunker Hunt, once the disfavored son, rose greatly in his father's estimation because of his handling of the food-division troubles, and came to have more access to Hunt than any other member of the family.

In any case, unbeknownst to either of his Dallas families or his secret family in Atlanta, Hunt decided to rewrite his will. This new last testament was dated February 24, 1971, and its signing was witnessed by three long-time Hunt employees, but Hunt did not reveal its contents to any of his kinfolk.

About this time, Hunt finally gave up hope of reviving his ailing food business. At the suggestion of Bunker and Herbert and with the help of a Hunt Oil employee named Bill Bledsoe, Hunt auctioned off almost all of the processing plants belonging to HLH Products. Since the plants were in as bad a shape as Tom Hunt had reported, their sale did not bring in very much money. In fact, having invested nearly $35 million in the plants, Hunt had to let them go for only $9 million, or a net loss of $26 million. Added to operating losses of $45 million, that made the total losses of HLH Products a staggering $71 million. The only portion of the food division that remained operative was a $2-million drug and cosmetics plant in Dallas that continued to do business as HLH Sales. Hunt's dream of building up another business from scratch had to be written off as a failure.

Meanwhile, Rothermel, Curington, and Brown mounted a counterattack against Bunker and Herbert. The government might not have a criminal case without the testimony of Kelly and McCann, but the three ex-employees had little doubt that the Hunts were ultimately responsible for the tap on their telephones. Rothermel's wife, Joyce, who was a psychiatric nurse, answered Hunt Oil's suit against her husband with a $1.5-million suit against Herbert Hunt for invading her privacy, personally and professionally, by wiretapping her telephone. Curington and Brown responded to Hunt Oil's suit against them by putting out a long list of countercharges and accusations. Claiming that H. L. Hunt himself had authorized any food-business side deals they may have entered into as compensation for their low salaries, the two former Hunt men loosed stories about Hunt's secret family by Frania Tye Lee, his gambling, his political activities, and even his son Hassie. They also made allegations about purported tax frauds by Hunt, sexual exploits by him and other members of the family, tainted food products supposedly sold to ghetto stores by HLH Products, and illegal Mexican labor allegedly employed on Hunt's Indian Hot Springs resort.

Rothermel loosed several allegations as well. Portraying the wiretap caper as part of an internal feud over Hunt's will, he told a *Houston Chronicle* reporter in an interview, "The first six children are well taken care of in trust funds. Margaret and Hassie have millions. As do the others. However, the other four children from his second marriage had only about $3 million all told in trust funds. That's why I used my influence on Hunt to change his will. And the first family didn't like it at all."

Claiming he intended to write a tell-all book about his experiences at Hunt Oil, Rothermel went on to say that Hunt had sanctioned "all our side deals," and that he had kept his boss informed of "everything going on." Rothermel added, "We made money for him, too." As to why he resigned, Rothermel claimed, "I just couldn't take it any more. I couldn't work for a man playing God."

Although the Hunts later protested that many of these accusations were false, the real damage was in having such matters, even the true ones, brought out at all. There were surely a host of embarrassing skeletons hidden in H. L. Hunt's closet, skeletons with which the other members of the Hunt clan were all too familiar. But Curington's and Brown's statements took something of the form of the question "When did you stop beating your wife?" There could be almost no satisfactory response to such a question or to the statements of Curington and Brown. It was as if the two former aides were saying, "Okay, come on and sue us. But if you do, be ready to cover all this ground and more." It was a no-win situation for the Hunts. A blood bath seemed imminent.

The Hunts responded to the counterattack by trying to make a deal. This alleged deal was supposed to have been arrived at in late 1970, just prior to the filing of Curington's and Brown's laundry list of disclosures about H. L. Hunt. Once again, Senator Eastland was said to have played a part. In fact, according to later public statements by an attorney for Bunker and Herbert, word of the purported deal "came from Eastland's office." The essence of the deal called for the Hunts to drop their civil suit against Rothermel, Curington, and Brown and the government would drop its plans to prosecute the wiretappers. What the Hunts would get from such a deal was clear—the obviation of any criminal charges against them. But what about the government's side of the deal? According to the Hunts, what the government wanted out of the deal was to save Rothermel, who the Hunts had come to believe was a high-ranking government agent, most likely in the employ of the CIA. The Hunts never said exactly who Eastland's office talked to in making these arrangements, but prosecutor Will Wilson later denied having a part in the deal.

At any rate, the Hunts did arrive at a settlement with Rothermel, Curington, and Brown in May of 1971. As part of the settlement agreement, the Hunts dropped their civil suit against the three former aides, and Mrs. Rothermel dropped her invasion-of-privacy suit against Herbert Hunt. Fidelity and Casualty Company of New York, the bonding company, agreed to pay the Hunts $100,000. The parties further agreed "never to give interviews of any kind, directly or indirectly, to the news media (press, magazine, radio, or television) with reference to each other or with reference to each other's family, and further [agreed] never to sell, publish, or cause to be published, directly or indirectly, communications, stories, books or articles of any kind with reference to each other or with reference to the members of each other's family nor to voluntarily disclose this Agreement or any portion thereof." The signers of the agreement included H. L. Hunt, the children of the first family except Hassie, the three former aides and their wives, two food brokers, the bonding-company man, and the lawyers for all concerned.

With the signing of the settlement agreement, the court records in the Hunt civil suit, including the statements by Curington and Brown, were put under seal. That seemed to end everything—or at least end legal matters—once and for all. The presiding judge remarked as a sort of postscript: "A lot of dirty laundry came out."

Alas, the government, which was not party to the above settlement agreement, did not make good on its alleged part in the deal. The Justice Department had been undeniably lackadaisical in its pursuit of the wiretap case. In fact, some fourteen months passed between the time of Kelly's arrest and the signing of the settlement agreement among the Hunts, the bonding company, and H. L. Hunt's former aides. Yet, during that period, there had been no indictments against Kelly, the Hunts, or anyone else associated with the wiretapping. Nor, for that matter, had there been any indictments against any of the alleged food-division embezzlers despite the Hunts' persistent urgings. But the government had not forgotten about the wiretap case or the possible involvement of the Hunt brothers in it. The prosecutors were just moving slowly. On May 12, 1971, a federal grand jury in Dallas indicted Jon Joseph Kelly and Patrick W. McCann III for illegal wiretapping. The deal, if there ever had been any deal, was off.

Once again, there was a scramble behind the scenes. Exactly who did what to whom was obscured by conflicting allegations and admissions, but Kelly once again ended up being represented by Dallas attorney Charles Tessmer, with the Hunts paying the legal fees. Tessmer reportedly wanted to have B. H. Timmons, a former assistant U.S. attorney, represent Pat McCann. But since Timmons had worked briefly on the wiretap case before entering private practice, he could not oblige. Timmons's replacement was Emmett Colvin, a deep-voiced, articulate man who was a good friend of Tessmer's. Tessmer and Colvin were the best defense talent in Dallas, the finest local counsel that money could buy. Yet both Kelly and the government would later allege that Tessmer and Colvin's primary goal was not defending their clients, but protecting the people who were paying their fees—Bunker and Herbert Hunt.

Having languished for so many months, the wiretap case began to move forward with astonishing speed. On August 19, 1971, Kelly and McCann were convicted of wiretapping. Neither man chose to give the government a detailed description of their wiretapping activities. Neither man named their paymasters. On September 9, 1971, Kelly and McCann were sentenced to three years in federal prison. Although they remained free pending their appeal, both men became increasingly worried that they really were going to jail, regardless of previous assurances to the contrary. Meanwhile, the grand-jury investigation of the wiretapping was continuing. The next in line for indictment appeared to be W. J. Everett, but the prosecutors seemed determined to trace the line of responsibility all the way to the top.

Both Kelly and the government later alleged that Herbert Hunt, attorney Charles Tessmer, and attorney Ralph Shank bought Kelly and McCann's silence at their wiretapping trial by promising to pay them in cash for each month they spent in jail. After Kelly and McCann were convicted, Herbert Hunt, Shank, and Tessmer allegedly reiterated their offer: the Hunts would pay them each $1,250 a month for every month they spent in prison—provided they did not talk. A short time later, B. H. Timmons allegedly informed W. J. Everett that he would be indicted soon, and offered Everett $800 per month in prison as payment for his continued silence.

The wiretappers thought the money sounded fine, but none of them particularly liked the idea of having to go to prison to collect it. Their cooperation had become a very negotiable commodity. They could trade it for Hunt money. Or they could trade it for government leniency. Perhaps, if they played their cards right, they could even get both. Everett reportedly rejected the money out of hand, saying he did not want to go to prison. Kelly and McCann waivered.

Then the government got a toehold. Following Kelly's conviction, the Probation Department requested him to make a statement detailing his wiretapping activities. Kelly called Tessmer for advice, but Tessmer was out. Then Kelly called Houston defense attorney Phil Greene. Greene told Kelly to go ahead and make his statement. Kelly followed Greene's advice and described the wiretapping story, including the Hunts' involvement, to the Probation Department.

Kelly later claimed that when Herbert Hunt and Ralph Shank learned what he had done, they were furious at him. According to Kelly, Herbert was especially angry because the Hunts had paid Kelly's legal fees. Kelly claimed that Herbert and Shank made it clear to him that he should not make any further statements about the case. Shank then allegedly reassured Kelly that his conviction would be reversed.

A short time later, Kelly contacted Charles Tessmer and told him he needed a job while his case was on appeal. Tessmer relayed the message to the Hunts, and Kelly received a phone call from Houston industrialist E. J. Hudson. Hudson, who was an old friend of H.L.'s and Bunker's, hired Kelly as the $700-per-month night security man at the Hudson Engineering offices in Houston.

At this point, Kelly and McCann apparently began to play both sides. While he was talking to the Hunts about hush money and jobs, Kelly was also negotiating with the government through his cousin and attorney Jerry Patchen. The subject of the negotiations was the possibility of Kelly testifying before the grand jury under a grant of immunity. Patchen told the government Kelly would not testify unless W. J. Everett was granted immunity also. Tessmer allegedly told the government that if Kelly was called before the grand jury, he would take the Fifth Amendment and say nothing.

Judge Robert M. Hill forced the issue off center on December 13, 1971.

Judge Hill granted Kelly immunity and ordered him to testify before the grand jury. Kelly refused and was cited for contempt. Judge Hill suggested that Kelly get another attorney because of Tessmer's apparent conflict of interest in representing Kelly while being paid by the Hunts.

Kelly took Judge Hill's advice. When he returned to Houston, he contacted famed criminal defense attorney Percy Foreman. Though now in his seventies, Foreman still had a reputation as the premier attorney in Texas and maybe the entire country. His record showed over 250 capital murder trials and not one defendant lost to the death penalty. Once when asked what he thought of the fact that convicted cattle rustlers served more time in Texas prisons on average than convicted murderers, Foreman replied that he thought things were as they should be. "I've known a lot of men that deserved to be shot," Foreman said, "but I've never known a cow that deserved to be stolen."

Kelly had met Foreman in connection with an unrelated case several months before. He knew Foreman's price was high, but he hoped that the old war horse might take his case at a reduced rate as a favor. Kelly later claimed that he explained his predicament with Charles Tessmer being paid by the Hunts, and asked Foreman to take over his representation in appealing Judge Hill's contempt citation.

Kelly said that Foreman agreed to take the case for a down payment of $1,000, and told Kelly that he was a fool to have let Tessmer represent him when Tessmer was tight with the Hunts. Kelly claimed that Foreman instructed him to pay his legal fees only with his own funds, not the Hunts'. Kelly raised the $1,000 by taking out a loan cosigned by a friend, and paid Foreman his down payment.

Then the plot began to thicken. A few days after conferring with Kelly, Percy Foreman telephoned E. J. Hudson, the Houston industrialist who was a long-time friend of the Hunts and Kelly's present employer. According to notes Hudson made of the conversation, Foreman said that $1,000 was not enough money to represent Kelly. In order to do the job, Foreman would need a much larger fee, say in the $50,000 range.

Hudson dutifully jotted notes of Foreman's points, and told him he would get back in touch.

Foreman then allegedly told Kelly that he would not have the time to represent him and dropped his case.

In the meantime, Hudson relayed Foreman's message to Bunker Hunt. Bunker and Ralph Shank discussed the pros and cons of hiring Foreman and finally decided to go ahead with it. On January 3, 1972, Ralph Shank telephoned Hudson and asked him to go ahead and pay Foreman the $50,000 he wanted. The next day Bunker called Hudson to confirm the fee decision. According to Hudson's notes, the Hunts had gotten Kelly back in the position he had been in with Tessmer. "Foreman can't front case," Hudson wrote in his diary, "but can control Kelly."

A short time later, Hudson paid Foreman the $50,000 in a cashier's check, and Foreman once again became Kelly's lawyer.

Although they did not deny paying the money to Foreman, the Hunts, Hudson, and their attorneys later claimed that the payment was not a bribe. They said that Kelly knew the Hunts were paying Foreman, just as he had known that they were paying Tessmer. In fact, they claimed that Kelly came to the Hunts looking for legal-fee money for his defense. The Hunts also later denied that their payments to Foreman, their payments to other attorneys in the case, and their offer of money to the wiretappers constituted an attempt to silence the wiretappers or an effort to obstruct the course of justice in any way.

In any event, the lid that had stayed on top of the wiretapping caper began to come off. On January 14, 1972, the grand jury returned a sealed indictment against W. J. Everett. The private eye was now officially on the hot spot and by no means committed to remaining silent if his silence meant jail time. Meanwhile, Pat McCann and his attorney Emmett Colvin were negotiating with the government for a grant of immunity. On January 19, after being promised immunity, McCann gave Assistant U.S. attorney Andrew Barr the tape he had made of his first telephone conversation with Bunker Hunt back in November of 1969.

When Ed Hudson got word that McCann was talking to someone, he called Percy Foreman. According to Kelly, Foreman then told Kelly that he must avoid testifying at all costs and intimated that if Kelly crossed the Hunts, they could be dangerous. Nevertheless, Kelly's cousin and part-time attorney Jerry Patchen was at that very same time telling Barr that Kelly was coming around and might soon be willing to testify. On February 3, 1972, the Fifth Circuit set aside Kelly's contempt citation. By all appearances, Foreman had accomplished what Kelly had originally hired him to do.

Back in Houston, Percy Foreman met the recently indicted W. J. Everett. According to Ed Hudson's notes, Foreman called Hudson and told him that he could "control" both Kelly and Everett for an additional $50,000. Foreman also warned that it looked like the government was going to indict the Hunt brothers and that they should "take all steps" to avoid an indictment. Hudson relayed Foreman's message to Bunker Hunt, noting in his diary, "Purpose in paying Foreman is to avoid indictments of Bunker and Herbert. . . . Kelly safe but McCann out of control.

A few days later, according to Hudson's notes, Foreman claimed he could "control" both McCann and Everett for an additional fee. After getting approval from Bunker to pay Foreman up to $75,000 more, Hudson managed to get Foreman to do the job for only $50,000 more. On February 18, 1972, Bunker wrote Hudson an IOU for $100,000 on the back of a piece of stationery from the Garden of the Gods Club. Hudson then got a cashier's check for $50,000 and paid it to Foreman.

Things remained quiet temporarily. Kelly later claimed that he told Foreman he wanted to testify under a grant of immunity in the hopes of getting a deal from the government. Kelly claimed Foreman responded by telling him that the Hunts had the means to hire a Mafia assassin if they were double-crossed, and advised, "The government can't help you if you are dead."

Foreman, for his part, later denied making any such threatening statements to Kelly. Though admitting to having contacted Hudson in connection with the wiretapping cases, Foreman also denied any impropriety or effort to obstruct justice such as Kelly alleged. Foreman claimed that in requesting money from the Hunts he was merely "promoting a fee," lawyer parlance for trying to obtain appropriate compensation for services rendered, and not trying to "control" anyone.

McCann also seemed ready to make a government deal. Barr granted McCann immunity, but Barr's Justice Department supervisor Henry Peterson overruled the grant of immunity. Peterson's stated reason was that the Fifth Circuit had not yet affirmed Kelly's conviction in the wiretap trial, and granting immunity at this stage might prejudice the case. McCann's attorney Emmett Colvin kept negotiating with Barr in an effort to arrive at an acceptable immunity agreement. Still, no one actually testified to anything.

The Hunt wiretap case escalated to an even higher level of intrigue in April of 1972, when John Connally hosted one of the most memorable barbecues in Texas political history. The barbecue was for President Richard M. Nixon, then about to begin his re-election campaign, and it was given under the auspices of Connally's newly renegade Democrats for Nixon. The Hunts and Connally had first met through a third-generation connection: H. L. Hunt's grandson Al Hill, Jr. had served with Connally's son John B. Connally III in the Texas Air National Guard. Bunker Hunt and John Connally the Elder first met in early 1971, when the Libyan government of Colonel al-Qaddafi nationalized the oil interests of Bunker Hunt's partner, British Petroleum. Bunker feared that he might be next and hired Connally to represent him with the Libyans for a reported ten-year, $75,000-a-year retainer.

Bunker and H. L. Hunt arrived at Connally's 1972 barbecue in a demonstrator Lear jet loaned to them by a hopeful airplane salesman. Bunker was said to have reproached Nixon at the party for the State Department's inaction in the face of the left-wing Libyan government's moves to nationalize oil companies operating in the country. Later, it was suggested that the Hunts may also have said something to Nixon about the Justice Department's handling of the wiretap prosecution. The basis for that suggestion was the fact that Bunker, Senator James Eastland, and Deputy Attorney General Richard Kleindienst agreed to meet at Eastland's ranch in Mississippi.

The gathering at Eastland's ranch was later described by sources close to the participants as "a friendly luncheon." Eastland admitted asking Kleindienst about the Hunt case, but insisted that all he asked for and got was a "status report" on the case. The fact that Kleindienst had been nominated to replace John Mitchell as attorney general and the fact that Kleindienst's nomination first had to be approved by Senator Eastland's Judiciary Committee caused some observers to wonder if subtle background pressure—or something more tangible—had accompanied Eastland's friendly inquiries. Convicted wiretapper Pat McCann later suggested in grand-jury testimony that Eastland had been paid a $50,000 or $60,000 bribe to intervene on the Hunts' behalf. Testimony by attorney Jerry Patchen also alleged a $50,000 or $60,000 bribe.

Although Eastland and Bunker Hunt denied that any bribe was made, Eastland acknowledged that he and Bunker were close friends and that he had sold Bunker some Charolais cattle at a reduced price. But the senator also pointed out that Bunker had not even contributed money to his campaign.

At any rate, following the luncheon at Eastland's ranch, the Hunt brothers' fortunes took a turn for the worse. On June 12, 1972, the Fifth Circuit upheld Kelly's and McCann's convictions for wiretapping. This, in turn, freed Henry Peterson to sign the grants of immunity the two wiretappers had been angling for. At the same time, Kelly came across a remarkable discovery—Ed Hudson's notes of his conversations with Bunker Hunt and Percy Foreman. Kelly discovered Hudson's notes one night while performing his security duties at Hudson Engineering. Kelly claimed he spotted the diary containing the notes on top of Hudson's desk. Inside the diary, in meticulous detail, Hudson had recorded the details of cash payments and backroom maneuvering, all of which, Kelly believed, were designed to make Kelly, McCann, and Everett the fall guys for the Hunt brothers.

Kelly removed Hudson's diary from Hudson's desk and took his find to his attorney-cousin Jerry Patchen. A short time later, Kelly was "terminated" from his job at Hudson Engineering, but the wiretap case had already taken on a new dimension. Now there was a possible basis not only for wiretap charges against the Hunts, but obstruction-of-justice charges against the Hunts and a whole string of big-name Texas attorneys.

Events began to move quickly. Kelly angrily fired Percy Foreman, informing the silver-haired old master that he now wanted to testify before the grand jury and scoring Foreman for failing to get him immunity in exchange for his testimony. On July 24 and 25, 1972, Jon Kelly and Pat McCann testified before the federal grand jury investigating the wiretap case. The following month, W. J. Everett and Clyde Wilson also appeared before the grand jury. The noose seemed to be closing around the necks of the Hunt brothers.

Then there was a mysterious lag. A month passed. Then another. And another. And still there were no signs of progress in the case. Some observers later speculated that the holdup may have been due to developments in an even more famous wiretap caper. On June 17, 1972, just about the time Kelly had discovered Hudson's diary, a team of burglars and wiretappers was caught breaking into the offices of the Democratic National Committee in the Watergate complex. Like the Hunt case, the Watergate case was growing from a crime into a cover-up of the crime that resulted in the committing of still more alleged crimes.

The Hunt case was like a Texas-style private-enterprise version of Watergate. In ordinary times, the Hunt case might well have been forgotten, shunted aside. But these were not ordinary times. A new morality and a new cynicism were sweeping the land. If the discovery of the Watergate burglars and the subsequent political fallout delayed Justice Department action on the Hunt case, the national mood assured that the Hunts would not be forgotten.

Sure enough, on March 2, 1973, over three years after Kelly's arrest, a federal grand jury in Dallas returned criminal indictments against Nelson Bunker Hunt, William Herbert Hunt, Clyde Wilson, and Morgan Watson. The charge: illegal wiretapping.

The Hunt brothers were both angered and intimidated by the indictments. This was the first time any member of the family had ever been slapped with criminal charges. Their high-level connections had not come through for them. The government had reneged on its supposed deal. Adding further insult to the whole affair was the fact that the government had taken no action against the men whom the Hunt brothers felt were the real villains—Rothermel, Curington, and Brown. While Bunker and Herbert were under indictment for wiretapping, the alleged perpetrators of the losses and embezzlements at the food division were not being brought to justice at all.

With no choice but to face the charges against them in court, Bunker and Herbert began shopping around for a good wiretap attorney. Meanwhile, their aging father went about his eccentric ways almost as if the demise of HLH Products and the wiretapping indictments of his sons were nothing but episodes in a bad dream.

CHAPTER 13

WHERE THERE'S A WILL

YOU really had to hand it to the old man: for all his faults and failings, he never quit. The times could pass him by. His business affairs could slip out of his control. His mental and physical balance could get shaky. But he never stopped his all-out pursuit of life. He never ceased being himself. H. L. Hunt the octogenarian of the early 1970s was just as much his own man as was June Hunt the footloose young gambler of the early 1900s. Right or wrong, in touch with the real world or living an illusion, he always did exactly what he felt like doing. He was always full of surprises. And he was always showing off his special talents, especially for the ladies.

Take the time pretty young Rena Pederson of the *Dallas Morning News* came out to interview him at Mount Vernon. It was early one morning in September of 1972, over a year after the auctioning off of the HLH Products processing plants. Hunt was sitting at the dining-room table, munching handfuls of grapes, dates, apricots, and pecans from an array of bowls set out in front of him. Now and again, he would take a sip from one of several glasses of fruit juice and cups of bouillon interspersed with the bowls of fruit and nuts.

Pederson sat nearby with a photographer and Hunt's wife Ruthie. The subject of the interview was Hunt's health diet, and Pederson was diligently taking notes as Hunt reeled off his standard litany of tips in between bites and gulps of breakfast.

"Avoid anything made with white sugar or white flour," he told her. "Eat plenty of apricot seeds, dates, and pecans, and . . ."

All of a sudden, Hunt slipped out of his chair and dropped to the floor. Landing like a cat on all fours, he began to crawl around and around the dining-room table on his hands and knees. Slowly at first. Then faster and faster. Soon he was lapping the dining-room table with astonishing speed.

"I'm a crank about creeping!" he shouted gleefully as he passed reporter Pederson's chair.

Never breaking his pace, Hunt continued his frenzied crawl around and around the dining-room table.

"Don't go too fast," pleaded Ruth, mindful of her husband's recently reinjured bad back.

"Yes, please slow down," the *Dallas Morning News* photographer chimed in. "I want to get your picture."

Hunt obliged the photographer's request, and came to a skidding halt at the south end of the dining room. With his sparse white hair, his crisp French cuffs, his tie, and his business-suit pants, he looked both ridiculous and oddly dignified as he posed for the camera in his infantile "creeping" posture. His long-traveled blue eyes sparkled with childish delight as the photographer snapped his picture.

"They never can keep up with me," Hunt cackled when the photographer was done. The thought seemed to please him immensely.

"Yahoo!" he whooped, pushing himself up from the floor.

The sound of his own shout also seemed to give Hunt great satisfaction. Returning to his place at the table, he victoriously ordered up a date for all present and set about extolling the virtues of "creeping."

As Hunt explained to reporter Pederson, "creeping" was his favorite form of exercise. He considered it far superior to running, swimming, golf, or tennis, and even better than yoga, which he also practiced. In the course of "creeping," Hunt maintained, a person worked the heart, the lungs, and all the important muscles of the body all at the same time. No other exercise could claim so thorough an effect. Just as creeping was the primary means a newborn infant used to develop its body, so creeping was also the best possible means for an adult to maintain a grownup body.

"I have lots of money," Hunt chuckled as he finished his explanation, "so they call me the 'Billionaire Health Crank.' Heh, heh, heh."

Of course, as Hunt went on to admit, he took his title very seriously. Having won recognition as the "world's richest man," he now wanted to become the world's longest-living man. The record, he said, was held by a Russian. The communists claimed their man had lived to be 167. Though he would have to live eighty-four more years to make it, Hunt figured he had a pretty good chance of bringing the record back home to America. He was still energetic and strong and had plenty of things left to do. He compared himself to the Hunzukuts of the Himalayas who played polo into their one-hundredth year. Instead of getting his exercise on horseback, Hunt simply got it on his hands and knees. He was also benefiting from a special daily "dietary supplement" he had just begun to manufacture. His new pills were composed of steer muscle, alfalfa, and Spanish moss.

As reporter Pederson could tell, this was H. L. Hunt at his happiest— the eternal wildcatter, the immortal individualist, the Last White Hope, proving his extraordinary powers one more time. Unfortunately, not all of Hunt's mornings were quite so merry. As one relative observed, he continued to have "his good days and his bad days." On his good days, Hunt could be charming, cute, mischievous, unexpectedly brilliant, and thoroughly beguiling. But on his bad days, he could also be moody, cross, temperamental, forgetful, impatient, intolerant, and thoroughly unbearable. And it was almost impossible for those around him to predict which days would be good and which would be bad.

Hunt still drove himself to work six days a week, but things down at Hunt Oil Company were not as before. With the divestiture of the food division, Hunt Oil's financial situation was improving dramatically. Since the company no longer had to pick up $10 million to $12 million annual deficits, the oil and gas division was accumulating enough capital to drill new wells. Possessed of energy reserves and real-estate assets worth upward of $130 million, Hunt Oil was getting back in the oil business and beginning to grow again. But Hunt Oil's success was less the result of what Hunt did than the result of what he did not do. The absence of the food division alone accounted for the company's turnaround. And parting with the food division was something Hunt had done only after much turmoil, persuasion, and financial loss. Operation control of Hunt Oil was no longer in the hands of Hunt or a circle of his personal aides, but under the supervision of his sons Bunker and Herbert and his nephew Tom, the ones who had finally convinced him to do something about HLH Products. They, not Hunt, were the architects of Hunt Oil's recovery. At the same time, though, they were all preoccupied with the management of other longstanding and much larger financial interests. Thus, H.L., Hunt Oil Company, and the small drug and cosmetics division still left over from the HLH Products sell-off tended to take a back seat to the big family money plays of the early 1970s.

The divestiture of the food division also marked the decline of LIFE LINE as a propaganda organ. The organization's broadcasts remained on the air, and Hunt continued to contribute to LIFE LINE's chest. But with the demise of its largest single sponsor, LIFE LINE got less and less air time, until it became a mere echo of its former self. Hunt remained as staunchly anticommunist as ever, but he seemed to lose interest in what was once his consuming passion. Hunt's son Bunker later testified that there was also a decline in threats against H. L. Hunt's life that happened to coincide with the decline in Hunt's public profile and with the departure of Hunt Oil security chief Paul Rothermel, implying that he believed his father's former aide may have exaggerated or even fabricated dangers in order to keep his own job secure.

Instead of being consumed with LIFE LINE, Hunt spent much of his time talking and writing. With his columns now published by twenty-two dailies and thirty-seven weeklies, Hunt had plenty to keep himself occupied. An aide recalled that the boss had four favorite subjects. The first three were aloe vera, his Indian Hot Springs Ranch, and the Texas Rangers, of which he became an honorary member. The fourth and most favorite was himself. As one associate put it, with only slight exaggeration, "He was interested only in H. L. Hunt." Hunt could and often did sit and tell stories about himself and his adventures for hours. For a number of years, he had been looking for someone to write his life story. He made overtures to Houston oil writer James

A. Clark and to several comely female reporter/researchers in the Dallas area, but he never seemed able to make a satisfactory contractual arrangement with anyone. Having already written bits and pieces about his life in his columns and letters to the editor, Hunt finally decided to get a couple of researchers and write his autobiography. Typically, he wrote not just one book, but two.

Hunt published his two works, *Hunt Heritage* and *H. L. Hunt Early Days,* in 1973 under his Parade Press label. Both books were paperback, about 150 pages in length, and priced at one dollar. On the cover of *Hunt Heritage,* there was a montage drawing of H. L. Hunt as a young man, H.L. as an old man, an oil rig, a refinery, a Model T at a gas pump, and an ocean-going ship. On the cover of *H. L. Hunt Early Days,* the montage showed a drawing of Hunt at later middle age, a drawing of MacArthur, and a huge offshore oil platform on a barge, all against an American-flag background.

"The distance between Nichols Prairie above Vandalia, Illinois, and Dallas is short if you gauge it by jet airliner speed, but it has been a long and eventful journey for me," Hunt wrote in *Hunt Heritage.* "The frame buildings of Vandalia, the closest community of size near my birthplace in Carson Township were a far cry from the skyscraper canyons of a great metropolis. Today, at my present age of eighty-four, as I write the story of some of my endeavors, I like to think that my head is in a cloud of constructive dreams, here in my 29th floor office in Dallas, but that my feet are still on the ground back in Carson Township in Fayette County, Illinois." Hunt admitted, "That may sound like a lot of stretching," but went on to opine: "If you are to progress as individuals, and as the greatest nation of all, it will take a lot of constructive dreaming, a lot of constructive work, and a lot of treading in the firm soil of practicality and patriotism that we inherited from our parentage."

Both autobiographies turned out to be considerably watered-down versions of Hunt's history and adventures. They were distinguished less by what Hunt said than by what he left out. Hunt gave detailed genealogical information about his family forebears, but only sketchy information about his own generation, his wives, and children. Frania Tye Lee's name was never even mentioned. He gave sketchy and self-serving accounts of his early oil days, the Dad Joiner deal, and Facts Forum. He made no mention of such misadventures as the circulation of Reverend Criswell's anti-Catholic sermon, the scandal at HLH Products, or the true circumstances of his three-family patriarchy. Instead, Hunt devoted his texts to making his own myth. In one book, he claimed to have been able to read the newspapers at the age of three. In the next book, he could accomplish the feat by the age of two. He told of his early facility with numbers and his card tricks, but not much of his gambling exploits. In both autobiographies, Hunt departed from his account of his own life to deliver long political essays, health tips, or accounts of one of his favorite subjects besides himself.

Hunt also kept searching for new ways to get his political philosophy across to the nation through a religious vehicle. One of the projects he considered most seriously was a 1970 TV film called "Miracle of America," which starred singer Pat Boone. Ole Anthony, a Texas businessman, politician, and theologian, was handling the money-raising effort for Boone's special. Having heard that H. L. Hunt was a great fan of Boone, Anthony decided to solicit a contribution. He finally tracked Hunt down at the Louisiana State Fair in Shreveport, where he found the old man selling aloe vera beneath a tent.

Anthony told Hunt about Boone's "Miracle of America," and the old man immediately became excited. Pat Boone was his ideal image of what a young American should be—pure, clean, and lily white. Hunt put down his aloe vera and rushed over to the local television station to screen Anthony's pilot tape of the show.

When H.L. and Anthony arrived at the television station, they found that the station's videotape player (VTR) was already in use. In fact, the VTR was being used to help broadcast the show that was on the air. Hunt was furious. He wanted to see "Miracle of America" at once. He demanded that the station stop the show in progress and put on the network show so that he could use the VTR to watch the pilot of this marvelous new Christian show. Astonished by Hunt's audacity and awed by his reputation, the station manager acquiesced to his demand.

Hunt and Anthony then nestled down in the station's screening room to watch the show. When Pat Boone's image came on the screen, Hunt choked up and began to cry.

When the screening ended, Hunt promised Anthony he would personally raise the money to finance the show. Anthony at first thought Hunt meant he was going to raise the money from some of several personal bank accounts, but this was not the case. Hunt intended to raise the money from other wealthy men—specifically his own bankers. He gave Anthony a notebook containing the names of about fifty bank presidents, and instructed him to telephone the men and invite them to Shreveport for a screening of the show. Hunt said he was sure all of them would want to contribute.

Anthony did as Hunt instructed, but only twelve of the fifty bankers showed up for the screening. Once again, Hunt was furious. He called up his Dallas office and ordered that his deposits be withdrawn from every bank whose president had not answered his invitation to the screening. But for all his fury, Hunt was not able to squeeze a single dime from the bankers who did see the pilot.

Hunt then turned to the members of his family. He took Anthony back to Dallas, and with somewhat less immediate success than he had enjoyed back in Shreveport, commandeered another VTR at the local Channel 4. Hunt then called up all the members of his two Dallas families and instructed them to come to the Channel 4 screening room at once. Most of the members of the two families did show up. When they had settled into their chairs, Anthony screened "Miracle of America." After the tape ended and the lights had come on again, Hunt launched into one of his spiels about the menace posed by the hippies and the Rockefellers. His tirade went on for what seemed like two hours. The entire family simply sat motionless, listening, as if they were almost afraid to move. Finally, Hunt stopped talking, got up from his chair, and left.

Hunt's involvement with "Miracle of America" proved to be a metaphor for most of his other political projects during the early 1970s. After all the fuss he made over soliciting contributions, Hunt was not able to raise a single cent for the film and did not see fit to give any of his own money either. The show did go on, but without the financial assistance of H. L. Hunt.

Undeterred by such fiascos, Hunt kept trying to find new ways to promote his political views. One of his dearest ambitions was to enlist the aid of his first-family sons in his political projects. This was no easy task. Hunt's sons did share his basic arch conservatism, and in earlier years had given their annual tithes to Facts Forum and LIFE LINE. But "the boys" were clearly embarrassed by their father's excessive zeal and cornball political style and did their best to keep their distance. This, also, was no easy task. In 1972, for example, Hunt decided that the best possible candidate for president of the United States was his son Lamar. As one Hunt Oil employee of the era explained, "Mr. Hunt thought Lamar was popular because of his sports enterprises." Reasoning that Lamar could translate that popularity into votes, Hunt tried to persuade his son to throw his hat in the ring. Lamar balked. Recognizing the ridiculousness of his father's proposal, he told Hunt that he would not run and would not serve even if elected. Hunt took his son's reaction as mere personal modesty and kept putting pressure on him to become a candidate. Finally, Lamar had to write his father a letter asking him to "please drop the subject" and never bring it up again.

Rejected by his sons and largely unheeded by the American public, Hunt continued to foist his political ideas and his health tips on whomever else would listen. These often turned out to be his own employees. Any innocent young landman or secretary who happened to be in the boss's office when he was struck by hunger for the midday meal would find himself or herself in for an unforgettable experience. Hunt would make an offer the employee could not refuse—to join the boss for lunch. Having been roped into sharing Hunt's peculiar repast, the employee would then have to sit for upward of an hour as Hunt lectured about the communists, his style of health foods, his belief that he had powers of extrasensory perception, and other favorite subjects, while eating oranges, apples, dates, pecans, coleslaw, and melon from atop a tablecloth of newspapers. Some employees claimed to have enjoyed Hunt's stories. Others found them nothing but an incoherent waste of time. Still, it was hard for even the most brusque and cold-hearted listener not to at least feel a twinge of sympathy for the white-haired octogenarian who for all his money seemed to have nothing left but his memories, dreams, and self-made myths.

Ironically, some of Hunt's self-made myths were true. He did look good for his advanced age. He had plenty of vim and vigor, fire and lust. One thing he never seemed to tire of was chasing skirts. Even into his eighties, Hunt always had an eye for the ladies and a well-known weakness for well-endowed young secretaries. One former aide recalled seeing Hunt at age eighty-two catching sight of a particularly well-built Hunt Oil secretary who was leaning over to file some papers in a nearby cabinet. Hunt bent over to the floor, bad back and all, so he could be sure to get a good look.

Still the archetype of frugality, Hunt showed but few visible signs of his wealth in these years. Perhaps the most significant one was the purchase in 1971 of a brand new dark blue Lincoln Continental to replace the Oldsmobile 88 he drove in the late 1960s. Hunt bought himself another new blue Lincoln in 1973. Meanwhile, Hunt Oil Company replaced its remanufactured World War II bomber with a 1969 Lockheed Jet Star. But apart from these few transportation luxuries, Hunt's life style remained as spartan as ever.

Despite his advancing years, Hunt seldom took a vacation. (He believed the fight for freedom, as he put it, was too important for vacations.) In fact, according to his wife Ruth, Hunt took only three vacations in his entire working life. One was a planned three-week visit to Europe which lasted three months. The second was a month-long trip to South America. And the third was a brief stay at his Palette Ranch in Wyoming. The Wyoming ranches were also a favorite vacation spot of his children and grandchildren. In addition to affording plenty of good hunting and fishing grounds, the Hoodoo Ranches had horse gear and cowboy guides for pack trips into the mountains. Hunt himself was not one for pack trips, but the younger generations of Hunts found them perfect relaxation from city life.

One self-made myth Hunt never stopped believing was that his son Hassie would one day recover from his illness. Hunt was consumed by this belief. If an employee was under fire for some reason and wanted to divert the boss's attention, all he or she had to do was ask, "How's Hassie?" The question would invariably stop Hunt in his tracks.

"He's getting better," Hunt would say. "I saw him today, and he's getting better."

In truth, Hassie was not getting any better. Still unable to do much more than eat, sleep, and stroll around White Rock Lake, Hassie would sometimes come down to the office with his father and merely stare silently at the surroundings or deliver obtuse one-liners such as, "Sometimes they let me make my own decisions." But Hassie's father never gave up hope of finding a "cure." Among other things, Hunt wrote memos to, or at least for, his son, listing various psychotherapeutic drugs that he thought might "cure" him. In one such memo, dated October 12, 1971, Hunt declared, "Hassie Hunt recovered completely from mental trouble about October 1, 1971, while using the chemical VALIUM, one tablet every morning and a second tablet if and when he thought he should take the second tablet. Constructively, H. L. Hunt."

Despite Hunt's optimistic prediction/assertion, Hassie did not recover completely or even partially. But Hunt kept on believing that Hassie was improving. Hunt included a recent photograph of Hassie beside a recent photograph of himself in *H. L. Hunt Early Days.* The photographs showed the two in dark suits and bow ties. There was no mention of Hassie's illness or Hunt's attempts to "cure" him, only the caption: "H. L. Hunt and his eldest son Hassie; the two once won a father-son 'lookalike' contest."

For all his lustiness and braggadocio, Hunt had many fears. One of his greatest worries, for example, was that he was physically shrinking in height as he got older. "My grandmother lived to be ninety-seven and kept getting smaller," he told an interviewer. "When she died, she was no higher than this table." Though Hunt was starting from a height of six feet, he was planning to live considerably beyond the age of ninety-seven, and the prospect of continued shrinkage at the rate his grandmother suffered was not appealing.

Besides being worried about shrinking, Hunt became deeply concerned about being regarded as "silly." He knew that much of the public and many of those around him, including members of his own family, considered his habits and views to be exactly that, and this, to him, was the most unkind cut of all. Better to be hated and despised to the very core than to be dismissed as a daffy old man. Craving new confirmation that he was not, in fact, just another senile nut, Hunt often put his employees on the spot by asking their opinions of his ways.

"I'll bet you think this is silly," he would say when he had cornered one of his men for a health-food lunch.

Lucky was the employee who could both think to say, "No, sir, Mr. Hunt," and then buttress his reply by telling the boss how healthy he looked, what good color he had in his cheeks, what energy he seemed to possess, and how his diet must have a great deal to do with all of that.

More than anything, Hunt feared losing his touch—or, rather, having people believe he was losing his touch. He wanted to convey the impression that he was still the world's greatest oilman, the patriarch without whom none of the family fortune would have been possible. Hunt seemed especially concerned with impressing this on the members of the first family, whose business activities he kept checking up on by means of his employee "spies." In point of fact, Hunt had virtually no oil-business activities of his own by this time, and was rarely required to make an important executive decision. Nevertheless, he continually resorted to endearingly transparent acts of trickery and subterfuge to leave the opposite impression. On one occasion, for example, an aide had just finished getting approval on the sale of a small real-estate property when Hunt's son-in-law Al Hill came into the office. The aide started to go, but Hunt called after him.

"You think those leases will be all right?"

The way Hunt was talking, it sounded as if he and his aide had been discussing some oil leases, not the real-estate sale. Quick to pick up on what was happening, the aide stammered that he thought the leases would be just fine, then left. As the aide recalled afterward, "There aren't any oil leases. Mr. Hunt was just trying to show his son-in-law he was still playing the game."

The real player in the Hunt family during the early 1970s was still Nelson Bunker Hunt. Despite the fallout caused by the wiretapping caper, Bunker continued to pursue one giant business deal after another, diversifying his fortune in oil, real estate, cattle, and even sugar and pizza parlors. Bunker's interests circled the globe and extended to four continents. His ventures in-

volved the use of some of the world's most modern technologies and the
interplay of some of the century's most complex and epochal political developments. But through it all, Bunker continued to operate with the instinctual,
shoot-from-the-hip approach he inherited from his old man. That approach
brought him a fair amount of success, but it also brought on at least one major
disaster.

Bunker began the decade with an ironic problem: he had too much
money. Through the late 1960s and early 1970s, income from his great Libyan
oil field continued to flow in at a rate of $30 million per year. There was
nothing wrong with that except that Bunker's income had no place to go. Oil
prices were then at the pre–Arab-oil-embargo level of $3 per barrel (and even
less in some areas of the world), so the idea of simply reinvesting that great
cash flow in more oil and gas exploration was not particularly attractive.
Consequently, Bunker began looking around for alternative investments. The
choices he came up with proved to be doozies.

At first, Bunker put most of his money into real estate. He bought ranches
in Oklahoma and Montana, cattle stations in Australia, horse farms in Kentucky, England, Ireland, France, and New Zealand. Having invested in the
Alaskan North Slope oil play via the Getty-Hunt consortium, Bunker positioned himself to profit from the expected Alaskan real-estate boom by buying
up large tracts in downtown Anchorage. Bunker further increased his holdings
by purchasing an estimated 20,000 head of cattle, becoming the world's largest
breeder of Charolais cattle. Either personally or through one of the many
family companies, Bunker also invested in oil and gas leases in Canada, New
Zealand, the North Sea, and the United States. (Though he did not plan to drill
many of the leases immediately, they stood as his wager that oil prices would
one day rise to what he considered more appropriate levels.) According to
Hunt insiders, Bunker's total real-estate holdings in the United States
amounted to more than 1 million acres. His foreign holdings, including the vast
Australian cattle stations, amounted to over 4 million acres.

With over 5 million acres of the earth under his ownership, Bunker was
well situated to cash in on the real-estate boom of the 1970s. But investing in
land was somehow not enough. Bunker still had his eye out for other lucrative
cash havens, places where his great Libyan income could flow in and multiply.
The place he picked was the silver market.

Bunker's interest in silver began one day down at the Hunts' Circle T
Ranch outside of Dallas. The year was 1970, and Bunker was sitting in one of
his favorite places, the kitchen, talking to New York commodities broker
Alvin J. Brodsky. A short, excitable man, Brodsky had flown down to Texas
to make what would turn out to be one of the most important sales pitches
of his career. His method was simple but graphic. As the cattle grazed outside,
Brodsky gestured at the items in the room—the tablecloth, the utensils, the
food, and he asked a single question.

"Bunker, do you believe you're going to have to pay more for these things
next year than you did this year?"

Bunker allowed that he did.

"Well, then," Brodsky said, "you should consider silver."

Simplistic as it may have sounded, Brodsky's pitch jived perfectly with Bunker's financial situation and his total world view. Like oil prices, silver prices were then relatively depressed. In fact, silver was at a historic low of only $1.50 per ounce. But Bunker believed that silver might be in for an enormous increase in price. The inflationary future Brodsky illustrated at the Circle T was one main reason. Bunker personally believed that inflation would grow worse. More generally, he also believed that life on earth—politics, living standards, population—was going to grow worse, too, and he saw plenty of evidence to support his view: the war in Vietnam, turmoil in the Middle East, and riots on American streets. On an even more personal level, Bunker also faced the possibility of future nationalization of his Libyan oil field by the radical Libyan leader Colonel Muammar al-Qaddafi as well as the prospect that the family wiretapping caper (then in the process of unraveling) would blow up in his face.

Alvin Brodsky was not the only person who recommended silver. There was Bunker's former prep-school roommate Ted Jansey and Dallas silver brokers Don and Scott Dial. As these and other silver bugs reminded Bunker, it was then illegal for Americans to buy gold. That left few attractive precious-metal alternatives for a U.S. citizen who believed the world was going to hell in a hack. So shortly after hearing Brodsky's pitch at the Circle T, Bunker and his brother Herbert began buying silver.

They bought slowly at first, making purchases in 5,000- and 10,000-ounce "penny packets" mostly through Bache, the brokerage house with which Brodsky was associated. The total amount of these investments was only a few hundred thousand dollars, small change by Hunt standards. The initial results, however, were the sort Bunker and his brother could readily appreciate. Between 1970 and 1973, the price of silver rose 110 percent to $3 an ounce.

In the meantime, trouble broke out in Libya. It all began as Libyan dictator Colonel al-Qaddafi started making noises about nationalizing his country's oil fields. The Libyan oil operators, most of whom were major oil companies, began meeting to discuss ways to combat the expected threat. In January of 1971, Occidental chief Armand Hammer and John J. McCloy, an attorney with close ties to the Rockefellers, the major oil companies, and the eastern-establishment foreign-policy elite, drafted a pact called the Libyan Producers Agreement. Also known as the "safety net," the agreement called for all the oil companies operating in Libya to present a united front in dealing with the Libyan government. The agreement further stipulated that if one company was nationalized, the other companies would help defray the loss by contributing percentage shares of their Libyan production as well as "fall back" oil from the Persian Gulf.

Bunker was naturally suspicious of the "safety net" agreement. The way he saw it, anything drafted by an eastern-establishment big-oil-company law-yer like McCloy was bound to be full of trouble. Bunker was sure the major oil companies had some ulterior motive in wanting to get the independents like himself to join in the agreement. Indeed, one of the important "fringe benefits" of the "safety net" was that it provided a way for the major oil companies to meet regularly to discuss world oil prices without violating antitrust regulations. Bunker seriously doubted that the majors would stand by their "safety net" pact if push came to shove in Libya. But in the interests of maintaining harmony, he was finally persuaded to sign it.

The first major test of the "safety net" agreement came in December of 1971, when al-Qaddafi nationalized the Libyan interests of Bunker's partner, British Petroleum. The reason given for the nationalization was that the British government, which owned half of BP, had sided with Iran in a dispute between Iran and Iraq over the ownership of an island and the sale of some jet fighters. The dispute had nothing to do with Libya except that Colonel al-Qaddafi supported Iraq's side.

Bunker now faced a dangerous double bind. Under the "safety net," he and the other oil producers were obliged to compensate BP for its lost production. In addition, the terms of Bunker's partnership agreement with BP called for him to pay BP 18,000 barrels of oil per day as compensation for BP's expenses as operator of the field. But the Libyans were making compliance impossible. After allowing Hunt technicians to come in and operate the Sarir field, they demanded that Hunt continue to market BP's share of the crude. Bunker refused, both on principle and on the grounds that marketing BP's share might expose him to hot-oil suits. According to Hunt insiders, Bunker tried to leave BP's share of the Sarir field in the ground until the crisis could be resolved. Then Bunker's technicians were expelled, and Libyan technicians took over the production of the field. Although Bunker continued to get his oil, he was no longer able to operate the pipeline valves. At this point, Hunt insiders later claimed, Bunker began to ship compensation oil to BP in keeping with the "safety net" agreement, but the takeover by the Libyan field technicians prevented him from sending BP its full share of Sarir crude.

In the fall of 1972, the Libyans started a new round of demands. Now they wanted not just royalty payments, but 51-percent participation in all Libyan oil operations. Both the major companies and the independents feared taking a next step. Should they stick to the "safety net" agreement and remain a united front? Or should they fend for themselves as best they could? Most companies, including Bunker's, tried to do both. While publicly stating that they would not concede to the Libyan demands, the companies privately attempted to cut their own separate deals. In November of 1972, for example, Bunker's lawyer Ed Guinn met secretly with the Libyans and proposed that the Libyans buy Bunker out for two years' production. The Libyans angrily refused, saying they did not have to buy their own oil, and ended the meeting. The following month, December, the Libyans shut down the Hunt wells completely.

It was at this point that Bunker turned to the fabled John Connally for help. Hired for a $75,000-a-year retainer for ten years, Connally became Bunker's chief Libyan negotiator. The former Texas governor demanded that the Libyans submit to arbitration over Bunker's shut-in wells. The Libyans, who seemed to be moved by Connally's mere presence, agreed to let Bunker resume production in January of 1973. The Libyans then concentrated their negotiating efforts on other oil companies. Connally appeared to have done the trick.

Unfortunately, Bunker's days of grace were numbered. The Libyans soon managed to get ENK, the Italian national oil company, to agree to a 51-percent participation agreement. In April, they telegrammed Bunker Hunt and called on him to match the deal. Bunker ignored the telegram. Then on May 17, 1973, John Connally resigned as Bunker's Libyan representative to become an unpaid adviser to President Nixon. Connally's resignation apparently emboldened the Libyans to act against Bunker Hunt. On May 24, 1973, Bunker's wells were shut in. The following month, Bunker's Libyan oil production was formally and completely nationalized. To add insult to injury, the Libyans also claimed that Bunker owed them an additional $17 million in royalty payments. Libyan dictator Colonel al-Qaddafi characterized his action against Bunker as "a slap on America's cool, arrogant face."

Both friends and foes would later argue that the nationalization of Bunker's Libyan holdings was largely Bunker's own fault. One former Hunt employee pointed out that other companies producing oil in Libya "played the game" with the Libyan government by spending portions of their production on building new schools and hospitals in their host country in addition to paying the required royalties. "Bunker," said this former associate, "kept all his profit for himself." Thus, Bunker and the supposedly public-welfare-oriented al-Qaddafi regime were not on the best of terms when Libya's quest for a larger share in its oil production began.

According to other observers, Bunker's downfall was caused by his own greed and intransigence. "Bunker probably could've kept from being nationalized," observed a man formerly associated with Hunt and several other of the oil companies operating in Libya, "if he hadn't taken an arbitrary position. But he did take an arbitrary position. His position was that they weren't going to take him over—either fifty-one percent or one-hundred percent or even twenty-five percent. His position was that he was going to fight them. It's been proven over the years that fighting the Libyans is a big waste of time." As this source and others pointed out, the other oil companies operating in Libya negotiated more flexibly, accepted the 51-percent-participation demand, and continued to operate profitably in Libya for years afterward.

Bunker naturally saw the situation in a different light. As far as he could tell, his demise had been precipitated by the fact that he had generally obeyed both the spirit and the letter of the "safety net" agreement. It was fine to say in hindsight that he could have negotiated his own deal with the Libyans, but the whole idea of the "safety net" had been for the oil companies to present a united front. Bunker now expected—or said he expected—the other oil companies to stand by him, present a united front, pay him compensation oil, and make him a part of any eventual settlement. More than that, he and BP published full-page advertisements in the pages of the world financial press warning that they would send lawmen to stop the unloading of any Libyan oil lifted from their former holdings.

The other companies did not exactly do Bunker's bidding. On the contrary, each retired to ponder how best to save its own interests. Representatives of the major companies met in New York and London in gatherings known as "the McCloy group" and "the London policy group." The major oil company men eventually determined that the only viable option was to concede to 51-percent participation. The independent oil company chiefs reached the same conclusion. Armand Hammer of Occidental, the most dynamic independent oil company head, led the pack. In June of 1973, just a few weeks after Bunker's nationalization, Hammer announced that Oxy had agreed to give the Libyans 51-percent participation and to accept lower annual production rates in return for the right to remain in the country.

Oxy's concession was the crack that broke the dam. One by one the other Libyan operators followed suit, each negotiating its own essentially similar participation agreement with the Libyans. None of the companies made Bunker a part of its new arrangements. Not surprisingly, the "safety net" agreement became a shambles. Some companies, Exxon among them, did pay compensation oil to Bunker and BP, but most did not. In defiance of Bunker's advertisements, Coastal States Corp. of Houston, which was not party to the "safety net" agreement, bought a cargo of Sarir crude from the Libyans and shipped it to Virginia. Bunker sent U.S. marshals to prevent the ship from unloading, but Coastal States eventually got a court injunction against the marshals, unloaded the crude, and commenced trading lawsuits with Bunker.

It soon became clear that Bunker's ouster from Libya was not just a personal problem. The fact that the oil companies who were party to the Libyan producers' "safety net" agreement abandoned their united front had dramatic consequences for the entire world. Al-Qaddafi's success in splitting the oil companies' negotiating cartel emboldened Saudi Arabian oil minister Yamani and other leaders of the Organization of Petroleum Exporting Countries to demand similar arrangements for themselves. Though events in Libya were by no means the only factors involved, their eventual upshot was the Arab oil embargo in the fall of 1973, the quadrupling of world oil prices, and the emergence of OPEC as the dictator of the global economic order.

Back in Dallas, Bunker Hunt rankled with bitterness toward all concerned. Al-Qaddafi's action in Libya had cost him a fortune. And if Libya's radical young dictator was the primary arch villain, Bunker believed his fall was caused by devils much closer to home. He accused the other oil companies of making him "the sacrificial lamb," the test case to see how far the Libyans would go in following through on their demands and threats. He also accused the U.S. State Department of continuing to do nothing to alleviate the Libyan situation. "The State Department is a big joke," declared Bunker's attorney Ed Guinn shortly after the nationalization. "They're more concerned about what somebody in Bombay or some other such place might say than they are

in protecting the American people's business interests abroad." Although
Exxon had ostensibly lived up to what Bunker claimed were its obligations
under the "safety net" agreement, Bunker privately blamed the Hunts' supposed arch enemies the Rockefellers for orchestrating the actions of the oil
companies and the inaction of the State Department.

Publicly, Bunker went after the big oil companies. In the spring of 1974,
Bunker filed the largest antitrust suit in history, alleging $13 billion in damages
at the hands of fourteen oil companies, among them Mobil, Texaco, Standard
Oil of California, Shell, Gulf, Occidental, Conoco, Atlantic Richfield, and
Gelsenberg of Germany. Bunker's suit contended that the companies "attempted to monopolize the importation and sale of Persian Gulf, Libyan and
other Mediterranean crude oil into the United States" and conspired to refuse
to supply Bunker with oil and to prevent him from resuming production in
Libya after his nationalization. In his complaint, Bunker claimed that he and
BP had spent $250 million developing the field and had paid $500 million in
"taxes and royalties" to the Libyan government. He claimed among his losses
in-the-ground oil assets exceeding $4.2 billion and a reasonable expectation of
five-year future profits of $650 million. A few of the companies settled Bunker's
claims out of court, but most denied everything, and prepared to defend
themselves at trial.

While Bunker went after the major oil companies, Bunker's former partner BP turned around and filed a £36 million ($76 million) lawsuit against
Bunker in England. At issue was the 18,000-barrel-per-day extra share BP
claimed it was due under its operating agreement with Bunker Hunt. Bunker
claimed he had been unable to get this oil to BP because of political pressure
from the Libyans and had, therefore, let it build up in storage tanks until a
solution could be reached. But BP claimed that despite the Libyan's pressure,
the time had come to pay up. Given the venue of the suit in England and BP's
part ownership by the British government, it was likely that the English courts
would be inclined to uphold BP's claim. That fact carried serious implications
for Bunker Hunt. As an American citizen, Bunker could try to appeal or
simply ignore the decision of the English courts. But Bunker had considerable
personal property in England, namely his highly successful horse farms and
racing stables, as well as large real-estate holdings in other parts of the British
Commonwealth. If BP wanted to collect, they had merely to attack Bunker's
assets in England.

Despite all these problems, Bunker had quite a bit to show for his abortive
adventure in Libya. For one thing, his net profits from 1967 to 1973 amounted
to an estimated $150 million, exempt from U.S. taxes because of the foreign
tax credit. With the negotiating help of John Tiggrett, an American deal maker
of international renown, Bunker was able to reach a $40-million turnaround
in the Libyans' claim that Bunker owed still more money to them in royalties
after his ouster. Instead of Bunker having to cough up another $17 million, the
Libyans agreed to pay Bunker $20 million as compensation for oil-production
equipment that had been commandeered in the process of nationalization.

Still, Bunker hardly had reason for rejoicing. He had lost what was probably the biggest oil field he would find in his life. The world political situation and the U.S. economy were tumbling into disarray. Inflation was eating away at the money he had made in Libya. And on top of everything else, the Justice Department had by this time indicted him and his brother Herbert for illegal wiretapping.

With his world apparently crumbling all around him, Bunker decided to go heavily into silver. This time he and his brother Herbert—aided by second-family in-law Randy Kreiling, a commodities expert—began buying into the market with what would soon come to be known as the typical Hunt style. The key elements in their strategy were size, secrecy, and surprise. Working through Bache and a variety of other brokers, they purchased not just penny packets, but millions and millions of ounces. Their first huge order was a 20-million-ounce December-1973 contract. Other big orders followed, and by early 1974, the Hunts had accumulated contracts totaling 55 million ounces, or about 7 to 9 percent of the total estimated world supply. That gave them more silver than anyone on earth save a handful of national governments and the silver exchanges themselves.

Bunker and Herbert placed their orders with a great deal of concern for confidentiality. Secret buying strategies were common in the commodities futures markets, where leaks of a big purchase can send prices skyrocketing. But the Hunts had more than the usual big futures play in the works. Most silver traders fell into two types: hedgers and speculators. Hedgers, who were often users of the commodity itself, bought both "long" and "short" positions to protect themselves against price swings in either direction that may throw their cost projections out of whack. Speculators bought mostly "long" positions or mostly "short" positions (but not both), depending on whether they believed the price would go up or down. In general, the futures market was not designed to be a substitute for the "cash" market, where the actual commodity was transferred with each sale and purchase. Thus, there was an implicit bias toward the hedgers, a fact that only increased the scale of risk Bunker and Herbert were taking.

There was another dramatic and unique feature to the Hunts' silver play. Most silver traders dealt only in paper, not actual metal. When their silver futures contracts matured, they sold them for a profit or loss, without ever physically handling the silver itself. Since they bought on margin, silver traders only had to put up a percentage of the actual purchase price to secure their contracts; in 1973, the margin requirements were only 5 percent of the total purchase price. The Hunts, however, were taking *delivery* on their contracts, all 55 million ounces worth. This meant they had to put up roughly $160 million—in cash. Taking delivery on all that silver also meant that they had to store it somewhere. And this, in turn, necessitated the second and most secret phase of their silver-buying scheme, an operation they discussed only in code.

Although the Hunt brothers would later deny the existence of this operation, sources familiar with the caper claimed that the Hunts' great silver roundup began with a secret shootout at the Circle K Ranch. The property of H. L. Hunt's second family, the Circle K was a 2,500-acre spread located east of Dallas. As the straw bosses for the operation, second-family in-law Randy Kreiling and his brother Tilmon reportedly recruited a dozen cowboys from the Circle K by holding a shooting match to see who were the best marksmen. The winners received a special assignment: riding shotgun on the Hunts' horde of silver.

With guns in hand, the Circle K cowboys reportedly flew to New York and Chicago aboard three chartered 707s. The planes came from a nationally known charter company, but the name of the firm was covered with tape so that the only visible identifying marks were the planes' registration numbers. The aircraft landed in the dead of night. A short time after their arrival, a convoy of armored trucks arrived from the New York and Chicago exchange warehouses. Inside were 40 million ounces of silver bullion. The transfers took place almost wordlessly. There was no joking around or grab-assing—just serious loading. When the planes were full, the cowboys climbed in, and the charter pilots got clearance for takeoff. Their destination: Zurich.

Upon their arrival in Switzerland, the Hunt planes were reportedly met by another convoy of armored trucks. The cowboys and the armed guards transferred the silver from the planes to the trucks. Then the bullion was driven to six secret storage locations in Zurich. Five of the storage locations were in bank vaults, among them the vault of Crédit Suisse. However, the Hunts' silver horde was too much for the available bank vaults to handle. The excess bullion had to be stored in the coffers of a Swiss warehouse named Freedlager.

The costs of this alleged transatlantic storage operation were considerable. Chartering the three 707s involved nearly $200,000. On top of that, average storage costs for silver amounted to half a cent per ounce per month. For the 40 million ounces stashed in Europe and the 15 million ounces still in exchange warehouses in Chicago and New Jersey, the annual storage charges amounted to some $3 million. Still, flying the bullion to Switzerland was cheaper than bringing it home to Texas, where the Hunts would have had to pay a 5-percent franchise tax to the state. More importantly, having his silver locked away in Swiss banks reportedly added to what Bunker wanted out of the deal most of all: a sense of security about his wealth.

For all his precautions, Bunker could not keep his silver-buying scheme a secret for long. In the spring of 1974, word hit the trading floors of the world that a mysterious Texan named Hunt had just taken delivery on more silver than any single buyer had purchased in recent memory. The price of silver rose to over $6 per ounce. Veteran traders were in a panic. Even as they frantically asked each other "Who's Nelson Bunker Hunt?" they whispered that the man was about to corner the market.

In most modern markets, talk of a corner would have been dismissed as just that—talk. The classic definition of a precious-metals corner was when an individual holds enough bullion and enough futures contracts to have a monopoly on the total supply—and thus effective control of the price of both bullion and futures, since anyone who wanted the metal would have to come to him. Few people or groups had the skill or, more importantly, the financial resources to pull one off. Indeed, the last time anyone cornered the silver market was when the Bank of England accomplished the feat in 1721.

But as the veteran traders knew, silver was potentially more vulnerable than other commodities. Unlike gold, silver has a wide range of industrial uses (most notably for photographic film stocks and X-rays) as well as a value in jewelry making. Annual production in 1974 was only about 245 million ounces, while annual consumption was about 450 million ounces. Exactly how much the total world supply amounted to was the critical unknown factor. Estimates ranged from 600 million ounces to 800 million ounces. Of that total, only 200 million ounces was believed to be available for delivery against silver-futures contracts. While silver from tea sets, silverware, and other sources had a way of coming out of the woodwork in times of high prices, many traders believed that it would take a lot less than 200 million ounces to corner the silver commodities market. But how much less? Had Bunker Hunt found the magic formula? Was he now ready to cash in?

In April of 1974, Bunker stopped in New York to visit the floor of the Comex for the first time. When he walked onto the floor, all activity came to a halt. The traders dropped what they were doing and simply stared at the overweight, bespectacled Texan in the cheap blue suit. Later that day, Bunker granted a rare interview to a reporter from the financial journal *Barron's*. Although he politely refused to reveal the size of his silver holdings, Bunker did give the world a glimpse of his long-term intentions. As he put it in typically twisted syntax, "Just about anything you buy, rather than paper, is better. You're bound to come out ahead in the long pull. If you don't like gold, use silver. Or diamonds. Or copper. But something. Any damn fool can run a printing press."

After this auspicious first appearance in New York, it was Bunker who soon appeared to be the fool. Silver peaked at $6.24 an ounce, then dropped back into the $3 to $4-an-ounce range. The going price of silver was now a little bit above the average price the Hunts paid for their 55 million ounces, but the storage charges were gradually eating into the Hunts' profits while their silver bullion sat in the vaults without generating any income. The market expected that the Hunts were merely short-term speculators who would try to bail out once the price peaked and started to turn against them. But the market was wrong. The Hunts were in silver for the long pull. Still believing that the price of their bullion could ultimately go nowhere but up, they held onto their bullion right through the price recession.

While Bunker coped with the volatilities of his oil and silver interests, his steadiest business was his "hobby," race-horse breeding. Nelson Bunker Hunt farms, by now blessed with some of the best bloodlines money could buy, kept producing champion after champion. Bunker's success with horses was due in part to his ability to have trainers like Charles Willingham and Jim Shannon, both of whom were known as the best in the trade. But credit was also due to Bunker himself. One of Bunker's best horses was Cannonero II, the biggest money-winning horse in 1971. Even better was Dahlia, who won both the French and English championships in 1973. Sired by Vaguely Noble, the prize-winning colt Bunker bought in the late 1960s, Dahlia became the first horse in history to win over $1 million in purse money. Because of his decision to avoid Triple Crown races like the Kentucky Derby in favor of racing on the European circuit, Bunker's name was not well known to racing fans in his own country. But he was rapidly becoming one of the best-known figures on the international racing scene.

Not surprisingly, the so-called "horsy set" considered Bunker an outsider, which he was. Most disturbing, from the horsy-set's point of view, was that Bunker Hunt did not show signs of easy assimilation. Unlike the equine establishment, Bunker had a down-home, easygoing, sort of unkempt style. He was iconoclastic and apparently proud of it. The horse people were, of course, glad to take Bunker's money when he came around offering them premium prices for their horse flesh. But now they were becoming a bit uneasy. This N. B. Hunt had bought up hundreds of horses. He had amassed one of the best-quality stables in the world. The horsy set could only wonder what would happen when N. B. Hunt was ready to become a big horse seller as well as a big horse buyer.

Despite, or perhaps because of, his Libyan nationalization and his wire-tapping indictment, Bunker tried to maintain a low political profile during the early 1970s. He held to his right-wing views and gave money or other support to a variety of arch-conservative organizations, but he did his best to keep his own name out of the public view. One former member of Young Americans for Freedom whose chapter had been allowed to use the Hunt Oil Company conference room for a board meeting observed that Bunker "seemed to be put off by his father's zeal—the way he went about things." Bunker gave money to the YAF on an issue-by-issue basis. (His brother-in-law Al Hill was on the advisory board.) Bunker also continued his financial support of the John Birch Society and became attracted to the preachings of Dr. Peter Beder, a traveling lecturer devoted to warning the country about the alleged evils of the Trilateral Commission. Dr. Beder's message, like that of the John Birch Society, was based on a conspiratorialist view of history, which held the Rockefellers (sponsors of the Trilateral Commission) responsible for America's supposed drift toward socialism and whatever else the right-wing considered wrong with America.

Because of his affection for these extreme points of view, Bunker's political support became viewed as a public liability by mainstream politicians and conservatives trying to "go for the center" of the political spectrum. Bunker's biggest known political favorite in the early 1970s was still George Wallace. In 1971, Bunker bought a table at a $50-a-plate Dallas fund raiser for Wallace and invited the former Alabama governor and intended presidential candidate home for a fried-chicken dinner. But according to former Wallace campaign finance man Tom Turnipseed, Governor Wallace did not want to accept Bunker's invitation for fear the press might find out and perhaps further identify him with the John Birch Society or some other ultraright group. In the end, Wallace did accept Bunker's invitation, but only after his aides convinced him they could keep news of the dinner out of the press.

Such, then, was the world of Nelson Bunker Hunt in the early 1970s. International oilman, silver speculator, champion horse breeder, vast landowner, right-wing political financier, and doomsday believer—these were but a few of the roles Bunker played. His name was not yet a household word. But, like his father before him, Bunker was becoming well known in many fields. He was, as *Dallas Morning News* reporter Earl Golz described him, a "hot news item."

While Bunker made the headlines, his brother Herbert continued his own lower-profile, moneymaking ways. The partner in many of Bunker's big ventures, Herbert was the steadying force of the brother-and-brother team. If Bunker was the creative visionary of their business schemes, Herbert was the detail man, the fellow who made sure that things were actually carried out and done right. He was also the more intellectual of the two. Where Bunker made decisions mostly on instinct and after talking to a few people he considered knowledgeable, Herbert liked to buttress his instincts with reading. Concentrating mostly on trade-related titles and business biographies, he read at least one book per week and many periodicals. Indeed, as he later admitted, one of the things that increased his own interest in the silver market was a book he read in 1973 called *Silver Profits in the Seventies* by Jerome F. Smith. Smith's book argued that the world was on "a collision course with chaos," and warned that "only the individual can protect himself from the forces of destruction." In Smith's view, the only way for an individual to protect himself was by converting paper money into "real money," to wit, gold and silver. Smith also advised that the metal should be held in silver bars stored in Switzerland, a precaution he advised as a hedge against a possible Soviet invasion of the United States. Although the Hunt brothers effectively denied it, informed sources later claimed that they followed Smith's prescription virtually to the letter.

Although often cast in the role of Bunker's shadow, Herbert spent about 45 percent of his time tending to his own personal ventures. In the early 1970s, the ambitious real-estate plans he had been working on in North Dallas for eighteen years came to fruition. His Hunt Properties had now acquired over 6,000 acres in what was one of the sunbelt's prime urban development corridors. Thanks to Dallas's boom, the value of the land skyrocketed. Herbert commenced to cover his vast properties with shopping centers, housing tracts, and office parks. At the same time, he began developing 3,500 acres in suburban Lewisville, Texas, and various commercial and industrial tracts in Florida and California. All told, Herbert's real-estate assets grew in worth to over $500 million.

Still primarily an oil man, Herbert also concentrated on developing oil and coal leases in North Dakota and on building Penrod Drilling. His success with Penrod was particularly impressive. The worldwide offshore drilling boom he had banked on proved to materialize beyond all expectations. Penrod's fleet grew to over seventy land and sea rigs. Herbert extended the company's operations from the Gulf of Mexico to the North Sea, the Persian Gulf, the Mediterranean, Australia, and Brazil. Penrod's clients included not only the Hunt family's array of companies, but corporate giants like Chevron and Shell. Just as H. L. Hunt had concerned himself with oil-business technology (like the salt-water injection wells in the east Texas field) and with social planning and personnel planning (like his flexible-work-week plan), so Herbert prompted Penrod to introduce the first turbine-powered offshore drilling rig and the first five-day work week in the drilling industry.

Herbert's most sensational deal was one he worked in partnership with Bunker: the Hunts' takeover of Great Western United, the nation's largest sugar refiner. The Great Western deal actually began as a minor stock deal. Having become interested in commodities, the Hunts were hoping to find a way to play the sugar market via the stock market. On the basis of little more than a call and a visit from one of their brokers, the Hunts bought $3 million worth of Great Western United stock. A short time later, they bought another $6 million worth. Only then did the Hunts discover that the company they had bought into was racked by serious management problems. Top executives were feuding. Although Great Western Sugar was making record profits, there was an alleged fraud in Great Western's real-estate division, and the company's Shakey's Pizza Parlor chain was on a downtrend.

Instead of backing off, Herbert and Bunker decided to charge ahead. In early November of 1974, after borrowing part of the necessary funds from the trust of their mentally incapacitated brother Hassie, they launched a $30-million tender offer for a 51-percent controlling interest in Great Western United. A short time later, Bunker and Herbert became chairman and president of Great Western United, and Hunt lieutenant G. Michael Boswell was installed as the company's chief operating officer.

The takeover of Great Western United marked a new phase in Hunt-family business history. For the first time, the family, or at least two of its members, owned a public corporation. The puzzling question was why Bunker and Herbert had bothered with the takeover. Owning a public corporation brought a host of disclosure and reporting requirements, which was why the family had heretofore kept all of its enterprises privately held. There were much more direct ways—like the commodities exchanges—for playing sugar prices, if that was what "the boys" really wanted to do. The Hunts' legal counsel recommended against the takeover. As one associate observed, "When you analyzed it, Great Western United could only have hurt them."

But Herbert and Bunker simply decided to ignore their own legal counsel. The reason, as Herbert all but admitted afterward, had more to do with the brothers' egos than anything else. "We felt that really our reputation was on the line with the public," Herbert admitted to a trade-industry reporter afterward, adding that the reputation the Hunts wanted to protect was "for being prudent businessmen and doing things right." One former Hunt associate put it even more succinctly: "Bunker and Herbert wanted to show the world they were businessmen, not just inheritors."

Bunker and Herbert also seemed determined to show the world they were just as tight with their money as their father had been. Fearing that someone was always trying to take advantage of them because they were Hunts, they were known to haggle multimillion-dollar deals down to the last penny. In the early stages of the Great Western United takeover attempt, for example, Herbert raised the Hunts' initial offer a mere 50 cents per share and declared that the time for compromise was past. On another separate deal, Herbert and the man he was negotiating with were only $40,000 apart on a multimillion-dollar deal when Herbert announced he would go no further.

"Come on, Herbert," the other man cajoled. "What's forty thousand dollars to a family like the Hunts'?"

"How do you think we got to be the Hunts?" Herbert replied.

While Bunker and Herbert did all their wheeling and dealing, Lamar still got the most publicity because of his sports interests. As Herbert revealed in one interview, "All through our school years, everybody knew Lamar as my younger brother. Now that he's involved in the sports world, every time I meet somebody, they say, 'Oh, you're Lamar's brother.' " Though he continued to invest in oil deals with his brothers, Lamar did not take part in their dramatic commodities and stock plays. Instead, he preferred to remain off on his own, dealing with his sports teams and other entertainment enterprises.

As Lamar always hastened to admit, his sports ventures were "not big-profit situations." The value of his football team, for example, was appreciating, but even with sellouts every game of the season, the Kansas City Chiefs would be lucky to generate as much as $1 million in net profits. Compared to a big oil deal, that was a relatively small return. But sports was still the arena in which Lamar would distinguish himself. Lamar's signature, with the "L" in his first name written much larger than the "H" in Hunt, was itself symbolic of his motivation. As Dallas graphologist Connie Gilmore observed in D magazine, "the fact that the L is much larger than the H shows that he wants the recognition to be directed at him personally, disassociated from any laurels tied to the family name or heritage."

At the same time, Lamar continued to be concerned with running his enterprises in a moneymaking fashion. Though evidently more secure and, in his field, more accomplished than his brothers, Lamar was still determined to show he was a businessman, not just an inheritor. Sometimes that required decisions as difficult as those in any other venture. His Kansas City Chiefs were a good case in point. After winning the Super Bowl in 1970, both the players and their popular coach Hank Stram lapsed into resting on their laurels. The Chiefs did not win any more Super Bowls and soon even fell from atop the division standings. Attendance at Arrowhead Stadium also declined. Lamar realized that part of the team's problem was Coach Stram's relationship to veteran players from the Super Bowl days who were hanging on past their prime. Though he, too, personally liked Stram, Lamar took the step he had to take and fired him. His move was not cold-hearted, just tough-minded.

"The reason he's successful is not that he's an easy man to deal with," Dallas Toronado soccer star Kyle Rote, Jr. said of his team's owner about this same time. "If he feels I don't deserve fifty dollars more, I honestly believed he would stay up into the early hours to argue the point."

Lamar's toughness paid off on the bottom line. Though not big-profit situations, the score card of his teams looked pretty good. Tennis was booming, and WCT was rising in popularity and paying for itself financially. Soccer was still slow in catching on, and the Chiefs were slipping, but football was a revenue producer. Although Lamar's balance sheets showed mixed won-lost records, all his teams made respectable showings.

In addition to looking after his professional football, soccer, basketball, and tennis teams, Lamar found a way to cash in on the amateur sports and recreation boom. The name of his venture was called Lakeway World of Tennis, and it was a tennis resort development set by the waters of a shining lake just outside the city of Austin. Lakeway quickly became one of Texas's most popular recreation spots.

For reasons that may have had a great deal to do with family heritage, Lamar was a reluctant celebrity. Like his brothers, he was put off by the cornball ways his father hawked aloe vera and the H. L. Hunt brand of politics. But during the early 1970s, Lamar did grant a few personality interviews and came out of his shell a bit. At one point, he even agreed to do a television commercial for Hart Schaffner & Marx clothing. Other celebrities in the series included Jack Nicklaus, O. J. Simpson, Bing Crosby, and Ricardo Montalban. Lamar endured eight hours of filming in his quarters at Arrowhead Stadium in Kansas City, making self-deprecating wisecracks and improvising the assiduously dull script he had been given. When the filming was over, Lamar remarked, "Well, we're finished in more ways than one. Hart Schaffner & Marx may be, too."

Interestingly enough, Lamar's grandest gesture during the early 1970s was the purchase in late 1970 of the North Dallas mansion of famed wheeler-dealer Jim Ling. Priced at a hefty $1.5 million, the house was an enormous French chateau–style affair set on 2.6 acres full of duck ponds, fountains, and statuary. The Lings had remodeled the house after buying it from the estate of a deceased cotton and oil broker in 1961. They added a recreation area and a master-bedroom suite, and adorned the dining room with gold-printed white wall fabric, mirrors, elaborately carved moldings, crystal and gilt chandeliers, and a twenty-six-place mahogany table with Louis XIV chairs. These home improvements reportedly constituted one of the budget items that caused Ling's financial demise. Somewhat better equipped to carry the load, Lamar and his wife Norma kept the statuary, the fountains, and the duck pond, and added what was becoming an impressive art collection, including a Rubens, a Breughel, a sixteenth-century choirbook stand, seventeenth-century Van Cleve bronzes, a pair of sixteenth-century Dutch globes, and assorted ivory and wood carvings. The Hunts also kept the fabulous wrought-iron gates the Lings had installed at the front entrance to the mansion. One of them featured a large capital "L" which had, of course, stood for "Ling." Rather than replace it with a capital "H," the Hunts let the "L" remain on the gate where it came to stand for "Lamar."

The first-family daughters, Margaret and Caroline, had almost as much money as their brothers, but they both continued to keep much lower profiles. This was particularly true of Caroline. She did not get involved in wild speculations like Bunker and Herbert or in highly visible sports enterprises like Lamar. She stayed out of politics. Instead, she was content to raise her family and leave the operation of her money, most of which was in the Caroline Hunt Sands Trust Estate, under the guidance of the faithful staff down at Hunt Oil. Caroline had been blessed with a good share of the Hunt luck. She did not seem to need to gamble on exotic deals or get especially anxious about finding new drilling prospects. Her trust estate just kept finding oil and her wealth kept building steadily and without fanfare. The only blemish on Caroline's life résumé was a marital problem. In 1973, she and Loyd Sands were divorced. Caroline subsequently married Hugo "Buddy" Schoellkopf, the affable and easygoing scion of one of Dallas's oldest families. Still, Caroline's profile was so low that it was not unusual to hear otherwise conversant social observers ask incredulously, "Is she a Hunt?"

Few people—at least few people in the know—asked the same question about Margaret Hill. The Hills had been socially prominent for some time now, what with their ownership of the Garden of the Gods Club and their membership in Dallas's most prestigious country clubs. Margaret did not play a part in the day-to-day business of the family companies. But she was always on hand when something big was in the works and never hesitant to express her opinion about business or family matters. Like Caroline, she stayed out of her brothers' wild speculations in favor of steady oil and gas drilling development. She seemed to regard her younger brothers as a bit reckless and was constantly on guard that they might make an imprudent decision affecting one of their joint interests like Placid Oil Company. If there was serious doubt about H. L. Hunt's competency, there was no doubt about Margaret's. Bunker and Herbert might have control of the day-to-day operations of the family companies, but in the first-family circle, they would still defer to her by virtue of seniority. Irreverent Hunt Oil employees referred to her as "the big boss."

As a whole, the first family of H. L. Hunt came through the early 1970s with typical Hunt luck. There were some tough losses, especially the nationalization of Bunker's Libyan oil field. But there were also some significant gains, among them certain windfalls that promised to make the family far richer in future years. One was the 1973 Arab oil embargo, which touched off a round of price increases that would multiply the value of the Hunts' oil and gas reserves many times. Another piece of Hunt luck was a successful gas well Placid Oil drilled in the Dutch sector of the North Sea. Although it would take several years to bring the gas on stream, initial indications were that the Hunts had found a gas field potentially worth hundreds of millions of dollars.

The first family also enjoyed a certain amount of social success in the early 1970s. Because of their relative lack of charitable contributions, the Hunts were still regarded as outsiders by Dallas society. But the first-family children and their spouses were more readily accepted than was H. L. Hunt. They also did more for charity than they were generally credited for. Bunker's wife Caroline, for example, belonged to the Dallas Women's Club, worked as a volunteer dental assistant at the Children's Medical Center, and taught Bible study at Highland Park Presbyterian Church. Herbert's wife Nancy also taught Bible-study classes, was active in the Day Care Association and Suicide Prevention, and was on the city's Crystal Charity Ball Committee.

The one truly dark cloud that continued to hang over the first family was Bunker's and Herbert's indictment for illegal wiretapping. Shortly after being charged, the Hunt brothers had hired Philip J. Hirschkop of Alexandria, Virginia, to defend them. A liberal young Jewish lawyer whose clients included black militant H. Rap Brown, the controversial Church of Scientology, and a long list of antiwar activists, Hirschkop was the opposite of the Hunts in every way. But he was also regarded as one of the nation's experts on wiretapping law. Teasing each other about their political differences, Hirschkop and the Hunts developed an unusual mutual affection for each other as they plotted their defense.

One of their first moves was to take the offensive in the press. Hirschkop publicly accused the government of reneging on its alleged 1970 "deal" not to prosecute the Hunts if the Hunts dropped their lawsuits against H. L. Hunt's former aides Paul Rothermel, John Curington, and John Brown. Hirschkop also wondered aloud why the government was so anxious to prosecute the Hunts when the Hunts had provided the government with evidence allegedly showing that Rothermel, Curington, and Brown had perpetrated a "massive embezzlement" of Hunt Oil's food division. Why wasn't the government going after them? One reason, Hirschkop suggested, was that Paul Rothermel was a government agent, possibly attached to the CIA, who had been assigned to watch the Hunts because of their politics. Hirschkop added that the CIA especially begrudged dropping the charges against Bunker Hunt because he had three times refused the agency's request to place an agent in his Libyan oil operation.

In April of 1973, Bunker and Herbert pleaded not guilty to the wiretap charges, but Houston private eye Clyde Wilson and phone man Morgan Watson entered guilty pleas. Private eye W. J. Everett entered a guilty plea several weeks later. That added three more names to the list of witnesses potentially damaging to the Hunts. In late July, Kelly and McCann, now more embittered than ever, began serving time in federal prison at Texarkana. Two and a half months later, Kelly filed a $101-million civil damage suit against Percy Foreman, the Hunt brothers, and Ed Hudson, alleging they had conspired to keep him quiet in order to save the Hunts. The suit, in turn, prompted the government to mount an investigation of possible obstruction of justice—i.e., cover-up—charges against the Hunts, Hudson, and attorneys Foreman, Shank, Tessmer, Timmons, and Colvin. Instead of growing cold with the passage of time, the Hunt case was growing hotter and hotter.

Much to the Hunts' chagrin, the Hunts and their hired wiretappers were not the only ones to face government prosecutors. In July of 1974, a federal grand jury finally returned criminal indictments against John Curington and John Brown. The two men were charged with mail fraud in connection with $17,000 worth of money allegedly embezzled from Hunt Oil. H. L. Hunt himself ended up testifying against his former aides before the grand jury. Curington and Brown produced a letter dated 1965 and signed by them, Rothermel, and H. L. Hunt in which Hunt authorized his employees to make side deals as compensation for their low salaries. But Hunt testified that he had not authorized such deals and had not known about them or the brokerage companies Curington and Brown had set up in connection with their deals. Hunt lawyers claimed Hunt had been tricked into signing the purported authorization letter.

The Hunts also protested that Paul Rothermel, whom they considered one of the kingpins of the alleged embezzlement scheme, was not indicted along with Curington and Brown. Instead, the government granted Rothermel immunity from prosecution in exchange for his grand-jury testimony against Curington and Brown. The essence of that testimony was that H. L. Hunt had been misled in signing the authorization letter, that Hunt had affixed his signature to the document as it was handed to him amid a pile of other routine correspondence. Hunt lawyer Phil Hirschkop loudly complained that the government was favoring Rothermel because, according to Hirschkop, Rothermel was a government agent. The Justice Department did not need Rothermel to disprove the authorization letter, Hirschkop contended, because the government knew "the thing was typed on a typewriter that wasn't manufactured until two years after the so-called letter."

Hirschkop also complained about the fact that the government had taken four and a half years to indict Curington and Brown, and did so only after Hirschkop threatened to prompt a Senate investigation. On top of that, Hirschkop groused, Curington and Brown were charged with only $17,439 worth of mail-fraud violations when Hirschkop had "personally" given the U.S. attorney "a file almost six inches thick with proof of one of the worst massive embezzlements in history."

The prosecutor in the Curington and Brown case, assistant U.S. attorney James Rolfe, merely shrugged off Hirschkop's allegations and pressed forward with his case. Rothermel, for his part, would not reply to Hirschkop or comment "on what role I might have played for the U.S. government." But Rothermel added, "Certainly I wasn't due to be indicted on anything."

While all these charges, countercharges, and verbal pyrotechnics added to the drama of the Hunt wiretapping case, they did nothing to remove the indictments hanging over the heads of Bunker and Herbert. The government remained just as determined as ever to prosecute the case. The Hunts had few alternatives except to cop a plea or try their luck in trial. As attorney Hirschkop worked to delay the wiretapping case until the government could try Curington and Brown, the Hunts kept insisting on their innocence and preparing to have their day in court.

H. L. Hunt's second Dallas family lived a much less sensational life than the first family during the early 1970s. They did not own sports teams or live in fabulous mansions. They did not try to corner the silver market or breed race horses or build a drilling empire. Younger and less well endowed financially than the first family, the second-family children were at earlier stages of life and their interests were on a different scale. But in their own way, the second-family children also distinguished themselves—both from their half siblings and from run-of-the-mill rich kids.

With their father's energy and drive and their mother's concern for other people, the three girls all turned strongly to religion and the helping professions. Swanee, the youngest, married a young minister named Mark Meeks and moved to Europe, where her husband entered a theological seminary. Later, Swanee and her husband returned to the United States, and took up residence in Denver, where Swanee began studying for a doctorate in pastoral care, and Mark became pastor of a Presbyterian church and a local leader of Amnesty International. The couple also became directors of an urban retreat for emotionally disturbed persons. Helen, the middle one, studied psychology and counseling at SMU and taught school for a year in predominantly black South Oak Cliff High School. Helen then married an ambitious young man named Randy Kreiling, who wrote her poetry even as he was wheeling and dealing in commodities, and settled down to raise a family.

June, the oldest, chose to remain single, continued her work with First Baptist Church, and launched a career as a professional singer. June's father did his H. L. Hunt best to promote her career, a fact which may or may not have helped. June did not cut any hit records, but she did get off to a good start with a USO tour of Vietnam in 1972. Thereafter, she became both a singer and a featured Christian youth speaker who sometimes shared the pulpit with evangelist Billy Graham.

In an interview with the *Dallas Times Herald,* June called her career "a permanent investment in people's lives . . . an insurance policy that will pay off time and time again." She naturally attributed her decision to become a youth leader and singer to a higher influence. ("God prompted me to enter this field of work," she said. "He knew all along what was going on, only He didn't tell me ahead of time.") But June also gave credit to her parents, especially her often-difficult father, for bringing out the best in her. "My father is the type who gives an assignment, regardless of whether you think you're capable of doing it," she reported. "I've learned not to question reasoning, but to go beyond myself and find out how things are done. I've learned I can accomplish most anything I set out to do. My parents were quite demanding, but what I thought was a disadvantage is actually an advantage."

Although June Hunt sometimes made headlines as the millionaire's daughter turned religious entertainer, the real star of the second family was June's older brother Ray. Having grown up a clean-cut young man with a budding young family of his own, Ray used to confide to his friends that he believed he had a lot of his old man in him. But Ray also had a lot of his mother in him, a fact that made him want to do well and also do good.

Despite being a rich man's son, Ray Hunt did not have it easy. His particular struggle centered around his status at Hunt Oil Company and, by extension, his status within the ranks of Popsy's patriarchy. Ray was under terrific pressure from many sides. Some of the pressure resulted from having to demonstrate his self-worth in spite of being the boss's son. Some of the pressure resulted from H. L. Hunt's nonpressure; Hunt did not try to guide Ray at every step as he had tried to guide Hassie, but left the young man to do what he pleased, a fact that sometimes compounded the difficulty of getting started in business and in life. But the greatest pressures Ray faced came from his half brothers. Bunker and Herbert were still suspicious of Ray's possible involvement in changing Hunt's will and Ray's formerly close relationship with Paul Rothermel. Bunker and Herbert also were resentful about Ray's refusal to assist in their wiretapping caper. Ray's half brothers seldom treated him as a member of the same family. They told associates that Ray was "different." They did not socialize with him or invite his participation in their deals.

Since Bunker and Herbert were in operational control of Hunt Oil Company at this time, this left Ray out in the cold. Though "protected" from his half brothers' enmity by Hunt's trusted counsel George Cunyas and given the title of vice president, Ray was simply not a factor, not a power down at Hunt Oil during the early 1970s. As one former Hunt employee put it, "He'd drill a few peanut deals with his trust fund, but that was about it."

True to family tradition, Ray took an active interest in conservative politics. But unlike his father and half brothers, Ray was not a far-right-winger. His politics were mostly mainstream conservative and mostly Republican. He listed among his major political activities being a member of the 1972 Dallas coordinating committee for Democratic Texas governor Dolph Briscoe, being chairman of Young Men for Bush in George Bush's 1970 U.S. Senate race, being chairman of Young Men for Collins in Jim Collins 1970 Republican congressional race, and being a poll watcher in the 1968 general election. Ray was also credited with founding the Aardvark Society, a conservative young people's economic dinner-discussion group. But he did not become an avid campaigner for LIFE LINE or a member of groups like the John Birch Society.

Effectively shut out of his half brothers' politics and business, Ray turned to a new field: investing in real estate. In the pre–Arab oil embargo days of the early 1970s, real estate was a better investment than oil. H. L. Hunt himself had said as much in public on at least one occasion. It was hardly a state secret. The Arab oil embargo had not yet taken place, and oil prices were at a depressed $3.50 a barrel. Real estate, on the other hand, was enjoying an unprecedented boom, both historically and in the short term. Investing in raw land and development was the new road to riches for young dreamers of the American dream. Like the oil business in the early days, real estate was an industry in which a little cash and a lot of credit could go a long way. Leverage was the name of the game. Location, location, and location were the three most important criteria in evaluating the worth of a piece of property. Prices were spiraling ever higher as property was bought and sold on the theory that there would always come along a "greater fool" who would pay an even higher price. Dallas was one of the epicenters of this real-estate frenzy. Everything from downtown buildings to vast prairie land was up for grabs. The air vibrated with the excitement of big money deals.

Ray Hunt hit the jackpot. His first real-estate deal was a family-style recreation ranch near Lewisville, Texas, which he bought with a friend in 1969. He did not do anything with the Lewisville land except hold it and enjoy it. The ranch was a good investment, but it was not something that would shake the earth. Ray's second real-estate deal was. Like his father and half brothers before him, Ray relied on his instincts, his intelligence, and his luck in making this big deal. He also relied on size, secrecy, and surprise, qualities that reaffirmed him as a true Hunt. At the same time, Ray showed he had some very special stuff of his own, qualities that set him apart from other members of his family.

Ray's big deal began innocuously enough in May of 1972, when he purchased 20 acres of land around the old Union Terminal in downtown Dallas for $2.3 million from the Teamsters Union pension fund. The land itself was nothing special. Ray's tract was part of a once-glorious section of the city then deep into the cycle of decay. The courthouse, Dealey Plaza, the *Dallas News* building, and a few landmarks of the old Dallas were nearby, but the core of the modern downtown area was several blocks to the east. A dreamer and previous owner named Jack Isaminger had once had vast urban-revitalization plans for the land, but Isaminger was never able to translate his dreams into reality, and the Union Terminal area had not "done anything" in years.

Ray originally looked at the land around Union Terminal as an investment he would simply hold with minimal improvements in hopes of selling it to a developer at a later date. Or so he would claim. But, he did intend to see that his "long-term investment" made a profit. He knew that for the land to appreciate it had to be developed or sold to a developer who would really transform it. Ray believed that one reason the area had not been developed was that it was cut up into a "mishmash" of small tracts. The property lines were so numerous and so oddly angled that looking at a map of the area was like looking at a broken mirror. Some of the property, including an old hotel, was owned by independent companies or individuals. Many of the parcels were owned by the city of Dallas. Realizing that both he and the city were "in it for the long pull," Ray decided to have a talk about the area with city manager George Schrader.

Schrader was one of the most powerful urban officials in Texas. No one elected him to office. He never had to conduct a campaign or curry favor with the voters. He was responsible only to the mayor and city council, who could fire him by vote. A diminutive man with an unsmiling face, Schrader had the look and air of an accountant. In a city long run by and for businessmen, George Schrader was like a senior vice president charged with managing the municipal corporate body in all its aspects. Schrader could not pass laws, but he could propose them. More than that, his day-to-day management decisions set policy for the city both before and after it was certified into law. Schrader ascribed to the prevailing philosophy that what was good for Dallas businessmen was usually good for Dallas, too. So when Ray Hunt approached him to discuss the future of the Union Terminal area, Schrader was already receptive to investigating any proposal that might give the land new economic life.

Schrader and Hunt met one day in the summer of 1972, just a few weeks after Ray's acquisition of the Union Terminal area property. Out of their meeting came a commitment to explore ways in which the area might be developed to the benefit of both the public and the private sectors. A few days later, Schrader informed Ray that it would be all right to hire planners to make a formal land-use study so long as the planners were not paid by the city and the city was not legally or morally obliged to adopt the plan. That was pretty much the first official go-ahead, obligations or no. At no time did Schrader or Hunt inform the mayor or the city council of the project. Instead, they elected to proceed in strictest secrecy, disclosing their inquiry to no one.

Ray hired a team of twenty urban planners. The team began with a proposed site of some fifty-two acres and three sets of considerations—the natural constraints of the area, the activities the private sector could establish in the area, and the activities the public sector could establish in the area. Month after month, the planning team worked away at their assignment. They drew and redrew streets and parks and sports arenas. They inserted office buildings, hotels, shops, and restaurants in between the streets and the railroad tracks, then switched everything around to look at other possible combinations. Finally, more than a year later, the proposal was ready.

Schrader disclosed his dealings with Ray Hunt to the press—and to Dallas public officials—for the first time with a dramatic announcement on October 15, 1973. He informed the citizenry that he was recommending that the city of Dallas join in a partnership with Ray Hunt to develop the Union Terminal area. This was no "urban renewal" in the usual sense. The city was not handing out a government grant or spending federal matching funds. Rather, the city of Dallas, with its "corporate hat on," would be acting just like a professional developer. The plan called for the city to swap about twenty acres of land with Ray Hunt and build some $38 million worth of streets and other improvements, including a "community center" that would be capable of serving as an indoor sports arena. Hunt, in turn, would spend $172 million in several phases through 1988, with the first phase due to open in 1978. Among Ray's contributions to the project would be the building of a 1,000-room luxury hotel, a 600-foot "theme tower," and an array of office buildings, shops, and other facilities. The idea was that the city's public-sector activity developments and Hunt's private-sector activity developments would complement each other or, as Ray later put it, "create a synergism" that made the whole project more than just the sum of its parts. Hotel patrons would be attending events at the sports arena, city employees would be patronizing the shops and restaurants in the area, the flow of people would intersect and commingle, and new economic life would be pumped into what was then a slum.

Schrader's announcement created multiple shock waves throughout the city. The idea of a partnership between city government and a private developer was unprecedented, even in businessman-dominated Dallas. But what was even more startling—and to some, disturbing—was Schrader's statement that Hunt, the city manager's office, and a twenty-member planning team had been working on the proposal for over a year without informing the mayor or the city council of their negotiations. Schrader justified the secrecy by explaining that the negotiations were "delicate" in nature and would have been impossible if made public. Schrader reminded the press that his recommendation as city manager did not constitute final approval of the project. "The city has made no commitment, and no funds have been spent," Schrader said. "The council still will have to decide all that."

While the council and the citizens of Dallas considered the Union Terminal proposal, Ray and Schrader went about advancing each other's interests just as if the project had already been approved. Ray and the city engaged in at least a dozen separate transactions involving the Union Terminal that were conducted without general public notice or approval. In essence, the entire real-estate package was purchased and put together, pending only council approval on the transactions involving the city's share of the project. One of these transactions was a "secret party" transaction in which Ray Hunt fronted for the city in acquiring an old hotel property at a bankruptcy sale held shortly after Schrader made his first public announcement of the project. As the city attorney openly conceded, Ray's action helped the city acquire the hotel property at a bargain price, and the city helped clear the transaction by waiving the back taxes owed on the property.

The ongoing deals between Ray Hunt and the city were not illegal, but they were unusual. The fact that Ray and the city were partners—or, rather, proposed partners—seem to throw all the ordinary ethical considerations out of whack. Since the city and Ray were supposed to be acting together as co-venturers, the city's help could not be labeled mere favoritism. At the same time, Ray undeniably got special advanges by virtue of the fact that his partner was city hall itself. Ray had a partner who did not have to apply to city hall for tax settlements or physical improvements precisely because his partner was city hall. Ray Hunt could not only look to the city for help, he had the power of the city—or at least the city manager's office—behind him all the way.

The Dallas city fathers did not waste a great deal of time pondering the new ethics and questions raised by putting the city in partnership with a private developer. Despite some initial grumbling about being "left out in the cold" during the planning stages, the city council deemed the project "good for Dallas." Led by Mayor Robert Folsom, a developer who advocated bringing pro basketball and hockey teams to the city, the council brought the matter to a vote in February of 1974, four months after Schrader's first public announcement. The project passed 9 to 2.

Having won council approval, Ray demonstrated a unique sense by naming the project Reunion. The name had many connotations. On the one hand, it was meant to stand for the remaking of the Union Terminal area. But intentionally or not, it also referred to the long-lost La Reunion colony that once nestled on the banks of the Trinity River not far from where Ray's development was located. Founded by a group of artisans and intellectuals in the 1840s, La Reunion was a utopian socialist community dedicated to experimenting with new social forms. The colony eventually failed, but when it did, its highly talented founders moved into Dallas and gave the nascent little town a badly needed injection of culture and intellect. It was a strange thing, to say the least, for any member of the Hunt family to associate with socialism, even if only in name and across more than a century of history. But Ray Hunt seemed to appreciate both the subtle ironies and the richness of the name. Reunion would stand for both a joining of government and private enterprise and for a fusion of the past with the future. Asked why he did not name his project "Hunt Plaza" or some other such title bearing the family name, Ray replied, "I don't believe in monuments."

As an added historical touch, Ray called the company he formed to handle his project Woodbine Development. Woodbine was, of course, the name of the prolific oil sand Ray's father had encountered beneath the Dad Joiner leases in east Texas. Situated atop a complex of geological structures, Dallas was where the Woodbine sand outcropped on the surface like ordinary rock. Since the Woodbine had been a lucky sand for H. L. Hunt in the quest for riches beneath the earth's surface, Ray hoped that the name Woodbine would be lucky for him now as he tried to make his own fortune above the earth's surface.

Ray conducted the ground-breaking festivities for Reunion on October 22, 1974, a bright and sunny Tuesday. As the *Dallas News* reported, the event had "all the hoopla of a political rally." It began with a morning train ride from the old White Rock Station out by Mount Vernon into the old Union Terminal. Ray, George Schrader, Mayor Folsom, and a host of other Dallas officials were on board, chugging through the city like politicians did back in the days of Abraham Lincoln. When the train arrived at Union Terminal, the passengers were greeted by the Kimball High School marching band and a crowd of 200 people. The station was bedecked with red, white, and blue bunting, just as in an old-fashioned presidential campaign. Everyone applauded and cheered, and the band struck up a song.

The ground-breaking for the Reunion project marked a major turning point in the history of thirty-one-year-old Ray Lee Hunt and the Hunt family as well as in the development of downtown Dallas. Ray was in the Reunion project to make money. He made no pretentions to the contrary. In fact, he emphasized it. But he was also doing something that directly and tangibly promoted the growth and, presumably, the well-being of Dallas. That made Reunion a semicivic undertaking as well as a business. And for a son of H. L. Hunt, this was most unusual. Many civic-minded citizens considered H. L. Hunt and his clan a blight on the Dallas landscape. The Hunts created employment, to be sure, but as far as the general public knew, they did relatively little to boost or enhance the civic good. For all his political writings and speeches and broadcasts, H. L. Hunt was not even a factor in local elections. But Ray Hunt was different. In the eyes of many Dallasites, he was the first Hunt who cared for someone other than himself.

Immediately, young Ray was in demand for all sorts of boards. Unlike his half brothers, who were generally excluded from the better Dallas society clubs, Ray, the illegitimately born son, was already a member of the prestigious Idlewild, Terpsichorean, Calyz, and Dervish Clubs as well as a member of three country clubs (Bent Tree, Royal Oaks, and the Dallas Athletic Club) and a board member of the Dallas Petroleum Club, the Chamber of Commerce, the North Texas Commission, the Museum of Fine Arts, and the SMU Alumni Association. Ray accepted these positions graciously and, like any good former high-school class president, took his board work seriously. It would still be years before even the first phase of his ambitious development project would be a functioning reality. But Ray Hunt was already emerging as one of the up-and-coming new leaders of Dallas. That image was further enhanced in early fall 1974 when it was disclosed that Ray was the principal backer behind a new city magazine to be called *D, the Magazine of Dallas.*

The good publicity Ray got for Reunion did nothing to enhance his status with his half brothers. If anything, Ray's success only seemed to accent the differences between them. Ray's style was suburban north Dallas and Royal Lane Baptist Church. The first family's was the more exclusive Park Cities and Highland Park Presbyterian Church. More fundamentally, the first family still bore resentment against the second. As far as Bunker and Herbert were concerned, Ray was still unproven, still wet behind the ears. But amidst the continuing ill will, a bridge did begin to form between the first family and the second. That bridge was personified by one Randall A. Kreiling, the husband of Ray's sister Helen.

Randy Kreiling was a handsome and ambitious man in his late twenties. The product of a middle-class family from Peoria, Illinois, he first demonstrated his flair for business by taking a $10,000 stake his father had given him and running it up to $1 million in the commodities market. Randy wrote poetry to Helen Hunt when he was courting her at SMU, but once he got married and into the real world, he was strictly business. "Randy was a buccaneer, a swashbuckler, just like H.L.," a friend recalled. "He wanted to take big risks and make big money."

As it developed, square-jawed Randy Kreiling had his own reunion project in the works: a reunion between the first and second families of H. L. Hunt. Randy naturally concluded that the best way to achieve such a reunion was through moneymaking deals that benefited both sides. Having impressed Bunker and Herbert with his skill in commodities, Randy went to work for the two first-family brothers on a full-time basis. He played important behind-the-scenes roles in their silver buying (as one of the straw bosses for the alleged overseas silver transfer) and in the takeover of Great Western United. Randy also demonstrated a flair for Hunt-style eccentricity in some of his undertakings. One of his pet projects was a scheme to cross beef cattle and buffalo to create what he hoped would be a new supermeat called "beefalo." While he was playing the role of financial go-between, Randy also tried to play the role of peacemaker. "On social occasions out at Mount Vernon, Randy was sort of a peacemaker between the two families," one friend recalled. "He always saw himself as the linchpin."

In part because of Randy Kreiling's mediating role, relations between the first and second families did improve. There were no dramatic epiphanies or tearful reconciliations, but the first family did seem more willing to live and let live, especially while Randy was making Bunker and Herbert some money. As time passed, the first family even managed to gain a certain sense of humor about their father's polygamous ways and propensity for secret families. One sign of this was a true story Herbert told about a long-haired, ill-kempt young man who appeared in his office one day claiming to be an illegitimate son of H. L. Hunt. Appalled at the idea of being related to such a scraggly, hippie type, Herbert determined to put the young man's claim to a quick test.

"Take off your shoes and socks," Herbert ordered the young man. "I want to see your feet."

Startled by Herbert's request, the young man did as he was told. But when he had exposed his feet, Herbert delivered some disappointing news.

"You don't have it," Herbert announced conclusively. "You can't be who you say you are."

"Don't have what?" the young man asked.

"The Hunt toe," Herbert replied. "All the Hunts have little toes that curl under and in. It's a genetic trait that comes from Dad."

As proof of what he was saying, Herbert then took off his own shoes and socks, and displayed his Hunt toe.

Sadly, the young pretender put his shoes back on and left.

Of course, such easily resolved encounters were rare. The first family still felt fundamentally estranged from H. L. Hunt despite their attempt to alert him to the troubles in the food division. The pain of the old man's polygamy and eccentricity cut sharp and deep. And the first family tended to blame their estrangement from Hunt on the second family. In point of fact, the second family did nothing to exacerbate that estrangement except exist. But that in itself was enough. The first family saw the second as illegitimate intruders and definitely not of the same class. At their best, the first family regarded the second-family children more like cousins than half siblings. At their worst, the first family regarded the second-family children as what they literally were, bastards.

All this put the second family in a vicious double bind. Like other rich kids, they faced the task of establishing their identities independently of the family name, proving to the world that they were real people in their own right regardless of being the children of H. L. Hunt. At the same time, they were put in the position of having to show their half brothers and half sisters that they were full-fledged, bona fide Hunts who were worthy of the name for more than the mere fact that they, too, had the Hunt toe. These conflicting demands made for an impossible situation, and it was a credit to the second family that they attempted to weather their difficulties with considerable poise and grace, not to mention a remarkable lack of bitterness. Still, despite the "bridge" provided by Randy Kreiling, the gulf between the first and second families remained as wide and turbulent as ever.

While H. L. Hunt's two Dallas families moved increasingly into the limelight, his secret family by Frania Tye Lee remained unrecognized by the patriarch and unaccepted by the first and second families. Known to the Dallas branches of the family simply as "the Lee people," they lived lives sharply in contrast to those of the rest of the Hunt clan. Where both the first and second families were blessed with generous shares of the Hunt money and the Hunt luck, Frania's side of the family seemed to have relatively little of either. Though Frania's children still showed they had a great deal of their old man in them, their adventures were almost like a cruel parody of the first and second families' exploits.

With his sister Haroldina still troubled by mental illness in Atlanta and his brother Howard now suffering from cancer in Houston, Hue attempted to carry the family banner as best he could. Believing himself to be gifted with the Hunt brand of high intelligence, Hugh attempted to make his mark in the field of education by founding the first Montessori school in Atlanta, which he and his wife continued to operate through the 1960s and early 1970s as their eight children grew. But Hugh continued to be beset with financial problems, most of which involved real estate. Unlike his half brothers, who were relatively liquid when the 1973–1974 real-estate crunch hit, Hugh was overextended. According to his own financial accounting, he was caught holding $26 million worth of property and quite a few notes.

"Money started getting tight," Hugh recalled afterward. "I sold some properties and took cash and second mortgages. Then people stopped paying second-mortgage payments. I was in the position of having to pay on second mortgages."

For a while, Hugh was able to borrow money from the Reliance Trusts. Then the trustees refused to lend him more. Hugh sold off some more properties and moved his wife and eight children to a big house on seven acres outside Potomac, Maryland.

Hugh's reasons for leaving Georgia may have been many, but court records show that in going north he was also leaving the venue of a whole spate of legal problems. Filed in counties of the Atlanta area where long lists of plaintiff and defendant lawsuits, including one in which the judge cited him for contempt and, in his absence, ordered his arrest. Most of the suits filed against Hugh involved alleged nonpayment of debts and bills or disputes over real estate.

Hugh's finances remained shaky. In an August 1973 financial statement, Hugh listed a schedule of his real-estate acquisitions and sales from 1958 to 1973 which showed net holdings worth over $13 million and profits of over $12 million in the twelve-year period. Hugh gave his income from real estate as $100,000 a year and his trust income as $75,000 a year. He listed his total assets at slightly over $10 million, including $7.5 million in real estate, $54,000 worth of stocks and bonds, and $30,000 worth of oil royalties. Hugh even said his net worth was over $8.3 million. But he listed cash on hand as only $1,534. Hugh's major company, National Homeowners Sales Service Corp. of Georgia, had even less cash. In a December 1973 financial statement, Hugh gave the company's assets as $1.6 million but showed cash on hand of only $68.32 and net losses of about $3,000 for the six months of June to December 1973. Hugh determined to weather his financial problems, but things did not look good.

In the meantime, Hugh decided to "semiretire" from real estate to become a "philosopher." He did not consider this a radical departure from some of his past experiences. He had, after all, attended Harvard Law School for two years and founded the Montessori school in Atlanta. He had also tried his hand at writing. One of the results was a December 1971 white paper entitled "The Purposes of the Defense Services in a Constructive Culture by H. R. Lee." Hugh's eighteen-page tract was in essence his own regurgitation of his father's right-wing views. Hugh even used H.L.'s political term "constructive" while illustrating his points with children's-textbook-style charts and drawings. He now determined to expand on his working through further reading and research.

Hugh's attempt at wheeling and dealing and at politics were clearly attempts to impress and get close to his father. Still troubled with identity problems stemming from his unusual family situation, Hugh went through another series of name changes, finally taking the name Hugh Richard Hunt. But for all his effort, Hugh seemed to make only minimal headway with his father. Hugh continued to show up at the office from time to time, and when he did, Hunt would always consent to see him. Sometimes the two would go to lunch or attend a political speech of some sort. Hunt also continued to underwrite Hugh's 1964 loan of $350,000 for a failed movie venture. But Hugh did not attain equal financial status or equal stature to his half siblings in the first and second families.

Frania Tye Lee entered the public eye only once in the late 1960s and early 1970s. That was in 1968, when a controversy erupted over Theater Atlanta's production of *Red, White, and Maddox,* a spoof on Georgia's conservative governor Lester Maddox. A conservative herself as well as the theater's land-lady, Frania evicted the Theater Atlanta group amid howls of protest from the director. She subsequently reopened the theater for a less liberal local troupe, but only after her dispute with the former tenants made her the center of hot controversy in the Atlanta arts world.

When the Theater Atlanta controversy subsided, Frania seemed to be drawn into herself still further. Although she was now pushing seventy, a number of Atlanta's more mature bachelors considered her quite attractive. But Frania was not inclined to marry. Her heart, according to one friend, still belonged to H. L. Hunt despite all the years and all the troubles.

Ironically, it was Frania's displeasure with Hunt that almost brought her story out into the open. Or so she later claimed. The catalyst was the publica-tion in 1973 of H. L. Hunt's two autobiographies, *Hunt Heritage* and *H. L. Hunt Early Days.* Frania's son Hugh, then age thirty-nine, had brought her a copy of one of the books. Frania found that Lyda Bunker Hunt's family history was written up in the books. So was Ruth Ray Hunt's family history. There were even a few photographs of Ruth in the books, and a mention of Hunt's trip to the Florida real-estate boom in 1925. But Frania and her children were not even mentioned, not once. It was as if they did not exist.

Frania became upset. According to her recollection of the 1942 settlement, it was understood that H.L. would never deny the existence of Frania's branch of the family. His autobiographies, by failing to mention her, in effect did just that. With Hugh in the room, Frania called up her old friend and former attorney Wright Matthews and told him about Hunt's autobiographies. For the first time in Hugh's memory, he heard his mother refer to his father as "Franklin Hunt," the name under which Hunt had allegedly married her back in Tampa, Florida, nearly half a century before.

"I want to start a lawsuit immediately," Frania informed Matthews after telling him about the omissions in Hunt's autobiographies.

Matthews, who was then in his late seventies, had to beg off. He told Frania he was too old to take on a case like that and advised her "to wait."

Frania held back on whatever plans she may have had to file a suit and waited to see if Hunt would keep his alleged promise to recognize her and her children in his will.

Back in Dallas, H. L. Hunt celebrated his eighty-fifth birthday on Febru-ary 17, 1974. He did not look well. His hair was wispy and white, his cheeks hollow, his complexion pale. His spine and shoulders were badly hunched over because his back was hurting him, and he would not see a doctor about it. The pain often put him in terrible moods, and occasionally put him in a wheelchair. He wore a Vicks-saturated bib under his shirt at all times, but he was still quite susceptible to colds. He continued to go down to the office every day, but his eyesight had gotten so bad that he finally consented to let a chauffeur drive him downtown and back.

Like the aging King Lear, Hunt was troubled by the internecine turmoil within his empire. He harbored nagging doubts about the love, loyalty, and competency of his offspring. But he did not allow his doubts to drive him crazy. Although Hunt did add one minor codicil to his February 1971 will, he did not make any major late-life revisions as far as his family members were concerned.

What did bother the old man was the prospect of dying. No longer convinced he would outlive the Hunzukuts or the 167-year-old Russian, Hunt began to fear the undertaker. At home with Ruthie, the one hymn he absolutely could not bear to hear was "Swing Low, Sweet Chariot."

As his body got older, Hunt, the lifelong sinner, tried to repent. All along he had banked on being able to outlast his misdeeds. Now he feared they might be catching up with him and decided to hedge his bets. One of the most touching episodes in this repentance was Hunt's encounter with singer Pat Boone in early September of 1974 at the Fairmont Hotel in Dallas. Boone, whose trademark was white buckskin shoes and an All-American-boy purity, had long occupied a very special place in H.L.'s heart. To Hunt, Boone personified everything that was good and right and Christian about America. A few years back, the very sight of Pat Boone in the film "Miracle of America" had brought Hunt to tears. Though he had to be pushed into the reception in a wheelchair, Hunt had no intention of missing the chance to see Pat Boone in person. When the moment came, Hunt's eyes once again began to tear.

"Pray for me, will you, Pat?" Hunt asked his singing idol with a sob.

Boone, himself a little overwhelmed by Hunt's reaction to their meeting, promised that he would. When Boone looked down at Hunt's wheelchair, he saw the old man had worn a pair of tattered white bucks in his honor.

On September 13, 1974, while he was working at his desk at Hunt Oil Company, H. L. Hunt collapsed. He was rushed to Baylor University Medical Center in Dallas. Baylor staffers later reported that Hunt was suffering from a "virus" with a touch of "pneumonia," but no further details were released.

Hunt remained in the hospital as September became October. On October 8, 1974, a family spokesman reported that "Mr. Hunt's condition is stable now," and that he was "better today." But Hunt did not keep getting better. Instead, he took a turn for the worse and grew weaker as the weeks passed. Soon he was unable to speak or move much at all. Those family members who came to visit could only sit beside the bed and hold his hand. Finally, on Friday, November 29, 1974, Haroldson Lafayette Hunt died. The official cause of death was not disclosed, but the most reliable reports coming out of his hospital room were that his heart had simply stopped.

The death of H. L. Hunt provoked as many different reactions as his life. Naturally, the newspapers were among the first to make their reactions public. The *Dallas Morning News,* a faithful conservative voice in Texas for more than a century, was the most praiseful of its late subscriber and "Letter to the Editor" writer. In an eight-paragraph editorial, the *News* lauded H. L. Hunt for helping to "conquer frontiers that opened up new dimensions of American life: The petroleum powered age of technology." The *News* said Hunt had come on the scene when the nation needed "doers and risk takers" and had fulfilled that need. "As an oil 'wildcatter,' he took the risks, all the time instead of just dreaming of doing." The editorial noted, "His success, and his financial rewards, exceeded even the most lavish of the American dreams," but quickly added, lest that sound too greedy, that Hunt "unlocked the earth's petroleum riches for man's use." The *News* editorial opined that "the American dream continues to shine" because of the successes of H. L. Hunt, and concluded, "Hopefully this nation will always have such men of courage—doers and risk takers—to pursue that dream, to the benefit of the country and the world."

An insightful, double-edged, but still affectionate obituary came from *Texas Monthly* writer Bill Porterfield. After recounting some of the dizzying estimates of Hunt's wealth, Porterfield declared that he, for one, was "not hung up on his money. . . . What I liked about old H. L. was the originality and richness of his character." Porterfield noted that *Fortune*'s most recent list of America's big rich did not feature flamboyant wheeler-dealers, but "a parade of pedestrian types who have cornered the market on faucets and tire treads" and "people who purvey pet foods and discount clothing." H. L. Hunt, on the other hand, was a different breed. "He was many men in one, multitudinous and contradictory," Porterfield wrote. "Good and bad, but on a larger scale, right out of Ayn Rand. In an age of midgets and conformists, he was a rogue who broke rules and cut a large swath and then, at last, lay down with a smile and allowed the ubiquitous and unctuous preachers to make him a monument to nobility. He knew they would because he knew human nature."

Outside Texas, H. L. Hunt's passing did not receive such sympathetic notices. In an obituary that began on page 1, the *New York Times* described Hunt as "one of the world's richest men . . . a militant anti-Communist and an ultraconservative." The *Times* recalled Hunt's role in circulating Reverend Criswell's anti-Catholic sermon in the 1960 presidential election, the unsubstantiated rumors that had swirled around Hunt following Kennedy's assassination in Dallas, and several oft-told stories about Hunt's rise to riches, his gambling, and his early days in oil. The *Times* labeled Hunt's politics as "probably counterproductive" and noted that he was a man who made no "munificent gifts to worthy causes." The *Times* obituary ended by reporting that former aide Rothermel had said he had resigned from Hunt Oil Company because he "couldn't work for a man playing God."

Perhaps the sharpest reaction to Hunt's death came from conservative columnist William F. Buckley, Jr. Having once feuded with Hunt in life, Buckley now buried Hunt as if with vengeance. He declared that Hunt had done more harm than good to the conservative movement in America. He pronounced again that Hunt's books were silly. He scorned Hunt's supposed contribution to the American dream by accusing him of having given capitalism "a bad name, not, goodness knows, by frenzies of extravagance, but by his eccentric understanding of public affairs, his yahoo bigotry, and his appallingly bad manners." In Buckley's estimation, H. L. Hunt's death was not an occasion for mourning but for relief—one of the right wing's most counterproductive old dinosaurs was finally out of the way.

Meanwhile, back in Dallas, H. L. Hunt's two recognized surviving families kept their reactions mostly to themselves. Because of the patriarch's two-and-a-half-month-long illness, no one was really surprised when the end came. Now that he was gone, his families marked his passing with everything from sobs of grief to sighs of relief. It was hard not to feel ambivalent, for H. L. Hunt had been an ambivalent figure to all his families, a husband and father who lavished both comfort and pain, love and neglect, a strangely endearing but always incorrigible man who had lived and died a mystery even to those he lived with. At the same time, it was hard for Hunt's two Dallas families not to feel anxious—anxious about the bad feelings that existed between them, anxious about what each would get in H.L.'s will, anxious about the future of the Hunt empire and their relative places in it. But all these were very complicated, intense, and volatile issues, the sort of things that should only be discussed in private. So instead of venting their true reactions in public, the Hunts simply prepared for H.L.'s funeral with as little fanfare as possible.

This was not an easy task. As it turned out, the Hunts received quite an outpouring of public and private condolences. News of H.L.'s death was on the radio shortly after it occurred on Friday morning. By Friday afternoon, slow-moving lines of cars were driving back and forth on Lawther Drive in front of Mount Vernon; each motorist would brake for an extra moment as he passed the house, pausing to acknowledge the passing of the former owner. Meanwhile, flowers, telegrams, and telephone calls flooded the Hunts' homes. Friends, acquaintances, associates, employees, and admirers expressed their sympathy from all over the country and around the world. Many wanted to know where they could contribute to a fund for the deceased. A Hunt family spokesman told the local newspaper that "Mr. Hunt would prefer that everyone make a contribution to his own favorite charity rather than offer any memorials to him."

H. L. Hunt's funeral took place on December 2, 1974, which was the Monday following his death. The service was held in the cavernous First Baptist Church, and it was a good thing that it was. More than 1,800 people filed by Hunt's open casket. This procession did not pass without incident. One man, whom church officials said was an ex-convict whom H.L. had once befriended, stopped in front of the casket, drew a rapierlike blade from a sheath disguised as a walking stick, and saluted Hunt's body. Fortunately, the man then put away his blade and left.

Heads also turned when Hunt's son Hassie arrived in the company of his attendants. It wasn't anything Hassie did that caused people to stare, but the fact that he looked so much like his father. The resemblance between the two had always been striking. Now it seemed eerie, especially to those who had known H. L. Hunt but had never met his mentally troubled son. But Hassie simply walked down the aisle like other mourners, stopped in front of the casket, and wept. Then he walked back down the aisle and took up a place in the back of the church.

A short time later, the organist played "God Bless America," and the Reverend W. A. Criswell led the members of Hunt's Dallas families onto the stage. Reverend Criswell closed the casket, and the Hunts sat down in the left front pews. Then he announced that Hunt's daughter June would sing a song her father had loved well. The song was about Jesus.

"I shall know him," June sang, "by the print of the nails of his hands." Her warm, well-trained voice filled the entire church. She managed to smile throughout the song.

When June had finished, Reverend Criswell read from the Scriptures. Dr. James Draper, the associate pastor, followed with a prayer for Hunt and his survivors. Then, to the astonishment of many of those present, Draper called for the Hunts who had not accepted Christ to do so, obviously intending his message to the children of the first family, who were not members of First Baptist. Draper extended the same invitation to anyone else in the audience who might not have accepted Christ. However, no one seemed inclined to come forward, at least not then.

Beverly Terrell, a Hunt family friend, sang another hymn. Brother Criswell informed the audience that it was the last hymn H. L. had heard on the radio before his death. The words went in part: "Voices of a million angels could not express my gratitude. . . . All that I am and ever hope to be . . . I owe it all to thee, God."

Then Sidney Latham, Hunt's former attorney, political mentor, and Hunt Oil vice president, rose to deliver the eulogy. Latham was now an old man. He knew the secrets and the excesses of H.L.'s life as well as anyone. However, he described Hunt as one of the finest Christians he had ever known, and tried to put Hunt's unspoken faults in the proper perspective: "H. L. Hunt moved in and about the timberlines of life where the timid fear to venture." Latham called Hunt one of the most misunderstood men who ever drew public comment. He recalled Hunt's dedication to the American way and his great success in business. But Latham said that the happiest moment in Hunt's life was the Sunday night back in 1960 when he, Ruthie, and their children had joined the First Baptist Church. "He said it was the best and biggest trade he had ever made. He said he had traded the here for the hereafter, and he was pleased."

When Latham finished, Reverend Criswell returned to the pulpit and gave those assembled his Bible-beating best. "Worthy, noble father," Criswell cried, "sentimental about his home and children . . . good to them beyond compare . . . especially to the child who was not well. . . . Oh, yes, I often referred to him as Mr. Golden Heart."

Criswell went on and on, pumping out phrase after staccato phrase which described H. L. Hunt as a man too big for one life, a man of mythical talents and the wisdom of Solomon. Finally, Criswell brought his oration to a sentimental close.

"Haroldson Lafayette Hunt," he intoned, "living giant with a gentle touch . . . *au revoir, auf wiedersehen,* till we meet again."

With that, the service ended. The family members filed out of the church and drove over to Hillcrest Memorial Park, where H. L. Hunt's casket was lowered into the ground next to the grave of his first wife, Lyda. The monument that marked the spot was a simple, flat piece of rose granite set on the family plot. There was no epitaph or fancy statuary, only the inscription:

HAROLDSON LAFAYETTE HUNT
FEB. 17, 1889–NOV. 29, 1974

CHAPTER 14

LIFE AFTER H.L. (Part One)

H. L. Hunt's will was filed for probate on Tuesday, December 3, 1974, the day after his funeral. As *People* magazine later reported with typical Holly-wood-Goes-to-Texas style, the will was a real "stunner." In that simple eleven-page document, Hunt left his Mount Vernon home and all of his stock in Hunt Oil Company to his second wife Ruth, and named thirty-one-year-old Ray Hunt, his only son by Ruth, the sole independent executor of his estate. Hunt's other major bequest was some Louisiana oil leases referred to only as "my Louisiana properties." Hunt left six-fourteenths of these properties to the six children of the first family and four-fourteenths to the four children of the second family. He left the remaining four-fourteenths to his four children by Frania Tye Lee. However, Hunt did not refer to Frania or their children by name. He simply willed their share to "Reliance Trusts." Finally, Hunt also included a challenge clause which said that anyone who disputed the will would automatically "lose and forfeit all right to any benefit and all right and title to any property" that might be due them under the will.

The public reaction of H. L. Hunt's heirs resembled the calm before the storm. In interviews with the media following Hunt's death, both Dallas families intimated that they thought the will was fair. In a February 17, 1975, *Business Week* story, for example, Lamar was quoted as saying that since his father had left the bulk of his personal estate to his wife, Ruth, "it was a natural thing for Ray to be the person who looks after it." However, Lamar added that Ray's position as executor of the estate "does not mean that Ray will run the business. He will be making an orderly transition, a change to whatever happens. He will have the responsibility of making decisions in relationship to Dad's property, but Dad's operation was much simpler [than the rest of the family operations]. . . . Hunt Oil, which was my dad's company, will be run basically by employees of the company. We all will continue to operate out of the Hunt Oil office."

Despite this public display of harmony, the first family was privately furious about what their father had wrought in his last will and testament. On the one hand, they professed to be disturbed about the allegedly shoddy legal form of the document, especially the fact that the will included no sophisticated provisions for avoiding taxes. Being older and more experienced in business, they felt that one of them, not their younger half brother Ray should have been named executor of their father's estate. But the first family's real displeasure was emotional. By making Ray the sole executor of the estate, the will left the impression that H. L. Hunt had passed the mantle of family leadership to him instead of to Bunker and Herbert, his oldest active first-family sons. Although the first family already had nearly twenty times the amount of money the second family received under the will, they seemed to feel that a share of the H. L. Hunt estate was somehow equal to a share of their father's heart. Since the will gave them only six-fourteenths share of the "Louisiana properties." The first family was still suspicious that someone other than their father—most likely Rothermel and/or Ruth—had helped Hunt compose the will. Despite the automatic disinheritance clause and the risk of washing a lot of H. L. Hunt's dirty linen in public, the first family seriously considered challenging the will in court.

Ruth and her children had an opposite reaction. To them, H. L. Hunt's will read like the fulfillment of the Biblical prophecy predicting equal justice for both "the last" and "the first" on reckoning day. Despite the document's lack of legal sophistication, one-half of the estate did pass to Ruth tax-free by virtue of the fact that she was Hunt's wife. In getting a majority share of Hunt Oil, the second family got a nest egg that was then worth around $110 million to $130 million; due to the Arab oil embargo and the rising price of oil, the value of that nest egg was rapidly appreciating all the time. But money was by no means the only consideration. Perhaps even more importantly, by naming Ray his sole executor, the will gave the second family a final stamp of recognition and approval. Even friends of the first family had to smile on the second's good fortune. "The will was fair despite what Bunker and the others thought," said one family friend. "Ray and his mother and sisters got no more than they deserved. They're still not nearly as wealthy as the older group, but the will did something for them that money could never do: it made them legitimate."

The same could not be said for the will's treatment of Frania Tye Lee and her children by H. L. Hunt. Just like Hunt's previously published autobiographies, the document failed even to mention Frania and her offspring by name. As far as the world knew, Frania and her children were still not the heirs of H. L. Hunt. Hunt's will also left the Lees on the short end financially. The will did leave each of Frania's children an equal pro rata share of Hunt's "Louisiana properties," but the total value of their share was at best a few hundred thousand dollars. The other families, either through the will or through prior transfers to their trusts, had received millions and billions. To make matters worse, Hunt's death had come at a time when Frania's son, forty-year-old Hugh, was in especially dire financial straits. Hugh's major corporation, National Homeowners Sales Service, was on the verge of bankruptcy, and he was still a few hundred thousand dollars in debt to his father from his ill-fated movie deal. Hugh still had some attractive real-estate properties and an income from the Reliance Trusts, but he also had eight children to feed and clothe and a slew of money-related legal problems to handle. And now his father was no longer around to help him out with a loan. Hugh and Frania discussed Hunt's will and what to do about it. Finally, Hugh decided it would be worth his while to go to Texas and pay a call on his half brothers. He had hopes they could discuss the situation and perhaps work something out.

Back in Dallas, Ray Hunt was discovering what a double-edged inheritance he had received. As sole executor of his father's estate, he now gained even more public recognition as the up and coming leader of Dallas. Perhaps his most prestigious honor was being elected president of the Dallas Petroleum Club in February of 1975, not quite three months after his father's death. Still shy of his thirty-second birthday, Ray was the youngest president in the club's history. He was also the second member of the Hunt family to hold the post, Herbert having served as president in 1970 at the age of forty-one. Ironically, as the *Dallas Morning News* pointed out in reporting Ray's election, Ray was "not usually thought of as an oil man." In contrast to his father and half brothers, Ray had made his public reputation in real estate, not oil. Ray was not even the president of his own company. As the *Morning News* story noted, Ray was still officially only a vice president and director of Hunt Oil Company. In the wake of H. L. Hunt's death, the post of president of Hunt Oil Company remained unfilled.

Had the press or the public been aware of the behind-the-scenes battles Ray was fighting at Hunt Oil Company, his election to the Dallas Petroleum Club presidency might have seemed more ironic. Ray had control (via his mother) of a majority of Hunt Oil Company stock. But he did not yet have control of the company. For weeks after his father's death, things remained in a state of uncertainty. Most of the uncertainty concerned the first family's future relationship with Ray and with Hunt Oil Company. The first family still owned an 18 1/2-percent stock interest in Hunt Oil Company. Bunker and Herbert still had offices on the twenty-ninth floor of the Hunt Oil headquarters in the First National Bank building. Hunt Oil still provided administrative services for all the first family's companies, trusts, partnerships, and personal accounts. Ray presumed that the first family would want these arrangements to continue, but he could not be sure. The problem was that Bunker and Herbert would not talk to him about the situation. Ray telephoned his half brothers daily. A secretary always took Ray's messages. But Bunker and Herbert never returned Ray's calls.

The reason for the first family's uncooperativeness was their still poisoned feelings about their father's will and the ascendancy of the second family. By Christmas of 1974, their tempers had cooled somewhat. They had decided to drop the idea of filing a legal challenge to the will. But the first family did not like the idea of being in any way "under" Ray or anyone else in the second family, even if it was only under the same roof or the same corporate umbrella. The decision they faced was not whether to separate themselves from the second family, but how and when.

The first big move was made in January of 1975, some two months after H. L. Hunt's death, when Bunker and Herbert began forming a new company called Hunt Energy Corporation. The original purpose of Hunt Energy was to explore for oil and gas in the United States. Now that the allowable price for domestic crude had risen to over $8 per barrel, the Hunts believed that a U.S. exploration program could be almost as lucrative as foreign ventures. After directing an aide to work up a $100-million exploratory budget, Bunker and Herbert named themselves chairman and president of the new company, installed a few loyal employees as a skeleton staff, and began looking for geologists and landmen to comprise an exploration team. The brothers also began to look around for office space for their crew. About this time, the first-family-owned Placid Oil Company, which had been headquartered on the twenty-fifth floor of the First National Building, was moving to new offices on the fourteenth floor. Bunker and Herbert decided to convert Placid's old offices into the new headquarters of Hunt Energy.

In keeping with the first family's post-mortem attitude toward the second, Bunker and Herbert did not bother to announce the formation of Hunt Energy to Ray. In fact, they purposely kept him in the dark and instructed their top people to do the same. Ray's daily telephone calls kept coming but remained unanswered, as if that would somehow make them go away.

But Ray Hunt was not about to go away. Bunker and Herbert could avoid him all they wanted, but they could not change his status as sole executor of the estate and heir to their father's majority stock in Hunt Oil. Nor could they keep the formation of Hunt Energy a first-family secret. There were simply too many employees with loyalties and counterloyalties to H. L. Hunt and both his Dallas families, too many eyes and ears with access to the gossip mill, to keep such a thing quiet forever. When Ray got wind of Hunt Energy, he tried even harder to reach Bunker and Herbert. They still refused to return his calls.

Stymied by his half brothers' silence, Ray tried to enlist the help of his half brothers' employees, most of whom were or had been employees of Hunt Oil Company, too.

"They're forming another company, and they won't talk to me about it," Ray confided to one. "You've got to keep me informed."

Ray's efforts produced few results. His daily telephone calls to Bunker and Herbert were still futile. Bunker and Herbert went on their merry way, putting together the beginnings of Hunt Energy and keeping whatever long-range plans they may have been formulating vis-à-vis Ray and Hunt Oil Company to themselves.

Finally, Ray was able to get through to one of his half brothers' aides. The young heir's voice was full of desperation. It was now early February of 1975, nearly three months since H. L. Hunt's death, and Ray had yet to sit down with his half brothers to even begin discussing the many estate matters of mutual concern, much less the formation of Hunt Energy.

"I've *got* to talk to them," Ray implored the aide.

By now, that much was becoming clear to everyone in the upper echelons of the Hunt organization—everyone except Bunker and Herbert. When the brothers were advised for the umpteenth time that Ray urgently needed to see them, Bunker feigned surprise.

"Ray wants to see us?" he asked disingenuously. An outsider would have thought Bunker had just heard about Ray's calls for the first time. Then, his tone filled with mock seriousness as he glanced over at his brother Herbert.

"Well, I guess we better go see him, then," Bunker said.

With that, Bunker got up from his chair and headed straight for Ray's office. Herbert followed close behind. After weeks of nonresponse, seeing Ray seemed to have all of a sudden become the most important thing in the world.

The meeting that ensued was the first time the two families had gotten together on anything since H. L. Hunt's funeral. But it was also the beginning of a formal separation between the first family and the second family. Bunker and Herbert informed Ray that they would be moving their personal offices from the twenty-ninth floor to the space they had chosen for Hunt Energy on the twenty-fifth floor. They also said they would be moving all the first family's companies, trusts, and accounts out from under the Hunt Oil servicing umbrella and reorganizing them under the umbrella of Hunt Energy, which would become the first-family holding company.

Because of the first family's continuing 18 1/2-percent stock interest in Hunt Oil, it was agreed that Bunker and Herbert would retain seats on the Hunt Oil board of directors. But Ray, who controlled 80 percent of the Hunt Oil stock, would assume the title of president, which their father had vacated at death. Ray would retain operational control of Hunt Oil and remain in the existing Hunt Oil headquarters offices on the twenty-ninth floor. Finally, the two sides agreed to assist each other in making the transition to this new arrangement as orderly as possible.

Having thus agreed to go their separate ways, the first and second families arrived at a temporary truce. There was still much bad blood between them and several important unresolved financial matters. But at least they had reached an accommodation.

No such accommodation was reached between the two Dallas families and the Lees. Hugh arrived from Atlanta shortly after the funeral. Day after day, he kept showing up in the Hunt Oil offices asking to see Bunker. But Hugh got nothing for his efforts but a long wait. Bunker would not acknowledge him or talk to him. Neither would Herbert, who often saw people Bunker turned away. Rather than accept or even reject their half brother, Bunker and Herbert treated him as if he did not exist. Ray Hunt, meanwhile, met with Hugh, but made it clear that as executor of the estate, he was bound to abide by the strict provisions of the will.

Rejected by both Dallas families Hugh went back to Atlanta and advised his mother that if they wanted to get anything out of the H. L. Hunt estate, they would probably have to file suit. Frania, by this time, was no longer as gung ho about filing suit as she had once been. She told her son that her marriage to "Franklin Hunt" might be hard to document because Hunt had told her back in the early 1940s that all records of their marriage had been destroyed. A short time after her marriage to John Lee, Frania and Lee had gone to Tampa to see if what Hunt said was true. Just as Hunt had predicted, Frania and her new husband found nothing.

Hugh, the former two-year Harvard law student, pointed out that the failure of his mother's search with Lee did not necessarily mean a record did not exist. Perhaps they had looked in the wrong place. Maybe the records for that year had been moved or misfiled. The only way to know for sure was to go to Tampa and have a look. So, with a sense of hope and a sense of trepidation, Frania and Hugh decided to set out on a journey through the long, buried past to see what they could find.

Meanwhile the members of the first family had all but forgotten about the Lees and were now turning their attention to a much more pressing matter: Bunker and Herbert's trial for wiretapping, which was due to begin in Lubbock in September of 1975. The situation looked chancy. In the five years since the Hunt-hired wiretappers were first arrested, the Watergate scandal had erupted and President Nixon had resigned. The entire world had been informed about wiretapping in expletive-deleted detail. All this would make it very difficult for the Hunt brothers to convince a jury that they had been ignorant of the law when they had hired the wiretappers, even though their acts had been committed over two years before the Watergate break-in and only one year after the federal law prohibiting wiretapping had gone into effect. Besides, ignorance of the law, which was the brothers' first line of defense, was really no defense.

The chances for the Hunts' second line of defense, (their claim) that they had not wiretapped with "evil intent," looked better. In March of 1975, John Curington and John Brown were convicted of mail fraud in connection with the alleged embezzlement schemes. Over the Hunts' loud protests, the government tried the two men for only $17,000 worth of proceeds from what the Hunts claimed was a multimillion-dollar rip-off and had granted Paul Rothermel immunity from prosecution. When sentencing time came, Curington and Brown were given probated sentences, which meant that neither man had to spend a day in jail. The Hunt brothers were not happy about that. But they also realized that the mere fact that Curington and Brown had been convicted —and thus labeled as criminals by a court of law—greatly enhanced the credibility of their own claims that they had wiretapped only to protect their aging father from the evil men ravaging his empire. Of course, the convictions of Curington and Brown said nothing about Paul Rothermel. Despite all the Hunts' allegations, Rothermel was never prosecuted or indicted on any charges in connection with the HLH Products case, and he continued to maintain that he was innocent of any wrongdoing.

Ironically, the Hunt brothers' chances for acquittal on the wiretapping charges now depended even more heavily upon their relationship with the second family. Defense attorney Phil Hirschkop planned to portray his clients as basically honest and well-meaning businessmen and family members who had only had their father's interests in mind, not greedy motives of their own. Most important was making the Lubbock jury believe that the brothers' wiretapping was done to stop the alleged thefts and not to thwart the second family's inheritance, as Paul Rothermel had suggested. Consequently, as Hirschkop explained to his clients, it was essential that the first family put aside any animosity toward the second. The two groups must submerge their differences and show up in Lubbock presenting a united front.

At the same time, Hirschkop advised, Bunker and Herbert needed to clean up their own personal public images. They had to come out of their private shells and talk to the media just like regular "good ole boys" who happened to have a rich daddy and a whole heap of money themselves.

To help accomplish their task, the Hunts hired Denver public-relations man Claude Fleet. Hirschkop and Fleet taught the Hunts to beam beauty-contest smiles, to give gushy personality-profile interviews to the media, and to relax around each other in public. Slowly, the two Dallas families began to become one.

But even as Bunker and Herbert tried to gear themselves up for making successful courtroom appearances, they also had to prepare for the worst. If convicted of wiretapping, they faced not only possible fines but possible time in prison. As a result, they had no choice but to make contingency plans for running the empire in the event of their extended absence.

In July of 1975, about two months before the Lubbock trial was scheduled to begin, the Hunt brothers were dealt another severe blow: a federal grand jury indicted them for obstruction of justice in connection with their alleged efforts to keep the private eyes who did the actual wiretapping from naming them as paymasters. Indicted along with them were their friend E. J. Hudson and attorneys Ralph Shank, Charles Tessmer, B. H. Timmins, and Percy Foreman, all prominent and well-respected figures on the Texas business and legal scenes. Reports of grand-jury appearances by Senator James Eastland and former Attorneys General John Mitchell and Richard Kleindienst had circulated in the press for months, but none of these men was named in the indictments or implicated in the alleged obstruction of justice. Nevertheless, newspapers and other media in and out of the state seized upon the obvious comparison—this was Watergate Texas style. First, there had been the wiretapping. Now the Hunts and their associates were charged with the cover-up.

With a second set of indictments now hanging over their heads, the Hunt brothers approached the Lubbock trial for wiretapping with even greater anxiety. Fortunately for Bunker and Herbert the first and second families' pretrial public-relations work paid off. When the two families arrived in Lubbock, they looked like one of the most harmonious collections of kinfolk in

America. In addition to the two defendants, the Hunt contingent included brothers, sisters, wives, cousins, children, and in-laws. Between sessions, Bunker, Herbert, and Lamar stood around chatting amiably with their half brother Ray. Tom Hunt, the affable and loquacious first-family cousin, held press conferences to explain the former aides' alleged embezzlement schemes and to show that they bore no ill feeling toward Bunker and Herbert for wiretapping his own phone in the process of trying to catch the real culprits. The women posed arm in arm for group photographs, with Lamar's strikingly attractive wife Norma providing the centerpiece. "We've determined to help show we're a family that sticks together," Norma Hunt told the press.

With the skill of a summer-camp counselor, attorney Hirschkop brought the entire Hunt clan into the trial process. During jury selection, he invited each of the family members to grade the potential jurors and encouraged them to voice their opinions when the group returned to their motel after court. When the trial began, Hirschkop got permission for Ruth Hunt, one of the defense witnesses, to remain in the courtroom where the jury could see her. At recess times, all the Hunts trooped off together for strategy sessions or family meals. But the Hunts also took care not to appear depressed or aloof. They kept smiles on their faces and exchanged pleasantries with the U.S. marshals about such things as "the place with the great blueberry muffins" and the need to cushion the court benches. The "just plain folks" show apparently had its desired effect.

"They sure don't act like rich people," one court employee told a reporter early in the trial. "That's what I call making the best of a bad situation."

Things went almost as smoothly onstage as off. Hirschkop hammered away at his main themes—his clients' ignorance of the law and their lack of "evil intent." Private investigator W. J. Everett testified that he had warned Bunker that the Hunts could be in trouble "criminally and civilly" if they got caught, but Hirschkop got Everett to admit he did not enumerate the dangers and illegality of wiretapping beyond that statement. Both defendants took the stand and told their story in their own words, denying that Everett had warned them wiretapping was illegal, contritely affirming that if they had known wiretapping was against the law, they never would have done it. Lamar and Tom added supporting testimony about the losses plaguing HLH foods and the difficulty in convincing H.L. that his closest men were betraying him. To dispel any suggestion of an internal family feud, Ruth testified that she, too, had tried to warn H.L. about his aides' betrayal.

Hirschkop followed all this by presenting a string of character witnesses chosen to impress a typical west Texas jury. One was the pastor of Highland Park Presbyterian Church in Dallas. Another was Campus Crusade founder Bill Bright. However, the most impressive of all from the jury's point of view was E. J. Holub, a former star linebacker for Lamar's Kansas City Chiefs and an alumnus of Lubbock's own Texas Tech University. A gargantuan man, Holub showed up at the courthouse without wearing a jacket or tie as the judge's rules required. The only coat the defense could find for him to wear was several sizes too small. But the misfit worked to the Hunt's advantage. With his arms sticking out of the sleeves of the coat, Holub looked even bigger and more imposing than he already was. His calm, hometown-boy assertions that the Hunt brothers were good people who even enjoyed an occasional game of touch football appeared to be just the sort of thing the jury needed to be told.

If there was any remaining doubt about the humanity of the defendants, the Hunt brothers probably dispelled it with their own behavior in court. Herbert broke down and cried while testifying about the way his late father was betrayed. His performance was dramatic and, by all appearances, genuine. In what was obviously not a calculated move, Bunker, well known as a heavy sleeper among his own family, actually dozed off while he sat at the counsel's table listening to the trial proceed.

After a week of testimony, the case finally went to the jury. Federal prosecutor Frank McCown left the jury with a warning to keep the alleged financial motives of the defendants in mind. "The Hunts would have you believe the Hunts wiretapped only to catch crooks and thieves," McCown said, adding, "the only thing they were concerned with was money. Dollars and cents."

Hirschkop countered with a final plea for sympathy on "just plain folks" grounds. Admitting his clients' affluence, Hirschkop told the jury that the Hunts "love and hate, they laugh and cry like you and I. I don't believe a jury anywhere would convict them of their wealth."

The jury took less than three hours to reach a verdict—not guilty.

The Hunts erupted into a spontaneous celebration, with the entire contingent of brothers, sisters, children, and in-laws joining in. Lamar even went so far as to order champagne. "It's been a long trial for everyone," he told the press.

It had also been a costly trial. The Hunt brothers' legal fees for the four years since wiretapper Jon Kelly's arrest amounted to over $1 million, a fact that did not escape Bunker's attention even amid the joy of his acquittal.

"If we'd been just ordinary folks, Herbert and I would have been in real trouble," Bunker told a reporter. "We can afford it. But my heart goes out to all the ordinary people, poor people, middle-of-the-road people who can't afford to hire counsel to defend themselves. The government can call out a whole array of talent to prosecute a case, but many defendants can only afford to plead guilty or nolo contendere."

The victory in Lubbock set the wheels of justice rolling in the Hunt's favor. Seven months later, in April of 1976, attorney Hirschkop arranged for a most generous settlement of the obstruction-of-justice indictments against the two brothers. The government dropped its charges against Herbert Hunt. Bunker Hunt entered a plea of nolo contendere to a charge that he "did knowingly misbehave" by making offers of monthly payments to prospective witnesses (i.e., wiretappers Kelly, McCann, and Everett) for not testifying about the Hunt brothers' role in the wiretapping. Bunker paid a $1,000 fine, and that was it. Attorneys Tessmer and Timmins also pleaded nolo contendere and paid $1,000 fines. Charges against attorney Percy Foreman, attorney Ralph Shank, and Houston industrialist E. J. Hudson were eventually dropped.

On leaving the courtroom after entering his plea and paying his fine, Bunker commented that the arrangement "seems reasonably fair to me," and told the press, "I probably made some honest mistakes." Herbert simply declared, "I wasn't guilty, and I'm just glad the government arrived at the same conclusion."

The plea-bargaining arrangement on the obstruction-of-justice charges closed the wiretap caper for Bunker and Herbert. The only remaining legal action against them was the $101-million civil suit filed against them back in 1973 by embittered former wiretapper Jon Kelly, and that suit was destined to languish until it was settled out of court.

Unfortunately for the Hunts, the end of the wiretap caper did not mark the end of the clan's internecine war. On November 11, 1975, just six weeks after the Lubbock trial and exactly fifty years to the day after her alleged wedding to H. L. Hunt, Frania Tye Lee filed suit against the H. L. Hunt estate in a Shreveport, Louisiana, federal court. In her suit, Mrs. Lee asked to be declared the "putative" (or commonly accepted) wife of H. L. Hunt. She claimed that she had married Hunt in Florida, lived with him for almost nine years in Shreveport and Dallas, and bore him four children before she discovered that he was already married to someone else and was the father of another family. Her petition mentioned the 1942 settlement agreement and the income she still received, but alleged that Hunt had violated the agreement by failing to keep an unwritten promise to name her and her children on an equal basis with his first family when he wrote his will. As compensation for all this, Mrs. Lee asked to be awarded one-half of all the community property H. L. Hunt had accumulated between 1925 and 1934, the years of their alleged marriage, and all the subsequent fruits of that property. Because Louisiana law prohibited inheritance by illegitimate children, Frania's son Hugh filed a separate but related suit in Baton Rouge, Louisiana, asking that he and his siblings be declared the legitimate heirs of H. L. Hunt.

The filing of the Lees' lawsuits did not receive the sort of publicity that had attended the wiretap case. In fact, there was scarcely a mention of it in any of the Dallas, Shreveport, or Atlanta papers. But as H. L. Hunt's two Dallas families quickly realized, Frania's suit could be even more embarrassing than the wiretap caper if it ever went to trial. This time, however, it was Ray Hunt who was on the hot seat, not Bunker and Herbert. As sole executor of the estate, Ray was the named defendant in Frania's lawsuit. It would be his responsibility to handle the suit and, if possible, to dispose of it before it ever got to trial.

What was uncertain was whether the first family would come to Ray's aid with a show of solidarity similar to the one in Lubbock. In the glow of Bunker and Herbert's acquittal, Ray told a reporter that he hoped the Lubbock trial would finally quiet the rumors of a Hunt family feud. "There never was any feud," Ray said, "but we couldn't really respond to the rumors on advice of attorneys." That, of course, was not exactly true then, and it was not exactly true now.

Whether or not Ray wanted to call it a feud, the relationship between the first and second family hardly approached harmony. The first family still bitterly resented the second, and still felt displaced in both their father's affections and the estate. The fact that the second family had ably supported the first in Lubbock did not end those feelings—it only made them lie dormant. Whether the outside threat posed by Frania Tye Lee and her branch of the H. L. Hunt patriarchy would prompt another courtroom reunion of the two Dallas families was an open question.

In the meantime, the first and second families simply tried to go their separate ways. They both retained their offices in the First National Bank building, but they made their headquarters on separate floors and tried in every way to differentiate Hunt Energy Corporation from Hunt Oil Company, and the first branch of the family from the second. This did not prove difficult, for the two groups were different in age, style, and almost every other way except, of course, surname.

In mid-March of 1975, several months before his trial for wiretapping, Nelson Bunker Hunt left Dallas with a tourist-class plane ticket and high hopes of finding a kindred spirit in the Middle East. When Bunker arrived in London, he and aide Bill Bledsoe changed to reserved first-class seats on a flight for Tehran. This was not usually Bunker's custom, flying first class. But on this particular day Bunker flew first class for a very good reason. When he arrived at the Tehran airport he would be met by his friend Mohammed Pahlevi, the shah's brother, and he wanted to make the best possible impression. Bunker had a business proposal for the Iranians: he wanted them to buy silver.

That fact that Bunker was soliciting an outside partner was in itself unusual. But, then, so was Bunker's financial situation. The scions of one of the country's best-known oil families, Bunker and Herbert were now more interested in silver than anything else. They were also in something of a cash squeeze. By this time, the Hunt brothers had owned the better part of their 55-million ounces for about a year, but the price was languishing around $4. However, Bunker still had confidence in the long-term outlook for the metal. He believed that if he could get another big buyer to join him in the silver market, a big buyer like the Iranian royal family, prices might begin to rise again—maybe even catch fire.

As the world would eventually learn, this sort of thinking was vintage Bunker Hunt. A pessimist about politics and society, he was an eternal optimist about his business investments. In true Hunt family tradition, he liked to think big, trust his instincts, and take big risks in the hope of a big return. He was also the sort of person who believed that the rules that applied to ordinary people did not apply to him. Even though he was slightly more conventional and detail-oriented, Herbert followed Bunker in almost every respect. Together, they made a most controversial pair. Some regarded them as the personification of everything that was still right about America, gallant archetypes of individual capitalism and the free-enterprise system. Others, however, saw the Hunts as representing everything that was wrong with capitalism, as throwbacks to an unpleasant era of exploitation and greed: Bunker and Herbert were the robber-baron brothers, classical "capitalist pigs." In either case, few could deny that the Hunt brothers seemed driven to acquire and acquire until they cornered the market in whatever field they were in. As aide Bill Bledsoe later remarked in reference to Bunker's dealings in everything from horses to silver, "He doesn't just want some of it. He wants it all."

Upon his arrival in Tehran, Bunker was ushered via chauffeur-driven limousine to an appointment with the Iranian finance minister, Hushang Ansary. A distinguished looking man in his fifties, Ansary listened as the great-girthed Texan sitting in front of him suggested that the Pahlevi family invest in several million ounces of silver. Ansary had never heard of Bunker Hunt and asked, by way of financial background, how much money Hunt had made in the previous year.

Bunker looked stumped. He really did not know how much he made, not exactly. He did not like to count his money—mostly because he thought it was bad luck. Besides, what he reported as personal income for tax purposes and what he regarded as available income for Hunt family investments were two vastly different figures.

"Fifty million dollars," Bunker said finally. Then he glanced at Bledsoe for reassurance. "Isn't that about right?"

Bledsoe nodded dutifully, not knowing whether it was or was not, but guessing that it had to be at least that.

Mr. Ansary looked a little skeptical. Bunker's hesitation seemed to put him off. The meeting ended without a firm commitment.

Choking and headachy from the Tehran smog, Bunker caught the next plane out, which happened to be bound for Zurich. Along the way, Bunker decided that he might as well go to Paris and see his race horses. Then he got another idea. Why not try the Saudis?

When he landed in Zurich, Bunker sent Bledsoe to telephone the family's Middle East expert in New York, Benjamin Harrison Freedman. A friend and contemporary of the late H. L. Hunt, Freedman was a long-time right-wing activist who had many Arab friends (including King Faisal) in part because he was well known as an anti-Zionist Jew. As such, Freedman was typical of the Hunt family's informal brain trust, an amazing assortment of mostly arch-conservative and often slightly eccentric wizards of science and pseudo-science ranging from economics to climatology.

Through Bledsoe, Freedman advised Bunker to slow down. King Faisal was currently occupied with a visit from U.S. secretary of state Henry Kissinger, who was then trying to bring peace to the Middle East through "shuttle diplomacy. All the Middle East was aware of Bunker's trip to Tehran, Freedman said; to fly right over to Saudi Arabia would only offend King Faisal by making him seem second to the shah. Freedman urged Bunker to fly back to the United States first and allow him to then make an appointment for Bunker to see the king in the latter half of April. That way, Bunker could show the proper respect for the king by coming directly from his home country. Freedman assured Bunker that he could arrange a private audience with Faisal and added that after seeing the king, Bunker would probably be referred to the Council of Ministers.

Freedman further cautioned that the political situation in the Middle East could reach a crisis point within the next forty-eight hours. He predicted that Kissinger would come back from his trip "with his tail between his legs without accomplishing anything." Faisal, Freedman said, was actually trying to be friendly to the United States and to reduce oil prices, but the American public and some of the news magazines, *Harper's* in particular, were making statements to the effect that the United States should occupy Saudi Arabia. Opining that those opinions sounded like they were coming from the Defense Department, Freedman went on to say that Bunker could well be "the link" between China, the Middle East, and the United States because he was "an international fair-haired boy." Exactly how Bunker, who had no interests in China, would act as a "link" to that country, Freedman did not say.

Bunker followed Freedman's advice. He went on to Paris to see his horses, then flew back to the United States while Freedman made arrangements for an audience with King Faisal in three weeks' time.

Then on March 25, 1975, King Faisal was assassinated by his deranged nephew. The assassination of the king brought Bunker's silver play to a halt. With little hope of finding another big buying partner any time soon, Bunker was forced to return his attention to the most pressing matter before him: his upcoming trial for wiretapping.

Following their acquittal in the Lubbock wiretapping trial, Bunker and his brother Herbert picked up their global silver play once again. This time, they got into the market not through their own individual accounts (which still held 55-million ounces of bullion and sizable futures contracts), but through Great Western United, the public company the Hunts acquired about the time of H. L. Hunt's death. Originally intended as a vehicle through which to play the sugar market, Great Western was turning into an albatross. During the first year of the Hunt's ownership, the bottom fell out of the sugar market, and Great Western suffered a decline in revenue of $100 million. Convinced that they could reverse some of Great Western's losses by getting the company into precious metals, the Hunts had the company sell its sugar futures and start buying silver futures. By the spring of 1976, Great Western's trading company was out of all commodities except silver. Later that year, Great Western took delivery on some 20 million ounces of silver bullion.

At this point, Bunker concocted one of his most cosmic schemes: a plan to trade the 20 million ounces to the Philippines through Great Western. The

Philippines would then send Great Western raw sugar for its refineries and exchange the silver for Saudi crude. With the Arabs into the silver market for $100 million, the price of silver would rise, Great Western would have sugar, the Philippines would have oil, and all sides would be happy. Or so Bunker hoped. In an effort to make Bunker's plan work, Herbert went over to the Philippines to negotiate the deal with President Marcos, and got a favorable response. But the International Monetary Fund, which lent a great deal of money to the Philippines to buy crude, said it would not recognize silver as part of the country's national resources. In effect, the IMF ruling meant that the 20 million ounces of bullion would be worthless in trying to get loans. With that, Bunker's scheme fell through. Great Western sold its bullion in early 1977 for $88.5 million, thus offsetting a substantial part of the revenues lost due to the collapse of the sugar market. Still, the company continued to operate in the red.

After the sale, the Hunt brothers took Great Western out of the silver-futures market, but not out of silver. Now they began using their newly acquired public company to go after one of the most precious metal prizes: the largest silver mine in America. Owning the nation's biggest silver mine would be like the crown on the Hunts' silver empire. As a working mine it was a productive asset in its own right. What's more, its estimated reserves of over 30 million ounces would give the Hunts a base lode in the United States to complement their stash in Europe. Finally, as the owners of an operating mine, the Hunts would qualify as commercial users of silver, and would thus be exempt from the trading restrictions applicable to futures-market speculators. Although this would later seem to be a most important benefit, it was a factor that the Hunts, incredibly enough, said they did not consider at the time.

Located near Kellogg, Idaho, the Big Creek mine was owned by a publicly traded company called Sunshine Mining. In the spring of 1977, Bunker and Herbert launched an attempted takeover of Sunshine Mining through Great Western. Sunshine's management opposed the takeover, and a complicated flurry of litigation ensued. When the dust settled, the Hunt brothers emerged with 28 percent of the stock for $19.5 million and a settlement agreement stipulating that they could acquire the rest of Sunshine's stock at no less than $15 a share, or about $60 million. Thus assured that the nation's largest silver mine would soon be theirs, the Hunt brothers installed a lieutenant—G. Michael Boswell, the former president of Great Western United (which had by now been renamed Hunt International Resources)—as the new president of Sunshine. Bunker and Herbert then turned their attention to other things.

One of those things was the Hunt family's invasion of another commodities market: soybeans. Though soybeans and silver were as ostensibly unrelated as fire and water, Bunker and Herbert forged a very definite connection between the two commodities. As usual, the connection involved money. Because the Hunts were unable to find another big buyer to join them in the silver market, they were still in a relative cash squeeze. But they refused to sell out or sit on the sidelines while other deals passed them by. Unable to get the price of silver to move, they decided to borrow against their bullion and invest that cash in other big commodity plays. Such a strategy involved a double risk. If the silver kept declining and their other plays also failed, they would be in more of a pinch than ever. But, then, big risks were just the thing that got the Hunt blood stirring.

Once again, the Hunts based their wheelings and dealings on the advice of a family brain-truster. In the case of soybeans, this expert was Dr. Iben Browning, a climatologist working out of Albuquerque. Sometimes referred to as Bunker's personal weatherman, Browning was actually an independent scientist consulted by clients ranging from commodities brokers to the Central Intelligence Agency. Browning believed that by studying long-term weather patterns, he could explain a wide range of historical phenomena like wars and population movements and could predict future events, particularly crop shortages. Like other Hunt experts, Browning generally believed that things were getting worse, and in the summer of 1976, he predicted that deteriorating climate changes in South America would lead to a world soybean shortage.

Bunker heard a variation on the same theme during a Chicago luncheon with a group he described as "a bunch of long-haired professional types who worked for the big food companies." According to Bunker, the longhairs were bullish on soybeans. "They all said to a man that beans had to go up because of the world protein shortage, and I believed them," Bunker recalled. Bunker's interest was heightened by a couple of tips he heard a short time after the luncheon. One said that Brazil, one of the world's largest soybean producers, was going to limit exports and impose a 5-percent tax on soybeans in order to conserve a supply for its own population. Another tipster told Bunker that the U.S. Department of Agriculture wanted the price of soybeans, then about $7 a bushel, to rise to $11 a bushel in order to prevent a shortage. Further investigation revealed that estimates of the U.S. soybean supply predicted a spring 1977 stock of only 65-million bushels compared to a stock of 245-million bushels in the spring of 1976.

Recognizing these warnings as a clue to making some big bucks, Bunker and Herbert began buying "long" soybean futures contracts with bank loans secured by silver-bullion receipts. The legal limit on soybean-futures contract holdings by an individual or group was 3 million bushels, but by the spring of 1977 the Hunt brothers had acquired 6 million bushels worth in their names and another 18 million bushels worth in the names of their children, for a total of 24 million bushels or roughly one-third of the total estimated U.S. supply. The Hunt brothers later claimed that neither they nor their children were acting in concert, but the evidence was overwhelmingly to the contrary. Ranging in age from nineteen to twenty-five, the Hunt children had never invested in commodities before February 1977. When the soybeans play began, each of the children had less than $100,000 in his or her individual bank account. But thanks to millions of dollars of timely interest-free loans from their fathers, the Hunt children were able to buy up huge quantities of soybean futures contracts at the same time their fathers stocked up on soybeans as well. Bunker and Herbert kept daily position sheets showing all the family's soybeans holdings, the day's price, and the prices at which the Hunts' contracts had been purchased.

By April of 1977, the Hunts' position sheets showed that soybean prices had jumped from $6 per bushel to over $10. The position sheets purposely did not show the Hunts' net gain (Bunker and Herbert believed it was bad luck to count their winnings before they were reaped), but if they had, they would have put the family ahead by roughly $96 million.

It was at this point that the Commodity Futures Trading Commission (CFTC) stepped in. The CFTC first prodded the Hunts behind the scenes to reduce their holdings in line with the 3-million-bushel limit. But the Hunts sold off only 2 million bushels and indicated they would not sell off any more. Then the CFTC decided to go public with the Hunt matter. Declaring that the Hunts had flagrantly violated the 3-million-bushel limit on futures contract holdings by any one individual or group and were "in a position to squeeze or manipulate the market," the CFTC not only filed suit against the Hunts, but took the unprecedented action of revealing the family's 22-million-bushel position to the press. Prices dropped about a dollar a bushel, then stabilized.

Bunker and Herbert were furious. Even as the CFTC accused them of attempting to manipulate prices upward, they accused the CFTC of trying to manipulate prices downward. The Hunts complained that they were once again the victims of government harassment emanating from the eastern establishment.

"There are literally dozens of family in-groups in Chicago if not elsewhere in the country," Bunker said, "who trade soybeans or trade grains, and the government has never tried to say that they're all trading together. I think the reason, frankly, they jumped on us is that we're sort of a favorite whipping boy, you know. We're conservatives, and the world is largely socialist and liberal. And as long as they want to jump on somebody, they want a name and they want somebody that's on the other side."

The Hunts vowed to fight the CFTC all the way. True to their word, they not only ordered their attorneys to prepare a legal defense, but began holding family information sessions to acquaint their children with the intricacies of commodities trading.

In the end, the Hunts managed to hang on to their contracts and take delivery on the soybeans. A federal judge in Chicago did rule that the Hunts had violated the legal limits, but decreed that there was no remedy that could be applied. Still bitter, the Hunts continued to protest that the government's unprecedented disclosure action had cost the family millions of dollars in losses. The government disagreed. Noting that soybean prices remained well above the $6-per-bushel level at which the Hunts had entered the market, the government claimed the Hunts made about $40 million on the deal. In either case, the soybeans caper had one undisputed result: the confirmation of the Hunt brothers' reputation as black knights of the nation's commodities markets. Though they did not know it then, that reputation would soon come back to haunt them.

At the same time that they were stirring up the silver and soybeans markets, Bunker and Herbert were making less publicized but no less controversial names for themselves in the oil business. Here, again, much of their strategy revolved around the "cash squeeze" resulting from their heavy (and nonincome-producing) investment in silver. Though the Hunt brothers were far from broke, they did not have the ready cash to get into the sort of $100-million-per-year drilling programs they wanted to get into. Consequently, Bunker and Herbert decided to do something no family member had done since H. L. Hunt broke up with Pete Lake back in the mid-1930s: take on outside investors. Among those they solicited were CB radio magnate Andy Andros, a prominent Philadelphia investment banking firm, and the German company Norddeutsche Vermogensanlage. In most cases, the individual investors went in on a well-by-well basis and paid one-third of the costs of a particular well for one-quarter of the proceeds, a typical oil-business arrangement called a "step-up." The German group, however, put up $50 million for a fifty-fifty exploratory drilling partnership.

The Hunt brothers also raised a few million more in oil-drilling funds by forming an oil-business subsidiary of Hunt International Resources (the former Great Western United), which they called Impel. Since the Hunts were 60-percent owners of the publicly held parent corporation, each dollar Impel spent was 60 cents their own and 40 cents that of the other stockholders.

Unfortunately, the famous Hunt luck did not seem to rub off on all the Hunt brothers' nonfamily partners and investors. The Andros group drilled an estimated twenty dry holes. The German group drilled about forty. There were angry mutterings from some of the investors and suspicions that the brothers might be holding out their best deals. One or two of the investors even threatened to file suit. When the Hunts suddenly began to hit a few wells, the grumbling subsided but the bad blood remained. Impel, the publicly held company, did not fare well either. Its first-year loss from drilling operations was $6.7 million. Its second year loss was even higher.

Even those critical of the Hunts marveled at the brothers' willingness to take big risks and drill for oil in exotic and difficult places. Though Hunt Energy was a family operation to the core, it and the companies affiliated with it were always in the vanguard of the industry, always drilling deeper and going after bigger fields than any other independent operators in the world. Penrod Drilling, for example, was constantly adding new rigs in an expansion program that would eventually bring the company's total fleet to over 90 strong. In addition to operating 37 rotary land rigs in the United States and several offshore jack-up rigs in the Gulf of Mexico, Penrod also commanded 5 semisubmersible offshore rigs used for drilling in the hostile waters of the North Sea, off the coast of New Zealand, and in the Mediterranean and the Persian Gulf. Larger and sturdier than the jack-up rigs, these semisubmersible units did not have legs that reached to the ocean floor, but semisubmersible ballasts that held the drilling platform in place. Costing upward of $50 million apiece, these rigs could function in water over half a mile deep and drill wells as deep as 17,000 feet below the ocean floor. The going rental for Penrod's offshore rigs was $50,000 to $60,000 per day, a figure that multiplied to give the Hunts an annual gross income of over half a billion dollars from Penrod alone. But according to former insiders and the public record, the Hunt brothers were easy to deal with only when things were going their way. When things turned against them, they sometimes threatened to sue or failed to pay up on time. For example, when the New Zealand government considered charging a $3-per-barrel energy tax on any production found offshore, Bunker threatened to file a $100-million lawsuit and the proposal was dropped. When a venture with Dome Petroleum in Canada's far-northern Beaufort Sea resulted in a $36-million dry-hole bill for the 1976 drilling season, the Hunts simply refused to pay. In March of 1977, Dome filed suit for the $36 million. The Hunts eventually managed to settle the Dome suit out of court, but in order to pay the drilling bill, they had to sell off half of their one-half interest to Gulf Oil. The sale proved a costly one. Dome subsequently made a huge oil well in the Beaufort Sea. Though the inaccessibility of the area meant that actual production would be many years away, the field's potential was gauged to be worth billions of dollars. By selling part of their interest, the Hunts gave up part of their share in that expected bonanza.

Of course, like their father before them, Bunker and Herbert did enjoy their share of the Hunt luck. In early 1976, after six years of preparatory work, Placid's enormous North Sea gas discovery finally came on stream. Production that first year was 193 million cubic feet per day, or the rough equivalent of $140 million per year in gross income, and that was gauged to be perhaps half of the field's full yearly potential. Though Placid had invested an estimated $360 million in the North Sea, it appeared likely that the field would pay out in less than three more years. From that time forward, the first-family trusts would have another incredible bonanza on their hands.

The Hunt brothers also had good luck back in the United States. In 1977, a consortium of Hunt companies drilled into the 22,000-foot-deep Tuscaloosa sand in Louisiana on a lease called (appropriately) Profit Island and found oil and gas deposits whose worth one former insider placed at nearly $1 billion. Unfortunately for Bunker and Herbert, the cash squeeze caused by their silver dealings forced them to apportion the deal not only among themselves but among the trusts of their sister Caroline and brother Hassie.

The Hunts' robber-baron image also extended to Bunker's horse racing and breeding operations. In fact, in the wake of his silver and soybeans plays, rumors began circulating around the horsy establishment that Bunker was out to corner the world blood stock market. The rumors came backed by a certain amount of hard evidence. By the late 1970s, Bunker claimed to own 500 to 600 horses worldwide, but associates placed the true size of his stable in the 800-to 1,000-horse range. Because he was becoming well known as an extraordinarily big buyer, he was thus becoming a source of great anxiety for other breeders. Bunker bought many of his horses under the names of friends and business associates. (At the famous Keeneland, Kentucky, horse sale, for example, he made purchases in the name of A. J. Brodsky, his silver broker, and in the name of his friend C. W. Smith.) Often Bunker would simply lend his friends the money to buy the horses, then take ownership or control of the horse after the sale. On occasions when he was selling, Bunker sometimes wound up as a silent partner in the syndicate that purchased the horse. This was the case, for example, in 1976, when a Bunker Hunt–owned colt by Triple Crown–winner Secretariat fetched a world record price for an unraced colt. Bunker ostensibly sold the colt to a Canadian syndicate, but wound up a few days later with some $500,000 worth of the syndicate himself.

Bunker's secret trading practices alarmed the horsy establishment even more. By buying under assumed names and buying back his own horses, Bunker was building a monopoly on blood lines, inflating the prices of the thoroughbreds, and generally giving the horse world a bad name. Or so the establishment believed. In a move aimed directly at Bunker Hunt, the Keeneland Association, governors of Kentucky's most prestigious horse sales, introduced new rules for identifying buyers designed to "enable us to get away from the fictitious names on the sales summary which leave a bad taste in everyone's mouth." (The French racing establishment also passed a rule aimed at Bunker which required owners who raced in France to stable their horses in France as opposed to places like England and Ireland, where Bunker kept most of his mounts.) Snubbed socially by the established breeders, Bunker was criticized by the racing press and deprived of the prestigious Eclipse Award title of "Horseman of the Year" despite breeding and racing exploits that most objective observers felt were clearly deserving of it. But like him or not, the horsy establishment had to deal with Bunker: he had too many fine horses to be ignored. As *Washington Post* turf writer Gerald Strine observed, "When Hunt used to buy from the established breeders, they didn't mind his ways. But now that they have to buy from *him,* they do mind."

One of Bunker's few noncontroversial investments in the late 1970s was his participation in George Steinbrenner's syndicate to buy the New York Yankees. Usually content to leave investing in sports enterprises to Lamar, Bunker remained in the syndicate only a short time and then sold out.

Like their late father, both Bunker and Herbert displayed double-sided personalities. They were one way in business situations, another way in non-business situations. Though hardly in the Mafia's league for toughness, they sometimes seemed to make a special point of showing that they were no pushovers. Just as H. L. Hunt had run Hunt Oil with the help of a former FBI agent, Bunker and Herbert ran Hunt Energy with the help of Tom Whitaker, a former FBI agent who had investigated the losses and alleged embezzlements at HLH Products. They also paid their employees relatively low salaries considering the multimillion-dollar deals they were constantly making. In fact, the highest nonfamily salary of record in the Hunt organization was only $125,000, with most top men earning much less. Paranoid that their employees were constantly trying to steal from them, the Hunts cracked down on everyone from suspected paper-clip thieves to suspected executive self-dealers. When a secretary was caught stealing less than $1,000 worth of items, the

Hunts pressed criminal charges and had her sent to prison. When Bunker's aide Bill Bledsoe resigned after thirteen years with the Hunts citing conflict of interest, the Hunts filed a nasty civil suit against him and unsuccessfully tried to press criminal charges. Thereafter, the Hunts required executives to sign an agreement not to make outside investments in any areas in which the Hunts might have an interest, and to submit their annual income tax returns to an independent audit.

Though reputed to have eyes for the ladies themselves, the Hunt brothers insisted that their employees be strictly faithful to their wives. In fact, when Herbert got word that a part-time consultant was philandering with someone else's wife, he dispatched a private eye to follow the man. (As it turned out, the episode degenerated into a replay of the Keystone Cops, with the cuckolded husband and the private detective chasing the consultant through a department store with a gun waving and department-store security in an uproar.) When asked why he took so strong a measure, Herbert replied that he did not want people working for him who played around.

But even as the Hunt brothers showed a hard-ass attitude in business, their other side could be quite charming, childlike, charitable, and, in the most oft-used phrase to describe them, "surprisingly down-to-earth" in nonbusiness situations. In fact, while Herbert quietly continued to give his time to the Boy Scouts, Presbyterian Hospital, and Highland Park Presbyterian Church, Bunker made international headlines in early 1977 by agreeing to help raise $1 billion for Here's Life, an affiliate of Bill Bright's Campus Crusade for Christ. Bunker then put his money where his mouth was by pledging over $10 million of his own cash to Here's Life. Brother Herbert chipped in another $1 million of his money. Later, Bunker agreed to provide $5 million in financing for the movie "Jesus" so that Here's Life could use it in its overseas crusades. Bunker and Herbert also joined their first-family siblings in giving $3.5 million toward a new spire for Highland Park Presbyterian Church in memory of their mother Lyda Bunker Hunt. While these gifts did not match the philanthropy of many other Texas millionaires, they added up to quite a bit more than the Hunt family had ever given to charity before. Eschewing the pretentiousness often associated with wealthy men, the Hunt brothers usually seemed more at home dining at some local hamburger joint than in the city's finest restaurants and, despite their propensity to deal in big sums with big-name people and corporations, almost never "put on airs." As one friend observed, Bunker was known to talk to virtually all classes of people, from the queen of England to the lowliest stable hand.

The period following H. L. Hunt's death also marked something of a political coming out for Bunker Hunt. Though still highly secretive about many of his associations, Bunker did join the John Birch Society's national council in 1976, which made his affiliation with the Birchers open for all to see. With Bunker's financial backing, which an informed source placed in the $250,000-a-year range, the Birchers attempted to modernize their image and pitch by renting space in suburban office buildings and putting together snappy audio-visual displays. Rumors persisted that the Birchers were behind all sorts of secret schemes, but the available evidence suggested the organization was primarily involved in decrying the eastern establishment–communist conspiracy and in soliciting new members.

Bunker's conspiratorial world view made him an easy prey for all sorts of paranoid theorists, spokesmen, and "educational" entrepreneurs. Requests for participation, support, and, most of all, money flowed constantly across Bunker's door. To the dismay of some more conventionally minded associates, Bunker entertained and eventually supported a number of these petitioners, even though they were only hucksters of fear. As one result, the name of Nelson Bunker Hunt began to be bandied about the dark and lonely councils of the far right in much the same way that the name of H. L. Hunt had been bandied about years before. His name was on the lips of intelligence officials, gun runners, paramilitarists, neo-Nazi watchers, and anonymous night callers. Bunker was whispered to be the secret financial angel behind almost every group from the Republican party rightward. Still others alleged he had his own right-wing paramilitary groups—his own private army—in the deserts of California. But no proof of the existence of Bunker's private army or his other supposed paramilitary involvements was forthcoming.

Although his greatest fame lay ahead of him, it was already clear by the late 1970s that Bunker Hunt was emerging as the successor to his father's myth. He was a character no novelist could invent: the very embodiment of the Texas-rich legend and yet, at the same time, a conglomerate of contradiction that defied the usual stereotypes. A tightwad like his late father, he wore cheap suits and searched for fallen change in seat cushions as if he were looking for the largest silver vein. But he also committed himself to such unconventional projects as an expedition to find Noah's Ark and a venture in manufacturing two passenger helicopters that literally never got off the ground. He was photographed with the queen of England and did business with heads of state all over the world, but he remained downhome enough to talk with horse trainers and ranch hands as if he were their next-door neighbor. Because, as one friend put it, "he just likes characters," he was known to associate with all sorts of promoters, hucksters, prophets of doom, and even an occasional reputed Mafioso, including one well-known gambler with whom he considered buying a cruise ship to convert into a floating gambling casino.

Capable of bumbling such simple tasks as counting a few hundred dollars' change or making one-way airline reservations, he often resembled an overstuffed teddy bear or an overgrown good ol' boy. He also had a sense of humor. When a *Sports Illustrated* writer asked him why he departed from his usual attire to don a morning coat and top hat for the English Derby, he replied, "I guess it's a case of 'monkey see, monkey do.' "

Time and again, Bunker echoed the almost wacky anti-Semitism formerly attributed to his father. He told one reporter, for example, that he was not prejudiced against Jews, but added, "They are a little different, like a Chinaman or whatever is different; you do have to say that." One of those differences, in Bunker's view, was intelligence. He definitely believed that Jews were smarter than everyone else and was not above using their smarts when it was to his business advantage. As he told one associate: "Never look a gift-Jew in the mouth." Despite such retrograde sentiments, one of Bunker's best friends in Dallas was M. B. Rudman, a flamboyant Jewish oilman who wore flashy clothes and plumed hats and ran an exercise ranch often populated by attractive young ladies.

Strangely enough, Bunker also harbored a prejudice against Phi Beta Kappas. He once told a business associate that he was leery of hiring Phi Beta Kappas because, "they all turn into communists." Bunker's prejudice on this score turned out to be particularly ironic when one of his daughters graduated from college magna cum laude and Phi Beta Kappa.

Bunker's most obvious excess was food. According to one family member, the weight on his 5-foot 11-inch frame ballooned to 300 pounds, but he continued to indulge in cheeseburgers, chocolate milk, pies, and, most of all, ice cream. Yet despite his hefty size and his tendency to be a heavy sleeper, he was full of energy and was remarkably light on his feet; he tried (with varying success) to maintain a regimen of jogging and racquetball, and occasionally visited the Golden Door "fat farm" in Escondido, California.

Although he sometimes came off as a fat, squinty-eyed bumbler, he was sharp and crafty and gifted with the same natural mathematical mind his father had. He could, for example, reel off the bloodlines and racing statistics of his horses and the depth and production figures of his oil wells as if he were reading from a book. He also had extraordinary bursts of creative vision. "Bunker has flashes just like the old man used to have," observed one family member. "Sometimes he's brilliant. The rest of the time you wonder whether he's really there with you or not."

Bunker naturally shied from comparisons to his late father. "I never had any ambitions to top my father, because he was a phenomenon," Bunker said in one interview. "Of all the fellows I ever met, he was the smartest." But at the same time that he claimed "money never really meant anything to me," he added that his chief goal was "to do well to make a profit, because that's how you judge success or failure in life, in business." Much like his father, Bunker regarded money as important not so much for the luxuries it could buy, but because money was "how they keep the score." When a reporter asked if the Hunts had entered the soybeans market because they thought the trading action was "great fun" and "enjoyed playing the game," Bunker answered with a succinct "maybe."

With the exception of Herbert, who worked more closely with his older brother than ever, the rest of the first-family siblings tended to stay out of Bunker's big deals, especially his speculative ventures like soybeans and silver. Despite invitations from his brothers to join them more actively in the oil business, Lamar remained largely preoccupied with his sports and entertainment enterprises and his art collecting. Caroline and Margaret left their interests mostly in the care of husbands and sons. At the same time, though, the interlocking boards of directors of the first-family trusts kept all five active siblings dependent on each other. Often, the signatures of each of the first-family children were needed to complete even the most routine lease assignments. As a practical matter, the entities owned by the first-family trusts, especially giant Placid Oil Company, were not run at "arm's length," as the Hunts sometimes publicly claimed, but, according to several present and former insiders, were closely controlled by the Hunts personally.

The formal organization of Hunt Energy reflected one aspect of the family pecking order. Though Bunker and Herbert were chairman of the board and president, Margaret, Caroline, and Lamar were on the board of directors. There was no doubt that Bunker, the family's oldest active male, was the boss in terms of general operations. As one top employee remarked at the time, "I am amazed by the leadership Bunker shows around his brothers Herbert and Lamar. They more or less accept the leadership, and Bunker obligingly takes the role as the big ol' chubby bear that he is and tells the others what to do." But on the matters of most importance, especially big deals concerning the jointly owned Placid Oil Company, all the first-family members had their say. In these instances, Margaret Hunt Hill, the oldest of all the first family children, often acted as the real chairman of the board of the family. As one insider observed, "When she took the floor, they listened to her very obediently, and even Bunker and Herbert were quiet."

Still, there was some obvious resentment of Margaret on the part of her younger brothers. Bunker and Herbert seemed to believe that Margaret was getting too old and too conservative in her business ideas, and was intent on giving the other members of the family a hard time. As another insider observed, family meetings tended to follow a basic pattern: "Bunker says, 'I know how it is; it's like this.' Margaret says, 'No, it's like this.' Herbert says, 'No, it's like Bunker says; I took notes.' Lamar says, 'Why do we always have to go through this?' And Caroline doesn't say anything."

Despite their internal differences, one of the first family's strongest traits was the ability to submerge disagreements into a solidly united front against outsiders. The first family was particularly solid in its stand against two other families: the Rockefellers and the second Dallas family of H. L. Hunt. Though an outsider might see many similarities—a powerful patriarch, a family history intertwined with American history, a surname synonymous with money itself —the Hunts could only see the differences between themselves and the Rockefellers. To them, the Rockefellers represented the opposite of everything worth making money for, the epitome of the corrupt and conspiratorial eastern establishment, the social and political antithesis of the Hunt family. The first family, like H. L. Hunt before them, blamed the Rockefellers publicly and privately for everything from Bunker's expulsion from Libya to the unseemly drift of American politics. As one of the first-family wives commented to a friend on the subject of the Rockefellers, "The only thing we have in common is taxes." The first family often seemed to wish the same was true of themselves and the second family, from whom they continued to keep their distance, save for the "bridge" between them in the person of Randy Kreiling.

Ironically, the one area in which the first family actually surpassed their late father was in making money. By the late 1970s, Placid Oil Company had production placed by insiders at the equivalent of 100,000 barrels per day, annual gross revenues of more than $350 million, and oil and gas reserves estimated to be worth upward of $4 billion. And Placid was just the largest of a vast array of assets the Hunts controlled. There was also Penrod Drilling, whose assets were easily worth $500 million. There were family real-estate holdings worth almost $1 billion. There were 55 million ounces of silver, vast coal leases, and an assortment of miscellaneous enterprises ranging from the sugar refinery and the Shakey's Pizza Parlor chain owned by Hunt International Resources to Lamar's soccer team and a company that made dimmer switches. Divided among roughly 150 corporations, partnerships, trusts, and individual accounts under the Hunt Energy umbrella, these interests provided employment for over 8,000 people. All told, the value of the Hunts' assets was in the $6-billion to $8-billion range.

Few other non-Arab families were even in the same league. The Mellons of Pittsburgh had huge stakes in Gulf Oil, the Mellon Bank, and Alcoa, and these corporations were worth tens of billions more than the Hunt family fortune. The Rockefellers, likewise, owned great stakes in Exxon and the Chase Manhattan Bank, the country's largest corporation and one of its largest banks. But both the Mellon wealth and the Rockefeller wealth were diffused over several generations. Recent biographers of the two families gauged the Rockefellers' and the Mellons' personal wealth to be in the $5-billion range. In addition to being greater, the Hunt wealth was still concentrated in the second generation. And thanks to the ever-escalating prices of oil and real estate, the Hunts' assets were growing more valuable all the time. As one Hunt family attorney observed, "The children of H. L. Hunt are richer than their old man ever was."

"Given the choice between luck and intelligence," Ray Hunt liked to say, "always take luck."

Ray's line was the property of his late father, but Ray kept it alive right on through the late 1970s by quoting it frequently. Ironically, Ray was never presented with the opportunity of having to make a choice between luck and intelligence—he had both, as he quickly showed. In early 1976, for example, some representatives of Sabine Corp., an oil firm, came to the Hunt family offices trying to sell a 15-percent interest in a British North Sea drilling deal spearheaded by Mesa Petroleum. The Sabine people stopped at Bunker Hunt's office first. But Bunker was out, so the Sabine men decided to show their deal to young Ray. Ray snapped it up—for Hunt Oil, not Hunt Energy.

"In the space of one week, we bought in and were drilling," Ray boasted later.

The price for Hunt's 15-percent interest was a real bargain—only $50,000. The risk was well worth taking. In the spring of 1977, the first well came in.

It was a whopper. Total potential reserves in the field were estimated to be as much as 500 million barrels, of which 15 percent or an estimated 75-million barrels would belong to Hunt Oil. Although this oil was still in the earth, not to mention under the cold North Sea, it was in many ways far better than U.S. greenbacks in the bank, for the price of oil kept rising and dollars kept shrinking. As oil prices spiraled up to $12 and then to over $20 and $30 per barrel in the coming years, Hunt Oil's share of the North Sea find rose in value, too. The more conservative estimates placed the Hunt interest at $200 million. Other estimates reckoned it be worth potentially as much as $1 billion. Veteran oilmen inside and outside the Hunt organization were amazed. The North Sea find had more than doubled the reserves of Hunt Oil Company. And this was basically Ray's first international oil venture.

"Damn it," grumbled one old wildcatter, "he's got his father's luck."

Although he did not have the same kind of eccentric genius his father and half brothers sometimes demonstrated, Ray showed a steadier, more reliable kind of smarts. He liked taking big risks in business, but he also liked to take reasonable steps to reduce his risks. He was not the type to invent a cosmic scheme to corner the world supply of some essential commodity, but he was not likely to get himself in expensive legal battles with government agencies either. Ray believed that the rules did apply to him. He also believed that the best way to build his company was to move decisively but carefully.

Ray's style immediately became apparent in the way he modernized Hunt Oil Company after his half brothers split off to form Hunt Energy. Right off the bat, Ray hired himself a brain trust of bright young men who also had top-level corporate experience. The foremost of these was Walter Humann, a former LTV executive who became a vice president of Hunt Oil. Humann and others like him helped Ray consolidate the second family's diverse operations —oil and gas, the remnants of H. L. Hunt's old drugs and cosmetics company, various timber and farm properties, and Ray's real-estate interests—under a better organized corporate umbrella. The whiz kids also introduced modern methods of management and operating efficiency. Thanks to this influx of fresh faces, the once-geriatric offices of Hunt Oil Company began to hum with a vibrant new energy.

At the same time, Ray did not discard all of the old organization just for the sake of change. General counsel George Cunyas, who was only in his late forties when H. L. Hunt died, remained on board as Ray's legal adviser, too. A variety of older and equally trusted Hunt Oil employees, many of them men and women who had been with the Hunt organization for twenty and thirty years, also kept their jobs at Hunt Oil or got new ones under the revised organization. Ray made sure that the old-timers were properly taken care of. He picked up quite a few medical bills that were not covered by the company's medical plan, instituted a new medical-benefits plan, and had Hunt Oil begin paying for 100 percent of the employees' pension plan rather than only a part of the plan, as in his father's day. Ray also raised the overall salary scale from its antiquated level to a more reasonable range. Hunt Oil did not become the place to get rich quick, but top executives began to earn upward of $100,000 per year rather than $20,000 or $30,000 per year, as in his father's day. Not surprisingly, H.L.'s youngest son quickly began to win the admiration and allegiance of the people who worked for him.

Ray's best move, in the opinion of both veterans and newcomers, was getting Hunt Oil Company back into the oil business. In addition to jumping into the North Sea deal with Mesa Petroleum, Ray geared Hunt Oil up to buy leases of its own in the North Sea and to get oil-finding efforts rolling in the United States. He hired new geologists and new landmen, and gave Hunt Oil a decent exploration budget for the first time in years. When he took over the helm at Hunt Oil, Ray learned the company had about 100,000 acres of offshore leases. Within a few years, Ray upped the total to 1 million acres. Ray did not have the kind of money his half brothers did. He could not afford to lose $40 million on dry holes in a single shot. But like his brothers, he did have the capacity to look for oil virtually anywhere in the world. And unlike the majors, he was not hamstrung by an unwieldly corporate bureaucracy. Whenever a good deal came in, Ray's inclination was to take a piece for Hunt Oil Company if he possibly could, even when the company was already over its exploration budget. "Don't worry," he would tell his men. "If it's a good enough deal, we'll find the money to get in it."

Before long new deals and news of new discoveries were flowing through the Hunt Oil Company offices almost as fast as in H. L. Hunt's halcyon days. The old-timers could not help but get excited: Hunt Oil was playing in the big leagues again!

Ray also got Hunt Oil back into other facets of the energy game. Uranium had been one of his father's interests back in the early 1950s, but, once again, H.L. had been way ahead of his time. The energy crisis and the proliferation of nuclear power revitalized the need for uranium. Ray got Hunt Oil in on the action by cutting a deal with Dallas-based Energy Resources whereby Energy Resources would provide the uranium leases and Hunt Oil would provide high resolution drilling technology which would cut the time needed to develop the leases by 60 to 80 percent.

In addition to supervising the building of his Reunion project, Ray began getting into other big real-estate deals in the Dallas–Fort Worth area. Like the official U.S. Census takers, most developers regarded Dallas and Fort Worth, which were some thirty-two miles apart, as part of a single great regional city, which was sometimes referred to as the Metroplex. Ray liked the Fort Worth portions of the Metroplex because they had not been as fully developed as the Dallas end. Fort Worth impressed him as being a place full of potential. As a result, Ray's real-estate arm, Woodbine Investment, bought up over 2,000 acres of prime real estate in the Fort Worth area and began making plans for large future developments.

As Dallas continued its sunbelt-style boom, Ray's media interests prospered and proliferated. *D* magazine, the flagship of Southwest Media Corp., gained a monthly circulation of over 60,000 readers. Though modest in number compared to the readers of the city's two major dailies, the *D* readers represented the highest-income and highest-spending groups in the city. Softer in editorial content than many of its counterparts; *D* did its share of hard-hitting articles. But the fact that it was owned by Ray Hunt created a prima facie conflict of interest which precluded any in-depth writing about some of the biggest players in the local game—i.e., the Hunts themselves and their Dallas business, political, and religious cronies. Though Ray generally refrained from influencing specific editorial policies, he did insist that the magazine not use "four-letter words" in its articles on the grounds that he did not want his mother reading a magazine which contained such expletives. Still, the publication's prodigious advertising and circulation revenues eventually reached some $3 million per year and made *D* one of the most prosperous city magazines in the country. Under the direction of *D*'s editor-publisher Wick Allison, a young and ambitious Republican activist, Southwest Media added a new magazine called *Texas Homes* to its stable. A glossy, four-color home and gardening magazine, *Texas Homes* also prospered, achieving a monthly statewide circulation of 100,000. Allison later bought a Dallas-based classical-music radio station for the company.

Just as in the old days, Hunt Oil Company functioned as an umbrella for Ray's diverse enterprises and for all the other second-family interests. However, after the first family split off to form Hunt Energy, the setup at Hunt Oil became much simpler. Instead of servicing some 200 separate accounts, Hunt Oil now looked after less than fifty. The two main branches of the company proper were the oil and gas division, which operated under the name Hunt Oil Company, and the real-estate division, whose operating entities included Hunt Investment and Woodbine Development (the company responsible for Reunion). There was also H. L. Hunt Sales, a cosmetics manufacturer still hanging on from the bygone food division. Separate from Hunt Oil Company proper but still under its service umbrella were the second family's Secure Trusts, the grandchildren's trusts, and the individual accounts of each second-family member.

Obviously, Ray could not stay on top of the daily details of all the Hunt Oil affiliated interests. Sometimes just being executor of the estate was a full-time job. His solution was, in the words of one associate, "to manage by exception." If a major problem arose in any particular area, he would rush to attend to it. But as a rule, he kept abreast of developments through regular reports, and let his lieutenants have broad operating powers. Ray routinely spent 80 percent of his own time on the oil business. Real-estate ventures, which were his individual claim to fame, consumed only 15 percent of his schedule. The remainder he devoted to his media and miscellaneous interests.

Ray's approach clearly paid off in financial terms. Throughout the late 1970s Hunt Oil Company grew and prospered as it had back in H. L. Hunt's best days. By the end of the decade, the fifty employees who had been left to run the company's Dallas headquarters had 150 new co-workers, all of them hired under Ray's management. Hunt Oil's domestic oil reserves, which had shrunk to around $100 million worth during H. L. Hunt's flirtation with the food business, were now worth over $300 million. The company's domestic production climbed from about $12 million worth per year to over $100 million per year. The total worth of the company's oil, real-estate, and miscellaneous assets was just under $400 million, *not counting the North Sea.* If the potential value of the North Sea reserves was figured in, Hunt Oil was worth $1 billion or more. Rising oil prices and the famous Hunt luck played a large part in Hunt Oil's success, but so did the leadership and management skill of Ray Hunt.

Besides running Hunt Oil, Ray also had to deal with the administration of his father's estate. As his split with the first family and Frania Tye Lee's recently filed lawsuit attested, this was no routine assignment. But in addition to these internal family matters, Ray also faced a threat from the tax men. Under the will and Texas community property laws, one half of Hunt's estate passed tax-free to Ruth. But the other half was subject to a 77-percent inheritance tax, 16 percent of which went to the state of Texas and the rest of which went to the IRS. The inventory of the H. L. Hunt estate that Ray's lawyers submitted to the Dallas probate court listed total Texas holdings of only $55,609,265. Of that amount, a little over $5.5 million worth was real estate, household furnishings, Mount Vernon (which was valued at $500,000), and ten vehicles, including Hunt's Oldsmobile 88, Ruth's Lincoln, a Buick Riviera, and a 1974 Chevrolet pick-up truck. The remainder of the estate consisted of Hunt's 80-percent stock interest in Hunt Oil Company, which Ray's attorneys valued at only $50 million, or slightly less than half the worth the best insider estimates gave it at the time of Hunt's death. Based primarily on the value of Hunt Oil's reserves, this estate appraisal might have seemed shockingly low to the public, but it was about par for the course as far as estate appraisals went. It was almost certain that the IRS would come up with a figure at least twice as high when it made its evaluation. Ray's task would be to try to work out a settlement somewhere in the middle.

In the meantime, Ray determined to solve his family tax problem by recapitalizing Hunt Oil Company. He hired the New York investment banking firm of Morgan Stanley to do an analysis of the company, then set about revamping Hunt Oil's stock structure. The net effect was to ensure that future appreciation in the value of the company would not flow to Ruth Hunt, who had inherited most of Hunt Oil's stock in H.L.'s will, but to entities controlled by Ray, June, Helen, and Swanee.

Even as he attempted great business and civic deeds, Ray tried to live what he called an "average" family life "despite the peculiar spelling of my last name." Upon taking over the presidency of Hunt Oil, he began to travel in the company of a bodyguard, a former Secret Service agent. He also kept his own home phone number out of the telephone book and worked to keep the names of his four young children out of the newspapers. But most other aspects of Ray's life remained the same. He continued to live in a spacious but hardly palatial home in North Dallas. In keeping with his father's example, he did not spend much on himself. He still wore neat but moderately priced business suits. He drove a '73 Buick for four years, selling it only when it was clearly on its last few miles. He compared the sale of his old car to "losing an old friend." He replaced it with an Oldsmobile.

With memberships in Dallas's most exclusive dance clubs, Ray was already far more sociable than his old man had ever been. But he did not become a high liver or a big party giver. A confirmed nonsmoker, he was also a nondrinker save for an occasional glass of wine. He kept in shape by jogging 2 1/2 miles per day at the Aerobic Center in Dallas. He attended Royal Lane Baptist Church on Sundays and found relaxation in hunting for wild game and being with his wife and kids.

Meanwhile, Ray began to get the kind of press not even a Hunt could buy. In an article on the Hunt family shortly after H. L. Hunt's death, *Business Week* portrayed Ray as *the* young comer of Dallas and the new breath of sophistication in the family empire. *Time,* in a story in the summer of 1977, played up Ray's civic-mindedness and the success of the Reunion project. The magazine entitled its story "The Nice Hunt," an appellation clearly implying a contrast between Ray and his father and half brothers. Born of a man who preached but seldom practiced the old American dream of uniting Christianity and entrepreneurial capitalism, Ray, the second-generation illegitimate son, was fulfilling that promise far better than any of his relatives past or present. He was not only financially successful, but also civic-minded, fair, courteous, kind, loyal, and true.

Ironically, the only doubt that Ray's admirers seemed to have about him was whether he might be too nice a guy. Was he really tough enough to handle the often nasty problems involved in running his father's empire? As one Dallas businessman told *Time* magazine in 1977, "He's the last one out of the elevator and the last one walking down the hall. But I'm not sure he can twist arms or kick butts the way he'll have to in order to run a good business."

Ray's mother and sisters also exemplified the "nice Hunt" image. One of Ruth Hunt's first acts after her husband's death was to donate a $1-million wing to the Baylor University Medical Center hospital in memory of H. L. Hunt. Under Hunt's will, Ruth, not Ray or his sisters, was the actual holder of the 80-percent stake in Hunt Oil. Though she left business matters to her son Ray, she was technically the richest member of the second family. But she did not all of a sudden put on airs. Her greatest luxuries were driving a Lincoln Continental Mark IV and going on trips to the Wyoming ranch in the Hunt Oil jet. Short and plump, she still had the sparkling eyes and ready smile of her youth. Only fifty-five years old at the time Hunt died, she had a long life expectancy and apparently intended to devote much of it to continuing her active work in and support of the First Baptist Church.

Ruth's daughter June, the only unmarried one of the second-family children, also carried the Hunt religious banner. Continuing her career as a Christian speaker and entertainer, she kept up a busy schedule of concert dates and public appearances, including work with the Billy Graham crusade. Like her father before her, June also tried her hand as an author. In 1975, her first book, *Above All Else,* was published by Fleming H. Revell Company of New Jersey. A religious autobiography, the book recounted incidents in June's childhood and religious-work career that illustrated her theme of "allowing God to *be* God in our lives." June dedicated her book "To my father, from whom I gained many insights which I didn't realize I was learning at the time."

Other than the inheritance tax collector, the two Dallas families of H. L. Hunt faced only one main obstacle to the enjoyment of their lives and fortune: each other. What friendly initiatives there were mostly seemed to come from the second family's side. Having testified in support of Bunker and Herbert at the wiretapping trial in Lubbock, Ruth tried to promote further good will between the two groups back in Dallas. Although H. L. Hunt had specifically willed her the Mount Vernon house, she made it clear that she still considered Mount Vernon home for both families. She opened up the place for social gatherings on traditional family occasions like Christmas and Thanksgiving and for special occasions like the tea she gave in honor of Herbert's daughters Barbara and Libby the year they made their debuts. Ruth also shared another treasured family property: the vast Hoodoo Ranches in Wyoming, where members of both the first and second families loved to go camping and hunting. In doing all this, Ruth was in effect attempting to play mother to both groups. Given the circumstances, this was virtually impossible, but her efforts were appreciated, especially by some of the younger, warmer-hearted members of the first-family clan. Said one: "Ruth tries."

None of the first-family children really responded in kind. They gladly accepted some of Ruth's overtures (especially sharing the ranch), but they did not make equivalent gestures in return, in part because many felt that all of it was in some form or fashion rightfully theirs. Much of the first family's longstanding resentment against the second family was really resentment against H. L. Hunt, but that did not make it go away with the old man's death. On the other hand, the first family did not burn all their bridges with the second. Bunker and Herbert continued to maintain their business relationship with second-family son-in-law Randy Kreiling, whom they regarded as a smart commodities trader and, therefore, a worthy fellow. But Kreiling, who still often ended up playing the role of peacemaker when testy moments arose, was really their only positive link to the second family. In public, both sides continued to deny that there was any kind of feud between them or ever had been and offered their widely publicized show of unity at the Lubbock trial as proof. But they could not hide the fact that they had basically gone their separate ways ever since. As one of Ray's sisters later admitted to a reporter, "We only see each other at weddings and at trials."

Oddly enough, one of the few nonbusiness things that bound the two families together was the common fate of having to combat lingering accusations about the Kennedy assassination. One such set of accusations was a movie called *Executive Action,* which blamed the assassinations of both

Kennedy and King on a crusty Texas millionaire in a white planter's suit. Another came from a Dutch journalist who claimed a dead friend had confessed to being the contact man between H. L. Hunt and Lee Harvey Oswald. Another was spawned by the statement of embittered former aide John Curington, who claimed to have seen Marina Oswald, wife of Kennedy's alleged murderer, in Hunt's office on the Saturday following the assassination. Still another was prompted by the appearance of a "Dear Mr. Hunt" letter signed "Lee Harvey Oswald." And another was started by a Soviet journal, which claimed that Hunt-family-financed killers shot President Kennedy, then escaped through drainholes in the street.

Significantly, none of the theories stood up for long under close scrutiny. The drainholes in the Soviet theory, for example, were only eight inches in diameter, hardly large enough to afford an escape hatch. The "Dear Mr. Hunt" letter was a many-generation Xerox copy, the authenticity of which was impossible to verify and easy to doubt. The story placing Marina Oswald in Hunt's office after the assassination was denied by Mrs. Oswald. The sensational story put out by the Dutch journalist was subsequently recanted by that very same journalist, who claimed he had made a mistake in his earlier report of his dead friend's words. Only *Executive Action* at least claimed to be fiction, although fiction based on real events. Through it all, the two Dallas families of H. L. Hunt kept on issuing denials that any of the Hunts had anything to do with the assassinations. And for what they were worth, these mutual denials were about the only points the first and second families seemed to agree upon.

The Hunts' uneasy truce ended with Randy Kreiling's downfall in the summer of 1976. The cause of Randy's demise was the same thing that had been his claim to fame: commodities dealings. Specifically, Randy was accused of using his knowledge of the first family's positions and his access to the second family's money to make trades that helped Randy Kreiling but did not help the Hunts. Whether or not Randy was actually guilty of any wrongdoing, the end result was clear: he lost his job with Bunker and Herbert. Later, Randy was divorced by his wife Helen. According to one insider, Ray Hunt did not approve or benefit from his brother-in-law's controversial trades and even took a strong hand in Kreiling's ouster. However, the episode only rekindled the first family's resentment toward the second, and before long the two groups were locked in another all-out fight.

This time, the fight centered on one of the few things that still brought the two sides together in any form or fashion: Hunt Oil Company. Although they no longer shared Hunt Oil's offices or serviced their many companies under its umbrella, the first family retained the 18-percent share of Hunt Oil stock that H. L. Hunt had transferred to their trusts before he died. The true value of this stock was itself destined to be a major point of disagreement, but there was no question that it was peanuts, mere table scraps, compared to the rest of the first-family interests. But they acted like protesting that 18 percent was the most important thing in the world.

They also acted as if their half brother could do nothing right. Under the first-family caretakership (after the food scandal but before H.L.'s death), Hunt Oil had languished while they concentrated their best efforts on their own wholly owned companies like Placid and Penrod. Under Ray's leadership, the company appeared to be well on the way to new prosperity, especially with the discovery in the North Sea. Still, the first family criticized Ray's management at every turn. They complained about the price Hunt Oil got for selling a farm in south Texas. They complained that Ray had more experience in the real-estate business than he did in the oil business and really didn't know what he was doing.

But the first family made its most bitter complaints about Hunt Oil's involvement in Ray's highly touted Reunion project. According to the story the first family told, Hunt Oil's involvement allegedly began in late 1974, about the time of H. L. Hunt's death, when Ray's project supposedly ran into serious financial difficulties. Faced with the prospect of losing all he had worked for in the downtown redevelopment, Ray turned to Hunt Oil for a loan. Later he sold the company a tract of land adjacent to the project as an investment. Bunker and his siblings, who owned land in other parts of downtown Dallas, did not take kindly to these alleged transactions. They complained that Ray's "Hyatt Regency," as they called it, was not a particularly good investment. They also complained that the rate of interest Ray would be paying was only 2.5 percent per year.

Ray's side of the story was much different. He insisted that Reunion had not faced serious financial problems and that there was no loan from Hunt Oil Company. What he had done was collapse Hunt Investment, a formerly separate real-estate venture, into Hunt Oil Company proper, but this was merely a reorganizational move. Reunion still stood on its own financial feet.

Whoever was right, the dispute over the Reunion matter proved to be the last straw as far as the first family was concerned. Bunker and his siblings demanded that Ray buy out their 18-percent interest in Hunt Oil so that the two families could separate once and for all. Ray balked. He claimed that he could not afford a buy-out at the time. In addition, Ray still did not know how much inheritance tax the estate would have to pay on its Hunt Oil stock. All he knew was that the IRS had recently refused to accept the oil-reserve figures the estate had submitted. He further pointed out that it would be hard to sell shares in a private company like Hunt Oil, especially minority shares, and suggested that the first family's 18-percent interest was really only worth about 12 percent. They retorted that their 18-percent stake was worth at least that and probably more precisely because it was a minority interest. Now more enraged than ever, they threatened to show their half brother exactly what they meant by filing a minority shareholder's suit if he did not come to terms.

The first-family war council convened in mid-February of 1977 inside the Hunt Energy Corporation conference room on the twenty-fifth floor of the First National Bank building. Outside the sky was lucent, and all of downtown Dallas fairly sparkled in the wind. But inside the conference room, there was an air of impending battle. Those present knew this was not just another

intrafamily spat. For in addition to summoning Tom Hunt and three trusted
aides, Bunker and Herbert had also brought in an outside lawyer they employed only on very special occasions: former Texas governor and perennial
presidential candidate John B. Connally. With Connally were two top men
from Vinson and Elkins, the giant Houston law firm in which he was a partner.

According to one of those present at the meeting, it was Connally who
best expressed the Hunt brothers' feelings in the process of giving them his
counsel. One course of action, Connally suggested, would be to tell the second
family that if they did not accept the first family's terms, the first family would
take them to the IRS over Hunt Oil's reserve estimates.

"If they want to play hardball," Connally reportedly declared, "we can
play hardball."

Connally's suggestion was typical big-time-Texas-lawyer talk, "saber rat-
tlin'," as it was known in the profession. Going to the IRS could easily backfire
on Bunker and Herbert. They were hardly in a position to be running to the
government when the government was usually running after them. But the fact
that they now seemed to consider Connally's suggestion seriously was a measure of how far their relationship with the second family had deteriorated.

As it turned out, Connally and the Hunts decided to hold off playing
"hardball" in favor of first attempting a "softball" solution. Connally offered
to meet with Ray himself to try to work out a settlement face to face. Despite
warnings from friends that going one on one with the likes of John Connally
would put him at a great disadvantage in the negotiations, Ray decided to
accept the offer.

The talks proved worthwhile. In December of 1977, after much haggling,
the two families reached a settlement. Under its terms, Ray agreed to transfer
a specified cluster of Hunt Oil properties (some oil leases, a pipeline in North
Dakota, and Florida timberlands) into a new subsidiary to be called Prosper
Energy. The first family agreed to then exchange their 18-percent stock in Hunt
Oil for full ownership of the properties in Prosper—provided, of course, they
could get a ruling from the IRS that the Prosper deal qualified as a tax-free
spinoff.

Unfortunately, this settlement did not end the Hunts' strife. For just as
they worked out the Prosper deal, they were faced with another, potentially
more explosive, family problem: the news that Frania Tye Lee's lawsuit appeared destined to go to trial after all.

Once again, the two Dallas families fell into bitter disagreement. The
argument was exacerbated by the first family's claim that Ray did not inform
them of their potential liability until a few weeks before the trial. Ray denied
the allegation. However, there was no question that the Hunts' liability was
substantial. Although Mrs. Lee's lawsuit was technically directed against Ray,
the estate's executor, and Hunt Oil Company, the holding company that
sheltered the second family's share of the estate, the community properties that
Mrs. Lee sought formed the basis for all the Hunt fortune. Before he died, H.L.
had transferred the bulk of the choice properties out of Hunt Oil and into
Placid Oil Company, which was owned by the first family through their Loyal

Trusts. By the time of the Shreveport trial, the gross annual income of Placid Oil was substantially greater than the total worth of all Hunt Oil. The first family feared that if Mrs. Lee beat Ray she might come after their own trusts.

In addition, the first family saw the specters of two old enemies, former Hunt Oil security chief Paul Rothermel and former aide John Curington, both listed as potential witnesses on Frania's side.

Bunker wanted a prompt out-of-court settlement for $8 million or $10 million. That way, he reasoned, Frania and her children would get what they really wanted, and all of them would avoid the embarrassment of a spectacular trial. At the same time, the first family would avoid the risk of having Frania come after their trusts if she was successful in her suit against Ray.

However, as Ray had already discovered, agreeing on a settlement was easier said than done. Frania's attorneys had set their sights on a figure in the neighborhood of $100 million. Negotiations went back and forth, but they refused to lower their demand. Ray's only alternative was to prepare to fight it out in open court and keep hoping for a breakthrough. But as 1977 drew to a close, those hopes faded rapidly. The trial was set for federal court in Shreveport on January 9, 1978, and it appeared that the judge was determined to begin on schedule.

Ray asked the first family to be there. He felt his lawyers could win the case on the law and on the facts. But he also expected that the aging Frania Lee would monopolize the sympathy of the court with her story of love and broken promises. What she had to say could be embarrassing, not just for him but for the first family and for the image of the one person they would always have in common, H. L. Hunt. It would be a tremendous help if the first and second families could show up presenting a united front, just as they had done in Lubbock with such great success.

This time, the first family balked. They still rankled with bitterness from their most recent Hunt Oil quarrels and did not feel they owed the second family anything, regardless of what had happened in the past. They regarded Frania's suit as Ray's problem: if he wanted to be executor of the estate, let him handle it. But the first family also realized that if Ray botched the case, they could lose millions, too. If putting on a show of solidarity in the court-room was what it took to prevent a rape of their own fortunes, then it only made sense to put on another award-winning public performance. Thus, with plenty of grumbling, the first family acquiesced to Ray's request.

Appropriately or not, it was about this same time that Ray announced that work on his Reunion project was running well ahead of schedule and that the project would be opening in the spring, also ahead of schedule. A few nights before Christmas, Ray turned on the geodesic ball atop the 500-foot-tall Reunion Tower for the first time and saw its lights shine above the Dallas skyline like a giant electric dandelion, brighter than all the stars.

When the Hunts arrived at the courthouse in Shreveport, Frania Tye Lee was already sitting at her counsel's table with her back to the door, her old head bobbing from palsy. She was attended by an entourage of four lawyers, two female legal assistants, two of the lawyers' wives, and a very big and dangerous-looking private investigator. Her son, Hugh Lee Hunt, waited outside in the witness room. Later, two of Mrs. Lee's seventeen grandchildren, Ron Cartledge and Mark Lee, arrived for the trial. Mrs. Lee's grandsons and the relatives of her witnesses took seats in public pews interspersed among the crowd like ordinary spectators.

For Frania's side, the case of *Lee* v. *Hunt* was already a potboiler. The mystery and intrigue had begun not long after Mrs. Lee filed her suit. Frania and her son Hugh went to Florida to search for a marriage license once again. This time they had found what they were looking for—almost. A voided entry in a marriage-license receipt record book showed the names "Franklin Hunt" and "Frania Tye" for the date November 10, 1925. But no sooner had the attorneys in the case of *Lee* v. *Hunt* made certified copies of the document than someone came along and sliced the original out of the record book with a sharp-edged instrument. Along with the disappearance of the marriage record came another startling development. According to Frania's son Hugh, nearly all of his mother's photographs and 16 mm film of H. L. Hunt in the old days was stolen from Mrs. Lee's Atlanta home. But as in the case of the marriage record, no culprit was apprehended. All this had been topped off by the dramatic reappearance of Frania's former fiancé Paul Kurz. Frania had thought Kurz was dead. But investigators for the Hunts had found him in Detroit as the owner of a brick company. In an effort to get Kurz to talk openly, the Hunt investigators originally told him that Frania was dead, and had named him as a beneficiary in her will. But Kurz had discovered the truth, and had fled to Frania's camp immediately. As the Shreveport trial opened, he showed up wearing a dashing beret, an overcoat, and a thin gray mustache, a witness for the plaintiff.

The first- and second-family Hunts, true to the form they mastered in Lubbock, arrived together and went right for the special seats across from the jury box which the judge had reserved for the families of both sides. In addition to his wife, his sisters, his half brothers and half sisters, and their wives and husbands, Ray was accompanied by four attorneys who sat at the counsel's table and four more who sat scattered about in the spectators' section. He had also brought along his aide, Tom Meurer, and a bodyguard named Walt Cogler, a former Secret Service agent. While Ray conferred with his army of lawyers, Bunker, Herbert, and Lamar stood outside in the hall with cousin Tom, a potential witness for the defense, and chatted nervously about the upcoming Super Bowl and other topics. Herbert offered a theory about lawyerly attire and its effects on juries—in essence, the darker the suit, the worse the effect.

"You notice that our lawyers are wearing the darkest suits," he observed prophetically.

Fearing the worst, the first-family brothers had brought along their by-now veteran counsel Phil Hirschkop. Attired in a trench coat, a gray LBJ-style Stetson, and brown Frye boots, Hirschkop patrolled the hall, chatting with his clients and grinning half mockingly at the surroundings.

Judge Tom Stagg convened the court a little after 9:00 A.M. on opening day, and after lecturing the press that this was "not a media event," he proceeded to run his court with a stopwatch. A tall, fiftyish Nixon appointee, born and raised in Shreveport, he had informed both sides that he had another trial set for the following Wednesday and intended to have this one finished before then. A case could have been made that Stagg had no business presiding over the lawsuit. He had revealed in one of the pretrial hearings that he had previously met some of the Hunts and had married the cousin of one of Bunker's prep-school roommates. Despite this revelation, none of the attorneys moved to disqualify him, and Stagg did not disqualify himself. As the trial progressed, however, he displayed a sympathy for the aging Mrs. Lee's ordeal that more than compensated for whatever pretrial affinities he may have had for the Hunts.

Jury selection, which was completed in only half a day, produced a panel of six with two alternates who were all lower-middle or middle class: a log hauler with a fifth-grade education, a high-school basketball coach, an unemployed Louisiana Tech graduate who lived at home with his parents, two working mothers (one a secretary, the other a hospital worker), an unemployed court reporter, an unemployed secretary, and a retired bowling-alley employer.

Frania's lead counsel Wallace Hunter went right to work. A gray-haired, spindly man who moved with quick, light steps, Hunter played heart-renderingly on the old themes of love, old age, and broken promises. He began by calling his own attractive red-haired wife to the stand for a nearly theatrical reading of Martha Kreeger's deposition describing the scenes at the Hotel Adolphus and finessed his way through one witness after another until he concluded with his touching examination of the plaintiff, his client Frania Tye Lee.

Frania gave a most remarkable performance indeed. With her gray head held straight and high, she retold her version of her childhood in Buffalo, her trip to Tampa, Florida, in 1925, her meeting with "Franklin" Hunt, the early years of their "marriage" in Shreveport and Dallas, and her discovery of Hunt's other family in 1934. She then went on to recount her move to New York, Hunt's attempts to convert her to Mormonism and legal bigamy, her embarrassment in Houston, her meeting with Lyda Bunker Hunt, and the stormy scenes of her final breakup and settlement with H. L. Hunt in 1942. Frania admitted signing a statement omitting any mention of her alleged marriage to Hunt, a statement she now claimed was full of factual errors. But she said she did so only because of certain unwritten promises Hunt allegedly made at the time.

"He promised me that in his will he would name me as wife, that he married me, that they're his children, and that he would leave the same amount of funds that the first family had," she told the court. The fact that Hunt's promises could only be fulfilled in his will explained why she had waited until after his death to file suit.

Portraying herself as a faithful woman unfairly wronged, Frania seemed to elicit sympathy with every line. Most notable was her testimony about Lyda Bunker Hunt, whom she met in 1940, as she (Frania) and Hunt were breaking up for the last time.

"Hunt did a lot of the talking," Frania recalled. "Both of us were strangers. We looked each other over. I arrived at the conclusion that Mrs. Hunt was the finest woman I ever met, and that every boy and girl would love to have her as their mother."

Frania also held fast under some intense cross-examination. For example, when the Hunts' attorney pressed her about swearing to the 1942 statement omitting any mention of her alleged marriage to Hunt, she replied, "Yes, I swore, but I signed that statement to protect Mr. Hunt from a bigamy charge. That was my contribution to his life."

"You say you swore to facts that were not true?" the Hunts' counsel asked.

"Yes."

"Doesn't that bother you to do that?"

"At that time I did that for the man I loved," Mrs. Lee answered with her voice rising. "And women in love are not philosophers, nor do they know the law that well."

"They know the truth, don't they?"

"Yes, but they make a lot of sacrifices. I was thinking not only of him, but of all the children."

Frania also withstood some more oblique questioning. At one point, for example, Case asked her about a Buffalo court case styled *In Re Francis Tyburski, an Infant Requesting Appointment of a Guardian.* Filed in 1924 when Frania was twenty, documents in the case had subsequently been destroyed in the course of the court's routine old-documents destruction program. Frania claimed that she could not remember what the case involved, and her attorney quickly rose to point out that the term "infant" in those days applied to any minor under the age of twenty-one. But in the wake of Case's questioning, the courtroom was filled with murmurings about this latest mystery.

With his client as her own best witness, plaintiff attorney Hunter concentrated on corroborating Frania's testimony with the testimony of other witnesses and what documents there were available. Along the way, he managed (sometimes unwittingly) to introduce some humorous moments into an otherwise grave proceeding. One occurred when Hunter called Helen Davis to the stand. A seventy-two-year-old maid who had worked for Frania during her residence in Shreveport in the late 1920s, Mrs. Davis testified that she "always thought" Frania and Hunt were married. On cross-examination, the Hunt defense counsel asked Mrs. Davis if she could identify the woman she knew as Mrs. Hunt in the courtroom. Mrs. Davis looked around the courtroom for a moment, then asked if she could stand up to get a better view. With the judge's permission, she scanned the courtroom for a full half minute. Finally, she pointed at Mrs. Lee, who was sitting at the plaintiff's table.

"Is that her?" Mrs. Davis said, giggling with glee. "Yes, that's her right there."

The courtroom broke up with laughter.

The Hunt defense counsel went on to ask Mrs. Davis if she had ever asked Frania if she and Hunt were married.

"No, no, sir," Mrs. Davis replied.

The Hunts' lawyer then asked if Mrs. Davis had ever seen folks who were not married "stay together."

"Well, I've seen colored folks stay together," Mrs. Davis replied.

Again, the courtroom broke up with laughter.

Hunter also came armed with a couple of hard shots. One was the threat of Hunt nemesis Paul Rothermel, whom he listed on his witness roster but did not call. Another was convicted felon John Curington, who did take the stand. After declaring that he bore no grudge against the Hunts despite all that had transpired, Curington proceeded to tell the court that H.L. had once admitted privately that he had married Frania. Curington added under Hunter's questioning that H.L. had also told him that he knew he had not fathered one of Lyda's children because he had been with Frania at the time. The judge and Hunter simultaneously stopped Curington from going any further, but the damage was done.

There were some serious defects in Hunter's presentation. Not the least was the appearance of Frania's forty-three-year-old son Hugh. Hugh's voice was weak and unconvincing, his gestures characterized by too much shrugging of the shoulders. Before anyone had mentioned Frania's tryst with Paul Kurz, Hugh was asked if he had any relatives in Cleveland. "No," he replied, pausing, "at least none that I know of." The courtroom erupted in smirking laughter the judge had to declare out of order.

Despite his shortcomings, Hunter put on quite a show. He was no Racehorse Haynes. He did not pretend to be. But he did manage to make Hugh and all the other plaintiff's witnesses appear, like himself, eminently human, if slightly flawed.

Chief defense counsel Donald Case, of the prominent Dallas firm of Jackson, Walker, Winstead, Cantwell and Miller, left just the opposite impression. A squat, cigar-chomping man with a croaky voice and an abrasive questioning style, he often seemed to draw more sympathy for the other side than for his own. To the courtroom observer, the defense also suffered from an apparent lack of preparation. They failed to take Hugh's deposition until less than a month before trial. They took no depositions at all from many of the other plaintiff's witnesses and potential witnesses, missing, among others, both Curington and Rothermel. They did not research the bigamy statutes until the morning of their cross-examination of Mrs. Lee, and then asked her if she had been advised of the statute of limitations governing Texas law, even though the alleged marriage was in Florida. On top of all this, they displayed no apparent theory of the case, no clear approach to attacking Mrs. Lee's claims.

Nevertheless, Case and his team did manage to score several important points. One was Frania's admission that she and Hunt never went out socially during their nine years together in Shreveport and Dallas, and that during that time Hunt never received any mail at the house. Case also got Frania to admit that she had heard of Dad Joiner and the Dad Joiner deal, and had even taken several trips with Hunt to the east Texas field, though Frania continued to maintain that "somehow" she still did not know her "husband" was H. L. Hunt. As the plaintiff side rested and the defense began, Case was able to cast further doubt on the missing "key" to the case: the mysteriously removed marriage-license record between Frania Tye and Franklin Hunt. As brought out in testimony, Hugh and Frania had discovered a voided entry in a Tampa marriage record book shortly before the trial. But once the lawyers in the case had made certified copies of the document, someone had come along and cut the original out of the record book. Apparently believing that the entry had been made far more recently than 1925, Case was unable to have the ink dated because of the original's disappearance. But he was able to put a handwriting expert on the stand who testified that the entry was written in different hand-writing than all the other entries in that record book.

The Hunts, meanwhile, tried to look calm and hold their tongues in the face of an increasingly bad situation. Ray's sister June did the best. Maintaining an expression of supreme compassion through most of the testimony, she remarked at one recess that she just hoped "things would work out the best for everybody." Bunker, on the other hand, seemed to suffer the most difficulty keeping his emotions in check. Noticeably disgruntled during the bulk of the proceedings, he would pace nervously during the breaks, often calling Phil Hirschkop or one of his relatives aside for a conference. The low point for him and most of the family was Curington's testimony about what H.L. supposedly said about the parentage of one of Lyda's children.

"I'll say this to the press," Bunker volunteered at the next break, "Curington may not have any animosity toward me, but I sure have animosity for him."

At the noon recess, the first family would generally troop off to the local Petroleum Club or, if the weather was bad, eat in the fifth-floor courthouse cafeteria. The second family (minus Ray, who would consult with his attorneys) favored a local hamburger stand, which, during the moments of their presence, suddenly had patrons whose wealth was greater than the total deposits in all the local banks. Both Hunt families assiduously avoided occasions to interact with "the Lee people."

Hugh, on the other hand, kept trying to establish an informal rapport. Once, when court was reconvening after a recess, he positioned himself in the hall so that anyone entering the room would have to pass directly in front of him. When Bunker approached, he suddenly extended his arm to shake hands. Somewhat taken aback, Bunker quickly pumped his outstretched hand, breathed an acknowledgment, and kept walking.

At the end of the day, Hugh would emerge from the witness room and join the attorneys and their entourage in escorting his mother back to the family headquarters in the Bossier City Holiday Inn just across the river from downtown Shreveport.

The Hunts, meanwhile, would repair to the Chateau Motor Hotel down the hill from the courthouse, where they had reserved the entire fourth floor. After showering and changing into more formal attire, the two families would gather separately, then meet together to discuss the progress of the trial. Visibly impatient with the way things were going, it did not take long for Bunker to make his feelings clear. At one point, according to several bystanders, he cornered a startled Don Case and started lecturing him on the evils of smoking, hoping that it might improve his courtroom performance.

"Oxygen," Bunker stormed. "You need oxygen. You're not getting enough oxygen to your brain."

Case could only reply that he had been smoking cigars all his life.

After two days of grueling testimony and Bunker's persistent urgings, Ray finally agreed to let Hirschkop explore the possibility of an out-of-court settlement. Hirschkop took his time. The following day he arranged an informal meeting with Hunter's co-counsel Roger Fritchie, a broad-shouldered, beefy man in his mid-forties. Fritche informed Hirschkop that Frania might be willing to come down from $100 million to $25 million. Hirschkop made no counteroffer, but said he would take the notion under consideration.

Two days passed, and Hirschkop did not reply. He would simply stride in and out of the courtroom conferring with his clients and taking notes on the testimony. He kept rebuffing attempts to start the talks again. Finally, Hugh Lee's anxiety bubbled over.

"Why won't you talk to us?" he asked Hirschkop at one point in the hall outside the courtroom.

Unable to think of anything to say, Hirschkop simply ignored him.

That night the intrigue of the negotiations intensified. While the two Hunt families were dining at the Chateau Motor Hotel, Mrs. Lee's grandson Ron Cartledge discreetly sat down at an unoccupied table nearby. A good half hour passed before any of the Hunts recognized who he was. When they did, Ron gave them a packet of letters from his Uncle Hugh and left.

The following day, Friday the thirteenth, Frania's attorneys rested their courtroom case. By this time, Hirschkop was ready to respond with an ultimatum. After a family conference at the noon recess, he told Frania's side that the Hunts would settle for $3.5 million but would not recognize Mrs. Lee as H.L.'s putative wife. He gave the Lees until 5:30 that afternoon to accept.

The deadline passed with no reply.

When court recessed for the weekend, the Hunts took off in different directions. Lamar and Norma flew down to the Super Bowl to watch the Dallas Cowboys beat Denver, Bunker headed for Houston to witness the birth of his third grandchild, Herbert and his wife returned to Dallas to plan the upcoming wedding of their son Doug, and Ray's sister Helen went home to check on her two small children.

Meanwhile, Ray remained in Shreveport to plot strategy with his attorneys. But the more he reviewed the week's testimony, the worse things looked. If things kept going the way they were, the Hunts could very well lose the trial and many millions of dollars, too. By the time his relatives returned to Shreveport on Sunday, Ray was ready to offer Mrs. Lee $10 million and to recognize her as his father's putative wife.

This time, the first family balked. The money part was all right, but they would hear nothing of conceding on the issue of marriage. Finally the two families agreed to let Hirschkop increase the Friday offer to $5 million.

Meanwhile, in Frania's camp, the tension was also building. Frania seemed to have been winning the war in open court, the struggle for the hearts of the jury and the spectators, but she had lost several important behind-the-scenes legal rulings. On the second day of the trial, out of the jury's presence, Judge Stagg had ruled that Mrs. Lee could not introduce evidence that the 1942 settlement agreement with Hunt was not intended to encompass her claim to community property. The next day, the judge had ruled that Mrs. Lee's claim of community property had to be restricted to the years 1925 to 1934, when she admittedly learned of Hunt's first family. Then, on the fourth day of the trial, the judge ruled that the jury would not be allowed to consider the claim that H. L. Hunt promised to acknowledge their marriage in his will and to treat her children equally with the children of his first marriage. The reason for this ruling was that Frania could not produce a witness to corroborate her claim against the deceased Hunt as required by the Louisiana Dead Man's statute.

As Judge Stagg later noted, "none of these rulings impaired Mrs. Lee's chances of establishing the putative marriage," but they did severely narrow her chances of voiding the 1942 settlement agreement. In order to have the 1942 settlement agreement thrown out, Mrs. Lee had to prove that Hunt "misrepresented, or failed to disclose, the value of the community property" back in 1942. She also had to come up with a convincing explanation of why she had waited nearly thirty-four years from the time the settlement was signed until filing her suit objecting to it. On top of all that, the defense had only begun to present its side of the case and was sure to have some damaging evidence in store.

With the weekend coming to an end, both Frania and the Hunts faced powerful inducements to reach a settlement. In Frania's case, the situation boiled down to weighing a chance for official legal recognition of her alleged marriage to H. L. Hunt against the possibility of getting a multimillion-dollar out-of-court settlement. As Judge Stagg noted later, "There was also the consideration that a substantial settlement would tend to confirm her claim in the public mind, thereby achieving some degree of recognition for her marriage." The Hunts, on the other hand, had to weigh the prospect of coughing up several million dollars in settlement money against the benefits of withdrawing the case from the public eye, avoiding the possibility of losing a partial judgment against their side if the case went to the jury, and obtaining a settlement that would end all future internecine litigation against the estate.

The following day, Monday, January 16, everyone showed up at the courthouse, but the proceeding never got under way. Instead, the Hunts and the Lees spent the morning in the judge's chambers trying to work out an agreement. By early afternoon, under Judge Stagg's auspices, they came to terms.

Under the settlement, the Hunts finally agreed to pay $7.5 million, a figure equal to exactly one-half of H.L.'s estimated community property at the time of the 1942 settlement in Dallas. The money would come in equal portions from the trusts of the first and second families. Some of the money would go directly to Frania and her attorneys, but the greater share would go to Mrs. Lee's children and grandchildren. In return, Hugh would agree to drop his suit to have himself and his siblings declared H.L.'s legitimate heirs. The Lees also agreed to sign still another blanket release to be drawn up by the Hunt family attorneys. Although Mrs. Lee would not be officially declared H. L. Hunt's "putative" wife, she would have the benefit (in status as well as money) of a settlement in her favor.

Meanwhile, the first and second families reached a settlement of their own. The main issue in the settlement was the trust of the first family's mentally troubled brother Hassie. Still extremely active in the oil business, Hassie Hunt's two trusts and the two operating entities bearing his name were worth in excess of $500 million, counting both Hassie's own oil and gas production and his trusts 8-percent share of Placid Oil Company and 12-percent share of Hunt Petroleum. Since the boards of Hassie's two trusts consisted of Margaret Hunt Hill, Caroline Hunt Schoellkopf, Al Hill, Sr., Herbert Hunt, Lamar Hunt, and long-time financial man John Goodson, the first family had effective control of Hassie's money. On occasion, such as in their takeover bid for Great Western United, the first family had provided itself with loans from Hassie's trusts. Throughout the Shreveport trial, the first family had feared that if Mrs. Lee were declared H. L. Hunt's putative wife, she and her children would have standing to challenge Hassie's will. They also feared that as Hunt's legally recognized second wife, Ruth Ray Hunt might already have standing enough to challenge Hassie's will and, therefore, could lay future claim to his estate. However, under the terms of their separate settlement, the first family got the second family and the Lees to agree not to challenge Hassie's will, thus insuring that when Hassie died, his share of the Hunt fortune would remain in the hands of the first family and its heirs.

While the judge's secretary was typing up the settlement papers, Frania and her grandson Ron Cartledge approached Bunker in the hall outside the courtroom.

"I just wanted you to know that I don't have any hard feelings about this," Mrs. Lee said. "I've always liked you kids."

Bunker merely nodded and smiled graciously.

At 2:35 P.M. Judge Stagg called the court back to order, had the marshal bring in the jury, and announced that an undisclosed out-of-court settlement had been reached. After instructing the parties not to comment on the settlement or the case, Stagg took the most unusual step of telling the courtroom audience how "impressed" he had been with Mrs. Lee's performance in the trial and the way she had endured the questioning.

"I also think it was a very gracious thing for the plaintiff to have spoken the way she did about Lyda Bunker Hunt," the judge informed the courtroom audience. With that, he adjourned the court.

Mrs. Lee acted like all her dreams had come true. By the time she reached the hall outside the courtroom, she had broken into a satisfied smile and was surrounded by eager reporters. Still, she declined to make any comment, although she clearly wished she could.

"Maybe later, maybe later," she said. "We have about three weeks of legal work ahead. They're warning me not to say a word." (The press later misreported her remark as "All in my favor, all in my favor.") Meanwhile, her attorney, Wallace Hunter, broke into tears of joy.

The first family's reaction was mixed. For folks who had just agreed to pay out their share of $7.5 million they did not seem very depressed, just tired and anxious to go home.

"No one likes to spend their life in court," Lamar's wife Norma observed.

"If everybody else is happy, I'm happy," Bunker remarked.

"They've got the wrong heroine," Herbert's wife Nancy protested, referring to the closing compliments Judge Stagg had paid to Mrs. Lee. "The real heroine was Lyda Bunker Hunt."

If the other Hunts appeared to be relieved by the settlement, Ray actually looked happy, almost buoyant. When he had finished his posttrial business in the judge's chambers, Ray came back into the courtroom, teased the waiting press about making a resounding statement, spread his arms, flexed his knees, and uttered a honey-voiced "No comment." But even without a comment, it was easy to see that Ray thought his side had actually gotten off pretty easy in the whole affair.

No one, however, stayed around long enough to ponder that notion or any of the other mysteries that still surrounded the case. By nightfall, the Lees were setting out for Atlanta, where they would await the final legal approval of the settlement, and the first-family Hunts were flying back to Dallas, where Bunker and Herbert would return to their exploits in silver. The next day Ray also returned to Dallas to get ready for the opening of his Reunion project. As they again went their separate ways, neither of the three families of H. L. Hunt knew when, if ever, they would all be gathered in the same place at the same time, but they could safely assume that if there were another three-way reunion, it would probably be in court.

CHAPTER 15

LIFE AFTER H.L. (Part Two)

ON February 25, 1978, Ray Hunt appeared in federal court in Shreveport with a cashier's check for $7.5 million. As stipulated in the agreement arrived at in Judge Tom Stagg's chambers a month before, the cashier's check was payable jointly to Frania Tye Lee, her lawyers, children, and grandchildren. All that remained was for Ray to hand over the check, and the case of *Frania Tye Lee* v. *The Estate of H. L. Hunt* would be closed. Or so Ray and just about everyone else connected with the case believed. But when Judge Stagg convened the proceedings that morning, Ray Hunt was socked with an unpleasant surprise: Frania's son Hugh was now delaying the signing of the final release papers on the grounds that he needed more time to consult his attorneys.

Several more weeks passed. Then it was disclosed that Frania had fired the attorneys who had represented her in the trial and in the settlement negotiations. The law firm of Durrett, Hardin, Hunter, Dameron, and Fritche retaliated by petitioning Judge Stagg to order Frania to abide by their 1975 employment-contract agreement or pay a minimum of $750,000 in legal fees. A short time after that, Hugh let it be known that he would not sign the final release papers at all.

Suddenly, the hard-fought settlement agreement among the three families of H. L. Hunt appeared to be off. Seventeen of the necessary signatures, including Frania's, had already been affixed to the final papers. The only holdout was Hugh. But Hugh's refusal alone was enough to derail everything. The two Dallas families were anxious to bury the case once and for all. But they were not about to pay over $7.5 million if they could expect more trouble from Hugh. Lawyers for the estate filed a motion asking Judge Stagg to enforce the settlement on Hugh.

Several more months passed as Frania hired herself some new attorneys. Finally, on the dark and rainy morning of December 7, 1978, the parties reconvened in Shreveport federal court. This time, the production was only a fraction of what had been done for the trial. Ray Hunt was there with at least five lawyers. Frania and Hugh and young Ron Cartledge were there with two lawyers. On hand to look after the first family's interests were two more lawyers, Phil Hirschkop and an assistant. Also present were Frania's trial attorneys, Wallace Hunter, Roger Fritchie, and Michael Cooper. But the rest of the family members, the brothers and sisters and wives and children, stayed at home.

A handful of media reporters showed up, so Judge Stagg invited the parties to conduct the hearing in the privacy of his chambers.

Once inside, attention quickly focused on Hugh and his refusal to sign the final release papers. Hugh admitted under questioning that he had been opposed to the settlement from the very beginning. At one point shortly after the end of the Shreveport trial, he had even commented to his attorney, "If I could get out of it, I would get out of it."

Hugh now claimed that the final documents drawn up by the lawyers after the Shreveport trial did not accurately reflect what the three families had agreed to back in January. In specific, Hugh complained that the agreement was too strict in forbidding the parties to discuss the case in public and that it failed to mention a promise to change the management of the Reliance Trusts. More ominously, Hugh also protested that the final agreement called for all three families to waive any future claims against each other's estates, when all he claimed to have agreed upon back in January was not to challenge the estates of other half siblings who died without a will. As one Hunt family lawyer noted, this suggested that Hugh was still after a slice of Hassie's estate, since he apparently wanted to keep the door open to challenge any half sibling's will.

The parties argued before the judge right through the morning, broke for lunch, then picked up again after lunch, with the Hunt estate attorneys grilling Hugh with questions and protesting to Judge Stagg that Hugh should simply be forced to sign the final settlement papers. Finally, about midafternoon, the two parties exhausted their arguments, and Judge Stagg closed the proceedings with a promise to issue a ruling in the case as soon as possible.

Several more weeks passed, and the first anniversary of the end of the Shreveport trial came and went without a word from Judge Stagg. Then the weeks became months, and still no ruling was forthcoming. The case of *Lee* v. *Hunt* remained in legal limbo. Hugh did not sign the final papers. And the estate did not release the cashier's check for $7.5 million. Meanwhile, the two Dallas families became preoccupied with much more earthshaking matters.

In February of 1978, just as the three-way family settlement agreement was beginning to fall through, Bunker Hunt happened to meet a very wealthy and influential Saudi Arabian sheik with the potential to help him in the silver market. The introduction came through the ubiquitous John Connally, whom Bunker had retained to negotiate a New Zealand oil-concession problem.

Connally, Bunker, and New Zealand prime minister Robert D. Muldoon were conferring one afternoon in the Mayflower Hotel in Washington, when Connally got word that his friend, Sheik Kahled Ben Mahfouz was also staying at the Mayflower. In fact, as Connally discovered, Sheik Mahfouz had taken an entire floor of the hotel, which he cordoned off with a contingent of forty security guards.

Upon learning that Bunker was interested in meeting some Saudis, Connally arranged an audience with Sheik Mahfouz after the New Zealand oil talks concluded. Like most other wealthy Saudis, Mahfouz had connections to the royal family, but he was not royalty himself. Rather, as a sheik, not a prince, he was one of that class of Saudis who had risen to wealth at the pleasure and munificence of the king. The Western mind might regard him as a feudal lord, but many Saudi bluebloods reportedly regarded him as *nouveau riche,* a wheeler-dealer with too high a profile. Nevertheless, Sheik Mahfouz's power was beyond dispute. He and his family controlled the National Commercial Bank of Saudi Arabia in Jidda, the desert kingdom's largest bank.

Connally and Sheik Mahfouz had established a symbiotic business relationship. Sheik Mahfouz had purchased an interest in the Main Bank in Houston, an institution in which John Connally happened to own a financial stake. The man the sheik had purchased his interest from was Saudi wheeler-dealer Ghaith Pharoan. The flamboyant Pharoan was Mahfouz's friend and Connally's client, but he was also the new owner of a stake in Bert Lance's National Bank of Georgia. Connally feared that even a remote association with Lance would damage his presidential hopes. Sheik Mahfouz bought out Pharoan's interest in the Main Bank to save embarrassment for Connally. By bringing Bunker Hunt and Sheik Mahfouz together, John Connally was performing one of his most fabled functions—that of deal maker.

The introductory meeting between Bunker and Mahfouz took place in Mahfouz's suit at the Mayflower. According to Bunker's aide Bill Bledsoe, who was present at the meeting, Bunker made a proposal to Sheik Mahfouz. In essence, Bunker said he wanted to invite some wealthy Saudis to join him the silver market.

Sheik Mahfouz appeared interested. No final commitment was given at the meeting, but plans were made to explore silver buying with some investors Mahfouz knew in Jidda.

Then, just as everything appeared to be going well, Bunker and Herbert suffered a series of costly defeats. The first occurred when Bunker's $13-billion lawsuit against Mobil and thirteen other giant oil companies in connection with his ouster from Libya was dismissed. Citing the Act of State doctrine, the judge ruled that the federal courts could not resolve a dispute arising from the actions of a foreign power, namely the Libyans. After spending an estimated $1 million in legal fees, the Hunts were left with no means of recovering the loss of their giant Libyan oil field. To make matters worse, Bunker then lost a $32-million judgment to British Petroleum, the government-owned oil giant. Like Bunker's suit against Mobil and the others, the BP suit turned on the actions of a foreign power, the Libyans, but the English courts did not see fit to dismiss the case on those grounds. Instead, the British made it clear that if Bunker did not pay up, the court might seize some of his assets in England, including his prize race horses stabled there.

Meanwhile, back in Dallas, more problems developed on the silver scene. Ironically, part of the problem arose from the fact that the price of silver finally began to move of its own accord. Responding at last to inflation and increases in other precious-metal prices, silver rose from $4 an ounce to $6 an ounce by January 1979. Prices continued a slow but steady climb toward the $8 mark through the spring and early summer.

By this time, G. Michael Boswell and the other young Hunt lieutenants in Sunshine Mining's management were turning hostile to the scheduled Hunt takeover via Hunt International Resources (HIRCO). Boswell and his men based their opposition both on personal and financial grounds. Complaining of heavy-handed treatment by HIRCO's managers, the Sunshine men claimed that the $15-per-share takeover price mentioned in the settlement agreement with the Hunts was a floor, not a ceiling. Boswell and his group made it clear they thought the price for Sunshine was now too low in light of the recent trends in silver prices. They wrote Sunshine shareholders a strongly worded letter, warning them, "DON'T GIVE SUNSHINE AWAY." Noting that Bunker and Herbert were taking out $42 million in personal loans toward the $79-million purchase price, the letter added,

CLEARLY, THE HUNTS, WHO KNOW A LOT ABOUT SILVER, WOULD NOT MAKE SUCH AN ENORMOUS PERSONAL LOAN UNLESS THEY FELT THE VALUE OF YOUR SUNSHINE SHARES WAS FAR IN EXCESS OF WHAT HIRCO WAS OFFERING YOU!

To the Hunt brothers, the Boswell letter was an act of high treason. He was, after all, *their* fair-haired boy. A bitter round of accusations and litigation followed, with the Hunts allegedly unleashing their private eyes to poke into the private lives of Boswell and the other "Sunshine boys." But Boswell's warning had its intended effect on Sunshine stockholders. After an unsuccessful tender offer, the Hunts finally dropped their takeover attempt and sold their shares in Sunshine back to a management trust. A few weeks later, they bought up the outstanding 40 percent of HIRCO still owned by the public, and took the company private.

In losing Sunshine, the Hunts lost the great silver mine they had lusted for. But their most sensational silver play was only beginning.

In the summer of 1979, just after the dust settled from the shootout over Sunshine Mining, Bunker and Herbert completed negotiations for their silver-buying partnership with the Saudis. On July 1, 1979, the partners incorporated a Bermuda-based trading company called International Metal Investment. The firm's registration listed four principals: Nelson Bunker Hunt, William Herbert Hunt, Sheik Mohammed Aboud al-Amoudi, and Sheik Ali Bin Mussalem. It was later disclosed that International Metal was interested in a variety of investments: gold, platinum, copper, even an oil refinery. But its main interest was silver. Far from just another offshore tax shelter, International Metal was the operating front for a secret partnership potentially capable of controlling the world price and supply of silver just like an OPEC of precious metals.

The participation of the two sheiks resulted from Bunker's John Connally connection. Like their mutual friend Sheik Mahfouz, both al-Amoudi and Ali Bin Mussalem were *nouveau riche* Arabs from Jidda. Both men had made their money in real estate when the late King Faisal parceled out some of the lands in the kingdom to allow those sheiks outside the royal family to share in Saudi Arabia's prosperity. According to the *Mid East Report* and other sources familiar with the two sheiks, al-Amoudi was worth about $300 million, while Ali Bin Mussalem was worth about $100 million. Although such wealth made them rich men by most standards, it hardly put them in the same league as the Hunts. What was more, by investing in silver, al-Amoudi and Ali Bin Mussalem were defying official Saudi business wisdom, which held that investing in precious metals put petro-dollars back in the hands of the West. Of course, as one international market observer noted, this same official wisdom had not prevented the Arabs from buying gold.

The equalizer, according to several accounts, were the sheiks' connections to the Saudi royal family. Known by conservative Arab financial men as high flyers, the two sheiks were not among the king's top advisers. But both al-Amoudi and Ali Bin Mussalem did know fellow Jidda resident Prince Faisal ben Abdallah al Saud. Prince Faisal happened to be the son of Prince Abdallah, the commander of the Saudi National Guard and a member of the kingdom's ruling triumvirate. Like Bunker Hunt, Prince Abdallah was a lover of fine horses and a billionaire many times over. Prince Abdallah could definitely afford to play in the same game with the Hunts. But like other highly placed Saudis, Prince Abdallah did not like having his name openly connected with business ventures, especially controversial ones. Although neither Prince Abdallah's nor Prince Faisal's names at any time appeared on the registry of International Metals, several knowledgeable sources suggested that they were the real money behind al-Amoudi and Ali Bin Mussalem.

The exact size of the International Metal Investment partnership was a closely held secret, but as subsequent events would prove, it was large enough to buy over 90-million ounces of silver bullion. At an average price of $10 an ounce, such a horde could be purchased on margin via silver-futures contracts for an initial cash outlay of some $45 million. But to take delivery on the bullion, as the partners intended to do, some $900 million in cash would be required. As fifty-fifty partners with the Saudis, Bunker and Herbert would be responsible for putting up roughly $450 million.

Where, given their cash squeeze, did the Hunts plan on coming up with that kind of money? The answer was contained in the question. The Hunts had some money free from the sale of their Sunshine stock. More importantly, they also had the 42-million ounces worth of futures contracts they had been rolling forward for the preceding several months. Those contracts settled daily. For every dollar-an-ounce increase, another dollar an ounce was credited to the Hunts' cash accounts. Since the price of silver had been rising slowly but steadily since the first of the year, the Hunts were now building up sizable surpluses in their accounts. The value of the 55-million ounces of bullion the brothers had reportedly bought back in 1973 and 1974 was also appreciating. With some 15-million ounces of that bullion still stored in U.S. vaults, the Hunts had handy collateral for cash loans. In effect, they could use their silver to buy more silver, pyramiding bar on top of bar.

The sources of the Hunts' silver-buying loans were some of the major financial institutions in the United States, Canada, and Europe. One loan was for $40 million and was made by a syndicate including the Bache Group (the parent of the Hunts' own silver broker), Continental Illinois Bank, and the Royal Bank of Canada. Another loan was for $233 million and was made by the First National Bank of Chicago, Irving Trust, and eight other large banks. In addition, the New York branch of Swiss Bank lent the Hunts $200 million and Citibank lent $17 million. While the exact circumstances of these loans would never be fully clarified, they were apparently made in defiance of Federal Reserve Board chairman Paul Volcker's request that banks not make loans for commodity speculation.

Appropriately enough, the Hunts formed a new subsidiary for their International Metal Investment partnership: Profit Investment. They chose the name not only for the obvious meaning, but also because of a long-lasting family superstition that names beginning with the letter "P" and containing six letters—names like Placid and Penrod—brought good luck to whatever venture they were associated with. According to later disclosures, Profit Investment represented the silver interests of not only Bunker and Herbert, but also their children, to whom they made over $150 million in personal loans, ostensibly for the purpose of buying silver.

The Hunt-Saudi silver buying began in mid-July of 1979 and began big. Working through both the Comex in New York and the Chicago Board of Trade (CBOT), the group purchased some 8,600 silver-futures contracts, the equivalent of 43-million ounces. All of the contracts were due for delivery that fall.

About the same time the Hunt-Saudi partnership was getting into silver, Bunker held an important horse auction: his first annual Bluegrass Farms sale. It so happened that Bunker held the sale on July 25, 1979, the same weekend as the prestigious Keeneland sale. By so directly placing his offerings of horse flesh in competition with those of Keeneland's, Bunker was effectively thumbing his nose at the horsy establishment that had been trying to regulate his secret buying and selling tactics. Rather than conform to the rules, Bunker had decided to make his own rules, to have his own sale, and he was one of the few breeders in the world whose stable was large enough and fine enough for him to get away with it. When the proceeds of the first annual Bluegrass Farms sale were tallied, Bunker came away with just under $13 million in gross sales. Some veteran turf observers grumbled that the total was probably at least 30 percent inflated, for it appeared that many of Bunker's sales were made to close friends and syndicate associates with whom he likely had buyback arrangements. (Later disclosures confirmed that Bunker had made millions of dollars in loans to a long list of horse-buying friends and associates.) But given the fact that the much longer-standing Keeneland sale grossed only $20 million that year, Bunker's sale certainly qualified as an impressive first effort.

But Bunker's first annual Bluegrass Farms sale was important for more than just multimillion-dollar horse trading. For at that sale, Bunker saw two men who would play large roles in the tumultuous events to come. One of the men was Naji Robert Nahas, a Lebanese Arab living in Brazil who owned twenty-three multinational companies and had made many millions speculating in coffee futures. It happened that Nahas was interested in horses. He bought eleven horses for roughly $1.1 million at the Bluegrass Farms sale. As Bunker told one turf writer at the time, "Mr. Nahas handles the Arab money in horses." Whether or not Bunker knew it at the time, Nahas was also interested in putting Arab money into silver.

The other man Bunker saw at his horse sale was Norman Waltuch. A big, burly fellow with close-cropped hair, Waltuch was not a member of the horsy set, but he was very much a member of the silver set. His occupation: trader for Conti Commodities Service. One of his newest big clients: Bunker Hunt's "friend" Naji Robert Nahas.

According to Waltuch's later testimony, Bunker approached the New York commodities trader at the Bluegrass Farms sale and struck up a conversation of mutual interest.

"What do you think of silver?" Bunker asked.

"I'm bullish on silver," Waltuch replied. "I think the silver market will go significantly higher."

The conversation continued for about ten or fifteen minutes on the prospects for silver, Waltuch recalled afterward. Then the two men parted.

A short time after the Bluegrass sale, Nahas and several associated accounts began buying into the silver market for 42-million ounces worth of futures contracts on the New York and Chicago exchanges. The buyers who entered the market with Nahas included Banque Populaire of Switzerland, a mysterious European front company called Gillian Financial, and Mohammed Fustock, a Saudi Arabian contractor known to be a close business adviser to Prince Abdallah. In addition to being friends and apparent trading partners with Nahas, these big buyers had two things in common: they kept their identities a secret from the marketplace, and they made their purchases through Norman Waltuch of Conti Commodities.

Still other foreign buyers, many of them Kuwaits and Bahrainis, also got into the silver market about this time. But instead of buying on the Comex and CBOT, these Arab investors did most of their trading on the European exchanges in London and Zurich. The vehicle for their trading was a company called Gulf Investment, which traded through the Arab consortium bank in Paris, but like the other foreign buyers, their identities remained secret.

As it turned out, Bunker's big silver dealings happened to coincide with some very well-placed political contributions. Those contributions included $4,250 the Hunts gave to Congressman Jim Collins of Dallas, $13,000 they gave to Congressman Larry McDonald of Georgia, $2,500 they gave to Congressman Steven Symms of Idaho, $5,500 they gave to Senator Jesse Helms of North Carolina, and $7,500 they gave to Senator Strom Thurmond of South Carolina. The Hunts had known Thurmond, Helms, and Collins for many years and admired the three for their conservatism. They had met Symms in connection with their interest in Idaho, among them the attempted takeover of Sunshine Mining. McDonald was, like Bunker, an avowed member of the John Birch Society. But all four lawmakers had one other thing in common with the Hunts —an interest in silver-related legislation. In December of 1979, Collins, Mc-Donald, Symms, Helms, and Thurmond all voted against a proposal that the U.S. government sell part of its 140-million-ounce silver stockpile, a move that would have flooded the market with government silver. In June of 1979, Collins and McDonald co-sponsored a bill that would have increased the federal silver stockpile by 50-million ounces, a move that would have helped increase silver prices as well. Though all five lawmakers denied any impropriety in their actions, Collins later admitted that he had personally invested in silver on the advice of the Hunt brothers and had made profits of $160,000 in silver-futures investments in 1978 and 1979. Collins and Symms also disclosed personal investments in a number of silver-producing and precious-metal companies, including, in Collins's case, three companies in which the Hunts also had stock interests. As Collins put it, "I am a believer in silver."

So, too, were Bunker and Herbert. Even as they made more big silver-bullion purchases, Bunker and Herbert had begun assembling a $20-million ancient coin collection, reputedly the largest and most complete in the world. They also bought Etruscan bronze statues from the fifth century B.C., Greek gold statuettes from the ninth century B.C., and Roman bronze statuettes from the second century B.C. Of course, these purchases were not inspired merely by a love of art for art's sake. Like their millions of ounces of silver bullion bars, these silver, gold, and bronze artifacts were "hard assets" whose value could be expected to appreciate as inflation increased and the dollar weakened.

Ironically, just as he was doing all this high-level wheeling and dealing, Bunker was also sending out an extraordinary invitation to most of the better-known Texas millionaires. The invitation informed recipients, "You, together with your wife or husband, if convenient, are cordially invited to be our guest at a very important meeting that could help determine the destiny of civilization."

As revealed on the front of the invitation in black letters, the sponsor of that urgent conference, which was to be held at the posh Loew's L'Enfant Plaza Hotel in Washington in late October, was Here's Life, a branch of the controversial and arch-conservative Campus Crusade for Christ. The host-committee list included such luminaries as Roy Rogers, former Nixon patron W. Clement Stone, two U.S. senators, the co-founder of Holiday Inns, the owner of the Dallas Cowboys, and, of course, Nelson Bunker Hunt. Having pledged to raise $1 billion for Campus Crusade, Bunker as now fulfilling his promise.

The recipients of Bunker's invitation could tell that the upcoming conference was as ambitious as his fund-raising effort. The invitation went on to promise that participants would "hear and discuss plans and strategies that are not only having a profound moral and spiritual impact upon many nations but are also a critical deterrent to the avalanche of evil that is threatening to engulf the world."

On April 15, 1978, while his half brothers were getting their silver play going and the settlement with the Lees was collapsing, Ray Hunt's anxiously awaited Reunion project opened with the kind of unbridled enthusiasm usually reserved for the weekend of the Texas-Oklahoma football game. The first of the structures to be completed was the 1,000-room Hyatt Regency hotel, a mountain of mirrored glass that was not just one crate-shaped column but a series of four-leveled cubist peaks. The other structure that opened was the 500-foot-tall Reunion Tower with its geodesic ball and revolving restaurant. Immediately after the official ribbon cutting, there was what the *Dallas Morning News* described as "about half an hour of chaos" as more than two hundred people rushed to buy a ride up the elevator in the tower's first thirty minutes of operation.

The "chaos" broke loose on an even larger scale that night when the tower put on a light show complemented by a massive fireworks display. With the rockets' red glare and bombs bursting in air, Reunion looked like the inspiration scene for the national anthem. Virtually all of Dallas came to an awe-struck halt. Motorists simply stopped in the middle of the streets. Traffic on the major freeways into and out of the downtown area did not move. Police reported thirteen major accidents and innumerable minor ones as people stared in wonder at the incredible celebration going on in the night sky.

Like most other large-scale Hunt family projects, Ray's Reunion project prompted its share of controversy. The night of the official opening, complaint calls flooded both Police and Fire Department switchboards for the duration of the light show. Later, complaints came in about the cost of riding up the Reunion Tower ($1.50), the food and service at the restaurant, and the bankruptcy sales of some of the properties in the Union Terminal area. Further controversy was probed when the city of Dallas sponsored a contest to name the new city sports arena to be built in the area, then scrapped all the contest entries in favor of simply calling the sports palace Reunion arena. But there were few complaints about the view of the city from the Reunion Tower or the view of Reunion from just about anywhere in the city. With the opening of the Reunion project, Dallas no longer had to look for a new symbol of the city's modern era—Reunion was it.

In true Hunt fashion, Ray took great pride in the financial accomplishments of his undertaking. As he often boasted, the $75-million first phase of Reunion, unlike so many other ballyhooed Dallas developments, opened ahead of schedule and under budget. The added plus, as Ray also was fond of pointing out, was that the once-blighted area was now paying over $750,000 a year in city taxes.

"It's the classic example of synergism: one plus one equals five," Ray told the *Wall Street Journal.* "Everyone comes out ahead in the game."

Ray's Woodbine Development followed up Reunion with announcements for other projects in the Dallas–Fort Worth area. Though not done in partnership with municipal entities, they, too, were conceived on a large scale. Among them, for example, was a forty-story office tower to be built in Fort Worth. Clearly, Ray Hunt had no trouble following one of his late father's chief commandments for success: think big.

While real estate continued to give him most of his publicity, Ray still devoted most of his time to increasing the oil and gas operations of Hunt Oil Company. The Hunt luck turned slightly sour for him in the North Sea when the British imposed environmental restrictions on the development of the Beatrice field. Instead of simply transporting the oil out by tanker ships, Ray and his partners would have to build a pipeline to the mainland, a project that would delay the onset of production by at least two to three more years. Mesa Petroleum, the original operator, sold out its interest in the field in the face of these delays, but Ray hung in, knowing that the value of his potential reserves was appreciating as the world price of oil kept rising. Meanwhile, Ray expanded the horizons of Hunt Oil Company into other areas. Perhaps his most surprising decision, given his family heritage, was going after an oil concession in the People's Republic of China. Bunker and Herbert had turned down an associate's suggestion that Hunt Energy attempt to get in on the newly opening China trade by remarking, "We don't want to turn into communists." But Ray suffered no such fears. As Dallas columnist Bill Porterfield observed, Ray recognized that "mutual interests are a heck of a lot more productive than mutual enmities," and would probably wind up making a good deal with the Chinese when all was said and done—regardless of whether his old man was turning over in his grave or not.

True to his father's tradition, Ray did keep Hunt Oil in certain farming and ranching interests. He even held onto the $2-million H. L. Hunt Sales, a vestige of H.L.'s old cosmetics firm. But Ray dropped the "beefalo" venture started by former in-law Randy Kreiling and generally refrained from his old man's corny promotional schemes.

Ray also continued to carry the family banner into what was for the Hunts a relatively unexplored area: the political mainstream. When his friend George Bush launched his 1980 presidential campaign, Ray quickly became a leader in the Dallas fund-raising effort. Ray and his wife Nancy also contributed the legal limit of $1,000 each, while Ray's mother gave a tea for Barbara Bush and 500 invited female guests. Departing from his usual behind-the-scenes political role, Ray also went out and personally campaigned for the passage of a Texas state constitutional amendment giving Texas cities new powers to finance urban renewal. Ironically, Ray's public identification with the proposal may have helped defeat it. Mention of the phrase "urban renewal" and the fact of Ray Hunt's support led some voters to suspect that the amendment was a pork barrel for Reunion. In actual fact, it was not, since the Reunion project was already fully financed under Ray's partnership with the city of Dallas. Nevertheless, Texas voters defeated the proposed amendment in a November 1978 referendum by a margin of 2 to 1.

Although Ray generally persisted in living up to the title "the nice Hunt," he did demonstrate a streak of his father's toughness. The signal incident as far as the public was concerned was a $1.55-million lawsuit brought against Ray's *D* magazine by former Dallas mayor Wes Wise. The focus of Wise's lawsuit was a *D* article entitled "The Unauthorized Biography of Wes Wise," which criticized the mayor's personal political style just before he he was due to stand for re-election. Wise won re-election, but charged *D* with libel. Rather than pay off Wise or print a retraction, Ray fought the suit in court for over four years. Finally, in February of 1979, a Dallas judge ruled that Wise, who was by now a former mayor, had no case and dismissed the suit.

Then Ray dropped a bombshell. In a countersuit filed in March of 1979, he charged Wise with extortion and illegal wiretapping. The essence of Ray's claim was that Wise had secretly tape-recorded a conversation between them prior to the publication of the *D* article with the intent of using it for extortion. In the case, Ray claimed, the taping constituted illegal wiretapping not because Wise had used a "bugging" device (which he had not), but because of Wise's alleged intent to use the tape recording for illegal purposes. In their taped conversation, Ray had told Wise, with whom he was then on friendly terms, that the editors of *D* had assured him that the article would contain no allegations of criminal wrongdoing and advised Wise that he would probably get more favorable treatment if he submitted to an interview with the author. Wise later used that conversation as his reason for filing suit against Ray (and not just *D* magazine) in his libel action. However, according to Ray, the secret tape actually absolved Ray of any guilt in the libel suit, so Wise decided not to use it in court. Instead, Wise allegedly demanded $500,000 to drop his suit. When Ray refused the demand, Wise allegedly edited the tape and sent it to Ray with an unsigned message which said, "Of course, there is more."

Ray's lawsuit carried some dramatic revelations about his toughness and the way he ran Hunt Oil Company. For one thing, it was disclosed that the reason Ray could confirm that the alleged extortion tape he received in the mail had been edited was because he, too, had taped the conversation with Wise. In fact, Ray had equipped his Hunt Oil office with an elaborate device which recorded all incoming calls. Ray's system was not illegal. (Under Texas law, it was permissible to record telephone conversations as long as at least one party to the call knew the call was being taped; knowledge of both parties was not required.) But, it was not the sort of thing one expected from "the nice

Hunt." Neither was the decision to reopen the Wise affair with such a vicious countersuit. According to *D* editor and publisher Wick Allison, that was precisely the point.

"He just wanted to show that he's not going to lie down and let people attack him because he's Ray Hunt," Allison said. "If someone attacks him, he's going to fight back."

Ray also showed his mettle in family matters. When the settlement with the Lees ran aground after the Shreveport trial, he had his lawyers press the judge to enforce the agreement. He also saw through the spinoff of the first family's interest in Hunt Oil into the newly formed Prosper Energy Corporation. With the completion of that spinoff, there were still numerous first- and second-family joint interests in various oil and gas properties, but the main operations of the two Dallas families were at last completely separate. Although Ray did not try to antagonize his half brothers or publicly disparage them, it was obvious that he welcomed the separation as much as they did. Thereafter, he and his publicity people spent a good deal of time and effort making clear to business associates and reporters that Hunt Oil and Hunt Energy were distinct and independent companies.

At the same time that he showed his strength, Ray also displayed an idealism that his father only paid lip service to. He was the kind of young man who said things like "I really think it's more or less the principles that are behind you that are important" and meant it. Ray had his father's zest for life. ("I hope I never retire," he told one reporter. "I hope I die when my parachute doesn't open at age ninety.") But he definitely had his own set of goals and priorities. As he put it, "I'd like to be able to look back and say, 'In my business activities, I enjoyed success. The activities that I was associated with were meritorious, meaningful, and significant, and hopefully improved the environment. I had worked with a small group of extremely qualified people and we all had a heck of a lot of fun in accomplishing our goals.' "

While Ray gained ever-increasing prominence as one of the new leaders of Dallas, his mother felt the double-edged sword of being the widow Mrs. H. L. Hunt. Ruthie Hunt had plenty to be proud of in the accomplishments of her son, in her grandchildren, and in her own life and religious work. But she also suffered her share of difficulties. Frania Tye Lee's lawsuit, for example, opened up the snarl of H. L. Hunt's family history and exposed Ruth to embarrassing publicity about her own unusual relationship with her late husband. Though not a recluse by any stretch, she generally avoided the public eye and did not grant interviews to reporters. One of the few exceptions was when she lost the family Bible one morning on the way to church. In an effort to get the Bible back, Ruth placed a small advertisement in the *Dallas Morning News.* The ad, in turn, led a reporter to telephone her requesting an interview. Ruth granted the interview in hopes the publicity might help in retrieving the Bible.

"It's so hard, I suppose, for others to understand why the Bible means so much to me," she told the *Morning News* interviewer. "But it's a part of myself, my memories, my family. There's been so much goodness in my life. Really so much. And the Bible reminds me of it."

Unfortunately, despite the ad and the short feature story that ran in the following Sunday's newspaper, Ruth never recovered her Bible.

Bunker Hunt's almost Biblical warning about the impending world apocalypse in the Here's Life invitation apparently went unheeded by the silver market in the fall of 1979. Having risen slowly but steadily all year, the price suddenly exploded from $8 to over $16 in only two months time. Part of the price explosion was undoubtedly attributable to the voracious demand of the new big buyers. But as the Commodity Futures Trading Commission (CFTC) itself later observed, the demand was also consistent with the worldwide demand for precious metals as a hedge against inflation and unstable politics. Gold prices had already been surging upward for months. Silver had remained relatively underpriced. Now it was catching up. On October 1, it closed at $17.88 per ounce.

Both the Comex and the CBOT flew into a panic. Trading was frenzied, then dried up as small investors scrambled for cover amid rumors that the new big buyers included the Hunts. Norman Waltuch, a respected but far-from-extraordinary trader, began to take on seemingly superhuman powers. Week after week, he would stride onto the trading floor in his bright yellow Conti trading jacket to place another big-buy order for his anonymous foreign clients. Soon Waltuch's mere appearance in the trading ring was enough to make the price of silver jump fifty cents an ounce. Finally, in November, Comex president Lee H. Berendt requested Conti to keep Waltuch away from the Comex silver ring.

The Hunt brothers later claimed that they did not discuss specific silver trades with each other, and maintained that they kept separate trading accounts. They also claimed they were not buying in concert with the so-called "Conti group," but in the midst of the tumult in the silver market, Bunker did meet twice with Norman Waltuch and Naji Robert Nahas. The first meeting occurred in Paris in September of 1979. The second meeting took place in Zurich in October. Though the details of the meetings were never revealed, Waltuch later admitted that the topic was silver.

By this time, U.S. commodities exchange officials and government regulators were growing extremely anxious about the silver market, and for more reasons than the individual antics of Normal Waltuch. The big buyers, which the CFTC specifically identified as the "Hunt group" and the "Conti group," kept buying futures, but they also kept taking delivery as their old contracts matured. The warehouses of the two exchanges held only 120 million ounces of bullion, and that amount was traded in the month of October alone. The Hunt-Saudi partnership, International Metal Investment, itself took delivery on some 40 million ounces. Combined with the Hunts' earlier purchases, this gave the group ownership of 62 percent of the stock in the Comex warehouse and 26 percent of the stock in the Board of Trade's vaults. International Metals also traded some of its futures for another 28 million ounces of silver not held by the U.S. exchange vaults. Conditions looked ripe for a "squeeze": that situation where there was simply not enough bullion available to meet the strict delivery terms of the contracts.

At this point, the CFTC and the exchange officials decided to have a talk with the Hunts. Explaining that they feared a squeeze, the exchange officials asked the Hunts if they would consider selling some of their silver.

The Hunts' answer was no. Bunker said that the new high interest rates, then around 16 percent, made him think twice about adding any more new "long" futures contracts to his holdings. But he also admitted that International Metal's strategy was to take delivery on its contracts, and that he and Herbert intended to hold onto what they had. Besides, as Bunker pointed out with typical understatement, "If you sell, you get into a tax problem."

On top of all that, Bunker and Herbert really did believe in silver as a long-term investment. For one thing, as he told the CFTC men, Bunker believed that the price ratio of gold to silver would eventually return to its ratio in Biblical times of 5 to 1. Even at the new high prices, the ratio was still more than 20 to 1, which made silver a good buy to his way of thinking. What was more, Bunker saw silver as the underpinnings of a new "hard money" economy. Bunker did not say that in so many words to the CFTC men and the exchange officials, but he did give them a glimpse of his basic apocalyptic vision when he revealed a previously undisclosed feature of his silver play: the fact that he was moving his metal to Europe. This time, he did not fly the bullion overseas in chartered jets with cowboy guards. As he told the CFTC, Bunker and Herbert simply traded 9 million ounces worth of metal they held in Chicago and New York exchange warehouses for an equal amount of bullion held by other traders in London and Zurich. The reason? As Bunker explained to the CFTC and the Board of Trade officials, he feared that the U.S. government might expropriate silver from American citizens just as it had expropriated gold back in the 1930s.

Despite having had meetings with Conti trader Norman Waltuch and Arab businessman Naji Nahas, Bunker also told the CFTC that the only Arabs he knew about in the silver market were Ali Bin Mussalem and Mohammed al-Amoudi, the two Saudi sheiks who were his partners in International Metal, though he did add that recent conversations with certain unnamed Arab acquaintances had led him to believe that other wealthy Arabs were investing in silver, too.

The Hunts politely informed the government and the exchange men that they wanted to cooperate. In fact, as proof of their good intentions, the brothers pointed to a recent deal they had made with Dr. Henry Jarecki of Mocatta Metals. The transaction was complicated, but in essence it allowed Jarecki to get Mocatta Metals out of a costly "short" position in silver by matching up "long" and "short" positions and selling the Hunts 23 million ounces of silver bullion and silver coins; the transaction also involved the release by Mocatta of over 10 million ounces of Hunt bullion the brothers had put up as collateral for earlier silver purchases. The Hunts claimed that this EFP ("exchange for physicals") transaction clearly showed they did not aim to "squeeze" the market—i.e., demand strict fulfillment of futures contract terms—but were willing to be flexible in their deal-making arrangements. On the other hand, the Hunts also made it clear that major reductions in their bullion and futures positions were out of the question.

Bunker's assurances that he was willing to cooperate as much as possible apparently mollified the CFTC officials. The CBOT, however, concluded that it was time to act. In a move aimed directly at the Hunts and the other big buyers, the Board of Trade raised the margin requirement and declared that silver traders would be limited to 3 million ounces of futures contracts. Traders with more than that would have to divest themselves of their excess futures holdings by mid-February 1980.

With that, the battle lines were drawn. Bunker let it be publicly known that he thought the CBOT was changing the rules in the middle of the game, and vowed to fight the limits all the way. Privately, he regarded the CBOT's action as another conspiracy against him by the eastern establishment. Among the conspirators, in his view, was Dr. Jarecki of Mocatta Metals, whom Bunker believed (despite Jarecki's subsequent denials) was out to get the Hunts in revenge for getting the best of their 23-million-ounce deal back in October.

For once, Bunker seemed to have a pretty good prima facie case for his conspiracy theory. The boards of both the Chicago and the New York exchanges were composed not only of "outside" directors but also of representatives of the major, usually eastern-based brokerage houses. (One such director was Dr. Henry Jarecki of Mocatta Metals.) Later testimony would reveal that nine of the twenty-three Comex board members held total short contracts on 38 million ounces of silver. With their $1.88-billion collective interest in having the price go down, it was easy to see why Bunker did not view them as objective regulators. At the same time, though, the CBOT restrictions made Bunker even more bullish on silver, because, as he put it, "they show a silver shortage exists."

Bunker appeared to be right. Through November and December, the price of silver rose faster than ever. By the last day of 1979, the price reached an astronomical $34.45 an ounce. Meanwhile, the Hunts' silver holdings kept increasing. By the end of December, the Hunts and their Arab partners held 90 million ounces of bullion, not counting the 40 million ounces the Hunts had allegedly stashed in Europe. The Hunt group also held about 90 million ounces worth of silver futures, most of them due for delivery in March on the Comex in New York.

During this period, Lamar, who had remained on the sidelines through most of the Hunt silver dealings, made some independent headlines of his own. On October 25,1979, while Bunker and Herbert were having their run-ins with the CFTC and the exchange men, the New York office of Sotheby Parke Bernet auctioned off *Icebergs,* a landscape painting by American artist Frederick Edwin Church for $2.5 million, the highest price ever paid for an American painting sold at auction. Although the winning bidder was officially anonymous, word soon leaked out that the buyer was Lamar Hunt. A short time later, it was disclosed that *Icebergs* had been loaned to the Dallas Museum of Fine Arts. According to one report, the loan apparently resulted from an expensive decorating error: when Lamar got the painting home to Dallas, he discovered that the masterpiece, which was over 9 feet long and 5 feet wide, was too big to go on the wall of his mansion.

Less publicized than his art dealings and the progress of his sports teams that fall was the fact that Lamar was also becoming more involved in silver. Back in the early summer, when Bunker was holding over 40 million ounces worth of futures contracts and Herbert was holding over 20 million ounces worth, Lamar's account showed only about 1.5 million ounces of futures contracts. But by the end of the year, Lamar began to increase his holdings to an eventual 9 million ounces worth. Though still a relatively small-timer compared to his brothers, Lamar soon had a $300-million interest in silver in his own right. One knowledgeable Hunt source attributed Lamar's increased participation to cajoling by Bunker and Herbert, who reportedly teased their little brother about "missing out" on their big silver play.

On December 19, 1979, after more than a year of deliberation, Judge Tom Stagg handed down a ruling in the case of *Frania Tye Lee* v. *The Estate of H. L. Hunt.* His opinion: that Hugh had "executed a binding contract" in agreeing to the settlement at the Shreveport trial and was now "obligate[d]" to sign the final settlement papers, and was so ordered to sign by the court. Noting that Hugh had refused to sign the documents at the hearing a year earlier, Judge Stagg extended "a brief opportunity to comply once more." But the judge added, "If Hugh has not executed the documents by 5:00 o'clock P.M. on Tuesday, December 27, 1979, the Court will direct the Clerk to execute them in his place."

Once again, Hugh refused to sign the settlement papers. Instead, he appealed Judge Stagg's order to the Fifth Circuit Court of Appeals, and filed a separate suit in Louisiana state court challenging H. L. Hunt's will on the grounds that Hunt's predeath gifts to the first and second families deprived Hugh and his siblings of their rightful share of the estate. Judge Stagg issued an injunction against Hugh's challenge to the will in state court, only to have Hugh's nephew Ron Cartledge write a letter asking Judge Stagg to step down from the case. As grounds for the recusation, Ron accused the judge of being a friend of Bunker Hunt and claimed that that might make Stagg "unconsciously prejudiced" against his side of the family. Rapidly running out of patience with these legal shenanigans, Judge Stagg agreed to holding a hearing on Ron's request.

Meanwhile, the $7.5 million in settlement money remained in escrow, and the settlement agreement in limbo.

As this family feud continued, Frania herself kept so low a profile that local reporters began referring to her as "the mystery woman of Atlanta."

Because of the front-page publicity of the trial in Shreveport, her name was virtually a household word in Atlanta. Everyone knew the outlines of her story and her relationship with H. L. Hunt. Yet very few people really knew her. And Frania seemed inclined to keep it that way. She kept on seeing personal friends and traveling about. But she did not grant any interviews to the press, and she did not engage in any of the public controversies or elegant social doings that had marked her earlier years in Atlanta. The only public reminders of her existence were occasional brief news stories about legal developments regarding the unfinished settlement.

Hugh also stayed out of the public eye, but not out of court. When not fighting the settlement agreement with the two Dallas families, he remained occupied with a whole series of separate legal and financial disputes, including the bankruptcy of his major corporation National Homeowners Sales Service. Nevertheless, Hugh found time to play father to the eight children he and his wife were raising on their ten acres outside of Potomac, Maryland, and to involve himself in a business venture aimed at producing a multipurpose van. Hugh also continued his "semiretirement" as a philosopher and educator. Among his favorite topics were Polish history and military history. Like his father, he was also interested in health foods, genetics, and family. He took pride in the fact that he had one son and one nephew studying medicine, another son studying aerospace, and another son entering college at the age of sixteen. Believing "only the strong survive," he once remarked, "We need to have 400 million people in this country as soon as possible."

After the Shreveport trial, Hugh also went through another name change. He changed his name to Hugh S. Hunt. "I went back to using the name 'Hunt' at my mother's request," he explained after the change. "She said, 'You were born a Hunt.' " The new middle initial Hugh adopted stood for Soltek, a name made up by Hugh himself. Each letter had its own significance. "So" meant "son of." "L" stood for Lewenduski, his maternal grandmother's maiden name. "T" stood for Tyburski, his mother's maiden name. "E" stood for Ella Rose Myers, which was H. L. Hunt's mother's name. And "K" stood for "Kelly," which was H. L. Hunt's grandmother's maiden name. Shakespeare might ask "What's in a name?" But Hugh S. Hunt knew: his whole family history.

As 1980 arrived, Bunker and Herbert Hunt saw an old nemesis rear its regulatory head. Having observed the big buying in silver for the past four months, the Commodity Futures Trading Commission staff finally decided that the silver positions held by the Hunts and the Conti group were "too large relative to the size of the U.S. and world silver markets." Subscribing to the philosophy that the futures market was not a substitute for the cash market, the CFTC determined that the time had come to stop Bunker's buying spree. A meeting to decide what to do was set for January 8, 1980.

Then the Comex stepped in. On January 7, the exchange announced new position limits restricting traders to no more than 10 million ounces' worth of futures contracts. The effective date of the limits was set for February 18. The day after the Comex announcement, the CFTC announced that it was backing the exchange's new limits.

Bunker was incensed. "I am not a speculator. I am not a market squeezer," he protested. "I am just an investor and holder in silver." Taking the offensive, he again accused the exchanges and the government of destroying the U.S. silver market by changing the rules in the middle of the game. "The market will move to Europe," he predicted ominously. "The silver market in this country is a thing of the past."

Strangely enough, the price of silver fell only one day in the wake of the Comex announcement, then started climbing even higher. Part of the reason for the continued price spiral, according to an after-the-fact analysis by the CFTC, was that Bunker kept buying silver. On January 14 and 16, the Hunts made agreements to take future delivery on 32 million ounces of silver (mostly in London) at various dates that spring. The largest of those contracts were with Englehard Minerals. On January 17, silver hit a record high of $50 an ounce.

Bunker could hardly be incensed about that. On that one day, the worth of the Hunts' silver-bullion holdings was nearly $4.5 billion. Since most of that silver had been acquired at less than $10 an ounce, they had a profit of over $3.5 billion. Bunker and Herbert had made twice as much money in the past six months as their late father had made in his entire lifetime—at least on paper. Of course, if Bunker actually sold all that bullion, he would face enormous tax consequences. The trick now was to figure a way to utilize those huge gains without having them decimated by the tax man.

As Bunker pondered that, the exchanges decided to impose their most stringent restriction yet. On January 21, the Comex announced that trading would be limited to liquidation orders only. There would be no more futures buying. The game was closing down.

The next day, the price of silver plunged to $34, a drop of $10 in a day. It stabilized shortly after that, and remained in the $34 to $39 range for the rest of the month. But in February, the price began to slide downward again. By that time, silver was literally coming out of the woodwork. In response to the new high prices, old ladies had been selling their tea sets. Families had been hocking their silverware. Coin collectors had been divesting themselves of their collections. In January and February alone, an estimated 16 million ounces of silver coins and an additional 6 million ounces of scrap silver had come onto the market. With the price of silver now dropping, some of those small sellers and small investors began complaining to the CFTC about the exchange restrictions.

Bunker, meanwhile, remained as bullish as ever. "Why would anyone want to sell silver to get dollars?" he asked in amazement. "I guess they got tired of polishing it."

Prudently or not, Bunker practiced what he preached. In early February, the Hunts took delivery of 26 million ounces of bullion from the Chicago exchange. That brought the brothers' total group holdings (including their partnership with the Arabs and their European silver stash) to slightly over 155 million ounces. Instead of selling his futures, most of which were set for delivery in March, Bunker simply rolled them forward into the months of May and September. He also bought a $4.25-million stake in Goldfield, a silver-mining concern, and a 6.5-percent stake in his own silver broker, the Bache Group. In late February, the Hunts made headlines in Dallas for an unusual precious-metals-based employee-benefits package. The plan provided that Hunt employees could take their bonuses in silver, gold, or cash, whichever was highest at the time the benefits were paid out. That was not the act of a. man who believed the price of silver was going to crater.

Neither were the things Bunker was doing behind the scenes. In late February, with the price now hovering in the $30 to $34 range, Bunker began another global search for a silver-buying partner. Despite the recent price slippages, the prospects looked good. The Kuwaitis and the Bahrainis in Gulf Investment had sold their silver near the top of the market for an estimated $22-million profit. Elated by their success, the group was ready to get back in the market again. They proposed a new venture in partnership with Bunker to be called Gulf Precious Metals. The intention of this new group was to raise another $500 million to buy more silver; of that total amount, Bunker would supply 10 to 20 percent.

Meanwhile, with the ready cash of Placid Oil, whose North Sea venture had reached payout and was now generating an estimated $200 million per year from the North Sea alone, the Hunts were making several large nonmetal investments. Placid bought the oil reserves of a company called Bodcaw for $190 million in cash, then purchased $100 million in stock in oil-rich Louisiana Land and Exploration Company. After that, Placid bought a 9.6-percent stake in coal-rich Gulf Resources and Chemical Corporation, then announced a $350-million tender offer for the rest of the stock. Gulf Resources' board voted against the tender, and the Hunts backed off.

Then rumors circulated that the Hunts had an even more prodigious takeover target: Texaco. Like cornering a modern market, taking over one of the Seven Sisters was almost too absurd for most people to think about. By one estimate, taking over the whole company would have cost $10 billion at prevailing market prices. Even the Hunts, with an estimated $4 billion in paper profits in silver, would be hard pressed to make that kind of play. But by that time, it seemed like anything was possible for the Texas brothers. So, while the purchases of Texaco stock by Placid were never confirmed, the rumors continued to circulate.

At the same time, the price of silver continued to drop. On March 3, it was at $35.20 an ounce; but by March 14, it was down to $21. One reason for the price drop was the rapidly spiraling interest rate; that not only strengthened the dollar but also raised the cost of buying on margin. Another reason was the fact that at January's $50 price, there were fewer and fewer people left who could afford to buy silver. Still another reason was the fact that world tensions had eased a bit, and the flight into precious metals as a haven from the apocalypse finally slowed.

For Bunker and his Arab partners, the continuing price drop spelled enormous trouble. It meant, for one thing, that the value of their already delivered silver bullion was decreasing rapidly. As $21 an ounce, the Hunts' silver was worth nearly $2 billion less than what it had been worth a few weeks before. That meant so much less collateral available for new silver-buying loans. Even worse, the declining prices meant that the Hunts had to keep coming up with more cash margin money to maintain their futures positions, which were in the 60-million-ounces range. By late March, their margin calls at Bache were in excess of $10 million per day.

Still confident that silver prices would turn upward again, Bunker refused to sell out. But despite his optimism, prices continued to drop, and the margin calls continued to mount.

Everything finally came to a head on March 25, 1980. Having been scrambling around Europe trying to find a way to make the silver market turn around before his cash completely dried up, Bunker suddenly realized that the end had come: the Hunts no longer had the resources to keep making their margin calls. Through an aide, Bunker sent back a cryptic one-line message for his brother Lamar to relay to brother Herbert. The message consisted of only three words: "Shut it down."

That afternoon, Bache called Dallas to inform the Hunts of a $135-million margin call due the following morning. Herbert responded with a stunner.

"We can't make it," he told his silver brokers.

The Bache people could hardly believe it. Had their biggest client reached the end of the rope? Still reeling from the thought of it, the Bache men told Herbert they would have to begin liquidating the Hunts' contracts. Herbert indicated that they should go ahead if that was what was required.

The next day, Bache sold off $100 million of Hunt bullion. It also contacted the CFTC. Bache told the commission that the Hunts' account carried an equity of only $90 million and that the brothers would probably lose another $86 million in the next day's trading. Combined with other recent losses of $40 million, that left a deficit in the Hunts' account of some $36 million. More important as far as the rest of the world was concerned, it was the kind of news that raised the specter of a full-scale financial disaster. Word that the Hunts' losses had imperiled the stability of a major brokerage house could drive the market into a panic.

CFTC chairman James Stone sounded the alarm to the government's financial heads of state. A short time later, fearing the worst, Stone, Volcker, SEC chairman Harold M. Williams and Deputy Treasury Secretary Robert Carswell began a round-the-clock silver-market monitoring session.

That same day, Bunker suddenly turned up in Paris. At 8:00 P.M. Paris time, which was 2:00 P.M. in New York, he released a remarkable announcement to the press via a Paris agency. His statement said that he and four Arab partners had acquired "more than 200,000,000 ounces of silver" and that the group was putting up its hoard to back the sale of silver bonds. The statement went on to say that the bonds would be distributed through "big European banks" (though it did not name any) and promised that the bonds would be in denominations of varying size, so as to attract small investors as well as large ones. Bunker's statement disclosed that his partners in the silver-bonds venture were Prince Faisal ben Abdallah, Sheik al-Amoudi, Mohammed Fustock (a Saudi contractor and adviser to the prince) and Naji Nahas, the Brazilian Lebanese who had purchased silver with the Conti group.

The announcement carried a host of intriguing ramifications. On one level, it appeared that Bunker Hunt had achieved the realization of an unstated dream—the creation of his own independent economy. Just as the governments of the world had issued currencies by virtue of the metal they owned, Bunker and his Arab partners were now planning to issue their own "hard" money backed by silver, even as the governments of the world were now issuing paper with no metal behind it.

In reality, Bunker's announcement carried a far more desperate message. The silver-bonds arrangements were obviously incomplete, or he would have been able to name the banks involved. With silver prices dropping and a personal financial collapse in the offing, Bunker was making a last-ditch attempt to raise cash and a last-ditch confirmation of the fact that he was still bullish on silver, moves he desperately hoped would stave off the coming debacle.

The next day, Thursday, March 27, the silver market collapsed. The price of silver opened that day at $15.80 per ounce. Then rumors started circulating that the Hunts had a $1-billion margin call and they were not going to be able to meet it. Subsequent rumors said that Bache was on the verge of going under. The price of silver plummeted to $10.80 an ounce. The debacle spilled over into the stock market on the strength of an additional rumor that the Hunts were selling off huge stock shares in Louisiana Land, Gulf Resources, and Texaco. The Dow-Jones average dropped a staggering 25.43 points, hitting its lowest level in five years. It looked to many like the sky was falling.

About that time, a second wave of rumors hit the streets. The Hunts would be able to meet their margin call after all. The price of silver remained at its $10.80 level, but the stock market rallied incredibly. Bargain hunters and other buyers brought the Dow-Jones back up to only 2.14 points below the level at which it had begun the day.

Shock waves from the silver crash reverberated around the world. For the little guy, there was reason for rejoicing: the break in silver prices was one of the first big price downturns in a long time. For investors who had gone short on silver, it was a time for raking in big profits: Armand Hammer, chairman of Occidental Petroleum, for one, reported a gain of $119 million in silver's slump. For investors who had followed the Hunts, there was reason for jumping out of windows: they lost millions that they could afford to part with far less easily than could Bunker and Herbert. But even for those who had remained on the sidelines, there was reason for grave concern. There had not been a day like Silver Thursday since the Great Depression.

As the world press tried frantically to reach him, Bunker made himself unavailable for comment. Shortly after making his silver-bonds announcement, he left Paris for Saudi Arabia to consult with his Arab partners. Having been billions ahead, he was now staring at billions in losses. The only thing he said before taking off was, "It'll all come out in the wash."

Bunker's prediction turned out to be more accurate than he might have wished. Instead of repeating Silver Thursday's debacle, silver prices rallied to $12 an ounce the next day. But Bunker and Herbert Hunt found themselves with some of the biggest losses in U.S. financial history. Since January, the value of their silver bullion had depreciated by nearly $4 billion. Because most of that silver had been purchased at under $10 an ounce, they were actually still a little bit ahead on their bullion purchases. But they had taken a tremendous beating in the futures market and on silver contracts they had purchased when the prices were in the $35-an-ounce range. The exact extent of the Hunts' troubles was hard even for them to determine, but it quickly became clear that their outstanding debts were in the $1.5-billion range, including a $665-million delivery contract with Englehard that they could not meet. These debts were due not only to Bache, the brokerage house that had apparently flirted with its clients' own disaster, but also to the Merrill Lynch and ACLI firms and to an assortment of domestic and foreign banks.

With much of their holdings pledged as collateral on loans that, in turn, had been used to buy silver, the Hunts and their bankers were in a double bind. The more the price went down, the more they owed, and the less their original collateral—the silver—was worth.

On the Sunday following Silver Thursday, Bunker flew in from Saudi Arabia to meet with Herbert and the Englehard people in Dallas. Since Bunker was fatigued, Herbert did most of the talking, and most of what Herbert had to say sounded pretty grim. Among other things, he informed the Englehard men that all the Hunts' silver was already pledged as collateral on loans or, as he put it, "all under water." Such a predicament might have seriously upset other mortals, but not Bunker Hunt. Confronted with his multibillion-dollar troubles, he simply observed that "a billion dollars isn't what it used to be."

Despite their ability to remain calm, the Hunts did not succeed in working out a deal with Englehard in Dallas. So that afternoon, they and the Englehard men flew to Boca Raton, Florida, where the heads of the nation's largest banks had gathered for a meeting of the Federal Reserve City Bankers Association. Volcker happened to be in town to give a speech to the association, and upon hearing of the Hunt-Englehard problem, allowed that he had no objection to their trying to negotiate a loan, despite his earlier disapproval of lending for commodity-speculation purposes.

Through the night and into the wee hours of the morning, the Hunts and the Englehard men negotiated with the bankers. Although he denied guiding or instigating the negotiations, Volcker reportedly sat in on some of the talks and at one point even appeared with a shirt over his pajama top to check on the status of the negotiations. But even under the benign gaze of the Federal Reserve Board chairman, the bankers could not come to terms with the Hunts. The brothers' maze of debts, commitments, and interlocking collateral was just too complicated. As one participant put it, "There were just too many loose ends."

Nevertheless, by the time the sun rose, the Hunts and Englehard had managed to reach an accommodation. Under the terms of the deal, the Hunts agreed to give Englehard 8.5 million ounces of silver and a 20-percent interest in their Canadian oil properties in the Beaufort Sea. Although carried on the books as worth about $275 million, the Beaufort Sea properties had a potential worth estimated at $600 million to $750 million. But the wells there had to come on production, and it would likely be years before they did. The Hunts just didn't know how much their deal with Englehard would cost them.

With the completion of the Englehard agreement, negotiations for a loan to the Hunts picked up again. Fearing that the Hunts' inability to pay their silver debts might cause more major tremors in the nation's financial system, Fed chairman Volcker gave his tacit approval to a plan to bail the brothers out. Under the terms of the deal, a consortium of banks, including First National Bank of Dallas and Morgan Guaranty of New York, agreed to lend $1.1 billion to a partnership composed of the Hunt brothers and Placid Oil, the most viable entity under the Hunt family corporate umbrella. The partnership, in turn, promised to use the money to pay off the Hunt brothers' silver debts.

The Hunts' loan did not come cheap. As collateral, Placid mortgaged substantially all of its oil and gas properties in Louisiana and the Gulf of Mexico, and its enormous gas leases in the North Sea. That was the equivalent of hocking the company's entire production, an asset estimated to be worth in excess of $6 billion. In addition, Bunker and Herbert contributed collateral in the form of 63 million ounces of silver bullion and coal properties worth an estimated $480 million. They also agreed not to speculate in the silver market until the 63 million ounces of silver they contributed to the partnership was sold off. "The terms of the loan were awful tough," Herbert said later, noting, "the collateral is probably eight or nine times as large" as the principal of the loan, or, in other words, on the order of $8 billion to $9 billion worth.

Bunker and Herbert also had to make some costly internal family financial arrangements. Fearing that Placid, the family jewel, might be left holding the bag if silver prices declined further, Margaret Hunt Hill, "the boys'" iron-willed older sister, insisted that her brothers put up even more of their own property to secure Placid's interest in the silver partnership.

"Margaret never liked the way Bunker and Herbert were wheeling and dealing," commented one knowledgeable source. "After the silver collapse, she put her foot down."

At one point in the internal family discussions, Margaret demanded to know just what Bunker had been trying to do with his silver play.

"Just trying to make some money," Bunker reportedly replied in a sheepish tone.

Now Bunker, Herbert, and Lamar had no choice but to mortgage some of their most personal possessions. The list of what they put up read like the inventory of an emperor's treasure chest: thousands of ancient coins from the third century B.C.; sixteenth-century antiques; Greek and Roman statuettes of bronze and silver; paintings by famous American landscape painters; fine porcelain birds; 500 race horses with names like Overdrawn, Extravagant, and Trillionaire; over 4 million acres of oil and gas leases, coal leases, and real estate; over 70,000 head of cattle; even lawn mowers, CB radios, water coolers, a Rolex watch, and a Mercedes-Benz automobile.

Even worse than these severe financial arrangements was the publicity that went with them. In the wake of Silver Thursday, Bunker's picture was on the cover of *Newsweek* magazine, and stories about his silver exploits with Herbert were on the front pages of newspapers all over the world. The Hunt brothers won more fame in eight weeks than their father had achieved in eighty-five years. But the media's images of the Hunt brothers were almost wholly unfavorable. With few exceptions, they were pictured as greedy, mean, and conniving. Many publications compared Bunker to J. R. Ewing, the fictional villain of the popular television series "Dallas." Playing upon Bunker's oversized girth, cartoonists depicted him as a pig wallowing in a sty full of silver. Even normally restrained business publications took their shots. The *Wall Street Journal,* for example, made a highly unfavorable editorial comparison between the late H. L. Hunt, whose acquisition of wealth served to increase the nation's oil production, and Bunker and Herbert, whose silver venture was merely a speculative play that did not produce jobs or anything else for anyone but themselves. In an unusually sharp editorial entitled "Too Rich to Fail," *Business Week* took the Federal Reserve to task for its loan bailout plan, "an arrangement that gives the Hunts what amounts to a second chance to benefit from a rise in silver prices." In *Business Week*'s view, there was "no excuse" for bailing out the Hunts. "They played a dangerous game for high stakes. They guessed wrong, and they lost. They should be forced to liquidate other assets and cover their losses—just as any speculator would have to do."

Along with being lashed by the media, the Hunts suffered from the enormous amount of public disclosure that accompanied mortgaging their possessions. For the first time in family history, the Hunt wealth was laid out in lists for all to see. The sheer richness and quality of the brothers' possessions, especially their numerous art treasures and coin collections, surprised even their fellow Dallasites. In the past, the family had been low keyed about what they had and, therefore, relatively carefree. From now on, they would have to spend more for theft protection and be even more security conscious.

The Hunts' mortgaging of assets also prompted a panic of sorts among their outside business associates. Rumors fed on rumors that the family was about to go broke, that the terms of their bailout loan would bring them to their knees. Finally, the Hunts felt compelled to issue a statement, saying that they were in fact going to remain solvent.

"Most Hunt ventures will this year show operating profits," Bunker, Herbert, and Lamar said in a joint statement. "A measure of this is that each of us personally will pay substantial income taxes in 1980. In addition, we project the same condition for 1981." As for the mortgages and the $1.1 billion loan, the Hunts' statement said, "Doing business on credit properly collateralized is a continuing part of the American business system." The Hunts also pointed out that their loan, unlike the billion-dollar loan made to bail out Chrysler Corporation about the same time, was not government guaranteed but secured by their own hard assets.

The near-panic caused by the Hunts' mortgages also prompted a public statement by their half brother Ray. In his press release, Ray noted that Hunt Oil Company and Hunt Energy were "entirely separate organizations" and that Hunt Oil "never speculated in the silver market" and was therefore "not in any way affected by recent fluctuations in the price of silver."

Even as they tried to reassure the world of their financial solvency, the Hunt brothers were beseiged with investigations by the CFTC, the SEC, and at least two congressional committees. After being cited for contempt of Congress for failing to answer one congressional subpoena and being recommended for a contempt citation, Bunker and Herbert showed up to testify before Congressman Benjamin Rosenthal's House Subcommittee on Commerce, Consumer, and Monetary Affairs. In that appearance, the brothers solemnly stated that they had not attempted to "corner, squeeze, or manipulate the silver market," and complained that they were the victims of market manipulation by the government regulators and the brokerage houses that were "short" on silver.

Speaking before a more than slightly awed panel of lawmakers, the brothers managed to brush off some of the more picky questions with downhome Texas one-liners. For example, when Bunker was asked how much the Hunts were worth, he replied, "I don't have the figures in my head. People who know how much they're worth usually aren't worth that much."

But the Hunts also made some statements that would come back to haunt them. One was Herbert's claim that he and Bunker had no "joint venture or joint enterprise" in silver, and that while they discussed silver in general at lunches and such, they did not even discuss their specific trades. "Let me make it very clear," Herbert said, "I look after my own investment in silver. I do not stay apprised of what my brothers own."

Herbert's incredible claim sounded like an echo of the Hunts' position in the soybeans squabble of 1977, but it had far more resonance because of the cataclysmic nature of the Hunt brothers' silver play. In addition to severely trying the Hunts' credibility with the public, the statement prompted embittered former Hunt aide Bill Bledsoe to come to the Rosenthal committee with some sensational countercharges. First, Bledsoe contradicted Herbert's claim that he and Bunker did not trade silver together. "The silver transactions are made by William Herbert Hunt and Nelson Bunker Hunt in concert," Bledsoe said. "They buy and sell silver together. It is more than just having lunch together. The business of Hunt Energy Corporation, the first order of business, is silver."

The House subcommittee immediately referred Herbert's and Bledsoe's directly contradictory statements to the Justice Department for investigation of possible perjury charges.

But there was more. In addition to his allegations about the silver deal, Bledsoe also made accusations about Hunt misdealings in the oil business. His most serious charges involved an alleged oil-field spy system that, as Bledsoe described it, was like a modern-day version of the spying system H. L. Hunt allegedly set up on the Deep Rock well when he was negotiating with Dad Joiner back in 1930. The key part of the system, Bledsoe claimed, was Penrod Drilling. No longer the small in-house drilling company H. L. Hunt had founded in the 1930s, Penrod was the world's largest privately owned drilling contractor with over seventy land and sea rigs in its fleet and at least fifteen more rigs soon to be on order. As a contractor for big oil companies like Chevron and Shell, Penrod had access to the drilling information developed by its clients, information that could be of great value to other oil exploration companies. The Hunts always insisted there was no conflict of interest in their ownership of Penrod and their own oil exploration companies. But according to Bledsoe, the Hunt brothers used Penrod to obtain confidential information from the drilling contractor's clients, then used that information to their own advantage before the clients could capitalize on the information themselves. In Bledsoe's words, "It was basically a way to cheat the major oil companies."

The way Bledsoe described it later, the Profit Island deal was one of the fruits of the Hunt espionage system. The chain of events allegedly began when tests on a well Penrod was drilling for Chevron outside Baton Rouge revealed "shoals" of oil and gas sands. Acting on that information, the Hunts quickly leased up the nearby Profit Island acreage under the name of John L. Copeland. The leases were later reassigned to Hunt Petroleum and two other family accounts before drilling commenced.

Bledsoe also had allegations to make about Impel, the drilling subsidiary of what was once a publicly held company, Great Western United. According to Bledsoe, the Hunts put Impel into high-risk deals off the coast of New Zealand and in Rankin County, Mississippi, in order to reduce the Hunts' personal exposure in the ventures. When this result in New Zealand was dry holes, Impel stayed in the venture, paying its share of the costs. But, according to Bledsoe, when the venture in Mississippi turned into a no-risk deal with the sale of a part-interest to a company who would pay all of the drilling costs, the Hunts took Impel out of the deal, assigned Impel's interest to their own personal accounts, and went on to profit from a gas field worth an estimated $500 million. According to Bledsoe and another former Hunt associate, the Hunt brothers also used Impel's geological staff to develop information on the Rocky Mountain "overthrust" belt, then grabbed up the best leases for the family's own personal accounts.

The Hunts responded to Bledsoe's charges with unbridled anger. Ignoring his attorneys' advice to keep silent on the matter, Herbert called a press conference and vowed to issue a line-by-line refutation of Bledsoe's accusations. He also handed out copies of Bledsoe's resignation letter which cited "conflicts of interest" as among the reasons for his departure from Hunt Energy. Noting that the Hunt brothers had filed suit against Bledsoe to recover allegedly "misappropriated" commissions, Herbert maintained that Bledsoe's statements were merely a self-serving counterattack on the part of the former aide.

By the early summer of 1980, things looked pretty grim for Bunker and Herbert. They faced a $1.1-billion debt with interest charges of $500,000 a day or nearly $200 million per year. Having already lost billions in paper profits, they stood to lose hundreds of millions more if the price of silver tumbled again. To make matters worse, they faced a market that believed they had to liquidate the 63 million ounces of silver they put in the partnership with Placid to comply with their loan agreement despite the Hunts' claims to the contrary. And though they claimed to have only 63 million ounces of silver left, their big purchases of 1973 and 1974 did not seem to be counted in the calculations. There may have been another 40 million ounces to cope with in their European stash. On top of all their silver troubles, the summer also brought unpleasant news on another commodities front. After three years of litigation the CFTC obtained a court ruling allowing it to seek "disgorgement" of all the profits the Hunts made in their 1977 soybeans play, profits the agency estimated at $30 million to $100 million.

The bottom line read just as badly in words as in numbers. Because of Bunker and Herbert, the Hunt name was more besmirched than ever. In their attempt to prove themselves as moneymakers in their father's image, they had ended up putting the better part of the family fortune in hock. In trying to build up a cache of silver that would see them through the apocalypse they believed was coming, they had brought down an apocalypse upon themselves.

On the other hand, the dark clouds over the Hunt empire contained some silver linings. At a price of $12 to $14 an ounce, silver was in the view of many analysts, drastically underpriced. While few predicted prices would shoot up to the $50-an-ounce mark any time soon, there seemed to be a good possibility that they could climb back to the $20 to $25 range. Should that happen, the Hunts would be able to pay off their silver debts with ease and wind up with some sizable profits. Moreover, the sheer size of the first family's nonsilver holdings made bankruptcy a remote possibility. Since H. L. Hunt's death, the value of the first family's assets had appreciated enormously, in part because they were invested in all the areas where prices were rising most dramatically —energy, real estate, and precious metals. At the height of silver's price, the Hunts controlled assets worth $12 billion to $14 billion. But even after the debacle of Silver Thursday, their asset worth was still in the $8-billion to $10-billion range. Even if the price of silver dropped to zero, the Hunts would have at least $6 billion to $7 billion in assets left.

Bunker and Herbert definitely felt the stress of the silver crash. According to friends, the affair at one point caused Bunker's legs to sweat and even made him lose a little weight. Yet, as one associate put it, "For a man who's just lost billions," Bunker looked "remarkably calm." Now hounded by press and photographers wherever he went, Bunker even managed some characteristic humor about his new notoriety. As he told one friend, "At least I know they're using a little bit of silver every time they take my picture."

Down but far from out, the Hunts remained bullish on silver. They told the press they believed silver prices would rise again—Bunker predicted that one day silver would reach $125 an ounce—and said they fully expected their financial situation to take care of itself. They also let it be known that they believed they had grounds for a lawsuit against the commodities exchanges for changing the rules in the middle of the game. With the smoke beginning to clear from the battlefield, the great silver play of 1979–1980 was looking less like a one-sided manipulation by the Hunts and more and more like a two-sided shoot-out, a pure power play in which the "shorts" and the eastern establishment had as much at stake as the Hunts. As Bunker put it in his appearance before Congress, "The game is not over."

True to Bunker's prediction, silver prices started to climb again a short time later. By midsummer 1980, prices were $16 to $17 an ounce, or roughly twice what they had been a year before when the Hunts and their Arab partners first entered the market together, and Bache, the brokerage firm that had apparently been pushed to the brink of collapse, was announcing record profits. Whether the Hunts would end up with big profits or more big losses was still hard to tell. But as Herbert admitted to one reporter, this midsummer price rally did put the brothers "slightly ahead." Coincidentally, it was announced about this same time that Bunker's fund-raising efforts on behalf of Here's Life, the religious organization that warned of an impending world apocalypse, had recently brought in some $20 million in pledges and contributions.

EPILOGUE

HASSIE Hunt looked like a ghost as he walked the shoreline of White Rock Lake in the fall of 1980. Now almost sixty-three years old and dressed in blue suit, white shirt, and bow tie, he was even more the spitting image of his old man as the world remembered him—the crusty old curmudgeon with wispy white hair and an impish grin. Violent and temperamental as a youth, Hassie was in his lobotomized and tranquilized old age gentle enough to be left in the company of the youngest Hunt grandchildren. Still, a male attendant stood nearby, keeping himself between Hassie and the lawn of Mount Vernon a few yards in the background.

How much Hassie could comprehend of the sound and the fury since his father's death no one really knew. But it would have taken the powers of extrasensory perception Hassie's late father attributed to him as a young man to foresee what was to come. With the most money, Hassie's branch of the clan, the first family, appeared destined to remain the richest, the most prominent, and the most controversial. At the age of fifty-four and fifty-one, Bunker and Herbert would probably command the first-family empire for most of the rest of the century. Since Placid, the first family's largest company, was held by the trusts, the first family hoped to pass it on to their heirs tax-free. If they were successful, that would mean that the Hunt empire would remain intact well into the second quarter of the twenty-first century.

But within this prospect of continuity were the seeds of demise. It was one thing for the five active children of the first family to run the empire by family council. It would be quite another for the nineteen members of the next generation to attempt the same thing. Some of the third-generation Hunts were showing signs of ability in oil, real estate, sports promotion, and even honeybee raising. But for the most part they all operated beneath the wings of their elders. Would a leader of H. L. Hunt's caliber, a bearer of his supposed "genius gene," emerge from the ranks? Or would the third generation be stifled from too long an apprenticeship beneath the second? And what about the near term? Would Bunker and Herbert come out of their silver play even richer than before? Or would the empire still be in hock by the time it passed to the next generation? Would the Hunts be successful in refuting the charges of their embittered former aide? Or was another major family scandal about to break loose?

And what about the second family? Though not as large, rich, or flamboyant as the first family, the second family promised to carry the Hunt banner for a long time to come as well. By the year 2000, Ray Hunt, the oldest of the second-family children, would be only fifty-seven years old, or just a few years older than Bunker was already. Would his North Sea deal turn into the bonanza he hoped for? Would Reunion continue to be a success? Would Ray be able to reach a low-tax settlement on his father's estate? H. L. Hunt had technically left his Hunt Oil stock to his wife Ruth. Would Ray be able to find a way to pass it on to his mother's heirs without further decimation by the tax man?

And what about Frania Tye Lee's branch of the family? Were the Lees destined always to be a cut below the other two families in status and several cuts below in wealth and fame? Would Hugh ever sign the settlement papers? Would Frania and her heirs get their $7.5 million? Would the three families of H. L. Hunt cease their feud and resolve their enmity?

If Hassie Hunt knew the answers to these questions as he walked the shore of White Rock Lake, he did not say. But whether Hassie was aware of it or not, there were only two real certainties in the Hunt family future. One was that the name Haroldson Lafayette Hunt would die with Hassie. Either out of respect or dread, none of H. L. Hunt's descendants had named their offspring after him. Hassie would be the last H. L. Hunt, at least for the foreseeable generations. But that did not mean that H. L. Hunt's name would be forgotten. For the second certainty in the Hunt family future was that the ghost of H. L. Hunt would haunt the earth for many years to come. Hassie and all his kin were living proof of that.

AFTERWORD AND ACKNOWLEDGMENTS

THIS book is the true story of H. L. Hunt and family. It is not an authorized biography. However, in the course of researching the book and the *Texas Monthly* and *Playboy* articles which preceded it, I was able to interview members of all three branches of the Hunt clan, among them Nelson Bunker Hunt, William Herbert Hunt, Mrs. H. L. (Ruth) Hunt, Ray Hunt, and Hugh S. Hunt. I also conducted over 250 interviews with relatives, friends, associates, avowed enemies, and present and former employees of the Hunts, and studied over 10,000 pages of court documents, film transcripts, media clippings, books, and photographs by and about the Hunts. This piece of writing is the product of research.

I have tried to tell a story, to portray and analyze as well as to report. But I have not tried to pretend omniscience. Rather, on matters of unresolved and important controversy in the story, I have attempted to relate, at least in summary form, the positions of the primary contending points of view. Because this is a true story, the facts and exact details are not always clear in every situation, not even to the participants. Consequently, I have tried to qualify the sources of my factual information where appropriate. Some of these references are in the narrative itself. Others are in the chapter notes, which follow.

This book could not have been written without the help of many people. Among those whose assistance, support, and inspiration have been most instrumental are Catherine Allen, Kathleen Anderson, Nancy Arn, John Bloom, Margaret Carroll, Rita Cobler, Robert Decherd, A. C. Greene, Michel T. Halbouty, Chappy and Ginny Hardy, Stu Henigson, Salah Izzeddine, John Makeig, David Moorman, Bill Porterfield, Jeanne Prejean, Allen Pusey, Dick Russell, Dorrance Smith, Henry Walker, Robert Wander, Shannon Wynne, and the staffs of the *Dallas Morning News*, the *Dallas Times Herald*, and the

Shreveport Journal. Special credits are also due my researchers Germaine Bourchard, Patti Everett, and Shirley Wetzel.

Several others deserve credit that cannot be expressed in words. My editors at *Texas Monthly*, William Broyles, Jr. and Gregory Curtis, first assigned me the Hunt project, guided me through three magazine articles which led to the publication of this book and, along with *Texas Monthly* publisher Michael R. Levy, stood by me at every turn. My first editor at *Playboy*, Terry Catchpole, not only gave generously of his own considerable Hunt research, but also helped me find order in the chaos of data and events. Jim Morgan, his successor at *Playboy*, did a remarkable job in carving a magazine article out of a mountain of manuscript drafts. Star Lawrence, my editor at W. W. Norton & Company, showed faith in this project when others did not, and masterfully steered the book to completion. My agent Bob Dattila provided both friendship and sound business counsel throughout. Finally, my erstwhile and understanding typist, Linda White Dossey, proprietor of The Typist in Houston, Texas, worked far beyond the call of duty from first draft to last.

To all those mentioned above, as well as to those who for reasons of space or requested anonymity cannot be mentioned, I owe my grateful thanks. However, any errors or shortcomings in this book are mine alone.

The Three Families of H. L. Hunt

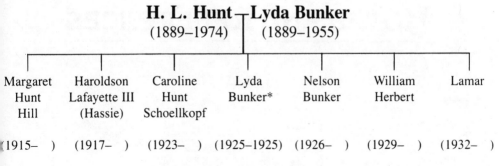

H. L. Hunt—**Lyda Bunker**
(1889–1974) | (1889–1955)

Margaret Hunt Hill	Haroldson Lafayette III (Hassie)	Caroline Hunt Schoellkopf	Lyda Bunker*	Nelson Bunker	William Herbert	Lamar
(1915–)	(1917–)	(1923–)	(1925–1925)	(1926–)	(1929–)	(1932–)

21 grandchildren, 14 great-grandchildren

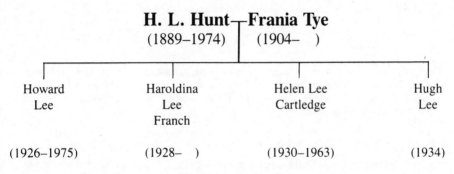

H. L. Hunt—**Frania Tye**
(1889–1974) | (1904–)

Howard Lee	Haroldina Lee Franch	Helen Lee Cartledge	Hugh Lee
(1926–1975)	(1928–)	(1930–1963)	(1934)

17 grandchildren

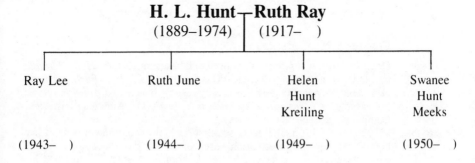

H. L. Hunt—**Ruth Ray**
(1889–1974) | (1917–)

Ray Lee	Ruth June	Helen Hunt Kreiling	Swanee Hunt Meeks
(1943–)	(1944–)	(1949–)	(1950–)

7 grandchildren

*died as an infant

NOTES AND REFERENCES

THE purpose of these notes is to give credit to particular works that were especially important in assembling the narrative of this book, and to provide additional substantiation for certain key points. For reasons of space, citations that are clear in the text are not repeated in the notes.

Page   **Chapter 1 H.L.'s Image**

15–20   Description of trial based on court testimony and personal observations of the author in case of *Frania Tye Lee* v. *The Estate of H. L. Hunt,* Shreveport, Louisiana, January 9–16, 1978.

21   " 'He was so very, very misunderstood.' " Author's interview with Ruth Ray Hunt.

21   "H. L. Hunt thought he carried a genius gene." Author's confidential interviews with former Hunt aide, former Hunt secretary.

Chapter 2 Hunt Heritage

22–39   Details of Hunt's forebears and childhood based, in part, on *Hunt Heritage* by H. L. Hunt (Dallas: Parade Press, 1973); *H. L. Hunt Early Days* by H. L. Hunt (Dallas: Parade Press, 1973); *Hunt-Bunker and Allied Families: A Genealogical Study with Biographical Notes* by The American Historical Company, Inc. (New York, 1946).

26–27   "She rewarded his mental feats by allowing him to continue nursing at her breast." Scenes and information based on author's confidential interview with former Hunt secretary. Also, *H. L. Hunt* by Stanley H. Brown (Chicago: Playboy Press, 1975), pp. 16, 24 ff.

29–30   Political information on Hash Hunt taken from *Vandalia Union,* October 11, October 25, and November 15, 1894. Also, author's interviews with local citizens, including historian Alenia B. McCord.

37–38   Description of June Hunt's card games based in part on H. L. Hunt's account in "Just Plain H. L. Hunt" by Tom Buckley, *Esquire* (January 1967).

Chapter 3 Luck, Lyda, and Oil

40   History of Lake Village, Arkansas, based in part on author's interviews with local citizens, including Sam Forte, Hal P. Sessions, *et al.* Also, *Hunt Heritage, H. L. Hunt Early Days* and "A Brief History of Chicot County" by Woodie Johnson Streett, *Arkansas Genealogical Records,* Vol. 78 (1972–73).

42 ff.   Description of H. L. Hunt's card games and haunts based in part on interviews with Forte and Sessions of Lake Village, local historian Brodie Crump of Greenville, Mississippi, and Frank Ciolino, Jr. of Greenville, Mississippi.

45–46   Description of H. L. Hunt–Lyda Bunker courtship and wedding based in part on author's interviews with Mattie Bunker Sessions, sister of Lyda Bunker Hunt.

46   Lyda Bunker's family background based in part on *Hunt-Bunker and Allied Families.*

47–48   Description of H. L. Hunt land speculating and poker playing based in part on Brown and Buckley works cited above.

49–50   Description of H. L. Hunt's departure for the El Dorado oil boom based on *Hunt Heritage* and interview with Sessions.

50–52   Description of El Dorado oil boom based in part on "The Discovery of Oil in South Arkansas, 1920–1924" by A. R. and R. B. Buckalew, *Arkansas Historical Quarterly,* Vol. XXXIII, No. 3 (Autumn 1974), 195–238.

51–52   Statistics on U.S. oil production, consumption, and drilling taken from *Twentieth Century Petroleum Statistics.*

52–55   Description of H. L. Hunt gambling halls and Ku Klux Klan encounter based on author's interviews with El Dorado residents J. S. Beebe, former El Dorado police officer Isaac A. Wilson, *et al.*

Chapter 4 Man with Two Families

58–61   Description of H. L. Hunt's early oil days, including wealth figures, based in part on *Hunt Heritage.*

61–62   Description of H. L. Hunt around barber shop based on author's interview with former El Dorado barber Bosco Holland.

63   Account of infant Lyda Hunt's death from interview with El Dorado resident Dick Dumas.

64   Song by H. L. Hunt recalled by Hunt in interview with Edwin Shrake, *Sports Illustrated,* Vol. 33 (September 7, 1970), 65.

64   Account of Frania Tye's childhood based on court testimony depositions in case of *Lee* v. *Hunt.*

65–68   Account of Frania Tye's meeting with Old Man Bailey and H. L. Hunt based on Frania Tye Lee testimony in *Lee* v. *Hunt.*

69–70, 73   Account of Frania Tye's life with H. L. Hunt based on her testimony in *Lee* v. *Hunt.*

73   Account of H. L. Hunt's decision to go to east Texas based on account in *Hunt Heritage,* pp. 75–76.

Chapter 5 The Dad Joiner Deal

75–103   Much valuable background information for this chapter has been drawn from *The Last Boom* by James A. Clark and Michel T. Halbouty (New York: Random House, 1972).

86–89   Description of Hunt-Joiner negotiations in Dallas based in part on H. L. Hunt's deposition in the case of *C. M. Joiner* v. *Hunt Production Co. et al.,* filed January 16, 1933, in Rusk County, Texas, district court.

Chapter 6 The Best Days

105   "The time we lived in Tyler." *Hunt Heritage,* p. 93.

105–106   Account of Hunt family life in Tyler based on author's confidential interviews with Hunt's former friends and associates.

106–107   Account of Hassie Hunt's youth based on author's confidential interviews with Hassie's former friends and associates. Also, accounts in Brown, various pages; Shrake; and *Hunt Heritage.*

107   Account of Bunker Hunt and his horse Lady based on Edwin Shrake interview with Bunker Hunt, "Knee Deep in Clover," *Sports Illustrated,* Vol. 44 (June 21, 1976).

108–110   Account of H. L. Hunt's exploits in Tyler based on Brown and author's confidential interviews with former Hunt associates.

112–113   Figures on Hunt wells in the east Texas field found in *East Texas Oil Parade* by Harry Harter (San Antonio: Naylor, 1934).

115   Poems written by H. L. Hunt introduced as evidence in trial of *Lee* v. *Hunt.*

117–118   Description of Hunts and Tyler Rose Festival based on author's confidential interview with former Hunt associates and articles in Tyler.

120   Account of Parade explosion based on Brown, pp. 147–50.

Chapter 7 Dallas

122   Footnote information from Shrake, *Sports Illustrated* (September 7, 1970).

123   Description of Dallas elite based in part on *The Super Americans* by John Bainbridge, 2d ed. (New York: Holt, Rinehart & Winston, 1972).

127–131   Account of Frania Tye's breakup with H. L. Hunt based on testimony in *Lee* v. *Hunt,* author's interview with confidential sources.

131–132   Account of Ruth Ray's childhood and early life based on *H. L. Hunt Early Days* and author's interview with Ruth.

134–137   Account of Hassie Hunt's breakdown and treatment based on author's confidential interviews with former Hassie Hunt caretaker, former H. L. Hunt personal secretary, and former Hunt aide. Information on Rosemary Kennedy lobotomy from *Jackie Oh!* by Kitty Kelley (Secaucus, N.J.: Lyle Stuart, 1978).

140   "Paranoid style" concept found in *The Paranoid Style in American Politics and Other Essays* by Richard Hofstader (New York: Knopf, 1964).

141–143   Account of H. L. Hunt's gambling exploits based on author's interview with former Hunt secretaries and former Hunt employer. Also, *Jimmy the Greek* by Jimmy Snyder with Mickey Herskowitz and Steve Perkins (New York: Playboy, 1975).

145   Reference to the "barefoot billionaire" found in "The Barefoot Billionaire," unpublished manuscript by former Hunt employee Ralph Lee.

Chapter 8 The Richest and the Rightest

150–151   Account of letter reaction to H. L. Hunt stories in *Life* and *Fortune* based on Brown; author's interview with former Hunt secretaries.

151   Transfer of Penrod Drilling account taken from "Trailblazer: Penrod Drilling Company Action Spans 43 Years," *Drilling-DCW,* Vol. 41, No. 9 (June 1980).

151   Secure Trust details taken from articles of incorporation, Secure Trusts.

151	Quotes from Hunt employees taken from Brown.
152–153	Quotes from H. L. Hunt taken from *Houston Chronicle* series by Saul Friedman, October 18, 19, 20, 21, 22, 23, 1964.
154–164	Much valuable information on Facts Forum and H. L. Hunt's ties to Senator Joseph McCarthy comes from eight past series in *Providence Journal-Bulletin* by Ben Bagdikian, January 1954, and reprint of series in *The Reporter* (February 16, 1954). Also, "H. L. Hunt—Portrait of a Super-Patriot" by Robert G. Sherrill, *The Nation,* Vol. 198 (February 24, 1964). Account of Hunt-McCarthy first meeting based in part on article in *Dallas Morning News,* April 5, 1952.
164–165	H. L. Hunt account of MacArthur presidential maneuvering from *Esquire* interview with Tom Buckley.
166–167	Account of H. L. Hunt dealings with Jimmy "the Greek" Snyder from *Jimmy the Greek, supra.*
171	Account of first-family reaction to discovery of H. L. Hunt's second and third families based on author's interviews with Nelson Bunker Hunt and William Herbert Hunt, and author's confidential interviews with other Hunt family members.
171–172	Account of Frania's children's experience from testimony of Hugh Hunt in *Lee* v. *Hunt.* Account of Frania's Atlanta years based on article in the *Atlanta Journal* by Yolande Guinn and Raleigh Bryans (January 12, 1978).

Chapter 9 Popsy and His Patriarchy

175–176	Details of Lyda Bunker Hunt will taken from filings in Probate Court, Dallas County, Texas.
176–177	Details of aftermath of Lyda's death based on author's confidential interviews with family sources. Details of Ray Hunt's confrontation with his father based on unpublished interview with H. L. Hunt by Dallas writer Jane Graham.
178	H. L. Hunt's version of decision to quit gambling from Tom Buckley interview in *Esquire.*
179	Allegations about H. L. Hunt gambling from sworn statement by former aide John W. Curington, filed March 5, 1971, in Dallas County District Court in connection with case of *Hunt Oil Company* v. *John W. Curington et al.*
179–188	Much valuable information and quotations on H. L. Hunt and LIFE LINE, Wayne Poucher, and HLH Products based on Sherrill, *supra.*
189	Description of H. L. Hunt at 1960 Democratic National Convention based on Buckley.
197	Estimate of Hugh Roy Cullen's gifts to charity from *A Saga of Wealth: The Rise of the Texas Oilman* by James Presley (New York: Putnam, 1978).
197–198	Figures on H. L. Hunt Foundation from Sherrill, *supra.*
212–213	Valuable details and information on Lamar Hunt and founding of the American Football League from unpublished interview with Lamar Hunt by Don Pierce. Also, *The Other League* by Jack Harrigan and Mike Rathet (Chicago: Benjamin, 1970); *The NFL's Official Encyclopedic History of Professional Football* by Tom Bennett *et al.* (New York: Macmillan, 1977).
214	Information on Frania Tye Lee's life in Atlanta based in part on Guinn and Bryans, *supra.* Author's interview with Hugh S. Hunt.
217–220	Some information and quotations on childhoods of second family based on account in *Above All Else* by June Hunt (Old Tappan, N.J.: Revell, 1975).
220–221	Information on Hunt family political contributions based on *Houston*

Chronicle series by Friedman, *supra;* Sherrill, *supra.*

Chapter 10 Welcome, Mr. Kennedy, to Dallas

223 ff. Internal Hunt memoranda on Kennedy assassination obtained from confidential source.

225–230 Information on "WELCOME, MR. KENNEDY" ad and Jack Ruby based on *Hearings before the President's Commission on the Assassination of President Kennedy* (the Warren Report) (Washington, D.C.: U.S. Government Printing Office, 1964), Vols. 1–26, various pages. Text of "WELCOME, MR. KENNEDY" ad from *Dallas Morning News,* November 22, 1963.

232 Account of events at Hunt Oil Company and on Hunt family based on author's interviews with former Hunt employees and Mrs. H. L. Hunt.

237–238 Information on the United States' secret war against Cuba based on "The Kennedy Vendetta" by Taylor Branch and George Crile III, *Harper's* (August 1975), p. 49.

239 ff. Excerpts from H. L. Hunt columns drawn from *Weekly Strength* (Dallas: HLH Products) and *Right of Center* (Dallas: Parade Press, 1971), both by H. L. Hunt.

Chapter 11 Just Plain Folks

247–248 Details of Hunt offices and Jack Anderson quote taken from *Houston Chronicle* series by Friedman, *supra.*

248 Figures on production of Black Lake field taken from author's interviews with former top Hunt employees. General production figures pre–Black Lake for Hunt Oil and Placid Oil taken from *New York Times* interview with William Herbert Hunt, August 24, 1964.

248 Figures on losses at HLH Products based on testimony by Tom Hunt, John Goodson, Tom Whitaker, W. Herbert Hunt, *et al.* in *United States of America* v. *Nelson Bunker Hunt and William Herbert Hunt,* Lubbock, Texas, September 16–27, 1975.

249–250 Account of Herbert Hunt's falling out with H. L. Hunt based on author's interviews with confidential sources.

256 Account of Jeane Dixon's dealings with H. L. Hunt based in part on author's interview with Jeane Dixon, and account in *My Life and Prophecies* by Jeane Dixon as told to Rene Noorbergen (New York: William Morrow, 1969).

259–261 Account of Hassie Hunt's return to Mount Vernon based on author's interview with Ruth Ray Hunt.

262 Account of Bunker Hunt and CIA in Libya based on filings in *United States of America* v. *Nelson Bunker Hunt and William Herbert Hunt, supra.* Also, author's interview with Hunt attorney Philip J. Hirschkop, and filings in *Nelson Bunker Hunt* v. *Mobil et al.*

268–269 Account of Lamar Hunt and AFL-NFL merger based on Harrigan and Rathet, *supra.*

269–270 Account of WCT founding based in part on author's interview with Dave Dixon.

274 Figures on Hunt Oil worth based on Hunt Oil Company financial statement, 1976, and author's interviews with former top Hunt employees.

274–275 H. L. Hunt interview with Mike Wallace taken from CBS "60 Minutes," Vol. 1, No. 14 (April 1, 1969).

Chapter 12 The Wiretap Caper

276–308   Account of HLH Products scandal and wiretap caper, including scenes and dialogue, based primarily on filings and court testimony in *United States of America* v. *Nelson Bunker Hunt and William Herbert Hunt, supra,* and filings and court testimony in *United States* v. *John W. Curington and John H. Brown,* Dallas, Texas, various dates, February and March 1975.

294   "I was lying to him about the bucket of acid." Author's interview with Jon Kelly.

298   Account of events after arrest of Jon Kelly based in part on filings and testimony in *Jon Joseph Kelly* v. *Percy Foreman et al.,* Houston, Texas; also, *United States of America* v. *Nelson Bunker Hunt and William Herbert Hunt,* Dallas, Texas, filed July 21, 1975.

300   Figures on food division from testimony in *United States of America* v. *Nelson Bunker Hunt and William Herbert Hunt, supra,* and author's interview with Bill Bledsoe.

306   Account of the Hunts at John Connally's barbecue based on *The Texans* by James Conaway (New York: Random House, 1976).

Chapter 13 Where There's a Will

311   Nelson Bunker Hunt statement regarding Rothermel in *United States of America* v. *Nelson Bunker Hunt and William Herbert Hunt, supra.*

316   H. L. Hunt's fear of shrinking reported in Shrake, *Sports Illustrated* (September 7, 1970).

318   Account of Hunt brothers' early silver purchases based in part on report by Charles Foley, *London Observer,* March 24, 1974. Also, *Wall Street Journal,* May 19, 1977.

318–322   Account of Nelson Bunker Hunt in Libya based on filings in Libyan oil suit mentioned above and author's interviews with confidential sources.

323–324   Account of Hunt brothers' silver round-up based on author's interview with confidential sources close to the principals. Also, sworn statement of former Hunt aide Bill Bledsoe before House Subcommittee on Commerce, Consumer, and Monetary Affairs, May 23, 1980. Hereafter referred to as Rosenthal subcommittee.

330–331   List of Hunt's coins and possessions, based on various filings with Dallas County clerk in connection with Placid Oil silver loan arrangement, May 1980.

341   Anecdote about the Hunt toe from author's interview with Herbert Hunt.

343   Hugh Hunt financial records filed in U.S. District Court, Alexandria, Virginia, March 5, 1975.

347–349   Account of H. L. Hunt funeral based in part on "H. L. Hunt's Long Good-Bye" by Bill Porterfield, *Texas Monthly* (March 1975).

Chapter 14 Life after H.L. (Part One)

352–354   Account of split between Hunt Oil and Hunt Energy based in part on author's interviews with former top employees.

360–362   Account of Hunt exploits in silver based in part on sworn statement of Bill Bledsoe, *supra.* Also, memoranda by Bill Bledsoe and author's interviews with confidential sources.

365–367   Account of Hunt oil-business activities based in part on sworn statement of Bill Bledsoe and author's interviews with confidential sources.

367–368 Account of Nelson Bunker Hunt's horse-buying tactics based in part on "Keeneland Seeks to End Mystery of Who's Who at Yearling Sale" by Gerald Strine in the *Washington Post,* July 16, 1976.

373 Recent biographies of Mellons and Rockefellers include *The Mellon Family: A Fortune in History* by Burton Hirsch (New York: Morrow, 1978); *The Rockefellers: An American Dynasty* by Peter Collier and David Horowitz (New York: Holt, Rinehart & Winston, 1976).

380–381 Account of Hunt family battle over prosperity based on author's confidential interviews with present and former top Hunt associates involved in the negotiations and various documents pertaining to those negotiations, including internal memoranda and Hunt Oil Company 1976 financial statement and schedules.

381–383 Account of Hunt family's internal negotiations based on author's confidential interviews with sources involved.

383–392 Account of Shreveport trial and settlement based on court testimony in *Lee v. Hunt,* personal observations of the author, and author's interviews with confidential sources. Also, Judge Tom Stagg's Memorandum Ruling of December 19, 1979.

Chapter 15 Life after H.L. (Part Two)

393–394 Account of breakdown of settlement in *Lee* v. *Hunt* based on author's interview with confidential sources and Judge Stagg's ruling of December 19, 1979, *supra.*

394–395 Account of Hunt-Connally-Mahfouz meeting based in part on sworn statement of former Hunt aide Bill Bledsoe. Also, author's interviews with confidential sources.

398 Figures on Hunt loans taken from filings with Rosenthal subcommittee.

398–400 Figures on Hunt 1979–1980 silver purchases and those of the Conti group taken from *Report of the Commodities Futures Trading Commission on Recent Developments in the Silver Futures Markets* (Washington, D.C.: U.S. Government Printing Office, May 1980), hereafter referred to as the CFTC report.

398–400 Account of Hunt horse-sale and silver-related conversations based on Norman Waltuch's testimony before Senate agriculture subcommittee, Senator Donald W. Stewart, chairman, June 26, 1980. Also, "A Bluegrass Record" by Joseph P. Pons, Jr., *The Bloodhorse,* Vol. CV, No. 32 (August 4, 1979).

400 Hunt political contributions and details based on articles in *Chicago Sun-Times,* June 28, 1980.

405 Waltuch's meetings with Hunt mentioned in Waltuch testimony, *supra.*

405–407 Figures on Hunt and Conti groups' holdings and account of meetings with CFTC from CFTC report, *supra,* and memoranda submitted to Rosenthal subcommittee April 15, 1980, by CFTC commissioner Read P. Dunn.

407–408 Figures on Hunt brothers' silver holdings from CFTC report.

414–415 Account of Hunt loan negotiations based in part on "Englehard's Not-So-Sterling Deal with the Hunts" by Peter W. Bernstein, *Fortune* (May 19, 1980).

415 Details on Hunt loan arrangements from filings in Dallas County and filings with Rosenthal subcommittee.

INDEX